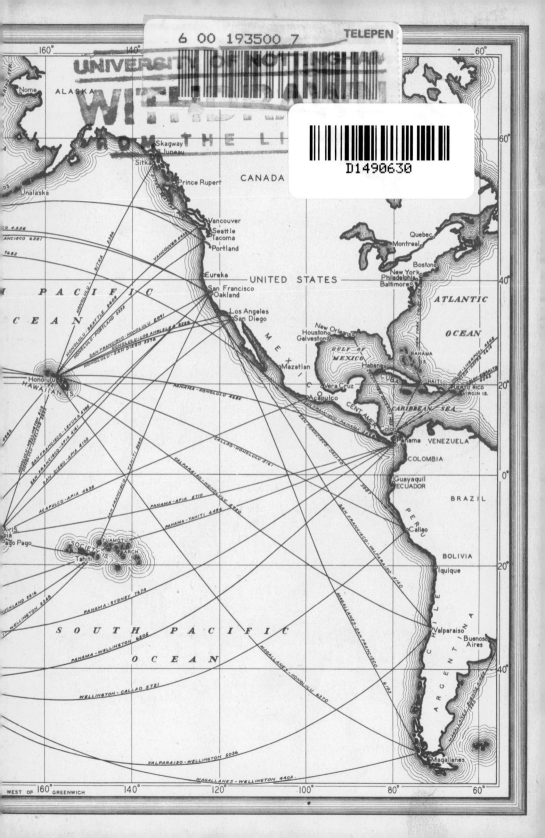

Maritime Trade of Western United States

STANFORD BUSINESS SERIES

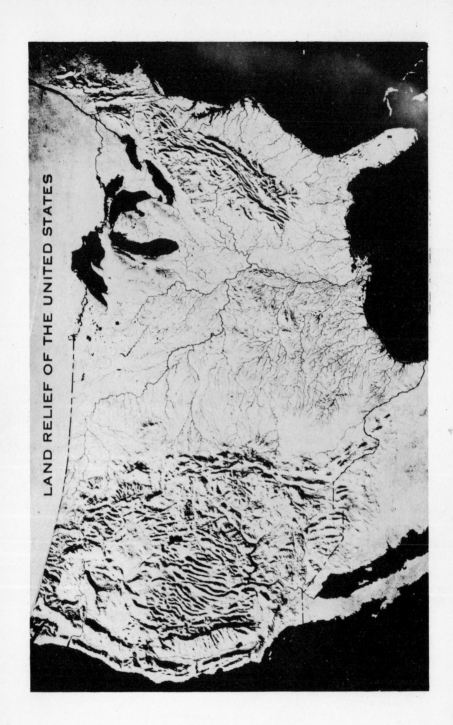

LAND RELIEF OF THE UNITED STATES

Maritime Trade of
Western
United States

By ELIOT GRINNELL MEARS

*Professor of Geography and International Trade; Stanford
Graduate School of Business; Organizer and Former
Chief, American Trade Commissioner Service*

STANFORD UNIVERSITY PRESS
STANFORD UNIVERSITY, CALIFORNIA

London: Humphrey Milford   Oxford University Press

STANFORD UNIVERSITY PRESS
STANFORD UNIVERSITY, CALIFORNIA

LONDON: HUMPHREY MILFORD
OXFORD UNIVERSITY PRESS

————

THE BAKER AND TAYLOR COMPANY
55 FIFTH AVENUE, NEW YORK

MARTINUS NIJHOFF
9 LANGE VOORHOUT, THE HAGUE

THE MARUZEN COMPANY
TOKYO, OSAKA, KYOTO, SENDAI

————

Preface

The time seems at hand for the preparation of pioneering shipping studies centering about the geographical background and development of important areas. With the knowledge that definite researches of this type had not been formulated, the American Council of the Institute of Pacific Relations in 1928 asked the writer to explore the possibilities involved in a study of transpacific shipping. Preliminary attempts to formulate the problems immediately encountered everywhere (*a*) the maze of nationalistic propaganda, (*b*) a stark confusion of the mercantile and national defense motives, and (*c*) a mass of undefined, uninterpreted, and conflicting statistics. At the outset, the logical attack upon the problem appeared to be a regional analysis. In this way, it has been possible to treat this definitive Pacific area as an entity and subject it to concrete analysis, and thereby to discover features in the situation which are often improperly emphasized or even largely overlooked. Accordingly, a study of transpacific shipping[1] was prepared and published for the biennial session of the Institute of Pacific Relations meeting at Kyoto in September 1929. An extension of the subject into the history and activities of shipping conferences and the nature of government subsidies in Pacific trades was presented by the American Group at the Banff session (August 1933) under the title *Regulation and Promotion of Pacific Shipping.*[2] This paper has been incorporated in this larger study.

This volume, it is believed, makes a contribution to knowledge in that it brings together the salient features in the shipping activities of the American Pacific Empire. But it goes farther by providing a much-needed interpretation of this pertinent material. Furthermore, and of possibly greater immediate interest to the student and certainly of intrinsic worth to shippers and traders, it presents analyses

[1] *San Francisco's Trans-Pacific Shipping* (New York, 1929), 105 pages.

[2] "Studies in Conflict and Control," *Regulation and Promotion of Pacific Shipping* (New York, 1933), 71 pages.

of the main points of weakness and strength in all the relevant statistics: for example, the writer endeavors to show why the various official figures from the United States Shipping Board (now United States Shipping Board Bureau of the Department of Commerce), the Corps of Engineers of the War Department, the Bureau of Navigation and Steamboat Inspection, the Bureau of Foreign and Domestic Commerce, the Panama Canal, and the local harbor boards do not and cannot agree. It is far from easy to extract from these little-understood and often contradictory statistics a clear and reliable picture of shipping and trade. Unless the student, business man, or legislator is sufficiently concerned to ferret out and to weight the actual trade facts, it is not surprising at all that the ignorance and misconstruction of the facts lead to uneconomic and futile shipping wars. As a result, public and private enterprise become intermeshed —and upon a world-wide scale.

The author is under particular obligations to numerous organizations and individuals. Special mention should be made of the assistance rendered by Mrs. Georgianna M. Weber and Mr. Vernon D. Wickizer in the drafting of certain sections of this study in its early stages.

The graphs and maps have been prepared by Mr. P. Stanley King of the Food Research Institute, Stanford University. The author has found especially useful the maps made by the late Professor J. P. Goode and issued by Rand, McNally & Company.

Shipping companies, chambers of commerce, officials, and port authorities have given excellent help. Of untold aid has been the hearty co-operation of officials of the Shipping Board, the Department of Commerce, the Treasury Department, the Corps of Engineers, and the Panama Canal Board. On special trips to Washington and New York, the author has secured valuable information not accessible in published form. Of the many persons to whom the author is under especially heavy obligations are Dr. James T. Shotwell, of Columbia University, and Dr. Carl L. Alsberg, of Stanford University, who have served successively as chairman of the International Research Committee of the Institute of Pacific Relations. The author is exceedingly appreciative of the assistance rendered by Professor William Hawley Davis and other members of the staff of the Stanford University Press.

The publication of this volume in its present form has been made possible by the support of the Carnegie Endowment for International Peace.

ELIOT GRINNELL MEARS

STANFORD UNIVERSITY
January 10, 1935

Table of Contents

APPENDIX

xi

LIST OF TABLES

Contents

LIST OF ILLUSTRATIONS

Maritime Trade of Western United States

I. Foreword

"As concerning ships, it is that which every one knoweth, and can say, they are our weapons, they are our ornaments, they are our strength, they are our pleasures, they are our defence, they are our profit; the subject by them is made rich, the kingdom through them strong, the prince in them mighty; in a word, by them in a manner we live, the kingdom is, the king reigneth."—*The Trade's Increase*, London, 1615.

Ocean shipping, more than any other international activity, is involved in propaganda. Private groups, acting through influential trade and regional organizations, are ever on the alert to keep people advised relative to those political actions at the nation's capital which the trade organizations consider inimical to them; the various governmental agencies are vitally concerned in the maintenance and promotion of military and naval interests, upon a national as well as a commercial basis; and local chambers of commerce are blatantly provincial in their outlook. As a result, there exists today no public or private organization which has as its function that of providing unbiased and interpretative information as to seagoing trade.

The tremendous importance of vessels as carriers merchandise, gold and silver, mail, and passengers cann be exaggerated, since the greatest highway of travel is sea. Oceans not only provide the only earth surface f from political control but also offer the superior advant of an unimpeded course of transit at low cost to and every world port, thus constituting the prime means of e ing an exchange of the commodities of commerce. The of international trade, including agricultural products industrial raw materials, semi-manufactures, and m; tured goods, moves by water rather than by land.

Nowhere is this situation more potently evident the American Pacific Coast states, where, in 1930, t of Engineers of the War Department estimated

1

commerce of Pacific Coast ports during the calendar year at 118,409,000 short tons, valued at approximately five billion dollars, and the United States Shipping Board recorded a traffic of 76,386,484 cargo long tons. Admiral H. I. Cone, Chairman of the United States Shipping Board, stated before the Twentieth National Foreign Trade Convention (Pittsburgh, April 1933) that the value of American seaport water terminals utilized for foreign trade was nearly one billion dollars, the shipyards alone representing an investment exceeding one hundred million dollars; and the book value of our overseas merchant fleet he stated to be $628,000,000. The seagoing American fleet consists of about 1,700 vessels of one thousand gross tons or more, aggregating nine and one-half million tons, and 600 American-flag ships operating on seventy regular lines in foreign trade. And since Section 500 of the Transportation Act (1920) commits the United States to a definite policy of encouraging water transportation, there is every reason to believe that American maritime trade can be compared to a lusty infant, unaware of its powers of growth and adaptation.

The magnitude of world shipping in United States ports appears most vividly in statistical form. During the fiscal year 1930 in the foreign, intercoastal, and non-contiguous trades approximately 6,000 vessels made 65,000 entrances and clearances in the carriage of 118,000,000 tons of cargo and 2,500,000 passengers; during the fiscal year 1933 approximately 3,600 vessels of the world fleet made 41,000 entrances and clearances in the carriage of 55,000,000 cargo tons and 1,400,000 passengers. For the twelve-year period, 1921–1932 inclusive, the United States Shipping Board reported that our water-borne commerce was served by 351 domestic ports, 420 ports in United States possessions, and 2,814 foreign ports, a total of 3,585 world ports engaged in transporting an aggregate of 2,053 separately classified commodities valued at nearly $83,000,000,000 and exceeding 1,000,000,000 cargo tons. An increase in world tonnage from 45,404,000 gross tons in 1914 to 67,920,185 tons in 1933, and 65,576,612 gross tons in 1934, discloses the magnitude of sea transport.

The dominant purpose of this study is that of discovering and interpreting significant trade trends. A fair criticism

might be made at once that the period under discussion is too brief to indicate a trend, since the statistics of the United States Shipping Board, the main source, appeared first in the year 1922. Furthermore, ever since the spectacular opening of the Panama Canal in August 1914 there has been a succession of abnormal periods of war and peace, political and economic changes, drastic monetary and currency regulations, and violent fluctuations in the quantity of trade and in prices. Thus we encounter serious difficulty. For example, the Department of Commerce reports that the American production of crude petroleum was nearly as great in 1933 as the average of the period 1926–1930 but that values thereof declined nearly 85 per cent; exports of gasoline were reduced one-half, with values reduced nearly 75 per cent; and the quantity and value of raw silk each declined 70 per cent. The year 1933, moreover, has proved unsatisfactory not alone because shipping statistics were not published until late in 1934, but also because within this calendar year a stated number of United States dollars purchased 56 per cent more domestic goods but actually 36 per cent less foreign goods in December than in March. What year or years are most satisfactory for yardsticks?

Indexes of general industry and trade compiled by the Twelfth Federal Reserve District (California, northwestern Arizona, Utah, Nevada, Idaho, Oregon, and Washington), based upon the 1923–25 annual average as equivalent to 100, make it appear that 1930 is more normal than any subsequent year, with little to choose between the 1932 and 1933 calendar periods. Thus, for the years 1930, 1932, and 1933, respectively, the indexes for manufactures were 102, 58, and 63; minerals 90, 57, and 54; building and construction 67, 37, and 42; carloadings 96, 57, and 58; bank debits 131, 74, and 69; wholesale sales 93, 55, and 56; department store sales 111, 74, and 70, and automobile sales 97, 34, and 48.

The year 1930 turns out to be the most representative or, negatively speaking, the least unrepresentative single year. Using 1924 as an average, the shipping freight rates index numbers compiled by the Chamber of Commerce of the United Kingdom give this range: 1927, 93–104; 1928, 90–113; 1929, 75–93; 1930, 62–71; 1931, 62–74; 1932, 58–69; and 1933,

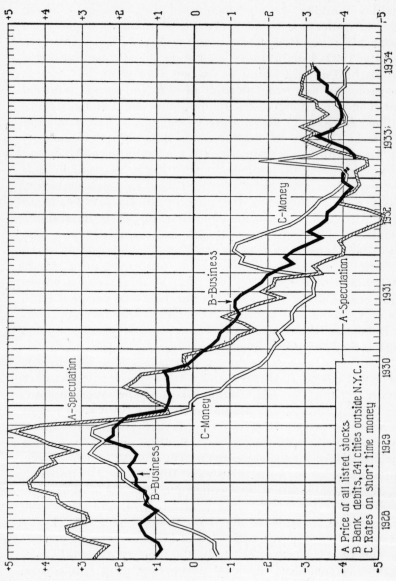

Fig. 1.—Harvard index chart, from *Review of Economic Statistics*, July 15, 1934. (Courtesy of the Harvard Economic Society.)

58–70. Statistics for the foreign and intercoastal trade of the Twelfth Federal Reserve District, compiled by the Federal Reserve Bank of San Francisco, using the 1923–25 average as equivalent to 100, give the indexes of total foreign trade values as follows: 1927, 120; 1928, 130; 1929, 140; 1930, 107; 1931, 71; 1932, 47; and 1933, 47. Similarly for indices of total intercoastal trade, the year 1927 stands at 98, 1928 at 87, 1929 at 97, 1930 at 86, 1931 at 71, 1932 at 54, and 1933 at 70.

Thus, with no series of years sufficiently numerous or typical to be designated a trend, the author, compelled to make a definite choice, has focused this study on the year 1930 as perhaps the best recent period under consideration. The graph, reproduced as Figure 1, through the courtesy of the Harvard Economic Society, substantiates the author's selection of 1930 as the focal year.

In order to provide the reader with more up-to-date information, despite its limited value upon a long-time basis, the author has embodied the results of the period 1929 to 1932 in chapter xv, "Cargo Tonnage Changes." Included as well in that chapter is certain detailed information not available elsewhere in the book.

The sections of the book may be grouped under the following heads: (1) Geographical and historical background (chapters ii–vi); (2) Statistical considerations (chapter vii and Appendix D); (3) Coast ports and services (chapters viii–ix); (4) Trades, by regions (chapters x–xiv); (5) Passenger and other non-commodity traffic (chapter xvi and Appendix B); (6) Shipping conferences (chapters xvii, xviii); (7) Subsidies (chapters xix, xx); (8) Résumé and conclusions (chapters xxi, xxii); (9) Exhibits of shipping services (Appendixes A and C and numerous exhibits in the text); (10) Maps, graphs, and tables, separately listed in the Table of Contents; (11) Selected bibliography.

The writer's attitude throughout this study combines that of a historical geographer and that of an economist. The farther one delves into the forces operating behind the shipping scene, the clearer it becomes that technical and business advances must be considered in retrospect. Remarkable inventions and discoveries in the combined field of communication and transportation have been a high light of twentieth-century progress. The speeding-up process, so easily recognizable in the technological field, has been geared into an economic system which has not been prepared for these changes. To illustrate from maritime developments, the "windjammer" has practically disappeared; likewise the familiar "tramp" is becoming old-fashioned; while the "liners" operating regularly upon scheduled routes are reckoned to comprise 70 per cent of the present world's tonnage as compared to but 36 per cent in 1913. Vessels built during the past decade have been much larger, more commodious though with less cargo space, less well adapted for general freight, and speedier. The enhanced speed of the new ships brings all seaports closer together, hence correspondingly less carrying capacity is needed for the same quantity of commodities. Yet world shipping tonnage has been increasing at a far more rapid rate than cargo tonnage. In 1913 and 1933, respectively, the volume of international trade was identical, its value had declined over 25 per cent, but the vessel tonnage gained 45 per cent in the two decades. Here is the crux of the immediate world shipping dilemma.

Maritime trade, therefore, depends far more upon the nature and volume of commerce than upon ship operation. Ship routes have a tremendous effect upon trade routes, especially since unlike the railway there is no fixed highway to be developed and maintained, moreover, at the expense of the carrier. But similar to the case of the railway, the traffic aspects are paramount. The shipping business is essentially a trade problem, and as such its activities are controlled by the requirements of commerce rather than ships. For this reason, in this volume the author has neglected related and highly important features of shipping such as navigation, operation and costs, labor unions and wages, port and harbor facilities, International Load-Line Convention, International Convention for Safety of Life at Sea, and national defense. While the writer is a staunch believer in the wisdom of an American merchant marine because of the accruing advantages in restraining excessive freight rates, promoting desirable trade routes and international exchange of commodities, and, in general, assuring American shippers fair treatment when their interests clash with those of foreigners, this study is not chauvinistic in its conception or execution. Rather, it is conceived that the real purpose of the merchant marine is to transport; hence there must be some quantity relationship between the vehicle of transport and the goods to be carried. The shipmaster reckons in terms of cargo tons; the trader in terms of value. The reader of this book must understand that there is neither theoretical nor practical correlation between these units of quantity and price.

Shipping is essential to trade, and trade is essential to shipping. One is unthinkable without the other. Nothing is so international as a vessel, for unlike the manufacturer or banker who can transact business by radio, telephone, or mail in his home office, the ocean carrier makes the actual trip and solicits foreign business on the ground. An exaggerated economic protectionism would destroy international shipping. No one realizes this truth so keenly as the ship owner. President Roger D. Lapham of the American-Hawaiian Steamship Company, at a recent meeting of the Chamber of Commerce of the United States, stated: "I do not pretend to be an expert in world economics, but it seems perfectly obvious to me that the American shipowner in foreign trade cannot expect to secure full cargoes for his ship unless it is made more possible for the American exporter to send his goods abroad, and more possible for the exporter abroad to sell his goods here." Normally, we export over one-third of our production of cotton, phosphate rock, sardines, linseed, raisins, prunes, apricots, apples, naval stores, kerosene, lubricating oils, tractors, and copper; in this foreign trade the Pacific Slope has an important share. Since we export certain commodities in order to import other commodities, and likewise import in order to export, trade demands become mutual. Ship economy does not permit profits upon one-way cargoes; therefore it becomes essential to consider both the commodity and the regional features.

The Pacific Coast states of California, Oregon, and Washington, together with the non-contiguous territories of Hawaii and Alaska, constitute the Western sea empire of the United States of America. To this littoral the interior Far Western states of Montana, Idaho, Wyoming, Utah, Nevada,

Colorado, New Mexico, and Arizona constitute a tributary area. Excluding American Samoa, Guam, and the Philippines, which are aligned with the Orient rather than with the Western Hemisphere, the sector so delimited has been construed by the author as "Western United States." The history of this large sector is recent, and serves well to portray the influence of past events upon present and potential sea-borne trade.

The world shipping situation, particularly since the early years of the twentieth century, must be understood in broad outline, at least, by the student of American maritime history. Land exploration and exploitation, wars, scientific discoveries and inventions, and economic changes of an international character underlie the number, type, and nationality of seacraft. For an industry which has the Seven Seas as its sphere of influence, these phenomena have an immediate and far-reaching percussion. Especially is this condition true of a nation which depends mainly upon foreign vessels for the carrying of its overseas freight and passengers. Therefore, the reader of this volume should grasp early the following significant developments in world shipping during by far its most important period, namely, the years 1910 to 1935. What are the overshadowing factors?

First, the opening of the Panama Canal in August, 1914, revolutionized trade and shipping routes and stimulated a vast amount of cargo traffic hitherto not available.

Second, the World War's effects were epoch-making and disastrous to the shipping industry. Consider how the huge war profits earned by neutral shipowners, to some extent by belligerents, have been dissipated by heavy purchases of vessels at prices too high to permit them to be operated profitably, a dearth of cargoes, the tremendous slump in immigrant traffic, a worldwide economic depression, and the keenest kind of national rivalries. Great Britain and Ireland still lead the world in number and tonnage of vessels, but the position is far less striking than formerly, with an actual decline of 6.7 per cent in gross tonnage of steamers and motorships; in comparing 1934 with 1914, while the United States sea fleet increased 382.2 per cent, Japan's increased 138.5, Norway's 103.4, and Italy's 101.0 per cent; furthermore, the percentage of steam and motor world tonnage from 1901 to 1934 changed as follows: Great Britain 50.2 to 27.4; United States 4.2 to 15.2; Japan 2.2 to 6.3; Norway 3.4 to 6.2; Germany 10.1 to 5.7; France 4.4 to 5.1; Italy 2.7 to 4.5; Holland 2.1 to 4.1.

Third, the growth in American shipping since the creation of the United States Shipping Board in 1916 has been the greatest factor in mercantile marine circles. At the outbreak of the war, the United States had only six steamers in the transatlantic trade and nine in the transpacific trade, a total of fifteen ships of 155,000 gross tons capacity. Documented tonnages for foreign trade amounted to 792,000 tons in 1910 and 1,076,000 in 1914 (contrasted with 6,303,000 gross tons in 1930). The percentage in value of our waterborne foreign trade carried in American vessels amounted to 89.7 per cent in 1830, 72.5 per cent in 1850, 35.6 per cent in 1870, 12.9 per cent in 1890, and 8.7 per cent in 1910 (compared to 34.7 per cent in 1930 and 35.4 per cent in 1933). At the behest of the war allies, the United States embarked upon a most costly trial-and-error and rapid program which entailed the building of 2,000 vessels at a cost of three billion dollars; these ships, now mostly scrapped, have proved a tremendous burden to the United States taxpayers, a sum which has been estimated by an astute shipping executive, Sir Norman Hill, to represent a loss of 1,000 million pounds sterling, which is equivalent to one-half of the loans made to the Allies. During the heyday of ship construction, ownership, and operation by the United States Shipping Board, foreign governments protested bitterly in the interests of their nationals but not less vehemently than private American shipowners who had, moreover, to compete with their own government, at their own expense, and without the assistance of official intervention. The Shipping Board has now ceased to operate ships, better competition has been introduced into this American industry, and the Shipping Board, as such, was abolished by presidential order in 1933 and recreated as a Bureau in the Department of Commerce. But this heritage has been an extremely unsettling influence in deep-sea shipping since 1916.

Fourth, the substitution of oil for coal as ship fuel has

gone on so rapidly that nearly 4,000 steamers are fitted for using either oil or coal; but the employment of coal exclusively has dropped from 89 per cent of total gross tonnage in 1914 to 52 per cent in 1934. This increasing dependence on oil has affected seriously the trade and shipping situation of Great Britain for the reason that outgoing cargoes of coal, both merchandise and bunkers, have been a leading factor in the supremacy of the British merchant marine. Cheap petroleum available at American Gulf and Pacific ports, especially the latter, diverts a vast amount of shipping to these regions.

Fifth, the types of vessels have changed greatly. Less than two per cent of the aggregate tonnage is in sailing crafts, and 54 per cent of these are under United States registry. The rapid growth in motorships is evident by the increase from 730,000 tons in 1914 to 10,893,000 tons in 1934 in the case of steam-turbine engines, and from 220,000 tons in 1914 to 10,605,000 tons in 1934 in the case of internal reciprocating engines. It is noteworthy that over one-third of the total Norwegian, Danish, and Swedish tonnage is in motorships; 15.3 per cent for Great Britain and Ireland; and 5.6 per cent for the United States. A significant feature is that only 5.6 per cent of United States seagoing tonnage is under five years old, compared to 10.6 per cent for Great Britain and Ireland, 12.7 per cent for Japan, 15.8 per cent for Holland, 17.4 per cent for Denmark, and 25.3 per cent for Norway. Despite this absence of the most modern vessels, the United States flag waves over 17.69 per cent of the ocean-going steam and motor tonnage, compared to 36.72 per cent for Great Britain and Ireland, 7.23 per cent for Germany, 6.83 per cent for Japan, 6.04 per cent for France, 5.29 per cent for Italy, 5.06 per cent for Holland, 3.28 per cent for Norway (low because of high proportion of tankers), and other countries 11.56 per cent. Great Britain and Ireland and the United States lead in tonnage broken up during the past ten years; nevertheless, from the standpoint of the most up-to-date types of vessels, Great Britain and the United States have not kept pace with certain other countries, notably Japan and Norway.

Sixth, economic and social happenings of vast import are

made evident by a slowing down in the world's rate of population increase, an increased industrialism on the part of all countries, monetary and financial restrictions and difficulties everywhere, and a pronounced trend toward economic nationalism. As a result of these developments, the temporary status of world trade and shipping is in need of great improvement. The realm of the Pacific is receiving a consideration in 1934 which was not even dreamed of in the year 1914.

Seventh, owing to the maladjustment of vessel tonnage and cargo offerings aggravated by wide differences between countries with respect to standards of living as reflected in shipbuilding costs and their maintenance, the leading industrial countries have embarked upon strong programs of shipping protectionism. Not less striking than the ship subsidies granted by the United States are the clear reversals in British policies from commodity free trade to safeguarding duties and in launching a novel tramp subsidy program. Great Britain, France, and Italy are among the countries which continue subsidies to secure the Atlantic "blue ribbon," and Japan is building up the speediest and most modern fleet in Pacific waters. Subsidies and bounties have always been troublesome features in world shipping, and they had reached a serious stage of development at the end of 1934.

Eighth, the vessel as a means of transport, still challenged by land carriers, now faces a new problem in air travel. The dramatic flight of the Lady Southern Cross from the Antipodes to San Francisco Bay by Sir Charles Kingsford-Smith and Captain P. G. Taylor in November 1934 is an augury of future possibilities. This hop of 7,350 miles took practically the same time as the Overland Limited between San Francisco and Chicago. One of the leading Coast steamship companies is now taking a direct interest in the transpacific aviation business. Along with the evolution in means of overseas transport, there is the pressing question of a greater governmental participation in the regulation of conferences and rates with respect to coastal services, near-by foreign trades, and overseas traffic.

Maritime developments of the American Western Empire cannot be divorced from the world picture.

II. Shipping and Trade Position of the Region

Last of the great oceans to be invaded by the prows of trade, the Pacific provides the trade routes for half of the world's population. Over its millions of square miles, an area almost as large as all other oceans combined, ships of all types, sailing under many flags, set their courses for ports in far-away lands. On the densely populated Asiatic side of the Pacific live peoples old in history and civilization but young in political, economic, and social development as measured by twentieth-century standards. With resources of unknown magnitude, as yet little exploited, with an enormous labor supply and a great potential market, these members of the human family have just begun to take advantage of the more progressive features of Western civilization.

Of the great continents surrounding the Pacific, those on the American side are the far less densely populated but industrially the further developed. Favored by the absence of extremes of temperature, violent storms, and persistent fogs, rich in natural resources, this world of the Pacific, now only partially exploited, is in many respects the most promising economic sector of the world. Most advanced industrially are the Pacific Coast states of California, Oregon, and Washington. These, together with the important non-contiguous territories of Hawaii and Alaska, constitute the Western-sea empire of the United States of America.[1] Handicapped to a certain extent by mountain barriers and stretches of desert wastes which separate them from the highly developed and thickly populated regions of Eastern United States, the American Pacific Coast states comprise a world frontier region having its major paths of commercial contacts along ocean rather than land routes.[2] The building of the North American transcontinental railways and the

[1] See Table 1, opposite. The Philippines, Guam, and American Samoa, which are under the virtual direction of the military departments of the American government, are aligned with the Orient rather than with the Western Hemisphere.

[2] See frontispiece.

12

TABLE 1

AREA, POPULATION, AND DENSITY OF AMERICA'S WESTERN EMPIRE, 1930*

	Area (sq. mi.)	Population (thousands)	Density (per sq. mi.)
Far Western States			
Pacific:			
California	158,297	5,677	36.5
Oregon	96,699	954	10.0
Washington	69,127	1,563	23.4
Total Pacific	324,123	8,194	25.8
Mountain:			
Arizona	113,956	436	3.8
Colorado	103,948	1,036	10.0
Idaho	83,888	445	5.3
Montana	146,997	538	3.7
Nevada	110,690	91	0.8
New Mexico	122,634	423	3.5
Utah	84,990	508	6.2
Wyoming	97,914	226	2.3
Total Mountain	865,017	3,702	4.3
Territories			
Alaska	586,400	59	0.1
Hawaii	6,407	368	57.5
Total Western Empire	1,781,947	12,323	6.9
Continental United States	3,026,789	122,775	41.3
New England	66,424	8,166	131.8
Middle Atlantic	102,554	26,261	262.6
Western Empire as percentage of total continental United States and incorporated territories	49	10	

* From Bureau of the Census, *Population,* 1930.

Panama Canal have, to be sure, overcome some of Nature's barriers and both have immeasurably facilitated communication with Atlantic lands, but in respect to intercourse the Canal is by far the more significant.

Distance, formerly the greatest barrier to world intercourse, is being rapidly diminished by modern invention. Transpacific steamers and motorships now regularly make the voyage from Yokohama to San Francisco on an adver-

tised schedule of twelve or thirteen days. To appreciate
how far the days of the Spanish transpacific galleon of the
end of the seventeenth century have been left behind, one
must read such accounts of voyages across the Pacific in
those days as this:

> The voyge from the Phillipine islands to America may be call'd
> the longest, and the most dreadful of any in the world; as well
> because of the vast ocean to be cross'd, being almost the one half of
> the terraqueous globe, with the wind always a-head; as for the
> terrible tempests that happen there, one upon the back of the another,
> and for the desperate diseases that seize people, in seven or eight
> months lying at sea, sometimes near the line, sometimes cold, some-
> times temperate, and sometimes hot, which is enough to destroy a
> man of steel, much more flesh and blood, which at sea had but
> indifferent food.

The Far East and the Far West grow nearer each year.
In fact, Californians sometimes refer to the "Far East" as
the "Near West." The Panama Canal has made new neighbors for the Pacific States so that now the trade with Western
Europe constitutes 20 per cent of their total, an intercourse
impracticable prior to the completion of the Canal.

Evidence of the growing importance of the American
Pacific States, not only in the Pacific world but in the Atlantic
as well, is provided by its growth in foreign trade. In 1929,
the total value of this commerce (1.1 billion dollars) was
four times as great as it had been in 1913, sixteen years
earlier, and nine times that in 1900.[4] Making allowances for
price changes, the growth is still more than 200 per cent.
Even in 1931, when trade had shrunk and prices had fallen
severely, the value of the business was approximately four
times that of the total imports and exports for 1913. Whereas
the foreign trade of the Pacific States more than trebled
between 1913 and 1929, as shown in Table 2 (p. 16), the inter-

[3] From Churchill's *Collection of Voyages and Travels,* translated from
the Italian, an account of the voyage of Gemelli Careri in 1697–98, reprinted
in Chapman's *A History of California* (1921), p. 91.

[4] To measure accurately the growth in Pacific Coast maritime commerce
is a far from simple task, as will be apparent from chapter vii. Values of
imports and exports through Pacific Coast customs districts, too, although
available for many years back, are subject to the vagaries of changing price
levels, a distortion particularly marked during the eventful years of world-
wide political and economic disturbances from 1914 to the present date.

national commerce of the world increased only 65 per cent during the same period and that of the whole United States only about 125 per cent.

Further, whereas in 1913 the foreign trade of the Pacific States area accounted for 6.4 per cent of the aggregate value of United States foreign trade, by 1929 this percentage had increased to 11.6 per cent, or nearly double its former importance.[5] Of the thirteen leading seaports of the world, reckoned on the basis of entrances of seagoing vessels in the foreign and coastwise trades, six are on the Pacific Ocean: Los Angeles, San Francisco, Singapore, Hong Kong, Shanghai, and Kobe. Captain Robert Dollar once stated: "This is an era of the Pacific. It is growing, and it is going to grow. The surface has not been scratched." But the phenomenal growth in the sea trade with the Pacific Coast states is, in fact, only a reflection of the new importance of the Pacific Basin. In 1913 the international trade of the countries of this Basin amounted to approximately six billion dollars, or 14 per cent of the total world trade; but in 1929, when aggregate world commerce had grown from 41 billion to 67 billion dollars, the share of Pacific countries increased to 14 billion dollars and represented 21 per cent of the total international commerce of the world.

From a shipping point of view, the tonnage of cargo involved in this exchange is, within certain limitations, of more significance than the value of the commodities entering into trade. These limitations largely determine the type and speed of vessels engaged in trade and the routes they follow. From 1922 onward it is possible to trace the growth in ocean-borne foreign trade in terms of volume through the several Pacific ports.[6] Figure 3 (p. 18) shows the growth, both absolute and relative, of the tonnage of Pacific Coast foreign trade

[5] Part of this relative increase is a reflection of the immense growth in raw silk imports from the Orient via Pacific Coast ports. A considerable percentage of such receipts, although actually landed on the Pacific Coast, are recorded as imports at other customs districts, so that in all probability the increase in actual Pacific Coast foreign commerce was much greater than these data indicate. (Consult chapter vii and Appendix D.)

[6] This period is scarcely long enough to establish any but the most general trends; nevertheless, the current position of the American Pacific Coast in the carriage of ocean-borne foreign commerce is clearly portrayed.

TABLE 2

Value of Exports and General Imports at Pacific Coast Customs Districts, 1900–1930*

(Thousand dollars)

Calendar Year	Exports					General Imports				
	Total Pacific†	Los Angeles	San Francisco	Oregon	Washington	Total Pacific†	Los Angeles	San Francisco	Oregon	Washington
1900 (fiscal)	72,167‡	2,739§	40,368	8,344	17,903	60,141‡	1,571	47,870	1,811	7,149
1907 (fiscal)	92,030¶	855	33,027	12,092	43,659	91,140¶	2,213	54,095	4,192	25,353
1913 (fiscal)	146,856	1,391‖	66,021	13,632	62,548	128,895	3,771‖	62,502	3,285	51,474
1922 (calendar)	312,357	23,553‖	145,099	51,006	90,071	430,152	24,941‖	170,815	7,809	218,219
1923 (calendar)	371,572	39,635	160,432	52,510	116,088	480,679	32,517	166,685	10,120	262,158
1924 (calendar)	447,310	73,477	173,441	62,865	134,760	477,302	40,591	146,335	10,676	270,286
1925 (calendar)	427,475	78,944	183,292	41,935	120,557	526,969	44,453	196,537	12,429	261,874
1926 (calendar)	518,888	103,645	186,773	78,494	147,570	548,102	49,571	210,139	13,714	261,880
1927 (calendar)	506,125	120,574	174,555	78,732	129,513	510,569	47,140	199,999	14,208	239,284
1928 (calendar)	561,007	141,899	201,265	63,879	150,817	504,695	54,351	198,275	12,124	229,024
1929 (calendar)	595,015	166,329	206,018	66,060	153,874	523,543	63,685	212,678	19,700	216,774
1930 (calendar)	449,260	149,911‖	147,568	46,787	102,655	343,446	52,088‖	155,564	10,977	113,708

* Data from Bureau of Foreign and Domestic Commerce.

† Including Alaska and Hawaii.

‡ Includes Humboldt (California), and Arizona.

§ All exports were from San Diego.

¶ Including Humboldt, California.

‖ Including San Diego, which was a separate customs district through 1922; recreated a separate district on June 20, 1930.

FIG. 2.—Map of United States Pacific Coast and the eleven Western states.

(excluding Alaska and Hawaii). Because of the great outward movement of petroleum, there is shown the volume of non-tanker cargoes, as well as the total trade.

Clearly there has been a remarkably rapid growth, both absolutely and relatively, in the maritime foreign commerce

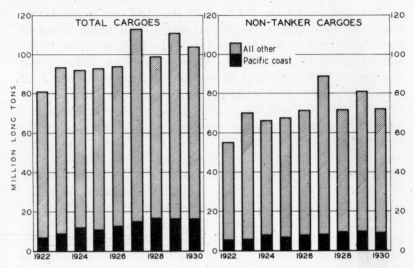

Fig. 3.—Growth in volume of United States foreign cargoes (total non-tanker), 1922–30.

of the American Pacific Coast within the short period which these data cover. The annual average foreign trade of the United States for the three years from 1922 to 1924, inclusive, was 88.6 million long tons; for the years from 1928 to 1930, inclusive, the average was 105 million long tons. The corresponding figures for the Pacific Coast were 9.2 million tons and 16.5 million tons, respectively. Thus United States total commerce showed on the basis of weight an approximate gain of 18.6 per cent, while Pacific Coast foreign commerce during the same time gained 81.1 per cent. The comparison is even more striking when made between Pacific Coast foreign commerce and all other American foreign commerce, as follows:

GROWTH IN OCEAN-BORNE FOREIGN COMMERCE

(*Long tons*)

	1922–1924 (3-year average)	1928–1930 (3-year average)	Percentage Increase
Pacific Coast states............	9,192,000	16,647,000	81.1
United States except Pacific Coast	79,378,000	88,373,000	11.3

In other words, the tonnage of Pacific Coast ocean-borne exports and imports has grown more than seven times as rapidly as that of the remainder of the United States in the period under review. Pacific Coast commerce suffered less decline in 1930 than that of either the Atlantic or the Gulf coasts. In fact, it practically maintained its 1929 volume. In 1922 the total volume of Pacific Coast foreign commerce (6,653 thousand long tons) represented 8.3 per cent of the United States total; in 1928, when the volume had much more than doubled (16,810 thousand tons), it constituted 16.9 per cent of the aggregate; and in 1930 it represented 15.8 per cent of the total United States foreign commerce.

In volume of cargo handled the American Pacific Coast is of less importance in the total United States import movement than in the export movement.[7] Characteristic surplus products of the region are more bulky than American export surpluses in general, but the same situation is not true of imports. Even on transpacific routes, imports into Pacific ports constitute decidedly less than half the total inward movement into the United States. Pacific ports, then, serve primarily the land areas naturally tributary to them, and, in spite of their favorable location with respect to the Orient, only moderate amounts pass through which do not originate in or are not destined for the Pacific and Mountain states.[8]

Foreign commerce of the West Coast is decidedly unbalanced, with an outward movement of more than four times the weight of imports. Even eliminating cargoes in tankers, most of which are petroleum exports, the volume of exports is considerably more than twice that of imports

[7] In total volume of commerce (domestic as well as foreign), however, the difference is not so great. In 1929, Pacific Coast ports handled nearly 46 million cargo tons, or 29 per cent of the entire outbound ocean movement of the United States; the approximately 38.5 million tons of incoming cargo represented 24 per cent of the country's total.

[8] Allowance must be made, however, for the fact that statistics in terms of weight tend to underemphasize cargoes of small bulk and high value. Since this type of cargo, of which silk and tea are prime examples, is precisely the sort most likely to utilize the Pacific gateway as the shortest route between eastern United States and the Far East, whereas the bulk products follow the all-water routes with minimum transshipment, the importance of Pacific ports as gateways is undoubtedly greater than the figures indicate. For further details, consult chapter xvi.

TABLE 3

WEIGHT OF CARGO OF WATER-BORNE FOREIGN TRADE, BY UNITED STATES DISTRICTS, 1922–1930*

(Thousand long tons)

District	1922	1923	1924	1925	1926	1927	1928	1929	1930
Total imports	44,682	43,296	40,899	43,135	44,686	42,183	47,395	50,985	46,642
North Atlantic district....	26,018	24,270	22,351	24,069	26,449	25,860	29,309	33,807	30,609
South Atlantic district....	1,090	1,561	1,725	2,082	2,165	1,577	1,615	1,630	1,734
Gulf district	11,024	10,029	9,889	8,539	8,185	6,094	6,325	6,754	4,786
Pacific district	1,814	2,524	2,585	2,602	2,712	2,835	3,027	3,185	2,888
Great Lakes district......	4,736	4,912	4,349	5,843	5,175	5,817	7,119	5,609	6,625
Total exports	42,502	49,080	52,261	49,666	68,140	56,935	58,829	57,475	48,009
North Atlantic district....	18,669	20,715	20,696	20,817	33,994	18,648	17,710	16,278	12,521
South Atlantic district....	786	927	822	1,082	1,354	1,126	707	916	786
Gulf district	10,584	10,599	12,805	12,420	13,304	13,935	15,025	16,075	13,716
Pacific district	5,465	8,472	9,360	8,355	11,450	13,316	13,441	13,593	11,744
Great Lakes district......	6,998	8,367	8,578	6,992	8,038	9,910	11,946	10,613	9,242

* Calendar years. Data from United States Shipping Board.

(Table 4, p. 22). Until comparatively recent times the foreign trade of the entire United States was characterized by a heavy export balance, more because of the preponderance of raw materials among exports and of manufactures and other relatively high-priced products among imports than because of the so-called "favorable balance" usually recorded in terms of value.

The Pacific Coast districts contributed 11.7 per cent of total United States exports, according to value, in 1930, compared with 8.7 per cent in 1925, while the figure for North American ports remained stationary. The imports according to value accounted for 11.2 per cent of the total in 1930, compared with 12.5 per cent in 1925, largely owing to the terrific drop in the value of raw silk despite the increase in the actual volume imported; while the imports at North Atlantic ports accounted for 60.6 per cent of the total in 1930, compared with 62.8 per cent in 1925.

According to recent figures, however, the volume of imports into the United States, exclusive of the Pacific Coast, has been in excess of the corresponding figure for exports in six of the nine years from 1922 to 1930, inclusive. This reflects the rapid industrial development of the country and the dwindling exportable surpluses of primary materials. On the Pacific Coast a parallel shift is only beginning, and the resources as well as the requirements of the region suggest that it will be many years before the inward movement from abroad will approximate the outward movement.

Not only do exports from the Pacific States greatly outweigh imports into them, but also the rate of increase of the former is much more rapid than for the latter. In terms of long tons, exports between 1922–1924 and 1928–1930 increased by about 120 per cent, while imports increased only 45 per cent during the same period. Because the volume of outbound cargoes is much greater than that of inbound, the Pacific Coast is obliged to contend with the disadvantage of a large movement of vessels in ballast or with only partial cargoes.

Ships on the run from San Francisco and Seattle to Yokohama and Shanghai carry to the Orient much heavier cargoes than they bring back. In exchange for cheap and bulky

TABLE 4

PACIFIC COAST EXPORTS AND IMPORTS, TANKER AND NON-TANKER, 1922–1930*

(Thousand long tons)

Year Ending June 30	All Foreign Commerce			Exports			Imports		
	Total	Non-Tanker	Tanker	Total	Non-Tanker	Tanker	Total	Non-Tanker	Tanker
1922..........	6,653	5,660	993	5,222	4,276	946	1,431	1,385	46
1923..........	8,866	6,103	2,763	6,544	3,796	2,748	2,322	2,308	14
1924..........	12,059	7,938	4,121	9,500	5,386	4,114	2,559	2,552	7
1925..........	11,039	7,008	4,031	8,505	4,474	4,031	2,534	2,534	..
1926..........	12,518	7,929	4,589	9,909	5,336	4,573	2,609	2,593	16
1927..........	14,819	8,844	5,975	12,004	6,099	5,905	2,815	2,745	70
1928..........	16,810	9,888	6,922	13,926	7,093	6,833	2,885	2,796	89
1929..........	16,610	10,171	6,439	13,498	7,158	6,340	3,112	3,014	98
1930..........	16,521	9,576	6,945	13,345	6,477	6,868	3,176	3,099	77

* Data from United States Shipping Board.

raw cotton and cotton goods from America they bring back small and relatively expensive bundles of raw silk and silk goods. In place of rough fir and pine lumber exported from the Pacific Northwest, they bring back lacquer ware. Westward they carry bulky flour, canned goods, petroleum, and machinery, but find for return cargo only drugs, wood oils, matting, toys, and art goods. In 1928, the value of United States exports to Asia reached a peak of 655 million dollars, while imports from Asia were valued at 1,169 millions—a trade stimulated because they entered largely duty-free. The peak value of imports occurred in 1929 when merchandise worth some 1,280 millions entered the United States from the Far East, although exports to that region were valued at only 643 million dollars. Translated into units of weight, in recent years the United States has been sending approximately 6.5 million tons of cargo to the Orient and has been receiving only some 1.5 million tons from there. If Australia were added, the outbound movement amounts to over eight million tons and the inbound to considerably less than two million tons.

Were it not for this problem of outbound cargoes, which are far heavier than the inbound cargoes, the situation on the Pacific, as well as on routes of less importance, would not be so serious. Of the ten or a dozen maritime courses across the Pacific Basin, the one from the Panama Canal along the California-Oregon-Washington-Alaska Coast to Yokohama is of major importance not only because of the character and wealth of exchangeable goods of the countries bordering it but also because it traverses the shortest distance between these points—the Great Circle route (see azimuth chart, Fig. 4, on page 29). In order to offset the disparity in cargo volume, a number of round-the-world freight services, most of them westbound, have been inaugurated.

Ships either from the Pacific Coast or from the North Atlantic sailing via Panama, with petroleum, lumber, dried fruit, wheat, or machinery, exchange their cargoes for half their bulk in the rarer, more expensive goods of the Orient and then may continue via Singapore to India and load the jute needed for the American farmer's grain sacks and so complete their voyage to New York. Or vessels from the

North Atlantic may return partially in ballast and pick up
lumber, grain, and flour for the United States East Coast
from the Pacific Northwest. European liners sailing via Suez
to China and Japan with bulky cargoes likewise must travel
light across the Pacific to the Pacific Northwest, where they
load with bulky commodities and continue home via Panama, thus completing a round-the-world trip.

Other means of overcoming this difficulty which have
been tried or suggested, together with the interesting effects
on the ocean freight-rate structures, are considered in subsequent chapters. A similar disparity in cargo volume is
found in the routes from the Pacific Coast of North America
south via the Panama Canal to the United States Atlantic
Coast and to Europe. Here again the bulky raw materials
of low unit value, such as lumber, lead, zinc, barley, wheat,
canned and dried fruits, and petroleum, from the Pacific
States, outweigh the more expensive but less heavy finished
and semi-finished products—machinery, hardware, textiles,
and refined petroleum—of the industrial Atlantic seaboard
and northwestern Europe, and here again the unbalance is
of prime importance. Atlantic Europe is the second largest
factor in the foreign trade of the Pacific Coast, while in
recent years the domestic intercoastal movement has
amounted to about 12 per cent of all Pacific States water-
borne commerce.

In addition to the North Pacific Great Circle route, the
intercoastal lane through the Panama Canal, and the northwestern Europe route, there are several other ocean tracks
on the Pacific which touch the North American West Coast.
The North Pacific to South Pacific traffic of the Americas is
one of ever-growing importance. Here too the trade is unbalanced, for our lumber and petroleum outweigh the commodities which Latin-American countries send us.

Similarly, on the route from the North American West
Coast to Australia via Hawaii the exchange is one-sided, with
exports of California petroleum and Northwestern lumber
accounting for the bulk of the trade. In addition to the ten
natural sea lanes across the Pacific, four of which include the
Pacific Coast states, there is another route, unnatural from
a distance standpoint, from San Francisco and Los Angeles

to China and Japan, via Honolulu. This 800-mile deflection is justified by the growing importance of Hawaiian trade and of the attractions of scenery and excellent climate.

Hawaii and Alaska, the two non-contiguous territories which complete the Western United States sector, send their products almost exclusively to the mainland. Hawaii, in addition to being the chief factor justifying the circuitous San Francisco–Los Angeles–to–Orient route, is a port of call off the North Pacific Great Circle course. Alaskan traffic to the north and Hawaiian traffic to the south provide the leading feeders to this main transpacific artery. Alaskan trade centers in Puget Sound ports; Hawaiian trade centers in California, particularly San Francisco. Fish and fish products, copper, and gold are the chief items from Alaska, while sugar and canned pineapple are the principal commodities from the Hawaiian Islands. Both territories take a wide variety of general merchandise in exchange. For the fiscal years 1928–30 the foreign trade of these territories amounted to only 3.4 per cent of the total cargo tons of their ocean-borne commerce, owing to the preponderant traffic with the national mainland.

The Philippines, acquired at the end of the last century as a result of the Spanish-American War, are also, for the time at least, a part of our American Pacific Empire. Politically as well as geographically, however, their relation to continental United States is far less close than is that of Hawaii. Trade with the Philippines is still classed as foreign trade, and independence for this Asiatic territory is now indicated.

From a shipping point of view, it is unfortunate that such a large part of the maritime commerce of the Pacific States is unbalanced. Ship operation is most profitable when holds are filled with freight on both outbound and homecoming passages, just as operation of modern passenger liners is more profitable when they carry their full complement. Yet unlike that of the Atlantic the passenger traffic on the Pacific, although growing, has never been of large proportions or of enough significance to justify the existence of liners for the purpose of carrying passengers alone. Freight, then, is the chief reliance of Pacific ships. The nature of the lands bordering the Pacific, the skills of their peoples, and their natural resources have dictated the character of its trade. The disparity, as far as tonnage is concerned, is not new; in fact, it has been present almost from the beginning of modern transpacific trade. During the past decade, however, it has become greater than ever. The volume of exports from the Pacific States has been increasing from two to three times as fast as the volume of imports, thus accentuating a condition which makes profitable operation of ships in transpacific trade much more difficult. However, the consideration of dry cargoes alone makes this factor appear not so unfavorable, and, of course, the kind of tonnage and space are not always synonymous terms.

Thus far the growth in the foreign trade of the American Pacific States area has been indicated and mention has been made of the cargo movements both outbound and inbound on the various principal trade routes. Before proceeding further it is perhaps well to obtain a summary view of the ocean-borne commerce of the region from a cargo point of view, in order to show the relative importance of its foreign trade. In the analysis of foreign commerce of the region it is desirable to have a more concrete view of the relative importance of various overseas areas in the maritime intercourse of the American Pacific States.

The total ocean-borne commerce of the United States Pacific Coast is divided somewhat as follows, the percentage being based on an average of the cargo tons of traffic during the three fiscal years 1928, 1929, and 1930:

Trade	Percentage of Total
Coastwise	65.0
Foreign	19.7
Intercoastal	11.9
Non-contiguous	3.4

The important part played by intercoastal trade (see Appendix Table X) as compared with foreign trade is strikingly evident on the Pacific Coast, far more so than for the nation as a whole, as appears from an analysis of Table 5. Clearly coastwise trade is the largest single element in the water-borne commerce of the region, but it is also the element for which existing data are least satisfactory. In terms of tonnage of goods shipped and received, total domestic waterborne commerce, according to the best information available, has aggregated well over 60 million long tons in each of the last six calendar years.[9] Of this amount some three-fourths consists in coastwise movement along the Pacific littoral.[10] The balance is mainly intercoastal, but there are annually from 2.5 to 3.0 million tons of cargo also shipped between Pacific ports of continental United States and the non-contiguous territories of Alaska and Hawaii. In official records all three transits are classed as coastwise trade of the United States.

. From many points of view, however, the strictly coastwise trade can be disregarded in a study of the maritime intercourse of the region. Coastwise trade is local traffic to and from United States Pacific ports, and while it is undoubtedly of internal importance and looms large in total water-borne commerce, it is, nevertheless, of less economic importance to the region than its trade with foreign countries, the Atlantic seaboard, and the territories of Alaska and Hawaii. The shipping and trade problems are obviously greatly different and of smaller import in maritime development in the instance of purely coastwise movements. Therefore, chief attention in this study is given to foreign commerce and to the protected intercoastal and non-contiguous trades.

Now these protected trades present quite different problems, and must be treated separately. Foreign commerce is affected directly by artificial restrictions imposed by various nations or as a result of economic forces of an international character. Currently, the foreign commerce of the Pacific States region is predominantly with East Asian countries, both on a tonnage and on a value basis. As has been noted, Atlantic Europe is the second most important over-

[9] This figure counts both receipts and shipments in Pacific coastwise trade, which introduces a large element of duplication as far as actual commodities transported are concerned.

[10] The word coastwise is used here and in general throughout this volume in its geographical and not its official sense, to denote movement between United States ports on the same seaboard. The nature of coastwise shipping of the Western frontier is shown in chapter x.

TABLE 5

CARGO TONNAGE OF FOREIGN AND INTERCOASTAL COMMERCE, UNITED STATES AND PACIFIC COAST PORTS, 1928–1930*

(Thousand long tons)

	Total United States Ports†			Pacific Coast Ports (Actual)			Pacific Coast (Percentages)		
	1928	1929	1930	1928	1929	1930	1928	1929	1930
Total commerce	120,069‡	123,320‡	111,052‡	28,592	30,143	26,807	23.8	24.4	24.1
Inbound	59,105	63,770	59,228	7,223	7,904	7,013	12.2	12.4	11.8
Outbound	70,326	70,101	60,868	21,369	22,239	19,794	30.4	31.7	32.5
With foreign countries§	106,224	108,460	97,293	16,467	16,778	14,870	15.5	15.5	15.3
Imports	47,395	50,985	47,562	3,027	3,185	2,905	6.4	6.2	6.1
Exports	58,829	57,475	49,731	13,440	13,593	11,965	22.8	23.6	24.1
Intercoastal	......	......	......	9,362	10,551	9,044	.....	.....	.....
Inbound	9,362	10,551	9,044	2,675	3,164	2,542	28.6	30.0	28.1
Outbound	9,362	10,551	9,044	6,687	7,387	6,502	71.4	70.0	71.9
With noncontiguous territories‖	4,483	4,309	4,715	2,763	2,814	2,893	61.6	65.3	61.4
Imports	2,348	2,234	2,622	1,521	1,555	1,566	64.8	69.6	52.1
Exports	2,135	2,075	2,093	1,242	1,259	1,327	58.2	60.7	62.9

* Data from United States Shipping Board. Coastwise trade other than from Atlantic and Gulf to Pacific and vice versa is not included.

† Continental United States.

‡ Duplication in intercoastal trade is eliminated.

§ In showing trade of Continental United States ports, Philippine Islands, Virgin Islands, and Canal Zone are included with foreign countries.

‖ Alaska, Hawaii, Puerto Rico, Guam, Samoa.

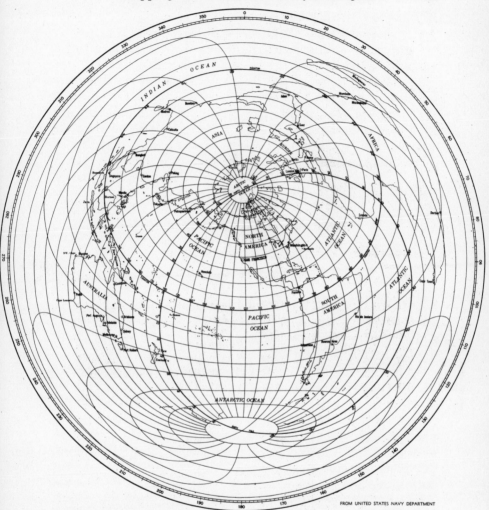

Fig. 4.—Sailing routes according to azimuth chart. Scale, one inch equals 5,000 statute miles.

seas foreign area in the trade of the Pacific Coast. Together, these regions account for approximately three-fourths of the total. If Australasia is added, the third most important factor, over four-fifths of the Coast's overseas foreign commerce, in volume as well as in value, is accounted for. Latin-American countries follow in the order shown in Figure 6 (p. 31),

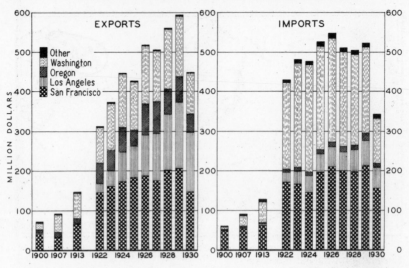

F_{IG}. 5.—Value of exports and general imports at Pacific Coast customs districts, 1900–1930.

which depicts the relative importance on a tonnage basis of the general world areas with which the Pacific Coast states have commercial relations.

Commodities involved in these various trades, the changes during the past decade in the movements in both directions, together with trends showing the relative importance of regions, are discussed in detail in subsequent chapters. In passing, it is desired only to point out that the combined movement reflects the system of economic specialization, prevalent in most of the world today, whereby the surplus output of commodities which can be produced at the greatest actual or relative advantage is exchanged for similar surpluses produced elsewhere. The character of these opposite streams of trade is naturally modified by restrictive legislation in the several countries. To date, outward shipments from the American Pacific States region are mainly primary products, including foodstuffs (Table 6, p. 32). Among receipts are found a wide variety of manufactured products and certain raw materials which cannot be obtained locally. In contrast, no one or two commodities dominate the inbound movement.

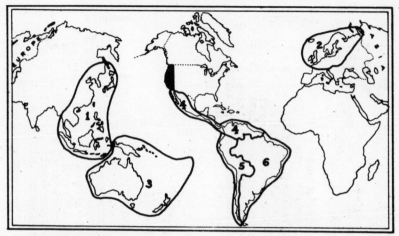

Fig. 6.—Relative importance of overseas foreign regions in the trade of United States Pacific states area.

	COMBINED IMPORTS AND EXPORTS	
	Total Dry Cargo	Value of Total Cargo
1. Eastern Asia (China, Japan, the Philippines, and the East Indies)	45.6%	55.9%
2. Atlantic Europe (United Kingdom, Havre-Hamburg range, and Baltic Europe)............	27.9%	21.6%
3. Australasia (Australia, New Zealand)..........	8.7%	6.0%
4. Mexico, Central America, and north coast of South America	4.9%	6.4%
5. West coast of South America..................	4.6%	2.4%
6. East coast of South America..................	3.0%	2.9%
7. Other regions	5.3%	4.8%
	100.0%	100.0%

Incoming cargoes from foreign countries are of great diversity, since the whole world is drawn upon to supply the requirements of a region advanced in material civilization and cosmopolitan in population. Even with the adoption of a commodity classification which combines many related products it is necessary to list a large number of such groups before even half the volume of imports into Pacific ports is represented. In value of imports, however, there is a somewhat greater concentration, but it is not possible to name the two or three most important commodities in import trade, because those which lead in volume are far down the

TABLE 6

Principal Commodities Imported and Exported, Pacific District, 1922–1930*

(In thousand cargo tons, 2,240 pounds)

Commodities	1922	1923	1924	1925	1926	1927	1928	1929	1930
Imports									
All commodities	1,431	2,322	2,559	2,534	2,610	2,815	2,885	3,112	3,176
Sugar and molasses	51	109	76	101	74	89	104	113	119
Paper stock	16	30	36	44	43	45	49	74	74
Coal and coke	211	297	134	160	177	155	132	120	127
Ores and metals (crude)	139	142	183	212	261	302	297	271	317
Logs and lumber	96	283	467	362	364	390	345	341	414
Nitrates, potash, fertilizer	55	102	80	87	99	109	105	133	118
Vegetables and products	100	157	144	217	174	167	217	282	277
Fruits and nuts	91	146	140	164	179	197	252	317	270
Coffee	71	70	80	68	75	70	83	77	78
Paper manufactures	69	119	137	127	114	125	133	110	134
Iron and steel	40	89	71	39	43	178	146	169	127
Chemicals	34	25	15	53	47	21	22	25	38
Other metals and manufactures	..†	112‡	214‡	172‡	187‡	137	127	120	110
Meat, fish, and dairy products	12	42	34	48	49	43	62	67	78
Jute manufactures	37	36	41	31	42	31	42	23	23
Exports									
All commodities	5,222	6,544	9,500	8,505	9,909	12,004	13,926	13,498	13,345
Tanker cargoes	946	2,748	4,114	4,031	4,573	5,905	6,833	6,340	6,869
Grain	1,564	902	1,111	686	855	1,222	1,509	1,010	900
Flour	329	395	585	215	237	258	328	411	350
Ores and metals	132	52	53	52	102	145	43	25	68
Petroleum products	59	168	263	421	476	525	626	707	856
Logs and lumber	1,521	1,450	2,461	2,084	2,556	2,751	3,328	3,377	2,925
Vegetables and products	69	49	26	26	37	43	43	67	45
Meat, fish, and dairy products	44	92	102	125	123	132	99	128	123
Fruits and nuts	111	218	214	261	319	378	404	578	392
Cotton	55	27	88	66	50	83	29	76	96
Copper	..†	37	59	84	90	23	87	84	53
Chemicals	18	34	37	37	36	38	85	99	133
Machinery and vehicles	12	20	52	25	30	42	45	59	53
Paper	..§	..§	..§	..§	..§	69	81	99	110
Iron and steel	13	10	30	6	7	32	57	58	41

* Fiscal years. Data from United States Shipping Board.　　§ Not given for years noted.

† Less than one thousand tons.　　‡ Figures are for copper only.

list in rank by value, while those of greatest aggregate value do not bulk very large in terms of volume (see Appendix Tables VIII and IX).

RELATIVE IMPORTANCE OF OVERSEAS REGIONS, PACIFIC DISTRICT,
FISCAL YEAR ENDING JUNE 30, 1930*

(Tons)

	All Imports†	All Exports	Tanker Exports
United Kingdom	83,940	2,249,311	1,014,104
North Atlantic and Baltic Europe	73,530	52,952	7,700
Havre–Hamburg	504,667	896,823	355,268
South Atlantic–Europe	3,914	67,226	46,768
West Mediterranean	25,878	63,677	.....
East Mediterranean and Black Sea	25	18,864	10,644
West Indies	21,716	120,553	96,755
Mexico	101,293	345,291	228,988
Central America	122,408	630,962	505,391
North coast of South America....	23,246	5,038	.....
East coast of South America.....	61,993	350,622	203,884
West coast of South America.....	212,139	1,031,601	762,317
West Africa	.....	.....	3,000
South and East Africa...........	251	50,690	10,362
Australasia	64,149	1,294,580	600,563
East Indies	77,496	189,417	55,871
India, Persian Gulf, and Red Sea	64,748	86,014	7,533
East Asia	845,279	4,692,292	1,951,405
Pacific Canada	870,565	1,185,983	997,835
Atlantic Canada and Newfoundland	18,464	10,300	10,300
Grand total	3,175,701	13,345,196	6,868,688

* Data from United States Shipping Board.
† Tankers accounted for merely 76,380 tons.

The outstanding factor in the tremendous growth in volume of exports from Pacific ports in so short a term of years is the rapid development of the southern California oil fields. Nearly three-fourths of the total tonnage gain registered in exports has been due to this single commodity. In 1922, tanker cargoes constituted less than one-sixth of total exports from Pacific Coast ports; in 1925 they amounted to nearly one-half of this volume; and in 1930 they amounted to over one-half the aggregate tanker and non-tanker exports (see also Appendix Table VIII).

The great importance of this oil to shipping far more than offsets the disadvantage of the increasing disparity in westbound and eastbound cargoes, which has been the principal contributing cause of the growing tonnage difference. Ever since the sailing vessel was driven from the seas by steam, fuel has been a factor in the determination of trade routes. The development of oil-burning steamships and motor ships has meant that abundant oil-bunkering facilities on a route are now generally of greater significance than abundant coal. The great size of the Pacific means long trade routes: from San Francisco, for example, Yokohama is 4,536 nautical miles away, nearly twice the distance from Halifax to London; Honolulu is 2,091 miles; Sydney is 6,744 miles; and Panama is 3,256 miles.[11] With coal as the fuel, much income-producing cargo space had to be utilized for storing sufficient fuel, sometimes enough to make a round trip, because of inadequate coal-bunkering facilities. With oil, bunkering for the whole trip is entirely feasible because not only is less weight in fuel required for the same trip but also oil may be stored in spaces not available for cargo. Labor and operating costs also are reduced. The immense petroleum resources of the American Pacific Coast are thus a factor of incalculable importance to the profitable pursuit of trade and shipping in the Pacific Basin.

In the merchant shipping business there are other very real and pressing problems. No cost-reducing expedients or efficiency-increasing instruments can solve the problem of a great excess in world shipping tonnage above the requirements of trade. Low operating costs and subsidies are elements in the situation, but they are only the determinants of survival, i.e., which ships will continue in business and under what flags they will operate. The World War offers a facile means of accounting for almost any current development in political, social, and economic activities. It did, as a matter of fact, contribute to the importance of the Pacific Basin, but it is also responsible for the unhealthy condition of world maritime shipping today.

11 See map of sailing distances, Fig. 4.

The seaports of England and Western Europe, prior to the war, had built up an immense warehouse, or entrepôt, trade. To a considerable extent the exchangeable surpluses from the far corners of the world were brought there and redistributed in accordance with regional needs. For over four years war interfered seriously with this type of enterprise. In consequence, regions of mutual surplus and deficiency established direct trade connections with each other, as exemplified by Australian wool, rubber from Malaya and Netherland India, and spices from many tropical lands. The closing of the Suez route in particular diverted streams of commerce to transpacific lanes. Two of the leading world powers, Japan and the United States, were also Pacific powers, and their comparatively slight preoccupation with the war throughout the greater part of its duration left them free to avail themselves of commercial opportunities created by the absorption of European energies in this conflict. The Panama Canal, which became available just as the war was in its beginnings, reinforced these developments.

The growth of maritime commerce on the West Coast is partly a reflection of population increases, but even more it represents the steady development of new trade routes made possible by the Panama Canal, which stimulates not only direct trade with Europe, with the Caribbean, and with the east coast of South America, but in addition transpacific shuttle services with intercoastal transshipment via Panama for goods destined for, or leaving, points on the Eastern seaboard. Such transshipment finds its economic justification in the fact that vessels not suitable for the long transpacific routes may be advantageously used for the intercoastal leg of the journey.

Rapid growth in population and consequent economic development on the Pacific Coast of the United States, and to a less extent in Canada, Mexico, and Central America, have played an important part in bringing to an end the long preoccupation of the people of the United States with lands bordering on the Atlantic. Population on the Pacific Coast has grown more rapidly in recent years than in any other part of the United States. Statistics show that in California alone the gain in population was 2,401,288 in the ten years

ending 1930. Likewise manufacturing development has progressed phenomenally; branch plants of Eastern and Mid-
western companies have been established on the Coast to
serve the expanding domestic market and also to be advantageously situated for trade with the inviting Pacific world
outside.

Increasing density of population under the Western
scheme of life almost inevitably brings industrialization and
an abandonment of that economic self-sufficiency by which
a simpler social organization can maintain itself. Industrialization, in turn, certain to foster commercial intercourse
with outside areas, creates the characteristic interdependence of regions where the economic life is based on an
advanced development of the division of labor. This international division of labor depends upon many things. It is
influenced, for example, by the distribution of natural resources, the scale of production, the proprietary control of
machinery and instruments of transport, the tariff policies
of the trading countries, and the state of the currency.

Some of the more fundamental of these factors will be
examined in subsequent chapters. Some are permanent influences shaping the character of commercial activity and
intercourse, such as the distribution of natural resources.
Others are inconstant in character, such as the currency and
tariff policies. Just now, as the nations of the world are in
the throes of an economic depression of a magnitude and
severity seldom if ever experienced before, the two factors
just mentioned loom exceedingly large. The fall in world
prices of commodities has affected all trade statistics expressed in terms of value, but the abandonment of the gold
standard by practically all of the world has created temporary perhaps but certainly severe problems for farmers,
manufacturers, foreign traders, and shipowners of all countries. Nationalism at present dominates world politics.

Before one has gone very far in a study of the maritime
problems of the American Pacific States this matter of competition assumes sizable proportions. Competition takes on
various aspects, involving regions, carriers, and commodities. Economic principles involving joint cost and substitute
products can never be overlooked. Competition in its many

aspects and ramifications is woven through all discussion of economic activity, especially trade. Since the World War, all nations have entered a period of even more intensified economic competition. True, a few strong nations take the lead and others must follow in self-defense. Witness the disastrous results of the short-sighted tariff policy of the United States, and the newfangled uses of quotas, embargoes, and other governmental devices to retard the natural flow of world commodities. In the short space of a few years almost insurmountable barriers have been built around most of the countries of the world. Trade is discouraged and shipping business lags.[12]

Without mention of further complicating factors, for enough have been mentioned to show that a study of the maritime intercourse of the American Pacific area cannot be made without regard to the multitude of economic and social forces at work in the world, we may now tie together a few threads of introductory thought.

It cannot be denied that the center of the world's trade is definitely shifting to the Pacific, and with accelerating speed. Between 1910–11 and 1928–29, exports from Europe to the United States increased 169 per cent and United States exports to Europe increased 185 per cent; at the same time imports from Asia increased 563 per cent and exports to Asia 806 per cent.[13] This growth in trade was not accompanied or caused by a corresponding increase in population. It did, however, follow significant developments in means of transportation and communication. The facilities of commerce increased in number and efficiency, but still transpacific cables are scarce in comparison with the number across the Atlantic and press rates on the Pacific are eight times higher. The radio has now been added to the cable, and steamships

[12] Another form of this economic warfare and a current expression of nationalistic tendencies is the scramble for control of such commodities as oil and rubber. Governments are participating more directly than ever in this game, and raw materials are becoming increasingly the stakes of diplomacy. Railway and mining concessions are other objects creating competition of one form or another between nations and generating their share of distrust and ill-will.

[13] Although European trade has declined in relative importance, it still dominates United States foreign trade.

have multiplied, but distances across the Pacific are still great despite the fact that freight and passenger vessels from Tokyo to New York cover the distance in less than three weeks, whereas eighty-five years ago it required from eight months to two years to travel between the Pacific Basin and New York or London.

It is reasonable to expect the great increase in United States trade with Asiatic countries to be reflected in the commerce of Pacific ports. Yokohama is 12,273 nautical miles from London and 9,656 from New York, but only 4,500 miles from North American Pacific ports. Largely because of the distance factor, the Coast states must inevitably acquire an increasing percentage of the Pacific trade expansion. This has occurred and is occurring now. Despite disturbed world economic conditions which have resulted in drastic declines in general world trade, the record of transpacific commerce is superior to that of other trades. The dollar value of United States exports to all markets declined one-third in 1931 as compared with 1930, but exports to all Asiatic countries fell off only 19 per cent and those to India, China, and Japan decreased only 10 per cent. From the standpoint of volume, American exports declined by more than 20 per cent from 1930 to 1931, but the combined exports to British India, China, and Japan registered an actual gain of more than 6 per cent.

The growth in importance of the Pacific area in trade and that of the American sector of this area, it has been observed, has not taken place without the introduction of new problems. As the East and the West are brought closer together these complicating factors are bound to appear. It is only by an intelligent appreciation of these problems and by honest grappling with them that satisfactory trade relations will result. As the Pacific steadily increases its participation in the world's maritime commerce, it is likewise participating in the wider drama of human history. If the Orient is open to influence from the industrial civilization evolved in Western Europe and the United States, the same contact which brings that influence opens the West to modification by the East. The comparative freedom and ease of travel today is breaking down the barriers of cultural isolation, just as improvements in transportation for commodities have broken down economic frontiers.

Western United States is thus greatly deserving of study not only because of its own unquestioned place in world economy but also because it is the most progressive section

TABLE 7

RANKING OF PACIFIC CUSTOMS DISTRICTS IN TRADE WITH FOREIGN
COUNTRIES, BY COMMODITY VALUE, 1930*

Country	Los Angeles		San Francisco		Oregon		Washington	
	Exports	Imports	Exports	Imports	Exports	Imports	Exports	Imports
Europe								
Azores and Madeira..............	..	..	..	2	..	..	..	..
Czechoslovakia	..	..	2	..	5	..	..	..
Denmark	..	..	5	5	..	..	..	..
Finland	..	..	5	..	..	..	..	..
France	..	..	..	5	..	..	..	..
Gibraltar	2	..	3	..	..	..	..	..
Greece	..	..	5	..	..	..	..	..
Irish Free State.................	..	..	5	..	2	..	..	..
Italy	..	..	..	5	..	..	..	..
Malta, Gozo, Cyprus............	3	..	..	..	4	..	..	..
Netherlands	..	..	..	..	..	..	5	..
Norway	..	..	4	..	..	..	5	..
Poland	..	4	5	..	4	..	..	..
Rumania	2	..	3	..	..	..	..	..
Sweden	..	..	5	..	..	..	..	..
Switzerland	5	..	4	..	..	..	..	..
United Kingdom	5	..	..	5	..	..	..	..
North America								
Canada	..	..	..	..	..	..	..	5
Central America	..	..	..	..	..	..	..	..
Costa Rica	5	4	3	2	..	..	..	..
El Salvador	4	2	2	1	..	..	..	5
Guatemala	4	4	3	3	..	..	..	..
Honduras	4	..	3	..	..	..	..	..
Nicaragua	..	5	3	2	..	..	..	..
Panama	3	3	5	4	2	..	..	..
Mexico	5	..	..	..	..	..	..	..
West Indies								
Trinidad and Tobago..........	3	..	..	5	..	..	..	..
Dominican Republic	..	..	..	4	..	..	..	..
Netherland West Indies.......	4	..	..	..	..	..	..	..

* Calendar year. Data from Bureau of Foreign and Domestic Commerce.

TABLE 7 (*Continued*)

Country	Los Angeles		San Francisco		Oregon		Washington	
	Ex-ports	Im-ports	Ex-ports	Im-ports	Ex-ports	Im-ports	Ex-ports	Im-ports
South America								
Argentina	3	..	..	..	..	..	..	..
Bolivia	5	..	4	..	..	..	..	..
Brazil	..	..	..	3	..	..	..	..
Chile	2	..	..	..	..	..	..	3
Colombia	5	5	3	2	..	..	..	..
Ecuador	..	4	4	3	..	..	3	..
Paraguay	4	2	3	4	..	..	..	..
Peru	..	..	3	2	4	..	2	..
Asia								
Arabia	..	..	3	..	2	..	..	..
British India	2	..	..	5	..	..	..	..
British Malaya	3	2	2	4	..	..	..	..
Ceylon	5	5	2	3	..	..	..	..
China	4	..	5	2	..	..	..	3
Netherland East Indies								
Java and Madura	4	..	2	5	..	..	..	..
Other Netherland East Indies	2	..	3	3	..	4	..	..
Hong Kong	3	5	4	2	5	..	1	..
Iraq	2	5	3	..	..	..	..	..
Japan	3	..	5	3	..	..	4	2
Kwantung	5	5	4	3	2	4	1	1
Persia	2	..	5	..	..	..	..	..
Philippine Islands	4	..	2	3	..	..	3	..
Siam	4	5	2	2	..	..	3	..
Asiatic Soviet Union	4	..	2	..	..	..	1	3
Oceania								
Australia	4	..	2	3	..	..	..	..
British Oceania	..	2	1	1	3	3	4	..
French Oceania	4	..	1	1	5	..	2	..
New Zealand	3	..	2	3	..	..	..	..
Africa								
British Africa—East	..	4	3	5	..	..	..	..
Gold Coast	3	..	..	..	..	..	..	..
Nigeria	4	..	..	..	..	..	..	..
Algeria and Tunisia	..	..	..	5	..	..	..	..
Other French Africa	..	..	..	5	..	..	..	..

of the nation. The present study undertakes to comprehend one conspicuous feature of the economic life of the American Pacific Coast. This region, cut off from easy land communi-

TABLE 8

RELATIVE IMPORTANCE OF ATLANTIC, GULF, AND PACIFIC DISTRICTS,
IMPORTS AND EXPORTS WITH FOREIGN REGIONS, TOTAL AND
NON-TANKER CARGO, 1930*

(Thousand long tons)

Foreign Regions		Imports			Exports		
		Atlantic	Gulf	Pacific	Atlantic	Gulf	Pacific
Total cargoes, all regions.....................		34,940	5,636	3,176	15,457	15,571	13,345
Non-tanker cargoes, all regions...............		20,900	3,501	3,099	14,031	8,518	6,477
United Kingdom	Total	1,358	129	84	2,580	3,104	2,249
	Non-tanker	1,333	30	66	2,213	1,408	1,235
North Atlantic and Baltic Europe	Total	1,500	37	74	682	954	53
	Non-tanker	1,486	37	74	574	382	45
Havre-Hamburg Range	Total	2,482	604	505	2,812	4,482	897
	Non-tanker	2,414	490	468	2,258	2,389	542
South Atlantic Europe	Total	593	23	4	193	566	68
	Non-tanker	593	23	4	114	235	20
West Mediterranean	Total	1,019	77	26	1,252	1,392	64
	Non-tanker	1,019	65	26	1,155	812	64
East Mediterranean and Black Sea	Total	757	26	...†	419	245	19
	Non-tanker	752	10	...†	419	217	8
West Indies	Total	9,572	1,903	22	1,715	1,580	121
	Non-tanker	3,133	787	22	1,675	678	24
Mexico	Total	1,408	727	101	157	131	345
	Non-tanker	128	196	99	157	113	116
Central America	Total	640	669	122	468	253	631
	Non-tanker	640	660	122	668	197	126
North Coast South America	Total	5,974	481	23	299	88	5
	Non-tanker	231	350	23	299	68	5
East Coast South America	Total	1,440	242	62	1,504	740	351
	Non-tanker	1,436	242	62	1,485	604	147
West Coast South America	Total	2,923	272	212	308	54	1,032
	Non-tanker	2,602	272	212	308	51	269
South and East Africa	Total	303	12	...†	309	150	51
	Non-tanker	303	1	...†	248	112	40
Australasia	Total	262	22	64	298	138	1,295
	Non-tanker	243	11	64	298	138	694
East Indies	Total	734	64	77	254	...†	189
	Non-tanker	663	3	77	254	...†	134
East Africa	Total	950	128	845	1,098	911	4,692
	Non-tanker	900	106	826	1,098	877	2,741
India, Persian Gulf, and Red Sea	Total	756	125	65	199	46	86
	Non-tanker	756	125	65	199	11	78
Pacific Canada	Total	355	12	871	17	25	1,186
	Non-tanker	355	12	871	17	25	188
Atlantic Canada and Newfoundland	Total	1,642	61	18	686	671	10
	Non-tanker	1,641	61	18	613	167	...
West Africa	Total	271	20	...	208	43	3
	Non-tanker	266	20	...	178	33	...

* Fiscal year. Data from United States Shipping Board.
† Less than one thousand long tons.

cation eastward by mountains and deserts (see Frontispiece), has found its destinies peculiarly tied up with the
sea. Even the completion of the transcontinental railway in
1869 and the subsequent addition of some half-dozen other
rail routes giving overland access to the East have lessened
but not destroyed its supreme dependence on the Pacific
Ocean. Its products were, and to a considerable extent still
are, crude materials, for which the effective area of distribution is narrowly limited without cheap ocean shipping.
A perusal of Table 7 discloses the ranking of the Pacific Coast
customs districts in American foreign trade, while Table 8
provides comparative information upon three continental
coastal districts.

The sea is the focusing point for our study of the development of American foreign trade. Over four-fifths of United
States imports and exports enter and leave the country by
vessel—a ratio which is somewhat higher than for the combined world foreign trade. The development of the Pacific
Coast is principally a maritime orientation now as always,
and with the growth in population and material wealth
which is inevitable, ocean shipping will become increasingly significant.

III. Geographical Influences

What is "Western United States"? The answer is not simple, since one's personal background molds so largely the conception of direction and distance. Within the borders of the United States there can be no question regarding the inclusion of the coast states of Washington, Oregon, and California, or the interior states of Montana, Idaho, Wyoming, Nevada, Utah, Colorado, New Mexico, and Arizona. There are, to be sure, some features in common between these Far Western states and those classified in the federal census as the West North Central (Minnesota, Iowa, Missouri, North Dakota, South Dakota, Nebraska, and Kansas) and the West South Central (Arkansas, Louisiana, Oklahoma, and Texas); but, perhaps arbitrarily, the writer has excluded this central area from his conception of "Western United States" and has confined his consideration to the eleven Pacific and Mountain states, together with the two noncontiguous territories of Alaska and Hawaii.[1]

This Western region comprises nearly half the total area of continental United States and incorporated territories, but includes only one-tenth of their total population.[2] On the basis of population density this region ranks low in comparison with the rest of the United States. Yet this very fact is an index to the tremendous possibilities for growth in the number of its inhabitants (Table 9). True, millions of acres of the western border are incapable of supporting human life, but the vast remaining lands offer a potential habitation for many times their present number. Little Hawaii, with her system of plantation economy, already has one of the

[1] There was solid truth rather than facetiousness in the following comment by Paul Shoup, president of the Southern Pacific Railway Company, at the annual meeting of the Chamber of Commerce of the United States held in San Francisco in May 1932: "The farther east one goes, the farther the West begins. I remember a gentleman in the Southern States telling that, having been born in New England, he felt assured as a boy that the West began in the western part of New York. He knew that to be the case because an Indian chief advised him that the Indians came out of the Rocky Mountains of Indiana and pursued the bison in the neighborhood of Lake Erie."

[2] See Table 1 (p. 13) and Fig. 7 (p. 45).

TABLE 9

POPULATION OF PACIFIC SEABOARD STATES AND NONCONTIGUOUS
TERRITORIES, 1850–1930*

Year	California	Oregon	Washington	Alaska	Hawaii
1850	92,597	13,294	.....	.....	......
1860	379,994	52,465	11,594	.....	......
1870	560,247	90,923	23,955	.....	......
1880	864,694	174,768	75,116	33,426	......
1890†	1,213,398	317,704	357,232	32,052	......
1900	1,485,053	413,536	518,103	63,592	154,001
1910	2,377,549	672,765	1,141,990	64,356	191,909
1920	3,426,861	783,389	1,356,621	55,036	255,912
1930	5,677,251	953,786	1,563,396	59,278	368,336

* Data from United States Census.

† Includes population (325,464) of Indian Territory and Indian reservations, specially enumerated in 1890 but not included in the general report on population for 1890.

densest populations of the world. The snow fields of Alaska must remain a barren waste, but the Pacific States, and to a much less degree the Mountain States, can accommodate a greatly increased population.

The total money cost of the Pacific States to the United States was less than $60,000,000. Historically, the Oregon Territory became a part of the Union through discovery and occupation; for the rest of the Pacific West the United States gave $27,267,622 for the Louisiana purchase, plus $25,000,000 for California and the rest of the Mexican cessions, plus $7,200,000 for Alaska. The Oregon Territory, the title to which was established in 1846, consisted of 286,541 square miles, while the Mexican cession (1848), which did not include the Texas annexation of 1845, amounted to 529,189 square miles. Out of this region California was admitted to statehood in 1850, Oregon in 1859, and Washington in 1889.

The Pacific littoral is of outstanding importance in any study of maritime commerce. The leading historian of the Pacific Coast, Hubert H. Bancroft, described in *The New Pacific* the setting of this virgin region at the close of the nineteenth century in the following terms:

The coast line of the United States on the Pacific and Arctic oceans is twice as long as that of the Atlantic. California has about 800 miles

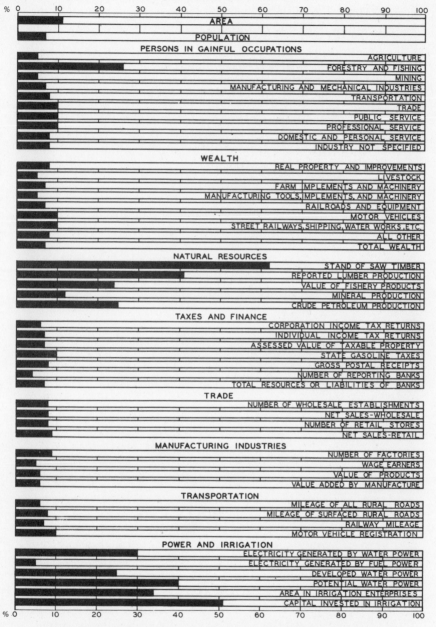

Fig. 7.—Statistics of three Pacific Coast states expressed as percentages of the total for United States. Data from Appendix Table I.

of coast line, with but few harbors as compared with those of the eastern side of America, or with those of the eastern side of Asia. Oregon's great harbor, the beautiful Columbia, extends hundreds of miles inland, while Washington, British Columbia, and Alaska, each has a plentiful supply of safe ports. Besides the harbors of San Francisco, San Diego, and Humboldt, there are many anchorages along the coast of California where vessels can lie in safety in calm weather.

It is of more than ordinary interest, therefore, to have available basic data for California, Oregon, Washington, Alaska, and Hawaii. Table 10, and detailed economic statistics which appear in Appendix Tables V and VI, should prove useful by providing area and population comparisons not only within this region but also with the developed New England and Middle Atlantic sections and entire continental United States.

TABLE 10

AREA AND POPULATION OF THE PACIFIC NORTHWEST BY PRINCIPAL
ECONOMIC DIVISIONS, 1930*

Section	Land Area		Population	
	Square Miles	Percentage of Total Northwest	Number	Percentage of Total Northwest
Western Washington ...	24,531	8.7	1,103,899	35.8
Eastern Washington ...	42,305	15.1	459,497	14.9
Western Oregon	29,460	10.5	770,813	25.0
Eastern Oregon	66,147	23.5	182,973	5.9
Northern Idaho	21,099	7.5	119,940	3.9
Southwestern Idaho	27,750	9.9	124,351	4.1
Western Montana	69,694	24.8	321,147	10.4
Total	280,986	100.0	3,082,620	100.0

* Data from *Commercial Survey of the Pacific Northwest* (1932), Bureau of Foreign and Domestic Commerce.

The significance of shape as an attribute of area is often overlooked, yet the distribution of the land and water mass is frequently of more significance than the aggregate number of square miles. Particularly is this factor consequential in the Pacific Empire, where Alaska is balanced on the Arctic Circle, Hawaii is by the Tropic of Cancer, Washington and Oregon are situated between latitude 42° and 49° and longi-

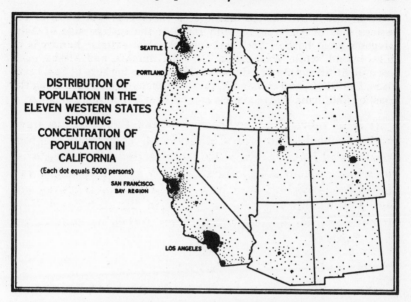

DISTRIBUTION OF
POPULATION IN THE
ELEVEN WESTERN STATES
SHOWING
CONCENTRATION OF
POPULATION IN
CALIFORNIA
(Each dot equals 5000 persons)

SEATTLE
PORTLAND
SAN FRANCISCO.
BAY REGION
LOS ANGELES

FIG. 8.—Map of eleven Western states showing density of population.

tude 116° and 125°, and California between latitude 32° and 42° and longitude 114° and 125°. The extreme east and west points in Washington are 360 miles apart, the north and south 240 miles apart; Oregon has a similar width but is less than 150 miles from north to south; and California has a breadth varying from 150 to 350 miles and an abrupt southeastern prolongation which places Los Angeles east of Reno, Nevada, giving a median length of about 780 miles, and a coastline of over 1,250 miles.

The areal extension and topography of California, which make possible nearly every conceivable climate, furnish the chief explanation of the ability of the state to grow nearly every type of temperate and subtropical crop. They largely explain the diversity of California's economic life in contrast to that of the other states of the Union (not excepting Texas) and the Pacific Northwest. Thus, Dr. E. D. Merrill, former Dean of the College of Agriculture of the University of California, has stated that, in the development of California agriculture, which has been limited to a period of seventy-five years, it is noteworthy that, with the exception of sugar cane, every major crop grown from Maine to Texas is cultivated in California.

Far Western topographical conditions have a most direct influence upon methods of transport (see Frontispiece). The lofty Sierra and the Rocky Mountains are natural barriers to overland communication between the Pacific Coast and the rest of the United States, in spite of the fact that the historical development of the country as a whole has been typically in an east-and-west rather than a north-and-south direction. The traffic situation on the Pacific Coast is distinctive, since the Sierra and the Rocky Mountains extend in a general north-and-south direction and act as barriers to the easy movement of commodities on an east-and-west course, while the all-water boundary of the Pacific Coast states produces sharp competition between rail and water carriers on the Pacific route.[3] As a result of the frequent and adequate coastwise service between the Canadian and the Mexican border, the railway rates between focal points such as San Francisco and Los Angeles are sometimes less than to intermediate points. There is a certain amount of freight, however, particularly of a high-grade or perishable character, which is transported by railways within the Pacific district. A recent development of marked and growing importance, however, is the truck-handling of agricultural products to terminals in competition with the railways. To illustrate, apple receipts at Seattle during the 1932–33 season for transshipment by water amounted to 588 thousand boxes by truck from Yakima, compared to 110 thousand boxes the previous season; and from Wenatchee this movement amounted to 239 thousand boxes in 1932–33, compared to 12 thousand in 1931–32. This new departure is all the more significant in that splendid roads have made possible the carrying of this fruit by highway over mountainous country.

The states west of the Mississippi River, generally speaking, are served more cheaply from the Pacific Coast than from the Atlantic Coast. The population living in the Great Plains constitutes approximately one-fifth of the population of the United States. The trade advantage of the Pacific

[3] S. Daggett, *Principles of Inland Transportation* (1928), chapter xi.

Coast states is far more marked in the case of the eight inter-mountain states situated between the Great Plains and the Coast, namely, Montana, Idaho, Wyoming, Nevada, Utah, Colorado, New Mexico, and Arizona. From the standpoint of either geography or economics the state lines are unsatisfactory measuring units, since resources and occupations are governed by regional rather than political boundaries.

Some measure of the vast extent and latent possibilities of the eleven Far Western states can be gained from the latest census figures: with an area amounting to 38.2 per cent and a population 9.1 per cent of that of the entire United States, this region accounts for 13.7 per cent in value of crops, 15.7 per cent in mines and quarry products, 9.9 per cent of the number of manufacturing establishments, 6.6 per cent of the wage-earners, 8.3 per cent of the primary horse-power, 7.2 per cent of the value of products, and 42.9 per cent of the lumber production, while possessing 98.7 per cent of United States standing timber, 16.9 per cent of its railroads, 17.8 per cent of its highways, and 13.5 per cent of its automobile registrations. Of the tangible wealth of the United States, 11.6 per cent is found in these Western states, with 8.4 per cent of the bank resources and liabilities, while 22,452 manufacturing plants spend $3,100,000,000 for cost of raw material, and retail purchases total $6,900,000,000 for the nearly 12 million population.[4] This Western region constitutes a geographic unit. True, the interior states have four seasons, the Coast states mainly two; and the former consist largely of plateaus and mountains, with desert areas and isolated fertile lands, while the latter have a topography of even loftier mountain-peaks, deserts, land below sea-level, and valleys composed of marvelously rich soil. Also the average elevation of the interior states is about 4,000 feet, compared to approximately 1,000 feet for the Coast states. Yet, despite the abundant rainfall west of the Cascades, not only their eastern slopes but the West as a whole is seriously deficient in rainfall; hence the need of irrigation and dry farming over most of the area.

4 The foregoing statistics obviously take no account of the outlying possessions, which are properly included in the American Pacific Empire.

These eleven Western states are likewise a fairly homogeneous economic unit. The Mountain states are the great grazing and mining sections of the country. The spring-wheat region of the Dakotas extends westward through Montana, Idaho, Washington, and Oregon. The forest, hay, and pasture industries of the Pacific Northwest are continued far into the western half of California, and the coast and interior valleys of the Golden State right to the Mexican border provide the rich Pacific subtropical crop region. Timberlands and hydroelectric supply abound in the Pacific Northwest and in California. Metallic mining is still an active industry in California. For the region at large, coal in Wyoming, Utah, and Colorado (with an inferior grade in the Northwest) and petroleum in California furnish other leading sources of energy.

Statistics are not needed to show that this Western area is clearly a geographical entity, that its economic and social existence is governed by regional rather than political boundaries, and that its future development is based primarily upon co-operative effort rather than upon rivalry in all lines of productive enterprise.

No better indication of the areal unity of Western United States can be evidenced than the extremely intimate and natural connections between the mainland and the far-off territories of arctic Alaska and tropical Hawaii. The industrial, trade, and shipping channels are predominantly with the Coast states.

Another feature of the region is its geographical concentration. The topography limits the number and character of transportation routes as well as the distribution of population. The length of the tide shoreline from Mexico to British Columbia is 3,765 statute miles,[5] yet six ports (Los Angeles, Port San Luis, San Francisco, Portland, Tacoma, and Seattle) in the fiscal year 1931 handled 87 per cent of the volume of foreign exports, and six ports (Los Angeles, San

---

[5] Detailed figures are California 1,555, Oregon 489, and Washington 1,721 statute miles. The tide shoreline of the United States Atlantic Coast is 11,679, and that of the Gulf Coast 6,418 statute miles. Corresponding figures are 15,132 statute miles for Alaska (a figure similar to that for the Atlantic and Pacific mainland coasts combined) and 810 statute miles for Hawaii.

Francisco, Portland, Tacoma, Port Angeles, and Seattle) handled 95 per cent of the imports. Other evidences of concentration appear in the few centers of large population. According to the last official census there are only six cities (Los Angeles, San Francisco, Oakland, Seattle, Portland, and Denver) of over 250,000 people, and but five other cities (San Diego, Long Beach, Salt Lake City, Spokane, and Tacoma) of more than 100,000 population. In this western section San Francisco occupies the most central position,[6] with other metropolitan cities, including Seattle, Spokane, Portland, Los Angeles, San Diego, Denver, and Salt Lake City, serving as increasingly important focal points.

With what resources is the American Pacific area endowed? What supports its population; what has contributed toward its development; and what does it produce in sufficient quantities to bring about a surplus that may be exchanged with other peoples, other countries, for commodities which they may be in a more advantageous position to produce? What are these commodities? In other words, what does the region possess in greater abundance than can be consumed by its people and what does it need from outside sources either to sustain life according to present standards of living or to extend economic activity?

Plants of one kind or another furnish about 73 per cent of the value of the chief products of the world, and animals account for another 15 per cent, so that about 88 per cent of all primary production is closely dependent upon climate, relief, and soil.[7] The chief elements of climate are temperature and rainfall. Temperature is dependent upon latitude and altitude, as modified by sea and land breezes. The relative positions of mountain ranges and sea breezes determine rainfall. Climate, then, may be said to be a joint product of latitude, altitude, ocean currents, winds, and mountain-range location. Although topography, taken in connection with existing wind and ocean currents, is largely responsible for diverse, sharp contrasts, the height and direction of the

---

[6] San Francisco is 2,408 statute miles from Honolulu, 1,499 statute miles from Sitka, 946 miles from Denver, 592 miles from Salt Lake City, 521 miles from San Diego, and 926 from Seattle.

[7] E. Huntington and F. E. Williams, *Business Geography* (1926), p. 15.

mountain systems in the various parts of this coastal region have more influence upon local climate, both rainfall and temperature, than has the latitude.

Perhaps no region presents such marked climatic contrasts in such close proximity as does the Pacific West. To the stranger the rapid changes are almost unbelievable. Dr. O. E. Baker, recent president of the Association of American Geographers, vividly describes the situation thus:

The Pacific coast is a unique part of North America—in mildness of climate, in magnificence of scenery, in majesty of forests, in kinds of crops grown, and, to a lesser extent, in the character of the people and their attitude toward life. Passing over the mountains from the hot Imperial Valley, occupying the Colorado River delta, with its cotton and cantaloupes, grown largely by aid of Mexican labor, to San Diego and Los Angeles, with their balmy and equable climate, their art and culture, is like going from Egypt to Italy. Likewise, climbing over the mountains from Reno, Nevada, to Sacramento and San Francisco, is almost like an airplane trip from Angora, Turkey, to Milan and Bordeaux, but briefer. Farther north, the traveler crossing the Cascade Mountains from the Yakima or Wenatchee valleys to the Puget Sound cities will find the change in climate as great as in going from Tashkent to Liverpool or Glasgow, but the trip requires only a few hours. Still farther north, traveling from Edmonton, Alberta, to Prince Rupert, British Columbia, is like a journey from Samara or Kazan, U.S.S.R., to the west coast of Norway.[8]

The entire American Pacific slope, for a varying distance inland, falls under the benign influence of the Pacific Ocean, avoiding extremes of heat and cold. This moderating influence is felt from the coastal plain of Alaska on the north, where the waters of the Japan Current give southern Alaska a warmer winter than Washington, D.C., down to San Diego with its monthly mean temperature varying only from 54.3° in January to 68.7° in August. As a result, these Pacific Coast seaports are never icebound, and enjoy uninterrupted navigation throughout the year.

High mountain walls rim the Pacific on its eastern side, leaving only a narrow strip between mountain and sea. In consequence, the land areas draining into the immense Pacific Basin are comparatively limited, being, in fact, only one-fourth as extensive as those draining into the Atlantic;

[8] O. E. Baker, "Agricultural Regions of North America," *Economic Geography*, April 1930.

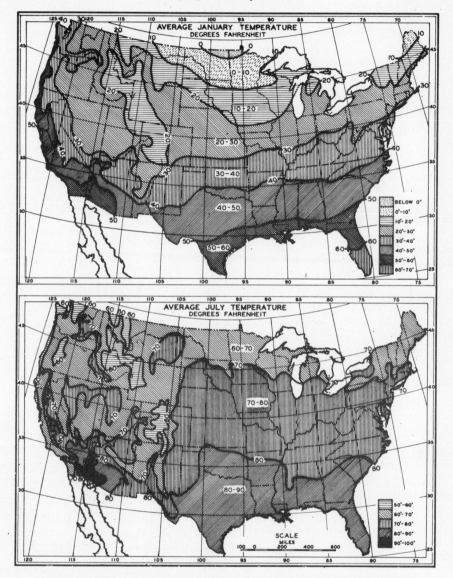

Fig. 9.—Map showing temperatures in United States for January and July.

yet the Pacific Ocean itself covers more than one-third of the entire surface of the earth—an area greater than that occupied by all land now above the level of the sea. This system of highlands crosses over from Asia in the north, following the Aleutian volcanic chain, and makes its appearance at the Alaska mountains, which closely parallel the shore, but then breaks into two ridges which follow the entire coastal strip of Pacific North America to the end of Lower California. The easterly line appears in northwestern United States as the Cascade Mountains; in California the continuation of the same system is known as the Sierra. Between these elevations and the continuous coastal ranges lie a series of north-south valleys, including the Puget Sound depression area and the Sacramento, San Joaquin, and Imperial valleys, which, together with numerous smaller lateral valleys adjacent, provide the principal agricultural areas of the Pacific Coast states.[9]

The influence of these mountain systems on climatic conditions and hence on economic resources of the region can hardly be exaggerated. They arrest the moisture-laden winds from the Pacific, exacting from them, especially in the more northerly latitudes, a heavy precipitation on seaward slopes. The Cascades and the Sierra store up a wealth of summer irrigation water and of hydroelectric power in the huge snow packs which gradually melt and provide a run-off in months of scanty or no precipitation. The gentle upward slope of the Sierra on their western side serves to extract the greatest possible rainfall for the land on the ocean side of their ridges. Were it not for the Sierra Nevada most of California would be a desert land. At the same time they shut out the cold winter winds from the north and the east and thus permit the tempering effect of the ocean to bring mild winters. One striking result is a citrus belt in the Sacramento Valley, in the latitude of New York, where, in fact, oranges ripen earlier than they do four hundred miles to the south.

High land immediately adjacent to the American Pacific Coast is responsible in large part, also, for the comparative infrequency of good natural harbors. The gradually sloping coastal plain of the Atlantic Basin contains many rivers of

[9] The northerly valleys are the result of subsidence of the earth's crust, while those of California were once arms of the Pacific Ocean and have gradually been filled up with soil washed down from the mountains on either side.

large size which empty into the sea and which provide at their mouths excellent harbors. On the Pacific littoral, on the contrary, harbors of this character are almost entirely lacking. The Columbia River system alone provides comparable facilities, and even in this case the mouth of the river is not suitable for an ocean port, with the result that the maritime outlet for the basin is upstream about one hundred miles from the open sea. Strictly speaking, therefore, there is no first-class natural *ocean* harbor from Puget Sound to San Francisco, a distance of some 767 miles. And from San Francisco southward it is necessary to sail about 450 miles before the attractive natural harbor of San Diego is encountered. Pacific South America is almost destitute of ports sheltered from the open sea. This geographic fact has had an important influence on the distribution of population and on land as well as ocean routes of communication.

In all of North and South America there are only seventeen land gateways into the Pacific, and of these the ten across the United States and Canada are the only ones which figure noticeably in international trade. In South America there are only two railways across the steep mountain slopes; in Panama there is only the short isthmus line, now of minor importance; in Central America and Mexico there are two roads each; in the United States, there are seven transcontinental arteries; and in Canada there are three. The relative amount of interference which these mountain ranges offer to land traffic is roughly proportional to the heights of the passes it is necessary to use. The Chile-Argentine line, for example, cost for construction over $300,000 a mile and faces an annual deficit despite high rates. The more recently completed Bolivian line presents the same condition. In comparison, the western mountain barriers of the United States are lofty but comparatively narrow. The Union Pacific, for example, cost only some $30,000 a mile to build.

The nautical geography of the Pacific States, which cannot be treated in detail in this study, must take account of the rugged and mountainous coast. Among the distinctive features of coastwise navigation are the depth of water, such that the 100-fathom curve lies at an average distance of less than 10 miles away from land, the difficulty of securing an-

chorage and shelter, the marked contrast in weather between
May to October and October to May, the temporary interference from fog, the marked contrast between tides during
the two high waters and the two low waters daily, and the
unusual variation in winds and currents.

Important as are the mountains in influencing the climate
of the American Pacific Coast region, latitude also affects
both temperature and rainfall. Roughly, between Sitka,
Alaska, and San Diego the rate of temperature change averages about .95° for each degree of latitude in January and
about .65° in July, and an annual average change of .8°.
What it means to the West Coast states to lie with the broad
Pacific Ocean to their windward may be appreciated by comparing these temperature changes per degree of latitude
with those prevailing on the Atlantic Coast, where is found
a change of 2.7° in January and 1.1° in July.

More marked is the effect of latitude on rainfall. The north
Pacific coastal strip is normally drenched with rain throughout the cool months of the year, and some rain falls in the
summer as well. Proceeding southward, both along the coast
and in the interior valleys, average annual rainfall declines

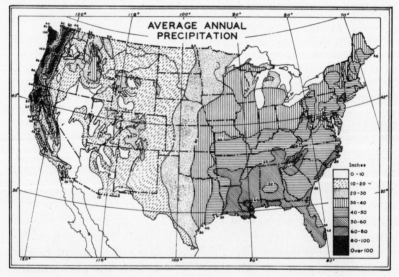

Fig. 10.—Map of United States showing average annual precipitation in
inches.

rather consistently. The coastal strip proper in Washington and Oregon receives from 50 to well above 100 inches of rainfall annually, which declines to about 22 inches in the latitude of San Francisco and to approximately 10 inches at San Diego. Inland there occurs a similar reduction in rainfall from north to south, ranging from between 40 and 60 inches in the Willamette Valley to about 18 in the Sacramento Valley, and declining to less than an inch in parts of the Imperial Valley. East of the Sierra desert conditions prevail in many places, and even eastern Washington and Oregon have extremely scanty rainfall.

A quotation from James Bryce stresses human geography along with the physical features of the Western frontier:

> What America is to Europe, what Western America is to Eastern, that California is to the other Western States. The characteristics of a new and quickly developed colonial civilization are all strongly marked. It is thoroughly American, but most so in those points wherein the Old World differs from the New. Large fortunes are swiftly made and not less swiftly spent. Changes of public sentiment are sudden and violent. The most active minds are too much absorbed in great business enterprises to attend to politics; the inferior men are frequently reckless and irresponsible; the masses are impatient, accustomed to blame everything and everybody but themselves for the slow approach of the millennium, ready to try instant, even if perilous, remedies for a present evil.
>
> These features belong more or less to all the newer and rougher commonwealths. Several others are peculiar to California—a State on which I dwell the more willingly because it is in many respects the most striking in the whole Union, and has more than any other the character of a great country, capable of standing alone in the world. It has immense wealth in its fertile soil as well as in its minerals and forests. Nature is nowhere more imposing nor her beauties more varied.[10]

In California, temperature differences are far less pronounced during the course of a year than are those of rainfall. Marked seasonality in rainfall is due to its location between the zones of the westerlies and the trades. This seasonality in rainfall has important effects on vegetation, and hence on types of agriculture. Only plants which can withstand a long summer's drouth are indigenous, except in the northwest corner of the state, which belongs climatically

[10] James Bryce, *The American Commonwealth* (1907), II, 425.

with Washington and Oregon. The vital dependence of California upon rainfall—and on snows packed in the mountains —is everywhere apparent. Water is the key to the agriculture of the state and to its economic development. Fortunately the Sierra receives the heaviest snowfall of any region in the United States.[11] Winter rains at lower levels provide amply for agricultural requirements for many months, but when the long, dry, hot summer months come, the melting snow from the mountains saves the growing crops from destruction. Even this slower run-off from melting snow does not usually last all summer, but the impounding of surplus waters in reservoirs is a solution which is gradually being applied to California's water problem, and this solution, or an alternative, must in the future be applied much more systematically to enable the state to realize its potentialities.

Gold gave the first great impetus to California's economy (Table 11), but, despite the recent gold-mining boom, it no longer occupies its former position with respect to the wealth of the state. California's major resources now lie in agriculture, in petroleum, in redwood and pine forests, and in scenic and climatic attractions which bring thousands of tourists annually into the state. Among these productive forces agriculture stands pre-eminent and supplies the framework for the entire economic structure of California.

The pastoral era of agriculture characteristic of the Spanish-Mexican régime was appropriate only for sparse population and comparatively undeveloped communities. The grain era which followed it, in the northern valleys where it proved possible, made for a better utilization of the resources which nature gave to California. But this era, too, fell far short of realizing the agricultural potentialities of the region, and it remained for large-scale irrigation to pave the way for the intensive cultivation of the soil in vineyard, orchard, and truck garden.

There is no state in the Union where a greater diversity of agriculture is possible or is practiced than in California. Some 188 commercial crops, exclusive of live stock and live-

[11] Snowfall in the higher Sierra Nevada often measures from 400 to 500 inches and has been known to total 884 inches (United States Weather Bureau, *Climatological Data of the United States,* Vol. I, 1906).

TABLE 11

GOLD AND SILVER PRODUCED IN THE WESTERN STATES, INCLUDING
ALASKA, IN TERMS OF RECOVERED METALS, 1848–1931*

State	Period	Gold Value	Silver (fine ounces)
Arizona	1860–1931	$ 159,833,188	$ 205,479,871
California	1848–1931	1,852,354,387	85,404,568
Colorado	1858–1931	720,301,766	660,127,833
Idaho	1863–1931	137,889,762	333,668,941
Montana	1862–1931	309,344,425	631,874,414
Nevada	1859–1931	459,717,619	541,191,602
New Mexico	1848–1931	37,629,582	53,055,053
Oregon	1852–1931	103,242,000	4,056,671
South Dakota	1876–1931	298,155,521	7,883,626
Texas	1885–1931	95,073	22,772,523
Utah	1865–1931	139,657,325	585,475,176
Washington	1860–1931	30,482,780	9,307,090
Wyoming	1867–1931	1,250,819	70,336
Total		$4,249,954,247	$3,140,367,704
Alaska	1880–1931	398,824,000	17,178,544
Grand total		$4,648,778,247	$3,157,546,248

* Data from Bureau of Mines (Charles W. Henderson, compiler).

stock products, are grown in the state. Such diversity brings unexcelled economic advantages in the greater stability of wealth and income for the region as a whole. A sizable export business in both raw and processed agricultural products has been developed (see Appendix Tables IV and VI), and many branches of agriculture are becoming increasingly dependent upon foreign markets for disposition of surpluses. The variety of California's agricultural production is at once a product of marked variation in soil and climate and of the circumstances which give its population a highly cosmopolitan character.

Except for the narrow depression at the Golden Gate, the great Sacramento–San Joaquin valley of California is shut in on all sides by mountains. Some 500 miles in length and from 20 to 50 miles in width, it comprises more than 18,000 square miles. Its sheltered position converts it into a huge orchard and vineyard, with the northern end admirably adapted also to wheat-growing and to the production of

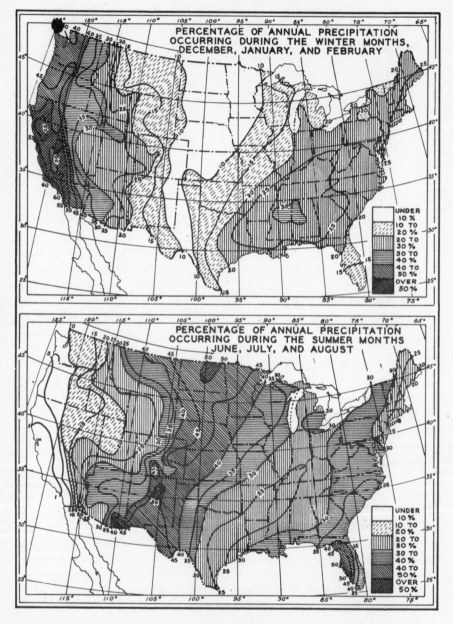

Fig. 11.—Maps of United States showing percentages of annual precipitation during the summer and winter seasons.

many vegetables in the rich delta lands. Deciduous fruits thrive throughout the central region and in the spur valleys leading from the hills into the main floor of the Great Valley. In addition to the interior valleys of California the coastal valleys, warmer in winter and cooler in summer, and enjoying considerably more rainfall, contribute greatly to the agriculture of the state. Among these the Santa Clara and Salinas valleys are of great agricultural value.

In the extreme south the once desolate wastes of the Imperial Valley have been converted, largely within the present century, into one of the most productive agricultural regions in the country with the aid of the turbulent waters of the Colorado River. From here come the earliest spring vegetables and fruits, matured before the frost is out of the ground in many parts of the East.

One of the strongest branches of California horticulture is the citrus-fruit industry. While there is a fair-sized citrus belt in the San Joaquin Valley, the bulk of the production comes from the southern counties around Los Angeles, lying outside the Great Valley, between the mountains and the sea. This region is likewise a great producer of English walnuts and almonds.

California fruits and vegetables have gained so wide a reputation that it is easy to overlook the fact that the first important agricultural industry—live stock—is still one of the state's major sources of wealth. Beef cattle, dairy herds, sheep for wool and meat, and the highly specialized poultry industry all flourish in the several districts where topography, climate, or other natural and man-made conditions provide the requisites for successful operation. Because of the live-stock industry, hay and forage crops lead in value all other crops of the state, even including citrus fruits.

California ranks far behind the Pacific Northwest in lumber production, but the forest resources of the state are nevertheless extremely valuable. The heaviest timber stand in the world is in the redwood belt in Humboldt and Del Norte counties. More extensive are the pine forests on both the western and the eastern slopes of the Sierra and to a lesser extent in the Coast Ranges. Of redwood and sugar pine California has a monopoly, and finds it profitable to ship large amounts out of the state in exchange for other varieties of lumber. Since the Coast has no commercial stands of hardwood, it must have recourse to outside supplies of this material.

At present the outstanding factor in mineral-oil production of the United States is the petroleum industry of California. Its enormous output accounts for not far from one-third of the total. The bulk of the mineral-oil resources of California are concentrated within a fairly small district in the southern part of the state. Four counties, Los Angeles, Kern, Orange, and Ventura, account for practically the entire output. These resources have been of incalculable advantage to southern California in fostering industrial and commercial development, as a supplement to the rich agricultural resources of the region. With oil and natural gas now ample to supply power and heat for transportation, industry, and homes, the long-felt handicap from lack of coal has been compensated for. Both railways and steamships serving the Pacific region have adapted themselves to this abundant fuel, and the motor car and the airplane continue to rely mainly on petroleum products.

In addition to the mineral-oil resources of California, developed and undeveloped hydroelectric power from mountain streams and irrigation projects increases greatly the means by which the population of this state may employ the forces of nature in its service. California leads all other states in the production of hydroelectric power, as it does in the production of mineral oil. Even with the present large exploitation of the energy from falling water, it is estimated that the potential water power of California amounts to five times that produced by existing plants.

Maritime fishing is an economic asset by no means unimportant to the people of California, for in respect to quantity it is first and in value second among the states in the Union; from an export standpoint, California passed the state of Washington a decade ago. Cannery fish, including tuna, sardines, and mackerel, are the most important, although a large variety of market fish are also caught.

California possesses two remarkably fine natural harbors, San Francisco and San Diego. The former, located midway of the Pacific Coast, attracts the most diversified commerce of any large American port outside New York. When Nature gave to southern California the huge oil fields which have contributed so greatly to the economic development of that region, she failed to create an adjacent natural harbor to serve the industrial life thus made possible. As far as is humanly possible, man has made good that deficiency, and the port of Los Angeles is now one of the greatest oil-shipping and timber-receiving ports in the world.

Among the natural resources of California which play a significant part in shaping the economic and social life of the people, the climatic and scenic facilities for recreation must not be overlooked. Tourist trade from outside adds greatly to the wealth of the state, as indeed it does to the picturesque West as a whole. What these same facilities mean in health and well-being to the residents themselves is a kind of value not reducible to a monetary basis.

A century ago California was practically uninhabited. Dr. Katherine Coman is the authority for the following statement:

A census of foreigners taken in 1840 enumerated sixteen foreigners at Yerba Buena, all Americans, thirty-one at San Jose, mostly British subjects, ten at Branciforte [now Santa Cruz], American hunters and sailors, thirty at Monterey, English and American merchants, as many more of the same class at Santa Barbara, twenty-three at Los Angeles, American traders and French fruit growers, but only seven at San Diego, the former resort of the drogher ships. The urban population in 1846 was between four and five thousand, e.g., San Jose 600 to 800, Los Angeles 1,250, Branciforte 470, Santa Barbara 900, Monterey 500, Yerba Buena 800.[12]

During the gold rush more than 80,000 people came to California, and by 1850 the inhabitants numbered 92,600. Thereafter began the steady climb upward of this figure, hastened after 1869 by the completion of transcontinental railway lines and after 1900 by the rapid expansion of the automobile and the resulting good-roads movement. Between 1910 and 1920 the state gained a million inhabitants; in the next decade the increase was two and a quarter million, or 65.7 per cent, while the rate of growth for the entire

[12] K. Coman, *Economic Beginnings of the Far West* (1912), II, 378.

nation was only 16 per cent. No other state in the Union gained so many new inhabitants in this decade, and no other made a percentage increase even half as great. California now ranks sixth in population among the forty-eight states.

In the Northwest states, and in northern California, where heavy annual rainfall is added to mild climate, are to be seen some of the most magnificent forest growths of the world. Few trees anywhere attain the size and majesty of the Douglas fir, while none compares in these respects with the redwood, which occurs nowhere except in California. These immense timber resources long seemed inexhaustible, and they were exploited with reckless waste. Some of the damage done through soil erosion and the like is irreparable, but much may still be done to turn the remaining forests into perpetually renewable assets as in Europe.

In these more northerly latitudes plentiful rainfall likewise provides abundant forage to support live-stock and dairy industries. Oregon is forging to the front as a producer of cheese. Inland valleys not entirely cut off from the tempering influence of the ocean afford excellent regions for the growing of fruit, protected alike from frosts and from destructive winds. Because of cool, moist summer climate, such valleys as the Puget Sound and the Willamette are especially adapted to the growing of berries and small fruits, as well as to general farming. Even in the valleys east of the Cascades irrigation water from those mountains has made possible the development of fruit-growing in the extremely rich volcanic soil which characterizes such regions as the Wenatchee and Yakima valleys, while farther east wheat-production is an important contribution to the agricultural resources of the state and to its exportable surpluses. Table 10 (p. 46) provides a regional grouping of homogeneous sections in the Pacific Northwest.

The mountainous regions of the Pacific Northwest accumulate glaciers and snow packs which provide water not only for irrigation but also for power. Most of the water-power resources of the country are centered in this area. Climatic conditions are highly favorable to a continuous production of power through interconnection of plants. The prodigality with which water-power resources have been bestowed throughout the Pacific Coast region compensates in measurable degree for the previously mentioned scarcity there of high-grade coal and provides a basis for building up a highly industrialized civilization.

Innumerable potentialities for natural harbors, the limits to the development of which rest only on the resources of the hinterland and the territories which can best be served by such ports, were created in the age when the North Pacific Coast sank sufficiently to drown the valleys which are now covered by the waters of Puget Sound. Seattle and Tacoma have had so far the greatest growth among Puget Sound seaports. Apart from the resources of their hinterland, special advantages accrue to Puget Sound ports because of their location on the Great Circle route to the Far East and their proximity to Alaska. Nearer to Yokohama by several hundred miles than any other major seaport of the United States, Seattle and Tacoma enjoy a flourishing trade with Japan and northern China. The importance of Seattle as a silk-receiving port has rested chiefly on this distance factor. The Canadian boundary line excludes natural tributary territory and also makes for intensive competition on each side of the frontier.

Puget Sound ports are at a disadvantage because they are hemmed about by mountains, the chief limiting factor to their growth, making access to the interior and to the East relatively difficult and expensive. To some extent this is true of the entire Pacific slope and it is one of the reasons why the Panama Canal has proved of such tremendous significance to the region. The river port of Portland, a great lumber-shipping terminal, however, is more advantageously situated. Varied products of the Columbia Basin find their natural outlet at Portland. Water-level routes constitute the lines of least resistance to the flow of traffic. The gap in the Cascades cut by the Columbia River makes this route the only one which does not involve more or less arduous mountain climbing. It is difficult to foretell how much, in the long run, this advantage may mean to the upbuilding of Portland as a great commercial center, for it is only a comparatively few years since channel-dredging converted Portland into a first-class port for ocean-going vessels.

Nathaniel J. Wyeth, who claimed to have originated the

first American settlement in Oregon, stated that when he
arrived on the lower Columbia in 1832 there were no Americans there, nor anyone having an American flag. "So far as
I know, there had not been since Mr. Astor retired from the
Coast." The population of the Pacific Northwest, however,
has not grown as rapidly as that of California. In 1850 Oregon Territory was credited with 13,000 inhabitants. Ten
years later the state of Oregon had 52,000 and Washington
Territory 11,000. By 1900 the two states supported 930,000. In
fifty years, therefore, they gained about 900,000 inhabitants.
When these figures are contrasted with the population
growth of that part of the Mississippi Valley region which
was settled at about the same time as the Oregon country, the
influence of two great mountain barriers and intervening
semi-desert country upon migration in the absence of special
or spectacular events is clear.[13] The 1930 Census shows
Washington as having slightly over one and one-half million
inhabitants and Oregon almost one million. The two states
together thus support almost exactly 2,500,000 people, or
slightly over 2 per cent of the nation's population, on an area
comprising 5 per cent of the country's domain.

A leading geographer, J. Russell Smith, predicts a brilliant
future for the Pacific Northwest, pointing out that "there is
no location for power resources in Europe or even in the
Eastern United States to rival it."[14] The average temperature
of the coastal strip and that of the Puget Sound and the
Willamette Valley are held to be almost ideal for the maximum productive efficiency of human labor, and the abundant resources in water power, timber, minerals (including
those from Alaska), and location with respect to Oriental
trade are counted on to provide materials with which to
work. If this prophecy is correct the Northwest will some day
be a country of dense population; certainly the abundant

[13] The region once known as the Oregon country includes also Idaho and
a small part of Montana. The rate of population growth for Oregon and
Washington alone, therefore, is slightly greater than the foregoing figures
indicate. In comparison, the four states of Iowa, Kansas, Minnesota, and
Nebraska gained more than six million inhabitants between 1860 and 1900,
with a total population in the later year of six and one-half millions.

[14] J. R. Smith, *North America* (1925), p. 612.

resources and superior population augur a most promising future.

To become aware of the earlier development of California as contrasted with the Northwest, as well as the relative lack of uniformity, one should find useful data in the accompanying Table 12, which records the course of foreign trade in two selected regions covering a period of three-quarters of a century.

TABLE 12

FOREIGN TRADE GROWTH, SAN FRANCISCO AND WASHINGTON CUSTOMS
DISTRICTS, 1860–1933*

(Thousand dollars)

Year or Yearly Average	San Francisco		Washington	
	Exports	Imports	Exports	Imports
1860.	4,868	7,367	63	...
1865.	9,988	15,802	633	12
1870.	13,992	15,983	428	35
1871–1875.	19,476	25,459	497	30
1876–1880.	27,718	29,798	486	33
1881–1885.	41,740	39,109	1,647	109
1886–1890.	33,035	44,344	2,708	417
1891–1895.	32,365	43,557	5,627	1,068
1896–1900.	36,607	40,443	13,948	6,399
1901–1905.	37,751	38,188	30,708	9,907
1906–1910.	32,758	49,226	38,567	23,409
1911–1915.	60,154	63,760	57,711	50,200
1915–1920†	186,317	197,613	222,702	206,862
1921–1925.	158,275	155,500	110,361	214,213
1926–1930.	183,236	195,351	136,886	212,134
1931.	112,257	85,776	67,269	55,344
1932.	82,201	58,228	36,679	37,325
1933.	84,512	55,554	35,289	28,282

* Data from Bureau of Foreign and Domestic Commerce. Exports (including re-exports) and general imports of merchandise.

† Period July 1, 1915, to December 31, 1920.

Features of the Alaskan situation are a coastline of 18,211 miles and coast ranges of 14,000 feet, perpetually snowclad. Recent and potential discoveries, however, which counteract the influence of the cold climates in the growing of crops and the conditions of habitation, are certain to bring fresh wealth to considerable parts of the present undeveloped area.

It has already been noted that the Pacific coastal plain of Alaska is extremely narrow, even non-existent in many portions, with mountains coming directly down to the sea. In fact, the almost continuous islands from Vancouver northward to southern Alaska, which make possible the inside passage, are the tops of mountains partly drowned by the subsidence of the coast. The shore is likewise deeply indented with fiords, even more so than the Norwegian coast, made by glacial action and the result of land sinking. This gives a tremendously long shore line and naturally turns the attention of men seeking a livelihood to the fish with which these waters abound. Paramount are the salmon fisheries, which still yield enormous catches each year in spite of the reckless methods employed. The salmon catch was worth more than thirty million dollars in 1930—Alaska's greatest annual item of income. Some restrictions are now imposed on the size of the salmon catch in Alaskan waters which may save this economic resource from being destroyed as it has been on the Atlantic. Other fish are not negligible in importance. Halibut, cod, and herring contribute substantially to the income of the Northwest states and of Alaska.

A small group of islands in the Bering Sea, the Pribilof Islands, yield the bulk of fur seals, which are killed in limited numbers under international agreement between the United States, owner of the islands, and Canada, Russia, and Japan. Under this protection the herds are rapidly being restored after almost complete annihilation.

In spite of the fact that the Alaskan forest belt between the shore and the high mountains is extremely narrow, southern Alaska possesses important timber resources, particularly pulp woods. This forest strip is a northerly continuation of those which add so greatly to the wealth of the Coast states and the Province of British Columbia.

The great valley of Alaska, the Yukon, opens into the Bering Sea. It is cut off by the mountains from the tempering influence of the Pacific and is subject to the greatest extremes of temperature. Summers may be very warm and winters bitterly cold. A temperature record of 100° north of the Arctic Circle seems truly astonishing until one remembers the almost continuous daylight of those latitudes in the summer. Rainfall is relatively light. Here is a vast region of forest and grasslands, close to the Arctic Circle, where the long hours of sunlight during the summer promote extraordinarily rapid growth.

Furs and gold have been the chief resources of the white people who have penetrated these regions. The native inhabitants originally supported themselves mainly by fishing, until white traders gave them a market for pelts. The Klondike gold rush was only less spectacular than the California gold rush a half-century earlier. There is undoubtedly still much gold in Alaska, as well as wealth in other minerals, not only in the Yukon but also in the mountainous regions of western Alaska. The greatest coal resources of the Pacific Coast are located here, awaiting population and industrial development to make their exploitation practicable. The same forces will extend to other mining in regions which now lie untouched.

Many foresee a great agricultural future for the Yukon Valley similar to that of Finland, to which it is often compared. All vegetables requiring cool weather flourish astonishingly, and grain-growing has likewise been pursued successfully. Live stock and dairy products, however, probably offer the greatest agricultural potentialities of this region as they do of Finland. Even farther north, in the tundra region of Arctic Alaska, conditions are favorable to animal life, and vast herds of reindeer have been raised and marketed both for food and for hides in regions little suited to anything else.[15]

Agriculture in Alaska on anything but a limited scale doubtless awaits population growth of the western continent to the point where lands of milder climate and more accessible location have reached the limits which they can support. When this will be no one can possibly foresee, for the reason that neither of the two major factors, rate of increase in population or agricultural technique, is fixed.

[15] There were estimated to be over 700,000 reindeer on farms or ranges in Alaska in 1930 as compared with 93,000 in 1920 and only 22,000 in 1910. These animals far outnumber all other Alaska farm animals. Of cattle and milk cows there were only 2,500. The government maintains a Reindeer Experiment Station at College, Alaska, under the Bureau of Biological Survey of the United States Department of Agriculture.

FROM CALIFORNIA PACKING CORPORATION

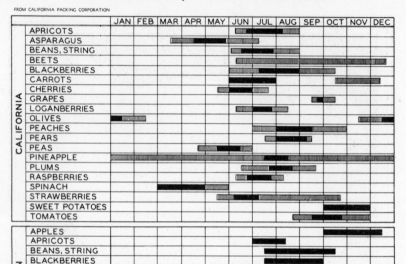

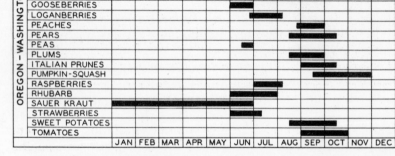

Fig. 12.—Canning seasons for various agricultural commodities of California, Oregon, and Washington.

Population statistics of Alaska show how slowly it is growing. According to the Census of 1930 this territory contained fewer inhabitants in that year than in 1910, when the effects of the Klondike gold rush had not yet entirely disappeared. In the earlier year there were 64,356 inhabitants, while in 1930 the number was 59,278. The latter figure represents a small increase, however, from the 1920 level. Approximately half of the racial make-up is white; the others are mostly Indians and Eskimos.

Because of its intimate economic and social connections with the mainland, Hawaii is considered a part of the Amer-

Fig. 13.—Map of Alaska.

ican Pacific Empire. The location of the islands gives them considerable importance as the crossroads in transpacific trade. More than ten million tons of shipping called at Hawaiian ports during each of the past three years.

The Hawaiian Islands are of the volcanic type, apparently formed by a series of submarine lava flows and by the elevation in this plateau of a number of volcanic cones.[16] The group consists of eight islands of some size and a dozen or more small, rocky islands, some scarcely more than reefs. Volcanic activity is still present in Hawaii, where is located Kilauea, the world's greatest active volcano.

[16] The islands of the Pacific are of two types, continental and oceanic. The former include those islands which appear above the surface of the ocean as tops of partly submerged highlands and mountain peaks, which were formerly part of a continent. The latter are of volcanic origin, entirely unrelated to previously existing land-masses.

These islands lie in the belt of the trade winds, and because of their mountainous character there is a very sharp difference in rainfall between their windward and their leeward sides. Annual precipitation reaches 400 or more inches in some places, but the dry lowlands mostly have less than 25 inches annually. Rainfall is irregular but tends to fall more in the cooler months. Differences in temperature are likewise the result of topography, and the highest mountain tops are occasionally snow-capped. The Islands as a whole may be said to enjoy an even temperature, characteristic of mid-Pacific conditions, with a range in temperature between the monthly averages of only a few degrees.[17] These islands are fortunate in avoiding the violent tropical storms so destructive to life and property on many Pacific islands.

Their tropical climate, together with the distribution of rainfall, determines agricultural development. Generally speaking, the windward slopes are subject to such constant rainfall as to prevent cultivation, so that most of the crops are grown on the leeward sides where rainfall is usually too scanty for growth without irrigation. Water is obtained from wells and from conduits of one sort and another brought from the wet slope of the mountains. Sugar and pineapples, in the order named, constitute the chief commercial products of the Islands; sugar is the leading industry, and pineapples the most distinctive (see Table 13). Both are characteristically produced by large-scale enterprises and by the latest scientific methods. The former requires much more moisture than the latter. In consequence it is usually grown on the lower, less precipitous slopes where irrigation offers less of a problem.

The population of Hawaii has grown steadily since the beginning of the present century. In 1900 the inhabitants numbered 154,000. According to the Census of 1930, there were 368,000 persons living in that territory. In 30 years, therefore, the population of Hawaii increased 140 per cent.

[17] Nevertheless the height of the mountain peaks together with the marked differences in rainfall between windward and leeward slopes results in perhaps greater climatic changes than can be found anywhere else in the world within so limited an area. See United States Weather Bureau, *Climatological Data of the United States,* Vol. III.

As is to be expected from its mid-Pacific location and its history, the racial make-up of the Hawaiian Islands is extremely diverse. Of the native Hawaiians of pure descent there are now very few—less than 23,000 in 1930. Even by adding persons classed as Asiatic-Hawaiian and Caucasian-Hawaiian, the total barely exceeds 50,000. The Japanese are the dominant racial element, numerically speaking. In 1930 nearly 140,000 persons were included in this group, or 38 per cent of the total. While the Japanese element has nearly doubled in the last thirty years, it has lost slightly in relative importance.

TABLE 13

HAWAIIAN PINEAPPLE PACK, 1903–1930*

(Measured in cases)

Year	Total Hawaiian Pack	Year	Total Hawaiian Pack
1903	1,893	1917	2,607,031
1904	10,397	1918	3,847,315
1905	45,041	1919	5,071,976
1906	74,245	1920	5,986,982
1907	168,205	1921	5,262,503
1908	343,726	1922	4,770,239
1909	401,940	1923	5,895,747
1910	464,968	1924	6,825,904
1911	725,742	1925	8,728,580
1912	1,313,363	1926	8,939,590
1913	1,667,122	1927	8,879,252
1914	2,268,781	1928	8,663,056
1915	2,669,616	1929	9,210,240
1916	2,609,483	1930	12,672,296

* Data from *Western Canner and Packer*, March 20, 1933. World-production statistics for 1929, dealing with source, variety, and pack, are British Malaya (Spanish red, 1,700,000), Formosa (native, 840,000), Australia (Queen, 140,000), Puerto Rico (Spanish red, 96,800), Union of South Africa (Queen, 58,000), and Fiji (15,000). The Hawaiian product is classified as Smooth Cayenne.

Next to the Japanese in number are the Filipinos, with 63,000 in 1930. This is the fastest-growing group among all races in Hawaii, and is the only one except the Asiatic-Hawaiian group representing a greater percentage of total population in 1930 than in 1900. At the beginning of the century Filipinos constituted only 1.2 per cent of the inhabitants of Hawaii; in 1930 they accounted for 17 per cent.

Nearly all are employed on sugar plantations. The Caucasian group, excluding Caucasian-Hawaiian, now number approximately 80,000, with substantially the same relative importance in each of the last three decennial censuses. The Portuguese, who have been imported in large numbers for agricultural labor, are the most numerous within this group.

The preponderance of Asiatics in Hawaii is thus very great. This, too, is to be expected from the geographic position of the Islands. If continental United States is the melting-pot of Europe, our non-contiguous territory of Hawaii provides, in its 6,000 square miles, a smaller but not less significant laboratory for working out the possibilities of cultural and biological fusion of diverse Asiatic peoples.

In conclusion, applicable to the Coast states, Hawaii, and Alaska, the paramount geographical influence is the sea. Exploration and discovery came from the ocean rather than overland. It may be observed from the trails of the explorers, which are shown in Figure 20 (see p. 105). The Manila galleon, Salem clipper ships, trading-posts established by Astor, the gold rush, and the continental cut at Panama are eloquent illustrations. The covered wagon, the completion of the first transcontinental railway in 1869, and the great modern highways, which have caused a very great immigration from other parts of the country, have produced an indelible result on the development of Western America. However, it is fair to state that the chief contributions to this civilization have come from maritime influences and activities. The populations of the Pacific Coast states, Hawaii, Alaska, and, to a lesser extent, the intermountain states, look toward the horizon of the Pacific Ocean. The influence of the sea upon people's habits, methods of thought, and ways of living still proves to be of tremendous significance.

IV. Utilization of Economic Resources

The leading factor contributing to the present-day significance of the American Pacific region is the character of the area itself. Man is not attracted in great numbers to regions lacking in fertility. There is always a lure—abundance of natural resources in either the land or the sea, prospective wealth, or better living.

Of course, an area may be rich in resources and still remain undeveloped for years. Sometimes, as in Mexico, the topography of the country is the barrier to extensive exploitation. Sometimes, as in China, unsettled political conditions so increase the risks of capital as to discourage its entrance on any large scale. But within certain limitations the original impetus to settlement and population growth is the economic wealth of the country itself. Trade follows.

The kind of trade will be determined largely by the nature of the country's resources and the stage of their development; the amount of trade is dependent upon the activity of the people inhabiting the area. Their activity is the resultant of their racial heritage, type of civilization and government, the amount of competition which obtains, climatic conditions, and allied factors. Trade is not possible or profitable without population. In other words, the people of an area support trade and the character of the intercourse with other countries is largely determined by the economic well-being of that people, coupled with the resources of their land. If they have exportable surpluses they will seek to exchange these goods for others not provided or at least not produced readily within their own boundaries.

Everything that favors production likewise favors the accumulation of surpluses. If a country possesses rich level soil, navigable waters, favorable climatic conditions—all of which are necessary to the production of most animal and vegetable products that enter into trade or furnish raw materials for manufacture—its commerce with other nations will be of one type. If it possesses a rugged topography and abundant rainfall, lumber production and the growing of tree fruits will be favored and its trade will be of another type. A rugged topography with a dry climate usually favors the production of metals. A suggestive list of deficient and surplus commodities appears in the tabulated imports and exports in Appendix Table X and in the accompanying text Table 14 (pp. 78–79).

Although important as a factor in creating an exchangeable surplus, physical features alone will not insure this result. Density of population is important, as are the quality of the inhabitants of the region, their special aptitudes, energy, standard of living, and stage of civilization. But one needs no great amount of imagination to visualize the rôle that resources play in the setting for maritime inter course. An intelligent stock-taking of resources is hardly practicable without some consideration of the geographic factors and influences responsible for these resources. Such factors must be considered in relation to resources, but also with respect to the location of the area and its markets, and to the sources of supply of materials necessary for its economic development. The matter of distance itself may or may not be a barrier to exchange, but to a large extent it determines extent and character of shipping, types of carriers, and trade routes. As men increase the scope of their power to modify their environment, the rigidity with which their natural setting controls their social and economic institutions is progressively relaxed. Yet the limits are always there, fundamental in their influence, and inescapable in their ultimate implications.

In its broad outlines, the economic history of the American Pacific Coast from the Civil War onward is a not unfamiliar story. In the Northwest, lumber, grain, fish, and, later, fruits were the main lines of development. They, and their derivative industries, with some mining, occupy the major energies of the people today. The acquisition of Alaska was a great stimulus to Puget Sound development, since it opened an immense new territory tributary to that region. Hawaii was an important outpost of the United States even before the Pacific States were incorporated into the Union. The early missionaries from New England provided the leading moral, social, and economic influences there during the past hundred years, and their descendants are now the leaders in the affairs of that rich commonwealth.

Lumber resources of California are principally the sugar pine and the distinctive, decay-resisting redwood. The mineral-oil wealth of southern California has significantly abetted the growth of industrial and commercial enterprise in that part of the state and has profoundly influenced the trend of maritime communication facilities for the entire Coast. The fisheries of the Pacific littoral are extremely important. In both the Northwest and California, increasing density of population has brought with it countless new industries, some local in scope, and others of national importance.

By no means negligible in the present economic structure of the Pacific Coast, and particularly of California, is climate itself. Climate and scenic attractions have been capitalized to produce revenue from visitors, and to attract permanent residents from other parts of the country. Statistics suggest that one out of every ten visitors becomes a permanent resident. The increased population resulting from those who stay adds to land values and to commercial and industrial opportunities in the same fashion as does population growth elsewhere.

Climatic conditions have likewise been largely instrumental in building up what is perhaps the most widely distributed production of California—the motion-picture films. The large percentage of the time when weather is favorable to both outside and inside photography as well as the great variety of scenery within a comparatively small radius are the principal natural advantages which southern California offers to this industry. According to the latest census returns, motion pictures now rank second among California industries in value added by manufacture.

The scenic grandeur and climatic attractions of Western United States bring about a vast tourist industry which, from the standpoint of contribution to state wealth, may rank among the first three or four commercial enterprises. This industry, which Europeans designate as "tourism," is a natural development because of the presence of numerous

TABLE 14

WATER-BORNE IMPORTS AND EXPORTS OF PRINCIPAL COMMODITIES, CALIFORNIA, OREGON, AND WASHINGTON, 1927–1930*

(Thousand long tons)

Commodities	California	Oregon	Washington	Total
Imports, 1927				
Total	1,531	130	1,153	2,814
Vegetables and vegetable products	122	17	55	194
Coconuts and copra	133	21	1	155
Sugar	82	4	3	89
Coffee	65	2	3	70
Paper manufactures	99	1	25	125
Coal and coke	55	3	97	155
Iron, steel, iron and steel manufactures	159	20	24	203
Copper and copper manufactures	7	1	238	246
Miscellaneous metals	41	...†	113	154
Logs and lumber	145	1	233	379
Exports, 1927				
Total	7,747	1,696	2,561	12,004
Wheat	20	724	180	924
Barley	254	...†	1	255
Wheat flour	24	77	157	258
Meat, fish, and dairy products	72	6	52	130
Fruits and nuts	246	78	54	378
Petroleum and petroleum products	6,407	1	23	6,431
Lumber	196	766	1,789	2,751
Copper and copper manufactures	3	...†	91	94
Imports, 1928				
Total	1,631	146	1,108	2,885
Vegetables and vegetable products	102	9	35	146
Coconuts and copra	138	31	3	172
Sugar	98	3	3	104
Coffee	78	3	3	83
Paper manufactures	92	14	27	133
Coal and coke	48	4	80	132
Iron, steel, iron and steel manufactures	154	13	...	167
Copper and copper manufactures	5	...	233	238
Miscellaneous metals	16	...	118	134
Logs and lumber	121	2	222	345
Exports, 1928				
Total	8,824	2,120	2,982	13,926
Wheat	35	1,025	240	1,300
Barley	181	1	...	182
Wheat flour	34	95	199	328
Meat, fish, and dairy products	68	3	35	106
Fruits and nuts	330	32	42	404
Petroleum and petroleum products	7,451	1	7	7,459
Lumber	173	935	2,220	3,328
Copper and copper manufactures	5	...†	82	87

* Fiscal years. Data from United States Shipping Board. Not all commodities shown.

TABLE 14 (*Continued*)

(*Thousand long tons*)

Commodities	California	Oregon	Washington	Total
Imports, 1929				
Total	1,863	112	1,137	3,112
Vegetables and vegetable products	121	12	48	181
Coconuts and copra	134	32	3	209
Sugar	95	10	8	113
Coffee	73	2	2	77
Paper manufactures	80	8	22	110
Coal and coke	41	2	77	120
Iron, steel, iron and steel manufactures	149	11	30	190
Copper and copper manufactures	5	...	223	228
Miscellaneous metals	19	...†	109	128
Logs and lumber	133	1	208	341
Exports, 1929				
Total	8,672	1,976	2,850	13,498
Wheat	8	595	142	745
Barley	218	1	...†	219
Wheat flour	40	121	249	410
Meat, fish, and dairy products	85	5	37	127
Fruits and nuts	393	72	113	578
Petroleum and petroleum products	7,040	1	8	7,047
Lumber	183	1,150	2,044	3,377
Copper and copper manufactures	7	1	76	84
Imports, 1930				
Total	1,888	114	1,173	3,175
Vegetables and vegetable products	118	12	54	184
Coconuts and copra	141	28	3	172
Sugar	107	8	4	119
Coffee	74	1	2	77
Paper manufactures	105	3	27	135
Coal and coke	54	3	70	127
Iron, steel, iron and steel manufactures	120	15	17	152
Copper and copper manufactures	9	...	249	258
Miscellaneous metals	30	...	94	124
Logs and lumber	143	1	270	414
Exports, 1930				
Total	9,151	1,678	2,516	13,345
Wheat	4	541	119	664
Barley	219	...	...	219
Wheat flour	35	116	200	351
Meat, fish, and dairy products	93	4	34	131
Fruits and nuts	265	53	74	392
Petroleum and petroleum products	7,703	...†	21	7,725
Lumber	150	929	1,846	2,925
Copper and copper manufactures	2	...†	51	53

† Less than one thousand long tons.

national parks and scenic wonders found here. For the United States as a whole the amount spent by the migrant American population is estimated at between three and four billion dollars annually, of which the single item of motor-camping equipment constitutes over one-third of a billion. Using national figures, it appears that the tourist business is 51 per cent larger than the oil-production business and 60 per cent greater than the total value of American lumber products. Since the Western section of the United States has a far greater than proportional share in the tourist business, no consideration of the resources of the region can be undertaken without valuing properly the greater economic assets of Nature's attractions.

A knowledge of the geographical distribution of resources is necessary in order to understand the growth and prospects of America's Western Empire. The contribution which the Coast states make to total continental United States consists of 11 per cent of the area, 7 per cent of the population, 8 per cent of the wealth, 62 per cent of the timber stand, 41 per cent of the lumber production, 34 per cent of the irrigated area, 40 per cent of the potential water power and 25 per cent of the developed water power, 30 per cent of the hydroelectric power, 24 per cent of the fisheries, 25 per cent of petroleum production, 12 per cent of the minerals, and from 5 to 9 per cent of the manufacturing industry, according to the statistical basis. (Consult Appendix Table I for information dealing with Washington, Oregon, and California separately, and as a unit.)

The following tabulation, based on the latest census, which gives the figures for 1929, affords a comparative picture of the economic products of California, Oregon, and Washington in millions of dollars:

	Value (Million Dollars)		
	California	Oregon	Washington
Crops	538	89	145
Live stock	287	55	91
Fish	13	3	10
Lumber	65	101	151
Mineral	555	7	22
Other manufactures	2,938	299	617
Total	4,396	554	1,036

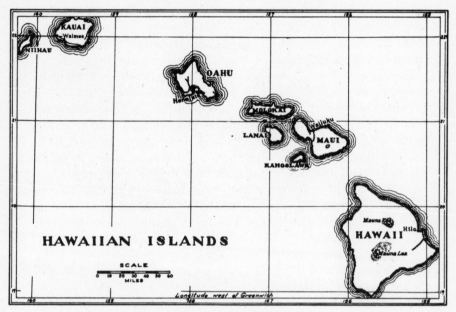

FIG. 14.—Map of Hawaiian Islands.

As may be observed from these statistics, California occupies a dominant position on the Pacific Coast. But, still further, the Golden State is outstanding in many respects among all states of the Union. A listing includes leadership in numerous horticultural products, such as citrus fruits, walnuts and almonds, prunes and plums, apricots, grapes, pears, peaches, olives, dates, figs, asparagus, lettuce, and cantaloupes. California also leads in the fishing industry, in gold-mining, in the tourist business, and in motion pictures. It is second among all states in mineral production and eighth in value of manufactures. California's ranking in leading industries is first in canning and preserving and in motion pictures; second in petroleum-refining and in planing-mill products not connected with sawmills; third in rubber tires and inner tubes, in coffee, and in spices; fourth in women's clothing; and fifth in lumber and timber products (not elsewhere specified), in bread and bakery products, and in printing and publishing.

The economic activities of Oregon and Washington are

dependent most of all upon the lumber industry; the largest timber stands are in Oregon. The Northwest is important also in dairy products, ranking third in the United States in production of cheese. Other important industries are the production of grain, flour, apples, sheep and wool, of fish, canning of all kinds, and in general the primary conversion of varied raw materials. In manufactures Washington ranks first and Oregon second in lumber and timber products, while Washington ranks fifth in wood pulp and sixth in flour-milling. It is a striking fact that, according to value of industrial output in California, canning and preserving account for 7 per cent and petroleum-refining for 15 per cent of the total state value, while in Washington as well as Oregon lumber and timber products make up one-third of the total value.

The Mountain States have the greatest deposits and the larger production of most basic metals. Arizona, Utah, and Montana are the leading copper producers. Utah produces 22 per cent of America's lead, Montana 18 per cent of the silver, Arizona 11 per cent of the silver and 10 per cent of the gold. Idaho produces one-seventh of the silver, and New Mexico 5 per cent each of copper and zinc. Colorado, Utah, and Wyoming have vast coal deposits, and Colorado has huge untouched oil shales. The grazing and live-stock industry, especially wool-growing, are important contributors to national wealth. Beet sugar from the Rocky Mountain States provides over one-fifth of the sugar marketed for consumption in the United States.

Hawaii is of rapidly increasing importance as a sugar-producer. On the basis of market sugar in the United States the percentage from Hawaii increased from a 10.4 average in 1922–1926 to 16.4 in 1932, as compared with 5.4 and 16.6 for the Philippines and 16.5 and 21.1 for continental United States. The insular regions of the United States doubled their share of United States sources of sugar over this short period, which provides an explanation, moreover, as to why the question of Philippine independence is of such importance not only to Cuba but also to Hawaii and the Mountain States. The shipments of sugar from Hawaii for refining in the San Francisco Bay area and the distribution of canned pineapples from Hawaii are its two main economic contributions to Western economy. Alaska has an integral place, principally because of her salmon canneries and her copper production. (Consult Appendix Table VI for detailed statistics.)

Exploitation of resources has been, and to a large extent still is, the history of maritime trade development in the American Pacific area. This statement is likewise true of British Columbia. Today metals, petroleum, and timber resources are being depleted. Yesterday, products of the sea rather than the land provided the great source of wealth and the incentive for long voyages and trading. The real beginning of economic enterprise in the region was made in the Pacific Northwest. Earliest of all fur trade was that in sea-otter and seal skins. Here the sea furnished not only the medium for transport but also the product itself. Ships from all parts of the world were drawn to the Pacific North American shores. Unlike contemporary ventures in California, the trade development which followed paved the way for permanent white settlement. Unfortunately it also opened an early chapter in the history of man's reckless exploitation of Nature's gifts.

Today the exports of petroleum products to foreign countries greatly exceed in both quantity and value the exports of any other commodity or group of commodities from the Pacific States area. Statistics by money value of Pacific Coast ocean shipments, which are available only for the portion entering foreign trade, do not begin to tell the story, yet in every year since 1924 they have constituted approximately half the total volume of the outgoing foreign commerce. In value they have amounted to from two-thirds to three-fourths the exports from the Los Angeles district and from one-fifth to one-fourth those of San Francisco. Figure 15[1] brings out clearly the position of tanker cargoes (mostly petroleum) in the field of Pacific Coast exports. Shipments of petroleum from the southern California fields have increased steadily, reaching a peak in 1930, when the

---

[1] Other Pacific Coast customs districts have relatively small mineral-oil exports. See Appendix Table IV.

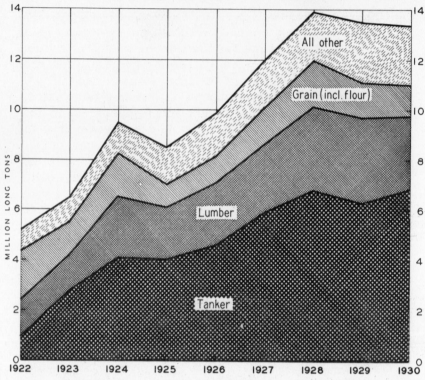

Fig. 15.—Nature of exports from United States Pacific Coast.

exports from Los Angeles harbor alone accounted for 35 per cent of the nation's total.

A natural resource like petroleum, which is neither replaceable nor suitably conserved, is rapidly exhausted. As long as these heavy exports continue, shipping in all probability will remain heavily unbalanced, since a great part moves in specialized types of vessels for which little return cargo is available. For the most part tankers are carriers devoted to the special task of transporting oil for concerns primarily engaged in mineral-oil production. While molasses, vegetable oils, and certain other liquids imported into the Pacific Coast also come by tankers, their movement is slight compared with bulk-petroleum shipments, and the labor of clearing the tanks for them is so great that little may be expected from that carriage in reducing the number of trips in ballast for returning petroleum tankers. Wet products, if brought in in bulk, are much more likely to come in tankers specially devoted to their carriage or to arrive by smaller lots in tanks built into general-cargo carriers.[2]

What has previously been said concerning the natural resources and the economic development of the American Pacific Coast provides a clue to the commodities which are produced in sufficient quantities to provide an exchangeable surplus. With some notable exceptions, this region is still largely in the exploitation stage of economic development, a stage in which the dominant products are raw or semi-raw materials and foodstuffs attainable without either intensive application of labor (except in growing certain fruits and vegetables) or complex industrial organization. Accordingly it is not surprising that those commodities which are most important among the outgoing cargoes in terms of quantity are also the principal ones in point of view of value. But this condition is not true of incoming cargoes.

To find the products which follow petroleum in importance in the export trade of the American Pacific Coast, it is necessary to turn from southern California to the Pacific Northwest. Before the discovery of gold, exchange of commodities between California and the Northwest was almost non-existent. California had supplied a large number of animals to assist in the establishment of a cattle industry in the Oregon country, but Oregon had little or nothing which could be disposed of in California. After 1849 conditions were very much changed, and here begins the coastwise exchange of goods so advantageous to both regions. Immense supplies of lumber as well as of all kinds of foodstuffs were required to provide for California's rapidly growing population, engrossed mainly in prospecting and mining. The Northwest country was able, and more than willing, to exchange some of her surplus of lumber and agricultural products for a share in California gold. But

[2] General-cargo carriers are handling an increasing percentage of bulk liquid cargoes by means of such compartments. Some petroleum products, of course, are exported in large volume by means of barrels or tins, particularly to the Orient.

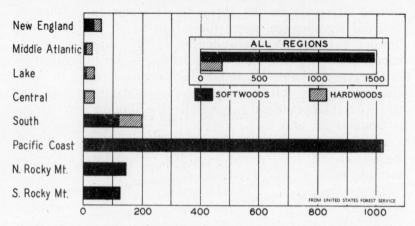

FIG. 16.—Softwood and hardwood timber stands in the United States.

many Oregon settlers turned gold-miners themselves, and for a while the lure of California gold bade fair to deplete the Oregon country of able-bodied men. Gradually, however, a returning tide set in, made up of both those who had been disappointed and those who had found fortunes and were now ready to spend. A major portion of the new wealth was devoted to much-needed agricultural and industrial developments. Thus, in two ways, Oregon gained a portion of the mineral wealth of California before the extent of her own resources was known.

The beginning of the lumber trade from the Pacific Northwest to California came as early as 1849. It was the Pacific Ocean which made that trade possible in the era before the advent of railroads or even roads of any practicable transport value over the mountain barriers separating the two territories. Lumber is conspicuously a commodity which demands cheap and extensive transportation facilities. With forests situated close to or with access to tidewater, sawmills grew up and flourished as a result of the brisk demand for lumber in California in the late '40's and in the '50's. Demand soon spread to southern California as well as in the San Francisco–Sacramento district, and San Pedro became an important lumber-receiving port.

The lumber industry is of prime importance to the Pacific Northwest. Over half of the total virgin timber in the

United States is in the three Coast states, a feature of unusual significance, since three-fourths of the American lumber cut and over nine-tenths of the superior grades comes from virgin stands. Washington is the ranking state in Douglas fir, hemlock, cedar, and spruce, Oregon in western yellow pine, and California in redwood, sugar pine, and white fir. The principal cut in both Washington and Oregon is Douglas fir, and in California it is western yellow pine. From the standpoint of lumber production in 1929, Washington ranked first among the states of the Union, Oregon second, and California (together with Nevada) fifth.

In the fiscal year 1922 both grain and lumber, including logs, were exported from the Pacific States region in greater volume than were petroleum products in bulk and in packages combined. Since that year, with the tremendously active California oil production, neither commodity has been a close rival of mineral oil in volume of outward shipments, yet both are still elements of great importance in the West Coast trade. Logs and lumber in recent years have ranked second, with a well-defined increasing tendency (Fig. 15). The average annual export for 1928–1930 was 3.2 million long tons, a gain of more than 75 per cent above the average for 1922–1924.[3] Present Coast exports of Pacific logs and lumber constitute 60 per cent of the total lumber exports from the United States.

Like petroleum, lumber represents the exploitation of a natural resource, the reduction of the magnificent stands of timber of the Pacific Coast states. Unlike petroleum, lumber resources may be restored by scientific methods, so that these states need not look forward to the time when this great industry will disappear from the region. The methods and rate of lumber production in the past have utterly destroyed much good timber land and have threatened exhaustion of the forest wealth of the Pacific in the

---

[3] The tremendous depression in the American lumber industry can be appreciated when one considers that the total production for 1932, estimated at 8,328 million board feet, was nearly 3,500 million feet less than in 1869, when the population of the United States was less than one-third of the present figure. Happily, there has been a great revival at the Pacific lumber mills of the United States and Canada during 1933 and 1934.

same fashion as in other parts of the country. Fortunately, however, wiser policies are gradually being adopted before it is too late. There is no reason why the Pacific Coast, and particularly the Pacific Northwest, may not in perpetuity find itself one of the world's greatest regions of surplus lumber production.

Closely allied to the great lumber resources of the Northwest are those of the pulpwood forests, upon which rests a rapidly growing paper industry in this region. While considerable paper and paper stock is imported through all the major Pacific Coast ports, exports are increasing steadily and rapidly, so that in both 1929 and 1930 the net import balance was comparatively small. In consideration of the great pulpwood resources of the Northwest, which extend through southern Alaska, and the superabundance of water power in the region, it is more than probable that in the future the Pacific Coast will rank among the world's net exporters of paper; even now, more than one-third of all paper exports shipped by water from the United States originate in this area.

After the decline of the hide-and-tallow trade, typical of the pastoral era of agricultural development in California, the northern part of the Great Valley became an immense granary where crops were grown and harvested before the summer's drought withered vegetation. At the same time the expansion of agriculture in the Oregon country added other large areas suited to the production of cereals. Accordingly grain early became one of the greatest products of the American Pacific Coast, adding much more to the permanent wealth of the region than was contributed directly by the spectacular yellow metal. In the export trade, grain and grain products now rank third in volume after petroleum and lumber (Figure 15, p. 84). Grain and flour exports combined have averaged annually well over a million long tons in the years covered by the reports of the United States Shipping Board; only once, in 1925, did the aggregate of the two fall below one million tons. In value, likewise, this group of products ranks high among the totals of all customs districts except Los Angeles (see Appendix Table IV). In the Oregon district, which is pre-

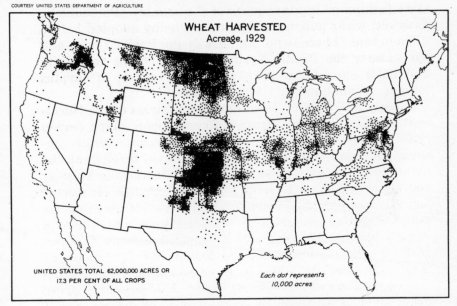

FIG. 17.—Wheat regions of the United States.

dominantly the port of Portland, wheat and wheat-flour exports have constituted more than half the value of all exports.

Portland holds the lead on the Pacific in the export of grain, a position which it owes largely to its location at the gateway of the wheat-producing region of the Columbia River basin. Because of its water-level route Portland enjoys a 10 per cent differential in rail rates from points embracing a large area in the lower Columbia and the Snake River valleys, including southeastern Washington, most of Idaho south of the Panhandle, and northeastern Oregon. Thus, from a mileage standpoint, it draws traffic which might appear tributary to Puget Sound. This situation is naturally unsatisfactory to commercial interests of Seattle and Tacoma, and repeated appeals have been made to the Interstate Commerce Commission for a removal of this differential. Nevertheless, Puget Sound ports likewise handle a heavy volume of wheat and flour exports, and the value of the two together is exceeded at the Washington customs

district only by those of lumber and of copper and its manufactures. The freight rate structure may be revised.

It cannot be said that exports of grain and flour from
this coast are showing any definite tendency toward increase
in the post-war period. They fluctuate sharply from year
to year, as may be seen from a glance at Figure 15 (p. 84).
The average for 1928–1930 is somewhat lower than that for
1922–1924, but, on the other hand, it is substantially greater
than that for 1925–1927. It is perhaps safe to prophesy that
grain exports from the Pacific area will probably move in
sympathy with those from the rest of the country, and, since
the national tendency is toward reduced exports of primary
foodstuffs, Pacific Coast exports of grain and flour are more
likely to pursue an irregular downward than upward course
over a long period of years. Currently, they account for
from one-fifth to one-seventh of the water-borne grain and
flour exports of the country.

The exports of wheat from the Pacific Coast states
amount to approximately one-fourth of the total United
States wheat exports. Mention should be made also of the
increasing cereal production in the Mountain States, particularly spring wheat. It is interesting to note that, while
the San Francisco customs district reports a considerable
export movement in grain and grain preparations, the dominant product among these is barley and not wheat, although
wheat flour is second in importance to barley among cereal
exports at this port. Rice, rice flour, and meal are also of
considerable volume among exports of such products from
the San Francisco customs district.

Barley cultivation in California increased from 890,000
to 1,500,000 acres from 1900 to 1910, when wheat nearly disappeared. An unusually favorable combination of soil and
climate yields an exceedingly high quality of malting barley,
raised in the great interior valley where the soil is too light
to produce high-grade wheat. Since about ten million bushels of this barley are exported annually to the United
Kingdom for use in the brewing industry, this commodity
provides an important sea trade.

In the Pacific subtropical region the value of agricultural
output is fully half that of all crops raised in the state,

although the acreage is only one-fourth. California is the greatest vegetable-producing state in the nation, and except for the portion furnished by Imperial Valley nearly all of the commercial crop is grown in the subtropical region. Until recently potatoes have been the leading crop; now the leading shipments are in the following order—lettuce, cantaloupes, potatoes, cauliflower, watermelons, tomatoes, onions, carrots, asparagus, and peas. The greatest money value is in the lettuce, cantaloupe, and asparagus crops. California contributes over one-sixth of the nation's acreage of fruits and nuts and over one-third of their value. Her exports constitute one-third of the dried-fruit products, one-half of the canned sardines, and over one-sixth of the entire canned pack. The live-stock situation in California is interesting because, while the production of cheese and poultry products is greatly in excess of state demand and dairy production and consumption are virtually balanced, there is a considerable deficiency in the supply of beef and pork, which are shipped in from neighboring states.

The intimate connection between energy resources and agriculture is shown by the greater use of electricity on California farms compared with that in other sections of the United States. Of the power used for agricultural purposes in California, 42 per cent is electrical and only 18 per cent is furnished by work animals, compared to $5\frac{1}{2}$ per cent and 60 per cent, respectively, for the country as a whole. Each farm worker in the state utilizes over three times as much power as the average for the United States, and for every hour of human labor used on California farms $1\frac{1}{2}$ horsepower hours are similarly employed. Advocates of agriculture and electrification point to the fact that the average net income of the California farm is larger than that of farmers in any other state and over twice the average for the United States (figures based on a survey made by the United States Department of Agriculture in 1924).

Since power and labor represent approximately 60 per cent of the total cost of producing national crops, further replacement of labor by machinery and the introduction of cheaper and more efficient mechanical units present one of the best means of reducing agricultural costs. In manu-

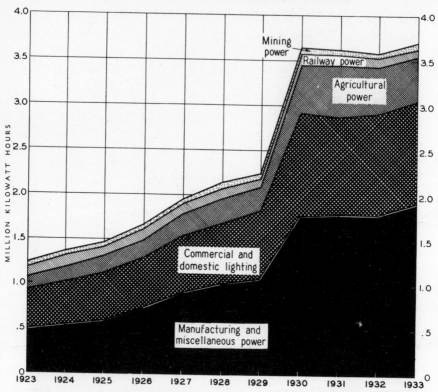

Fig. 18.—Chart showing growth of electric power. From Pacific Gas & Electric Company annual report.

facturing, electricity has proved the cheapest and most efficient form of power, and about 70 per cent of the total horsepower used in factories now comes from this source, compared to less than 6 per cent of the power on all farms.

The three leading groups of exports from the American Pacific Coast from the point of view of tonnage, namely, petroleum, lumber, and grain, have in the past moved largely in shipload lots. Adding together all tanker cargoes, grain, and lumber, but excluding flour and petroleum in packages, the exports of these first three classes constitute at the present time about 80 per cent of the tonnage of all Pacific Coast exports. With the exception of a small volume of highly manufactured lumber products, such as furniture, the commodities named are characteristically low-freight-

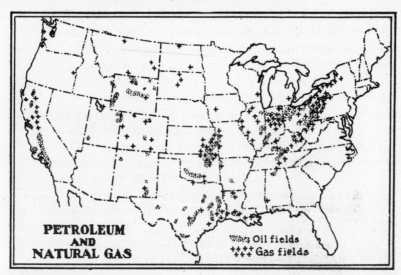

Fig. 19.—Map of United States showing fields of petroleum and natural gas.

rate products, and even flour and petroleum in packages may be so classed. Since grain and raw lumber are typically tramp-ship cargoes, this tonnage which such vessels lift at North Pacific ports helps to reduce the disproportion between outbound and inbound cargoes with which liner services have to contend. Thus tankers and tramp vessels operate to smooth out cargo inequalities, especially in the marked seasonal trade variations.

Fast liner services on the Pacific thus find a relatively small amount of highly profitable export cargo even in times of normal freight rates. Many of them are fitted with tanks for participation in the movement of petroleum in bulk.[4]

[4] Pacific Coast ports offer a marked contrast to those of the North Atlantic in the proportion of high- and low-freight-rate export cargoes. According to the United States Shipping Board, in the fiscal year 1930 there were 13.1 million long tons of exports, excluding tanker cargoes, from the North Atlantic district (as far south as, and including, Hampton Roads). Of this total, 7.8 million tons were classed as low- and 5.3 million tons as high-freight-rate cargoes. On the Pacific, of 6.4 million tons of non-tanker cargoes, 5.2 million tons were low-rate and 1.2 million tons high rate. The respective proportions were very similar in 1929. Exports from Gulf ports, on the other hand, resemble those of the Pacific much more closely than those of the Atlantic.

They likewise carry some grain, and lumber in its less crude forms. For large shipments of such products, however, they can scarcely compete with the low operating and overhead charges of tramp vessels.

Although of far less importance in bulk than the commodities already discussed, horticultural products are being exported from the American Pacific Coast in growing quantities. This movement is assuming considerable importance both as an economic asset of the region and as a source of revenue for the shipping companies. In point of view of tonnage the exports of fruits and nuts[5] have exceeded those of flour each year since 1924 and thus rank fourth among the groups of export products. In 1922 exports of these commodities from all Pacific ports were only a little over 100,000 tons, but by 1929 they had grown in volume more than five times and the average for 1928–1930 was two and a half times the average for 1922–1924. (See Appendix Table VIII.)

Data are not available to show how much of this movement was composed of fresh products carried as refrigerated cargo, but it is well known that the volume of such exports has been tremendous in recent years. The increasing number and frequency of sailings from Pacific ports of ships equipped with modern refrigerator space, visiting all world ports, is sufficient indication that such products are an important part of the outward cargoes of fast liners.

The problems of successful refrigeration of perishables in transoceanic voyages have not been entirely solved, and heavy losses are occasionally incurred through serious deterioration of commodities en route. Technical and chemical research are resulting in great advances in refrigeration facilities both on land and on water, and after ways and means have been found for reducing this cost materially a far larger amount of potential products can find ready markets.

Each of the major Pacific ports participates to an important extent in the export trade in fruits and related products. From the Northwest goes the bulk of the deciduous fresh

[5] This is the classification adopted by the United States Shipping Board. Presumably it includes dried as well as fresh fruits.

fruits, while California leads in citrus exports. Nevertheless it is somewhat misleading that in 1930 almost as many boxes of citrus fruits were listed among exports from the Washington district as were credited to the Los Angeles district. Clearly there is a considerable movement, presumably by rail, from southern California to Washington. It is certain that such shipments are almost exclusively destined to Canada, since Canada takes some 85 per cent of all oranges exported from the United States; but the method of tabulating overland exports is to credit them to the customs district where they cross the border (see chapter vii). Seattle appears to rank first among Pacific ports on the basis of fresh-fruit exports, even if allowance is made for the probable overland movement to Canada, some of which are doubtless transshipped to foreign destinations. This port handles the products of the great orchard regions of the Wenatchee and Yakima valleys. Apples are the largest single item among fresh fruit exports from the Pacific Coast, as they are from the United States as a whole. Washington produces one-third of all the commercial apples grown in the United States. In addition to the apple industry, Washington has a leading position in the pack of salmon and in the canned-fruit and -vegetable industry, and is the depository of the only important gold deposits in the Northwest section of the United States. The increasing dependence upon Northwest production is evident through a net decrease of 79,000,000 apple trees in the United States from 1910 to 1925, and a further decrease of 21,000,000 trees from 1925 to 1930, making a total decrease of 100,000,000 trees. The eleven Western states, on the other hand, produced two decades ago nineteen million bushels, while in 1932 they produced over fifty million bushels, an increase of 163 per cent. The number of bearing trees increased 10 per cent and the yield per bearing tree gained from an average of 1.5 bushels to about 4.3 bushels. According to the statistics of the International Apple Association, for the season of 1932 the Pacific Coast ports exported a total of 7,500,000 boxes, which represented two-thirds of the total exports from all North American ports.

The season for 1933 exceeded greatly a previous record,

since the Pacific Northwest exported 10,300,000 boxes of apples and 2,223,190 boxes of pears to all world markets, as against the 1932 totals of 9,986,490 boxes and 1,869,495 boxes, respectively.

The following tabulation, taken from the *Western Canner and Packer* for March 20, 1933, shows how the West ranks in the production of canned and dried fruits and vegetables:

	Value	Percentage
Total canned fruits (1931)	$ 98,324,169	......
Western output	75,300,188	......
Percentage from the West	....	76.5%
Total dried fruits	60,564,703	......
Western output	53,264,597	......
Percentage from the West	....	87.9%
Total canned vegetables	176,308,546	......
Western output	23,198,074	......
Percentage	....	13.1%

A number of prepared foods are also of considerable importance in Pacific Coast trade. Exports of canned and dried fruits and vegetables, fish canned or otherwise preserved, and condensed, dried, and evaporated milk all give evidence of the fact that this region is one of surplus food production, and that these surpluses, as far as they cannot be marketed advantageously in the fresh state, are prepared in various ways in order to increase the area where they may be distributed in edible condition. It is noteworthy that among ten main groups of products exported from the San Francisco customs district of sufficient aggregate value to warrant separate tabulation by the writer, seven fall within the class of foodstuffs, either fresh or prepared; from the Washington district, five out of ten are included in this category; from the Oregon district, two out of three; and from the Los Angeles district, two out of six. Except for grain, these food products represent a relatively intensive agriculture and, in most cases, the application of considerable labor in processing.

The chemical industry has likewise made relatively rapid progress on the Pacific Coast in the post-war years. Unless the basis of classification was changed to include among chemicals in later years certain products which were excluded in the beginning, exports of chemicals have increased in volume more than seven fold between 1922 and 1930. In the latter year they were reported to total 133,000 long tons. Although the Pacific Coast ships substantial and rapidly growing quantities of chemicals, it is also a region of imports for such products. It is significant that these imports do not appear to be increasing. If one may assume a reasonably consistent classification of a group which is difficult to define, then chemical imports and intercoastal receipts combined are not at the present time nearly so great in volume as exports. In terms of value, however, the situation is probably otherwise, since the more highly manufactured and expensive chemicals probably continue to come mainly from regions having more established chemical industries.[6]

Comparatively few other commodities are exported from the American Pacific Coast which are of outstanding importance from either the tonnage or the value standpoint. A fairly large but fluctuating quantity of ores and metals leaves this region, among which copper products lead. Most of the Pacific Coast copper exports are shipped from Puget Sound ports which have received ore and crude metal from Canada, Alaska, and the west coast of South America.

During the decade of the 1920's there was mined and shipped out of Alaska far more copper, in terms of value, than gold. Only within the last two or three years, when the declining price level reduced the value of copper and discouraged copper-mining operations, did the Alaska gold output, stimulated by enhanced price quotations, rise above that of copper in value.[7] Copper exports from Pacific ports, excluding Alaska, whose foreign trade is very small, aver-

[6] This point cannot readily be tested because of the wide variation in classification of chemicals between the statistics of the Department of Commerce and the United States Shipping Board. The former has a detailed list of specifically named commodities; the latter uses only the group term "Chemicals."

[7] Reduction of imported copper ores and the refinement of crude copper on the Pacific Coast yields a large surplus not only for export but also for domestic disposal in the eastern part of the country. For the most part this metal is shipped as refined copper in ingots, bars, et cetera, although some more highly manufactured forms are also exported.

aged close to 75,000 long tons in the 1928–1930 period, or about 20 per cent of the total copper exports from the United States.

A few further words upon the development of the resources of Alaska and Hawaii are necessary to complete the story of maritime trade progress through the exploitation of economic assets. Neither of these territories figures prominently in direct transpacific commercial relations, inasmuch as their intercourse is chiefly with the mainland direct, but they have played important rôles in the economic history of the American Pacific States region.

Neither politically nor economically was Alaska much of an asset to Russia. Ruthless hunting of fur-bearing animals rapidly diminished their numbers. Living conditions were almost intolerable, and natives and Russians alike died in great numbers from starvation and disease. The pitiful settlements in Alaska were utterly dependent on food from the south or across the sea. It was in the hope of establishing a supply colony that the Russians undertook settlement on the coast of California a few miles north of San Francisco Bay; they could not rely on being supplied by the residents of California, since Spain did not encourage commercial intercourse through the employment of foreign ships. Politically the retention of a foothold in North America promised to be costly and embarrassing, and the experience of the other European nations with their American colonies suggested that a Russian colony could not expect permanency.

The sale of Alaska to the United States was consummated in 1867. For thirty years thereafter its economic history was uneventful. Then came the Klondike gold discoveries on the Canadian side of the international boundary line with percussions throughout the Yukon Basin. The influx of prospectors was numbered in the tens of thousands and many an old "sourdough" still tramps over these forbidding regions, committed to a life in which all the hardships of yesterday and today are forgotten and endured on the chance that tomorrow may bring wealth and ease. Gold output steadily declined after the more accessible and easily found stream beds were worked. Permanent output usually depends on the industrial working of gold-bearing ores. Such ores are found in the coast district and without doubt exist in many other parts of Alaska. In a land which does not tempt prospectors to settle down and establish homes, gold mining, particularly placer mining, leaves little permanent impress on the economic development of the region. For a number of years the major volume of gold output has come from large, well-equipped mines, and the individual operator becomes a less important factor each season.

After a considerable period of neglect the United States government is taking a more active interest in the 600,000 square miles of arctic and sub-arctic domain. The Alaska Railroad has been built and is being operated by the government, although at a considerable loss; roads are being constructed; educational work in mining and agriculture is being fostered; experiment stations are being maintained; and great effort is being made to render the natives of the northern plains regions economically secure through the maintenance of reindeer herds.

In spite of vast resources in mineral wealth the sea continues to be Alaska's greatest asset, as it was in the first era of Russian exploitation. Nowadays the sea furnishes the salmon, instead of the sea otter and the seal—food instead of raiment. The total value of the salmon catch in 1930 was well over thirty million dollars, whereas the gold output was only eight and one-half million.

For the most part Alaskan salmon fishing and canning is a large-scale enterprise based on capital supplied from the states of California and Washington. The United States Bureau of Fisheries reports a world pack of canned salmon for the year 1933 amounting to 9,071,000 standard cases of 48 one-pound cans, which was distributed as follows: Alaska, 5,226,000 cases; Pacific Coast states, 1,137,000 cases; British Columbia, 1,265,000 cases; Siberia, 670,000 cases; and Japan, 773,000 cases. Thus, the Alaskan contribution represents nearly 60 per cent of the world's pack. This industry increases the income of Alaska mainly through the wages paid to native helpers. In general the profits made in Alaskan enterprises are distributed elsewhere, so that locally controlled capital does not increase rapidly.

The greatest handicaps to the exploitation of the resources which indubitably exist in Alaska are its forbidding
climate and its comparative inaccessibility. Except for the
strong gambler's urge which draws the prospector to such
regions, few men will choose so harsh a land in which to live
until driven by the pressure of population from more favorable areas, and the North American continent is far from
having reached that density of population.

When Captain Cook made the Sandwich Islands (Hawaii) a haven and a way station, the beginning of their rôle
at the crossroads of the Pacific appeared. Northwest fur-
traders also found them of inestimable value. Here was a
place to recuperate from the rigors of fur-hunting and trading among hostile Indians in northern waters. Here, likewise,
provisions could usually be obtained for the next venture.
The whalers who followed in the wake of the short-lived
fur trade also made Hawaii a base of operations. These
vessels put into Hawaii with cargoes of oil and bone, disposed of them to other vessels which were there awaiting
them, and ventured forth again.

Some enterprising trader discovered that sandalwood,
greatly prized by Chinese mandarins, abounded in the forests of Hawaii, and there ensued a very brisk and highly
profitable trade to supplement the failing income which
resulted from the waning supplies of sea-otter skins. Here
again greed for immediate profits all but stripped Hawaiian
forests of this fragrant wood, as it had succeeded in destroying the sea otter. After a comparatively short time, therefore, this commerce also dwindled to insignificant proportions.

An event extremely important to Hawaii from an economic standpoint occurred in 1875 when a treaty with the
United States was negotiated which granted free entry of
Hawaiian sugar into the United States in return for per-
mission to the American government to use Pearl Harbor
as a supply base or naval station. In 1887 Pearl Harbor was
ceded to the United States. Here were definite steps toward
both political and economic fusion.

During these years when American capital and enterprise had followed the missionaries into Hawaii, agricul-

tural resources had been developed and plantations estab-
lished with the energy of a people who had spread from the
Atlantic to the Pacific in the nineteenth century. In 1898
Hawaii was admitted to the Union as a territory.

The economic history of the Islands in the present century
has been one of steadily increasing population and agricultural output. Its greatest resource is sugar, and the prosperity of a large percentage of its people is bound up with
the rise and fall of sugar prices. Nearly a quarter of a
million acres are devoted to sugar cane. In 1929 and 1930,
in spite of low sugar prices, the annual value of sugar shipments to the United States was close to sixty million dollars.
Canned pineapples, valued at forty million dollars, came
next in importance. Other crops, including coffee, rice,
tobacco, taro, and miscellaneous fruits and vegetables, fall
very far behind sugar and pineapples in value of output.
A recognition of the greater degree of economic security
coming from a more diversified agriculture has not yet succeeded in displacing these two products from their position
of overwhelming importance. Plantation methods for both
products are highly developed and the agricultural technique employed is, in general, based on the best scientific
knowledge now available. In the case of pineapples, the
finished product is shipped from the country, while the
sugar industry extends only through the process of reducing
cane to raw sugar; refining plants on the mainland complete
the manufacturing process.

Summarizing the record and bringing it up to date, we
find that the outbound water-borne commerce of the American Pacific area consists in large measure of raw and semi-
manufactured products which the natural resources of the
region provide. In foreign, intercoastal, and coastwise shipments this condition prevails. For the most part, the greatest surpluses have come from resources which present rates
of exploitation will soon exhaust. If, and when, the petroleum fields of southern California are drained dry, that
industry will disappear from the region. If forest lands
continue to be as wastefully lumbered as in the past, they too
will before long be almost worthless. One great source of
wealth from the sea—namely, sea otters—was entirely de-

stroyed a century ago by unrestrained exploitation, while whales and seals were all but exterminated and salmon have been gravely threatened with the same fate.

The record of activities by which men have gained a livelihood in the Pacific world, romantic as it is in many ways, is one that contains many regrettable pages. Spectacular results in a short time may be achieved from economic activity which confines itself to "skimming the cream" from the great abundance of natural resources at hand. From the perspective of those who are threatened with a skim-milk inheritance the record of that achievement does not look so impressive. Remarkable as has been the economic development of the American Pacific Coast, as of the entire United States, self-congratulation needs to be tempered with analysis as to the price which is being paid for the wealth attained. Mining is a temporary industry, and the entire nation has been guilty of "mining" rather than "cropping" fields, streams, forests, and ocean.

And yet the first steps toward building up an economic life in the American Pacific world on a more permanent basis than that of pioneer exploitation have been taken, and the foundations are laid for the more complex industrial life which lies ahead. Reforestation is beginning to be practiced. The salmon and seal are under government protection to prevent extermination. Water, the leading economic resource of the Far West, has not been singled out for separate treatment. Extensive irrigation projects have made highly productive vast areas now capable of supporting relatively dense populations.

Manufacturing for local requirements is spreading to include a wider market where conditions are favorable. Notable among these are the fruit-and-vegetable processing plants, trade in the products of which has shown such pronounced growth in recent years. Paper mills, with access to vast and, if properly handled, perpetual supplies of pulp wood and cheap hydroelectric power, promise to convert this region into one of net surplus of paper, if they have not already done so. Similarly there are the beginnings of other industries, some based on imported raw materials such as rubber and vegetable oils.

The tourist industry, except as it may occasion additional forest fires or disfiguring structures in places of scenic beauty, is one which may be exploited to the fullest without reducing the permanent assets of the region. All these developments hasten the day when the Pacific Coast may live comfortably on current income instead of depleting dangerously the capital with which it has been so generously endowed by Nature. Until that day arrives, this region will not be assured a place of permanent importance in world economy, nor will its maritime potentialities be properly realized.

V. Beginnings of Seacoast Trade

An island upon which Bering's decimated crew spent the winter of 1741–1742, after their leader's tragic death, provides the setting for the first step in the exploitations by white men of the bountiful natural resources of the North American Pacific Coast.[1] After the Russian conquest of Siberia in the seventeenth century a great impetus was given to solving the problem of the geographic relation between the northeast coast of Asia and the American continent.

Bering's two expeditions proved to be large factors in the exploitation and eventual settlement of the Pacific Northwest and the Pacific Coast as a whole. His stranded crew found their winter island haven teeming with sea otter and other marine animals, the skins of which survivors carried home in the spring. The sale of these skins made them rich, and before long many a Russian adventurer made his way to the Commander Islands and beyond. The Russian system of levying tribute in furs on subject natives gradually spread throughout the islands and into the mainland of far northwest America.

For nearly forty years Russia enjoyed exclusive control of this profitable venture. Then out of the South Pacific sailed one of England's greatest explorers, Captain Cook, to settle the question for all time as to whether or not there existed a usable passage either to Hudson's Bay or to the Arctic Ocean and, incidentally, to take possession for Great Britain of all the new lands he visited. As late as 1776, then, Pacific North America was interesting to the British primarily because it might reveal a passage from sea to sea, and the accomplishments of Cook's voyage toward making this a land important in its own right were largely unanticipated by-products of the expedition.

Sea-otter furs were obtained at Nootka Sound on Vancouver Island, where Cook made a landing and later featured by the exploits of Lieutenant John Meares, and also in Alaska,

[1] Interesting speculations appear in an article by H. R. Wagner entitled "Apocryphal Voyages to the Northwest Coast of America," American Antiquary Society, *Proceedings*, 1931, Vol. IV, No. 1, pp. 177–234.

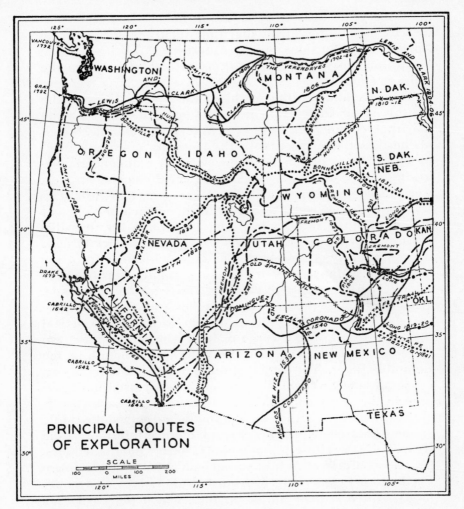

Fig. 20.—Map of Western United States showing principal routes of exploration. (Based upon *United States Geological Survey Bulletin 817.*)

where the expedition encountered not only natives obviously used to trading with white men but later the entrenched Russian fur traders. Stopping at Canton en route to England, the expedition found the demand for the furs so great and prices so high that the news spread rapidly. The published report of Captain Cook's expedition appeared in 1784, exactly 150 years ago. It made unmistakably clear the commercial possibilities of the maritime fur trade of the Pacific Northwest. Soon ships, chiefly American and British, began to appear in search of these skins so highly prized in the Chinese markets.

The revelation to the world of the potentialities of the Northwest fur trade came at a most opportune time for the maritime commerce of the new American Republic, which at the outset was faced with the necessity of complete reorganization as the result of the political realignments following the Revolutionary War. Protected colonial markets were then regarded as a thing of the past, and American traders with the Orient were handicapped because they had so few products to offer in exchange for the tea and silks of China. Yankee merchant adventurers were quick to seize the opportunity offered by the news which came out of the Northwest. Many a New England family fortune was founded on the rich and rapid rewards of the new trade. The "Columbia," the first American ship to circumnavigate the globe, sailed from Boston to the Northwest Coast and thence to China with a cargo of furs. On its second trip to the Northwest it discovered and entered the mouth of the Columbia River. The contribution of this vessel to American economic and political history can be expressed no better than in the words of Dr. S. E. Morison of Harvard University: "On her first voyage the Columbia had solved the riddle of the China trade. On her second, empire followed in the wake."[2] Massachusetts merchants early dominated the American effort in this trade to such an extent that the entire Pacific Coast came soon to regard Boston ships as synonymous with American ships, an idea which persisted long after the maritime fur trade had dwindled to minor importance.[3]

[2] S. E. Morison, *The Maritime History of Massachusetts, 1783–1860* (1921), p. 51.

[3] During the years of the Nootka affair, and after the settlement of the dispute, Yankee traders made great headway in the competition for the trade until finally they enjoyed the major share of it. Russian ships were excluded from Chinese ports, and the conflicting monopolies of the East Indian Company and the South Sea Company precluded competition from British traders. Japan was then still a hermit nation.

Originally focusing in the Northwest, the trade spread rapidly down the coast into California waters and California ports, where the economic foundation of an American Pacific Empire was unobtrusively laid from Vancouver Island on the north to Lower California on the south. There is no more spectacular chapter in the early history of transpacific maritime commerce than the brief era of the sea-otter trade. There is also, perhaps, no chapter which reflects more pitilessly the qualities of short-sighted greed which the pursuit of quick riches so often reveals in men.[4]

The economic history of the Pacific Coast is by no means all of a piece. In the light of the diversity of its political history, its geographic features, and its natural resources, this is not surprising. From the earliest period of white exploration and occupation one must distinguish between the Pacific Northwest and California. Before the American era political considerations were extremely important, although not solely so, and the mutual interdependence of political and economic factors up to that time makes it difficult to consider them other than in conjunction.

Spain, under whose auspices the New World was discovered and under whose flag, at one time or another, a greater part of the Western Hemisphere was held or claimed, dominates the early narrative of California. In the Oregon country, on the other hand, the direct influence of Spain was as slight as were her efforts to enforce her claim to sovereignty of that region; here the chief actors were the British, the French Canadians, and the Americans. Here, also, the curtain on the drama of white civilization rose somewhat later than in the Spanish settlements to the south, although the American participation was earlier.

The motif common to both regions, however, is the part played in the exploration and development of the entire Pacific Coast by the protracted search for a shorter passage to the Far East. The discovery of America did not put an

---

[4] The maritime fur trade of the Pacific was followed by land fur trade in the Northwest and also to a lesser extent in California. The Northwest trade was largely in the hands of the British, but the short-lived American venture around Astoria early in the new century helped to buttress the subsequent American claim to sovereignty of the region.

end to the search, but rather intensified the efforts of many nations bent toward finding an easier and shorter route to the fabled wealth of the Indies. Countless explorations were inspired in the three centuries during which this dream held sway. The contributions to geographical knowledge which they made paved the way for trade and settlement. For many years the North American Pacific owed its importance in the eyes of the commercial world to its location as a gateway to the East.

In what is now California the chief contacts with the outside world during the early decades of the nineteenth century came through Spanish ships, mostly from Mexico except for the Manila galleon. Trade contacts with non-Spanish ships prior to the beginning of the nineteenth century were slight. All such intercourse was prohibited by law until 1828, when Mexico removed the centuries-old restrictions. Nevertheless, since such trade was advantageous to the Californians, as well as to the Yankee and other ships which came into Pacific waters, the years of Spain's slipping grasp on the New World saw increasing violation of this prohibition. Foreign ships began to come with greater frequency, managed an entry on one pretext or another, and developed contraband trade of such proportions that the law against trading with foreigners soon appeared honored more in its breach than in its observance. There were too many products of which the Californians stood in need to enable them to withstand the alluring and varied temptations of these enterprising smugglers.

Yankees were prominent among these traders, and with the increasing absorption of Europe in the Napoleonic wars, American ships soon outnumbered all others. Among them were many fur traders, seeking the beautiful sea otter in southern waters as those in the northern latitudes became depleted. When the sea-otter trade declined, whaling attracted increasing numbers; by the 1830's, as those who have read Richard Henry Dana's classic are aware, a brisk trade in hides and tallow was flourishing between California cattle owners and the "Boston" ships. This trade was the backbone of the commercial intercourse on the Coast up to the momentous events of 1848 and 1849, and many a ranch owner acquired a handsome fortune from the thousands of cattle which his great landholdings supported.

Shortly after the beginning of the Mexican régime, Americans began to appear in California as more or less permanent members of the community. For the most part trade brought them there, both those who arrived from the sea and those who made their way overland. These first comers were mainly fur trappers or traders to whom a more settled life in richly endowed California made an appeal. Later, as the number of Americans in California increased, organized parties of emigrants to the Pacific Coast greatly accelerated the growth of the American population of California. Many parties which left the Mississippi Valley as a unit during the early years of the '40's divided upon reaching Fort Hall; some, usually the majority, turned north for Oregon, and the rest made their way across the Sierra to California.

Of tremendous assistance to these emigrants was the settlement of New Helvetia, near the confluence of the Sacramento and American rivers. This settlement was founded in 1840 by John Sutter, of German-Swiss extraction, who planned the ultimate creation of an independent state in the great California valley. His settlement was half-military in character, but its activities embraced a wide variety of agricultural and commercial projects. The location of New Helvetia made it of great assistance to parties entering California from northern or central routes, and many an exhausted, half-starved group found shelter and recuperation with this hospitable and versatile man.

Thus, year by year, during the '30's and '40's of the century, American settlers arrived in California, some by sea but more by land. Some became Mexican citizens; some married into Spanish families. Many acquired land and many pursued trade. Their influence, both on California and on the attitude of the people of the United States toward California, greatly affected the political events which packed the closing years of the first half of the century. Moreover, one of these immigrants, John Marshall, an obscure arrival from the Oregon country, was to be the instrument of an event more spectacular and more revolutionary to the economic and social fabric of the entire Pacific Coast than anything that can be imagined. It is an unusual historical coincidence that the two events, acquisition of Alta California by the United States and the discovery of gold, occurred almost simultaneously, each uninfluenced by the other.

The settlement of the Oregon boundary in 1846 and the acquisition of California from Mexico two years later gave the United States approximately 1,500 miles of coastline (or 3,700 miles, including all indentations) facing the Pacific Ocean. This new territory naturally stimulated a vastly increased interest in the Pacific. By this time, however, as a result of the Industrial Revolution, commerce and markets of Europe had gained tremendously in importance relative to those of the Far East and so, although the new territory faced the Orient, its most promising trade opportunities now lay in the opposite direction, in the domestic markets of the Atlantic seaboard and in Europe.

From a political as well as a commercial point of view it was apparent that communication facilities between the West and the East needed great improvement. A year after the acquisition of Oregon, steps were taken looking to the establishment of regular communication by water with the Oregon country. An act of 1845 authorized the Postmaster General to enter into contracts with steamship companies for the transportation of mails between American and foreign ports, and between American ports coastwise. Under this authorization a contract was made with the Pacific Mail Steamship Company for a monthly service between Astoria, Oregon, and the Isthmus of Panama, with calls at San Diego, Monterey, and San Francisco. This service, inaugurated in October 1848, shortly after the beginning of the gold rush,[5] connected at the Isthmus with the United States Mail Steamship Company having a contract for semi-monthly service from New York to Colon. The route became of exceedingly great importance to both temporary and permanent emigrants to California and stimulated the building of the railway across the Isthmus, begun in 1850 and completed in 1855.

---

[5] This unforeseen event made operations highly successful for the company and resulted in a supplementary contract in 1851 for semi-monthly service. See chapter xvii.

The Pacific Mail Steamship Company was not alone in undertaking to transport eager gold-seekers from the Isthmus to San Francisco. In 1849 there were twelve steamships making such runs, a larger number than were employed at that time between New York and Liverpool and New York and Havre combined.[6] The discovery of gold likewise stimulated intercoastal shipping via the Horn or the Straits of Magellan. In 1849 it was reported that as many as seven hundred vessels of all descriptions cleared for California from various ports on the Atlantic seaboard.

California gold was also responsible in large measure for one of the most romantic developments in the maritime history of the United States—the clipper ship. Originated in New York and brought to its highest perfection in the shipyards of Massachusetts, the clipper ship was the answer of Yankee ingenuity and daring to the need for fast and yet faster means of communication between the Atlantic and the Pacific shores of the young continental empire. The brilliant epoch of American maritime ascendancy was almost at its end, and it was more than fitting that it should close in the blaze of glory shed by the brief but dashing era when the clipper ship reigned supreme.

Apparently the "Sea Witch" was the first of its type to be sent around the Horn with men and goods for the gold fields of California. It arrived in San Francisco on July 24, 1850, after a run of only 97 days. For the few short years during which the operation of such craft was profitable one dazzling performance after another marked the voyages of the clipper fleet employed on the California route. There were 18 ships which made 22 runs of under 100 days between Atlantic ports and San Francisco in the decade between 1850 and 1860. Pre-eminent among them was the "Flying Cloud," built by the greatest of clipper-ship designers, Donald McKay, which, on her maiden voyage in 1851, reached San Francisco 89 days out of New York. Three years later she duplicated this performance, a record only once equaled by any other sailing ship.

[6] E. R. Johnson and collaborators, *History of Domestic and Foreign Commerce of the United States* (1922), p. 359.

The "Flying Cloud" was the fastest sailing ship in American history. Of the hundreds of clipper ships which traveled between the Atlantic Coast and California from 1849 to 1853 this was the most famous. Its record of less than ninety days between New York and the Golden Gate is remarkable, when one considers the frequent voyages made by other ships requiring ten months' time.

As with the early Northwest fur-trading craft, the clipper ships usually made their way homeward across the Pacific to China and thence around the world (see Figure 4, p. 29). In those days California offered little in the way of return cargo, whereas the costly teas and silks of China were ideal wares for these speedy ships to handle. Merchants offered them double and treble the freight rates that could be obtained by slower sailing ships. Morison says:

> Crack British East-Indiamen humbly awaited a cargo in the treaty-ports for weeks on end, while one American clipper after another sailed proudly in, and secured a return freight almost before her topsails were furled. When the Yankee beauties arrived in the Thames, their decks were thronged with sightseers, their records were written up in the leading papers, and naval draughtsmen took off their lines while in dry-dock.[7]

The clippers, however, were an answer to special conditions, and their relative costliness to build and to operate made them unprofitable luxuries on routes where normal freight rates prevailed. They were employed on the trans-atlantic run to Australia, but it was predominantly the California trade with which they were most completely identified and in which many earned their cost in one voyage. By the middle of the '50's, when the early frenzy of the California gold rush had died out and vessels trading to that coast no longer brought exceptional returns, the brief reign of the Yankee clipper was almost at its end.[8]

---

[7] S. E. Morison, *op. cit.*, p. 359.

[8] Two hundred and forty-six vessels put into San Francisco in 1856 with a total tonnage of 209,902. Eighty-one of these came from New York and forty-four from other Atlantic ports; forty-two hailed from China and twenty-two from Great Britain. The freight paid of this traffic amounted to $4,592,104, more by $500,000 than in 1855, but less than half the sum for 1853 ($11,752,104) (Ernest Seyd, *California and Its Resources*, London, 1858, pp. 72–74).

A valuable report prepared by Honorable Salmon P. Chase, Secretary of the Treasury, to Honorable Hannibal Hamlin, Vice-President of the United States and thus President of the Senate,[9] cites the British official records, which at that time segregated the trade of California from that of other United States ports. The British figures are given as follows:

Year	Imports from California	Exports to California
1856	$ 162,827	$2,226,937
1859	137,760	2,224,570
1861	3,414,968	2,085,691
1866	1,722,294	1,817,236

It is interesting to note that the trade of San Francisco in 1863 amounted to $13,000,000, exclusive of precious metals, with quicksilver, wheat, wool, hides, flour, and copper ore the leading products, and New York and Boston, Great Britain, and China the main destinations. During the years 1854 to 1863, inclusive, the treasure shipments were valued at $464,000,000, three-fourths of it sent to eastern ports of the United States and the rest largely to England and China. Despite the tremendous later importance of the agricultural and horticultural industries in the wealth of California, during this particular period the numerous activities affected by gold discoveries played the leading part in Pacific developments.

It would be difficult to exaggerate the extent to which the California gold rush altered and, in particular, expedited economic development on the entire Pacific Coast. The sudden inrush of fortune seekers from all parts of the world, and the millions in ready wealth which the more fortunate obtained, provided an impetus to material progress by no means confined to regions in the neighborhood of the mines. Thus the exploitation of another resource makes economic history and explains the course of Pacific maritime trade development.

The close of the clipper-ship era of California and transpacific trade is marked by the beginning of a new phase in

9 Report of Secretary of the Treasury, 38th Congress, 1st Session, *Executive Document 55* (1864).

the commercial relations of the Pacific Coast with the rest of the world. California discovered, as had Oregon previously, that grain may be turned to gold, and with a more certain return than comes to those who seek the elusive metal hidden in the waste places of the earth. Wheat and later flour began to leave Pacific ports, bound for the Atlantic seaboard and for the Far East. The first flour exports to Japan from the Columbia River district of which there is a record were made in 1857. Having largely left behind her the purely pastoral era of the Spanish-Mexican régime, California was well embarked on the next phase, in which grain-growing predominated. The West again had something to offer the ships of the world to replace the dwindling hide-and-tallow trade, by that time pre-empted by South America.

It is fascinating to learn from a leading historian, writing in 1882, of the rapid development of maritime activities on the Pacific Coast. Two quotations from John S. Hittell are noteworthy:

For twenty years after the discovery of gold at Coloma, the maritime traffic of this coast was extremely active. All the freight and most of the travel to and from California took the sea route. During the flush period of the placers, the miners and traders, whom they enriched, demanded large supplies of foreign products. To accommodate them, steamers more commodious, and large sailing-vessels swifter than any previously seen, were constructed. The California clipper was the name of the finest class of sailers on the sea. In 1850, San Francisco had become one of the greatest seaports, and its maritime commerce continues to grow, though much of its freight coming from and going to the Atlantic Coast, now takes land routes. . . . .

San Francisco is the only American seaport, except New York, that imports regularly from France and China, and the consumption of French and Chinese products is much larger on our coast, in proportion to population, than in any other part of the Union.[10]

Great changes have followed in both the domestic and foreign trade of the United States. Incalculably facilitated by the Panama Canal, round-the-world shipping services are a post-war revival, although now on a regular schedule,

---

[10] John S. Hittell, *The Commerce and Industries of the Pacific Coast of North America* (1882), pp. 195 and 207.

of those highly profitable ventures of Yankee merchant-seamen in the early days of the Republic. Long since has the merchant function been separated from that of the carrier. The clipper ship wrote finis to such undertakings. Changed, too, of course, are the wares borne across the seas, but, so far, the direction of the voyage remains the same. The world exchangeable surpluses are still so distributed as to make a westbound voyage around the world more productive of cargoes than one going in the opposite direction.

It is a far cry from the incredible cockleshells at the end of the eighteenth and the early years of the nineteenth century to the huge, power-driven liners of today. Many a sailing vessel under 100 tons manned by officers and crew no older than the present generation of college students then safely made its way around the Horn, across the Pacific, and through the dangerous, poorly charted, reef-and-rock-strewn waters of the Southern Seas during this bold era. The sailing fleet reached its culmination, however, in the clipper ships of the middle decades of the century; the age of steamships was already at hand. Substitution of iron for wood hastened the decline of the sailing vessel, and the building of transcontinental railways added to its burden of competition from faster means of transport. Nevertheless, sails survived longer in the waters of the Pacific than elsewhere, and the shortage of tonnage during the World War gave them one last brief period of significance before the final curtain on the romantic drama which was theirs. And now the steamship, which crowded sails from the sea, is fast being overtaken on the Pacific by the motor ship. California petroleum spells the difference between a profitable and a losing voyage on routes where coal is not abundant and distances are long.

But the story is only partly told if we fail to emphasize the tremendous importance of the opening of the Panama Canal on American and world history. The great importance of this maritime route can never be overlooked in Pacific Coast annals, and no better interpreter can be found than Professor Henry Morse Stephens of the University of California, who, as president of the Panama-Pacific Historical Congress held in the San Francisco Bay region in July 1915, uttered these telling words:

The completion of the Panama-Pacific Canal opens the fourth chapter in the history of the Pacific Ocean. Since the Asiatic and American peoples seem to have had no regular intercourse across the Ocean, even if occasional fishermen may have been blown from shore to shore by the winds, the first chapter opened with the coming of Europeans almost simultaneously to gaze upon the Pacific Ocean from both east and west, at the beginning of the sixteenth century. For about two hundred years the Ocean remained a Spanish lake, disturbed only by the intervention of adventurers, explorers, and pirates of other nations. Then came the second chapter, the chapter of conflict between the nations of Europe, which closed when the Spanish-American countries, the United States of America, and the Dominion of Canada occupied the American coast-line of the Ocean. The third chapter covers the greater part of the nineteenth century, during which Europe made spasmodic efforts among the islands and in China to secure a foothold, and the power of New Japan arose. This epoch now ends. The completion of the Panama Canal has brought Europe into closer touch with the Pacific Ocean; the old isolation of the American coast of the Pacific has come to an end; and new problems have arisen for merchants and politicians alike.[11]

The opening of the Panama Canal to traffic on August 15, 1914, brought to a close another epoch in the maritime history of the world. Old trade routes gave way to new; regions formerly cut off from each other by barriers to easy communication now found themselves measurably nearer to each other; commodities limited to local distribution found wide markets. When man completed what Nature had so nearly accomplished along the narrow isthmus between North and South America, mingling the waters of the Atlantic and Pacific Oceans, the foundation was laid for a new commercial era.

[11] H. Morse Stephens and Herbert E. Bolton, editors, *The Pacific Ocean in History* (1917), p. 23.

VI. Effects of the Panama Canal

Profound and world-wide changes in trade routes and international economic relationships have developed in consequence of the opening of the Panama Canal. Hubert H. Bancroft foresaw clearly the tremendous potential significance of this artery:

As to the necessity of the canal to commerce, or the feasibility of constructing it, the time had passed for such discussion. As to its relative value to one part of the world and to another, it will prove nearer of equal value to all than might appear at the first glance. Whatever helps London, helps all who do business with London, and that is all the world. I cannot say much for the intelligence of the midcontinent man who claims that because his town is not a seaport he will derive no benefit from a ship canal. Let him consider that an inter-oceanic waterway across any isthmus of America would make not only a seaport, but a Pacific seaport, of all the cities in the United States which are situated on or near navigable waters. From all the towns on all the principal lakes and rivers, lakes Michigan, Ontario, and Erie, rivers Ohio, Mississippi, and Missouri, and a score of others, vessels of medium tonnage will ply direct to San Francisco, Yokohama, Hongkong, Manila, Sydney, Valparaiso, and every other Pacific seaport; and where water communication is not already open for access to the sea, the canal once constructed such communication will soon be opened, and there will be such a revolution in the world's commerce as is now not even dreamed of.[1]

Construction of this strategic waterway aroused an immense amount of interest everywhere. The political, naval, and economic aspects were treated in a voluminous literature, largely of a speculative and rather ephemeral character.

Prophecy and accomplishment seldom seem to agree, and notably is this true of the seers living in the first two decades of the twentieth century. The attempt to forecast the national and international significance of this great American investment turned out to be impossible, especially with the unleashing of unprecedented social, political, and economic changes. In fact, a well-rounded picture of the effects of the Canal has yet to be given. This chapter makes no pretense

[1] H. H. Bancroft, *The New Pacific* (1900), pp. 385–86.

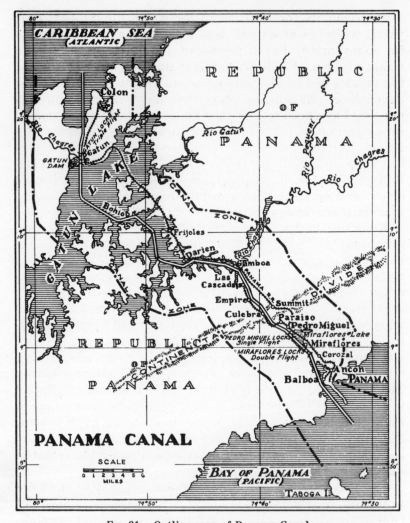

Fig. 21.—Outline map of Panama Canal.

of going beyond a discussion of some of its shipping developments to date.

On August 15, 1914, the first ship passed through the Panama Canal. At that time the attention of the civilized world was riveted on the appalling drama of war just under way in Europe. That conflict was to absorb more and more of the thoughts and energies of the world for the next four years, while its aftermath was to disturb normal progress for many more. For a period of four years the Panama Canal performed military service; since then it has been of far greater aid to all types of ocean vessels navigating the Seven Seas. The many years that have elapsed since its opening have been so extraordinarily packed with arresting developments in other fields that most people complacently accept its contribution. Nevertheless, the Panama Canal has been and continues to be an influence second to none in the industrial and commercial development of the Pacific slope, and certainly this continental artery dominates the maritime activities of the entire Pacific Basin.

Four hundred years elapsed from the time Balboa first glimpsed the Pacific and claimed its discovery for Spain before that great ocean was joined to the Atlantic by a waterway across the Isthmus between the two continents of the New World.[2] For centuries it was the preoccupation of rulers and adventurers to find what Columbus had sought when he discovered America—a shorter and easier passage to the Orient. Countless explorations by sea and by land were inspired wholly or partly by this dream, adventuring which continued well into the nineteenth century. Among the many projected routes, this narrow isthmus, with its inherent possibilities, was always prominent, and when it finally became evident, as a result of these explorations, that there was no open way between oceans from the Arctic Sea to the Straits of Magellan, attention and hope centered here.

As early as 1698 the Scottish venture officially called the Company of Scotland Trading to Africa and the Indies, but commonly known as the Darien Company, set out to establish colonies at the Isthmus. The express purpose of this undertaking was the development of a trans-isthmian route,

---

[2] A passage across the Isthmus is said to have been established by a Franciscan padre of the village of Novita, in what is now Colombia, which was purported to be navigable for canoes during the rainy season. While this passage, of course, can have had little or no commercial significance, its existence at so early a date is extremely interesting from a historical point of view. See Alexander von Humboldt, *Political Essay on the Kingdom of New Spain* (1814).

probably overland, which would immeasurably facilitate European trade with the Far East and likewise deliver control of world trade to those who held the key to this route. More than a hundred years later, and almost one hundred years before the opening of the Panama Canal, Bolívar, in his *Jamaica Letter,* expressed the same belief in the wealth and power which would come to Central American nations from "their magnificent position between two seas." He foresaw the necessity of a water passage, and prophesied not one canal but several.

Their canals will shorten the great ocean trade routes and bind Europe, Asia, and America together by commercial ties, bringing to their happy shores the tribute of the four quarters of the globe. Possibly they are the predestined site of the ultimate capital of the world, as Byzantium was in the ancient hemisphere.[3]

Bolívar was not alone in his belief in the future domination of world commerce by one or more Central American states which should owe their power to their strategic location as a gateway to all oceans. Many years later, Prince Louis Napoleon Bonaparte, afterward Napoleon III, utilized his enforced inactivity while a political prisoner in France to study the project of a Nicaraguan canal; he even obtained a concession from that government for the undertaking. In a pamphlet published after his escape to England he expressed his conviction that Nicaragua would gain through such a canal power and grandeur in the New World at least equal to that which Constantinople had enjoyed in the old.

Napoleon, for all his experience in affairs of state, lacked the clarity of political vision which the poet Goethe demonstrated twenty years later and which enabled the latter to foresee and to read the implications in the rapid territorial expansion of the vigorous young republic of the United States toward the Pacific. This great man of letters anticipated, with almost uncanny prophecy, the future course of events with reference to the construction and control of the Panama Canal. In 1827, Goethe, in conversation with a friend regarding the project of constructing a passage

[3] From Bolívar's *Jamaica Letter,* appearing in 1815.

through the Isthmus of Panama, made the following observations:

This much however is certain, if a canal could be built which would permit the passage of ships of all sizes from ocean to ocean, the entire world, both civilized and uncivilized, would reap countless benefits. But it would surprise me if the United States would miss the opportunity of getting such a work into their own hands. The westward tendency of this young nation will in the course of thirty or forty years have established it beyond the Rockies. New trading centers will spring up in the safe and roomy harbors on the Pacific coast for developing commercial relations with China and the East Indies. In that event it will not only be desirable but also necessary that both merchant vessels and men of war should have a quicker connection between the Atlantic and Pacific than is possible by a voyage around Cape Horn. I therefore repeat that it is absolutely necessary for the United States to build the inter-oceanic canal and I am sure that she will do so.[4]

Thus men of many nations and for many generations dreamed of a canal across the Isthmus; a number of dreams reached the stage of surveys and financing activities—the French attempt progressed even to the point of partial construction. It now seems in retrospect, as it did to Goethe in prospect, that once American control of a long Pacific coastline was assured it became inevitable that the United States should be the nation to fulfill these age-old dreams. Surely to no other country was an isthmian canal of such vital significance in both domestic and foreign affairs, politically as well as economically. Of the great variety of estimates ventured regarding the potential use of the Panama Canal, none was regarded as more authoritative than Professor Emory R. Johnson's conclusions, which appear in Table 15.

Substantial savings in distance, and consequently in time are naturally the paramount justification for a canal. Inasmuch as trade normally seeks the shortest route and as in the case of the Panama Canal the distances saved are so great, important modification of former ocean trade routes by it was to be expected. The two accompanying tables of distances (Tables 16 and 17) show that the three ports, New York, New Orleans, and Liverpool, which may be taken as

---

[4] J. P. Eckerman, *Conversations with Goethe,* quoted in *The Pacific Ocean in History* (1917), pp. 126–27.

TABLE 15

Vessel Tonnage That Might Have Used a Panama Canal, 1899 and 1910*

	1898–99	1909–10
Europe with:		
Western South America....................	1,771,858	3,148,400
Western Central America and Mexico.......	140,000	199,502
Pacific United States, British Columbia, and Hawaii	642,180	689,718
Pacific United States via Suez Canal.........	......	158,000
Oriental countries east of Singapore and Oceania	816,223	1,174,585
Eastern seaboard of United States with:		
Western South America, Pacific Mexico, and Hawaii	166,364	467,595
Pacific Coast of United States via Cape Horn	109,312	172,655
Pacific United States and Hawaii via American-Hawaiian Steamship Co.	......	363,426
Oriental countries east of Singapore and Oceania	908,140	1,500,000
Panama traffic	336,998	418,490
Eastern Canada with Alaska, Chile, and Australia	......	35,658
Total	4,891,075	8,328,029

* Data from Emory R. Johnson, *Panama Canal Traffic and Tolls* (1912), "Table I. Vessel Tonnage, Entrances and Clearances, Available Panama Canal Traffic, 1899 and 1910."

fairly characteristic of Atlantic and Gulf United States and North Atlantic Europe, all profit greatly from the Panama route in sailings to Pacific American ports and to New Zealand.

Conversely, of course, Pacific American ports and New Zealand gain in their American and European North Atlantic trade. New York and New Orleans likewise gain in trade to Japanese ports, Chinese ports north of Hong Kong, and Australian ports. Liverpool saves nothing in trade to Asia and none to any of Australasia except New Zealand. Sydney is nearly equidistant from Liverpool by Panama and by Suez.[5] In trade with Hong Kong and Manila, Atlantic ports as far south as Norfolk save little or nothing by using the

[5] Since Liverpool is only five hundred miles farther from Wellington via Magellan than via Panama, it derives no advantage from the latter route except through cargo-offerings and temperature conditions.

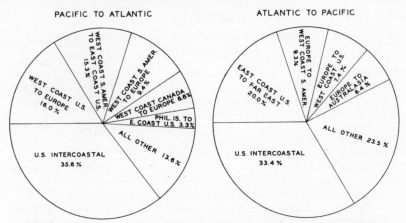

FIG. 22.—Panama Canal traffic percentages by principal trade routes.

Panama route rather than that via Suez; but south Atlantic and, particularly, Gulf ports of the United States profit by the newer interoceanic canal.

Except for brief interruptions by slides in the early years, the Panama Canal has now been in practically continuous operation for twenty years. At the close of business on June 30, 1931, approximately 65,000 commercial vessels had

TABLE 16

REDUCTION EFFECTED BY PANAMA CANAL IN DISTANCES FROM NEW YORK, NEW ORLEANS, AND LIVERPOOL TO PACIFIC PORTS, AMERICAN AND FOREIGN*

(In nautical miles)

Destination	From New York	From New Orleans	From Liverpool
San Francisco†	7,873	8,868	5,666
Honolulu†	6,610	7,605	4,403
Callao†	6,250	7,245	4,043
Valparaiso†	3,747	4,742	1,540
Yokohama	3,768	5,705	− 694
Hong Kong‡	− 18	1,919	−4,172
Manila	41	1,978	−4,421
Sydney	3,932§	5,444§	− 150‡
Wellington	2,493†	3,488†	1,564‡

* Data from United States Hydrographic Board.
† Difference between Panama and Magellan routes.
‡ Difference between Panama and Suez routes.
§ Difference between Panama and Cape routes.

TABLE 17

COMPARATIVE DISTANCES FROM NEW YORK (VIA PANAMA) AND
LIVERPOOL (VIA SUEZ) TO FAR EASTERN COUNTRIES*

Destination	New York via Panama Ports of Call	Nautical Miles	Liverpool via Suez Ports of Call	Nautical Miles
Yokohama	Panama and San Francisco ...	9,798	Aden, Colombo, Singapore, Hong Kong, Shanghai	11,678
Shanghai	Panama, San Francisco, Yokohama ...	10,839	Aden, Colombo, Singapore, Hong Kong ...	10,637
Hong Kong	Panama, San Francisco, Yokohama ...	11,383	Aden, Colombo, Singapore ...	9,758
Manila	Panama, San Francisco, Yokohama ...	11,548	Aden, Colombo, Singapore ...	9,701
Adelaide	Panama, Tahiti, Sydney, Melbourne	10,904	Aden, Colombo, King George Sound	11,142
Sydney	Panama and Tahiti	9,811	Aden, Colombo, King George Sound, Adelaide, Melbourne	12,235
Wellington	Panama and Tahiti	8,851	Aden, Colombo, King George Sound, Melbourne	12,989

* Data from United States Hydrographic Board.

passed through the Canal since its opening, with an aggregate net tonnage (Panama Canal measurement) of nearly 300 million and with cargo amounting to over 300 million long tons. The last ten of these seventeen years have accounted for over 80 per cent of the aggregate ship and cargo tonnage.

Traffic using the Panama Canal during the last decade has shown a marked increase. In the fiscal year ending June 30, 1923, the transits of motor vessels through the canal numbered 121 and their aggregate net tonnage (Panama Canal measurement) was 574,553 tons. This was slightly more than 3 per cent of the total traffic, which amounted to 3,967 transits totaling 18,605,786 net tons. From that time there was an uninterrupted succession of increases until 1928; following a slump during the next four years the statistics now record a gratifying recovery.

It is entirely safe to assume that if the World War had not come to disrupt world industry and trade, the tonnage and cargo totals for the entire period of operation would have been very much larger. The question whether or not a second canal is necessary, either a Nicaraguan sea-level passage or a double-lock system at the present Canal, has been discussed intermittently during the past five or ten years, but at present there appears to be no urgent necessity for a second canal.

Where has this great volume of commerce originated, and whither is it bound? An answer to these questions will contribute substantially to the problem of determining to what extent the various regions and classes of trade are the beneficiaries of the Panama Canal. Fortunately, the official statistics of Panama Canal traffic include a detailed analysis of the trade routes followed by all commercial vessels using the Canal, and the tonnage of cargo carried on each.

Of the three categories of commerce of the Canal, namely, American intercoastal, American foreign, and all other foreign, the United States is exclusively concerned with the first, which constitutes more than a third of the total; shares the second, which amounts to nearly two-fifths of the total, with other countries; and has no direct concern with the third, which accounts for the remaining quarter. This is the approximate status of Panama Canal traffic at the present time, and the prevailing ratios have not been markedly different throughout the post-war period except in 1924, when intercoastal traffic alone, weighted by huge oil shipments, accounted for half the entire volume of commerce.

Striking, if not unexpected, is the extent to which the Canal serves as an avenue for the domestic commerce of the United States. During the past few years intercoastal traffic has constituted a little over one-third of the entire volume of cargo passing through the Canal. On eastbound traffic, which constitutes almost three-fourths of the intercoastal movement, the proportion of intercoastal traffic to total traffic through the Canal from the Pacific to the Atlantic has averaged 41 per cent. No other trade connection using the Panama Canal even approaches the intercoastal route in volume of cargo or in tonnage of shipping.

American internal commerce has, of course, been subject to profound modification as a result of the new trade route. In 1911 the aggregate volume of water-borne intercoastal traffic by the several routes then available was estimated at only 800,000 tons. Transcontinental traffic on the railways in the same year was estimated at between five and six million tons.[6] Nineteen years later the volume of intercoastal water-borne traffic alone was approximately 10.5 million tons, or nearly twice the total rail-and-water shipments between eastern and western United States in 1911. In the same period the volume of freight carried by the leading (Class I) railways, excluding tonnage received from connecting carriers, increased less than 40 per cent. There can be no question that the Panama route has diverted an important volume of tonnage from transcontinental railways, but it should be stated clearly and forcefully that it has made possible the development of an immense flow of traffic that could not otherwise have moved to such distant markets. This huge cargo movement through the Canal, then, is possible only because of the recognized cheaper costs of water in comparison with rail transport. Table 18 records the national mercantile marines utilizing the Canal since its opening and testifies to the wonderful traffic success of this American artery.

Total American foreign trade through the Canal now accounts for about two-fifths of the aggregate cargo movement. Among the most important international commercial lanes which the Panama Canal serves are several between the United States and foreign regions. First in importance on this basis at the present time is the route between the west coast of the United States and Europe. A large vol-

---

[6] E. R. Johnson, *op. cit.*, pp. 54–58. Shipments classed in that report as transcontinental include a major portion of traffic that is not strictly transcontinental. In fact, probably less than one-fourth originates in, or is destined for, points east of Buffalo and Pittsburgh.

TABLE 18

COMMERCIAL TRAFFIC THROUGH THE PANAMA CANAL BY NATIONALITY OF
VESSEL, 1915–1930*

Nationality and Year Ended June 30	Number of Vessels	Net Tonnage (thousands)†	Tolls (thousands of dollars)	Tons of Cargo (thousands)
Total traffic:				
1915–1930, total	59,431	263,955	247,512	275,979
1916...............................	758	2,396	2,408	3,094
1917...............................	1,803	5,799	5,627	7,059
1918...............................	2,069	6,574	6,439	7,532
1919...............................	2,024	6,125	6,173	6,917
1920...............................	2,478	8,546	8,514	9,374
1921...............................	2,892	11,416	11,277	11,599
1922...............................	2,736	11,417	11,198	10,885
1923...............................	3,967	18,606	17,508	19,568
1924...............................	5,230	26,149	24,291	26,995
1925...............................	4,673	22,855	21,401	23,959
1926...............................	5,197	24,775	22,931	26,037
1927...............................	5,475	26,228	24,229	27,748
1928...............................	6,456	29,459	26,944	29,631
1929...............................	6,413	29,838	27,127	30,663
1930...............................	6,185	29,981	27,077	30,030
United States:				
1915–1930, total	26,583	127,558	119,150	136,597
1916...............................	213	653	724	849
1917...............................	404	1,239	1,238	1,476
1918...............................	567	1,704	1,714	2,098
1919...............................	784	2,257	2,327	2,759
1920...............................	1,129	3,791	3,806	4,547
1921...............................	1,210	4,862	4,785	5,163
1922...............................	1,095	4,972	4,867	4,951
1923...............................	1,994	10,209	9,474	11,055
1924...............................	2,947	15,807	14,483	16,654
1925...............................	2,326	12,271	11,302	13,080
1926...............................	2,432	12,565	11,540	13,711
1927...............................	2,685	13,915	12,720	15,242
1928...............................	2,753	13,753	12,646	14,249
1929...............................	2,700	13,326	12,300	14,076
1930...............................	2,885	14,534	13,221	14,499
British:				
1915–1930, total	17,048	77,334	73,163	75,621
1930...............................	1,536	8,007	7,198	7,573
Norwegian:				
1915–1930, total	3,084	11,331	10,237	12,884
1930...............................	371	1,660	1,410	1,808

* Data from *Report of the Governor of the Panama Canal.*
† Net tonnage is according to Panama Canal measurement.

TABLE 18 (*Continued*)

Nationality and Year Ended June 30	Number of Vessels	Net Tonnage (thousands)	Tolls (thousands of dollars)	Tons of Cargo (thousands)
Japanese:				
1915–1930, total	1,994	9,326	9,848	11,608
1930	163	803	851	1,010
Chilean:				
1915–1930, total	851	2,645	2,353	1,552
1930	46	164	154	106
Danish:				
1915–1930, total	928	3,471	3,302	4,625
1930	91	382	353	506
Dutch:				
1915–1930, total	1,246	6,008	5,451	6,148
1930	141	671	572	619
Peruvian:				
1915–1930, total	915	2,335	1,797	1,480
1930	2	9	10	13
French:				
1915–1930, total	1,140	4,746	4,805	4,657
1930	124	628	583	577
Swedish:				
1915–1930, total	869	3,605	3,032	5,172
1930	125	572	473	832
Spanish:				
1917–1930, total	373	1,220	1,179	863
1930	2	4	6	8
Italian:				
1915–1930, total	640	3,057	3,023	2,279
1930	66	429	385	264
German:				
1920–1930, total	1,946	7,303	6,528	8,067
1930	377	1,433	1,236	1,388
Miscellaneous:				
1915–1930, total	1,814	4,017	3,643	4,426
1930	256	684	625	827

ume of cargo annually leaves American Pacific ports for Europe; a much smaller, but still considerable, traffic moves in the opposite direction. In the fiscal year 1930 more than four million tons of cargo were shipped between Pacific ports of the United States and Europe, of which 83 per cent was eastbound. These four million tons constituted 13 per cent of the entire commercial traffic of the Canal. Commerce between the east coast of the United States and the Far East has likewise been facilitated by the opening of the Panama Canal; in 1930 two million tons of cargo were shipped between these two regions via the Canal, or 6.7 per cent of the aggregate cargo transiting this waterway. A number of other American foreign-trade routes using the Panama Canal show substantial volumes of traffic, including those between the east coast of the United States and the west coast of South America, Australasia, and the Philippines, and between the west coast of the United States and the West Indies and the east coast of South America (see Table 19, pp. 130–31).

United States imports and exports passing through the Canal during three recent fiscal years (1928–1930) constituted more than 38 per cent of total cargo tonnage using the Panama route.[7] Since American intercoastal traffic accounted for over 34 per cent of the total in the same years, the combined domestic and foreign commerce of the United States may be said to absorb nearly three-fourths of the total services to commerce which this artificial waterway performs. But it should be added that the foreign portion of United States trade necessarily involves other nations; hence the participation of other countries in Panama Canal traffic is obviously greater than merely the remaining one-fourth in which the United States does not figure. Notwithstanding these gains which have accrued to the trade of other countries, and they are great, they compare in no case with those which have come to the United States.

The number of transits for Panama and those for Suez are surprisingly similar. In 1924 the vessels passing through Panama numbered 5,230, compared with 4,763 through Suez. In 1930, the figures were 6,185 and 6,345, and in 1931, they were 5,529 and 5,621, respectively. For the fiscal year 1931 the Suez Canal traffic statistics were somewhat larger, with 45,000,000 gross tons and 33,000,000 net tons, compared with 37,000,000 gross tons and 30,000,000 net tons recorded by the Panama Canal. (The comparison is not exact, however,

[7] Since a small volume of cargo remains undistributed as to origin and destination in the official reports of the Panama Canal, the exact amount of American foreign-trade tonnage cannot be given.

TABLE

CARGO TONNAGE THROUGH PANAMA CANAL,

(In thousand cargo

Origin and Destination	Atlantic to Pacific		
	1928	1929	1930
Grand total	9,066	10,166	8,064
To west coast United States†	3,908	4,434	3,536
To west coast other North America	500	589	478
To west coast South America	1,234	1,578	1,192
To Asia	2,061	2,098	1,797
To Australia and New Zealand	1,363	1,468	1,061
From east coast United States	6,009	6,609	5,237
To west coast United States†	2,994	3,467	2,804
To west coast other North America	77	86	78
To west coast South America	366	427	311
To Asia	2,013	2,014	1,739
To Australia and New Zealand	558	615	305
From east coast other North America	619	772	614
To west coast North America	294	329	224
To west coast South America	97	179	151
To Asia	41	54	25
To Australia and New Zealand	186	210	214
From Europe	2,282	2,596	2,013
To west coast North America	933	1,024	756
To west coast South America	764	940	728
To Asia, Australia, and New Zealand	585	632	529
From east coast South America and Africa	156	189	200

* Calendar year. Data from *Panama Canal Record*.   † Including Hawaii.

since the tonnage measurements and other recording are
not identical.) Of the 4,994 vessels in commercial traffic
passing through the Panama Canal in the fiscal year 1933
there were 1,686 flying the American flag, 1,039 the British,
325 the German, 407 the Norwegian, 217 the Japanese, 80
the Dutch, and 66 the French; in the same period, of the
5,163 vessels passing through the Suez Canal 76 flew the
American flag, 2,829 were flying the Union Jack, 437 the
German flag, 329 the Dutch, 324 the French, 301 the Italian,

19

tons of 2,240 pounds)

Origin and Destination	Pacific to Atlantic		
	1928	1929	1930
Grand total	20,336	21,284	19,784
To east coast United States...............	10,745	12,079	11,144
To east coast other North America.......	1,224	1,076	1,072
To Europe	8,188	7,963	7,401
To Africa and South America.............	179	166	167
From west coast United States†	10,118	11,009	10,557
To east coast United States...............	6,873	7,545	6,983
To east coast other North America.......	498	217	294
To Europe	2,701	3,193	3,209
To Africa and South America.............	47	55	71
From west coast other North America......	3,265	2,367	2,372
To east coast North America.............	602	586	563
To Europe	2,629	1,765	1,786
To Africa and South America.............	34	15	23
From west coast South America.............	5,666	6,237	4,953
To east coast United States...............	2,859	3,260	2,718
To east coast other North America........	451	524	441
To Europe	2,258	2,358	1,722
To Africa and South America.............	98	95	72
From Asia and Australasia..................	1,286	1,671	1,902
To east coast North America.............	685	1,024	1,217
To Europe	601	646	684
To east coast South America.............	...	2	1

300 the Japanese, and 231 the Norwegian. A graph (Fig. 23, p. 133) contrasting Panama and Suez Canals provides a further world view.

To make certain broad comparisons between the two great world canals, the Suez and the Panama, it is interesting at this point to turn attention for a moment to the British position with respect to the Suez Canal. From a geographical point of view, the Suez serves almost equally well the European continent and the British Isles in providing a short route between the densely populated agricultural East and the industrial European continent. The commanding position of British shipping in Suez traffic can be explained principally by the necessity for sea communication between the British Isles and the Imperial interests to the east, with India occupying the central position. Furthermore, the leading part played by British shipping and trade in international affairs requires continuous use of this waterway.

A certain parallel may be traced in the American position with respect to the Panama Canal. Even as the Suez route is extremely important politically as well as commercially to Great Britain because of her far-flung possessions, so the American waterway is of distinct political significance to the United States because of her Pacific territory, which includes not only the continental states but also the outlying territories of Alaska and Hawaii, and the dependencies of Guam and American Samoa, and the Philippines. From a strategic standpoint, those countries which have both Atlantic and Pacific seacoasts have the closest interest in this seaway, since it provides an artery for both foreign and domestic intercourse.[8] Yet differences in area, population, resources, and economic development obviously produce corresponding differences in the degree to which these several countries are able to utilize the Panama route, quite apart from considerations of geographic location. In almost every way, the United States at the present time is in a position to avail itself of the services which this waterway affords more fully than any other nation. As far as the present and the future are concerned, it is not difficult to support the view that the Panama Canal is "first and foremost an instrument for the internal development of the United States and the expansion of her Pacific commerce."

Participation of nations in Panama Canal traffic may be

[8] The cargo-tonnage from the Canadian West Coast through the Canal increased from 181,000 long tons in 1922 to 3,525,000 in 1931; cargo destined for this region increased from 148,000 long tons to 967,000 in the same period. The Panama Canal is much more important to the west coast than to the east coast of Canada, since for the latter district the cargo originating on the east coast increased from 25,000 long tons to 111,000 and the destined cargo to that coast increased from 7,000 long tons in 1922 to 517,000 long tons in 1931.

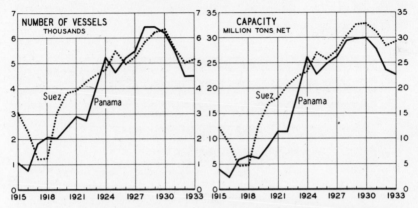

Fig. 23.—Comparative statistics, Panama and Suez canals, 1915–33. Suez Canal—calendar year data 1915–23 from *Commerce Yearbook,* 1931 (crop year data prior to 1924 not available); years ending June 30, 1924–33, from merchant marine statistics, United States Department of Commerce, 1933. Panama Canal—*Commerce Yearbook;* years ending June 30.

measured in terms not only of commercial cargoes but also of shipping, direct and indirect. Maritime countries like Great Britain and Norway are international carriers to the extent that their participation is not limited to the volume of cargo originating in or destined for their shores. To illustrate, over a sixth of the vessels in the British merchant marine in 1913 failed to include any port in the British Isles anywhere on their voyages. Merchant marines of such nations engage to a greater or less extent in indirect trade, which is trade between ports neither of which lies in the country whose flag the carrying ship flies. Because this trade is important to the shipping engaged therein, it must be given due consideration. Tonnage by nationality of commercial vessels using the Canal is the best available yardstick (see Fig. 24, p. 134).

In the fiscal year 1930 almost 30,000,000 net tons of commercial shipping passed through the Panama Canal. Of this aggregate 14.5 million tons, or 48.5 per cent of the total, were flying the American flag (see Fig. 24). Ranking second was the British flag, which appeared on 8,000,000 tons of shipping, or 26.8 per cent of the total. For the period 1922–1930, American ships have constituted one-half the total and

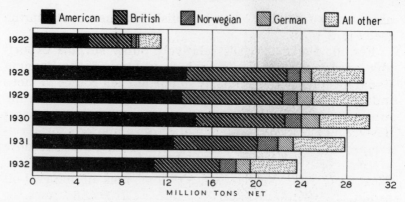

Fɪɢ. 24.—Nationalities of ships using Panama Canal, 1922, 1928–32.

British ships about 28 per cent. American and British ships combined, the latter including Canadian and Australian vessels, account for nearly four-fifths of all commercial ships transiting the Panama Canal in this period.

Leadership of American vessels is not surprising in view of the preponderance of American cargo tonnage, particularly intercoastal, to be described in chapter x. While British flag tonnage is not a close second, amounting to only a little more than half the American tonnage, the place of the British merchant marine in the carrying trade of the world and the fact that the British overseas dominions of Canada, Australia, and New Zealand are so located as to profit by the Panama route account for the comparatively large share of British shipping.

Throughout the post-war period there have been no other countries whose shipping averaged as much as 5 per cent of the total tonnage transiting the Canal. Japanese ships accounted for 7.6 per cent of the total in 1922 but have since declined in relative importance to less than 3 per cent. Norwegian ships have gained both absolutely and relatively during the period and by 1930 had attained an aggregate net tonnage of 1,660,000, or 5.5 per cent of the total. German tonnage through the Canal has made even more pronounced growth since 1922, increasing from 123,000 net tons in that year to 1,433,000 tons in 1930, when it constituted almost 5 per cent of the total—a reflection of that country's remark-

ably successful effort to re-establish her merchant marine
(see Fig. 3, p. 18).

For the Pacific Coast's relatively bulky surplus exportable products, such as oil, grain, and lumber, the Panama
Canal has given tremendously important sea routes to more
industrially advanced regions. In domestic trade alone the
intercoastal route has been a great stimulus to Pacific Coast
development, since it has opened Eastern markets for Western products which were formerly at a disadvantage because
of the more expensive transcontinental haul. During the
fiscal year 1930, nearly 3,400,000 long tons of mineral-oil
products and 2,200,000 tons of lumber left Pacific ports for
the United States Atlantic and Gulf ports. These two commodities have constituted more than half of all intercoastal
traffic and from 75 to 82 per cent of eastbound intercoastal
cargoes in the last four fiscal years. Table 20 (p. 136) shows
the commodity movement between the United States Atlantic Coast and the Far East.

While lumber and mineral oil dominate domestic commerce through the Panama Canal on the basis of tonnage, a
very wide variety of other products, more valuable per unit
of bulk, have also found the Panama route highly advantageous. From the Atlantic to the Pacific, in particular, the
list of commodities which move in substantial amounts is
a long one, and includes a large number of manufactured
and semimanufactured products from the more highly industrialized regions east of the Mississippi River. From the
Pacific to the Atlantic the Canal is of growing importance in
the shipment to Eastern markets of West Coast food products, notably canned goods, dried fruits, and sugar.

The intercoastal route via the Canal has affected economic progress of the Pacific slope not only directly through
providing cheap and expeditious water carriage but also
indirectly through the influence of water competition on the
transcontinental rate structure. Water competition, because
of the possibility of shipments around the Horn or across
Panama by rail, has always operated to set the upper limits
of rail rates on shipments between points on or near the
seaboards.

With the opening of the Panama Canal the seriousness

TABLE 20

Principal Commodities Transiting the Panama Canal between
East Coast of United States and the Far East, 1927–1930*

(In thousand long tons)

	1927	1928	1929	1930
Atlantic to Pacific				
Total	1,545	1,614	1,914	1,896
Ammonia	125	70	57	100
Automobiles and accessories..	16	23	57	47
Cotton	355	243	328	243
Iron and steel (includes railway material, iron, and scrap)	294	357	318	410
Mineral oil, crude and refined	263	339	330	305
Phosphates	103	149	193	309
Tobacco	46	41	82	73
Flour	13	15	66	36
Pacific to Atlantic				
Total	115	123	122	133
Glass, glassware, and porcelain	3	6	8	7
Vegetable oils, including wood and "others"	17	22	19	42
Rice	4	4	8	5
Tea	7	8	9	8
Wool	3	7	8	5

* Data from *Panama Canal Record*. Not all commodities shown.

to railway traffic of water competition was immeasurably increased by the lowering in cost and time and the improvement in quality of the interocean service. It is not practicable here to trace in detail the relations between the Panama Canal gateway and the transcontinental rail-rate structure.[8] It is worth pointing out, however, that the present transcontinental rate structure is highly advantageous to the Pacific area. The system of blanketing rates, in considerable measure the result of the alternate water route, followed by both eastbound and westbound traffic, gives this region a wide domestic market for its products on good competitive terms with other producing regions, likewise, an equally wide area on which to draw for the great variety of products it is not able to supply in adequate amounts from

[8] See 40 Interstate Commerce Commission 35; 46 I.C.C. 236; 48 I.C.C. 79; 74 I.C.C. 48.

its own resources. Such exceptions to the "long and short haul" clause of the Interstate Commerce Act as have been granted by the Commission have operated to the advantage of industrial and trade development of the Pacific slope by continuing the dependence of the Rocky Mountain territory on the commercial and jobbing centers of the Coast terminals. Many domestic manufacturers, too far from Atlantic or Gulf terminals to profit by the Canal route, have found it advantageous to maintain themselves in the Pacific Coast market by establishing branch factories there.

A statistical study, made by the United States Department of Commerce, dealing with transcontinental and intercoastal trade of the Pacific Southwest for the year 1926[9] makes available for the first time reasonably complete data of transcontinental rail traffic of a given region so that it may be compared with water-borne traffic to and from the same area. These figures do not tell the whole story of transcontinental traffic, as the region covered includes only California, Nevada, Utah, Arizona, and New Mexico. In 1926 something over 40 per cent of the aggregate transcontinental traffic of the Pacific Southwest both eastbound and westbound was carried by ships moving through the Panama Canal. Rail and water competition in the case of leading commodities, for another period, is illustrated by Table 21 (p. 138).

Because lumber, after petroleum the most important commodity by weight in intercoastal traffic, moves mainly out of Pacific Northwest ports, and since this commodity is one particularly suited to water transportation, it seems reasonable to believe that the percentage of water shipments to rail shipments in transcontinental trade is greater for the Pacific region as a whole than it is for the Pacific Southwest. This belief is strengthened by considering the great quantities of perishable foodstuffs in eastbound transcontinental rail shipments from the latter territory, which depend on rapid transport for successful marketing.[10]

[9] *Domestic Commerce Series* No. 25 (1929). The government arbitrarily includes in the term "Pacific Southwest" the states of California, Nevada, Utah, and Arizona, the greater portion of New Mexico, a small portion of western Texas, and the eastern part of Idaho.

[10] A further discussion of commodities moving coast-to-coast appears in chapter x.

Accordingly it is probably not far wrong to state that close to half of all transcontinental shipments now employ the Panama route. The development of faster ships will tend to increase this percentage still further; but as faster ships are more expensive to build and to operate, the rates charged by such carriers must necessarily be higher than those of slower ships, a condition which will limit the inroads they are able to make on the business of both their rail and their water competitors. In any event, it is clear that the Panama route has created a serious problem of readjustment for Western railroads.

TABLE 21

COMPARATIVE TRANSCONTINENTAL TONNAGE, RAIL AND CANAL*

Commodity	Tons by Rail	Tons through Canal
Ammunition	245	367
Cotton piece goods	3,271	10,925
Soda alumina sulphate	25	....
Lard and lard substitutes	4,003	4,118
Paint	6,597	8,104
Roofing material	5,845	4,541
Rosin	....	6,311
Soap	3,227	13,154
Soda	1,255	9,824
Iron and steel	156,085	779,369
Paper	14,918	25,194
Total	195,471	861,907

* Selected commodities moving June–November, 1923. Data from Interstate Commerce Commission, Fourth Section, Application No. 12436 (1926).

While existing data do not permit exact statements on the point, it is generally conceded that the Panama Canal route offers effective competition to transcontinental railroads only for traffic originating in or destined for regions within a few hundred miles of the coast. On the Western slope such a strip consists substantially of the three Pacific Coast states; and their commercial relations with all points similarly near the Gulf or the Atlantic seaboard are thus materially changed by the existence of the Panama Canal.

It has been estimated that the Panama Canal has effected

an average saving of ten dollars per ton on coast-to-coast commerce. What the aggregate savings may have been on the basis of this estimate cannot be calculated, since lower transportation costs have brought forth an immense quantity of tonnage that would not have moved except at the lower rate.[11] It is not necessary to make such a calculation, however, in order to appreciate the fact that from the point of view of domestic commerce alone, and even solely that of the Pacific States region, the Panama Canal is amply repaying its cost of construction and maintenance.

Next in importance to the Pacific Coast of the United States, after the intercoastal route, is the trade with Europe through the Panama Canal. The Canal has meant for the Pacific slope excellent communications with the markets of Europe and a further broadening of outlets for characteristic products of the region. Mineral oil, lumber, and foodstuffs constitute the main shipments to Europe. It has meant, likewise, that the Canal has made it possible for this region to obtain from Western Europe a wide variety of products which can move usually by ship at lower rates than by combined water-and-rail carriage to Western United States.

Very low rates westbound from Europe to the Pacific Coast of the United States are in effect because the disproportion of tonnage in the two directions is extreme: eastbound traffic is about five times as great as westbound. As a result, even such low-grade commodities as cement and sand may move 8,000 miles in successful competition with similar products originating in the East or the Middle West, while rates from Europe are often lower than the corresponding intercoastal rates. Whatever may successfully enter this country from Europe over existing tariff and other governmental barriers is now available to Pacific Coast regions at prices little above those at which they can be offered

---

[11] These gains may be subject to some deduction through the fact that blanket transportation rates lead to multiplicity of competing points and consequent cross-hauling that involve an element of social waste, even though accompanied by pecuniary gains to the individuals concerned. This point, of course, brings up the whole question of rate-making theory, which clearly cannot be pursued here.

in Eastern markets, and normally below those available in the populous central states of this country.

The extent to which this European trade has been facilitated can be appreciated by a comparison of pre-war and post-war trade. In the last three fiscal years before the opening of the Panama Canal, the value of the trade of the Pacific Coast customs districts with the United Kingdom averaged about twenty million dollars annually. In the two years 1929–30 this trade averaged one hundred and ten million dollars. Even allowing for the difference in price levels between the two periods, the exchange of commodities appears to have increased perhaps fourfold.[12] Correspondingly great or even greater relative changes have taken place in the value of Pacific Coast trade with France, Germany, and the Netherlands. These increases are very much more rapid than that registered by foreign commerce for the entire United States, and substantially greater, likewise, than the gain in the aggregate foreign commerce of the Pacific Coast.

The story of the service of the Panama Canal to the Pacific region of the United States is largely, but not fully, told in intercoastal and European trade. The volume of traffic moving between this coast and the West Indies and the east coast of South America is likewise of sufficient size to warrant separate tabulation, although compared with the tonnage moving on the two first-mentioned routes the latter two are of minor significance.

There are, of course, certain ways in which the Panama Canal has operated to the disadvantage, temporarily at least, of economic progress in the Pacific area. If this artery has enabled the Pacific Coast to face east, it has likewise facilitated the westward facing of the Atlantic areas. The very transport agencies which extend the market for Western products likewise extend the market for those of the East, and the newer, less experienced industries of the Pacific Slope face, with every improvement in facilities, a reduction in the special advantage which they enjoy in neighboring

[12] No exact calculation can be made, since the general indexes of import and export prices are not necessarily applicable to trade between Pacific ports and specified foreign countries. The export price index, using 1913 as 100, was 125 in 1929 and 113 in 1930. The import price indexes for these two years were 119 and 97, respectively.

markets. Not only domestic industries of the Eastern and Middle Western areas but also those of Europe have been given readier access to Pacific Coast markets; therefore industrial growth of the latter must confront strong competition in the very heart of its home territory.

Similarly, the former strong advantage which the Pacific Slope, as compared with that of the Atlantic Coast, enjoyed in transpacific trade has been greatly reduced for Japanese ports and those of China north of Hong Kong.[13] Shipments between Eastern United States and Eastern Asia and Australasia which used Pacific ports as a gateway in order to save time move in part via Panama direct to their Atlantic destinations. Fine wool from Australia and carpet wool from China are leading examples. Even silk, which has normally moved over the fastest possible route irrespective of freight rates because of its extremely high value per unit of bulk, has recently been moving in increasing volume direct to Eastern mills by ship through the Panama Canal. To whatever extent such services supplant those discharging cargo at Pacific ports for transshipment either by rail or by intercoastal vessel, the Oriental trade at Pacific ports will obviously suffer and the profits which have accrued from handling such traffic will decline.

On the other hand, there is a considerable but unknown quantity of goods transshipped intercoastally at Pacific ports which would have moved via the Suez Canal between Atlantic ports and the Far East if the Panama Canal had not been opened. Purely intercoastal ships are, in general, of a less expensive type to build and to operate than those suited to long transoceanic voyages. The latter may thus be employed on strictly transpacific services with a moderately quick turnaround through the use of these "feeder" services.

In no way can one appreciate better the actual rôle played by Panama in maritime geography than to read the world shipping record for a single week in January 1934 which is reproduced in Table 22.

[13] Hong Kong and Manila are each about equally distant from New York via Panama and via Suez, so that the opening of the Panama Canal did not bring them any nearer to New York than they have been since the first overland rail connection in 1869.

TABLE 22

Movements of Ocean Vessels through the Panama Canal, January 15—January 22, 1934*

Atlantic to Pacific

Ship	Nationality	Line (Charterer or Operator)	Port From	Port For	Cargo Nature	Tons
Franconia	Brit.	Cunard Line	New York, N.Y.	Round the world	Passengers only	...
Hanley	Amer.	Interocean S.S. Corp.	Boston, Mass.	Everett, Wash.	Steel, general	857
Helga	Dan.	J. Lauritzen	Cardiff, Eng.	Chile	Ballast	...
Nokomis†	Amer.	United States Navy	Norfolk, Va.	Balboa, C.Z.	Ballast	...
John D. Archbold‡	Amer.	Standard Ship. Co.	New York, N.Y.	Los Angeles, Calif.	Ballast	...
J. L. Luckenbach	Amer.	Luckenbach Line	Boston, Mass.	Seattle, Wash.	Ballast	...
Langleecrag	Brit.	F. Carrick & Co.	Pt. Royal, Jam.	Vancouver, B.C.	Ballast	...
Kafiristan	Brit.	Nitrate Corporation	S. Shields, Eng.	Chile	Ballast	...
Dakotan	Amer.	Amer.–Hawaiian Line	Boston, Mass.	Tacoma, Wash.	General	2,081
San Marcos	Amer.	Quaker S.S. Line	Albany, N.Y.	Portland, Ore.	General, coal, lubricating oil	2,768
Gulfpenn‡	Amer.	Gulf Refining Co.	New York, N.Y.	Los Angeles, Calif.	Ballast	...
Baru§	Pan.	Elliot Ship. and Land Co.	Cristobal, C.Z.	Panama, R.P.	Ballast	...
Sally Maersk§	Dan.	A. P. Moller	La Romana, Santo Domingo	S. San Francisco, Calif.	Sugar	4,868
Stanford§	Nor.	J. B. Stang.	Mobile, Alabama	Yokohama, Japan	Scrap steel	8,003
Ensley City	Amer.	Isthmian S.S. Lines	New York, N.Y.	Seattle, Wash.	Steel, general	8,226
Pacific Shipper§	Brit.	Furness, Withy & Co.	Manchester, Eng.	Vancouver, B.C.	General	264
Chilore	Amer.	Ore S.S. Corp.	Baltimore, Md.	Cruz Grande, Chile	Ballast	...
City of Brisbane	Brit.	Ellerman Lines	Tampico, Mexico	Adelaide, Austr.	General	7,053
Ionic	Brit.	Shaw, Savill & Albion.	London, Eng.	Wellington, N.Z.	General	5,366
Deebank	Brit.	Mersey Paper Co.	Liverpool, Eng.	Sydney, Austr.	Newsprint paper	4,657
Mercury Sun‡§	Amer.	Gulf Refining Co.	Chester, Pa.	San Francisco, Calif.	Ballast	...
Sambu‖	Pan.	Elliot Ship. and Land Co.	Cristobal, C.Z.	David, R.P.	Kerosene	77
Bennekom	Neth.	Royal Neth. S.S. Co.	Hamburg, Ger.	Corral, Chile	General	1,173
Hannibal†	Amer.	United States Navy	Norfolk, Va.	Balboa, C.Z.	Ballast	...
Edward Luckenbach	Amer.	Luckenbach Line	Boston, Mass.	Tacoma, Wash.	General	1,756
Lundby§	Dan.	A/S Motortramp	London, Eng.	Los Angeles, Calif.	Ballast	...
Taijin Maru§	Jap.	Ocean Transport Co.	Savannah, Ga.	Vancouver, B.C.	Ballast	...
Valverde	Ital.	Soc. Italiana de Nav.	Philadelphia, Pa.	Antofagasta, Chile	Ballast	...
Queen City	Brit.	States Marine Corp.	Tampa, Fla.	Osaka, Japan	Cotton, phosphate	7,700
Trematon	Brit.	Hain Steamship Co.	Nuevitas, Cuba	Hongkong, China	Sugar	7,100
No. 223‖	Amer.	United States Navy	Cristobal, C.Z.	Balboa, C.Z.	Ballast	...
No. 353‖	Amer.	United States Navy	Cristobal, C.Z.	Balboa, C.Z.	Ballast	...

Brandanger§	Nor.	Westfal, Larsen & Co.	Rosario, Arg.	Vancouver, B.C.	General	3,020
Marie Bakke§	Nor.	Knut Knutsen O.A.S.	Gothenburg, Swed.	Valparaiso, Chile	General	2,191
President Johnson	Amer.	Dollar Line	New York, N.Y.	San Francisco, Calif.	Machinery, general	3,046
Quebec City	Brit.	Reardon-Smith Line	Cardiff, Eng.	Vancouver, B.C.	Ballast	....
Tijuca†§	Nor.	Wilh. Wilhelmsen	Swansea, Eng.	Los Angeles, Calif.	Ballast	....
Sorvard§	Nor.	Long Is. Mach. & Eq. Co.	Jacksonville, Fla.	Moji, Japan	Scrap iron	6,531
Kinai Maru§	Jap.	Osaka Shosen Kaisha	Savannah, Ga.	Kobe, Japan	General, cotton	5,908
Ionic Star	Brit.	Blue Star Line	Newcastle, Eng.	Vancouver, B.C.	Ballast	....
Absaroka	Amer.	McCormick S.S. Co.	Philadelphia, Pa.	Seattle, Wash.	Iron, steel, general	2,680
Santa Maria§	Amer.	Grace Line	New York, N.Y.	Valparaiso, Chile	General	1,744
C. A. Canfield‡	Amer.	Standard Ship. Co.	New York, N.Y.	Los Angeles, Calif.	Ballast	....
Santa Teresa	Amer.	Panama Mail S.S. Co.	Philadelphia, Pa.	S. San Francisco, Calif.	General	2,922
Sambu||	Pan.	Elliot Ship. and Land Co.	Cristobal, C.Z.	Balboa, C.Z.	Ballast	....
J-10✕	Amer.	United States Army	Cristobal, C.Z.	Balboa, C.Z.	Ballast	....
No. 101✕	Amer.	United States Army	Cristobal, C.Z.	Balboa, C.Z.	Ballast	....
Tacoma	Ger.	Hamburg-Amer. Line	Hamburg, Ger.	Portland, Ore.	General	4,855
Reynolds	Brit.	Bolton S.S. Co.	Baltimore, Md.	Taltal, Chile	Ballast	1,815
Fella§	Ital.	Nav. Libera Triestina	Venice, Italy	Vancouver, B.C.	Steel, corn, general	4,015
Robin Goodfellow	Amer.	Luckenbach Gulf Co.	Houston, Tex.	Tacoma, Wash.	Steel, corn, general	....
Innesmoor§	Brit.	J. J. Moore & Co.	Marseilles, France	Vancouver, B.C.	Ballast	....
San Gil	Pan.	United Fruit Co.	Mobile, Ala.	Pto. Armuelles, R.P.	Ballast	3,612
La Plata Maru§	Jap.	Osaka Shosen Kaisha	Montevideo, Uru.	Kobe, Japan	General	....
Salinas‡	Amer.	United States Navy	Cristobal, C.Z.	Los Angeles, Calif.	Ballast	....
W. S. Miller‡	Amer.	Shell Oil Company	Fall River, Mass.	San Francisco, Calif.	Ballast	....
Athelmonarch‡§	Brit.	Nisho Company	Hull, England	San Luis Obispo, Cal.	Ballast	2,585
La Paz§	Brit.	Pacific Steam Nav. Co.	Hull, England	Valparaiso, Chile	General	1,582
Arizonan	Amer.	Amer.-Hawaiian Line	Boston, Mass.	Portland, Ore.	General	8,243
Oakmar	Amer.	Calmar Line	Baltimore, Md.	Seattle, Wash.	Steel, general	242
Durazzo	Ger.	Hamburg-Amer. Line	Cristobal, C.Z.	Guayaquil, Ecuador	General	3,247
Hororata	Brit.	N. Z. Shipping Co.	London, Eng.	N. Plymouth, N.Z.	General	707
Brynjes§	Nor.	Canadian Transp. Co.	St. Pierre Miquelon	New Westminster, B.C.	Whiskey	....
Stensby§	Dan.	Canadian Transp. Co.	Pto. Colombia	Vancouver, B.C.	Ballast	....
Clarissa Radcliffe	Brit.	Nitrate Corporation	Baltimore, Md.	Arica, Chile	Ballast	1,686
Chas. H. Cramp	Amer.	Argonaut S.S. Line	New York, N.Y.	Seattle, Wash.	Lubricating oil, gen.	5,618
Siljestad§	Nor.	Fern Line	Houston, Tex.	Japan	General, cotton	....
Corsair÷	Amer.	J. P. Morgan	New York, N.Y.	Galapagos Is.	Ballast	951
Willkeno	Amer.	Williams S.S. Corp.	Baltimore, Md.	Seattle, Wash.	General	....
Utacarbon†	Amer.	Union Oil Co.	Boston, Mass.	Los Angeles, Calif.	Ballast	....
Sveajarl§	Swed.	Knutsen Line	Gothenburg, Swed.	Los Angeles, Calif.	Ballast	....
J. M. Danziger†	Amer.	Standard Ship. Co.	New York, N.Y.	Los Angeles, Calif.	Ballast	....

* Data from the *Panama Canal Record*, February 15, 1934. Record from midnight to midnight.

† Survey ship.   ‡ Tanker.   § Motorship. || Motor schooner.   ✕ Launch.   ÷ Yacht.   ¶ Sub-chaser.

TABLE 22—Continued

PACIFIC TO ATLANTIC

Ship	Nationality	Line (Charterer or Operator)	From	Port For	Nature	Cargo Tons
San Blas	Pan.	United Fruit Co.	Puerto-Armuelles, R.P.	Mobile, Alabama	Bananas	1,200
Baru§	Pan.	Elliot Ship. and Land Co.	El Real, R.P.	Cristobal, C.Z.	Bananas	105
Sambu‖	Pan.	Elliot Ship. and Land Co.	Darien, R.P.	Cristobal, C.Z.	Bananas	21
Mathew Luckenbach.	Amer.	Luckenbach Gulf Co.	Seattle, Wash.	Mobile, Alabama	General	6,098
Pomona	Amer.	Weyerhaeuser S.S. Co.	Seattle, Wash.	Boston, Mass.	Lumber, general	10,000
Geo. H. Jones‡	Amer.	Standard Ship. Co.	Los Angeles, Calif.	Chelsea, Mass.	Fuel oil	10,876
Ranapo‡	Amer.	United States Navy	Los Angeles, Calif.	Norfolk, Va.	Fuel oil	11,259
Gulfcrest‡§	Amer.	Gulf Refining Co.	Los Angeles, Calif.	New York, N.Y.	Fuel oil	14,386
Nordbo§	Dan.	Anglo-Can. Ship. Co.	Vancouver, B.C.	Manchester, Eng.	Kerosene, furnace oil	7,641
Atlanta City	Amer.	Isthmian S.S. Lines	Hilo, T.H.	Baltimore, Md.	Pineapples, sugar	8,702
California	Ital.	Nav. Libera Triestina	Vancouver, B.C.	Genoa, Italy	General	8,516
New Orleans§	Amer.	Roosevelt S.S. Co.	Manila, P.I.	Baltimore, Md.	General	6,947
Salinas‡	Amer.	United States Navy	Los Angeles, Calif.	Cristobal, C.Z.	Gasoline	3,373
Shohei Maru§	Jap.	Mitsui & Co.	Iloilo, P.I.	New York, N.Y.	General	5,558
Silverfir§	Brit.	Silver Line	Manila, P.I.	New Orleans, La.	Sugar, coconut oil	7,670
Meton‡	Amer.	Shell Eastern Pet. Co.	Los Angeles, Calif.	Sewaren, N.J.	Kerosene	10,065
Santa Barbara§	Amer.	Grace Line	Valparaiso, Chile	New York, N.Y.	General	4,095
Forbes Hauptman	Amer.	McCormick S.S. Co.	Pt. Townsend, Wash.	New York, N.Y.	General	5,874
Moveria§	Brit.	Donaldson Line	Vancouver, B.C.	Glasgow, Scot.	Frozen, general	5,184
Californian§	Amer.	Amer.-Hawaiian Line	Portland, Ore.	Boston, Mass.	Lumber, general	9,075
Langleegorse	Brit.	Canadian Transp. Co.	Vancouver, B.C.	London, Eng.	Grain, lumber	7,523
Newton Beach	Brit.	J. Ridley Sons & Tully.	Vancouver, B.C.	London, Eng.	Lumber, wheat	6,975
Washington Express§	Nor.	Fruit Express Line	New Westminster, B.C.	Hamburg, Ger.	Fresh fruit	1,966
Hindpool	Brit.	T. A. Lee & Whitmore	Vancouver, B.C.	Hull, Eng.	Wheat	8,163
Emidio‡	Amer.	General Petroleum Co.	Los Angeles, Calif.	New York, N.Y.	Gasoline, fuel oil	9,408
Karamea	Brit.	Shaw, Savill & Albion.	N. Plymouth, N.Z.	London, Eng.	Frozen, general	6,700
Sambu‖	Pan.	Elliot Ship. and Land Co.	Panama, R.P.	Cristobal, C.Z.	Empty drums	4
Emergency Aid	Amer.	Pac.-Arg.-Brazil Line	Seattle, Wash.	Buenos Aires, Arg.	Lumber, general	3,993
Yuri Mari	Jap.	Kokusai Kisen Kaisha.	Pulupandan, P.I.	New Orleans, La.	Sugar	8,500
Geddington Court	Brit.	Canadian Transp. Co.	Vancouver, B.C.	Antwerp, Belg.	General	10,170
Llanover	Brit.	Chilean Nitrate Co.	Tocopilla, Chile	Azores e	Nitrate	8,072
San Simeon	Amer.	Quaker Line	Portland, Ore.	Philadelphia, Pa.	Lumber, general	5,703
Portmar	Amer.	Calmar S.S. Co.	Portland, Ore.	Baltimore, Md.	Lumber, general	5,440

Uyo Maru§	Jap.	Kawasaki K. Kaisha	Manila, P.I.	New York, N.Y.	General	7,032
Fordefjord§	Nor.	Chilean Nitrate Co.	Tocopilla, Chile	Savannah, Ga.	Nitrate	7,780
Svealand§	Swed.	Ore S.S. Corp.	Cruz Grande, Chile	Sparrows Pt, Md.	Iron ore	21,652
Golden River	Amer.	Amer.-Hawaiian Line	Seattle, Wash.	Charleston, S.C.	Lumber, general	5,706
Hertford	Brit.	Federal Steam Nav. Co.	Auckland, N.Z.	Glasgow, Scot.	Frozen, general	6,705
Eleanor Christenson	Amer.	Sudden & Christenson	Tacoma, Wash.	Baltimore, Md.	Lumber, general	6,951
Gen. Wm. M. Graham β	Amer.	United States Army	Balboa, C.Z.	Cristobal, C.Z.	......	.....
Abana	Ger.	North German Lloyd	Guayamas, Mex.	Bremen, Ger.	General	3,145
Salvador	Brit.	Pacific Steam Nav. Co.	Champerico, Guat.	Cristobal, C.Z.	General	215
Otira	Brit.	Shaw, Savill & Albion	Opua, N.Z.	London, Eng.	Frozen, general	3,661
Cali	Ger.	North German Lloyd	Guayaquil, Ecuador	Cristobal, C.Z.	General	1,068
Temple Bar	Brit.	Chilean Nitrate Co.	Iquique, Chile	Azores ε	Nitrate	7,750
Azumasan Maru§	Jap.	Mitsui & Co.	Moji, Japan	New York, N.Y.	General	6,797
S.C.T. Dodd‡	Amer.	J. B. Berry Sons Co.	Los Angeles, Calif.	Tiverton, R.I.	Kerosene, furnace oil	10,150
Chilcot‡	Amer.	Chile S.S. Co.	Los Angeles, Calif.	Philadelphia, Pa.	Fuel oil	7,346
Katrina Luckenbach	Amer.	Luckenbach Line	Seattle, Wash.	Boston, Mass.	General	7,154
President Pierce	Amer.	Dollar Line	Manila, P.I.	New York, N.Y.	General, cotton	3,906
Montgomery City	Amer.	Isthmian S.S. Lines	Kahului, T.H.	Baltimore, Md.	Pineapples, sugar	8,350
Tampa§	Nor.	Canadian Transp. Co.	Vancouver, B.C.	Hull, Eng.	Lumber, wheat	6,043
Brion	Neth.	West Indian S.S. Co.	Guayaquil, Ecuador	Cristobal, C.Z.	General	688
Katsuragi Maru§	Jap.	Kokusai Kisen Kaisha	Manila, P.I.	New York, N.Y.	General	7,033
Panaman	Amer.	Amer.-Hawaiian Line	Portland, Ore.	Boston, Mass.	General	5,097
Elmworth§	Brit.	Canadian Transp. Co.	Vancouver, B.C.	Dublin, Ireland	Wheat, lumber, gen.	8,173
Kwansai Maru§	Jap.	Osaka Shosen Kaisha	Iloilo, P.I.	Baltimore, Md.	Sugar, lumber	5,889
Wyoming	Fr.	French Line	Vancouver, B.C.	Antwerp, Belg.	General	7,485
Alaska	Nor.	Chilean Nit. Sales Co.	Antofagasta, Chile	Wilmington, N.C.	Nitrates	7,678
Justin	Ger.	North German Lloyd	Vancouver, B.C.	Bremen, Ger.	General	6,203
Nicoline Maersk§	Dan.	A. P. Moller	Dairen, Manchuria	Rotterdam, Neth.	Soya beans	7,480
Santa Cecilia	Amer.	Argonaut Line	Seattle, Wash.	New York, N.Y.	General	7,722
J. A. Mowinckel‡§	Danz.	W. Tankschiff Rhed'l.	Talara, Peru	Vallo, Norway	Crude oil	16,057
Japan Arrow‡	Amer.	Stand. Vacuum Transp.	San Francisco, Calif.	New York, N.Y.	Gas oil	12,722
Pennsylvania	Amer.	Panama-Pacific Line	San Francisco, Calif.	New York, N.Y.	General	4,790
Santa Rita§	Amer.	Grace Line	Valparaiso, Chile	New York, N.Y.	General	4,238
Tatsuno Maru	Jap.	Nippon Yusen Kaisha	Hinigaran, P.I.	Cristobal, C.Z.	General	7,638
Sambu‖	Pan.	Elliot Ship. and Land Co.	Darien, R.P.	New York, N.Y.	Bananas	26
Nurtureton	Brit.	R. Chapman & Sons	Vancouver, B.C.	Hull, Eng.	Wheat	9,380

§ Motorship.   ‖ Motor schooner.   ‡ Tanker.   β Mine planter.   ε For orders.

In summary, the Panama Canal has enabled the American Pacific States region to face eastward as confidently as its geographic location enabled it to face westward. Atlantic markets have been opened for all varieties of Pacific Coast products, and particularly those which are too bulky to stand high freight rates. If the time ever comes, as some eminent geographers predict, when the Pacific coast of North America will support the densest population of the Western world, it is safe to predict that the Panama Canal will have played the leading rôle in this achievement.

VII. Some Pitfalls in Shipping Statistics

While available statistics are absolutely necessary in order to discover the trends and details of sea-borne traffic, the searcher after information immediately encounters serious difficulties. He discovers that there are numerous bodies, official and otherwise, which regularly issue statistical reports, no two of which agree in classification of traffic or actual tabulated results. They are apparently contradictory, full of inaccuracies, and despite the excellent standing of the reporting organizations offer no sound basis of comparisons. To speak mildly, the whole situation becomes confusing, yet such business records are essential to the intelligent conduct of ocean commerce. It is with this thought clearly in mind that the writer inserts, at this place, a few words of suggestion and warning relative to the utilization of shipping statistics, at the same time making available to the student a more detailed analysis of the subject in Appendix D of this volume.

Where should one look for the best information? The answer to this is not simple, for it depends largely upon the special purpose of the inquiry. The most valuable statistical reports are issued regularly by the Shipping Board Bureau of the Department of Commerce (formerly United States Shipping Board), Bureau of Foreign and Domestic Commerce, Bureau of Navigation and Steamboat Inspection, Corps of Engineers for Rivers and Harbors, Panama Canal, local harbor boards, chambers of commerce, trade associations, foreign governments, and the League of Nations. What we find is that each set of statistics is designed for a particular purpose, with the result that more than one source usually must be consulted. Some examples of the need for caution which must be considered in using any figures are discussed in this chapter.

What is the California export trade in oranges? The answer would seem simple enough, yet our official figures are decidedly misleading. By a reference to the official trade returns for the calendar year 1930 we learn that the total United States exports amounted to over $11,000,000, but that of this amount less than $1,000,000 was credited to Los Angeles, the chief area of production. Over half the American exports are credited to Michigan, followed by the state of Washington, with even the Dakota customs district given a larger figure than Los Angeles. Obviously not only are these statistics meaningless as far as they fail to give the source of production but also the compilation of California exports is prejudiced to the extent of many million dollars. The Los Angeles Chamber of Commerce reports that the value of oranges shipped from Los Angeles Harbor amounted to $761,000, or $50,000 less than appear in the United States official figures. The impossibility of segregating outbound water movements from rail shipments across the Canadian and Mexican borders makes it hopeless, without recourse to unofficial figures, to proceed further with this statistical inquiry.

Another interesting example arises in the case of the export of prunes, owing to the fact that during the past few years approximately two-thirds of these exports have moved to Europe direct from the Pacific Coast instead of being transshipped as formerly through Atlantic ports. Unless due consideration is given to this factor of direct sailings, the trade and shipping statistics become decidedly misleading. Similar illustrations are readily available in the case of numerous other commodities which are now carried direct from the West Coast to foreign countries.

Statistics of water-borne commerce, gathered for different objectives and hence presented in different form, are of two main types. They may be purely transportation statistics, showing the place-to-place movement, or they may be statistics of trade, showing the commercial exchange of goods. It is important to recognize the distinction between trade and transportation statistics. Trade statistics may show either the immediate exchange between regions in which are located the seller and the buyer, or they may show the movement between the regions of origin and final destination. For convenience the former may be called immediate trade statistics, and the latter ultimate trade statistics. Immediate trade statistics are sometimes identical with transportation statistics and sometimes with ultimate trade statistics, yet often they are identical with neither. Thus there are really three overlapping types of records of water-borne commerce, but most of the available official statistics fall within either the first or the second class.

Vessel movements are recorded by the Shipping Board Bureau, the Bureau of Foreign and Domestic Commerce, the Bureau of Navigation and Steamboat Inspection, the Corps of Engineers for Rivers and Harbors, and local ports. In addition to purely transportation information, cargo-movement statistics are reported by the foregoing bodies with the exception of the Bureau of Navigation and Steamboat Inspection. These are the chief and only official sources of statistical data available for reviewing the record of maritime trade of the American Pacific States during the past decade.

Differences in method of compilation, in form of presentation, in terms and definitions, in degree of detail, and in object to be served render an attempt to reconcile the data from these several sources difficult if not futile. Each source must necessarily be used independently, bearing in mind the limitations imposed by the character of the data in each case, and using one series as a supplement to, rather than a check upon, another. In this way a reasonably well-rounded picture of the commerce of any region may be obtained.

Net tonnage of vessel entrances and clearances, reported by the Bureau of Foreign and Domestic Commerce as a measure of maritime activity, is unsatisfactory because of the meaning of the terms "in ballast" and "with cargo." The latter may mean slightly or fully loaded, and there is no method of determining from official reports which one happened to be the case. Furthermore, vessels reported as clearing a port with cargo may not have loaded any cargo at that particular port. Thus the port credited with an entry or a clearance of a vessel may not be entitled to it. Such records are misleading because of the practice of reporting vessels as "entering" at the first port where the whole or a part of their cargo is unladen and as "cleared" at the port where outbound cargoes were completed. Even this practice varies among customs districts, some reporting vessel movements regardless of cargo and others recording entrances or clearances on the basis of cargo loaded or unloaded.

Complications arise in determining the origin or destination of cargo when ships call at ports in many countries. In fact, entrance and clearance statistics do not show actual vessel movements for ports, customs districts, or foreign countries, owing to the methods of computation and tabulation. Even if it may be assumed that the port of the city of San Francisco, for example, so dominates the commerce of the San Francisco customs district that figures of the district are truly representative from year to year of the city, the method of crediting entrances to only the first United States port, and clearances to only the last United States port, involves a substantial understatement of the volume of vessel movement in and out of the district. A vessel leaving Vancouver and calling at Seattle, San Francisco, and Los Angeles en route to the United Kingdom via the Panama Canal would appear among the entrances from Canada at Seattle and among the clearances for the United Kingdom at Los Angeles. On the return trip following the same route, Los Angeles would be credited with the entrance and Seattle with the clearance. In both directions the fact that this vessel called at San Francisco to load or discharge cargo would be entirely omitted in the official figures.

Official statistics of vessel movements are unsatisfactory, therefore, not only because each vessel is credited with only one entrance and one clearance, irrespective of the number of ports visited, but also because of the prevailing system of failing to credit any port unless it happened to be the first continental port visited or the last continental port cleared for foreign waters. Seaports, therefore, which are visited first or last on a ship's journey, or are situated adjacent to a foreign country, make the best statistical showing. Thus the following table accords Los Angeles and the state of Washington a magnified importance in contrast with San Francisco and Oregon, respectively.

Ship movements for British Columbia are equally misleading. For example, in 1932 the customs department recorded arrivals of 2,148 vessels of 5,529,000 net tonnage from foreign ports at Vancouver, contrasted with 2,052 vessels of

TABLE 23

VESSELS ENTERED AND CLEARED IN FOREIGN TRADE, TOTAL AND PACIFIC
CUSTOMS DISTRICTS, 1928–1930*

(In thousands of net tons)

Customs District	1928		1929		1930	
	Entered	Cleared	Entered	Cleared	Entered	Cleared
Grand total	80,211	80,667	82,602	82,343	81,253	81,307
Seaports, total	62,809	62,331	66,853	67,030	66,499	66,500
Pacific coast, total.........	15,292	15,715	16,278	16,545	17,015	17,385
Washington	6,273	6,278	6,856	6,436	7,409	6,746
Oregon	927	976	929	939	533	709
San Francisco	1,996	2,457	2,075	2,529	2,092	2,414
Los Angeles	4,792	4,573	5,054	5,210	5,012	5,718
Alaska	362	267	321	239	301	235
Hawaii	942	1,164	1,043	1,192	1,319	1,411
San Diego	...	...	...	...	348	152

* Data from Bureau of Foreign and Domestic Commerce.

4,049,000 net tonnage at Victoria. Actually, approximately
50 per cent of the vessels inbound at Vancouver were of the
deep-sea type, compared to 20 per cent at Victoria. These
statistics issued by the Canadian Department of National
Revenue are therefore less satisfactory than those issued by
the Vancouver Harbour Board, which adopts the classification of vessels according to "deep sea," referring to all
vessels entering from ports beyond Cape Flattery; "foreign
coastwise," meaning vessels operating between Vancouver
and Puget Sound; and "coastwise," a term which applies
only to the province of British Columbia. On the basis of
shipping statistics, Victoria is placed far ahead of any port
in eastern Canada, while with reference to volume of exports for the year 1932 the figures for Victoria are 52,167
cargo tons, contrasted with 445,000 tons for New Westmin-
ster and 3,719,000 tons for Vancouver.

There are almost insuperable difficulties in providing an
adequate record of vessels and cargoes, owing to the fact
that a single vessel may be loaded or in ballast; it may have
cargo to be loaded or distributed at coastwise continental
United States ports, at foreign ports, at ports in non-contigu-

ous United States possessions; or it may carry cargo inter-coastally. For example, consider the recording difficulties involved in the round-the-world service of a Dollar liner which enters at New York with foreign cargo for Boston, Havana, Cristobal, Balboa, Los Angeles, San Francisco, Honolulu, and the Far East. Bonds required for dutiable foreign cargo for delivery at various ports mentioned are given at New York. On original clearance from New York, the vessel proceeds to Boston, where part of the cargo is discharged and additional cargo laden for various domestic and foreign ports. It then returns to New York, where additional cargo and/or passengers are taken on board for any port on its itinerary. On the second departure from New York the vessel clears for Havana, Cristobal, and Balboa direct; also to Los Angeles and San Francisco with residue foreign cargo; also with intercoastal cargo for same; to Honolulu with foreign and domestic cargo, also foreign and domestic cargo for Far East ports via domestic ports.

The point is that each of the foregoing "clearances" requires a separate set of documents even though all cargo may be in the same hold.

The statistics of vessel movements, therefore, are misleading with respect to the very facts they purport to represent, especially when their method of compilation is not clearly stated. Certainly no published official statistics of vessel movements can be safely relied upon to measure the comparative importance, in either foreign or domestic water-borne commerce, of the various ports of the United States. Nor do they serve as a correct guide to comparative maritime activity on the various trade routes in or across the several oceans. Accordingly, use should not be limited to merely one of them in the analysis of Pacific Coast maritime commerce.

Care must be taken in interpreting even official figures because of the local pressure which is always brought to bear in order to make the statistics as attractive as possible. New York has acceded to this pressure, since the Collector of Customs at the Port of New York supplements the statistics issued regularly by the Bureau of Foreign and Domestic Commerce with a current statement of entrances and clearances which includes both indirect and direct movements. While the writer is in hearty sympathy with the wisdom of issuing this specially-prepared statement, he would point out the confusion which arises by placing New York in a preferential position compared to other ports, through the issuance of a regular monthly statement such as that which appears in Table 24 (p. 154).

In the case of those communities which advertise a certain definite number of lines making calls, it should be admitted that no one has yet established any method of ascertaining how such services can be computed. To illustrate, is a joint service one line or two; is a round-the-world service one line or many lines; is a tanker service to be rated as a steamship line; and how are intra-port and river services to be listed? With reference to the Pacific Coast, mainly the same vessels call at San Francisco and Los Angeles except that San Francisco also possesses a few barge routes and several bay and river carriers, while Los Angeles has more tanker services.

Statistics for imports are frequently confusing, since little attempt is made to indicate whether the statistics provided show "imports for consumption" or "general imports." The distinction is that the total value of imports includes the value of merchandise entered for consumption, combined with that withdrawn from bonded warehouse for consumption. Beginning January 1934 the official statistics issued by the Department of Commerce show imports for consumption rather than general imports, whereas formerly general imports included the value of merchandise entered for immediate consumption, combined with the value of merchandise entered for warehouse. Thus, under the former method of compilation, the value of merchandise imported in a given month did not indicate the value of merchandise that entered in domestic channels of trade during that month, since merchandise entering a warehouse might be withdrawn for exportation later. Under the newly adopted method the monthly compilation of imports indicates the value of merchandise that actually entered into domestic channels of trade during the month in question, more satisfactory therefore for general purposes but confusing when

TABLE 24

REPORTED VESSEL ENTRANCES AND CLEARANCES, PORT OF NEW YORK,
APRIL 1934*

FOREIGN TRADE ENTRANCES

	Vessels	Net Tons
Foreign direct		
In ballast	15	141,239
Bulk cargo	43	125,691
General cargo	113	821,059
Total	171	1,087,989
Foreign via other ports		
In ballast	6	11,321
Bulk cargo	7	16,773
General cargo	75	307,645
Total	88	335,739
American direct		
In ballast	4	23,572
Bulk cargo	23	99,425
General cargo	90	388,199
Total	117	511,196
American via other ports		
Bulk cargo	1	3,450
General cargo	51	179,916
Total	52	183,366

DOMESTIC TRADE ENTRANCES

	Vessels	Net Tons
Intercoastal		
In ballast	..	....
Bulk cargo	14	67,902
General cargo	63	240,323
Total	77	308,225
Coastwise		
In ballast	3	10,795
Bulk cargo	5	14,362
General cargo	137	412,280
Total	145	437,437
Noncontiguous		
Bulk cargo	4	11,589
General cargo	23	69,628
Total	27	81,217

* Data from Collector of the Port of New York (from the *Journal of Commerce,*
June 18, 1934).

one attempts to make a chronological comparison of "imports."

It is scarcely necessary to point out that value figures over a series of years are comparable subject only to the limitations both of changing general price level and changes in unit value of the various constituent commodities. The present tariff law, moreover, makes provision for five alternative methods of determining the value of imports subject to ad valorem duty. As tariff laws change, the comparability of import figures over a period of years is affected. As it is, there is considerable error in the statistics of dutiable imports, more in statistics of free imports, and most of all in statistics of exports.

A consistent bias is found in dutiable-imports statistics, owing to the tendency toward understatement of value and that toward classification of merchandise so as to make it fall in the lowest possible duty group. Both value and quantity figures are, of course, understated as a result, but even so the import statistics are far better than the export. There are no legal penalties attached to the making of export declarations, and consequently they are often made carelessly. The United States is almost alone in recording the value of both exports and imports on an f.o.b. basis.

Another caution to be observed is that, in the Bureau of Foreign and Domestic Commerce reports, imports and exports by customs districts are treated differently. Exports are credited to the district where merchandise leaves the country. Export statistics, then, give no clue to the actual origin of commodities through the various customs districts of the country.[1] Imports are credited to the port of physical entry only when that point is also the place of technical entry for consumption or warehousing, since the importer designates his choice of the port of entry.

Perhaps the most striking instance of the shortcomings of this method of compilation for purposes of regional eco-

---

[1] Mention should also be made of the fact that total exports include domestic exports and foreign exports, and the latter include goods of foreign origin re-exported in the same condition as when imported without any processing designed to enhance their value. The quantity of foreign exports is relatively insignificant.

nomic analysis occurs in the case of silk. Until five years ago virtually all raw-silk imports into the United States were landed on the Pacific Coast, at either American or British Columbia ports. Consumption of this raw silk is mainly in the New York–New Jersey manufacturing area. Neither of these facts, however, is clearly brought out in the statistics of imports by customs districts. One seeking accurate information on the silk trade would surely be misled unless he had access to corrective information from other sources. During the calendar year 1929, for example, raw silk was reported among the general imports of sixteen customs districts. Among these, the following districts accounted for all but a small percentage of the total imports of 87,000,000 pounds:

District	Pounds Imported
Washington	29,911,994
New York	19,625,873
San Francisco	18,141,232
St. Lawrence	8,871,167
Buffalo	7,074,434
Oregon	1,681,996

From the point of view of direct ocean-transportation movements these figures are not representative for any district mentioned above. They greatly understate the receipts of raw silk at the three Pacific customs districts and to an even greater extent overstate the receipts by water at New York. In fact, the latter receipts were probably extremely small in 1929, although the current trend is toward all-water movement via Panama. Import entries at the Buffalo and St. Lawrence districts are presumably entirely overland rail movements, although not the entire rail movement of this commodity through these districts. Considering the silk movement from the standpoint of ultimate trade, on the other hand, the New York figures are far too small and the others entirely too large. There is no silk industry of importance elsewhere than on the Atlantic seaboard.

The commodity trade statistics in the instance of commodities which may move either overland by rail or intercoastally, therefore, must be used with caution. Table 25, which gives the total arrivals of raw silk in the United States according to the overland, Panama, Suez, and European routes for the years 1924 to 1933 inclusive, is an exceedingly important demonstration of the combined effect of reduced commodity prices and cargo rates in the diversion of the Coast's leading import from the transcontinental to the intercoastal route.

TABLE 25

RAW-SILK IMPORTS INTO THE UNITED STATES BY OVERLAND, PANAMA, SUEZ, AND EUROPEAN ROUTES, 1924–1933*

Year	Total Overland		Panama		Suez		European		Total Arrivals (Overland, Panama, Suez, and European) Bales
	Bales (All Ports)	Percentage of Total Arrivals	Bales	Percentage of Total Arrivals	Bales	Percentage of Total Arrivals	Bales	Percentage of Total Arrivals	
1924..	381,631	98.4	130	0.0	140	0.0	5,774	1.5	387,675
1925..	458,872	93.7	12,613	2.6	7,727	1.6	10,422	2.1	489,634
1926..	478,827	95.0	7,607	1.5	11,420	2.3	6,346	1.3	504,200
1927..	513,121	92.9	16,640	3.0	19,959	3.6	2,721	0.5	552,441
1928..	522,347	92.2	31,319	5.5	8,629	1.5	4,083	0.7	566,378
1929..	520,448	78.7	116,496	17.6	12,207	1.8	12,460	1.9	661,611
1930..	340,654	62.0	190,061	34.6	1,606	0.3	17,563	3.2	549,884
1931..	231,085	38.1	351,474	58.0	407	0.1	22,953	3.8	605,919
1932..	221,558	40.5	311,757	57.0	330	0.1	13,550	2.5	547,195
1933..	110,591	22.0	373,440	74.2	125	0.0	19,250	3.8	503,406

* Data from the Federated Textile Industries, Inc. Percentages approximate.

The foregoing information, together with that which appears in Table 32, chapter viii, p. 191, unfortunately bears no reference whatever to the official "port of entry" as recorded in the customs figures, such as those already cited for the year 1929. How much of this actual transportation movement appears in the directory under statistics accredited to a particular port is a mere matter of conjecture. Examples can be drawn from other commodities such as wool: for illustration, the largest shipment of wool which has been received at San Francisco for over seven years arrived from Australia in June 1933 for transshipment to Eastern states immediately upon arrival. A personal investigation discloses that this entire movement is credited as an import of the Port of New York, although none of it arrived there by water. San Francisco loses all credit.

Classification of items varies greatly in the official statistics of water-borne commerce. The Bureau of Foreign and Domestic Commerce reports, designed to be helpful to the manufacturing and merchant firms, use the quantity units known to the various trades involved. Shippers, however, who are more interested in volume movements, are unable to extract such information from these reports as they might if, for example, the different articles moving in exports and imports were all recorded in terms of a common unit of weight.

Shipping Board Bureau reports, on the other hand, are compiled with a different objective. They are designed to be useful to shippers and hence involve greater emphasis on tonnage, particularly bulky commodities of relatively low value but moving in large quantities. As the number of such products is obviously limited, the Board's classification of items is restricted, which leads to a grouping of different commodities within the same class, frequently obscuring the facts regarding the movement of individual items of some importance.

For example, the word "provisions" may cover grain and grain products as well as all other substances used in the manufacture of food. A commodity class entitled "grains" may be shown separately and may include all products thereof for both human and animal consumption. In many cases, raw materials and their finished products are included within the same class. The term "textiles" may include raw wool, cotton, or other fibrous materials as diverse as jute and silk, together with their manufactures. There is no complete uniformity from year to year, even for individual ports, and the varying importance of different commodities at different ports has led to an adoption of a commodity grouping for each port more or less specialized to suit the statistics. These facts render it difficult to make comparisons between ports and between years.

Then, too, the inclusion or exclusion and interpretations of such items in imports and exports as bunker fuel, ships' stores, and bullion and currency are not standardized. Gold and silver are important items on the Pacific Coast, and it makes a real difference whether or not they are taken into account. In American statistics, each commercial transaction appears only once, hence the official figures can give no indication as to the amount of port-to-port traffic. Domestic-commerce statistics are, in fact, quite unsatisfactory; the foreign-trade movements only are covered in official reports with anything like satisfactory completeness and accuracy. Nowhere other than in the reports of the Board of Engineers for Rivers and Harbors is there a record covering all types of ocean-borne trade, and the questionable nature of some of these statistics has already been suggested.

The Bureau of Foreign and Domestic Commerce reports alone provide commodity statistics covering the trade of and with noncontiguous territories of the United States. Although the reports of this Bureau are the most detailed available on commodity movements in foreign trade, nowhere is a three-fold classification by article, customs district, and country available which would make possible a full analysis of the commerce of any district. The "origin" of shipments in foreign countries is often merely the country from which immediate shipment was made rather than the country of production. Nations with major seaports thus appear to have more industry and trade than they actually do have and other important areas appear to have little. In strict accuracy such statistics do not represent the direct transportation movement between ports of the United States and foreign countries, the immediate trade relations, or even the exchange of goods produced by the countries specified. Hence, one needs to be wary.

Likewise, the Shipping Board figures, because they consider only seaport terminals, give no clue to the original or ultimate destination of goods. They are, however, extremely valuable in that they permit tracing port-to-port movements from and to the United States. But where alternate routes over different oceans are available for traffic moving between widely separated ports, these statistics fail to give any clue to the proportion of the traffic following each route. For example, the percentage of the trade of Atlantic United States with the Far East moving via Suez and the part going via Panama cannot be determined, nor can the use of Suez be compared with that of the Cape of Good Hope.[2]

Because the Department of Commerce reports are classified by customs districts rather than by ports, the nearest approach to the imports and exports at Portland or Seattle are the Oregon and Washington customs district figures. In each instance a number of fairly substantial cargo movements at other ports within these states are included, so that if it were desired to follow the lumber movement, for example, from any of these ports, it would be necessary to use other sources, principally the reports of the Shipping Board or the War Department.

Even in the Los Angeles district, several complications arise in determining the petroleum exports of the port of Los Angeles. According to the Bureau of Foreign and Domestic Commerce 45,773,888 barrels of all classes of petroleum (other than greases, wax, asphalt, and coke) were exported from the Los Angeles customs district during the calendar year 1929. No conversion factor is given for reducing this figure to a weight basis in order to compare it with the report of the Shipping Board on the port of Los Angeles for the fiscal year 1929 or with that of the War Department for the calendar year. The latter shows an export of 6,687,859 short tons of bulk and package petroleum, exclusive of bunker oil, while the former reports 5,330,958 long tons. After allowing for the different unit employed, the War Department's figure for the calendar year is still substantially larger than the Shipping Board figure for the fiscal year.

Raw-silk imports into the San Francisco customs district amounted to 9,070 short tons (18,141,232 pounds) in the calendar year 1929. The War Department reports a total of 15,316 short tons for the port of San Francisco alone. The Shipping Board does not show silk separately in its returns, but reports an import of 94,652 long tons of textiles into

[2] The Osaka Shosen Kaisha, for example, has been operating its round-the-world service westward via South Africa and the Panama Canal, while other round-the-world services use the Suez Canal and the Panama Canal. Some movement, likewise, still takes place around Cape Horn instead of by the more direct Panama route.

San Francisco, including all Bay ports, in the fiscal year 1929. Clearly, there are many problems encountered in any attempt to analyze and integrate the water-borne statistics of the entire United States or the Pacific Coast section.

, Reports of intercoastal traffic by the Shipping Board and by the *Panama Canal Record* should tally closely, since both cover the fiscal year and are in terms of long tons. Yet a comparison of the two sources for three years is as follows:

1927	United States Shipping Board	*Panama Canal Record*
Atlantic to Pacific............	2,609,763	2,822,598
Pacific to Atlantic............	7,557,589	8,039,804
1928		
Atlantic to Pacific............	2,382,170	2,576,399
Pacific to Atlantic............	7,290,534	7,657,300
1929		
Atlantic to Pacific............	2,989,029	3,184,141
Pacific to Atlantic............	6,907,589	6,992,632

Such instances might be multiplied indefinitely. Thus, exports of cotton from the Galveston customs district, including Houston, Dallas, and Texas City, amounted to 977,935 long tons in the calendar year 1929 according to the Bureau of Foreign and Domestic Commerce, but the United States Shipping Board reported an export movement of 1,143,595 long tons of cotton in the fiscal year 1929 from these three seaports.

American port statistics, as compiled by harbor boards, chambers of commerce, and other local bodies, are usually unsatisfactory. Their methods of compilation seldom agree. A careful investigation into the statistical procedure followed at numerous ports bears every evidence that the figures are on the whole honestly compiled, but there is no standardized statistical procedure. Thus, in answer to the writer's request for information regarding intercoastal trade, eastbound trade, and foreign trade, the San Diego Chamber of Commerce writes: "We would very much like to know the actual condition, and the actual facts are so far from being known we dare not hazard a guess." The most complete figures, made possible through a remarkable degree of co-operation with the steamship lines, are provided at the Port of Los Angeles. The Los Angeles Chamber of Commerce issues daily reports taken from the custom-house records, not depending therefore on either the Shipping Board or Department of Commerce figures, which arrive too late for their business purposes. The comptroller of the Los Angeles Harbor Department calls attention to the serious difficulties involved in providing satisfactory figures, but advises that "as regards the commerce statistics situation in general I have no hesitancy in stating that this Department exerts its best efforts toward compilation and publication of honest, dependable data as to commerce thru the port." The Board of State Harbor Commissioners at San Francisco has records of its own piers, while statistics for ship tonnages of the port are kept by the Marine Department of the San Francisco Chamber of Commerce. The statistical reports issued by the Board of State Harbor Commissioners are good.

At Portland the Merchants Exchange compiles statistics for the Commissioner of Public Docks. The Tacoma Chamber of Commerce depends upon the harbormaster's office, which advises that "reports are gathered from various sources, some being sent in by shippers, manufacturers, and dock operators, some taken from manifests in dock and customs house offices here, and others are gathered in various ways." The Seattle Chamber of Commerce writes:

> You will notice that these State figures include only the foreign and intercoastal waterborne commerce. There are no records kept of the coastwise statistics for this state, which leaves the records of the waterborne commerce incomplete for Washington, as they are also for California, Oregon, and Alaska. The State of Washington is at a disadvantage in comparisons of statistics because there seems to be no uniformity in the keeping of statistics by various ports in the State. There is no law compelling the compilation of these statistics; therefore the carriers are inclined to keep this information confidential.

The Corps of Engineers for Rivers and Harbors depends entirely, as to at least one large West Coast port, upon the statistics provided by the local chamber of commerce. It is apparent, therefore, that these diversified statistical practices do not make a satisfactory port-by-port comparison,

although, within the limits of what the figures are intended
to convey, these records are usually of distinct value.

The Bureau of Foreign and Domestic Commerce issues
multigraphed statements giving the annual export trade by
states. These figures are widely quoted but are distinctly
misleading since the commodities which they represent are
not necessarily produced in that state, nor do these figures
give a complete record for any state. The following table
gives the reported information for the years 1928, 1929, and
1930.

TABLE 26

REPORTED EXPORTS BY STATES, 1928–1930*

Rank	State	1928	1929	1930
1	New York	$861,578,924	$956,755,282	$698,659,077
2	Texas	817,002,082	657,559,600	506,083,298
3	California	345,436,658	380,344,112	304,876,298
11	Washington	121,638,132	126,744,522	86,667,880
17	Oregon	69,271,988	70,208,381	52,239,619
35	Arizona	13,105,944	14,438,868	8,849,792
40	Montana	6,814,817	5,680,894	4,303,010
42	Colorado	3,419,934	4,001,887	3,238,588
43	Hawaii	3,955,464	3,738,352	3,157,912
45	Idaho	2,282,991	1,956,019	1,243,944
46	Wyoming	2,703,557	1,451,983	1,115,452
48	Utah	647,152	1,006,411	644,094
49	New Mexico	2,105,133	1,517,886	558,044
51	Nevada	416,107	543,679	328,211
52	Alaska	933,795	559,465	248,223

* Data from Bureau of Foreign and Domestic Commerce.

The Department of Commerce designates this information as based upon states of original shipment as noted by
shippers in the making out of export declarations. The scant
value which attaches to these figures can be readily appreciated when it becomes recognized that the sole basis of
calculation is the place where the export declaration was
prepared. The statistics for the interior states considerably
underestimate actual conditions—there are no statistics anywhere which provide a satisfactory indication of this export
traffic. Hence these figures do not represent either the
locality of production or the port of departure.

Some sources utilize a calendar-year basis and others a fiscal-year basis, so that a direct comparison between the United States Shipping Board reports (which use the former method), for example, and the Bureau of Foreign and Domestic Commerce reports (which use the latter method) is inadvisable. In using the statistics of water-borne commerce, a much more important and useful category of water-traffic statistics than the vessel-movement data, further complications merit our attention.

Reports made by the Chief of Engineers, United States Army, do not indicate whether vessels were with cargo or in ballast, and involve no separation of foreign, coastwise, and intercoastal movements; thus there is some question regarding the reliability and worth-while nature of certain statistics. The United States Shipping Board reports exclude vessels that are under 100 gross tons, while those issued by the Governor of the Panama Canal are, of course, primarily an indication of the utilization of the Canal for the shipping on important trade routes.

The deadweight ton, which is probably a closer approach to the carrying capacity of the ordinary cargo vessel than the net ton, is used in the reports of the *Panama Canal Record* and the United States Shipping Board; but the Bureau of Foreign and Domestic Commerce uses the net-ton unit (calculated by measuring the internal carrying capacity of a vessel, after deducting space for crew and engines, and allowing 100 cubic feet to each ton), and the War Department has still another method of calculation. Since rules of vessel measurement are not standardized and the practices of official bodies compiling statistics are not uniform, comparisons are obviously not facilitated.

Equally frequent cases are encountered in which no comparison at all is possible between sources because of differences in forms of tabulation. On the whole, it is perhaps more satisfactory not even to attempt reconciliation, because of so many fundamental differences, but to use each source for what light it appears able to throw on whatever problem is at hand. That is the procedure followed in this research project.

In Appendix D will be found a more detailed analysis of

official sources, an account of the methods used in compilation and presentation, and, in general, a critical evaluation of available series of data. In the present chapter the purpose of the writer is merely to mention some of the cautions which must be observed with reference both to understanding the statistics of any one official body and to attempting comparisons. Unnecessary confusion all too often appears in the careless use of terms, units of measurement, proper names, and so on.

There is a vast need for better methods of gathering and reporting maritime trade statistics. The various statistics issued by any one country are difficult to bring into harmony, and the problem of bringing international statistics into accord is a much more difficult proposition. The United States government has from time to time endeavored to establish a more unified classification of trade and shipping statistics, but actually little has been accomplished to date. It is unfortunate that the Advisory and Technical Committee for Communications and Transit of the League of Nations, at its session held in Geneva late in 1933, decided for financial reasons to postpone indefinitely its important project for unifying transport statistics.

Despite the foregoing glaring weaknesses in maritime statistics, it cannot be too strongly emphasized by the writer that existing American statistics from numerous sources set a general standard of individual excellence and compare most favorably with those prepared by any country. They constitute the raw material of shipping intelligence.

VIII. Leading Coast Ports

In this chapter, the emphasis is on the location, facilities, and activities of the outstanding Pacific Coast ports. For reasons discussed in the preceding chapter, a rating of these ports will not be attempted here because of the impossibility of establishing satisfactory standards which would meet the acceptance of students and men of affairs alike.

Port development takes place in accordance with trade requirements and along the path of favored traffic routes. The presence of natural harbor facilities is not enough. A port of importance never evolves without favorable trade conditions, but a good harbor is, nevertheless, an important factor in port growth. Favorable trade conditions are a resultant of many more factors, among which the tributary territory (hinterland) is of prime importance in port development. In examining the position of the leading Pacific Coast ports, then, consideration must be given to such factors as the productivity, the topography, transportation facilities and rates of the back country, and, finally, the virility of the local population. These underlying conditions determine the nature and extent of the commerce of particular ports, and also their competitive relations with other water terminals.

The American Pacific Coast has relatively few great ports, but among these are numbered several of the finest harbors in the world, where deep, sheltered bays, virtually landlocked, provide space which is capable of handling a far greater amount of traffic than it does at present. The Puget Sound region, for example, is in reality a series of harbors connected by deep water, many of which have already had more or less development. San Francisco Bay is sufficiently large to hold many times the present navies of the world. Because of the mountainous and semi-arid character of much of the land adjacent to the Pacific shoreline, however, the major ports on the Coast have as yet developed only a fraction of the commerce which they are able to handle.

In the earlier chapters it was shown that in comparison with European countries or even the Atlantic seaboard of the

United States, the Pacific Coast is not favored with many natural terminals for maritime development. Europe, for example, has a well-developed port for every 64,000 square miles of land area. On the American Pacific Coast there are only five ports that may be termed "well developed," or one for each 200,000 square miles of land. Of course, this is not exactly a fair comparison, because as population increases and trade grows ports are developed even though they appear to have few advantages. But it is significant that with 40 per cent of the total coastline of the United States the Pacific Coast has but three natural harbors and one man-made harbor of first importance.

Were the Pacific area totally undeveloped industrially this paucity of ready-made harbors would not matter so much, but in 1929 Pacific Coast ports of the United States handled 27 per cent of the total ocean-borne trade of the United States through 4 per cent of the country's ports.[1] Up to a certain point, the greater the volume of traffic in a port, the more efficient its operation becomes, but thereafter the law of diminishing returns becomes operative and additional growth is undesirable. Congestion slows up traffic so that port costs begin to mount. There is reason for the belief that the ports of San Francisco and Los Angeles are approaching a condition of congestion, which is not surprising in view of the well-known tendency for trade to concentrate in a few large ports and also due to the small number of developed ports on the Coast in relation to the volume of traffic handled.

With the growth of trade many small ports come into existence, since they are more favorably situated with reference to producing areas. These secondary ports are export regions, but seldom figure in the import trade. The large cities, on the other hand, are important marketing centers; hence in addition to handling their share of export trade a few water terminals account for the vast preponderance of merchandise imports on the Pacific Coast.

In forecasting the relative growth of present large and

[1] Atlantic seaboard ports handled 54 per cent of the total volume of traffic, twice that of the West Coast, and Gulf ports 19 per cent of the total.

small ports, important consideration must be given to the intrinsic advantages offered for interdependent land, air, and water transportation. We know that those localities which provide the best facilities for a "break in transportation" have the most logical chances for future expansion.

A bird's-eye view of the shipping commerce of the leading Coast ports appears in Table 27 and Figure 25.

TABLE 27

COMMERCE OF PRINCIPAL PACIFIC COAST PORTS, 1929

Pacific Ports	Thousand Short Tons (2,000 lbs.)*				Thousand Cargo Tons (2,240 lbs.)†	
	Imports	Exports	Coastwise		Imports	Exports
			Receipts	Ship-ments		
Total	*4,149*	*17,918*	*39,471*	*36,428*	*3,185*	*13,593*
San Diego	41	11	877	29	31	8
Los Angeles	728	7,886	5,354	14,938	685	6,054
San Francisco Bay.......	1,430	4,012	19,078	6,871	1,194	2,482
Long Beach	102	345	493	1,572	...	...
Portland	137	1,500	2,650	1,004	109	1,377
Grays Harbor	2	818	186	1,192	2	611
Tacoma	446	858	1,422	1,488	391	667
Seattle	475	663	4,880	1,945	445	718
Everett	143	230	973	818	8	217
Honolulu .:.............	108	11	1,055	802	...	...

* Data from *Annual Report of the Chief of Engineers,* United States Army.
† Data from United States Shipping Board.

The aggregate water commerce of Pacific ports is around 110,000,000 tons annually. Of this volume California ports account for about three-fifths, with San Francisco and Los Angeles dominating the shipping. Although San Diego handles an exceedingly small proportion of Pacific Coast or California commerce, it has one of the three natural harbors found in the Pacific States, and so is destined to have a more important place in the shipping of the region. Discovered in 1542 by Cabrillo, San Diego harbor was first to achieve prominence in the early history of Pacific North America; its slower development has been due to the absence of those spectacular events that attract population, the limitations

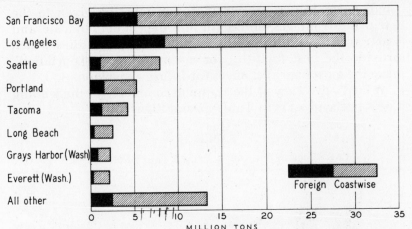

FIG. 25.—Water-borne commerce of United States Pacific Coast ports, 1929.

until comparatively recent years upon such essentials as an adequate water supply, the relatively smaller wealth of the back country, which is still largely undeveloped, and the competition of Los Angeles.

Port development at San Diego did not really begin until about twenty years ago. In the past decade its commerce has increased several hundred per cent. At the present time San Diego is the headquarters of a separate customs district; before 1922 also it was a separate district, but between 1922 and 1930, or throughout most of the period with which the present survey is concerned, its foreign trade was included with that of the Los Angeles district in the official statistics published by the Bureau of Foreign and Domestic Commerce. San Diego's trade and shipping statistics, therefore, are too meaningless to justify a chronological tabulation here.

By far the greatest portion of the maritime commerce of San Diego consists of coastwise receipts from other Pacific ports (772,000 tons out of an aggregate of 900,000 tons in 1930, according to the report of the local harbor department). More than three-fourths of these receipts are accounted for by mineral oil and lumber. Fish and fish products are its most important coastwise outgoing cargo, but total less than

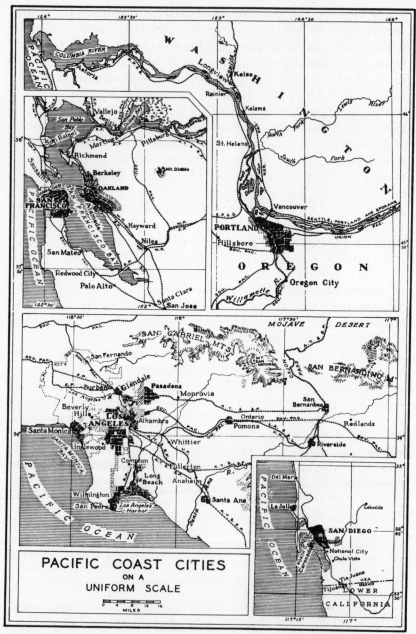

FIG. 26.—Maps of Portland, San Francisco, Los Angeles, and San Diego.
(For Puget Sound ports, see Fig. 28, page 189.)

5 per cent of the volume of coastwise receipts. It is not surprising that San Diego's foreign trade is predominantly with Mexico, with Europe ranking second.[2] Total foreign trade in the fiscal year 1930 amounted to 60,000 tons, according to the local harbor report, and to 37,000 according to the United States Shipping Board.[3]

Because it is the most southerly Pacific Coast port, San Diego enjoys certain geographical advantages in the matter of distance, especially for southbound and eastbound cargoes. A total of thirty-seven lines serve the port, but only about twenty make it a regular port of call. Two railroads serve the port, both parts of important transcontinental trunk systems, and numerous truck lines. Rail rates are the same as those applicable to other Pacific Coast ports and ocean rates on all lines calling at the port are the same as those from other Pacific ports to the same destinations.

A large portion of San Diego's hinterland is mountainous or desert and slightly developed. Southern Arizona, New Mexico, northern Mexico, including Lower California, and southern California (particularly Imperial Valley) comprise the natural tributary lands; but except for Imperial Valley on both sides of the border and parts of Arizona the country is unexploited. Given adequate water, much of this land, especially in northern Mexico, could become a rich agricultural region. Although mineral wealth is known to exist, except in Arizona these resources have not been exploited. The city of San Diego itself cannot support a large population on its existing water resources; yet population is a factor vital to trade. From the completion of Boulder or Hoover Dam on the Colorado River, San Diego as well as Los Angeles will derive great benefit.

Because of the rate structure San Diego can and does

[2] Through lack of direct steamship service, both eastbound intercoastal and foreign, the bulk of the foreign trade is transshipped through Los Angeles harbor and is often entered as coastwise movement. Thus an indeterminable amount of the commerce reported as coastwise is actually intercoastal or foreign.

[3] Some of the discrepancy is due to the fact that the unit of measurement of the Shipping Board is the long ton while that of the San Diego Harbor Board is the short ton. In the present chapter more use is made than elsewhere of local statistics.

draw grain and cotton from the San Joaquin Valley for export and may thus compete on even terms with neighboring ports. Cotton and cottonseed products have become important in exports to foreign countries. The great importance of the harbor at San Diego at present is as a naval base rather than as a commercial seaport. San Diego possesses many natural advantages for overcoming the present obstacles to her maritime trade development, including the absence of any neighboring competitive ports south of the California-Mexican boundary.

Ninety-seven nautical miles to the north of San Diego are the ports of Los Angeles and Long Beach, which, from an economic standpoint, may be considered as a single port area. Discovered in the same year as San Diego by Cabrillo, what is now Los Angeles was visited by several Spanish explorers, each of whom apparently applied a different saint's name to the region until in 1609 the name San Pedro was finally decided upon; and so this harbor was known for 300 years. Until the completion of the government breakwater and the annexation (1909) of the harbor to the city of Los Angeles a quarter of a century ago, the port had little commercial importance. Beginning with the opening of the Panama Canal, however, development of the harbor has been rapid, a striking instance of man's ingenuity and foresight in coping with Nature's barriers. In this instance, harbor facilities were practically non-existent; it was necessary to build them. In addition to the large government appropriations, the citizens of this community expended over $25,000,000 for port development. And then came the tremendous asset of the mineral-oil wealth in southern California. That exploitation is the key to the growth of the port of San Pedro.

Petroleum tanker cargoes dominate the export movement from the Pacific States area to almost every part of the world. Most of the movement is through Los Angeles harbor, a movement so great as to place this port near the top among United States ports on the basis of weight of cargoes handled.[4] Prior to the opening of the Panama Canal,

---

[4] In 1930, Los Angeles ranked third, after New York and Duluth-Superior, in aggregate volume of water-borne commerce. See also chapter xv.

total foreign trade at San Diego was nearly as important as that at Los Angeles, and the exports of the former port surpassed those of the latter several-fold. According to a report of the Chief of Engineers, United States Army, total traffic at Los Angeles harbor, both foreign and coastwise, amounted to 1,728,000 short tons in the calendar year 1913. Of this, by far the greater part was coastwise. By 1920, statistics from the same source indicate a growth in total traffic to well over 4,000,000 tons, of which less than one-fifth, or about 750,000 tons, was foreign. Another seven years' growth brought water-borne commerce at Los Angeles up to 26,000,000 tons, fifteen times that reported fourteen years earlier.

TABLE 28

PRINCIPAL EXPORTS AND IMPORTS OF LOS ANGELES, 1913 AND 1926–1931*

(Thousand dollars)

	Fis-cal 1913†	Calendar Years					
		1926	1927	1928	1929	1930†	1931†
Exports (total)	...	103,360	120,396	141,652	165,849	149,567	92,284
Fish, fresh and preserved................	...‡	1,551	2,752	2,519	3,696	2,911	911
Citrus fruits	...‡	1,259	3,369	2,006	5,579	1,594	4,909
Cotton, unmanufactured	...‡	8,281	13,265	17,213	28,072	19,952	14,966
Petroleum products	...‡	76,532	82,572	95,147	95,602	96,730	51,005
Oil-well machinery	...‡	2,908	3,168	3,187	3,611	2,781	1,262
Borax	...‡	878	2,133	3,187	2,708	2,856	3,178
Imports (total)	...	49,571	47,140	54,351	63,685	52,088	39,882
Fish, fresh and preserved................	36	1,015	2,378	2,581	3,685	3,758	1,512
Oil seeds	...‡	1,753	359	293	1,009	3,767	3,765
Oil cake and meal.......................	...‡	528	1,215	1,522	1,514	879	207
Coffee	163	4,442	4,275	4,820	4,797	3,171	3,273
Rubber	...‡	11,103	6,960	9,153	13,101	8,981	5,138
Coconut oil, inedible....................	...‡	1,126	1,264	1,618	1,295	0	42
Cotton, unmanufactured	...‡	5,613	2,548	3,922	4,906	1,221	1,003
Wood and manufactures.................	408	1,525	2,152	1,737	1,986	1,826	1,136
Paper	...‡	2,862	2,986	2,580	2,399	3,660	2,475
Iron and steel manufactures.............	49	2,491	3,671	3,943	3,074	2,374	1,450
Fertilizer	268	1,549	1,183	2,028	1,779	1,481	1,640

* Data from *Foreign Commerce and Navigation of the United States.* This table excludes foreign merchandise, transit, and transshipment movements.

† Including San Diego, which was a separate customs district in 1913 and was recreated a separate district on June 20, 1930.

‡ Not listed separately.

The growth in traffic at Los Angeles has been more rapid than that of any other important port on the Coast. Even within the six years from 1925 to 1930 inclusive, the tonnage of its commerce increased steadily from 18.3 million long tons to 28.1 million tons (see Appendix Tables III and IV). In 1930, for the first time, the official figures of total weight of water-borne commerce at this port exceeded those of San Francisco. Recent trends at the two ports suggest that unless petroleum production declines appreciably this change in rank is not merely a temporary trade fluctuation but is likely to be maintained for many years. The striking feature is that a development of the harbor since 1924 has been from that of a crude-oil shipping port to one which now ships approximately 80 per cent of the refined oils. Table 28 provides a list of leading foreign trade commodities.

Because of the overwhelming importance of mineral oil in Los Angeles' water-borne commerce the disproportion between the volume of outgoing and incoming commerce is exceedingly marked, with the former approximately three times the latter. This lack of balance is especially marked in foreign commerce, with a volume of exports nearly ten times that of imports. In 1930, total exports from Los Angeles amounted to 6.4 million tons. Exports other than petroleum were less than 400,000 tons, with imports in excess of 675,000 tons. A similar, but less extreme, preponderance of mineral-oil products prevails in the domestic water-borne commerce of Los Angeles.

In value, total foreign trade of the Los Angeles customs district has made the remarkable increase from slightly over $5,000,000 in 1914 to $229,000,000 in 1929, a 45-fold gain. Even allowing for the higher price level, the expansion may be termed phenomenal. During the same sixteen years, the foreign traffic of the Pacific Coast as a whole increased more than fourfold (see Appendix Table V). Greatest percentage gains occurred in Los Angeles commerce between 1922 and 1924, and in the export trade. Practically all of this increase of over two million tons in two years is accounted for by petroleum exports, when the southern California oil fields were coming in on a huge scale (see Appendix Table IX for more detailed information).

Nevertheless the rapid growth which the port has registered is not entirely the result of an equally rapid exploitation of irreplaceable petroleum resources. Exports other than petroleum have gained steadily since 1922 and in 1930 were nearly seven times as great as in 1922 (see Appendix Table IV). The growth in import trade has been less consistent, but the increase in the same period was more than threefold. Intercoastal and coastwise receipts have likewise registered substantial gains in recent years, and the volume of the former is now greater at Los Angeles than at San Francisco. No other export from Los Angeles, however, approaches oil in volume, and only lumber among imports has attained a volume in excess of 100,000 tons. Contrast this with the five or six million tons of petroleum exported annually, and the complete domination of oil in tonnage is evident. Compare this petroleum-export volume with the 315,399 tons exported in 1922, and then the magnitude of the expansion in this commerce may be appreciated. Although petroleum products account for 65 per cent of the total commerce of the port, they constitute only 22 per cent of the reported value.

On the basis of bulk shipments entering into the trade of the port, lumber holds second place. Lumber has been an important factor in the traffic of the harbor from earliest times, most of it originating in the Pacific Northwest and entering the coastwise trade. Imports of metals and metal manufactures have also increased substantially since 1922. Both these items are a partial reflection of the rapid growth in population in and around the city of Los Angeles and the consequent increase in construction activity for industrial, commercial, and residential purposes. Imports of fertilizer help to supply the needs of the rich and important agricultural region of southern California. Imports of paper have also reached substantial proportions. On the whole, four-fifths of all imports are raw or semi-raw materials required by the industries of the southland (see Appendix Table IV).

The list of Los Angeles exports other than petroleum products is comparatively short. Paper stock and paper manufactures, cotton, and fruits were the principal items sent abroad in sufficient volume during the period to warrant separate tabulation. Certain commodities have been important in one or two years but unimportant in others.[5] Cotton exports are irregular in volume, without any apparent relation to the size of the California cotton production for corresponding years, but an upward trend is unmistakable. The cotton exported from Los Angeles is grown in the San Joaquin and Imperial valleys, Arizona, Texas, and other cotton states.[6] Cotton and petroleum alone constitute approximately four-fifths of the total value of exports from Los Angeles and a much greater percentage of the volume. Citrus fruit exports, likewise, are a noteworthy contribution to outbound cargoes from Los Angeles.

Crude rubber, nearly all of which comes from the East Indies, leads the list of imports, and along with cotton imports reflects the rapidly growing rubber-goods industry of southern California. Official statistics do not indicate clearly the extent to which this industry is participating in the country's export trade in rubber manufactures. The Pacific Coast is well located for the development of a rubber industry from the standpoint of both raw materials and markets. The disproportion of outbound to inbound transpacific cargoes tends to produce low ocean rates westbound, while the rapid increase in population in California and the high level of automobile ownership there make for a strong regional demand.[7]

Exploitation of mineral-oil deposits in this region has stimulated the growth of a local oil-well-machinery industry.

---

[5] For example, over 50,000 long tons of borax were exported from Los Angeles in the fiscal year 1928, but this product was not mentioned separately in the returns of the Shipping Board for earlier years. The same is true of 55,000 tons of gypsum imports in 1928.

[6] Most of the cotton produced in the Pacific Southwest is of superior, long-staple quality. It is exported to Japan and the United Kingdom for use in high-grade cotton manufactures. The export movement through Pacific ports accounts approximately for the cotton output of this region, and in 1930 foreign shipments reached nearly 91,000 long tons.

[7] The demand for tires in the Pacific Coast states, particularly in California, is probably greater, in relation to the number of automobiles registered, than in any other part of the country. Because of the equable all-year climate, and relatively long distances between centers, cars are customarily driven a higher mileage per year here than elsewhere. Also the great influx of nonresident motorists spending weeks or months on the Coast greatly adds to the sales of locally produced tires.

The combined value of exports of such machinery from Los Angeles for the three years 1926–1928, inclusive, exceeded in value the exports of citrus fruits from this customs district during the same period.

It is to be noticed that both fish and unmanufactured cotton are exported and imported in appreciable amounts through Los Angeles. Canned sardines constitute the principal fish products exported, and fresh or iced tuna fish accounts for most of the fish imported. (See Appendix Tables IV and VI for more detailed information.)

Los Angeles itself is served by three important trunk-railway systems which have either their own connections with the port some twenty miles distant or utilize the jointly controlled belt-line railroad connecting them with all steamship lines. Five trunk and local railways serve the port, and motor-carrier services are numerous and especially well developed in this area. About eighty steamship lines now make Los Angeles harbor a regular port of call. The hinterland has a huge asset in the number of population in addition to the rich petroleum deposits it contains. Agriculture, which has become specialized but highly developed in southern California, provides such specialties as citrus fruits, which enter prominently into water-borne commerce. Favored by a rich territory, rapidly increasing population, and a superior climate, Los Angeles will continue to grow.

Although maritime commerce of this important port is not diversified but heavily dependent upon a few special commodities, it has, largely because of oil, a signal value to many countries of the world. The United Kingdom, Japan, Mexico, and China are the most important customers or suppliers in foreign trade. Most countries with which the port deals are primarily customers, for, as has been noted already, the outbound movement far exceeds the inbound movement.

Notwithstanding the heavy dependence upon a limited resource of Nature for the time being, it is altogether probable, with the development of the tributary country agriculturally and industrially, that the trade of Los Angeles harbor will become greater, more diversified, and better balanced. No small credit is due the initiative of those loyal

residents who visualized the potential rôle of a world port
in southern California and then proceeded to supply this
need.

Coastwise from Los Angeles harbor to San Francisco
Bay, a distance of 368 nautical miles, ships pass two ports
of comparatively small importance. San Luis Obispo, while
it has an ocean-borne commerce of considerable volume, is
almost exclusively engaged in the shipment of petroleum,
of which at least two-thirds is sent to Latin American ports
and the rest to Pacific Canada. In 1930, outbound traffic
amounted to 1,670,000 long tons and inbound traffic to less
than 30,000 tons. Practically all the latter was accounted for
by American and Canadian coastwise freight.

Monterey, which figured prominently in early California
history, serves as a shipping-point for petroleum and, in
smaller volume, for canned fish. Its receipts are largely of
a miscellaneous character, chiefly products for local consumption. Commerce of the harbor is almost entirely domestic to and from Pacific Coast ports. The fishing industry,
centered at Monterey itself, is most important in the city's
economic life today. A large fleet of small boats engage in
local fishing, supplying fresh sea food for San Francisco
and other markets and raw materials for the local canning
industry.

More than one hundred fifty years after Vizcaino's stop
along the shore to which he gave the name of Monterey Bay,
an overland expedition from San Diego set out in 1769 and,
after revisiting Monterey, finally discovered the great Bay of
San Francisco. One hundred ninety years earlier Drake had
spent a few weeks not far from the Golden Gate, but it had
remained for Portolá to discover it—a remarkable fact in
view of repeated explorations during two centuries, all
of which were at least partly inspired by the desire to locate
a passage from the Atlantic to the Pacific and obviously
necessitated a close scanning of the shoreline for promising
entrances.

The San Francisco Bay area includes a number of separate port cities, notably Oakland, Alameda, and Richmond,
and several smaller upper Bay ports. Oakland, a rapidly
growing port with excellent warehousing facilities for dried

fruit and other perishables, will benefit greatly from the Bay bridge. The upper Bay ports are principally devoted each to a single product, such as Crockett to sugar for receiving and refining, but most of them serve oil-refineries. Sacramento and Stockton are interior points serving a rich agricultural and timber region, and, while properly belonging to the wider Bay area, they can be considered as distinct ports. However, for present purposes the region will be considered as a whole, and attention will naturally be concentrated on the port of San Francisco. Since the days when the gold rush first crowded the Bay with a forest of masts, San Francisco, by most tests, has been the greatest port of the Pacific Coast.[8] Because of its central location, its exceptionally fine harbor, its well-balanced diversified commerce, the port of San Francisco enjoys certain competitive advantages over other Pacific Coast ports. In the matter of geographic location alone, it has the advantage of being the main gateway for the central Pacific Coast area and the adjacent hinterland. San Francisco is second to New York as the home of American vessels (Fig. 27, p. 180).

Rich adjacent agricultural lands, plus industrialized centers, plus population, make for a certain stability in maritime commerce. Whereas Los Angeles trade is dominated by petroleum, Seattle by silk, and Portland by lumber and grain, that of San Francisco includes canned and dried fruits and vegetables, cotton, leather, automobiles, minerals, coffee, sugar, copra, tea, fibers, tin, machinery, and many other commodities which might be termed general merchandise. While Los Angeles has a larger population and a vast local market, it does not offer the shortest route between the northern area and the Atlantic and Middle Western states. A great diversity in cargoes may logically be expected for a major distributing center like San Francisco, which is also the financial center of the West for somewhat the same reasons.

[8] Because of the silk movement through Puget Sound ports the value of total commerce credited to the Washington customs district was greater than that of San Francisco from 1923 to 1926, inclusive. The ranking of ports by official statistics of vessel entrances and clearances has little significance, for reasons explained in chapter vii.

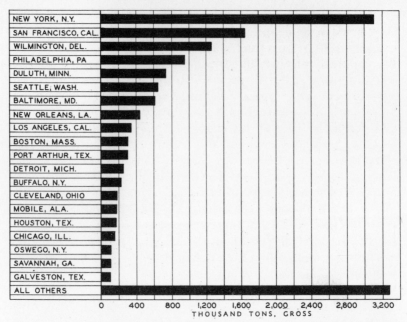

FIG. 27.—American merchant marine tonnage documented at each of the principal ports on December 31, 1933.

Commerce that inevitably follows, plus the intrinsic advantages of a fine harbor, have made this port the general shipping center of the Coast as well. Like those of Los Angeles, its wharves are served by a belt-line railroad which connects the waterfront with four transcontinental rail systems having their Western terminals in the Bay region and with neighboring industrial centers. To be more precise, these rail terminals are on the eastern or "continental" side of the Bay, and herein lies an advantage for such port cities as Oakland and Richmond, where manufacturing has been extensively developed and maritime growth has been rapid in recent years. The rapid development of Oakland is shown by an increase of 25 per cent in the water commerce of 1933 as contrasted with the previous year, including a movement of over two million tons of lumber. The Oakland port authorities report that during 1933 the vessels calling at the various Oakland terminals numbered 4,049 deep-water ships with a

TABLE 29

PRINCIPAL EXPORTS AND IMPORTS OF SAN FRANCISCO, 1913 AND 1926–1931*

(Thousand dollars)

	Fiscal Year 1913	Calendar Years					
		1926	1927	1928	1929	1930	1931
Exports, total	66,021	184,149	172,038	199,542	204,514	146,028	110,672
Canned milk, condensed, dried, and evaporated	156	4,065	3,516	4,124	4,342	3,186	2,058
Fish, fresh and preserved............	3,582	6,855	5,656	7,018	8,024	4,792	3,361
Grains and grain preparations.......	5,589	12,448	20,179	15,625	14,394	10,643	7,277
Canned vegetables	551	2,138	2,162	2,693	3,471	2,292	1,743
Fresh fruit	345	1,537	2,038	2,476	2,418	3,092	3,595
Dried fruit	4,596	18,507	22,622	27,437	20,210	19,509	21,695
Canned fruit	4,616	17,191	17,100	20,887	21,813	16,194	15,823
Wood and wood manufactures†.....	2,332	6,887	7,910	6,903	7,714	3,096	1,992
Petroleum products	7,104	47,770	35,011	40,675	45,500	31,867	21,080
Motor cars	649	1,444	2,429	4,987	4,768	2,980	1,397
Imports, total	62,502	210,139	199,999	198,275	212,678	155,564	85,776
Nuts	265	1,471	1,978	2,961	2,011	1,613	1,489
Coffee	4,828	31,572	26,116	29,352	30,362	24,525	19,643
Tea	3,496	2,951	2,875	2,779	2,468	2,200	1,864
Sugar	489	6,368	7,239	8,953	4,647	4,829	3,493
Copra	1,205	14,373	12,333	13,541	12,878	10,702	4,496
Vegetable oils, inedible	541	10,262	8,670	8,488	8,994	7,038	3,492
Jute and jute manufactures.........	2,616	8,617	6,185	7,483	6,359	6,596	2,868
Silk, raw	24,759	82,537	82,573	76,152	92,193	54,242	20,269
Paper	450	3,577	4,124	3,712	2,941	4,033	2,989
Tin	1,291	2,076	2,015	2,022	2,265	1,228	744

* Data from *Foreign Commerce and Navigation of the United States.* This table excludes foreign merchandise, transit, and transshipment movements. Not all commodities shown.

† Excluding cork and pulp woods.

net registered tonnage of 8,502,596, against 3,621 vessels with a combined net tonnage of 7,918,080 during the previous year. Connection with the great inland valleys of California and points east is facilitated by the use of these ports, and often the amount of handling necessary is reduced. Over forty truck-transport services function as feeders and distributors for the port of San Francisco itself, and approximately eighty steamship lines make it a regular port of call.

Total water-borne commerce of San Francisco (including San Francisco Bay ports) has averaged slightly above 25,000,000 long tons in five recent calendar years (Appendix

Table III). Considerably over half of this total is accounted
for by coastwise trade, in which receipts are twice as great
as shipments. The result is, according to this record, that
San Francisco's aggregate incoming commerce is considerably in excess of its outgoing, although the volume of
outgoing foreign as well as intercoastal commerce is substantially greater than incoming.[9]

If petroleum is eliminated, since it moves largely in
tankers, an almost even balance between the volumes of
incoming and outgoing foreign commerce results. This is
highly advantageous to San Francisco from a shipping standpoint, since it tends to eliminate the movement of ships in
ballast and hence makes possible more profitable steamship
operation and lower rates. Another significant feature of
the commerce of the port of San Francisco, aside from tanker
cargoes, is that its foreign trade is characterized by a relatively smaller percentage of low-grade bulk commodities
of the type that usually move in shipload lots (see Appendix
Table IV). Consequently, San Francisco is an attractive port
for liner services, a fact which is reflected in the large transoceanic passenger traffic through the port.[10]

Between 1913 and 1929 the value of San Francisco's
foreign trade increased from some $128,000,000 to a peak
of approximately $419,000,000 or more than a threefold ex-
pansion. The foreign commerce of the Pacific Coast as a
whole, however, increased four times during the same period
(see Table 64, p. 414). In 1913 San Francisco Bay's foreign
commerce constituted 47 per cent of the Pacific area's total,
but ten years later, and until 1926–1927, Puget Sound ports
(Seattle, primarily) took the leadership, largely because of
the growth of silk imports into that customs district. In recent years the San Francisco customs district has again led
all other Pacific ports, as well as Hawaii and Alaska, in the

[9] An unknown percentage of this commerce classed as coastwise is
interport between various points on San Francisco Bay; unfortunately the
only available statistics cannot be regarded as satisfactory.

[10] That is, large in comparison with Pacific ports but not with Atlantic
ports. In contrast with other Pacific Coast ports, San Francisco is far in
the lead, handling nearly 70 per cent of the total transoceanic passenger
business of the entire Coast (Appendix B).

value of foreign trade. (See Table 33, p. 196, for more specific data.)

Though petroleum does not dominate San Francisco commerce as it does that of Los Angeles, it is, nevertheless, San Francisco's most important export in both quantity and value. Furthermore, tanker cargoes, which have increased nearly six times in value since 1914, now account for roughly a fifth of total exports in value and about one-half in volume. Excluding petroleum, approximately 90 per cent of the value of remaining cargoes and approximately 60 per cent of the volume are accounted for by food products. Chief food exports are dried, canned, and fresh fruits, vegetables, fish, grains, condensed and evaporated milk, and so on. Important amounts of lumber, paper, metals, chemicals, salt, and manufacturing products are also exported; but petroleum, fruits and vegetables, and grains account for three-fourths of the total volume of exports (see Table 30, p. 186).

Imports are more diversified. Since 1924 total receipts of nuts have led all others in cargo tonnage. These imports are mainly for the vegetable-oil industry and have grown tremendously since the pre-war era. They reflect the great extension in the use of vegetable oils in the United States, which has resulted in the establishment of an important vegetable-oil industry on the Pacific Coast. This region is advantageously situated to receive Oriental and tropical oils, but tariff restrictions have largely eliminated from Pacific Coast imports all but coconut oil from the Philippines and copra, both of which are admitted free. Large quantities of the latter are brought in to be crushed and refined in local plants. San Francisco and Portland are the most important oil-crushing centers on the Pacific Coast.

Cane sugar and coffee, both tropical products, enter San Francisco in substantial amounts. In addition to receiving the major sugar output of Hawaii, the American Pacific Coast imports substantial quantities of sugar not only from the Philippines but also from Central America and the Caribbean. Imports of sugar and molasses together have varied widely from year to year, but for the period 1928–1930 they have averaged above 100,000 long tons. Adding to this total the receipts from Hawaii, over 700,000 tons, it becomes clear that there is a sugar-refining industry of large proportions on the Pacific Coast. The San Francisco Bay industrial area is the center of this industry, with the largest single refinery in the world located at Crockett.

Silk has accounted for as much as 40 per cent of the total value of imports into the customs district in recent years, with San Francisco ranking second to Seattle in this respect among United States ports and now nearly on a par with the northern district. Jute and jute manufactures are also imported to the extent of seven or eight million dollars. The volume of paper imports, which exceeds by more than fifty per cent that of lumber, now accounts for about 70,000 tons. (See Appendix Table IV for more detailed information.)

Most of the commodities which have been mentioned come from half a dozen countries, and, in turn, the best markets are to be found among the same nations. Japan, the Philippine Islands, China, the United Kingdom, Australia, and Pacific Canada account for about three-fifths of the foreign trade of San Francisco reckoned by either volume or value. The British countries are the best customers, while the largest incoming supplies arrive from Japan and the Philippines.

For many years San Francisco dominated the import and export trade of the Pacific Coast, but a change was inevitable with the development of the eleven Far-Western states. While the port has lost relative importance not only within San Francisco Bay but with respect to other Pacific ports, its progress has nevertheless been marked, and the division of its trade, which in many cases meant not merely a diversion from one port to another but also the sharing of new commerce, is an entirely healthy phenomenon. The strategic location of San Francisco is sufficient in itself to insure great constructive developments. Its future is dependent upon the conception of an interlocking metropolitan area, and not as a series of independent localities. San Francisco is the only United States port owned and operated by the state.

The only port of note on the coast from San Francisco to the Columbia River is the northern California port of Eureka, noteworthy chiefly for lumber exports, which reached the figure of 58,000 tons in 1930. The most important port between San Francisco Bay and Puget Sound is Portland, located on the Willamette River, approximately one hundred miles inland from the mouth of the Columbia River, and about six hundred and fifty miles by sea from San Francisco. Vessels plying to and from Portland must pass Astoria, situated near the sea, which is chiefly a lumber- and grain-exporting port, which does not as yet have sufficient general cargo to justify regular schedules by liners.

The growth of Portland is closely linked with the development of navigation on the Columbia River, which was discovered and only partially explored in 1792 by Captain Gray. By 1824, the settlement of the Oregon country was such as to make the Columbia River a main artery of commerce. Then, as now, exportable surpluses of wheat flour, lumber, and salmon were the basis of the maritime trade. Improvements to navigation of the river made possible a growth in deep-sea commerce from some 1.5 million tons in 1909 to 5.3 million tons in 1929. Yet because these few products account for practically all the outgoing commerce, most vessels attracted to the port of Portland are single-purpose cargo carriers. Unlike the San Francisco Bay and Puget Sound ports, Portland does not share greatly in the westbound transcontinental export traffic.

Tributary territory to Portland is rich in natural resources but somewhat limited in area, owing to the mountain barriers encountered in attracting commerce. In freight-rate advantages, however, the territory is somewhat greater, since all of Oregon, southern Washington, southern Idaho, and northern Nevada falls within an area where Portland enjoys an important traffic differential. Four transcontinental railroad lines serve the port, with connections to Washington and California.

Oregon is economically heavily dependent upon the lumber industry, as evidenced by the employment of about 60 per cent of all industrial workers in this or allied occupations. Fruit- and vegetable-canning, the second most important industry, has grown rapidly, but the export movement in canned goods is relatively small. Population and industrial development of the hinterland is not yet great enough to support a large and diversified commerce in both direc-

TABLE 30

PRINCIPAL EXPORTS AND IMPORTS OF OREGON, 1913 AND 1926–1931*

(Thousand dollars)

	Fiscal Year 1913	Calendar Years					
		1926	1927	1928	1929	1930	1931
Exports, total	12,575	78,466	78,725	63,875	66,060	46,784	28,507
Wheat and wheat flour..............	9,180	51,583	54,348	34,750	33,774	24,693	11,518
Fresh fruit	...†	2,884	1,962	3,206	3,170	3,476	3,377
Wood and wood manufactures‡.....	2,593	15,486	15,395	18,669	18,519	11,544	7,976
Imports, total	3,204	13,714	14,208	12,124	19,700	10,977	5,535
Coffee	270	1,260	731	1,102	820	648	592
Sugar	...†	281	281	553	671	584	549
Copra	...†	2,351	2,882	2,972	3,678	3,056	1,294
Vegetable oils, inedible..............	...†	1,876	1,550	515	30	13	...§
Jute and jute manufactures.........	869	1,712	1,749	1,809	1,266	1,213	766
Paper	...†	25	823	818	135	144	281
Iron and steel manufactures.........	79	599	567	559	486	431	316

* Data from *Foreign Commerce and Navigation of the United States*. This table excludes foreign merchandise, transit, and transshipment movements. Not all commodities listed.

† Not listed separately.
‡ Excluding cork and pulp woods.
§ Less than one thousand dollars.

tions. Portland remains essentially an exporting port, with outbound commodities in both foreign and intercoastal trade greatly exceeding in weight those which enter. (See Appendix Table IV for further material.)

In volume of ocean-borne commerce Portland ranks close to Tacoma, and occasionally exceeds the latter. Its growth has been more consistent during the past six or seven years. In foreign commerce, however, Portland's maritime commerce is substantially larger than that of Tacoma. Some sixty steamship lines regularly serve the port, as well as others operating on irregular schedules, particularly wheat-carriers, since this movement is highly seasonal. Wheat goes principally to United Kingdom and European ports, while the lumber movement is westbound to the Orient. Portland owes its importance as the principal wheat port in large measure to more favorable rail rates for Columbia-basin growers than are enjoyed by Puget Sound ports.

Although grain shipments fluctuate considerably from

year to year, there appears to be a tendency for Western grain to move through Pacific ports more than in the past. This tendency, plus the importance of lumber in the economic life of Oregon, should continue to provide Portland with a large volume of cargo. As industries are developed in the hinterland, more general cargo should be available for shipping. To illustrate, 567,795 boxes of fresh pears were exported from Portland during 1933, as compared with 189,077 boxes in the previous year. This establishes Portland as the leading Pacific Coast exporting center for boxed pears.

Navigational and terminal facilities have been provided, the district is relatively freer from fogs than other important Pacific ports, and with the evolution of population growth and additional communication lines it is reasonable to believe that the potential advantages of this area may be more fully realized.

Less than 200 miles north of the mouth of the Columbia River at Astoria, vessels plying between Portland and Seattle reach the entrance of the Strait of Juan de Fuca from which the port of Seattle is located some 125 nautical miles inland to the east and south. This strait is the great sea entrance north of San Francisco Bay, a distance of some 682 miles by sea. From Portland or Astoria, northbound vessels pass Grays Harbor, one of the several lumber-exporting ports in the region. Entering the Strait, Port Angeles is cleared on the south shore, and Victoria on Vancouver Island and the city of Vancouver are in the distance. To the south lies Everett, another important lumber-exporting port. Beyond Seattle, 19 or 20 miles distant and still on the Sound, is Tacoma.

All of this Puget Sound region shared the early attention given the entire Pacific Coast in the prolonged search for an interocean channel. After Spanish conquest and settlement had made reasonably well known much of the coast to the south, later explorations gave particular attention to more northerly latitudes in the hope of discovering a northwest passage. By the time such hopes were finally dispelled, a great deal of geographic information about the region had been accumulated and the fur trade had been exploited, as brought out in an earlier chapter.

It was not until the 1850's, however, that commercial shipping was really begun with the initial exports of lumber from the region. With the growth in population following the completion of the two northern transcontinental rail systems later in the century, Seattle and Tacoma were in a better position to develop maritime commerce. In 1896, the first direct regular steamship service to the Orient was established by the Japanese Nippon Yusha Kaisha line, operated in conjunction with the Great Northern Railway. Since then, progress has been rapid, with new services by various American and foreign companies. In recent years the aggregate water-borne commerce of the port of Seattle has averaged eight million long tons, and that of Tacoma about four million (see Appendix Table III). In volume of foreign commerce alone, however, Tacoma has been a fairly close rival of Seattle. Its foreign commerce of 992,000 long tons in 1930 was only 60,000 tons short of the Seattle total. Both ports have a large coastwise traffic, some of which is undoubtedly Puget Sound local traffic. Their commerce, like that of the Coast as a whole, is considerably heavier in the outgoing than in the incoming direction, but the disproportion is much less extreme than at Los Angeles. Export trade at these ports is largely in grain, lumber, fruit, and copper, but the imports at Seattle are much more diversified (Table 31, p. 190).

Thus far, in sketching the positions of various Coast ports we have given attention to geographic factors of importance but little to the significance of port location with respect to trade routes. Puget Sound ports have one outstanding natural advantage of great importance, especially in transpacific trade, in that they lie directly on the Great Circle Route from Panama to the Orient. The nearest Japanese port, Yokohama, is 4,255 miles from Seattle, less by several hundred miles than from any other American Pacific port. Seattle is closer than any other West Coast port to the leading entrepôts of eastern Asia. There is no question, therefore, that Seattle's location on the shortest route between the manufacturing centers of the United States and the dense population of the Orient gives her a distinct advantage with which rival ports must always reckon. Furthermore, the

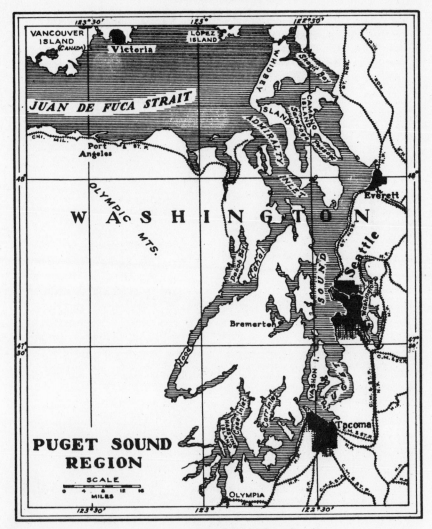

FIG. 28.—Map of Puget Sound.

nearest Alaska port, Ketchikan, is only 649 miles distant along the same course. It is not strange, then, to find Seattle and Tacoma, particularly the former, the major distributing points for Alaska traffic.

Immediately tributary to Seattle and Tacoma is a rich country with abundant mineral, forest, and agricultural

TABLE 31

PRINCIPAL EXPORTS AND IMPORTS OF WASHINGTON, 1913 AND 1926–1931*

(Thousand dollars)

	Fiscal Year 1913	Calendar Years					
		1926	1927	1928	1929	1930	1931
Exports, total	62,548	146,845	128,787	150,001	153,240	101,951	66,638
Canned milk—condensed, dried, and evaporated	349	1,691	2,537	3,423	3,260	2,763	2,533
Fish, fresh and preserved	1,755	5,094	4,175	4,927	5,080	4,382	3,794
Wheat and wheat flour..............	13,828	19,616	21,852	19,946	20,058	13,752	9,830
Fresh fruits	1,141	4,364	5,260	6,878	10,156	9,202	8,832
Canned fruits	11	2,131	1,728	2,714	1,954	2,306	2,308
Tobacco manufactures	349	3,517	1,009	4,948	962	261	239
Cotton, unmanufactured	6,331	8,267	1,177	2,490	3,488	1,086	25
Wood and wood manufactures†.....	6,893	28,389	29,317	31,296	32,076	20,530	13,886
Copper and copper manufactures....	1,269	29,945	25,755	29,995	29,925	15,707	8,024
Motor cars	2,041	4,799	5,234	8,606	7,563	3,520	1,310
Imports, total	51,474	261,880	239,284	229,024	216,774	113,708	55,344
Nuts	133	1,455	1,544	1,700	1,343	323	471
Coffee	183	1,539	1,407	1,595	1,234	957	796
Tea	1,816	2,681	2,456	2,486	1,935	1,588	1,252
Silk, raw	30,230	198,254	175,441	167,964	150,931	62,195	26,880
Wood and wood manufactures†.....	705	7,963	9,593	8,716	9,490	6,839	3,805
Paper	743	3,838	4,528	5,300	5,255	4,656	4,512
Copper, crude	4,234	16,091	14,941	15,802	20,252	13,448	6,128

* Data from *Foreign Commerce and Navigation of the United States.* This table excludes foreign merchandise, transit, and transshipment movements. Not all commodities listed.

† Excluding cork and pulp woods.

resources which are being opened and developed. The climate of the region is most favorable for the development of the Northwest country. Transportation facilities are ample by both land and sea, and terminal facilities keep pace with the needs of commerce. Two transcontinental railroads have their terminals at Seattle, and over 100 steamship lines serve the port. Connections with the Canadian railway systems are also enjoyed by both Seattle and Tacoma. The trading territory, which includes Alaska, extends as far east as Montana and as far south as California. Competition within these limits is principally between the Northwestern ports of Washington and Oregon. The completion of the Grand Coulee and Bonneville hydraulic projects will add greatly to the wealth of the Northwest.

Until the past few years raw-silk imports have been the

main factor in Seattle's large value of importations and are an important reason for the great shipping growth she has recorded during the past ten or twenty years. In 1910, for example, imports into the Washington customs district were valued at a little less than $29,000,000; in 1920 they had grown to $174,000,000, and in 1929 to $233,000,000. Exports, on the other hand, grew more rapidly during the earlier decade, which included the war years, but have declined since then, and in 1929 amounted to some $156,000,000. War-time prices of lumber and grains and the opening of the Panama Canal largely account for the increase from $30,000,000 in 1910 to the $228,000,000 which comprised the value of exports in 1920. (See Appendix Table V, Washington, for more detailed information.)

The tendency for silk, since the price decline, to take all-water routes to the Atlantic-seaboard manufacturing center has been noted elsewhere. Table 32 discloses the tremendous gains of California's ports at the expense of Seattle. Although raw silk from Japan gave Seattle a high value of imports, Seattle's volume of foreign incoming cargo has been relatively small. The distance factor, however, which gives Seattle and Tacoma a two-day sailing advantage over San Francisco and a three-day one over Los Angeles, should

TABLE 32

OVERLAND RAIL MOVEMENT OF RAW SILK ARRIVALS BY PACIFIC COAST PORTS, 1924–1933*

Year	Seattle		San Francisco		Vancouver		Los Angeles		Portland	
	Number of Bales	Percentage of All Rail	Number of Bales	Percentage of All Rail	Number of Bales	Percentage of All Rail	Number of Bales	Percentage of All Rail	Number of Bales	Percentage of All Rail
1924	248,084	65.0	46,621	12.2	86,926	22.8	...	...	...	...
1925	231,543	50.5	99,082	21.6	128,247	27.9	...	...	...	...
1926	252,540	52.7	107,210	22.4	119,077	24.9	...	...	...	...
1927	241,081	47.0	117,900	23.0	154,140	30.0	...	...	...	...
1928	245,278	47.0	133,224	25.5	143,845	27.5	...	...	...	...
1929	231,998	44.6	144,216	27.7	133,796	25.7	...	...	10,438	2.0
1930	120,129	35.3	109,890	32.3	101,102	29.7	7,292	2.1	2,241	.7
1931	74,402	32.2	70,417	30.5	76,617	33.2	9,649	4.2	...	...
1932	70,621	31.9	63,009	28.4	68,638	31.0	19,290	8.7	...	...
1933	30,825	27.9	29,319	26.5	31,115	28.1	19,332	17.5	...	...

* Data from The Federated Textile Industries, Inc.

continue to play an important part in the development of its maritime commerce, even though the relative importance of silk shipments continues at its present level. Commodities of small bulk but high unit-value will continue to seek the shorter routes to Eastern consuming centers of the United States. Tea is another example of such a commodity. It is possible that Seattle may again become the premier tea-entry port of the United States as a result of the reduction in the overland-freight rate to Middle Western and Eastern consumption centers. Related commodities are likely to be routed through Seattle or Tacoma, since these gateways have a natural advantage in expediting transportation; they should continue to be important transshipment ports.

Intercoastal shipments via Panama from Seattle consist largely of lumber and lumber products, paper, fish, canned fruit, and flour (see Appendix Table VIII, Seattle). In foreign trade, ships destined for Europe and South America carry chiefly lumber, fish, apples, pears, wheat, and flour. The same general commodities are exported to the Orient, plus manufactured goods from the interior of the United States. Imports from the Orient, aside from raw silk, consist of vegetable oils, bean cake, nuts, carpets and rugs, wool, matting, porcelain, jute cloth and bags, and tea.

Commerce of the port of Tacoma, unlike that of Seattle and Portland, is largely the product of lumber and wood-working industries within the limits of the city. Some 90 per cent of the approximately $95,000,000 of exports in 1929, both foreign and domestic, originated within the city. Only 15 to 25 per cent of Seattle and Portland exports so originate, showing that as a transshipping center Tacoma is of small importance compared with Seattle. Shipments of lumber and lumber products from Tacoma probably outrank those from every other port. In 1929 they were valued at $28,000,000. The important smelters at Tacoma have been mentioned in another connection; in a recent year, 85 per cent of Tacoma's import tonnage consisted of ores from British Columbia and South America. Practically all copper shipments are made by vessel. Copper exports increased steadily during the past decade and reached a total value of nearly $38,000,000 in 1929. Flour is another export which has increased in both volume and value during the decade. Total shipments during 1929 were valued at approximately $15,000,000. The tonnage of foreign imports into Tacoma is somewhat smaller than that into Seattle, while, on the other hand, imports from Alaska, California, Hawaii, and Atlantic Coast points are very much smaller. Tacoma's maritime commerce, although fairly balanced in value, is unbalanced in tonnage, especially if shipping from and to local ports is omitted from consideration.[11] (See Appendix Table IV, Tacoma, for more detailed information.)

Served by the same railroad systems as Seattle and by some 67 steamship lines which make regular calls, Tacoma enjoys the same freight rates and has the same back country already described for Seattle. Total commerce of Washington ports is between 30,000,000 and 36,000,000 tons annually, with a value in excess of a billion dollars. Only about a third of this value figure is foreign trade, perhaps no greater than similar trade of Washington's Canadian neighbors through the single port of Vancouver; and for Seattle and Tacoma alone somewhat more than 2,000,000 tons enter into foreign commerce, compared with over twice that volume for Vancouver. Although Vancouver does not fall within the American Pacific States area, it is nevertheless part of the great Puget Sound region and the only foreign port of importance situated on the North American Pacific Coast. Some mention of Vancouver is desirable, therefore, especially in the light of competition that exists with American Puget Sound ports.

Vancouver, located on the Strait of Georgia just north of the international boundary, 121 nautical miles from Seattle, is the third largest city of Canada. It ranks with Montreal as a leading shipping-port, and is the outstanding Canadian metropolis on the Pacific. With the opening of the Panama Canal it has assumed an entirely new and additional strategic position as a shipping-point for the agricultural products of a large part of western Canada and the forest products and ores of British Columbia.

---

[11] Coastwise imports for 1929 into Tacoma amounted to nearly 3,000,000 tons, compared to 860,000 tons for foreign exports. These receipts consist mostly of lumber in various forms.

Owing to the interruption of the World War, advantage was not taken of this new position until 1919. Since that time shipments of grain, lumber, fish, flour, and many other commodities have been sent to the United Kingdom and the Continent, greatly increasing the commerce of the port.[12] In 1919 no grain from Vancouver was destined for these markets; in 1928 almost 75,000,000 bushels, or 77 per cent of all grain shipments from Vancouver, were routed across to the Atlantic via Panama. Vancouver is one of the most swiftly growing and most vigorously developing ports on the Pacific Coast of North America, especially in her export trade.[13]

In the Oriental carrying-trade, competition between British Columbia ports and Pacific ports of the United States is keen. The old established passenger and mail services of the Canadian Pacific, as well as other lines, continue to hold their own, however, owing to the regularly available offerings of exports to China and Japan such as grain, flour, lumber, metals, pulp, fish, pilchard meal, and other products of local origin. Vancouver is well served with rail connections and is able to compete on favorable terms with United States Pacific ports. There is a large intercoastal lumber movement from British Columbia ports to the Atlantic seaboard and, as has been noted previously, a growing coastwise trade with the Pacific Coast states, particularly California. Lumber and pulp and paper production, followed by agriculture, mining, and fisheries, are some of the more important economic activities of British Columbia which find expression in commerce chiefly through the port of Vancouver. The maritime position of Vancouver is succinctly described in a recent issue of *Harbour and Shipping:*

[12] Peak volume of foreign water-borne commerce of Vancouver was reached in 1928, when the aggregate movement was over 5,600,000 tons; but in 1932 this movement still amounted to 4,876,933 tons, three-fourths of which was outbound cargo. In 1930, combined Seattle and Tacoma foreign trade totaled 2,044,000 tons, compared with 4,356,160 tons for Vancouver during the same year.

[13] The attractive residential city, Victoria, is not important industrially, and the isolated British Columbia ports north of Vancouver specialize in fisheries, lumber, and lumber products.

To a port such as Vancouver the efficiency and low cost of operation of ships is a vital matter; far more so than to ports situated on
the Atlantic Coast or elsewhere. The geographical situation of our
Pacific Coast is such as to provide a "long haul" to all the principal
markets of the world. Vessels must travel three times as far to get
to Europe from Vancouver as they do from Atlantic Coast ports.
The price received for merchandise exported from Pacific Coast
ports to Europe must compete with the price quoted by other ports.
The longer distance of the voyage from Vancouver makes the ocean
freight a greater factor in the total price. Thus if by means of greater
economies of operation, ships can carry goods at a lower rate, then
the long haul will benefit relatively more than the short haul. The
ocean freight constitutes a far bigger proportion of the "c. i. f." cost
from Vancouver than from imports with a shorter ocean voyage.

It is unfortunate that time and space are not available
for doing justice to the many small and growing ports which
are certain to figure conspicuously in the future development of the Pacific Coast. Many a promising lumber or
grain port in the Puget Sound region has received no mention, in order to conform to the policy of this chapter, which
is that of dealing with what are now the most important
ports of the region. Broadly speaking, a characterization
of any one of several smaller ports serves to describe many
others in the same locality. In order to help visualize
the future importance of numerous small ports, the reader
will wish to analyze Table 33, which records the volume of
foreign trade of Pacific Coast ports for the years 1922 to 1930,
inclusive, and provides a measure of the relative importance
of minor ports in total commerce, imports, and exports.

Bare mention has been made of terminal facilities, types
of ownership and administration of ports, and various other
matters, which apply more to a study of general port development, even though they must always be considered problems
of crucial importance in the entire water-transportation
problem. Nor has any attempt been made in this chapter
to place a valuation upon one port in comparison with
another—an impossible task, as pointed out elsewhere.[14]

[14] See the author's *San Francisco's Trans-Pacific Shipping* (1929), pp.
45–53, for a discussion of indices of port rivalry and the various standards
of measurement employed in ranking or rating ports.

TABLE 33

SUMMARY OF PACIFIC PORT COMMERCE, 1930*

Port	Imports	Exports	Coastwise	
			Receipts	Ship-ments
Pacific ports	3,838	15,467	35,295	33,818
San Diego, Calif.	51	14	799	24
Los Angeles, Calif.	716	7,359	6,412	13,725
San Luis Obispo, Calif....................	...	459	33	1,311
San Francisco Bay, Calif..................	1,275	3,091	14,914	6,007
Monterey, Calif.	...	...	171	37
Humboldt, Calif.	...	29	248	267
Long Beach, Calif.	68	471	1,159	2,341
Coos Bay, Ore.............................	...	137	34	378
Portland, Ore.	121	1,235	2,769	915
Other ports on Columbia and Willamette rivers	...†	267	166	351
Longview, Wash.	5	131	85	389
Grays Harbor, Wash.......................	2	469	241	748
Port Gamble, Wash.	...	23	1	255
Olympia, Wash.	3	238	84	461
Tacoma, Wash.	431	656	1,156	861
Seattle, Wash.	407	505	3,784	1,451
Everett, Wash.	145	159	316	771
Anacortes, Wash.	69	21	131	71
Bellingham, Wash.	46	85	194	640
Port Angeles, Wash.......................	175	1	202	133
Port Ludlow, Wash.......................	...	25	1	184
Honolulu, Hawaii	116	14	1,093	705
Kahului, Hawaii	5	...	276	161
Hilo, Hawaii	22	...	137	248

* Data from Annual Report of the Chief of Engineers, United States War Department.
† Less than 500 tons.

The purpose has been rather to set forth the factors that determine maritime development and create competition in shipping. Because the Pacific Coast, despite its paucity of good harbors and other water terminals, is only just entering upon its period of intensive development in comparison with the coastal zones in other parts of the world, the competitive aspects have not as yet acquired the proportions they undoubtedly will assume in the future. To date, the situation has been one of sharing an ever-increasing volume of commerce rather than of deflecting trade routes in one direction or another.

Each harbor, of course, has a distinct advantage in competition for traffic originating in or destined for territory immediately adjacent to it. Matters of port size, facilities, operating costs, and increasing congestion tend to penalize the larger ports. On the Pacific Coast, however, ports are relatively few and far between and the back country of each is comparatively undeveloped. The immediate hinterland at present, therefore, in this young growing country is much greater than it will be after the Coast becomes more industrialized. Competition is now based largely on traffic to and from the interior, although within the coastal zone similar conditions may be said to exist. For example, rail freight rates determine the direction of movement of certain products of the San Joaquin Valley in California; and the advantage of Portland in the matter of grain rates in the Northwest has been mentioned.

The interior region of competition extends east of Montana to the Atlantic seaboard and south of the Missouri River to the Gulf. That is very roughly the great area in which much transpacific commerce has its origin or its destination. Competition here is among Pacific ports as well as with Atlantic and Gulf ports. Freight rates tend to be equalized so that it is just as economical for a shipper to route his cargo in one way as in another. Competition takes the form of a struggle for favorable rail rates in inland traffic, but all important Pacific Coast ports are on an equal basis with respect to import and export transcontinental freight charges. Each port therefore competes for its trade on the basis of the shipping facilities it has to offer and its efficiency and economy in the land-and-sea interchange and handling of traffic.

These are some of the important artificial conditions affecting port development. Implied are ample land transportation facilities in addition to terminal facilities. Also, economic conditions must be such as to foster industrial development. These factors, combined with the natural advantages favoring the growth of commerce which were mentioned earlier—harbor free from hazards to navigation, strategic location on principal ocean-trade routes between areas of dense population, climatic conditions favorable to industrial development, and resources of back country sufficient to supply outbound cargo for vessels—all make for maritime-trade progress. Ports having the best combination of these factors will have a more evenly balanced outbound and inbound tonnage movement.

The ideal port, of course, is one having a balanced volume of traffic, even though an exactly even import and export movement is never found. Ports having large cargo-tonnage of a single commodity, usually of low value and requiring vessels of special design, are not so attractive to carriers as ports importing and exporting freight of general character of high value. Nor is a highly seasonal offering of cargo as attractive as a regular year-round volume, even though the latter is of more modest proportions. Cargoes of a diversified nature in sufficient quantities throughout the year make shipping profitable, and the port offering such advantages has no difficulty in attracting steamship lines. Unlike railways, ships can change their routes at will. They follow commerce. Ships call where trade offers.

IX. Types of Vessels and Services

In the discussion of Pacific Coast ports in the previous chapter a background has been provided for examining the types of vessels operating in these waters and the services they provide. Space does not permit here an extended discussion of the operations of liners and tramps, respectively, or the availability and utilization of the ocean carrier with respect to the carriage of passengers, cargo, mail, and express. In Appendix A will be found an up-to-date schedule of liner services on the West Coast, with prime reference to the transportation of passengers. However, all of the ships enumerated carry freight, and to most of them the latter business provides the main revenue.

Nowadays, relatively few vessels transport either passengers or cargo exclusively. Government transports, not numerous, yet numerous enough to be noted in mercantile marine circles, constitute another kind of service. A more important shipping service is available in the water-carriers owned and operated by industrial companies, specialized vessels, which are really transportation divisions of large firms but sometimes complicate the cargo situation by offering space to other shippers. Petroleum, steel, and fruit companies, which are leading examples, are listed regularly in *Lloyd's Register of Shipping;* and in Appendix C of the present volume appear the names and number of vessels of the largest American merchant fleets. It is worth while at this point to indicate the relative importance of this West Coast with reference to the American merchant marine, as shown in Table 34 (p. 200).

The Bureau of Navigation of the United States Department of Commerce is the official source for the record of all documented vessels "registered," "enrolled," or "licensed." According to the report covering the fiscal year 1933, 24,868 vessels aggregating 15,060,157 gross tonnage were registered, of which the Pacific Coast district contributed 6,462 vessels of 2,970,218 gross tonnage. Thus the Pacific Coast, which comprises the regions of California, Oregon, Washington, Alaska, and Hawaii, accounted for one-fourth of the total number of vessels and one-fifth of the gross tonnage. Ac-

TABLE 34

NUMBER AND GROSS TONNAGE OF DOCUMENTED VESSELS OF THE UNITED
STATES, 1850–1930, PACIFIC COAST DISTRICT AND TOTAL SEABOARD*

Year	Pacific Coast		Total Seaboard	
	Number	Gross Tons	Number	Gross Tons
1850†	.....	18,655	......	3,051,390
1855	.....	93,455	......	4,876,720
1860	.....	85,111	......	4,723,006
1865	.....	154,350	......	4,179,920
1870	1,136	190,398	21,420	3,163,597
1875	1,225	229,257	24,665	3,596,876
1880	1,143	272,361	19,290	2,989,140
1885	1,268	360,608	19,295	3,169,930
1890	1,402	428,391	18,734	3,066,988
1895	1,525	433,501	18,661	3,113,282
1900	2,217	612,904	18,749	3,340,796
1905	2,730	821,710	20,144	4,220,077
1910	3,574	936,591	20,658	4,459,264
1915	5,016	1,122,620	21,707	5,432,616
1920	6,512	3,326,285	23,362	13,065,104
1925	6,035	3,282,243	21,758	14,390,411
1930	6,466	3,226,597	20,787	13,131,044

* Fiscal years. Data from Bureau of Navigation and Steamboat Inspection.

† The first year that tonnage was reported for the Pacific Coast Division was 1849, with a gross tonnage of 722.

cording to ports, the ranking in number of vessels is Washington (Seattle), Alaska, San Francisco, Los Angeles, and Portland; the ranking in tonnage is San Francisco, Washington (Seattle), Los Angeles, Portland, and Alaska. With respect to number of vessels the regional ranking is Washington, Alaska, California, Oregon, and Hawaii; but on a tonnage basis the order is California, Washington, Oregon, Alaska, and Hawaii. In respect to the size of vessels the outstanding position of California is shown by these averages: California 1,284 gross tons, Hawaii 531, Oregon 477, Washington 243, and Alaska 43. Applicable to the Pacific Coast as a whole, the size of ships is twice that of the average for the country, and the ships which claim San Francisco as home port average approximately two-thirds larger than those registered from the port of New York, or 1,640 and 995 gross tons, respectively.

The shipping connections of the Pacific Coast ports in the foreign and non-contiguous ocean trades are well depicted in sailing lists. A convenient directory of steam services published currently by the weekly *Pacific Shipper,* classified according to intercoastal, coastwise, and foreign routes, appears in Appendix A, to which the reader is especially referred in the light of information to be presented in this chapter; likewise the *Shipping Register* and the *Official Steamship Guide* are reliable sources of ship sailings.

The types of vessels call for brief comment. In chapter v, dealing with the beginnings of seacoast trade, mention was made of the galleon and of the early cargo carriers. The transition from sail to engine has been a gradual process, and the "windjammer" has not as yet entirely disappeared. In local shipping in many parts of the world the sailing craft is still the predominant vessel; however, in maritime shipping the sailing-ship era has practically ended. The Alaskan "Star" packets have recently been laid up. (The Commissioner of Navigation records 86 sailing vessels of 110,085 gross tonnage for the Pacific Coast, out of the United States total of 1,227 vessels of 562,959 gross tonnage.) The Pacific Coast has resisted the trend as persistently as any other region, but only since 1929 has the last sailer in the salmon trade between California and Alaska ceased to operate; the lumber schooners, which are unique sailing crafts, now are equipped with engines.[1]

Conforming to strict nautical usage, when one commodity constitutes the predominant cargo in international tonnage its carriage is spoken of as a special "trade." From the Pacific Coast these trades are grain, lumber, and petroleum.

[1] Captain Kettle, the shrewd commentator in *Harbour and Shipping,* July 1932, remarks: "The decline and fall of the windjammer is nowhere more noticeable than in the port of Vancouver. Even as late as twenty years ago, as many as five could often be counted in the port at one time, loading lumber for the seven seas. Thirty years ago there were often as many as twenty-five or more ships awaiting cargo or loading lumber; but, be it noted, one large modern freighter often carries as much in a full cargo of lumber as ten to fifteen of the old-style windjammers carried. The early days of the export lumber trade were the beginnings of the port of Vancouver, and lumber must be regarded as the keystone of our port business, grain being a mere parvenu, dating from 1921 only, in the commercial sense, although there were a few experimental government shipments before that."

TABLE 35

Types of Vessels Employed in Transpacific Liner Traffic, Flag and Line, May 1929*

Flag and Line	Total Ships		Oil-Burning Steamers		Coal-Burning Steamers		Motorships		Speed of Ships		
	Number	Gross Tons	Number	Gross Tons	Number	Gross Tons	Number	Gross Tons	Over 14	12-14	Under 12
British											
Bank Line..........	8	40,892	2	10,423	1	4,713	5	25,756	..	8	..
Kerr..........	11	54,519	..	.....	..	.....	11	54,519	..	6	5
Union S.S.	9	77,215	2	15,973	5	36,638	2	24,604	4	2	3
Canadian Pacific..........	3	52,076	..	.....	3	52,076	..	.....	3	..	..
Blue Funnel..........	4	41,347	..	.....	4	41,347	..	.....	..	4	..
Total British..........	35	266,049	4	26,396	13	134,774	18	104,879	7	20	8
Danish											
Java Pacific..........	4	29,950	1	8,438	2	14,944	1	6,568	..	4	..
Total Danish..........	4	29,950	1	8,438	2	14,944	1	6,568	..	4	..
Swedish											
Trans-Atlantic of Gothenburg....	8	42,994	3	14,778	..	.....	5	28,216	2	2	4
Total Swedish..........	8	42,994	3	14,778	..	.....	5	28,216	2	2	4

American											
Matson	21	150,190	21	150,190					6	6	9
Matson-Oceanic	4	22,262	4	22,262							4
American-Hawaiian	10	65,737	10	65,737							10
Los Angeles S.S. Co.	4	36,037	3	25,357	1	10,680	1		2	2	2
Dollar A.M.L.	6	42,573	6	42,573							6
Tacoma Oriental S.S.	6	38,306	5	33,469	1	4,837	1				6
States	11	62,738	11	62,738							11
Dollar	17	218,604	17	218,604					11	6	
Kerr	2	6,864					2	6,864			2
Total American	81	643,311	77	620,930	2	15,517	2	6,864	19	12	50
Japanese											
O.S.K.	9	76,430	7	61,896			2	14,534	2	7	
N.Y.K.	15	137,324	5	58,903	10	78,421			5	10	
Mitsui	5	27,821	3	16,521			2	11,300		1	4
Kawasaki Dock	9	57,055	8	51,210			1	5,845		4	5
Total Japanese	38	298,630	23	188,530	10	78,421	5	31,679	7	22	9
Grand Total	166	1,280,934	108	859,072	27	243,656	31	178,206	35	60	71

* Data compiled by the author from the best available records.

TABLE 36

LUMBER SHIPMENTS FROM THE PACIFIC NORTHWEST (MARCH 1934)*

Vessel	Ton-nage	Loading Point	Destination	Cargo Feet
"Kokuryu Maru" (Jap.).........	4,459	British Columbia..	Japan	2,452,000
"Yahiko Maru" (Jap.)...........	3,885	Puget Sound	Japan	3,542,000
"Choyo Maru" (Jap.)..........	3,311	British Columbia..	Australia	6,731,000
"Ryoyo Maru" (Jap.)..........	3,650	British Columbia..	Japan	1,798,000
"Bright Star" (Br.).............	3,400	British Columbia..	Australia	3,639,000
"Nyhorn" (Nor.)	2,732	Grays Harbor	U.K./Rotterdam ..	1,095,000
"Massmar" (Am.)	3,600	Grays Harbor	Atlantic Coast.....	1,942,000
"Falstria" (Dan.)	2,771	Grays Harbor	Orient	2,021,000
"Shunsho Maru" (Jap.).........	3,914	Columbia River....	Japan	3,222,000
"Herman F. Whiton" (Am.)....	3,430	Columbia River....	Atlantic Coast.....	4,802,000
"Taibun Maru" (Jap.)..........	4,099	Grays Harbor	Japan	1,083,000
"Massmar" (Am.)	3,600	Columbia River....	Atlantic Coast.....	3,707,000
"American Oriole" (Am.)........	3,185	Puget Sound	Atlantic Coast.....	4,866,000
"Venice Maru" (Jap.)...........	4,013	British Columbia..	Japan	1,976,000
"Shohei Maru" (Jap.)..........	4,413	Columbia River....	Japan	3,600,000
"Juyo Maru" (Jap.).............	3,407	British Columbia..	Australia	3,801,000
"Ishin Maru" (Jap.)............	3,137	Grays Harbor	Japan	3,272,000
"Stjerneborg" (Dan.)	2,785	Columbia River....	China	4,334,000
"Everett" (Am.)	3,571	British Columbia..	Orient	1,593,000
"Iwatesan Maru" (Jap.)........	4,070	British Columbia..	Japan	1,795,000
"Jufuko Maru" (Jap.)..........	4,293	British Columbia..	Japan/Vladivostok	667,000
"Astoria" (Dan.)	2,594	Puget Sound	Japan	2,630,000
"Point Palmas" (Am.)..........	3,048	Grays Harbor	Gulf Ports	1,230,000
"Texmar" (Am.)	3,439	Grays Harbor	Atlantic Coast	782,000
"Scotland Maru" (Jap.).........	4,263	Grays Harbor	Japan	431,000
"Taian Maru" (Jap.)...........	4,326	Grays Harbor	Japan	1,265,000

* Data from *Daily Commercial News,* San Francisco.

Wheat shipments from the Pacific Northwest, barley from San Francisco, lumber from the Northwest, and oil from California ports feature this traffic. The incoming trades consist of sugar and pineapples, mainly from the Hawaiian Islands, carried by liners as well as by tramps, and bananas from Central America, transported on the new United Fruit vessels. The tanker vessels, associated usually with fuel oil, lubricants, and gasoline, are industrial carriers owned and operated by large oil companies. Fruit carriers frequently combine in their cargo grain and lumber, but for most commodities the vessel is devoted to only a single "trade." The refrigerator ship, which has revolutionized the transportation of fruits and vegetables, and the oil tanker are discussed later in this chapter. Other types of vessels which should be considered in passing are the transports of the Army and the Navy and the Panama Railroad Steamship Line ships. Both services are owned by the United States government. The American Steamship Owners' Association and large independent American operators continue to protest against this type of competition with private lines. An elimination or curtailment of these services would redound to the benefit of private American companies serving Pacific Coast ports.

Deep-sea vessels operating on the Pacific Coast are largely liners rather than tramps. Even before the war, when this type of ship operation had not gained the position in world maritime commerce which it now holds, predominance of liner services characterized Pacific shipping. It is estimated that, prior to 1914, at least half of the ocean commerce of the world was carried by general traders or tramp ships. This ratio, however, did not apply to Pacific commerce, since there the comparative regularity of bulk-cargo offerings throughout the year early favored the establishment of regular lines. Another factor operating before the war to the disadvantage of tramp shipping in this area was the low level of liner freight rates. Japanese lines, naturally prominent in transpacific shipping, were compelled by subsidy agreements with their government to maintain rates at levels designed to stimulate Japanese overseas commerce. This meant that competing lines had to meet these low rates, with the result that tramp ships found little opportunity to quote rates low enough to attract cargo away from the faster, more regular lines.

While abnormal conditions arising from the war caused a temporary stimulus to tramp shipping on the Pacific, later developments in the region, as elsewhere in the world, have been toward greater and greater relative importance for liner services. Before 1914, with the exception of a relatively small intercoastal trade via Magellan, steamship lines operating out of Pacific ports confined their operations almost exclusively to the Pacific Basin. There was little maritime commerce with regions not bordering the Pacific, except in so far as tramp shipping provided such a connection. Foreign-trade shipping, at that time, was predominantly transpacific shipping.

A survey of transpacific shipping is available which gives the tonnage of ships employed in regular service on these routes prior to the war and in 1916.[2] Before the war approximately 380,000 gross tons of shipping were employed more or less regularly in liner trade across the Pacific. Of this total about 150,000 tons, or 39 per cent, were under British registry, 128,000, or 34 per cent, under Japanese registry, and 80,000, or 21 per cent, under American registry. One German line, the Hamburg-American, was also operating a transpacific service from North Pacific ports to the Orient.

The disruption of normal commercial relationships during the war resulted in the withdrawal of a large percentage of European ships from transpacific trade. With the sale of the Pacific Mail steamers shortly after the outbreak of the war, the American flag likewise virtually disappeared from the carrying-trade of the Pacific. This left the field strongly dominated by the Japanese, so that in 1916, before the resumption of the Pacific Mail service, it was estimated that Japanese lines accounted for 55 per cent of the total. British shipping, which declined in absolute amount, constituted about the same proportion of the total as before the war, but American vessels accounted for only 2 per cent at that time. Total transpacific liner services, computed by these American officials at about 280,000 gross tons in 1916, are perhaps somewhat underestimated.

After the war shipping returned quickly to the Pacific. There is no doubt that the final as opposed to the temporary effect of this conflict was to increase the trade of this Basin. The closing of the Suez route during the war forced shipping and trade across the Pacific. Europe's four-year preoccupation with war resulted in a material diminution of entrepôt trade and the establishment of direct shipping connections between the respective countries of origin and destination. The United States and Japan, Pacific powers experiencing a rapid industrial development, were for the greater part of the war period relatively free to take advantage of the possibilities for commercial expansion which European withdrawal from trade had created.

[2] United States Bureau of Foreign and Domestic Commerce, *Trans-Pacific Shipping*, Miscellaneous Series 44 (1917).

With or without the war the Pacific Ocean was bound to experience a great increase in trade as a result of the opening of the Panama Canal and the development of Western North America. Since the completion of the Canal was almost simultaneous with the beginning of the war, it is not possible to segregate entirely the trade changes of which the Canal was the cause from those growing directly out of the war.

An early post-war study of transpacific shipping, undertaken under the initiative of the Carnegie Endowment for International Peace, reached the conclusion that by 1920 there were some 2.5 million tons of ships, including tramp vessels, operating in transpacific trade.[3] It should be stated at once that this estimate is not comparable with earlier or later figures, since it includes not only tramp shipping but also feeder services of unspecified volume in Asiatic waters. It seems probable that even so the total figure overstates the tonnage actually employed and that the volume of strictly transpacific liner services at that time was hardly more than one-third this figure.[4]

The new commercial lanes which the Panama Canal made possible have been utilized for the transportation of large amounts of goods between regions brought closer by this continental artery. For the American Pacific Coast this has inevitably meant a greatly augmented list of regular steamship services to almost every part of the world. A substantial number of regular services are maintained to Europe and to Caribbean and Atlantic ports of Central and South America. The international coasting-trade along the Pacific is likewise better served by steamship lines than before the war. The mammoth increase in tonnage employed by the United States intercoastal route since the opening of the Canal is depicted in chapter x (see also Appendix D).

Statistics available beginning with the year ended June 30,

---

[3] P. C. Crockatt, *Trans-Pacific Shipping* (1922).

[4] The estimate in the report puts the Japanese tonnage at 960,000, the British at 660,000, and the American at 750,000, with another half-million tons of tramp shipping of French, Russian, Italian, Portuguese, Norwegian, and Chinese registry. There are scarcely 750,000 tons of American shipping even now in operation on all Pacific Coast foreign-trade routes, and little tramp shipping flies the American flag.

1922, show the participation of American and foreign ships in the carrying of Pacific Coast foreign commerce. According to these figures American ships have not carried so much as 40 per cent of the weight of all exports and imports through Pacific Coast ports in any year covered by the data. In 1922 these ships accounted for 39 per cent of this movement, but the average for the period as a whole was under 35 per cent and in 1929–1930 they carried barely 33 per cent (see Appendix Table IX). Thus, for these nine years American shipping has not increased its relative importance in Pacific Coast foreign trade. In every year except 1922 British vessels have handled a volume of American West Coast import and export cargo almost as great as that handled by vessels of United States registry, and in 1928 the former even slightly exceeded the latter.[5] From year to year the British share fluctuates more widely than the American, and the former showed a definite loss in relative position during 1929–1930.

Pacific Coast carriers flying the American flag do not, at the present time, account for as high a percentage of imports and exports through that coastal district as do American ships as a whole in the aggregate foreign trade of the United States. In the three fiscal years, 1928–1930, the tonnage of total imports and exports carried in American vessels applicable to all domestic regions has been almost exactly 40 per cent. This would appear to indicate a weaker competitive position of American ships on the Pacific than elsewhere. As a matter of fact, however, among transoceanic liner routes Pacific Coast shipping under the American flag enjoys a greater participation than elsewhere. The stronger showing for the country as a whole is in large part accounted for by the performance of American ships in near-by foreign trade.

Another element in the situation is the fact that Pacific Coast exports include a greater proportion of crude materials commonly handled by tramp ships than does the foreign commerce of the country as a whole. Since there is virtually no tramp tonnage under the American flag, the percentage of

[5] The volume of American foreign-trade tonnage handled by foreign ships other than British is included in "all other foreign" in the Shipping Board reports, so that separate totals for other foreign countries are not available.

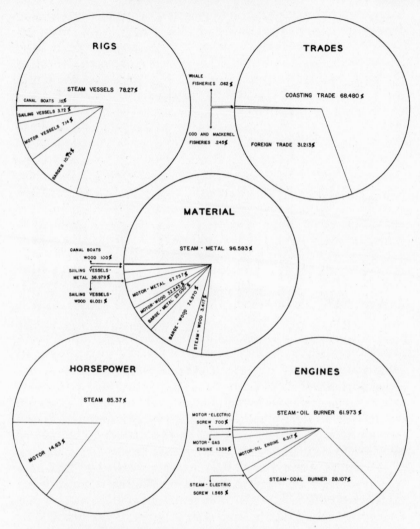

Fig. 29.—American documented merchant marine on June 30, 1933.

trade carried by American ships on the Pacific is correspondingly reduced, but the participation of the latter in the transport of the remaining cargoes is relatively great.

Figure 30 makes clear that the percentage of imports into
Pacific ports carried in American ships is almost uniformly

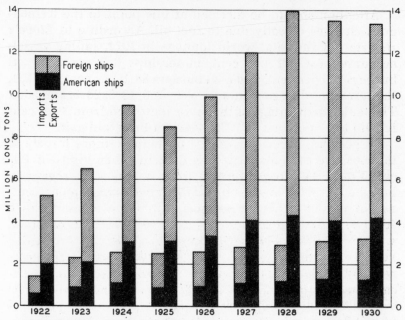

Fig. 30.—Cargo carried in American and foreign ships in United States Pacific Coast foreign trade, 1922–30.

greater than that of exports. In the carriage of commodities classed by the United States Shipping Board as low-freight-rate cargoes are included lumber and wheat, which move on tramp vessels in shipload lots. This largely explains why the participation of American ships in the outward carriage of low-freight-rate cargoes is smaller than in any other branch of the trade. American capital has not, in the last half-century or more, been attracted to tramp shipping when so many more profitable channels of investment were open—a not uneconomical situation, since this shipping is attractive only to countries poor in natural resources. In high-freight-rate cargoes, on the other hand, American vessels have handled on the average almost as high a percentage of the total as they have of any category of trade.[6]

6 A further explanation of the larger share of American ships in imports may be found in the fact that purchasers usually specify the route and carrier, with the result that American exports are likely to be shipped according to the instructions of foreign purchasers while American imports are normally transported according to the wishes of American buyers.

Attention should be directed at this point to the tremendous changes directly due to fuel oil. According to *Lloyd's Register,* of the total world tonnage in 1914, sailing vessels accounted for 8.1 per cent, motorships 0.5 per cent, oil burners 2.6 per cent, and coal burners 88.8 per cent; in 1931, the corresponding percentages were 2.0, 13.5, 28.5, and 56.0. The tanker percentage of the totals increased from 3 per cent in 1914 to 11 per cent in 1930, nearly a threefold gain.

In general, American vessels participate more largely in the carriage of tanker cargoes than in other kinds of Pacific Coast foreign commerce. This is true with regard to both the outgoing and the incoming movement. The percentage of tanker exports carried in American ships declined from 38 per cent to 31 per cent from 1922 to 1930, compared with an increase of from 17 per cent to 27 per cent for British vessels; the imports in Pacific Coast foreign trade have corresponding figures of 42 per cent and 40 per cent for American vessels and 21 per cent and 26 per cent for British vessels over this period (Appendix Table IX). The prevalence of industrial carriers among the tanker fleet undoubtedly accounts for the stronger position of American ships in this service.

The relative importance of American ships in the carriage of Pacific Coast international trade varies widely for the several trade routes over which this commerce moves (Appendix Table VIII). It may be observed that American participation is strongest in the trades near by and weakest in the transoceanic trades, a situation which likewise characterizes the water-borne foreign trade of the country as a whole. The American Bureau of Shipping in *The American Merchant Marine* (1933) observes:

At the present time one-third by value and 40 per cent by volume of our water-borne foreign trade is carried in American-flag vessels. This is three times the 1914 percentage but is still below the percentage required to maintain our position as a world power. Figured either per ton of exports or per capita, the United States has less ship tonnage in foreign commerce than any other maritime nation.

Such a showing is not unexpected, in view of the real advantages of proximity and the fact that none of the countries near by has a strong merchant marine, whereas several European countries and Japan have highly developed commercial fleets.

Among the more important trade routes those to the United Kingdom and Western Europe have the least relative employment of American shipping, to be explained by the participation, at this writing, of but one American-flag service from the Pacific Coast to Europe. In Pacific Coast trade with the United Kingdom, vessels of United States registry carry little more than 10 per cent of the total, while in the trade with Western European ports of the Havre-Hamburg sector, the present share of American ships is hardly 5 per cent.

Among transpacific trade routes, the one to East Asia is most important from the standpoint of volume of trade. On this route American vessels carry slightly under one-third of the aggregate volume of cargoes in both directions, about the average for all Pacific Coast trade, but more than one-half the imports. Much less important quantitatively than that of East Asia is the trade with the East Indies, which include the Philippines; here American ships make a somewhat better showing.

Mexico, Central America, north and west coasts of South America, and Pacific Canada, on the other hand, are all regions whose commerce with Pacific ports of the United States is preponderantly by ships of American registry. These regions are so located as to provide virtually an international coasting employment for American ships, a situation which co-ordinates extremely well with the fully protected domestic coastwise trade.

The writer has essayed the task of compiling a complete list of services currently operated from the American Pacific Coast to other parts of the world. (See Appendix A.) Advertised sailings in the first months of 1932 were largely used as the basis, and pertinent information was obtained regarding the vessels so tabulated. Use was made of records of individual vessels appearing in *Lloyd's Register, List of Merchant Vessels* (published by the United States Commissioner of Navigation), sailings advertised in *Pacific Shipper, Shipping Register, Marine Digest, Harbour and Shipping,* and *Daily Commercial News* (San Francisco), and of first-hand contact with the steamship lines. Such a list of ships can never be entirely accurate for the reason that ship operations are subject to frequent changes, even in the case of liner services, and no records are completely up to date. Some vessels are continually being transferred from one route to another, or are laid up or put into service according as seasonal or other variations in cargo offerings occur. Nevertheless, it is possible from a study of this kind to discover important and interesting facts regarding the character of facilities regularly offered on the Pacific Coast for maritime transport of cargo, passengers, and mail and miscellaneous services.

Since the period of this tabulation falls within an industrial era of severe depression throughout the world, liner tonnage serving the several routes must be regarded as subnormal. However, the recent decline in active ship tonnage on regular service is relatively small compared to the widespread force of the economic disorganization.

During the early months of 1932, according to this tabulation, there were employed more or less regularly in service from United States Pacific ports to all foreign regions approximately 2.2 million gross tons of shipping, compared to the estimated 2.5 millions already mentioned for the year 1920. Adding to this the volume of intercoastal shipping, which totals 900,000 tons but which includes some duplication with American-flag foreign-trade services operating intercoastally as one leg of a longer voyage, an aggregate of close to 3,000,000 tons of ships serving American Pacific ports, not including strictly coastwise carriers and those operating only to Alaska and Hawaii, is obtained.

Out of the 2.2 million tons of foreign-trade liner shipping, approximately 750,000 tons, or almost exactly one-third, are operated under the American flag. British shipping comes second with about 600,000 tons and Japanese shipping third with somewhat under 350,000. Thus the three flags ranking first before the war still predominate, which is a fact fully in accord with expectations. But the magnitude of shipping enterprise in this area has changed greatly, for American participation has advanced from third to first place.

TABLE 37

NET TONNAGE OF VESSELS ENTERED AND CLEARED IN FOREIGN TRADE,
1910–1930*

(In thousands of net tons of vessel capacity)†

Class	All Ports				Seaports Only
	1910–1914‡	1921–1925‡	1926–1930‡	1930	1930
Total entrances	46,619	66,292	79,062	81,253	66,329
American	11,328	29,644	30,314	31,866	24,520
Foreign	35,291	36,648	48,748	49,387	41,809
Per cent American	24.3	44.8	38.3	39.2	37.0
With cargo (total)	32,597	47,946	56,410	59,716	52,200
American	6,042	21,846	22,713	24,271	20,272
Foreign	26,555	26,000	33,697	35,445	31,928
In ballast (total)..................	14,022	18,346	22,652	21,537	14,129
American	5,286	7,798	7,601	7,595	4,248
Foreign	8,736	10,547	15,051	13,942	9,911
Total seaports	35,211	52,934	63,618	66,329	66,329
Total northern and Mexican borders	11,408	13,358	15,444	14,924	.....
Total clearances	46,579	66,653	79,759	81,307	66,372
American	11,590	29,554	30,709	31,560	24,088
Foreign	34,989	37,098	49,050	49,747	42,284
Per cent American	24.9	44.4	38.5	38.8	36.3
With cargo (total).................	40,404	51,468	63,085	63,315	53,379
American	8,996	19,681	21,340	21,715	17,622
Foreign	31,408	31,786	41,745	41,600	35,757
In ballast (total)	6,175	15,184	16,674	17,992	12,993
American	2,594	9,872	9,369	9,845	6,467
Foreign	3,581	5,310	7,305	8,147	6,526
Total seaports	34,965	53,553	67,345	66,372	66,372
Total northern and Mexican borders	11,614	13,099	15,414	14,935	.....

* Data from Bureau of Foreign and Domestic Commerce. Totals approximate.
† Net ton equals 100 cubic feet of space, excluding cabins, machinery, etc.
‡ Average for the period; data for 1910–1914 are for fiscal years ended June 30.

Another way of measuring the participation of various
countries in transpacific services is on the basis of the
number of vessels employed. Out of somewhere between 175
and 200 vessels operating above and below the Equator in

transpacific trade from American Pacific ports, American ships number one-third or more and have two-fifths of the gross tonnage. Five companies, operating eight lines, account for the good representation of the American flag. Thus in the Far Eastern trade the Dollar interests with their present wide ramifications control more than 60 per cent of the American tonnage serving Pacific ports. Table 38 and Figure 31 (p. 222) afford a valuable picture of our shipping.

TABLE 38

MERCHANT SHIPPING OF THE UNITED STATES, 1850–1930*

Year Ended June 30	Number of Vessels			Gross Tonnage (thousands)					
							Documented for		
	Total	Sailing, etc.†	Steam and Motor	Total	Sailing, etc.†	Steam and Motor	Foreign Trade‡	Coast-wise and Internal Trade§	Great Lakes¶
1850........	.....	.....	.....	3,535	3,010	526	1,586	1,950	198
1860........	.....	.....	.....	5,354	4,486	868	2,546	2,808	468
1870........	28,998	25,474	3,524	4,247	3,171	1,075	1,517	2,730	685
1880........	24,712	19,995	4,717	4,068	2,856	1,212	1,353	2,715	605
1890........	23,467	17,502	5,965	4,424	2,565	1,859	947	3,478	1,063
1900........	23,333	16,280	7,053	5,165	2,507	2,658	827	4,338	1,566
1910........	25,740	13,288	12,452	7,508	2,608	4,900	792	6,716	2,895
1914........	26,943	11,452	15,491	7,929	2,501	5,428	1,076	6,852	2,883
1918........	26,711	10,053	16,658	9,925	2,453	7,471	3,604	6,321	2,798
1920........	28,183	9,369	18,814	16,324	2,501	13,823	9,929	6,935	3,139
1921........	28,012	8,941	19,071	18,282	2,537	15,745	11,082	7,200	2,840
1922........	27,358	8,398	18,960	18,463	2,481	15,982	10,725	7,738	2,724
1923........	27,017	8,071	18,946	18,285	2,463	15,821	9,073	9,212	2,758
1924........	26,575	7,825	18,750	17,741	2,425	15,315	8,797	8,943	2,791
1925........	26,367	7,730	18,637	17,406	2,430	14,976	8,155	9,251	2,853
1926........	26,343	7,654	18,689	17,311	2,462	14,848	7,722	9,589	2,844
1927........	25,778	7,394	18,384	16,888	2,381	14,507	7,317	9,570	2,805
1928........	25,385	7,115	18,270	16,683	2,336	14,344	6,940	9,743	2,773
1929........	25,326	7,007	18,319	16,477	2,315	14,162	6,912	9,565	2,771
1930........	25,214	7,003	18,211	16,068	2,311	13,757	6,303	9,765	2,758

* Data from Bureau of Navigation and Steamboat Inspection.

† Includes canal boats and barges.

‡ Includes tonnage, formerly considerable but recently insignificant, engaged in whale fisheries.

§ Includes vessels engaged in cod and mackerel fisheries (36,478 tons in 1928, 38,903 tons in 1929, and 41,870 tons in 1930).

¶ Included in preceding column.

British shipping is also very important on these routes. Seven lines, mainly under British control and using principally British ships, operate transpacific services from United States Pacific ports, while the Canadian Pacific Steamship Company, owner of the important fast passenger-and-mail "Empress" ships, hails from Vancouver. The British lines touching American Pacific ports were employing, in the early months of 1932, about 40 ships, aggregating approximately 300,000 gross tons. Two of these lines call only at Los Angeles among Pacific Coast ports. Two lines, the Barber Line and the Silver-Java-Pacific, operate ships of both British and other foreign registry.[7]

Participation of Japanese ships in transpacific trade is likewise great, since this is one of the most logical routes for the operation of the strong Japanese merchant marine. Four lines now serve American Pacific ports, and a fifth calls at Los Angeles for bunkers only. Two of these lines, operating large express and passenger ships, make an exceedingly important contribution to shipping services of this type on the Pacific. It is somewhat difficult to distinguish liner from tramp services in Japanese sailings; hence the total tonnage of Japanese transpacific liner services is not easily stated. It is the writer's conclusion, nevertheless, that there is not a great deal of difference between the tonnage of British and of Japanese shipping on the Pacific.

A comparatively small number of ships of nationalities other than American, British, and Japanese operate regularly on these services; practically, only three Scandinavian lines require mention.

Transpacific services, including the round-the-world lines, continue to be the most important element in Pacific Coast sea trade, so far at least as the volume of tonnage employed is concerned. Including lines operating to Australasia there are now over 1.3 million gross tons of ships sailing on more or less regular schedule from American Pacific ports westbound. Thus we have the picture that approximately 60 per cent of all foreign-trade shipping operating out of Pacific ports crosses the Pacific Ocean.

[7] The estimate of 300,000 gross tons includes only the British vessels on these services.

There is considerable variety in the itinerary of these lines, some going only to Japan and North China, some to South China and the Philippines, and some still farther west to the Straits Settlements, the East Indies, and British India. A number of lines include sailings from one or more Pacific Coast ports to the Orient as one section of their round-the-world services. In general, two main routes are followed across the North Pacific—the northern route, along the Great Circle, which is considerably the shorter, skirting the Aleutian Islands, and the more southerly route via Hawaii.

On the outward voyage most of these transpacific lines operate from one port or a limited number of related ports. Thus there are the California transpacific services out of San Francisco and Los Angeles, the Columbia River services, chiefly from Portland, and the Puget Sound services from Seattle, Tacoma, and Vancouver; also combinations of the three. But on the homeward voyage, nearly all lines include San Francisco in their itinerary because this port is the destination of the greatest volume of cargo inbound to any Pacific Coast port. In addition to these services are several which go to the South Seas and Australasia, some of them, too, calling at Hawaii before crossing the international date line en route to ports below the Equator.

The unbalanced cargo movement between American Pacific ports and the Far East and its effect in encouraging the establishment of westbound round-the-world services will be discussed in chapters xii and xiii. Some of these lines serve both San Francisco and Los Angeles with outbound cargo space, while some call only at Los Angeles, so advantageously located with respect to such a route, with the further great attraction to shipping of its unexcelled oil-bunkering facilities. In the same fashion certain lines from Atlantic ports to the Orient via Panama have added Los Angeles as a port of call for cargo or for bunkers or for both. The happy accident of adjacent oil fields has been of incalculable importance to Los Angeles in building up a great seaport where virtually no natural harbor facilities exist. Despite excellent bunkering facilities available at other Pacific ports, the cheap fuel oil available at Los Angeles harbor benefits the entire coastal shipping.

One of the noteworthy developments in present-day ship operation which is particularly prominent on the Pacific is the rapid replacement of coal-burning steamships by oil-burning vessels. This is in line with world developments, since *Lloyd's Register* records that in 1914 steamers totaling 1,310,209 gross tonnage were equipped to burn fuel oil while in 1931 this figure had mounted to 20,002,307 gross tons, an increase of over 1,400 per cent.

There are many who predict that coal-burning steamers are destined to be almost completely supplanted by ships using fuel oil, either under boilers or in engines of internal combustion. Some believe, likewise, that the motorship has such pronounced advantages over either coal- or oil-burning steamships that it will eventually eliminate the greater portion of steam shipping. Mr. A. Loveday, Chief of the Economic and Financial Section of the League of Nations, offers this pertinent observation in his review of Professor Sven Helander's study entitled *Die Internationale Schiffahrtskrise und Ihre Weltwirtschaftliche Bedeutung* (appearing in *Weltwirtschaftliches Archiv,* October 1928):

> The whole of this analysis of supply is of very considerable interest and it is only to be regretted that Professor Helander did not follow it up further and consider in a little more detail the question of oil versus coal burning ships, types of engines, etc. In a later chapter he expresses the view that an increase in trade will tend towards a shortening of the average voyage, which will adversely influence the motor ship. If this is true it is likely to have considerable effect on, for instance, the relative efficiency of the British and Italian mercantile marines.

On the long transpacific runs oil-burning ships, particularly motorships, exhibit such marked economies in operation that the great majority of new ships designed for this trade are being constructed to burn oil. The scarcity of coal on the Pacific North American Coast south of Puget Sound and the abundance of oil in California make this shift in fuel highly advantageous. An oil-burning steamship has a much larger cargo-carrying capacity than a coal-burning vessel of the same size.[8]

[8] In the first place, two-thirds of a ton of oil will ordinarily supply the same number of thermal units as a ton of coal. In the second place, space

For the Pacific Coast, the United States Commissioner of Navigation reports that for the fiscal year 1932 there are 855 vessels of 2,473,484 gross tonnage which represent one-seventh of the American total in vessels and one-fifth reckoned in tonnage. The position of the Pacific district is more conspicuous with reference to motorships, since the number recorded is 3,923 of 274,486 gross tonnage, or one-third of the total American vessels and one-fourth of their gross tonnage.

For some time past motorship construction has approximately equaled, and has often exceeded, steamship construction in the world as a whole, and the transits of this type of ship through the Suez and Panama Canals have gained rapidly in recent years.[9] But among recent constructions of American ships the percentage of motorships has averaged considerably lower than for the other important maritime nations.

Out of total shipping of something over 2.2 million gross tons now operating in regular services in foreign trade from American ports on the Pacific, almost one million tons are motorships. If American-flag services are eliminated from these totals, since they employ almost no motorships, it appears that the other maritime nations find it advantageous to employ in Pacific Coast trade almost two gross tons of motorships to one of steamships. On the basis of the number of ships in operation, motorships account for four out of

on the vessel not otherwise usable for profitable purposes will serve for the storage of fuel oil. In the third place, fewer men are required to man the ship, so that crew quarters may be reduced and the additional space used for cargo. The motorship represents still further economies in the same direction and in other particulars (in part set off by higher initial cost), but the important factor on long voyages is to keep the bunker space as small a proportion of total deadweight carrying capacity as possible in order to release the maximum space for cargo. Because of the relatively small amount of space required on motorships for fuel and engine-room crew, many such ships bunker for the round trip, even on long voyages.

Many experiments are being made, however, in the field of steamships and in utilizing powdered coal. It appears likely that coal-burning steamships have a future as well as a past.

[9] Motorships using the Suez route in 1926 constituted only 9.4 per cent of total transits (in net tonnage) but 20.5 per cent in 1930. During the fiscal year 1931 motorship transits through the Panama Canal amounted to 40 per cent of the tonnage of all commercial ships using this waterway.

five vessels of foreign registry. Japanese and Scandinavian
lines are now relying almost entirely on motorships in their
transpacific services.

Among 175 or more ships sailing from one or more American Pacific ports to points in the Far East, more than 90 per
cent are oil-burning vessels, of which approximately half
are motorships. Although the United States has half as much
ocean-going merchant shipping as Great Britain, its tonnage
of motorships is barely more than one-fifth the British total;
it is about one-third that of Norway, whose total merchant
fleet, over 50 per cent motorized, is only one-third as great.

The majority of transpacific lines (those to the Orient,
to Australasia, and around the world) are provided with
commodious passenger accommodations. The traveler to
China or Japan now has the choice of a dozen lines for this
trip, including freighters which have desirable space for a
few passengers. Some of the newest liners compare favorably in size, speed, and appointments with the majority of
transatlantic passenger vessels. The express lines maintain
a schedule of from 12 to 14 days between Yokohama and
San Francisco, via Honolulu, and slightly longer on the
reverse trip. The major shipping companies on the Pacific
are bending their best efforts toward developing Pacific
Ocean travel in both its recreational and its other branches,
believing that such service has an integral part to play in
furthering the commercial and political importance of this
largest basin.

In tabulating the ships operated to the Far East on the
basis of age one finds that among American ships all but a
comparatively few were built between 1918 and 1922, a
period corresponding to the extensive war-inspired shipbuilding program of the United States. Very few of these
vessels, therefore, are less than ten years old, and equally
few more than twenty years old. Among foreign ships on
these routes, on the other hand, approximately half have
been built within the last five years, most of these as late
as 1929 or 1930. It is among these newly built carriers that
motorships figure so conspicuously. Consult Table 39.

In the early months of 1932 over a score of steamship lines
were in regular operation between Pacific ports of the

TABLE 39

VESSELS ACCORDING TO AGE, STEAM, MOTOR, AND GRAND TOTAL, JUNE 30, 1933*

Age of Vessel	Steam			
	Number	of Total Vessels Percentage	Gross Tons	of Total Gross Percentage
Five years or less...............	.160	2.93	531,488	4.51
Between 5 and 10 years.........	258	4.71	469,748	3.99
Between 10 and 20 years........	2,035	37.16	7,251,511	61.52
Over 20 years..................	3,023	55.20	3,534,908	29.98
Total......................	5,476		11,787,655	

Age of Vessel	Motor			
	Number	Percentage of Total Vessels	Gross Tons	Percentage of Total Gross
Five years or less...............	1,867	14.69	225,411	20.98
Between 5 and 10 years.........	2,381	18.74	253,585	23.60
Between 10 and 20 years........	3,692	29.07	468,831	43.62
Over 20 years..................	4,766	37.50	126,758	11.80
Total......................	12,706		1,074,585	

Age of Vessel	Total			
	Number	Percentage of Total Vessels	Gross Tons	Percentage of Total Gross
Five years or less...............	2,526	10.16	882,553	5.86
Between 5 and 10 years.........	3,766	15.14	998,652	6.63
Between 10 and 20 years........	7,762	31.21	8,569,300	56.90
Over 20 years..................	10,814	43.49	4,609,652	30.61
Total......................	24,868		15,060,157	

* Data from Bureau of Navigation and Steamboat Inspection.

United States and Europe. Some of these lines serve only United Kingdom ports, some serve only Continental ports, while others include both England and the Continent in their itinerary. As a general rule they call at all the more important Pacific Coast ports from Vancouver to Los Angeles (some including San Diego), thereby giving each port frequent European sailings.

These lines together were employing over 100 ships, aggregating some 800,000 gross tons. Approximately half of the total by number, and more than half by tonnage, are ships built between 1926 and 1930. All but a very few were constructed after 1915. In age they correspond closely to those employed on transpacific runs, if American ships are omitted from the latter.

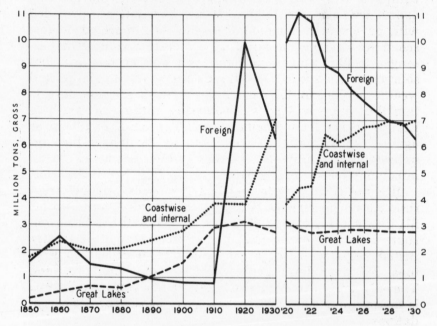

Fig. 31.—Merchant marine of the United States documented for foreign, coastwise, and Great Lakes trade.

While the advantages of oil-burning ships are not so pronounced on the Pacific Coast–European route as on transpacific runs, because of the relative abundance of coal in the United Kingdom and Western Europe, two-thirds or more of the vessels operated from Pacific ports to Europe use oil as a fuel. More than half of all ships on this route are motorships, although the proportion of motorships in the world's ocean-going fleet is less than 20 per cent. One British line operating to Europe has developed an interesting adaptation of its ships to fuel available on the route; among nine steamships employed on this run, six are convertible, burning either coal or oil. Consequently they bunker with coal at British ports for the outward trip to the Pacific Coast; and on arrival there they are converted to oil-burners and take on fuel oil for the homeward trip.

The vast majority of the ships operated to Europe are equipped with refrigerator space to handle the growing export trade in perishables. Many, likewise, are provided with passenger accommodations and are operated on fast schedules designed to build up a lucrative volume of passenger traffic, which has long been one of the principal sources of revenue to transatlantic liners. As population and wealth increase on the American Pacific Coast it seems certain that there will be an increasing volume of travel to Europe direct from Pacific ports. The chief handicap as against the transatlantic route will be the longer time required by the all-water journey, which seems to be an important factor also to Orientals visiting North America.

It is not surprising to find British shipping strongly represented in the services to the United Kingdom and Europe. Six lines serving United States Pacific ports on the European route are operated by British interests, using close to fifty British ships, which aggregate somewhat over 300,000 gross tons. No other flag is represented by more than two lines. The only American service between Pacific ports and Europe is by an industrial carrier offering no passenger accommodations.

In addition to these six British lines are two Norwegian, two German, one French, one Belgian, one Swedish, one Danish, one Italian, and one Dutch line, besides the American line already mentioned. Non-British foreign lines depend almost entirely on motorships; five European services are maintained exclusively by this type of vessel.[10]

10 The Holland-American line also employs motorships exclusively on this route, but since its service is maintained jointly with the Royal Mail Line, which uses half steamships and half motorships, it is not included among the five. The former company pioneered the Coast refrigerator services.

Among the ships now in operation on the Pacific Coast–
European routes, half have been built no earlier than 1926
and so are essentially up to date. This percentage is strikingly similar to that obtaining in the transpacific trade,
although the ships on the European route on the whole
average somewhat older. The one American line to Europe
has no vessel built later than 1921.

In addition to the transpacific and European services,
American and foreign steamship companies operate a number of lines to Central and South America, both east-coast
and west-coast. One Norwegian and one American line
maintain services between Canadian and American Pacific
ports and Brazil and Argentina. Both lines provide facilities
for refrigerator cargo and both carry passengers. The American service operates under a United States mail contract.
In connection with this service the latter company also calls
at West Indies ports, thus providing direct connection with
those ports as well as with the east coast of South America.
The Norwegian line at present operates southbound via
Magellan and returns via the Panama Canal.[11]

The American line operates steamships built in 1919 and
1920, while the Norwegian line is tonnaged mostly by motorships built in 1926 and 1929. Three American lines are engaged in shipping services from the Pacific Coast to Central
America, serving both west-coast and east-coast ports either
directly or via transshipment at the Panama Canal. Two
of these lines are also United States intercoastal carriers,
one operating between Gulf and Pacific ports and the other
between Atlantic and Pacific ports. All three lines hold
United States mail contracts under the Merchant Marine Act
of 1928; two of them have recently put into service new ships
built to maintain performance of these contract services.
No foreign lines are operating from the Pacific Coast to
Central America except as a part of a longer route elsewhere
mentioned.

For the west coast of South America there are at present

[11] Owing to a regular embargo imposed by Argentina on fresh fruits
between December 15 and May 1, this line transfers some of its ships during
these months to the Pacific Coast–European route. This embargo likewise
explains the outward routing via Magellan now followed.

only two lines in direct operation, one American and one Japanese. Both operate via Central American ports. In addition, several lines to Europe carry cargo for the west coast of South America for transshipment at the Canal, as do those to Central America. This route is believed to have suffered more severely than any other on the American Pacific Coast as a result of the current economic stagnation, and several lines formerly serving the route have entirely discontinued sailings.

One line, operating three Shipping Board motorships on bareboat charter, is maintaining a bi-monthly service direct to South Africa, calling at all important ports from Vancouver to Los Angeles, then proceeding via Magellan to Capetown and other South African ports. Homeward routes vary with cargo offerings. This line is not only the only one on the Pacific Coast operating Shipping Board vessels but also the only American line tonnaged exclusively or even principally with motorships.[12]

At the present time there are not far from 150 vessels, aggregating above 900,000 gross tons, and representing some fifteen lines, employed in American intercoastal trade through the Panama Canal from Pacific ports to those on the Atlantic or the Gulf. The majority of these lines operate ships not documented for foreign trade but serving strictly as domestic intercoastal carriers. The American-Hawaiian is the oldest and largest of these carriers. A number, however, transport cargo to and from Central America and Caribbean ports, at which they call en route between United States ports. The Dollar Lines operate intercoast, eastbound, as one section of their transpacific service, and westbound as a part of their round-the-world service. Almost without exception the intercoastal lines, always of United States registry, call at several American ports on both seaboards. It is noteworthy, too, that the leading American steamship line in the intercoastal trade and also the foremost figure in the round-the-world services both pioneered from San Francisco, where they still maintain their headquarters.

Most of the strictly intercoastal carriers are moderate-

12 This line has now (July 1934) ceased operation.

sized ships, averaging not far from 6,000 gross tons. Considerably over half were built in the peak era of American shipbuilding, between 1918 and 1922. Scarcely a half-dozen of all ships operated intercoastally have been built since 1922. All but a very small number, moreover, are steamships fitted to burn fuel oil under boilers. These vessels are predominantly freight carriers, and with few exceptions those which are provided with accommodations for passengers are the lines which also serve foreign ports en route between the two seacoasts.

One further group of maritime transport services on the Pacific remains to be considered — the coastwise carriers. This group includes not only those connecting ports in Washington, Oregon, and California but also those which serve Alaska and Hawaii. In addition to the lines which confine their operations strictly to Pacific coastwise trade, a number of the intercoastal carriers offer coastwise shipping facilities, since they call at many Pacific ports en route to and from Atlantic and Gulf ports. For this among other reasons, it is difficult to make a separate tabulation of Pacific coastwise services.[13] Those which serve only Pacific ports of the three West Coast states number approximately half a dozen, omitting very small lines of local scope. Two companies operate passenger and freight lines to Hawaii, in addition to a number of transpacific lines which call at the Islands en route. There are also several services to Alaska from Puget Sound ports.

In this purely coastwise maritime service there has been the least change as compared with pre-war conditions. The war, with its political and economic consequences, made vast alterations in Pacific Coast foreign-trade shipping and in American participation therein. The Panama Canal revolutionized intercoastal shipping. Along the Pacific Coast, however, no event has occurred to modify, in any pronounced manner, the normal course of local development.

The ships which serve the Pacific Coast for the inter-port carriage of goods constitute a vital branch of the transport

[13] See Appendix A for a tabulation of shipping companies operating in the various trades. A list of the coastwise lines appears on pages 249–50.

facilities of this region. The movement of lumber alone is great enough to justify a coastwise lumber conference which is separate from, though closely in touch with, the general coastwise conference. Passenger traffic is similarly of some importance, particularly the movement between California ports, and recreational travel during the vacation months.

Development of shipping facilities for the successful transportation of perishables over long distances is a matter of peculiar importance to the American Pacific Coast, as it is to any region (New Zealand, for example) where economic resources are suited mainly to the production of exportable surpluses of perishable commodities. The outstanding position of the American Pacific Coast in the growing of high-grade fruits and vegetables is well known. The successful utilization of this resource depends on cold-storage transportation facilities suited to the requirements of the several commodities transported. To learn what these requirements are, and to see that they are provided, has been the joint concern of growers, government agencies, and shipping companies. Note the list of services in Table 40 (pp. 228–29).

At the present time there is no steamship route from the American Pacific Coast on which there are not employed a considerable number of ships equipped with refrigerator space for the handling of perishable cargoes. In fact, both intercoastal and offshore ship lines are turning to "dry ice," or carbon dioxide crystals, as a new means of water-borne refrigeration. In particular, the lines to Europe are almost exclusively tonnaged by such ships, some of which have space for the carriage of more than 10,000 tons of refrigerator cargo (allowing 40 cubic feet per ton). Between 275,000 and 300,000 tons of such space are now available for the transportation of perishables on this route. Many ships serving the Orient and Australasia are also equipped with refrigerator compartments. On these routes, however, the average size of refrigerator cargo space per ship is very much smaller than it is on vessels bound for Europe. Hardly more than half the ships in transpacific trade offer refrigerator services, and the total space so provided probably does not equal 50,000 tons.[14] The lower standard of living pre-

14 Here, and elsewhere in this connection, the data refer to approximately January 1, 1932. Later information appears in Table 40.

TABLE 40

REFRIGERATOR SERVICES, PACIFIC COAST VESSELS*

	Number of Vessels	Total Refrigerator Capacity
Orient		
Dollar Line and American Mail Line	20	10,490
Kerr Steamship Company	13	14,900
Pacific Java Bengal Line	2	2,125
Nippon Yusen Kaisha	10	2,220
Barber Line	5	3,250
Bank Line	6	2,040
Oceanic and Oriental Line	3	450
States Steamship Company	3	12,000
Osaka Shosen Kaisha	13	3,829
Canadian Pacific	4	1,949
Mitsui Line	2	134
Maersk Line	2	428
West Coast South America		
Grace Line	5	825
Intercoastal		
Panama Pacific Line	3	5,400
Dollar Line†		
Grace Line	4	4,000
Coastwise and Alaska		
Pacific Steamship Lines	8	862
Alaska Steamship Company	2	447
Grace Line‡		
Hawaii		
Matson Navigation Company	14	4,960
Dollar Line§		
Canadian Australasian Line	2	2,950
East Coast South America		
Pacific Argentine Brazil Line	4	1,500
Blue Star Line¶		
Central America		
United Fruit Company**		
Grace Line††		
Mediterranean		
Navigazione Libera Triestina	4	2,625

* From *Pacific Shipper*, November 5, 1934. Space is in tons of 40 cubic feet.
† Westbound and eastbound, *see* Orient.   ‡ See Intercoastal.
§ See Orient.   ¶ See European.
** Subject to booking, refrigerator cargo accepted weekly from San Francisco
to Balboa.   †† See West Coast South America.

TABLE 40 (*Continued*)

	Number of Vessels	Total Refrigerator Capacity
United Kingdom, Europe		
Holland-America & Royal Mail‡‡.............	11	67,886
Blue Star Line............................	11	88,279
Donaldson Line	8	33,630
East Asiatic Company......................	3	6,647
French Line	8	4,900
Fruit Express Line........................	3	13,500
Furness Line	10	33,975
Hamburg-American Line	7	15,427
Interocean Line	8	16,975
Cascade Line	4	5,600
Johnson Line	3	3,578
North German Lloyd......................	6	14,816
Fred Olsen Line..........................	6	9,250
Reardon Smith Line.......................	1	1,000
Total	218	392,847

‡‡ North Pacific Coast Line.

vailing among most of the population in the Orient precludes for the present any extensive demand for imported perishable fruits and vegetables.

On the routes to Central America and the east coast of South America, vessels equipped with refrigerator compartments find some cargo for such spaces in both directions. Bananas are imported directly from Central America, and frozen meats from Argentina. A two-way traffic of this sort is naturally more profitable from the standpoint of ship operations than the almost exclusively one-way movement of refrigerator cargo prevailing on the routes to Europe and Asia. There is no present prospect, however, of any substantial return movement of perishables to the Pacific Coast from the regions now taking the greater portion of the outbound ocean cargoes of this character.

It is pertinent to quote the Pacific Coast Freight and Charter Market Report, issued by the General Steamship Corporation, Ltd., for April 2, 1934, to illustrate actual conditions:

A slight weakening in freight rates in one or two major trades was experienced during the month of March, although volume of business was fairly well maintained. The outlook for the coming month does not hold much hope for any great improvement in rates, but a good volume of business should continue.

A résumé of the various trades in detail follows:

GRAIN

China.—This market was the largest contributor to volume of business and quite a number of vessels, both American and foreign flag, were fixed for prompt loading, as will be noted from fixture list. Rates remained unchanged with American vessels securing in the neighborhood of $3.75 per ton and foreign vessels in the neighborhood of 11/– per ton. It is anticipated that this movement of Wheat will continue throughout the summer, which will provide a good outlet for tramp steamers, who may find themselves seeking cargo from the Pacific Coast.

Japan.—No full cargoes were fixed in this direction, but regular liners have been booking thousand ton parcels at rates in the neighborhood of $2.25, which is 25c lower than secured in previous months.

U.K.-Continent.—During the early part of the month several vessels were fixed from Pacific Coast to Europe at rates ranging in the neighborhood of 19/– to 20/6, depending upon ports of discharge, but the last half of the month saw a considerable falling off in business and at this time space is reported to be offering freely to Continental ports at 14/–. It is felt that this unsatisfactory state of affairs is only temporary, however.

Intercoastal.—Some inquiry was heard for American vessels on time-charter basis for Wheat to U.S. Atlantic or Gulf, but owners, in view of the scarcity of return cargoes, have been insisting on complete round voyages, to which charterers are at the moment unwilling to agree.

LUMBER

China.—Several full cargoes have been fixed on the basis of $5.75 to Shanghai, with up-River ports taking about $1.00 per M ft. additional. Also, one or two cargoes have been fixed to North China ports at rates in the neighborhood of $5.50 to $6.00, depending upon specifications.

Japan.—Demand on the part of Japanese buyers has fallen off and rates have accordingly trended downward to $5.25 on squares. It is believed that the situation is only temporary and another fortnight should see rates back to former levels of $6.00.

Australia.—Several vessels were fixed for full cargoes of lumber from North Pacific to Australia at undisclosed rates of freight for April/May loading. It is rumored that fixtures were made on lump sum basis, which if converted into rates per M ft. should work out in the neighborhood of $7.50, which makes for some little improvement in this section.

Intercoastal.—Full cargoes were conspicuous by their absence and no fixtures were made.

TIME CHARTER

Little or no business was effected in this section, as will be noted from fixture list.

TANKERS

A fair business was again done from California to various destinations in both clean and dirty trades, as evidenced by fixture list.

A list of reported charters for the month follows:

A LIST OF CHARTERS (MARCH 1934)†

WHEAT

"Leeds City"	2884 nrt	Portland	Shanghai	April	p.t.
"Snistad"	2453 nrt	Portland	Shanghai	March	p.t.
"Harperly"	2724 nrt	Vancouver	London/Hull	March	p.t.
"Artemisia"*	4088 nrt	Grain B.C.	Shanghai	April	p.t.
"Anglo Peruvian"*	3331 nrt	B.C.	U.K.	April	p.t.
SS "Kirkpool"	3012 nrt	B.C.	U.K.	March	p.t.
SS "Simonburn"	3242 nrt	Portland	Ireland	March	20/6
MS "Bronxville"	2973 nrt	Portland	Shanghai	M/Apr.	p.t.
MS "Skramstad"	2455 nrt	Portland	Shanghai	M/Apr.	p.t.
MS "Cape Horn"	3615 nrt	Portland	Shanghai	M/Apr.	p.t.
SS "Frumenton"	4059 nrt	Portland	Shanghai	M/Apr.	p.t.
SS "Margaret Dollar"	4351 nrt	Portland	Shanghai	March	p.t.
SS "Treworlas"	2867 nrt	B.C.	U.K.	March	17/3
SS "Innerton"	3241 nrt	Portland	U.K.	April	p.t.
SS "Melville Dollar"	4319 nrt	Portland	Shanghai	March	p.t.
SS "Illinois"	3362 nrt	Portland	Shanghai	March	$4.75
SS "Pennsylvania"	3522 nrt	Portland	Shanghai	March	$4.75
SS "Warlaby"	3013 nrt	Portland	Ireland	April	19/6
SS "Texas"	3533 nrt	Portland	Shanghai	March	$4.75
MS "Fernwood"	2727 nrt	Coos Bay	Shanghai	April	p.t.
"Harpasa"*	3035 nrt	B.C.	Liverpool	April	p.t.
MS "Nordbo"*	2732 nrt	B.C.	Hull	April	p.t.
SS "Aldington Court"	2979 nrt	B.C.	Dublin/Belfast	May	p.t.
SS "Dalcross"	2821 nrt	B.C.	London	April	p.t.
SS "Olovsborg"	3542 nrt	B.C.	England	April	p.t.

LUMBER

SS "Anglo Indian"	3400 nrt	B.C.	Australia	Ap/May	p.t.
SS "Harlingen"	3205 nrt	North Pac.	Australia	Mar/Ap	p.t.
SS Two unnamed		North Pac.	Australia		p.t.
SS "Fernwood"*	2750 nrt	North Pac.	Shanghai	May	p.t.

TIME CHARTER

MS "Brand"	2829 nrt	U.S.W.C./B.C.	U.K./Cont.	April	6/1½
SS "Artemisia"	4088 nrt	B.C.	Shanghai	April	£4400
MS "Beljeanne"	4285 nrt	North Pac.	U.K./Cont.	April	p.t.

† In this list, nrt = "net register tons"; p.t. = "private terms."
* Berthed for wheat, lumber, and general cargo.

TANKERS

SS "Athel" .... 10,000 fuel oil	Calif.	Japan	June	9/6
MT "Mijdrecht" ...... 10,000 t. clean	Calif.	Aus./Japan	Ap/Jun	12/–
				9/6
MT "Papoose" .... 70,000 bbls. gasoline	Houston	S.F./Tacoma	Mar.	70c
MT "Tamiahua" .....125,000 bbls. dirty 1 yr.	Calif.	N.H./Gulf	Apr.	56c
MT "Frank G. Drum". 78,000 bbls. dirty	Calif.	La Union		
		San Jose	May	22½c
MT "Corabank" ...... 13,000 t. clean 2 trips	Calif.	Aus./Japan	May	11/–
				9/6
MT "Attila" .... 12,000 t. clean 2 trips	Calif.	Aus./Japan	May	12/6
				9/6

MISCELLANEOUS

MS "Nordpol" .... Copra	P.I.	W.Coast Mex.	May	p.t.
SS "Jufuku Maru"..4293 nrt Empty cans	Seattle	Vladivostok	March	$4.90 M.T.

On the whole, therefore, the maritime connections of American Pacific Coast ports now embody direct routes and frequent sailings to every important trading region in the world. The merchant vessels so employed are characteristically new, up to date, and reasonably fast. On the most important routes half or more average less than five years in age. The ocean-going merchant ships of the world, on the other hand, include hardly 20 per cent built within the last five years. Such age comparisons, to be sure, are somewhat misleading, for the reason that a varying percentage, and at the present time a rather large percentage, of ships are always laid up; but these ships are predominantly the older, less efficient ones. Consequently ships in service on almost all routes will average less in age than the world's merchant fleet as a whole. Nevertheless, in this case the difference is great enough to warrant the assertion that Pacific Ocean commerce is attracting a rather more substantial percentage of the new vessels put into service than are routes in other parts of the world.

Within the last quarter of a century, it is true, there have been no startling reductions in record transpacific runs. As early as 1905 the steamer "Siberia" of the old Pacific Mail Line once made the voyage direct from Yokohama to San Francisco in ten days and ten hours. The present record between these two ports, via Honolulu, stands at 12 days, and from Manila, including all stops, the advertised schedule is twenty-four days. Nevertheless, even within the post-war period, there has been a definite reduction in the average time for transpacific voyages.

Increased speed is, of course, not less true of Atlantic shipping. The difference is that because of the much greater extent of the Pacific, the time and distance factor has in the past proved a greater barrier to cargo and passenger movements there than on the Atlantic. The increased speed brings current transpacific crossings close to the average time on the Atlantic some two decades ago.

The Pacific Ocean, to be sure, has not yet attracted for permanent employment any of the huge super-liners such as are found on the Atlantic, supported by the normally great volume of transatlantic travel. Perhaps the popular mania for palaces of over 50,000 tons attaining speeds of 22 to 29 knots may pass; certainly conditions since 1925 have made their operation decidedly unprofitable to their owners.

The persistent demand for larger and faster ships has the double effect of rendering obsolete a large percentage of the world's merchant marine and of imposing the necessity of making these more costly carriers profitable. The modern freighter carrying bulk cargo averages from 11 to 12 knots, and it is greatly to be questioned whether the cargo can pay for greater speed. Certainly tramps cannot be greatly developed in either size or speed. Some authorities advocate cargo lines of some 7,500 to 15,000 gross tonnage with speed of 15 to 16 knots and a certain amount of passenger accommodation available, but this type of vessel is suitable only for important routes affording regular cargo-and-freight offerings. Each route has its own requirements, so it is noteworthy that the Japanese are putting into service even speedier ships on the transpacific run.

It is probable that such ships will never be profitable on the longer transpacific runs. In any event, such a development clearly awaits a more definite shift in commercial and cultural interests from Europe to Asia than any yet in view. Speed, comfort, and even luxury for passenger travel is consistent with ships of half the size of the "Leviathan" (now obsolete because of its slow speed) and the "Majestic," even though the "Queen Mary" and the "Normandie" represent the latest word in vessel excellence.

X. Domestic Coastal Cargoes

A fair amount of goods was exchanged between Atlantic and Pacific ports of the United States by sea even before the construction of the Panama Canal, but this trade in no way compared with the magnitude of the present inter-coastal movement already referred to in chapter vi. Important as the intercoastal cargo traffic is to the American Pacific States, its volume is only 60 per cent of the total foreign trade of the region, while its rate of growth has been somewhat less rapid. Nevertheless the economic importance of domestic intercoastal commerce is greater than statistics indicate, for, unlike foreign trade, it has a certain stability and freedom from uncertainty due to the absence of artificial trade barriers.[1]

The accompanying table presents a statistical review of the intercoastal trade of the past two decades. Intercoastal, like foreign trade, is heavily unbalanced, and largely for the same reason. Exchangeable surpluses are for the most part bulky and of relatively low unit-value, while the lack of self-sufficiency in many lines of manufacturing demands an inbound movement from the eastern part of the United States of a very wide variety of manufactured products of high value but relatively small bulk. Consequently, the Pacific Coast annually sends to Gulf and Atlantic ports of the United States more than twice the weight of goods received from those points. For the short period for which data are available there is no apparent tendency for this disproportion to grow either less or greater. In the long run, however, there is little doubt that the intercoastal cargo movement in the two directions will become more nearly balanced because there are, fortunately, no tariff barriers to hamper regional exchange in domestic trade.

On the other hand, domestic commerce between the Eastern and Western seaboards of the United States, unlike most

---

[1] Domestic intercoastal trade is limited by possible state quarantine measures in the interests of excluding plant diseases and pests and, of course, by the persistent economic principle of comparative advantage.

foreign commerce, has a choice of the two routes, transcontinental railways and intercoastal steamships. Hence not all the products of which the Pacific Coast has a large exchangeable surplus will appear prominently among outbound intercoastal shipments, nor will all commodities for

TABLE 41

UNITED STATES INTERCOASTAL TRADE, TOTAL AND DIRECTION, 1914–1933*

Year	Actual Data (In Tons)			Indexes (1923–1925 Average = 100)		
	Total	East-bound	West-bound	Total	East-bound	West-bound
1914†........	748,809	402,442	346,367	16.1	11.2	32.6
1915........	1,490,349	702,043	788,306	13.3	8.2	31.0
1916........	152,001	54,361	97,640	1.4	0.6	3.8
1917........	205,593	174,565	31,028	1.8	2.0	1.2
1918........	797,362	702,086	95,276	7.2	8.2	3.7
1919........	1,372,095	1,119,207	252,888	12.3	13.0	9.9
1920........	1,061,652	644,833	416,819	9.5	7.5	16.3
1921........	1,841,565	924,851	916,714	16.5	10.7	36.0
1922........	4,032,369	2,057,638	1,974,731	36.0	23.9	77.4
1923........	13,046,970	10,059,152	2,987,818	116.8	116.7	117.2
1924........	11,118,793	8,853,616	2,265,177	99.6	102.7	88.8
1925........	9,338,174	6,941,053	2,397,121	83.6	80.5	94.0
1926........	10,922,607	8,266,500	2,656,107	97.8	95.9	104.2
1927........	10,908,464	8,182,983	2,725,481	97.7	95.0	106.9
1928........	9,763,331	6,848,088	2,915,243	87.4	79.5	114.3
1929........	10,843,963	7,469,076	3,374,887	97.3	86.6	132.3
1930........	9,561,698	6,866,178	2,695,520	85.6	79.7	105.7
1931........	7,871,392	5,705,140	2,148,252	70.5	66.2	84.3
1932........	6,002,511	4,300,664	1,701,847	53.8	49.9	66.8
1933........	7,858,793	5,957,296	1,901,496	70.4	69.1	74.6

* Data prepared by Twelfth Federal Reserve District, based upon the *Panama Canal Record*.

† Last five months.

which this region draws on Eastern United States sources of supply appear among water-borne receipts. In both directions the more bulky and less perishable products will choose the water route. Since a greater portion of the products of the Pacific Coast fall in these categories than do those of the East, a heavy eastbound balance results. As a matter of fact, transcontinental rail shipments are also unbalanced, and in the same direction.[2] In bulk, then, if not in value, the Pacific Coast region sends more to Eastern United States than it receives.

No statistics are available showing the division of total commodity exchange between the East and the West that is effected by ships in intercoastal trade and by rail across the continent. In chapter vi the writer has hazarded a rough estimate that probably as much as one-half of the combined East-and-West movements are by water. At present the percentage may be even greater, since the intercoastal route is heavily overtonnaged, hence competition is intense and instability in rates very marked. The Intercoastal Shipping Act of 1933, described further in chapter xvii, became effective on March 3, 1933. This law imposes federal regulation upon intercoastal carriers and is held to offer a partial solution of the problems now confronting the railways. This aspect is one which many of the shipping interests are most inclined to fear, although the need for rate regulation of intercoastal carriers is recognized. Although stabilization of the California coastwise trade on a uniform basis for all lines was tentatively achieved in 1933, there is still a certain amount of conflict of jurisdiction and authority among the United States Shipping Board Bureau, the Interstate Commerce Commission, and the California State Railroad Commission.

To reproduce an actual schedule of sailings, with detailed information relative to vessels, lines, ports of departure, and destination, affords the reader a vivid picture of the heavy intercoastal tonnage. A fortnight's record of departures, selected at random, is shown in Table 42 (pp. 238–39).

In 1846 the Oregon boundary dispute with Great Britain was settled, and a treaty was negotiated with New Granada (later Colombia) in which the latter guaranteed transit across the Isthmus to American citizens and American com-

[2] Mr. Edwin Selvin, editor and publisher of the *Business Chronicle* (Seattle), speaking before the Pacific Northwest Advisory Board (March 24, 1933), said that the long haul of empty box and refrigerator cars across the country paralleled loaded ships. He stated that statistics for three years ending with 1931 show that 51.4 per cent of the box cars loaded in the Pacific Northwest were hauled empty from Eastern sources and 7.7 per cent of refrigerators loaded East returned empty: these empty box cars coming West are the equivalent of nine thousand solid trains of approximately sixty cars, each moving without any compensating revenue.

merce on terms equal to those accorded citizens and the commerce of New Granada. Early in 1847, in order to facilitate communication between the Atlantic and the Pacific coasts, Congress authorized two mail contracts between New York and Oregon by way of the Isthmus of Panama, one for service between New York and Chagres, and the other between Panama and Astoria. Special steamships were constructed for these lines. Service began late in 1848, some months after the Mexican peace treaty which ceded California to the United States and after the discovery of gold had started a stampede of fortune seekers to the Pacific Coast.

These events, crowded within two short years, mark the beginning of domestic intercoastal trade. It was a trade born of necessity, since America's new Pacific empire lay beyond two great mountain ranges and an inhospitable desert land. That overland communication was possible had already been proved, but it was arduous. Clearly the sea must help to bind the new to the old. It was a trade destined to become of great significance to the future of the Far West littoral.

Had the California gold rush not coincided so nearly with American territorial acquisitions on the Pacific Coast, the development of intercoastal communications and commerce relations might have been far different. As it was, only eight days intervened between the discovery of gold and the signing of the treaty of Guadalupe Hidalgo. The sudden and tremendous increase in demand for passage to California was an incalculable stimulus to the improvement of facilities, and the progress made contributed substantially to the rapid economic development of the Pacific slope. Migration overland, around the Horn, or across the Isthmus focused the attention of the world on California.

In 1849 some 700 vessels cleared for California from various ports on the Atlantic. Twelve steamers made trips between San Francisco and Panama, a larger number than were employed at that time between New York and Liverpool and New York and Havre combined.[3] Two routes were

[3] Emory R. Johnson and others, *History of Domestic and Foreign Commerce of the United States* (1915), p. 359.

TABLE 42

EASTBOUND INTERCOASTAL SAILINGS (APRIL 16–APRIL 30, 1934)*

| From | | | | | | Vessel | Line | Due | | | | | |
San Francisco	Oakland Alameda Richmond	Los Angeles	Portland	Seattle	Tacoma			New York	Philadelphia	Boston	Albany	Baltimore	Norfolk
April 16	April 14	April 18	……	……	……	"Montanan" ……	American-Hawaiian ……	May 7	May 11	May 14	……	May 11	May 13
April 17	April 16	April 19	……	……	……	"Forbes Hauptman"†	McCormick Line ……	May 10	May 14	……	May 19	May 11	May 13
April 17	April 19	April 17	……	……	……	"Portmar"†§ ……	Calmar Line ……	May 8	May 11	May 14	May 11	May 17	……
April 19	April 18	April 21	……	……	……	"Harry Luckenbach"§	Luckenbach Line ……	May 5	May 11	May 11	……	……	……
April 19	April 17	April 21	……	……	……	"President Lincoln" ……	Dollar Line ……	May 10	May 15	May 18	……	……	……
April 19	April 18	April 21	……	……	……	"Panaman" ……	American-Hawaiian ……	May 11	May 13	May 21	……	……	May 13
April 19	April 18	April 21	……	……	……	"Santa Cecilia"§ ……	Grace Line ……	May 15	May 18	……	……	……	……
April 21	April 21	April 25	……	……	……	"Texan" ……	American-Hawaiian ……	May 17	May 21	……	……	……	May 20
April 23	……	April 26	April 17	……	April 14	"EleanorChristenson"	Arrow Line ……	May 13	……	……	……	……	……
April 24	April 23	April 26	April 19	April 14	April 14	"Losmar"§ ……	Calmar Line ……	May 24	May 16	May 19	……	May 24	……
April 24	April 23	April 26	April 18	April 14	April 14	"Lillian Luckenbach"†	Luckenbach Line ……	May 26	May 30	May 20	……	……	……
April 26	April 24	April 28	April 21	……	……	"Heffron" ……	Weyerhauser Line ……	May 31	June 6	……	……	June 3	June 5
April 26	April 25	April 28	……	April 18	April 18	"San Angelo" ……	Quaker Line ……	May 18	……	……	……	May 19	May 23
April 26	April 28	April 28	April 20	April 17	……	"American Star"† ……	Nelson Line ……	……	……	……	May 29	May 29	May 31
April 26	April 24	April 28	April 17	April 14	April 11	"Willhilo" ……	Williams Line ……	……	……	……	……	……	……
April 26	April 25	April 28	……	April 19	April 16	"Alaskan" ……	American-Hawaiian ……	May 15	May 22	May 25	……	May 27	……
April 27	April 26	April 28	April 23	April 23	……	"Santa Paula"§ ……	Grace Line ……	May 14	May 19	……	……	……	……
April 28	April 30	April 30	……	……	……	"California" ……	Panama Line ……	……	……	May 22	……	……	……
April 28	April 27	April 30	April 24	April 16	……	"Santa Cecilia"† ……	Argonaut Line ……	May 30	……	……	May 30	May 22	May 24
April 28	April 27	April 30	April 21	April 19	April 19	"West Cape"† ……	McCormick Line ……	May 18	May 21	May 24	……	……	……
April 29	April 28	May 1	April 23	April 19	April 19	"Lena Luckenbach"§ ……	Luckenbach Line ……	……	May 25	May 28	……	……	……
April 30	April 28	May 2	April 20	……	……	"Mexican" ……	American-Hawaiian ……	May 21	……	……	……	……	……

* Data from *Pacific Shipper*, April 16, 1934. Consult Appendix A, "Directory of West Coast Services," which omits non-passenger vessels.
† Loads Stockton. "Lillian Luckenbach" calls at Manhattan. § Calls Manhattan.

For Jacksonville, Fla., and Savanna, Ga.: "American Star," Nelson Line, and "Eleanor Christenson," Arrow Line, call here.
For New London, Conn.: "Willhilo," Williams Line, and "Sage Brush," Shepard Line, call here.
For Wilmington, N.C.: "Willhilo" and "Willboro," Williams Line, call here.
For Charleston, S.C.: "American Star," Nelson Line, "Alaskan" and "Missourian," American-Hawaiian Line, call here.
For Port Newark, N.J.: "Montanan," "Panaman," "Mexican," American-Hawaiian Line; "Portmar" and "Pennmar," Calmar Line; and "Sage Brush," Shepard Line, call here.
For Trenton, N.J.: "Heffron," Weyerhäuser Line, calls here.
For Bridgeport, Conn.: "San Angelo," Quaker Line, and "Willhilo," Williams Line, call here.
For Providence, R.I.: "Horace Luckenbach," Luckenbach Line, calls here.
For Portland, Me.: "Santa Cecilia," Argonaut Line, calls here.

GULF EASTBOUND SAILINGS

| From | | | | | | Vessel | Line | Due | | | | | |
San Francisco	Oakland	Alameda	Stockton	Los Angeles	Portland	Seattle			New Orleans	Houston	Mobile	Beaumont	Corpus Christi	Tampa
April 14	April 16	April 17	April 13	April 19	....	....	"Point Clear"....	Gulf Pacific....	May 7	May 11	May 15	....	....	May 18
April 24	April 23	April 23	....	April 26	....	....	"Robin Adair"..	Luckenbach	May 14	May 18	May 22	....	....	....
April 28	April 30	May 1	....	May 3	April 14	April 20	"Point Salinas"..	Gulf Pacific	May 21	May 25	June 1	....	May 28	....

followed across the Isthmus, one across Panama and one across Nicaragua.[4] The latter soon became the more popular as it cut several hundred miles from the journey. Still another route, by sea to Corpus Christi or Vera Cruz and thence overland across Mexico, was attempted by some hardy but poorly informed travelers, many of whom paid with their lives for the rashness of the undertaking.

No official statistics on the volume of intercoastal commerce moving around the Horn and across the Isthmus exist for the years between the beginning of such trade and the completion of the Panama Canal, but the early volumes of *Foreign Commerce and Navigation of the United States* contain data on the value of goods shipped between New York and San Francisco via the Isthmus of Panama; figures are likewise available, beginning with 1886, showing the movement of vessels between Atlantic and Pacific ports via Cape Horn. These incomplete returns provide the only basis for judging the status of intercoastal trade before August 15, 1914.

In marked contrast to the situation today, early coast-to-coast commerce was predominantly westbound. The Far West was then in that pioneer stage of development characterized by heavy dependence upon other regions, and there was little surplus to offer the more advanced Atlantic seaboard states.

The record of vessel movement between Atlantic and Pacific ports during the thirty years in which such data were reported shows that this trade route varied widely in importance from year to year, particularly in the Pacific-to-Atlantic movement (Table 43). In neither direction was there apparent any well-defined trend toward increase or diminution of ship tonnage. In most years, a large proportion of ships entering Pacific Coast ports from the North Atlantic seaboard did not return by the same route. Half or more of them are reported to have cleared for Europe,

---

[4] A railroad was started across Panama in 1850 and five years later was completed. Another had been projected by Mexico across the Isthmus of Tehuantepec as early as 1824, but a crossing at this point was not completed until 1894, far too late to share in the beginnings of intercoastal communications.

whence they returned to the United States,[5] like the old Northwest traders of the sea-otter era, following approximately the same routes as the clipper ships of a later period.

TABLE 43

VESSEL TONNAGE BETWEEN ATLANTIC AND PACIFIC PORTS OF THE
UNITED STATES VIA CAPE HORN, 1886–1916*

Year	Entering Pacific Ports	Leaving Pacific Ports
1886	67,660	16,843
1891	98,996	23,812
1896	71,090	53,143
1901	49,668	6,650
1906	76,983	62,595
1911	72,050	17,780
1916	55,127	64,567

* Excluding trade of Hawaii. Source: Bureau of Foreign and Domestic Commerce.

Reports of intercoastal traffic following the Isthmus route, in terms of value of cargo rather than of ship tons, show a similar disproportion between westbound and eastbound traffic. Following the completion of the first transcontinental railway in 1869, there was an apparent decline in the movement, particularly in the westbound direction. The railroads made available a better means of transporting the relatively high-grade products moving from Eastern states to the Pacific Coast, but they were not able to make similar inroads on the eastbound traffic via Panama inasmuch as it consisted largely of low-grade commodities dependent upon cheap water transportation for profitable distribution.

After the turn of the century both westbound and eastbound traffic increased, although the former did not entirely recover lost ground until the American-Hawaiian Steamship Company transferred its services from the Magellan route to the Isthmus of Tehuantepec, utilizing the Tehuantepec Railway for transfer of cargo from ocean to ocean. This

[5] Emory R. Johnson, *Panama Canal Traffic and Tolls* (1912), p. 34.

change greatly stimulated traffic in both directions. In the fiscal year 1912 the total westbound domestic traffic over both Isthmian routes amounted to about $54,000,000, or twice the value of the eastbound traffic.[6] In the Johnson report on Panama Canal Traffic and Tolls, a comprehensive tabulation of intercoastal water traffic of the United States is presented for the years 1906 to 1911 (see Table 44). According to this research, which contains the best available estimates of the traffic movement for those years, there was a 100 per cent increase from 1906 to 1911 in the tonnage of water-borne cargo moving between Atlantic and Pacific ports of the United States, including Hawaii. In the earlier years this traffic is estimated to have amounted to 560,000 tons, augmented five years later to 1,100,000 tons. Excluding the trade in Hawaiian sugar the cargo movement for the two years was 470,000 and 800,000 tons, respectively, of which the American-Hawaiian Steamship Line alone is reported to have handled in 1911 nearly one-half the total cargo tonnage. Johnson made an extensive study of the probable utilization of the Canal then under construction, taking foreign-trade routes into consideration as well as the intercoastal movement. It was estimated that over 8,000,000 net tons of shipping would have utilized the Canal had it been in service in 1909–1910.[7]

During the past decade the principal commodities leaving American Pacific ports for foreign destinations are likewise, for the most part, the leading commodities entering

[6] These records, however, are not strictly comparable with those for years prior to 1907, since they include domestic intercoastal movement at all Atlantic and Pacific ports instead of merely the movement between New York and San Francisco. These two ports, of course, were outstanding in intercoastal traffic throughout the pre-Canal period. A considerable intercoastal traffic with Hawaii also developed as a result of this new route, which is not included in the foregoing figures. For details, see *Foreign Commerce and Navigation of the United States,* 1907 to 1912, inclusive. These data do not appear in annual volumes after 1912.

[7] Refer to chapter vi, "Effects of the Panama Canal," which includes a great deal of relevant information. It is interesting to note the estimated relative importance of the several routes, and to compare these magnitudes with those now being recorded annually in the reports on the Panama Canal. Noteworthy is the extent to which the intercoastal movement after the completion of this waterway exceeded the most careful estimates.

TABLE 44

VOLUME OF INTERCOASTAL WATER TRAFFIC, 1906–1911*

(Tons of freight)

	1906	1907	1908	1909	1910	1911
Total coastwise traffic of Panama Railroad†	50,851	42,229	38,420	46,823	79,876	211,928
Atlantic to Pacific	25,914	26,944	23,258	38,095	46,394	96,420
Pacific to Atlantic	24,937	15,285	15,162	8,728	33,482	115,508
Coastwise traffic of Panama Railroad Steamship Line,‡ total	50,803	42,144	38,263	46,610	79,876	172,499
New York to Colon	25,866	26,859	23,131	37,910	46,394	66,922
Colon to New York	24,937	15,285	15,132	8,700	33,482	105,577
Coastwise traffic of Pacific Mail,‡ total	50,803	42,144	38,263	46,610	79,876	76,972
Atlantic to Pacific	25,866	26,859	23,131	37,910	46,394	29,080
Pacific to Atlantic	24,937	15,285	15,132	8,700	33,482	47,892
California-Atlantic Steamship Line (Pacific service),‡ total	.....	.....	.....	.....	.....	134,545
Atlantic to Pacific	.....	.....	.....	.....	.....	67,332
Pacific to Atlantic	.....	.....	.....	.....	.....	67,213
California-Atlantic Steamship Line (Atlantic service,‡ total	.....	.....	.....	.....	.....	39,018
Philadelphia to Colon	.....	.....	.....	.....	.....	28,488
Colon to Philadelphia	.....	.....	.....	.....	.....	5,487
New Orleans to Colon	.....	.....	.....	.....	.....	1,002
Colon to New Orleans	.....	.....	.....	.....	.....	4,041
American-Hawaiian Steamship Line,§ total (excluding Hawaiian sugar)	146,900	145,900	144,200	312,400	306,700	458,300
New York to Pacific ports	114,900	131,900	117,200	229,200	247,100	295,800
Pacific ports to New York	32,000	14,000	27,000	83,200	59,600	162,500
Hawaiian sugar	91,700	198,300	242,700	248,100	244,300	296,600
Tonnage via Cape Horn and Straits of Magellan,¶ vessel tonnage (entrances plus clearances), total	310,030	273,775	215,907	85,694	172,655	157,608
Atlantic to Pacific	169,787	191,432	159,725	52,873	117,147	117,007
Pacific to Atlantic	140,243	82,343	56,182	32,821	55,508	40,601
Approximate freight carried**	271,276	239,553	188,918	74,982	151,073	137,907
Total line traffic (excluding Hawaiian sugar)††	197,703	188,044	182,463	359,010	386,576	669,817
Total tramp vessel traffic‡‡	271,324	239,638	89,075	75,195	151,073	138,318
Total water traffic (excluding Hawaiian sugar)§§	469,027	427,682	371,538	434,205	537,649	808,135
Total water traffic (including Hawaiian sugar)	560,727	625,982	614,238	682,305	781,949	1,104,735

* Data from Emory R. Johnson, *Panama Canal Traffic and Tolls* (1912), pp. 50–51.　　　　　　　　　　† Annual Reports of Panama Railroad Co.

‡ Statement of E. A. Drake, vice-president Panama Railroad Co.

§ Statement of American-Hawaiian Steamship Co.

¶ United States Commerce and Navigation Reports, 1906–1911.

** Assuming 1¾ tons of freight for one net vessel ton, and dividing by 2, since each ship is counted twice—once as an entrance and once as a clearance.

†† Traffic of Panama Railroad Steamship Line, Pacific Mail, California-Atlantic, and American-Hawaiian Line.　　　　　‡‡ Total water traffic less total line traffic.

§§ Coastwise Panama Railroad traffic plus American-Hawaiian traffic plus traffic via Cape Horn and the Straits of Magellan.

into eastbound domestic intercoastal traffic. Those specialized products which the Pacific States produce in excess of local requirements find a ready market in the more densely populated and more highly industrialized sections of the

TABLE 45

INTERCOASTAL TRAFFIC OF UNITED STATES PACIFIC COAST WITH
PRINCIPAL ATLANTIC AND GULF PORTS, 1925–1930*

(Thousand long tons)

	Fiscal Years					
	1925	1926	1927	1928	1929	1930
Inbound, total	2,171	2,345	2,610	2,382	2,989	2,934
From Atlantic, total	1,863	2,032	2,250	2,029	2,475	2,312
Portland, Maine	11	10	24	25	27	23
Baltimore	627	766	821	746	940	833
Boston	77	88	103	89	102	90
Newark, New Jersey	90	101	...†	...†	...†	...†
New York	516	458	613	557	662	627
Norfolk, Virginia	97	58	56	59	73	63
Philadelphia	378	462	555	495	594	586
Jacksonville	34	12	9	10	17	23
From Gulf, total	308	314	360	353	514	621
Galveston	30	32	33	36	41	65
Mobile	135	112	112	120	206	297
New Orleans	94	106	140	110	166	141
Outbound, total	6,724	6,925	7,558	7,291	6,908	7,192
To Altantic, total	6,478	6,531	7,341	7,005	6,515	6,715
Portland, Maine	8	7	19	18	29	66
Baltimore	511	738	1,016	1,017	988	973
Boston	421	597	523	581	496	516
Fall River	247	481	219	119	...‡	41
Marcus Hook, Pennsylvania	71	19	10	17	13	...‡
Newark, New Jersey	90	116	...†	...†	...†	...†
New York	3,871	2,963	3,822	3,400	3,131	3,371
Norfolk, Virginia	33	35	67	124	60	80
Philadelphia	790	1,004	1,082	1,198	1,084	1,114
Poughkeepsie	76	71	69	99	76	83
Providence, Rhode Island	101	140	288	237	236	155
Charleston, South Carolina	87	68	37	42	34	31
Jacksonville	66	75	42	11	23	14
To Gulf, total	246	294	217	286	393	477
Galveston	19	11	17	4	4	3
Houston	18	38	55	50	69	109
Mobile	25	23	24	38	29	26
New Orleans	122	91	78	111	225	183

* Data from United States Shipping Board.

† Not listed separately, included in New York.   ‡ Not listed separately.

East. To some extent, also, outbound intercoastal traffic resembles inbound foreign traffic, since Pacific ports serve as a gateway for products from transpacific regions which are destined for Eastern markets via intercoastal carriers.

Principal commodities by weight in United States intercoastal trade for the year 1930 from the Pacific to the Atlantic were: mineral oil 46.1 per cent, lumber and hardwoods 30.0 per cent, canned foods 7.6 per cent, all other 16.3 per cent. Briefly, this presents the picture, as it exists today, of the distribution of outbound cargo traffic via Panama from the United States Pacific ports destined for the Eastern seaboard.

Petroleum products account for half or more of the volume of export trade from the Pacific Coast and for not far from half the water-borne intercoastal cargoes. In the record fiscal year 1927, for instance, somewhat more than half the volume of domestic traffic passing through the Panama Canal from the Pacific Coast of the United States to Atlantic and Gulf ports consisted of shipments of petroleum products.[8] Were it not for this one item, the traffic would be well balanced, since total receipts at three Pacific ports are approximately half their volume of shipments. Los Angeles, because of this heavy petroleum movement, greatly outranks all other Pacific ports in the weight of intercoastal

[8] Figures of intercoastal traffic published by the Panama Canal do not agree with those issued by the United States Shipping Board. The latter appear to be consistently smaller than the former. This may be accounted for in part by the fact that the movement of cargo in vessels under 100 gross tons is not included in the Shipping Board tabulation. In 1926, however, there appears to be a difference of a million tons in the intercoastal movement of petroleum as reported by the two governmental agencies. Such a wide divergence is hard to explain in view of the fact that both figures cover the fiscal year and both are in terms of long tons. Ordinarily very little petroleum would move in vessels under 100 gross tons. Figures for individual commodities reported by the *Panama Canal Record* might be expected to be smaller than Shipping Board figures for the reason that the former include a large class designated only as general cargo—"shipments of various goods are likely to be in excess of the aggregate tonnage of those reported during the year and shown in the annual summary because there is a natural tendency not to list small miscellaneous shipments, but to include these under the head of 'general cargo'; not infrequently no other classification is made of entire cargoes carried by vessels." (*Annual Report* of the Governor of the Panama Canal, 1929.)

traffic handled; in intercoastal receipts, likewise, Los Angeles stands first among Western seaboard ports.

Outbound intercoastal trade further resembles foreign-export cargoes from the Coast in that lumber ranks second in volume of shipments. The lumber movement has been well above two million long tons in each of the last four years. Many of the formerly great lumber-producing regions of the United States east of the Mississippi River have been sadly depleted and as a result this country is heavily dependent upon the forest resources of the Northwest. Participating in this trade are several North Pacific ports which ship little or nothing else. Grays Harbor and Everett, for example, now outrank all other Pacific ports in intercoastal lumber shipments (see Appendix Table VI). Together they accounted for approximately two-fifths of the total lumber movement during the fiscal year 1930.

Closely associated with the lumber industry is the wood-pulp and paper industry, which has attained prominence in foreign trade. Products of this industry are also rapidly increasing in importance among outgoing intercoastal cargoes. In 1930, paper and paper-pulp shipments together amounted to nearly 175,000 long tons (see Appendix Table IV).

Outlets for the surplus food products of the rich agricultural sections of the American Pacific region are found in Eastern domestic markets as well as in foreign countries. The tonnage of all food products shipped to Eastern United States from Pacific ports at the present time constitutes from 12 to 15 per cent of the entire movement, and the recent trend appears upward. Taking into account also the large volume of food moving east by rail, it becomes perfectly clear that the Pacific area is an important source of the nation's food supply.

Comparatively small quantities of perishable foodstuffs move by water, since the time factor is of sufficient importance to justify the more expensive transcontinental rail haul; however, canned foods of all kinds travel domestically via Panama and in even greater volume than they are shipped abroad (see Appendix Table VI). Dried fruits are also sent eastward in large amounts by the water route.

Sugar, shipped raw from Hawaii to the mainland for refining, is another commodity which moves in substantial volume by freighters to Eastern markets. While considerable
amounts of grain and flour are sent from the Pacific to the
Atlantic in domestic commerce, the relative importance of
these products is very much less on this route than in foreign
trade because of the immense grain-producing regions of
the central plains and the wide distribution of wheat-growing lands throughout the nation.

Now turning attention to the nature of intercoastal receipts in Pacific ports, the Atlantic-to-Pacific movement via
Panama, one finds that in some respects incoming cargoes
from Atlantic and Gulf ports of the United States resemble
the general character of all imports. For the past few fiscal
years the volume of receipts from the two sources has been
almost the same. In general, commodities received by the
intercoastal route include fewer raw or semi-raw materials,
and not many for which the United States depends on tropical and Oriental sources.

A few specific items and one broad group of commodities
stand out in the Atlantic-to-Pacific intercoastal traffic. In
1930, principal commodities or commodity groups according
to weight were as follows: iron and steel 41.8 per cent, tin
plate 4.4 per cent, sulphur 3.6 per cent, paper 2.3 per cent,
all other 47.9 per cent. This general distribution indicates
the approximate relative importance of various items in the
trade today.

The most important broad group of commodities supplied
by Eastern United States is that which embraces metal
manufactures of all sorts. Iron and steel products, including
railway materials and scrap, move inward at the rate of
well over a million long tons annually, a volume which
accounts for over one-third the weight of all intercoastal
receipts. Included in this category are structural shapes and
other iron and steel manufactures used primarily in public
works and building construction.

Related to iron and steel products is the considerable
item of tin plate, the receipts of which have been rapidly
increasing. Before 1928 this item was not reported separately; between 1928 and 1930 intercoastal receipts increased

from 48,000 to 140,000 tons. Tin plate is used in the manufacture of tin containers for canned foods and petroleum products, and the growth in shipments from the Atlantic is a reflection of the demand created by these expanding industries on the Coast.[9]

Among the more highly manufactured forms of metal products brought to the Pacific States from the Atlantic and the Gulf are automobiles and accessories and miscellaneous machinery and implements. In recent years these products have supplied approximately 100,000 long tons of cargo annually to carriers. In 1930 the volume of receipts at Pacific ports was 120,000 tons (see Table 7, pp. 39–40).

Over 100,000 long tons (1929–30) of additional incoming intercoastal shipments are accounted for by sulphur, most of it originating at Gulf ports and destined principally for the horticultural districts of the West Coast.

Despite the fact that the Pacific Coast produces such a large percentage of the nation's petroleum it also receives mineral-oil products in intercoastal trade. This movement, amounting to almost 100,000 tons in 1930, mostly from North Atlantic ports, is due to the Coast demand for special grades of Eastern oils which have a paraffine rather than the asphaltic base characteristic of Western oils.

Except for a certain amount of wool manufacture in Oregon and some jute, the textile industry is relatively undeveloped on the Pacific Coast and therefore must depend upon outside supplies to satisfy regional needs. Intercoastal carriers bring large amounts of textiles to the Coast, supplies which are supplemented by imports from abroad, although in time this industry doubtless will assume considerable importance on the Pacific seaboard.

Another commodity, lumber, of which the Pacific Coast produces an immense exportable surplus, is also shipped in from Atlantic and Gulf ports. This movement, however, is small in comparison with outbound lumber cargoes, and, as

---

[9] California has long been the leading producer of canned foods, especially fruits, in the United States. Oregon and Washington are also important states for the canning of fruits and berries. Washington, Alaska, and California together account for a large portion of the domestic production of canned sea products.

in the case of lumber imports from Asia, consists largely of hardwoods in which Pacific forests are deficient. Paper also is brought in intercoastal vessels, although much more is shipped out on this route. Some of this cross-hauling represents specialization in different kinds and grades of paper.

Although Atlantic ports send some coal each year to the Pacific Coast, the amount is not increasing because of the local presence of substitute sources of energy, petroleum, natural gas, and hydroelectric power. There are good coal deposits in Washington, also in Colorado, Utah, Wyoming, and British Columbia.

Likewise, as in the instance of petroleum, sugar, paper, lumber, and many other products, there is some criss-crossing of canned-food shipments. Certain kinds of canned fruits and vegetables produced near the Atlantic seaboard find markets in the Pacific area. Receipts of canned foods from the East by the Panama route amounted to 81,000 tons in 1929 and 74,000 tons in 1930. Eastbound shipments of canned products, it will be remembered, are in excess of a half-billion long tons annually.

Commodities and groups of commodities mentioned above arriving at Pacific ports from regions tributary to Atlantic and Gulf ports by no means exhaust the list of those included in the total of this movement. In fact they do not account for much more than two-thirds of the total volume. As we ascertained in chapter vii, statistics of intercoastal traffic in terms of value are not available. Included also in this traffic are a large number of miscellaneous products moving in relatively small amounts, some of them itemized in the reports of the Panama Canal, some grouped together as general cargo. Individually, most of these commodities are not important; collectively, however, they are so numerous and varied that they constitute a substantial portion of total intercoastal receipts from the Atlantic and Gulf sections.

The Pacific Coastwise Schedule, which appears currently in the *Shipping Register,* lists regular sailings by the following lines: American-Hawaiian Line, Chamberlin Steamship Company, Grace Line, Kingsley Company of California, Los Angeles Steamship Company, Luckenbach Line, Los Angeles and San Francisco Navigation Company, Los Angeles—

Long Beach Dispatch Line, McCormick Steamship Company, Pacific Coast Direct Line, Inc., Pacific Steamship Lines, South Coast Steamship Company, Sudden & Christenson. Information relative to intercoastal sailings appears in Appendix A.

Another class of water-borne commerce bulks very large in the region's total tonnage of maritime trade (which does not involve commercial relations outside of the United States). This is the coastwise trade, or the shipments between American ports situated between the Canadian and the Mexican borders. Although an exchange of goods between Pacific States and Alaska is designated officially as noncontiguous trade, in principle it might be classed also as coastwise trade.[10] In any event, the writer has chosen to include maritime commerce with the territory of Alaska in this category, just as he considered Alaska and Hawaii along with California, Oregon, and Washington as comprising the American Pacific States region.

While coastwise trade dominates Pacific maritime cargoes, judged solely on the basis of tonnage, there are no official statistics showing the commodity movement.[11] Although representing 65 per cent of the total traffic, it does not have a corresponding economic importance to the Pacific States region; hence, for this reason and the fact that official statistics are nonexistent, this trade will be considered here only briefly. In chapter viii, where the business of individual ports of the Coast was discussed, there was much more to say on this subject.

Since 1925 coastwise commerce of the Pacific Coast has apparently fluctuated within fairly narrow limits around 50,000,000 long tons annually. The data suggest normally a

---

[10] The writer has chosen to consider trade between the mainland and the Hawaiian Islands, also a noncontiguous trade, in connection with transpacific commerce in chapter xiii. But the reader should be advised that a very frequent "ferry" service and a combined trade reaching into the two-hundred-million-dollar class might perhaps more properly be treated in the present chapter.

[11] The figures published by the Board of Engineers for Rivers and Harbors, as previously explained, do not distinguish between intercoastal traffic, coastwise traffic, and trade with noncontiguous territory.

slight upward trend in the volume of these movements, since such an increase appears to be in line with developments in Pacific maritime commerce generally.

Coastwise commerce cannot be unbalanced, since the shipments of one Pacific port will, barring wreck, be the receipts of another.[12] For this reason, the total of 50,000,000 tons is twice the actual volume of goods exchanged. As far as individual ports are concerned, incoming and outgoing coastwise commerce must both be counted. From the standpoint of the volume of goods transported and of the commercial transactions to which that transportation was incident, the figure of 25,000,000 tons seems clearly correct for Pacific coastwise trade of the United States.

In view of the limitations in coastwise-trade data, it becomes necessary to turn to reports of traffic at the several localities published by local port and harbor authorities or Chambers of Commerce. Since only the largest ports compile and publish such information, the picture which they provide is necessarily incomplete, but it is probably sufficiently representative to indicate in a general way the commodities moving by the water route from one Pacific Coast port to another.

Los Angeles ships comparatively little in coastwise trade outside of mineral-oil products. The largest single item not included in that category is oranges, and the largest group of related products is vegetable foodstuffs. Even this foodstuff group, however, does not constitute as much in weight as one per cent of the petroleum shipments.

In Seattle's coastwise commerce, as in her foreign and intercoastal shipments, flour, grain, and lumber bulk large, but they do not occupy the same outstanding position in coastwise as in other trades. Paper shipments are also heavy,

---

[12] It is interesting to note in Appendix Table VI that coastwise receipts at Pacific ports are consistently much larger than coastwise shipments. No satisfactory explanation of this curious showing occurs to the writer, and none is offered by the responsible government agency. Shipments are en route for short voyages. Pilferage and other losses would tend to make receipts smaller than shipments. If the difference were one of value it could be accounted for by a practice of adding transport and other handling costs to outbound cargoes.

as are those of canned goods and potatoes. In general, there is a relatively greater diversification in this movement than in the other categories of outbound trade.

In the coastwise trade of Tacoma, lumber plays a dominating part, while grain and grain products and canned fruits and vegetables account for the major portion of the remainder. Coastwise shipments from Portland to a considerable extent resemble in commodity make-up those from Puget Sound. At both ports lumber ranks first in volume, with flour, canned goods, and paper accounting for a large share of the balance. In consequence, Washington and Oregon have very little maritime exchange, but each state has considerable water-borne commerce with California, whose surpluses are in the main different from those of the Northwest.[13]

Finally, the trade of the Pacific States with Alaska needs comment. In the last six calendar years the volume of water-borne commerce (other than that purely local) of Alaska has ranged from 700 to 800 thousand tons. In spite of unfavorable world economic conditions, Alaska enjoyed a somewhat greater commerce in 1930 than in any year covered by the author's data. Most of this trade is with the Pacific Coast states, particularly Puget Sound ports. The exchange is remarkably evenly balanced, i.e., Alaska sends annually to the United States, in cargo-tonnage, approximately as much as she receives.

In both quantity and value the most important commodity in Alaskan trade is fish, the total value of which is several times as great as that of its mineral shipments. Salmon alone constitutes about 90 per cent of the former. In the last two years, taken together, more than $83,000,000 worth of fish and fish products have been sent southward, mainly to Pacific States ports, out of an aggregate of $128,000,000 of all shipments. Metals, chiefly copper and gold, account for most of the remaining values.

---

[13] Statistics, official or otherwise, relating to the commodity make-up of coastwise shipments from and to San Francisco are not available, but it is probable that this trade, like the foreign trade of San Francisco, is more diversified than that of other Pacific ports.

Shipments from Pacific ports to Alaska are very much more diverse than they are in any other trade except that of Hawaii. Relatively undeveloped industrially, Alaska exhibits economic activities highly specialized along a few lines for which natural resources give it peculiar advantages. Consequently, the territory is far from self-sufficient and per capita trade is high. The scanty population makes a modest demand for a wide variety of general merchandise. In fact one of the important elements in the growth of Seattle is that it serves as a center of activity for supplies of this character destined for Alaska.

XI. Ocean Traffic with Canada and Latin America

Maritime trade with Canada, Mexico, Central America, and, to a lesser extent, South America can properly be classed under coastal traffic, since scant distinction is made between this type of business and domestic cargoes discussed in the last chapter. American vessels operating on the Pacific littoral or serving Atlantic and Gulf ports of the United States normally call at one or more foreign ports. Lines operating between continental United States and Alaska touch ports in British Columbia. The trade of the Americas, however, can be distinguished according to its domestic and its foreign character; therefore attention drawn to the salient features in the coast commerce with Canada and Latin America is helpful in understanding the economic developments taking place in California, Oregon, and Washington. American relations with Canada and Latin America are continually becoming closer.

While the European Continent still dominates the foreign commerce of the United States, its relative importance is decreasing, a change which can be explained by new trade contacts with the countries on the continents of Asia and America. Political changes in Cuba following the Spanish-American War, discovery of oil in Mexico, growth in the industrial development and expansion in the buying-power of Canada, and the increasing capacity of the United States to consume vast quantities of commodities like sugar and tropical fruits, which were formerly in the luxury class, have all contributed to this change in commodity trends. It is noticeable, too, that the greatest increase in trade occurs with countries closest geographically to the United States.

Highly important to the Pacific Coast region is western Canada, although Latin-American countries are becoming more and more prominent in its maritime trade. Latin America, however, is a broad term used to include Mexico and Central American countries as well as all of South America. Similar in trend to the foreign commerce in the United States, the export trade of the Pacific Coast to South America has expanded greatly, while the proportion of imports received from the continent to the south has remained almost stationary for half a century.

Of the total United States water-borne trade with Pacific Canada, all except a comparatively small amount is handled through Pacific ports. In every year since 1922 the exchange of commodities between Pacific ports of the United States and those of British Columbia has amounted to more than a million long tons, and in 1930 it passed two million tons (Table 11, p. 59). In volume, Pacific Canada ranks among the three most important trade regions in the foreign commerce of the Pacific States. In some years this district has ranked second, exceeding the trade volume with the United Kingdom. Although the trend in volume of imports from Pacific Canada has been upward, the rate of growth between 1923 and 1930 has been considerably less than that of exports.[1]

British Columbia is the only foreign region in this hemisphere sending a much larger volume of non-tanker cargoes to American Pacific ports than it receives. Total traffic between the ports above and below the international boundary line is fairly well balanced, but the elimination of tanker exports from United States ports leaves a heavy surplus of southbound cargo. In recent years, non-tanker imports from Pacific Canada have been some four or five times the volume of non-tanker exports to that region.

Obviously, then, petroleum exports constitute a very high percentage of the entire northward movement. In 1929 and 1930, tanker exports (nearly all petroleum) and exports of petroleum in packages accounted for 85 per cent by weight of all exports from American Pacific ports to those of British Columbia. Expansion of this trade has been more rapid than that in other export cargoes, and hence has been responsible for most of the increase in total exports to Pacific Canada between 1922 and 1930.

In addition to petroleum, a considerable number of miscellaneous products are shipped north, including iron

[1] Imports in 1922 were less than half those for 1923 and less than one-third those for 1924, so that an abnormal and unrepresentative increase would be indicated by making comparisons with statistics of the earlier year.

and steel manufactures, pigments, and chemicals. Both groups of commodities appear to be moving in increasing volume, but still this trade is so small that it is not of great importance. Some coal and coke, as well as lumber, are also exported to Canada, although the southbound movement in these same products is much larger. In the foodstuffs group, fruits and nuts are the principal items shipped from American to Canadian Pacific ports.

In view of the unequaled lumber resources of the American side of the border, it is somewhat surprising to note among imports from all foreign countries that lumber outranks all others on the basis of tonnage.[2] This leadership has been maintained without interruption for a decade.[3] The major portion of the lumber imports, and half or more of the imports of paper stock, enter Pacific ports of the United States from British Columbia, and are thus essentially a part of the great lumber industry of the Pacific Northwest.

Although the Pacific district of the United States is rapidly increasing its production and outward shipment of lumber and lumber products, paper continues to be imported in substantial quantities. In this total the mills of British Columbia are figuring more prominently than ever. Another explanation for the large inbound movement of these derivatives of the lumber industry is the heavy investment of American Coast capital in Canadian raw-material industries. From British Columbia come, therefore, both important lumber and paper imports, in itself a testimony to the international character of resources which extend over an area through which a national boundary line happens to run. The three items, lumber, paper stock, and paper, have aggregated not far from half the total volume of receipts at American Pacific ports from British Columbia since 1922 (Table 46). The significant statement has been made by a

[2] It should be remembered that the Coast region is deficient in most kinds of hardwoods, which must be shipped in from Eastern United States or from abroad to supply the growing furniture industry of the Coast. Virtually all lumber imports not coming from Canada originate in East Asia, mainly the Philippines; from these regions come mahogany and other cabinet woods.

[3] If paper stock (including pulp wood and wood pulp) be added, the lumber movement has exceeded other imports in weight since 1923.

leading banker of British Columbia, Mr. F. B. Fowler, to the effect that one out of every two newspapers published in the United States is printed on Canadian-made paper.

TABLE 46

VOLUME OF FOREIGN TRADE OF UNITED STATES PACIFIC COAST WITH PACIFIC CANADA, BY COMMODITIES, 1922–1930*

(Thousand long tons)

Commodities	1922	1923	1924	1925	1926	1927	1928	1929	1930
Exports—Total	373	555	659	688	742	879	961	1,058	1,186
Tanker cargoes	300	420	477	499	588	710	772	831	998
Petroleum in packages	+	19	62	22	3	11	35	56	43
Coal and coke	+	7	12	25	41	19	12	14	11
Logs and lumber	+	6	16	5	6	5	27	31	17
Fruits and nuts	9	14	13	16	14	15	16	16	13
Iron, steel, and manufactures	...	+	1	1	+	6	10	9	20
Pigments, chemicals, etc.	3	5	4	6	6	6	7	9	10
Imports—Total	279	614	915	871	882	977	884	872	871
Logs and lumber	60	240	417	321	305	329	285	278	335
Paper stock (including pulpwood)	9	16	16	23	27	22	21	30	36
Paper and manufactures	63	91	101	96	93	99	89	65	83
Coal and coke	52	80	65	89	92	88	70	64	59
Ores, metals, and manufactures	44	103	197	226	235	261	270	232	214
Animal, fish, and dairy products	4	26	19	34	24	20	15	9	11

* Data from United States Shipping Board. Not all commodities shown.

By raising recently the American tariff on lumber, the United States cut off almost completely British Columbia's largest export market for merchantable lumber shipments— the Atlantic Coast and California. The trade was faced with the problem of replacing this lost market, and has been fortunate in having two factors which contributed to a successful solution of the problem within the short space of one year: the political aid of preferential tariffs in Australia and Great Britain, and the economic aid of a vigorous market-extension campaign.

The Canadian-Pacific region is likewise an important source of copper and other ores and metals. Until recent years, total imports of metallic minerals into the American Pacific States increased steadily and averaged 100 per cent greater in 1928–1930 than in 1922–1924. Among raw and semi-raw materials, ores and metals are now second in im-

portance from the standpoint of weight in the imports. Like
the imports from British Columbia alone, imports of these
products from all sources have approximately doubled during the period between 1922–1924 and 1928–1930. For the
earlier period this average was slightly above 150,000 tons,
for the later nearly 290,000 tons. Imports of this type bear
witness to the growing industrialization of California, Oregon, and Washington, an industrialization which as yet,
however, is in too early a stage to find an important place
in outgoing commerce of fabricated products.

Centered at Tacoma, however, is one metal industry of
real importance to the Pacific Coast. This is the copper industry, drawing ores and crude copper mainly from Alaska,
Pacific Canada, Australia, and the west coast of South
America. Imports of copper into Tacoma alone have averaged well above 200,000 long tons in recent years, while the
value of crude copper imports into the Washington customs
district reached $20,000,000 in 1929.[4] The subsequent exports
of refined copper from Tacoma are heavy.

Canadian coal fields still supply a substantial volume of
cargo to ships sailing from British Columbia to Pacific ports
of the United States, but there is no apparent tendency for
this movement to increase. Imports of coal and coke were
formerly of much greater significance in Pacific maritime
commerce, both relatively and absolutely, than they are
at present. Dwindling receipts of these fuels are readily explained by the increased use of petroleum for both transport
and industry and by the development of hydroelectric power.

British Columbia is the principal coaling area on the
Pacific Coast, but the shipping now regularly serving Pacific
ports relies mainly upon oil, thus reducing to a minimum the
demand for coal-bunkering. Industrial plants also have
largely adapted themselves to the use of power from petroleum and hydroelectric resources close at hand, as have the
railways. As a result imports of coal from all countries into
the Coast states in 1929 and 1930 were scarcely half those of
1922 and 1923, when coal and coke imports outranked all

---

[4] The largest volume imported was in 1930 when 245,000 tons were
received, but the precipitous decline in the price of copper lowered greatly
the recorded value of these imports.

others in volume. About half the supply comes from British Columbia, the remainder from the United Kingdom and Continental Europe.

Pacific Canada, the United Kingdom, and Australasia are all included among the five or six most important regions in the volume of their trade with respect to the Pacific Coast ports of the United States. Since these countries rank among the leaders on the basis of aggregate trade, the British Empire is recognized as a factor of immense importance in the foreign commerce of the Pacific States as in that of the United States as a whole.

Between 1922 and 1930 these three regions accounted for an average of approximately one-third the aggregate volume of water-borne foreign commerce of the Pacific Coast. The combined tonnage of their trade was nearly 5.8 million long tons in the fiscal year 1930, and represented 35 per cent of total Pacific Coast foreign commerce. Absence of language barriers, free movement of peoples across the border, common business enterprises, coupled with other favorable factors tend, of course, to promote British-American commercial relations. Such initial advantages are exceedingly important in the early development of trade. Propinquity and cordial relations between peoples facing each other across the international boundary are sure factors in the building up of increasingly important maritime relations between the expanding Canadian-Pacific and American-Pacific regions.

Southbound international coasting trade of the Pacific States area is, on the whole, greater than that with Canada, although no individual trade region bulks so large.[5] Com-

---

[5] "The trade between the United States and the west coast of South America, comprising that through the Panama Canal, through the Straits of Magellan, and between the Pacific ports of the two Americas, was 50 per cent greater in 1923 than in 1914, measured by the net tonnage of ships entered and cleared. . . . . The great gain in American trade with the west coast has been almost entirely due to the chance which the Panama Canal offered for the direct import by the shortest navigable route of bulk exports to the United States and to the stimulus which the War gave to the export of these bulk materials and to the growth in the United States of the metallurgical and chemical industries." *Shipping of the West and East Coasts of South America with the United States and Europe,* United States Department of Commerce, Trade Information Bulletin No. 304 (1925).

merce with the west coast of South America ranks first among Latin-American trades, and has been growing somewhat more rapidly than total foreign commerce of the American Pacific Coast. Since 1925 the volume of commodities exchanged between the Pacific ports of the United States and of South America has been above one million long tons, and in 1929 it almost reached 1.5 million tons. In the latter year, as in several earlier years, this trade ranked fourth in volume among the twenty regional divisions of total foreign commerce with American Pacific ports (see Appendix Table VIII). Most of the total United States export tonnage to the west coast of South America originates in Pacific ports, but only a relatively small portion of imports is shipped to the region.

This route, like most others involving the Pacific States, is characterized by a much greater volume of exports than of imports and for the same reason, namely, heavy petroleum shipments from southern California. Even with the elimination of tanker cargoes, however, the remaining trade is still considerably heavier in the southbound direction.

Apart from petroleum exports, which constitute from two-thirds to three-fourths of all Pacific southbound shipments between the Americas, lumber constitutes a major portion of the remaining cargoes. If to these two commodities are added grain and flour, there is only a very small tonnage of other exports unmentioned. Trade with this region, then, exemplifies in striking fashion the characteristic dominant products of American Pacific Coast export trade.

The west coast of South America does not have a long list of commodities to send northward in return. As might be expected, the commodities sent are largely in the form of crude materials. First in importance is copper ore, bound for the smelters of the Puget Sound area, although some other ores and metals are also shipped in fair quantities. The great nitrate deposits of Chile provide needed fertilizing agents to support the intensive agricultural development of the Pacific Coast, notably in southern California.[6] A sub-

---

[6] "Paradoxical as it may seem, Chile until this last year exported nitrates to all nations of the world to aid them in production of wheat and

stantial and increasing volume of such products has been imported, the nitrates from Chile accounting for more than a third of the total. These products largely exhaust the list of important imports into the Pacific States from western South American ports.

The trade of Mexico and Central America with Pacific ports of the United States increases by more than a million long tons the total foreign commerce of the region. To these countries, as to most other customers, especially Central America, go large quantities of petroleum products. Exports to this region are almost entirely composed of tanker cargoes and petroleum products in packages. Imports from Mexico and Central America are not large, and are composed chiefly of miscellaneous tropical products, together with some ores and metals from Mexico. Trade statistics of Central America include a considerable movement to and from Cristobal, which is largely cargo transshipped at that port from or to ports lying east of the Panama Canal.

In earlier chapters, the influence of the Panama Canal on the maritime development of the American Pacific States region and two direct manifestations of this influence were recorded. One was the development of domestic intercoastal trade made possible by the Canal, and the other was the rise of European trades, largely a product of the same factor. A third direct and tangible bit of evidence is provided by the Pacific Coast trade with the east-coast countries of South and Central America and the West Indies.[7] Though not at present so important as the first two developments, this growth is a notable result of the new trade facilities afforded by the Panama Canal.

other cereals and then proceeded to buy wheat lavishly from these customer nations. The paradox has ceased. This year, with the demand for nitrates reduced to little more than a promise, Chile's government financed the farmers there to a bountiful supply of nitrate fertilizer for wheat acreages, and the result is that Chile will need only a slight amount of wheat. A tremendous crop, proportionate to acreage, was produced." *Pacific Shipper,* October 9, 1933.

[7] East- and west-coast shipments to and from Central America and Mexico are not segregated in the reports of foreign commerce by trade regions, so that it is impracticable to examine this particular portion of the trade in much detail.

Maritime intercourse with the east coast of South America has averaged well over half a million long tons since 1925. In 1928 this commerce reached a peak of over 1.2 million tons; five years earlier it had amounted to less than 240,000 tons and in 1922 to less than 40,000 tons. Exports are very largely tanker cargoes (petroleum) and lumber, with small shipments of food products and of miscellaneous manufactures. Imports from the east coast of South America consist of a considerable variety of foodstuffs. Coffee is usually the item of largest volume in this movement, although in some years grain occupies first place. In other years grain receipts from that region have been negligible.

While the American Pacific Coast is an area of great surplus production with respect to many varieties of foodstuffs, nevertheless it exhibits a substantial import movement in edible products of one kind or another. Among these, coffee undoubtedly ranks first in value. Coffee enters each Pacific customs district in substantial amount, but the imports at San Francisco are several times those of the other three districts combined (see Appendix Table IV, also chapter viii). Most of this comes from eastern and northern South America, so that the volume of imports largely represents the consumption requirements of the regions tributary to Pacific ports.

Commerce with the West Indies, much smaller than that with the east coast of South America, has thus far never amounted to as much as 200,000 tons. Exports from American Pacific ports to the West Indies are similar to those destined for the east coast of South America, principally petroleum and lumber, with small shipments of foodstuffs and miscellaneous manufactures. Imports from these Caribbean islands are almost entirely sugar and molasses. There has been a recent striking development in the commerce with Central America in which the banana boats of the United Fruit Company figure prominently.

The trade of the Americas is a future prize. Propinquity, which has been an important factor in past and present developments, will prove to be of even larger importance in the future. The surplus products of west-coast Canada are largely competitive with products of the United States

West Coast, while the commerce between the Pacific Coast states and South America is certain to be on a more reciprocal basis. The excellent opportunities afforded for the investment of surplus capital in the North, South, and Central Americas offer constructive and sure potentialities for expansion.

XII. Ocean Traffic with Europe

Foreign shipping through the Panama Canal has stimulated tremendously the contacts between the American Pacific Coast and transatlantic countries. Table 47 (p. 266) lists passenger liners operating between the Coast and Europe during a recent month. From the standpoint of the trade of the Pacific Coast, this new, direct connection is second in importance only to that involving the domestic intercoastal cargoes already described in chapter x. This foreign traffic is the direct outgrowth of the construction of a waterway between the two oceans. While other ocean trades have profited also, for example, that between the Pacific States and the east coast of South America, by far the greatest tangible results to the region of the Isthmus connection are to be found in the extension of intercoastal trade into the North Atlantic Ocean.

This European commerce, which in 1929 amounted to more than one-fifth of the total volume of water-borne foreign commerce of the Pacific States area, does not rank with that of the transpacific region, which accounts for a little less than half the total. There is the important distinction, however, that in comparison with that of Asia and Oceania the former is a virtually new trade, a trade founded substantially on the Panama route, whereas transpacific intercourse has an entirely different basis. Some appreciation of the rise of Pacific Coast maritime relations with the United Kingdom and Western European countries may be obtained by focussing our attention first upon the maritime trade with Great Britain, which has been the most important factor in this commerce.

During the three fiscal years prior to the opening of the Panama Canal, the value of the trade of Pacific Coast customs districts with the United Kingdom averaged about $20,000,000 annually. In 1929 and 1930 it averaged about $110,000,000 (Table 48, p. 267). Even allowing for differences in price levels between the two periods, the trade[1] has in-

---

[1] No exact calculation can be made, since the general indexes of import and export prices are not necessarily applicable to trade between Pacific

creased perhaps fourfold. Correspondingly great or even greater relative changes have occurred in the value of Pacific Coast trade with France, Germany, and the Netherlands. This growth has been very much more rapid than that recorded for total United States foreign trade with these same countries, and also substantially greater than the increase in the foreign commerce of the Pacific States area with all countries.

The more rapid growth of trade with Europe, for the Coast region in comparison with that of the country as a whole, is noteworthy. Europe has always been the outstanding factor in American foreign trade, and although still dominating it her relative importance is steadily declining. Over four-fifths of all United States exports went to Europe fifty years ago; just before the war this proportion had declined to three-fifths; and in recent years it has approximated two-fifths. Half of the value of importations into the United States came from Europe fifty years ago; today about 30 per cent of American imports are from that continent.

One of the outstanding tendencies in the foreign commerce of the United States, then, is the decline in the relative importance of Europe both as a customer and as a source of supply. Despite this marked trend, the importance of European countries to the Pacific States region has increased phenomenally, as indicated by the growth in trade since the opening of the Panama Canal. As a market, transatlantic countries are far more important to the Pacific Coast than they are as a source of supply, and the cargo movement between them has been correspondingly unbalanced.

Six out of twenty-seven European countries purchase 75 per cent of total United States exports to the continent. These countries—Great Britain, Germany, France, Italy, the Netherlands, and Belgium—are similarly the principal factors in Pacific Coast–European trade relations. Great Britain ranks

ports and specified foreign countries. The export-price index of the United States Department of Commerce, using 1913 as the equivalent of 100, was 125 in 1929 and 113 in 1930. The import-price indexes for these two years were 119 and 97, respectively. Another significant factor is that before 1915 considerable cargo originating on the Pacific Coast was credited to other ports.

TABLE 47

JOINT SCHEDULE OF SAILINGS, NORTH PACIFIC COAST–EUROPEAN PASSENGER CONFERENCE*

Vessel	Line	Dates of Sailing								Dates of Arrival				
		Vancouver, Victoria	Seattle, Tacoma	Portland	San Francisco	Los Angeles	San Jose	La Libertad	Panama Canal	United Kingdom Ports	Havre	Rotterdam	Copenhagen	Gothenberg
"California"	Libera	April 5	April 9		April 14	April 16		April 24	April 27					†
"Pacific Grove"	Furness	April 6	April 11	April 14	April 19	April 21			May 1	May 17				
"Delftdyk"	Holland-America	April 7	April 12	April 18	April 26	April 28			May 7	May 21		June 1		
"Seattle"	H.A.L.	April 11	April 17	April 21	April 25	April 27			May 7		‡			
"Amerika"	East Asiatic	April 13			April 22	April 24			May 3	May 20	¶May 22		May 27	
"Wyoming"	French Line	April 13	April 14		April 17	April 19	April 25	April 26	May 1		¶May 17	May 27		
"Margaret Johnson"	Johnson	April 14			April 17	April 20			May 3	May 19				May 28
"Canada"	Johnson				April 21	April 23			May 5	May 25				June 4
"Pacific Enterprise"	Furness	April 16	April 21	April 25	May 3	May 5			May 15	May 31	‡			
"Schwaben"	N.G.L.	April 21	April 27	May 1	May 5	May 7			May 17			June 17		
"Lochmonar"	Royal Mail	April 21	April 26	May 2	May 2	May 12			May 21	June 5				
"Cellina"	Libera	April 25	April 28	May 1	May 5	May 7		May 16	May 20					†
"San Francisco"§	French Line	April 27			May 1	May 3	May 10	May 11	May 14		May 30	June 9		
"Pacific Exporter"	Furness	April 30	May 5	May 9	May 17	May 19			May 29	June 14	‡			
"Portland"	H.A.L.	May 2	May 8	May 12	May 9	May 18			May 28	June 15				
"Annie Johnson"	Johnson	May 4			May 6	May 9			May 29	June 15				
"Europa"	East Asiatic	May 9			May 18	May 20			May 29			June 17	June 22	June 25
"Winnipeg"	French Line	May 11			May 15	May 17	May 24	May 25			June 14	June 23		
"Los Angeles"	H.A.L.	May 12	May 18	May 22	May 26	May 28			June 7	June 28				
"Pacific President"	Furness	May 14	May 19	May 23	May 23	June 2			June 12	June 15				
"Lochgoil"	Royal Mail	May 19	May 24	May 30	June 7	June 9			June 20	July 8		July 20		
"Tacoma"	H.A.L.	May 23	May 29	June 2	June 6	June 8			June 18		July 10			
"San Diego"§	French Line	May 25			May 29	May 31			June 11		June 27	July 8		
"Pacific Trader"	Furness	May 28	June 2	June 6	June 14	June 16			June 26	July 12				

* Data from *Official Steamship Guide*, San Francisco. This includes also international vacations aboard European liners via Panama Canal direct to Europe from the Pacific Coast.   § Third class only.
† Calls at Marseilles and Genoa.   ‡ Calls also at Hamburg and Bremen.   ¶ Calls also at Hamburg.

TABLE 47 (*Continued*)

PORTS OF CALL EAST OF PANAMA CANAL, NORTH PACIFIC COAST–
EUROPEAN PASSENGER CONFERENCE

East Asiatic Company.—Kingston, St. Thomas, Southampton, Rotterdam, Hamburg, Copenhagen, and Hull.
French Line.—Curacao, Havre, Bordeaux, Dunkirk, Antwerp, and Rotterdam.
Furness Line.—London, Liverpool, Manchester, and Glasgow.
Hamburg-American Line.—Curacao, Hamburg, Bremen, Antwerp, and Rotterdam.
Johnson Line.—Cartagena, Puerto Colombia, Plymouth, Hull, Antwerp, and Gothenberg.
Holland-America Line.—Puerto Colombia, Curacao, Kingston, Bermuda, Swansea, Liverpool, Southampton, London, and Rotterdam.
Libera Line.—Las Palmas, Palma de Mallorca, Marseilles, Genoa, Leghorn, Naples, Venice, and Trieste.
North German Lloyd.—St. Thomas, Hamburg, and Bremen.
Royal Mail Lines, Ltd.—Liverpool, Southampton, London, and Rotterdam.

second, after Japan, in the value of its commerce with Pacific Coast ports, and in five of the nine years between

TABLE 48

VOLUME OF FOREIGN TRADE OF UNITED STATES PACIFIC COAST WITH UNITED KINGDOM, BY COMMODITIES, 1922–1930*

(*Thousand long tons*)

Commodities	1922	1923	1924	1925	1926	1927	1928	1929	1930
Exports—Total	1,046	1,042	1,165	1,263	1,510	1,745	1,823	1,996	2,249
Tanker cargoes	88	218	375	506	523	724	620	783	1,014
Petroleum in packages	—	...†	...†	...†	...†	1	9	2	1
Grain in flour	778	550	525	412	626	602	734	570	586
Logs and lumber	30	56	67	95	90	102	171	244	326
Fruits and nuts	59	144	121	152	190	214	214	279	213
Copper and manufactures	...†	4	12	19	22	7	11	16	17
Pigments, chemicals, etc.	1	7	9	5	5	6	20	18	24
Miscellaneous metals	3	5	8	19	11	22	5	1	1
Vegetables and products	42	17	7	8	8	4	3	17	10
Imports—Total	103	204	158	96	92	71	81	93	84
Tanker cargoes	—	—	—	—	—	16	13	30	18
Coal and coke	52	85	33	47	51	7	32	36	46
Clay and manufactures	4	15	15	15	13	17	14	7	7
Iron, steel, and manufactures	3	57	41	11	...†	10	6	9	3

* Data from United States Shipping Board. Not all commodities listed.

† Less than one thousand long tons.

1922 and 1930 ranked second in volume. During the same period a 100 per cent increase in the volume of this Pacific

Coast commerce was recorded, and in 1930 the Pacific ports loaded more than one-fourth of all United States exports to the United Kingdom.

The disproportion between exports and imports, similar to the exchange of commodities between the American Pacific States and Australasia, is extreme in United Kingdom trade. Out of an aggregate commerce of over 2,000,000 long tons in 1929 and 1930, less than 100,000 tons were imports; in 1930 only 4 per cent of the combined movement in both directions consisted of incoming cargo (see Table 48). Even after the elimination of tanker exports, imports account for less than one-tenth of the volume of remaining exports. Furthermore, while exports have continued to grow in volume, since 1920, imports have shown a declining tendency, thus widening, at least for the time being, the discrepancy in cargo tonnage moving in each direction. In terms of value the disproportion is somewhat less marked. The average value of imports from Great Britain to Pacific districts in recent years has been around $7,500,000, and that of exports about $110,000,000.

Foodstuffs of one kind or another needed to feed Britain's dense industrial population have accounted for approximately half the total volume of shipments from Pacific Coast ports. Grain and flour, ranking first in five of the nine years from 1922 to 1930, have shown no consistent tendency toward increasing the proportion of total volume during the period. Export cargoes of fruits and nuts, on the other hand, have attained an average volume in the last three years of more than twice that of 1922–1924.

Neither petroleum nor lumber has been relatively so important among exports from the American Pacific Coast to the United Kingdom as in the foreign trade of the Pacific Coast as a whole, yet both have increased much more rapidly than have total exports to the United Kingdom. By 1930, tanker cargoes amounted to 45 per cent of the total outward movement. Exports of logs and lumber likewise increased steadily from 30,000 long tons in 1922 to ten times that amount in 1930. British imports of lumber from North American Pacific ports are relatively small even yet as compared with those from the hardwood ports of the Southern

States.[2] Gains in petroleum and lumber exports largely account for the doubling in total tonnage of American export trade to Great Britain between 1922 and 1930.

Outbound cargoes of copper and its manufactures, pigments, and chemicals destined for the United Kingdom have likewise grown greatly. The tonnage involved in each group of products is, however, still so small that it forms an insignificant part of the commerce via Panama on the Pacific Coast–transatlantic route (see Table 48).

Exports from the United Kingdom into Pacific Coast ports of the United States are almost negligible. Since 1924, furthermore, this trend has been irregularly downward. To-day, only some 5 per cent of the volume of all United States imports from Great Britain is absorbed by Pacific States. Coal and coke furnish the principal cargoes for incoming ships from England, with tanker imports, presumably mostly creosote, second in recent years. Small but widely fluctuating amounts of iron and steel manufactures are also received, as well as miscellaneous clay products. In neither group has there been any apparent tendency toward expansion in the years from 1922 to 1930. From the standpoint of quantity, variety, or value, the import trade from the United Kingdom, on the whole, is not significant.

In some respects Coast commerce with Continental ports between Hamburg and Havre, both inclusive, should be associated with that of trade with the United Kingdom. The majority of shipping lines operating services to Europe from Pacific ports call at both British and Continental ports. The character of the commodities exchanged is similar, although exports to the Havre-Hamburg range are very much smaller than those to the United Kingdom, while imports from the region are several times greater. Trade with these Continental ports has been increasing rapidly, even faster than Pacific Coast commerce as a whole, with the result that the aggregate commodity movement on this route is overtaking that of the British total with Pacific ports.

---

[2] The Ottawa Agreement has been largely responsible for a subsequent shift of West Coast lumber exports from the American to the Canadian side (consult chapter iv).

In 1922 and 1923 trade with the Havre-Hamburg range was only about one-third as great as that with the United Kingdom; at present it is nearly two-thirds the volume. If existing trends are maintained it will not be many years before the volume of Pacific Coast commerce with these continental ports exceeds that with British ports.

The character and severity of England's post-war industrial and financial readjustment problems are factors, perhaps temporary ones, in the slower growth of the commerce of that country. Another cause doubtless lies in the declining importance of British ports as entrepôt centers consequent upon the growing number of direct shipping services between countries of origin and those of ultimate destination: for example, Australian wool and Malayan rubber reach the United States largely by direct route. Such a change was perhaps inevitable, but it was certainly hastened by the World War.

Similarity of commodity movements between Pacific ports and those of the United Kingdom and Western Europe, respectively, is striking. The latter are highly industrialized regions with dense populations, needing raw materials, and not self-sufficient in the production of many foodstuffs. Both lack petroleum and timber resources. Both regions are producers of coal and iron. It is not surprising to discover that to the Havre-Hamburg range, as to Britain, there is the movement of grain and flour, fruits and nuts, petroleum and lumber (see Table 49).

Tanker exports, which have increased enormously since 1922, lead other commodities in volume even as they do in the outward shipments from Pacific ports to most other parts of the world. They do not, however, constitute so great a percentage in the Continental trade as elsewhere. Lumber exports, which rank second, have also increased manyfold during the past decade. Most of Europe's lumber imports from the United States, however, come from the Gulf States region.

Grain and flour cargo shipments to the Havre-Hamburg area reveal the same erratic variations from year to year that they do in Pacific Coast trades as a whole. Partly because so many parts of Europe have been growing, at excessive cost, sufficient wheat for domestic requirements, usually due to the protection afforded by high tariffs or quota restrictions, grain and flour are relatively less important in this trade than in that of Britain. Exports of

TABLE 49

VOLUME OF FOREIGN TRADE OF UNITED STATES PACIFIC COAST WITH
HAVRE-HAMBURG RANGE, BY COMMODITIES, 1922–1930*

(Thousand long tons)

Commodities	1922	1923	1924	1925	1926	1927	1928	1929	1930
Exports—Total	331	156	166	338	410	582	794	923	897
Tanker cargoes	15	26	46	94	121	176	148	300	355
Petroleum in packages.............	—	—	...†	...†	...†	...†	20	22	26
Grain and flour.....................	250	62	35	80	56	109	243	97	41
Logs and lumber...................	10	13	13	31	33	75	137	153	218
Fruits and nuts....................	32	26	36	55	70	95	107	196	99
Copper and manufactures..........	...†	13	8	46	53	14	56	50	31
Pigments, chemicals, and manufactures	...†	2	7	6	6	8	34	37	56
Imports—Total	128	183	301	376	389	439	423	462	505
Tanker cargoes	—	—	—	—	—	22	40	34	37
Paper stock	6	7	11	9	7	11	10	22	21
Coal and coke.....................	—	1	...†	8	25	59	27	17	22
Nitrates, potash, fertilizer.........	4	5	5	5	13	15	24	39	38
Clay and manufactures............	...†	1	5	5	6	16	21	12	12
Iron and steel manufactures‡......	35	26	16	22	28	154	136	148	121
Chemicals	1	5	8	44	35	10	7	15	21
Miscellaneous ores, and metals....	...†	25	56	75	98	10	11	10	3

* Data from United States Shipping Board. The Havre-Hamburg Range includes all Continental ports between Havre and Hamburg, both inclusive.

† Less than one thousand tons.

‡ The figures reported for 1926 and 1927 suggest that products earlier reported under miscellaneous ores and metals were transferred to the iron and steel category in 1927.

copper and chemicals in recent years have been considerably larger to Continental ports in the Havre-Hamburg sector than to the United Kingdom. The trade in both industries is a growing one, especially in chemicals.

Imports from this region are very much larger and somewhat more diversified than those from the United Kingdom. In 1930 they exceeded half a million long tons, as compared with 84,000 tons from British ports. Despite high protective barriers, imports are expanding more rapidly than exports.

As a result, if tanker cargoes are eliminated from consideration, the outbound and incoming movements are very nearly balanced, which compensates, to some extent, for the exceedingly light shipments from British ports, which are transported mostly by the same vessels. North Pacific–European liner services offer low freight rates on their westbound sailings, which has been a stimulus to the trade and partly accounts for the rapid growth (see Table 48, p. 267).

The Continental iron and steel export trade appears to be gaining rapidly in the Pacific market, in part at the expense of the British, and now constitutes the largest factor among imports from that region (see Table 49). Hampered in the development of its own heavier metal industries, by reason of lack of coal and ore deposits, the Pacific Coast depends heavily upon Europe and on eastern United States for a great variety of iron, steel, and other metal manufactures.

Imports of iron and steel and manufactures increased from an average of 67,000 long tons in 1922–1924 to 147,000 in 1928–1930, a gain of 120 per cent. Since practically all such imports come from Western Europe, including the United Kingdom, it becomes evident that low freight rates westbound on this route do not make it impossible for certain classes of semi-manufactured metal goods from Europe to compete with those from eastern United States in the American Pacific market. However, these products arriving from Europe are only a small fraction of those received by the intercoastal route from the Atlantic and Gulf seaboards.

Tanker cargoes, in the main creosote,[3] coal and coke, also potash and other fertilizers and chemicals, all move in relatively substantial amounts from Western Continental to American Pacific ports. In 1929 and 1930 fertilizers ranked second after iron and steel among the Coast imports. Clay manufactures and paper stock have been imported in considerable quantities in record years, but neither one as yet

---

[3] The reports of the United States Shipping Board from which these figures have been taken give no quantitative information regarding the commodity make-up of tanker cargoes. There is a large movement of creosote from the Netherlands to Pacific ports which comes as tanker cargo.

accounts for quite as much as 5 per cent of the total incoming movement on this route.

The commodity movement between the Pacific Coast of the United States and Western Europe as a whole may be summarized by reference to statistics of the Panama Canal for recent years (see accompanying Table 50). In general, this tabulation does not reveal the same amount of detailed information as the Shipping Board statistics, but owing to differences in classification it does help to complete the picture by emphasizing bulk movement. Petroleum products, grain and flour, lumber, canned food, and fresh and dried fruits dominate the outbound cargoes from Pacific ports to Europe. Iron and steel products, sand, cement, creosote, coke, paper, and pulp are the chief imports—all bulk products. The eastbound movement in 1929 and 1930 was over three million long tons, while the westbound, Atlantic to Pacific, was less than 700,000.

TABLE 50

PRINCIPAL COMMODITIES TRANSITING PANAMA CANAL BETWEEN THE WEST COAST OF THE UNITED STATES AND EUROPE, 1927–1930*

(Thousand long tons of cargo)

Commodities	1927	1928	1929	1930
Pacific to Atlantic				
Total	2,674	2,939	3,084	3,319
Grain and flour	990	1,225	806	688
Canned food	147	151	213	183
Fresh fruit	75	66	170	102
Dried fruit	91	126	162	95
Lumber, including hardwoods	153	287	354	535
Copper	64	74	72	51
Mineral oil, crude and refined	965	809	1,078	1,400
Atlantic to Pacific				
Total	527	577	669	698
Cement	29	28	57	71
Coke	65	53	49	60
Creosote	30	47	57	65
Iron and steel, including railway material and scrap	156	140	156	141
Paper and paper pulp	27	39	1	56
Sand and silversand	64	62	58	78

* Data from *Panama Canal Record.* Not all commodities shown.

Baltic and Mediterranean Europe are of minor importance in the volume of direct shipping with reference to the American West Coast, hence these other European regions are not treated separately here. Similarly, Western Asia and Africa are small customers. For further information, the reader is referred to the annual *Report on Volume of Water Borne Foreign Commerce of the United States by Ports of Origin and Destination* (Shipping Board Bureau, No. 42-32) and *Foreign Commerce and Navigation* (Bureau of Foreign and Domestic Commerce).

The American import tariff is doubtless an important factor in closing the Coast market to European producers. Applicable to the three Pacific States, the situation is significant. Foreign trade statistics of this region for the calendar year 1930 show that 88 per cent of the imports from Africa enter duty free, 84 per cent from South America, 80 per cent from Asia, 71 per cent from North America, 69 per cent from Oceania, and 42 per cent from Europe. It is interesting to compare these ratios of duty-free and duty-levied commodities with the trends in trade and shipping. Furthermore, the percentage of duty-free imports into the West Coast district is much higher than for the United States, because of the higher percentage of raw materials and crude foodstuffs which are not subject usually to the customs tariff. A recovery by European nations to their position in the Pacific area of a decade ago seems possible only if American tariff barriers are lowered sufficiently to place the transatlantic countries on an economic parity with the industrial region of eastern United States.

XIII. Ocean Traffic with Far Eastern Countries

Transpacific trade probably originated in 1565, less than three-quarters of a century after the discovery of America, and only thirteen years after the first white man set foot on the soil of Lower California. The Manila galleon, which sailed annually about the middle of the year from the Philippines to the Mexican Pacific port of Acapulco, was a prize of unequaled richness for any bold pirate or privateer who could capture her.

Traveling light on her westbound voyage, she was loaded beyond the point of safety on her eastbound trip with a great variety of costly and exotic merchandise gathered from many lands of the Far East. Many a fortune was made from a single trip. Until 1789 the Manila trade was a monopoly of tremendous importance from both a military and a commercial standpoint, but after that time the galleon's importance declined with the increasing appearance of competing ships of other countries, although sailings were not abandoned until 1815. For a time after the arrival of the Spaniards the trade with the foreign countries increased, but later and during a period of two hundred fifty years it was almost destroyed by the decree of the Spanish government restricting trade with Mexico, the channel through which commerce with Europe moved, to two sailing ships each year. During the latter part of the eighteenth century this restriction was removed, and transportation facilities improved by gradual stages until the Spanish-American War.

One of the motives which inspired the establishment of settlements in what is now the state of California was Spain's desire to provide protection from foreign depredation on her transpacific trade. The raids of Sir Francis Drake and other British privateers upon Spanish ships and towns in the Pacific also led to explorations of the North Pacific Coast as early as the end of the sixteenth century, with the object of founding a suitable way-station for the galleon. Usually sighting the American shore many hundreds of miles north of her destination, it was felt that a safe port somewhere in these higher latitudes would provide both an opportunity for needed recuperation after long months at sea and a base from which other Spanish vessels could operate and warn the approaching galleon of hostile ships. For this and other reasons connected with fears of foreign aggression attempts were made from time to time to push Spanish exploration and colonization northward. Yet a hundred years elapsed before any very substantial progress was made, and even then it was lower California and not upper California which witnessed the first white settlement. Nevertheless these numerous explorations added appreciably to knowledge concerning the land to the north; they paved the way for settlement when circumstances were more favorable.

It should be remembered that the Pacific Coast of North America first gained economic significance in the eyes of the European world because of its believed proximity to Asia. Even after more accurate geographic knowledge became general, this coast continued to be regarded as important mainly because it served as a gateway to the still highly profitable Oriental trade—of such importance as to incite diplomatic maneuvers by more than one nation. Less than a century ago, when the great central section became an integral part of the United States, it had already won a significance in its own right, quite apart from, and in addition to, the proved inherent advantages for Asiatic trade.

Distance and physical barriers militated against cheap overland communication, and the long unbroken coastline of the Americas intensified the isolation of the American Pacific Coast from Atlantic shores. These factors, in turn, tended to identify its maritime commerce very largely with Pacific Ocean commerce exclusively until the Panama Canal joined the two great seas. Both for this reason and because Pacific ports serve as a convenient gateway for American trade with the Orient, it is not strange to find that commerce with transpacific countries is of first importance in the maritime trade of the region.[1] This leadership is indicated by all

[1] In the term transpacific are here included Japan, China (including Hong Kong), Asiatic Soviet Russia, the Philippines, the East Indies, Australia, and New Zealand.

manner of measurement, whether in terms of quantity or value, or of the imports, exports, or total commerce. Since the opening of the Panama Canal, however, the dominance of transpacific countries in the foreign trade of Pacific States ports is much less marked than it was earlier, primarily because of the rise of European trades brought out in previous chapters.

Among the twenty trading areas classified by the United States Shipping Board reports the East Asian trade with Pacific ports so far outranks all others as to account for approximately one-third of the aggregate movement[2] (see Figure 32). This region ranks first in both imports and exports

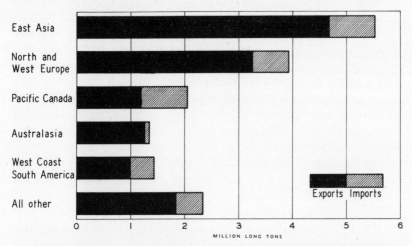

Fig. 32.—Regional distribution of Pacific Coast foreign trade, 1930.

separately, and in dry-cargo trade as well as in the total. In 1922 Pacific Coast commerce with East Asia was 3,000,000 long tons, out of an aggregate foreign trade of 6.7 million tons. In 1929 and 1930 the total trade had increased to an average of above 16.5 million tons, while that with East Asia averaged 5.6 million tons. Thus, while the exchange of goods between the American Pacific Coast and East Asia has

[2] East Asia, according to the Shipping Board designation, includes China, Japan, Union of Soviet Socialist Republics in Asia, and the Philippines.

increased nearly 100 per cent in this brief period, it has not grown so rapidly as the foreign trade of the Coast as a whole.

In value of imports and exports, countries in the East Asian region account for between 40 and 50 per cent of the aggregate value of Pacific Coast foreign commerce. In the foreign trade of the United States as a whole Asia has steadily grown in importance, so that now about 15 per cent of all exports are sent to countries in this region and about 30 per cent of the total imports of the United States come from these same lands. Table 51 lists the chief commodities.

The persistent increase in the importance of Asia is another of the outstanding trends in the foreign trade of the United States. Fifty years ago less than 2 per cent of the value of all American exports were taken by Asia; before the war the percentage had risen to about 6; and in 1931 it was 15.9, somewhat higher than the average of the past decade, which was nearer 11 or 12 per cent. A similar trend exists for imports. Close to 30 per cent of all imports come from Asia now, whereas before the war the proportion was about half as great and fifty years ago was only one-tenth of the value of all United States imports representing purchases from Far Eastern countries.

Not only does the American Pacific States sector exchange a greater volume and value of goods with East Asia than with any other trade region, but it accounts as well for a larger volume of the total foreign trade of East Asia with the United States as a whole than does any other American coastal district. According to volume, approximately 70 per cent of American exports to East Asia leave Pacific Coast ports. Mr. A. Bland Calder, United States Trade Commissioner at Shanghai, has made the following pertinent observation:

Our sales to China consist largely of staple products such as wheat, flour, cotton, tobacco, cigarettes, kerosene oil, dyes, lumber, commodities necessary for or in constant use by the populace. These items aggregate more than 75 per cent of our exports to China. These commodities in the run of a year's business are less affected by economic depression in China than are manufactured articles, luxury goods, machinery, or equipment lines. For this reason our trade has held up surprisingly well, whereas countries supplying chiefly manufactured goods to China have experienced a much heavier decline in sales than have we.

TABLE 51

VOLUME OF FOREIGN TRADE OF UNITED STATES PACIFIC COAST WITH
EAST ASIA, BY COMMODITIES, 1922–1930*

(Thousand long tons)

Commodities†	1922	1923	1924	1925	1926	1927	1928	1929	1930
Exports—Total	2,638	2,554	4,338	3,246	3,426	3,924	4,906	4,942	4,692
Tanker cargoes‡	434	767	1,045	1,285	1,044	1,240	1,814	1,767	1,951
Petroleum in packages.............	30	70	85	121	182	222	260	230	280
Logs and lumber...................	1,204	878	1,751	1,228	1,507	1,593	2,018	1,982	1,473
Grain and flour....................	575	524	1,030	247	301	443	411	478	534
Paper and manufactures...........	...§	...§	...§	...§	...§	48	55	76	76
Animal, fish, and dairy products..	15	48	55	69	64	60	53	50	51
Iron and steel, and manufactures	13	8	27	4	5	22	42	42	13
Copper and manufactures..........	...§	19	38	19	13	1	18	16	4
Other ores, metals, and manufactures	125	50	69	29	44	25	52	43	82
Automobiles	1	4	16	6	11	14	16	28	18
Tobacco	6	18	17	21	34	15	12	18	13
Chemicals	7	13	12	14	12	8	14	23	32
Imports—Total	453	739	668	741	688	734	760	784	845
Fruits and nuts.....................	59	116	113	126	102	143	158	153	113
Vegetables and products...........	75	145	133	189	147	147	180	224	228
Sugar and molasses................	37	86	54	84	62	55	71	41	70
Logs and lumber...................	27	38	42	35	47	51	54	57	73
Jute and manufactures.............	16	36	40	31	43	31	38	14	9
Cotton and manufactures...........	2	12	14	21	21	23	37	31	40
Silk and manufactures.............	2	22	19	25	26	29	29	32	33
Other textiles and manufactures...	17	72	69	52	48	45	42	45	48
Coal and coke.....................	29	2	...¶	...¶	...¶	—	3	...¶	—
Clay products	11	15	25	20	27	23	24	36	41
Rubber	1	1	2	5	11	10	5	14	12

* Data from United States Shipping Board.

† These figures are not strictly comparable for the several years because of slight changes in commodity classifications and because certain items in the reports from which these figures are taken may be included in "All other" until large enough to be shown separately.　　　§ Not reported separately.

‡ Mainly petroleum and its products.　　　¶ Less than one thousand tons.

For the combined movement in both directions, Pacific ports account for over 60 per cent of the aggregate volume of American foreign trade with East Asia. In terms of value, however, the dominant position of the Pacific Coast is not maintained. Considerably under half the national total is credited to Pacific customs districts, and this applies also to imports and exports separately,[3] which means, of course,

[3] For reasons pointed out in Appendix D, the statistics on value of imports credited to the several coastal customs districts heavily understate by an undeterminable amount the value of goods actually landed.

that the exports from the rest of the country to East Asia are far greater in unit value than are those from the Pacific Coast, a fact not surprising in view of the Coast's heavy exports of crude materials.

For many years Japan has ranked first among individual countries in value of foreign trade with Pacific customs districts, a position dependent to a considerable extent upon the silk trade. Before the war Japan stood first not only in total commerce but also in both imports and exports separately. Silk was not relatively so important in Japanese shipments to Pacific United States then as now.

In the fiscal years 1913 and 1914 the value of exports from the United States to Japan approached much more nearly that of imports than it has in recent years. While imports from Japan reached a peak in 1929 of 239,000,000 dollars, an increase of more than 300 per cent from the pre-war level, exports have grown scarcely half as fast, and Japan now ranks second in the value of exports from the Pacific Coast. This difference in rate of growth is largely accounted for by the rapid expansion in the silk trade, which was not correspondingly balanced by our exports to Japan. If the present direct movement of silk to Atlantic ports via Panama should presage a permanent alteration in trade routes in addition to the increasing transshipment by all-water travel, Japanese trade with American Pacific ports may be expected to decline considerably in relative importance.

Other transpacific trade routes which are of some importance in the foreign commerce of the American Pacific Coast are those of Australasia and the East Indies. To Australia and New Zealand, Pacific ports ship a greater volume of products, even excluding exports in tankers, than do the Atlantic and Gulf Coast ports combined. Pacific Coast trade with Australasia consists almost entirely, in both quantity and value, of outbound shipments. Since 1923 imports have declined greatly, while exports have increased consistently each year. In 1930 exports totaled almost 1.3 million long tons, over six times the size of the movement in 1922, and represented over 95 per cent of the total volume of traffic in both directions (Table 52).

Although comparatively large, exports are not diversified.

Tanker cargoes (all, or practically all, petroleum), petroleum in packages, and lumber account for 85 per cent of Pacific Coast exports to Australasia; and there appears to be no noticeable tendency for the trade to become more diversified.

TABLE 52

VOLUME OF FOREIGN TRADE OF UNITED STATES PACIFIC COAST WITH AUSTRALASIA, BY COMMODITIES, 1922–1930*

(Thousand long tons)

Commodities	1922	1923	1924	1925	1926	1927	1928	1929	1930
Exports—Total	198	401	528	709	943	1,042	1,243	1,291	1,295
Tanker cargoes	—	10	62	120	160	285	511	517	601
Petroleum in packages............	21	69	106	176	240	217	193	257	290
Logs and lumber..................	142	272	313	370	490	472	479	452	344
Fruits and nuts....................	...†	5	6	4	4	8	10	9	6
Paper manufactures	...‡	...‡	...‡	...‡	...‡	6	5	4	3
Imports—Total	114	163	60	45	45	27	37	58	64
Fruits and nuts....................	20	22	18	19	25	17	27	41	46
Wool	3	2	1	2	3	2	1	1	2
Hides, skins, and manufactures...	2	4	2	3	2	2	2	2	1
Coal and coke.....................	78	128	34	16	9	—	—	2	—

* Data from United States Shipping Board. Not all commodities shown.

† Less than one thousand tons.   ‡ Not reported separately.

Small quantities of fruits and nuts and an even smaller volume of paper products are exported to the region, but neither group of commodities accounts for as much as one per cent of the total volume of outgoing cargoes on this trade route.

Imports, although they have declined considerably below the level of 1922 and 1923, have shown signs of recovery during the past year or so. Largely responsible for the decline in imports during the past decade was the shrinkage in tonnage of coal and coke shipments. These cargoes in 1922–1924 accounted for well over half the total imports, but since 1927 no imports of this character from Australia have been recorded at Pacific ports. With the elimination of coal, fruits and nuts[4] have become the leading import from this region, constituting more than half the total during the last five or

[4] No doubt largely coconuts and copra from South Pacific islands, here included in the Australasian trade region.

six years. Wool in small amounts and hides and skins are also imported; neither commodity group gives much evidence of increasing. American Pacific Coast ports do not serve as the principal gateway for incoming cargoes from Australasia to the same extent that they do for outgoing commerce. Out of a total of some 350,000 tons of imports from Australia and New Zealand to the United States in 1930, only 64,000 tons arrived at Pacific ports.

Direct exchange of commodities between the East Indies and Pacific ports of the United States is not large. This region trades more with the Atlantic Coast than with the Pacific, particularly importing more merchandise from the Eastern States (see Table 8, p. 41). Again, tanker cargoes and petroleum in packages dominate the outbound movement from Pacific States, although some food products are also exported. Among the incoming cargoes fruits and nuts, as in the instance of East Asia, together with crude rubber, supply more than half the total tonnage. As already suggested, commodities from the East Indies are transshipped at Hong Kong or elsewhere, with the result that the actual exchange of commodities with this region is greater than the reports indicate. How much greater, of course, it is impossible to surmise from the official records. In an address at the Los Angeles Convention (1928) of the Association of Pacific and Far Eastern ports, Manager E. W. Latie, of the Tacoma-Oriental Steamship Company of Tacoma, made this observation:

Until recent years the great bulk of cargo for the United States originating in Java, Straits Settlements, Saigon, Bangkok, Rangoon, Penang, Colombo, and Calcutta moved to Hong Kong for transshipment. However, competition from direct services inaugurated during the last few years has substantially reduced the volume. Great quantities of gunnies from Calcutta still move through Hong Kong. This traffic is regulated and to a great extent controlled by the Calcutta Trans-Pacific Conference. However, the Silver Line, operated by the General Steamship Company of San Francisco, during the past year has inaugurated a direct service from Calcutta, Straits Settlements, and Java ports to San Francisco which has proved attractive to many shippers.

In value, raw silk far outranks all other commodities arriving at Pacific ports. In 1928 and 1929 it accounted for nearly half the aggregate value of all imports credited to Pacific Coast customs districts (see chapter viii). Since an undetermined but vast additional amount of silk is landed on the Coast and shipped overland in bond, and so credited as imports at other districts, its relative importance in transportation is far greater than the customs statistics indicate (chapter vii and Appendix D). From a commercial or industrial standpoint, as has been explained in chapter vii, silk imports represent almost entirely a transit movement, since there is no silk industry of importance on the Pacific Coast. Silk cargoes illustrate the principle that high-grade commodities tend to travel by the shortest route. The recent shift in the route for raw-silk imports from transcontinental rail haul to all-water through shipment via the Panama Canal, a decline from 98.4 per cent in 1924 to 22.0 per cent in 1933 in the case of the former, is explained by the precipitous decline in silk prices. Some idea of the extent to which this shift has occurred may be obtained from the following figures showing the percentages of total silk imports into the United States credited to Pacific Coast customs districts for the years 1926 to 1930.[5]

	1926	1927	1928	1929	1930
Percentage	69	64	66	57	43

Foreign trade of the Pacific Coast with China, while very much smaller than that with Japan in terms of value and somewhat less in terms of weight, is nevertheless large enough to rank China among the four leading nations in American Pacific foreign trade during the last few years (Appendix Table IV). Imports and exports are not far from a monetary balance in this commerce, and the trade, unlike that with Japan, is not dominated by a single commodity. In 1928 the total value of Pacific Coast trade with China, including Hong Kong, was approximately $122,000,000 and in 1929 it was only $10,000,000 less. The disturbed conditions in 1930 which affected all commerce, reduced this total to $71,000,000.[6] Except for beans and raw silk, the bulk of

[5] These percentages, it must be remembered, do not include all the silk actually landed at American Pacific ports.

[6] Canada, as well as the United Kingdom, outranked China in value of commerce with the American Pacific Coast in 1930, but if Hong Kong trade is added then China ranked third in 1930 also.

China's exports have been essentially by-products of a subsistence agriculture, and as such their prices do not necessarily bear any relation to costs of production.

The commodity make-up of American Pacific Coast exports to East Asia resembles to a marked degree that of general foreign exports to all countries. Lumber and petroleum far outrank all other products in volume of cargo; together they account for some two-thirds of total exports. In the East Asia trade, lumber (including logs) usually outranks exports of petroleum, which reverses the order which has prevailed in the Coast's foreign commerce in general. Recently China has been buying approximately two-fifths of all the Douglas fir exported. Although petroleum has a place of considerably smaller relative importance than it occupies in the total trade of the region, there is some evidence that its relative importance is increasing, and at the expense of lumber. In 1922–1924 lumber exports to East Asia averaged 40.2 per cent of the total cargo volume, but by 1928–1930 this percentage had declined to 37.6 per cent.

Another resemblance of East Asian trade to total Pacific Coast foreign trade lies in the fact that grain and flour exports to this region rank third after lumber and petroleum, and constitute a large but widely fluctuating percentage of the total. In 1929 and 1930 grain and flour cargoes averaged above 500,000 long tons. On the whole, the trend appears downward, the average volume for 1922, 1923, and 1924 being considerably higher than for any succeeding year.

Other exports to East Asia on a weight basis are relatively unimportant in comparison with these three groups of commodities. They consist mainly of miscellaneous manufactures, including iron and steel, copper and other metals, automobiles, paper, and chemicals. Such commodities, in the aggregate, have shown a less marked tendency toward expansion in volume between 1922 and 1930 than have total exports to East Asia from Pacific ports. This is an indication, however, not that the Far East is purchasing fewer of these commodities but that they are being supplied by other parts of the United States, notably the Atlantic seaboard. Exports of iron and steel products, automobiles, chemicals, etc., from the East Coast of the United States to the Far East have increased markedly during recent years (see Table 20, p. 136).

Imports from East Asia, in most years, account for less than one-sixth of the total Pacific Coast commerce with that region. After deducting exports in tankers from the figure of total exports, the outbound movement is still more than four times the volume of incoming cargo. This means a considerable operation of ships with only partial cargoes on the eastward transpacific run, although some of the surplus westbound traffic is carried by tramp ships with no fixed routes and some by westbound round-the-world liners.

East Asia sends to Pacific shores a variety of textile materials and textiles, including jute,[7] cotton, wool, and silk, but ranking first and second in volume, respectively, are vegetable products and fruits and nuts.[8] The latter group undoubtedly consists largely of coconuts and copra from the Philippines. Sugar and molasses arrive in considerable quantity from the same source, as do logs and lumber. The Pacific Coast is rapidly increasing its imports of crude rubber, which originate in the East Indies. In the Shipping Board records these shipments appear as imports from East Asia, since substantial amounts are transshipped at Chinese ports. The importation into Pacific ports from East Asia also includes varied clay products, especially china and porcelain, and the amount has been increasing rapidly in recent years, totaling over 40,000 long tons in 1930.[9]

Considered in its entirety, transpacific trade constitutes less than half the total volume of water-borne foreign commerce of the American Pacific States region. The trade with

[7] India sends, either directly or indirectly via eastern Asiatic ports, most of the jute received on the Pacific Coast. Carpet wools come mainly from China, while India, China, and Japan send cotton or cotton textiles. On the whole, the imports of these commodities have increased greatly during the decade 1920–1930.

[8] The term "vegetables and products" used by the United States Shipping Board cannot readily be broken down into its constituent elements, but probably includes vegetable oils.

[9] The weight of imports recorded in the statistics of the United States Shipping Board is gross weight, and hence statistics of commodities requiring heavy packing, such as porcelain and china, considerably overstate the actual quantity of the commodities themselves.

Hawaii is classed as noncontiguous, but conceivably might be listed as "transpacific." The proportion of total trans-oceanic tonnage (as distinguished from coastwise or inter-coastal commerce) accounted for by transpacific maritime intercourse cannot be measured accurately.

Again, one should be reminded that it is not possible to ascertain, with certainty, the route followed by cargoes shipped between Pacific ports of the United States and the Orient. Goods from ports in India, to a lesser degree Nether-lands India, may occasionally travel westward and reach American Pacific ports through the Suez and the Panama canals. The volume of such movement would necessarily be small because of the distance factor.

Clearly, maritime commerce is all-important to the terri-tory of Hawaii, and in its world-trade relations transpacific shipping is unavoidably involved. These relations at present are almost entirely confined to exchanges of goods with the mainland of the United States, particularly California and the port of San Francisco. In spite of the fact that the Ha-waiian Islands are at the "crossroads of the Pacific" and con-stitute one of our important "overseas" markets, their own foreign commerce is extremely small—less than one per cent, by weight, of their combined inward and outward ship-ments.

In the last six calendar years the volume of water-borne commerce (other than purely local) of Hawaii has ranged from 2.1 to 2.4 million long tons. In 1930, in the face of un-favorable world economic conditions, Hawaii enjoyed a somewhat greater commerce than in any previous year covered by the data. The commerce is well balanced, i.e., the annual volume of exports approximately equals the tonnage imported. Sugar (and molasses) and canned pineapple con-stitute all but a small portion of the total movement from the Islands to Pacific ports. If coffee is added to these two prod-ucts, the chief Hawaiian outbound trade is specified.

In contrast with the limited varieties of imports, mainland shipments to Hawaii are much more diverse, in fact more diversified than any other Pacific Coast trade. The Islands are not self-sufficient; economic activities are highly spe-cialized, hence they import small amounts of a great many

TABLE 53

JOINT SCHEDULE OF WESTBOUND AND SOUTHBOUND VESSELS, TRANS-PACIFIC PASSENGER CONFERENCE*

From Pacific Ports, 1931		Vessel	Line	Due						
Leave	Leave West Coast			Honolulu	Yokohama	Kobe or Osaka	Shanghai	Hong Kong	Manila	Singapore
June 1 Los Angeles	San Francisco 2	"Lurline"	Matson	June 7						
June 2 Vancouver	Victoria 4	"Empress of Canada"	Canadian Pac.	June 7	June 16	June 17	June 19	June 22	June 24	
June 4 Los Angeles	San Francisco 6	"Asama Maru"	N.Y.K.	June 11	June 20	June 22	June 25	June 27		
June 4 Los Angeles	San Francisco 8	"President Monroe"	Dollar	June 15		June 23	July 2	July 6	July 9	July 14
June 8 San Francisco	Los Angeles 9	"Malolo"	Matson	June 14						
June 9 Victoria	Seattle 12	"President McKinley"	American Mail		June 22	June 23	June 26	June 29	July 2	
June 9 Los Angeles	San Francisco 12	"Silverbeech"	Silver						July 6	July 27
June 12 Vancouver	Victoria 13	"Empress of Russia"	Canadian Pac.	June 18	June 27	June 28	July 1	July 4	July 7	
June 12 San Francisco	Portland 13	"General Sherman"	States		June 29	June 30	July 3	July 7	July 10	
June 15 Los Angeles	San Francisco 15	"President Coolidge"	Dollar	June 20	June 29	June 30	July 2	July 5	July 7	
June 15 Seattle	Vancouver 16	"Hikawa Maru"	N.Y.K.		June 29	July 2§				
June 15 Los Angeles	San Francisco 16	"Lurline"	Matson	June 21						
June 20 Vancouver	Victoria 20	"Niagara"	Canadian-Aus.	June 27						†
June 23 Los Angeles	San Francisco 25	"Taiyo Maru"	N.Y.K.	July 1	July 11	July 13§	July 16	July 20		
June 18 Los Angeles	San Francisco 22	"President Van Buren"	Dollar	June 29		July 12	July 17	July 20	July 16	July 28
June 22 San Francisco	Los Angeles 23	"Malolo"	Matson	June 28						
June 23 Victoria	Seattle 23	"President Jackson"	American Mail		July 6	July 7	July 10	July 13	July 13	
June 26 San Francisco	Los Angeles 27	"Mariposa"	Oceanic	July 2						‡
June 26 Los Angeles	San Francisco 29	"Silverguava"	Silver						July 22	Aug. 9
June 23 Los Angeles	San Francisco 29	"President Cleveland"	Dollar	July 5		July 17	July 20	July 23	July 21	
June 29 Los Angeles		"La Plata Maru"	O.S.K.		July 16	July 18				
June 29 Seattle		"Hiye Maru"	N.Y.K.		July 13	July 16				
June 29 Los Angeles	San Francisco 30	"Lurline"	Matson	July 5						
June 30 Vancouver	Victoria 30	"Empress of Japan"	Canadian Pac.	July 5	July 14	July 15	July 22	July 24	July 26	
June 30 Los Angeles	San Francisco 3	"Chichibu Maru"	N.Y.K.	July 8	July 17	July 19	July 24	July 28		
June 26 San Francisco	Portland 4	"General Lee"	States		July 20	July 21			July 31	

* Data from *Official Steamship Guide*, May 1934.   † Calls also at Suva, Rarotonga, Auckland, Wellington, and Sydney.
‡ Calls also at Papeete, Pago Pago, Suva, Rarotonga, Auckland, Wellington, Sydney, and Melbourne.
§ Calls also at Nagasaki or Moji.

miscellaneous products in addition to the leading export commodities of the Pacific Coast region.

In the foregoing pages, the importance of transpacific maritime trade to the American Pacific States region has not been overstressed, but the mere recitation of the facts has implied much. Because of the Panama Canal, which has made possible direct all-water connections between our Atlantic Coast and the Far East, to the West Coast the foreign commerce of the region has in some ways become less important; it has also become somewhat more diversified among countries, but not with respect to the commodities entering into the trade. Although transpacific intercourse is relatively less important than it was before the construction of the Canal, the significant fact remains that the largest maritime stake of the Pacific States region is around the Pacific Basin. One significant evidence of the intimate relationships across the greatest ocean is to be found in the regular, frequent sailings of splendid ocean vessels (see Table 53, p. 287).

Furthermore, the trend in the foreign commerce of the United States as a whole is continually magnifying the rôle of transpacific countries. No more than a review of the developments of the past decade has been attempted in this chapter. No issues, no problems, have been injected into the record, nor can forecasts or prophesies be accurately made. But the problems of the Pacific cannot be ignored. The entire future of maritime commercial relations hinges, to a surprising degree, upon how the peoples living on the further shores of the Pacific work out their own social, political, and economic problems.

XIV. Trade Setting of Oceania and the Orient

An adequate explanation of maritime trading activity of our American Pacific ports would involve an examination of the developed resources of each country with which they have commercial relations. Obviously, limitations of space and time will not permit going this far afield. But because the future of the American Pacific sector is so closely wedded to the future of Pacific Basin countries, it is vital to consider briefly some of the more significant factors in the trade setting of certain transpacific countries. Even though now some of these lands are not so important to the commerce of Pacific Coast ports as are certain European nations, nevertheless the past is behind us and the present is transitory. Any judgment of trends must be based on an appraisal of undeveloped as well as developed resources, and on human as well as material resources, as one endeavors to peer into the not too far-distant future.

In the South Pacific Ocean, the leading countries are Australia and New Zealand. Nine-tenths of Australia really belongs to the Indian Ocean Basin, but since the one-tenth draining into the Pacific holds four-fifths of the country's population and wealth, it is surely proper to consider Australia as a South Pacific land. Although this country on the fringe of the world is of approximately the same size as the United States, it has only six million people. The only important commercial area is situated on the one-fifth or Pacific side, which is cut off by a series of mountain ranges, generally called the Great Dividing Range, from the vast wasteland to the west and the Indian Ocean.

Offsetting some of the disadvantages of being located approximately halfway around the world from London or New York are the climatic advantages which accrue from isolation in the midst of an ocean. The 100- to 200-mile-wide eastern coastal slope of Australia receives abundant rain from the southeast trades, fairly evenly distributed throughout the year. Because north-to-south Australia covers some 19° of latitude, climate ranges from subtropical at the north to temperate at the south end of the coast. It is not surpris-

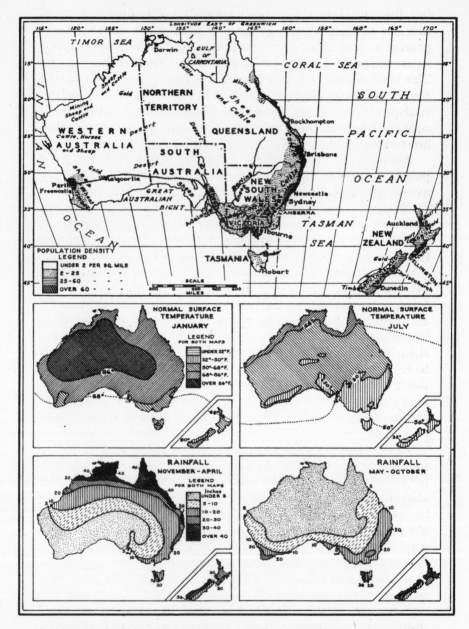

Fig. 33.—Maps showing population density, temperature, and rainfall of Oceania.

ing, then, in view of favorable rainfall and temperature conditions, to find varied crops. Wheat, wool, meats, dairy
products, and fruits (grapes, apples, berries, pineapples,
bananas, and oranges) are some of the principal products.
The land is also rich in mineral resources. Australia is still
the third largest gold-producer in the world, and the leading
coal-producer of the Southern Hemisphere. Silver, lead,
copper, tin, zinc, and iron are also mined in considerable
quantities.

Australia is inhabited by a homogeneous and energetic
people, mostly of British extraction. The scarcity of natives
avoids a race problem; economic and social conditions are
distinctly favorable. Most of the six million inhabitants live
in towns, and 40 per cent of them are in six cities. The great
strides made in navigation and in various communication
facilities during the past hundred years have prevented isolated Australia from becoming a backward country with
limited intercourse with the remainder of the world. Her
foreign commerce amounts to over a billion dollars a year,
an extremely high per capita trade similar in this respect to
Canada, but much less than that of New Zealand. The vast
sheep and cattle ranches are responsible for the large exports
to Europe of wool, frozen mutton, beef, and butter. Next to
wool, from the standpoint of value, the most important export consists of gold specie, which normally amounts to approximately twice the value of the outward trade in wheat
and flour.

Chief imports into Australia are textiles and clothing,
machinery, and other manufactured products. Although
large coal deposits at Newcastle and Sydney, situated by the
shoreline, have contributed to exports and aided Australia's
industries materially, these manufactures are of a fairly
simple type, such as tanning, dairy-products manufacture,
and canning and preserving. The stage has not yet been
reached when large amounts of raw materials are needed for
manufacturing purposes, although more complex processes
have now been well started. As an indication of the maritime
significance of Oceania, it is noteworthy that British, German, Dutch, Japanese, American, Canadian, and Norwegian
shipping companies maintain direct lines to the principal

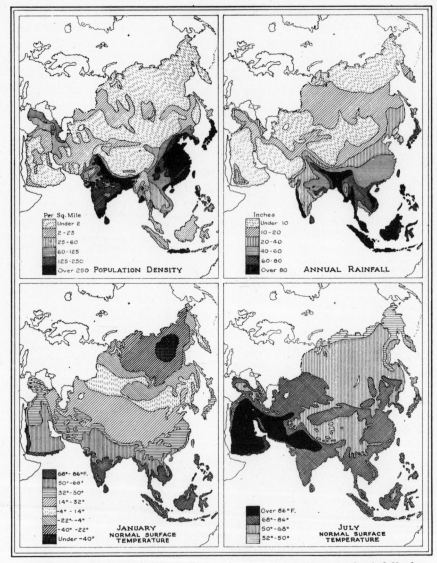

Per Sq. Mile
Under 2
2 - 25
25 - 60
60 - 125
125 - 250
Over 250   POPULATION DENSITY

Inches
Under 10
10 - 20
20 - 40
40 - 60
60 - 80
Over 80   ANNUAL RAINFALL

68° - 86° F.
50° - 68°
32° - 50°
14° - 32°
-4° - 14°
-22° - -4°
-40° - -22°
Under -40°   JANUARY
NORMAL SURFACE
TEMPERATURE

Over 86° F.
68° - 86°
50° - 68°
32° - 50°   JULY
NORMAL SURFACE
TEMPERATURE

FIG. 34.—Maps showing population density, temperature, and rainfall of Asia.

ports of Sydney and Melbourne, as well as the New Zealand ports of Auckland and Wellington.

A thousand miles or more southeast of the Australian Pa-

cific Coast is New Zealand, a British country whose eastern
slope resembles that of Australia in climate and products.
Two-thirds the size of California, it has a range of volcanic
mountains running the full length of the two main islands,
the peaks in the South Island attaining majestic heights and
in many ways resembling the Alps of Switzerland. Climate
is mild, cool and moist in many parts, snowfall and water are
plentiful, with rain coming usually from the westerlies off
the South Indian Ocean. A quarter of the country is forest
land, and much of the remainder is grass, which permits
grazing throughout the year. Like Australia's, its 1.5 million
population is largely British in extraction, culture, character,
and economic and social life. However, these British com-
monwealths have absolutely distinct identities. They are a
thousand miles apart, and an indication of the rivalry appears in the scant liking of the New Zealander for the name
"Australasian."

Most of New Zealand's exports are animal products—
wool, frozen beef and mutton, dairy products, and the like.
In the mountains are found considerable gold, iron, and coal,
and lesser amounts of silver, copper, and manganese. There
are tremendous food-producing possibilities, and because of
labor shortage and distance from foreign markets New Zealand is largely a sheep and cattle country. The same general
type of manufactured articles are imported as in the case of
Australia. The inhabitants of New Zealand are of a high
type, and the 50,000 Maoris living in their midst are a far
more advanced group than the natives found generally in
the South Seas.

North of Australia and New Zealand and thousands of
miles from the Pacific Coast states are lands inhabited
mainly by races having strikingly divergent origins, social
customs, languages, and civilizations. Not only do they differ
among themselves but practically all are alien to American
institutions and manner of living. Because of these marked
variances, maritime intercourse with them is hindered and
also aided. Hindered, because the native or cultivated wants
of Asiatic peoples for food, clothing, and shelter are not the
same as those of European races or of English-speaking
countries, although in some respects the desires of these

peoples have been greatly altered in relatively recent years
as a result of "economic penetration" of Western civilization. And at the same time aided, because their civilization
has developed certain arts and handicrafts which do not
flourish in the United States. True, many of the imports
from Far Eastern countries are in the nature of luxuries
rather than necessities, but because of America's industrial
growth and consequent advanced living standards her population can afford to buy these commodities. Other products,
particularly certain raw materials, are necessities. Aware of
this advanced state of material well-being in Western countries, Asiatics import American machinery and manufactured products in the hope that they may build in a similar
fashion and reap rewards in more physical comforts for the
masses of the people. They aspire to greater political and
economic strength among nations.

Now, as in the past, one of the chief factors in the political
and business relations of Pacific peoples with the world is
the interplay between forces making for Asiatic migration in
the quest of a better life, and the tendency of Europeans to
dominate Asia (in the quest also of material gains though of
a far more ambitious nature) but not to settle there. Until
comparatively recent years, Pacific countries did not have
ready access to the Atlantic world. Consequently, the maritime trade which developed among the various sectors of the
great Pacific Basin was confined largely within a single sea.
The longest shipping-routes were across the Pacific and the
bulk of the carrying tonnage remained in the Pacific.

Unlike the American side, where the sea meets the land
abruptly and coastal islands are rare and of little importance, the Asiatic coast is fringed by closely spaced islands
extending from Kamchatka through the Kurile, Japanese,
and Ryukyu islands to Taiwan, thence through the Philippines and the Moluccas to Papua, Thursday Island, and down
the Australian coast to Tasmania.

Compared with lands bordering the Atlantic, those of the
Pacific are difficult of access from the sea. They are characterized by abrupt mountain ranges rather than by coastal
plains. Across the Bering Strait, narrowly separating America and Asia, there is a long range of mountains running

southwest, gaining in altitude all the while until it joins the Himalayas at the west end of the great plateau of Tibet. The Himalayas projecting east and sloping to the south through the Malay lands to Singapore are the same range, sometimes submerged on its course, which features the extant shore of Australia.

Physiographically and climatically, the Asiatic mainland consists of seven fairly distinct regions: the Siberian coastal zone, the Chinese-Tibet plateau, Manchuria, North China, Central China, South China, and the Mekong Valley. In addition, Japan, the Philippines, the East Indies, Australia, New Zealand, and some thousands of lesser islands are contained within the great Pacific Basin on the Asiatic side. India, for present purposes, is added to the category of trans-pacific countries from the standpoint of commercial intercourse with the American Pacific States.

Size, shape, and position of Asiatic countries all combine to produce climatic variations and extremes. The prevailing westerlies of the most favorable latitudes do not appreciably modify the severity of the climate. Climate and topography both have a striking effect upon the peoples of this area and their trade relations with the world. Extremes of heat or cold occur at some time of the year in almost all of Asia and offer a serious deterrent not only to agriculture but also to the health and energy of the local population.

In the far north of the mainland lies the cold tundra belt, with few inhabitants, scant vegetation, and limited natural resources. From a commercial standpoint it may be dismissed from consideration. To the south is the Siberian coastal region, believed by some to have enormous potentialities and by others to possess so many disadvantages that its development will be indefinitely postponed. The latter view appears the more logical. One of the world's greatest timber reserves is found in this region, but because of the extremely cold climate the quality of the stands is not good, and, even if it were, the region lacks the capacity to furnish a steady growth. The forests, it may be noted here in passing, abound in bear, lynx, wolf, fox, sable, squirrel, hare, and ermine. The population of that Pacific slope is probably not over 1,300,000; most of these people are Cossack peasant im-

migrants living along the Trans-Siberian railroad and the
Amur. Mineral resources are only superficially known, yet
few geologists doubt that the southern part of the area contains large quantities of iron, coal, and petroleum and moderate amounts of gold. This much is known about Siberian
minerals: they exist in great variety.

In the Amur region to the south, horses, cattle, sheep, and
hogs are raised, and wheat, rye, barley, oats, soy beans, and
rice are grown to a limited extent. The fisheries hold some
promise of expanding enterprise, although this resource has
been largely exhausted, just as fur trapping is becoming a
vanishing business. The salmon fisheries off Kamchatka are
largely in Japanese hands. Although the region is probably
rich in mineral and timber resources and possesses hydroelectric power potentialities, it is sparsely populated, lacks
capital, and at present exports chiefly wheat, butter, hides,
and furs, none of which are of especial interest to the American Pacific states.

Farther to the south is Manchuria, now Manchukuo, about
two and one-half times the size of California, with 30,000,000
people, about 97 per cent of whom are Chinese. Manchukuo
is situated in the latitudes of Minnesota and Manitoba. In
the northern section heavy timber stands are to be found and
lumbering is active; iron, coal, and gold are mined; soy
beans, indigo, opium, tobacco, wheat, and barley are among
the chief crops. In 1929 Manchuria's 222,000,000-bushel production of soy beans represented 63 per cent of the entire
world production. Although the bean industry of this section
has not displaced the silk industry as China's largest export
factor, its products still account for a significant share of
China's total exports.

Japan, meagerly endowed with natural resources, looks
to Manchukuo for the coal and iron which she lacks. At
present the domestic steel industry relies heavily on pig- and
ingot-iron importations from the United States. In many
ways Japan proper is in a situation economically similar to
that of the British Isles, but, lacking wool, iron, and sufficient
coal, the nation must rely substantially on foreign importations to feed, clothe, and shelter her 64,000,000 inhabitants.
The country is unsuited for growing cotton, and sheep-rais-

ing was practically unknown until after the World War. Rice is the one great staple foodstuff, but not enough is grown for native consumption, with the result that rice grown elsewhere, including the Sacramento Valley, is often imported. Although some wheat, barley, and rye are grown, a deficiency in cereals is a normal occurrence. In the waters surrounding the Japanese archipelago marine life flourishes. The Japanese have learned to exploit these resources of the sea to a remarkable degree. Fishing is not confined to the immediate waters. Huge catches are made and an exportable surplus is produced which enters into external trade.

Latitude, mountain ranges, the Chinese monsoon, and two ocean currents largely determine the climate of Japan. Difference in latitude alone might explain the cold temperatures of the northern islands, which are in the same latitude as Vancouver, and the subtropical climate of Formosa to the extreme south, in the same latitude as the southern point of Lower California. Coupled with this range in latitude are a warm ocean current (the Japan Current) coming out of the South China Sea and washing the southeast shores of the islands as far north as Tokyo, and a cold south-bound current from the shores of Kamchatka which exercises a cooling rather than a tempering influence on the northern islands. Further, an extended range of mountains divides the islands approximately north and south, so that climatic conditions on the eastern and western slopes are quite different. On the western side, toward Asia, temperature extremes of hot and cold are more marked than on the Pacific side, but, even so, in Tokyo variations of from 12° to 98° F. are normal throughout the year, and the annual rainfall reaches 58 inches. The northern islands, being mountainous and cold, are sparsely populated and little cultivated. Honshu, the main island, is also mountainous and forested, but has a milder climate, especially to the south, and is intensively cultivated and densely populated.

Although her main islands are smaller than California in area, Japan supports as many as half the population of the United States in the country proper, with 26,000,000 more living in Formosa, which supplies the major portion of the world's camphor, Korea (Chosen), and Karafuto (Sakhalin).

Half of the population are farmers engaged in tilling small plots of land and living in small villages. The other half of the people live in urban localities, six of which have over 600,000 population. Japan's land resources consist of agricultural crops such as rice, beans, peas, barley, wheat, and sweet potatoes, all of which are grown extensively; mineral resources of copper,[1] with coal, petroleum, and iron found in only moderate quantities; and potential hydroelectric power resources which are rapidly being developed and offer promising possibilities.

Industrial development, although comparatively recent in origin, has made rapid strides, so that Japan now manufactures for her own use or for export the following products: pottery, glassware, machinery, tools, paper toys, textiles made of cotton, wool, and silk, and so forth. Raw silk, the most important item in the economic life of the country, continues to be the largest single factor in exports, accounting for 40 per cent of the total value. The United States takes nearly all of Japan's silk, and, in turn, Japan is a heavy buyer of raw cotton from the United States. Silk exports go far toward offsetting heavy imports of cotton, lumber, foodstuffs, iron and steel, and machinery.

Like the Seattle-Vancouver sector of the American Pacific Coast, the Yokohama-Osaka-Kobe sector of Japan is strategically situated on the Great Circle Route across the North Pacific, and this, the shortest navigation route between America and Asia, is naturally most important on this ocean highway. Not only from a cargo-originating and coaling-station point of view but also from a navigation angle the Yokohama region has an enviable geographic location. It is a natural gateway to China and the promising southeastern Asia area.

Despite her many advantages, however, the point should be stressed that Japan proper has little coal, iron, or petroleum, grows no cotton, and possesses very few domestic animals. Furthermore, her pasture land is limited, a situation

---

[1] Although more or less richly endowed with copper, the cost of production has so increased since the war that Japan now has a net excess of imports; most of these imports are from the United States.

which is subject to vast change with the exploitation of Manchuria. The food problem is always serious, the national debt is large, and taxes are high. Foreign trade is absolutely essential to her prosperity, and in this respect she is dependent upon three markets—China, the United States, and India.[2] The Japanese are an alert and progressive people—the active factor in the problems of the Far East, while China is the passive factor. Although not particularly gifted in inventiveness, they are avaricious readers, serious students, and people quick to adopt improvements in their economic life and institutions. For subsequent industrial development it appears that Japan will depend upon outside sources for textile fibers, except silk, for industrial metals, except perhaps copper, and for fuel. The big problem will be to find a means of paying for such imports.

On the mainland of Asia resides almost half the population of the world. There is to be found every conceivable type of topography, climate, and natural resources. Because of its relatively low latitude and heavy summer rains, southeastern Asia grows enormous crops. In many places two or three crops can be raised each year. Coal and iron are to be found in abundance, especially in China. Comparative freedom from storms, except in the summer typhoon seas, great rivers, and innumerable islands provide natural facilities for transportation. Water-power potentialities seem to be unlimited, yet the people have done very little to utilize their natural advantages—advantages which in some respects seem to surpass those of Europe and other favored sections of the world. Instead, famines are common, transportation and communication are largely of a primitive type, and the living standard of the mass of the people is wretchedly low.

The internal and external trade of the countries of the Orient is extremely inactive in comparison with that of the Japanese Kingdom. Industry, in the American sense, is

[2] During the last four or five years about 30 per cent of Japan's imports (by value) were from the United States, while over 40 per cent of her exports were purchased by the United States. China bought from 16 to 18 per cent of Japanese exports and supplied approximately 10 per cent of her imports. British India supplied another 13 per cent of imports and took in return 8 or 9 per cent of exports. The leading Japanese exports are raw silk and textile manufactures.

almost nonexistent. Manufacturing, except for an occasional plant operated by foreigners in order to prepare simple foodstuffs or semi-manufactured goods for export, is of the most primitive type. Many of the peoples are subjected to European imperialism, notably in British India and in British Malaya, Chosen (Japanese), French Indo-China, Netherlands India, and various dependencies and mandates. The Philippine Islands are under the jurisdiction of the United States, but are not to be classed as a possession. Siam, nominally independent, has been subjected to tutelage by Britain and France. Japan is the only truly independent state, since China, technically a sovereign power, has been subjected to internal and external pressure.

China proper falls into three fairly distinct sections, North China, Central China, and South China, corresponding roughly to the three ancient political divisions as well as to the climatic and topographic divisions. Extremes of heat and cold are more marked in the north and away from the sea; of the three divisions, South China has the least extreme climate. Like Japan, China has many fine harbors and in addition several great navigable rivers. Her people are less aggressive, more conservative, and less given to change than are the Japanese. They can endure much, are very patient—in short, they are perhaps the main passive factor in the Far Eastern situation. About 80 per cent of the Chinese engage in agricultural pursuits, farming small two- to eight-acre plots but securing fairly high yields. Vast mountainous and desert regions greatly reduce the areas under cultivation so that one finds the mass of the total population living in about one-third of the total area of the country. China is the world's largest producer of rice, soy beans, peanuts, tea, and tung oil, and is exceeded only by Japan in the production of raw silk and by the United States and India in the production of cotton.

North China differs from other sections in several ways. Writing of her people, Dr. Ellsworth Huntington, in *The Character of Races* (1924), makes this striking observation: "Another curious fact about China is that although the southerners are more progressive than the northerners, the northern cities have become more Europeanized than the southern." Meats other than pork are here common items of food; rice, except for a species of millet called "small rice," is not grown. The people inhabiting this area live on millet, wheat, barley, maize, soy beans, potatoes, and sweet potatoes, and rice is imported for the well-to-do. Nor is bamboo grown here; it is imported from the south. Owing to the coincidence of summer rains and high temperatures, North China grows several subtropical crops — tobacco, opium, silk, cotton, tea, and sugar. In North China is located Shansi province, which contains the world's largest known anthracite fields and also vast bituminous deposits as well as rich iron-ore beds, limestone, potter's clay, and salt.[3]

Through the center of Central China flows the great Yangtze-Kiang or Blue River, which is navigable to Chinese junks for some 1,700 miles from its mouth and for ocean steamers some one thousand miles from the sea. Tea, rice, cotton, silk, and bamboo are the principal products of this region. Carts, donkeys, and camels, used in North China, are rare; railways are of scant importance, being replaced by human beings and buffaloes as the chief modes of transportation. Most of the manufacturing of China is done in this section and 60 per cent of the country's foreign trade originates here, primarily because it contains most of the important treaty ports.

Shanghai is the most important trading-port in the Far East and by far the leading distributing-point for China. It now ranks after London and New York as the world's third port and after Chicago as the fifth largest city in the world. The concentration point of the two most important industries of China, cotton textiles and flour-milling, is located in Shanghai. Although China has begun to emerge from domestic handicraft industries, the factory system plays only a minor rôle as yet in the industrial life of the country.

[3] Estimates of the mineral resources of all China are speculative. The present view inclines to the belief that such resources have been greatly overestimated, owing to observers' having mistaken widespread surface occurrence for abundance. Closer examination seems to indicate that the greater number of orebodies known are small in extent and ill-adapted to large-scale mining operations.

Japan and Taiwan (Formosa), Hong Kong, and the United States supply most of the imports into the country, and in the same order of listing they buy the merchandise China has to export. At the Seventeenth National Foreign Trade Convention held in Los Angeles (1930), Mr. R. J. Cromie, the well-known publisher of the *Vancouver Sun,* observed:

> To my mind China is the greatest potential trader in the world today. Look at the size of China—four million square miles; China has a variety of climate ranging from 25 degrees north of the equator down at Canton, to 60 degrees north up in Manchuria and Mongolia— and producing in that range of climate every variety of crops and peoples, from semi-tropical fruits and small agile people in the south, to cereal and bean crops and big high-cheeked Manchus and Mongolians in the north; and China has about 425 millions of people.

South China is smaller in both area and population than North and Central China, the rugged character of much of its land making it unsuited for thick settlement. Around Canton in the delta lands, however, it is densely populated. Rice, sweet potatoes, corn or maize, peanuts, tea, beans, sugar cane, and green vegetables are all grown in its semi-tropical climate. Oranges, pineapples, mangoes, bananas, persimmons, coconuts, and similar fruits may be had in abundance. The mineral resources of this region are not well known, but ample supplies of coal and iron exist, particularly in the western highland province of Yunan, which in addition contains valuable copper and tin deposits.

The bulk of the commerce of South China, consisting of tea, silk, and vegetable oils, is handled at Hong Kong, a free port with a fine harbor, favorably located on the north side of the South China sea for handling the transshipments for Suez and Panama traffic.

South of China and east of India, stretching from the Tropic of Cancer south to the equator at Singapore, is the peninsula known as the Federated Malay States. This is really a mountainous continuation of the great Chinese plateau throughout its northern section with an eastern-and-western mountain rim running south. Much of the territory is forest jungle, a considerable part is grassland, and only the lands along the streams and in the deltas are extensively cultivated. In Indo-China, the largest colony of France,

Haiphong and Saigon are the chief seaports; the latter has a fine natural harbor through which over a million tons of rice are shipped in export each year. Rice, fish, rubber, tin, and teakwood are the chief exports of the area. Hundreds of thousands of Chinese have gone into Indo-China and now control a good share of the business activities. As in so much of the southeastern Asiatic region, the development of resources here has only begun. Further growth in modern transportation will mean much in the economic life of these peoples.

Between Indo-China and the Straits Settlements lies Siam, a country of eleven million people, with its leading activities centered at Bangkok, which is located on an island. Siamese products are similar to those of Indo-China, with rice the outstanding crop. There are numerous rice mills in the country, a few of them of modern type; most of these establishments are owned by resident Chinese. Tin-mining and teakwood-working are local industries furnishing export commodities.

British Malaya is noted as the world's leading export source of tin, and also for its vast production of plantation rubber. Other products, including rice and copra, are of minor importance. Because of the tremendous exports of rubber and tin, it is not surprising that the United States imports over 40 per cent of the entire exports of British Malaya. The imports come first of all from Netherlands India and second from the United Kingdom; the chief items are gasoline, rice, and miscellaneous goods, but the foreign trade figures are notoriously unsatisfactory, since Singapore has such an important position in the entrepôt trade of the Far East. The future of this strategically situated outpost rests mainly upon the world's demands for rubber and tin.

Between the Federated Malay States and Australia lie the East Indies, an archipelago extending over 4,000 miles from the west end of Sumatra to the east end of New Guinea. About 70,000,000 people live on the islands in this region, 42,000,000 in Java alone and 12,000,000 on the seven thousand islands in the Philippine group. Climate is tropical—hot and rainy. Except for the Philippines, northwest Borneo and eastern New Guinea (British), and eastern Timor (Portuguese), most of the archipelago is under the efficiently paternal Netherlands government. Java, an island the size of New York state, is the most highly developed and orderly tropical region of the world. Noteworthy local products are excellent crops of sugar, rice, tea, rubber, rattan, varnish, pepper, tobacco, and cinchona bark.

American trade with Netherlands India has increased enormously since the war. Automotive products have been in great demand, but these islands have also absorbed considerable quantities of canned goods, wheat flour, and similar products of the American Pacific Coast. Except for Java, however, the islands are only beginning their development. The rubber plantations in Sumatra will become a large factor in the world supply. The Philippines, on the other hand, produce abundant crops of coconuts, sweet potatoes, beans, bananas, sugar, rice, tobacco, and hemp. Most of their trade is with the United States. It is largely because of the absence of trade barriers with the United States on exports of sugar and other products that the Philippines may be given their independence.

Before the war and the opening of the Panama Canal most of the trade intercourse between the United States and British India was of an indirect nature, i.e., goods were shipped to Great Britain for transshipment. Now, especially the United States Pacific Coast has a more direct transpacific connection with India. Trade, of course, is predominantly with Great Britain; but the United States holds second place, followed by Japan. Since Great Britain seems reluctant to release or slacken her hold on India, boycotts of British goods are frequent and trade is diverted to other countries. Still, the total commerce of India is small in comparison with a population of some 351,000,000. America's part in India is insignificant compared with that of England, yet in the past the United States has imported more from India than from all of Latin America exclusive of Argentina and Cuba.

Wheat, barley, and rice, together with corn and millet, are the chief mainstay of the people. Sugar, cotton, jute, opium, indigo, tea, oil seeds, and tobacco are other important crops. Half of the value of India's exports is in raw cotton and

jute. Oil seeds and tea account for another 25 per cent of
the total. Her rôle in supplying the outside world with food
is of minor importance, since most of the food is needed at
home to provide a bare existence for her huge population.
Dependent as she is almost wholly on the summer monsoon
rains, crop failures are frequent. When rains are delayed
or do not last long enough, millions of people are deprived
of food, suffer, or die, and disease spreads rapidly. The
repeated famines of India are a great hindrance to her
material development, second in importance only to her
uneconomic worship of animal life. India's economic resources are rich and abundant.

A moderate amount of manufacturing has been started
in the cotton and jute industries, so that now some of the
country's exports are slightly or coarsely fabricated. Imports are mainly clothing (chiefly cotton), some silk, a small
amount of machinery, railroad equipment, automobiles,
paper, and so on. Per capita trade is small because of the
racial characteristics of the people and their economic and
social conditions. Partly because of the climate, in many
districts millions of natives have little energy or ambition,
which constitutes a human-resource deficiency. Population
is so dense in sections of the country that it is only with great
difficulty that a living may be gained from the soil. Some
Indians are good traders, but business capacity and mechanical ability are rare; consequently India is a country with
scant economic enterprise as yet except agriculture, but with
a bright industrial future. Since the war, the trade of the
United States with India has increased sixfold.

In the foregoing pages, the differences among the various
nations of the Pacific in resources, wealth, character of the
people, and stage of industrial development, all of which are
determinants of the character of domestic and foreign trade,
have been all too sketchily outlined. Nature's resources are
by no means equally distributed; consequently trading is
necessary, and trading involves the utilization of human
resources and the exploitation of natural resources.

By way of summary, the potentialities of the Far East
can be clearly pictured through the presentation of constructive population and economic information. Table 54,

based on official statistics for the year 1930, giving the area, population, density per square mile, length of railways, imports per capita, and exports per capita, presents a bird's-

TABLE 54

OFFICIAL ESTIMATES OF AREA, POPULATION, DENSITY, RAILWAYS, IMPORTS, AND EXPORTS FOR OCEANIA AND THE ORIENT, 1930*

	Area (Thousand sq. mi.)	Population (Thousands)	Density (Per sq. mi.)	Railways (Miles)	Imports (Per capita)	Exports (Per capita)
Orient						
China	4,300	462	110.4	9,507	1.3	0.9
Chosen (Korea)	85	21	247.1	1,710	8.6	6.3
India, British	1,108	351	173.4	41,724	1.9	2.6
Indo-China, French (1929)	285	21	74.6	1,488	4.8	4.8
Japan (proper)	147	64	437.4	12,187	11.8	11.0
Malaya, British	53	4	80.1	1,037	96.0	90.0
Netherlands India ..	734	61	82.8	4,596	5.5	8.0
Philippine Islands..	114	12	107.2	803	10.0	10.9
Siam	200	12	57.5	1,760	7.8	8.2
Total	7,026	1,008	143.5	74,812	....	....
Australasia						
Australia	2,975	6	2.2	26,605	98.5	91.9
New Zealand†	103	2	14.6	3,403	146.0	150.0
Total	3,078	8	2.6	30,008	....	....
Continental United States	2,974	122,775	41.7	249,433	24.5	30.2
World	50,892	1,992,500	39.2	763,462	14.1	12.8

* Data from *United States Department of Commerce Yearbook, 1931*, Vol. II.
† Area excludes outlying and annexed islands. Population includes Maoris.

eye view of the teeming situation for each country, and illustrates the tremendous possibilities for internal development and foreign trade as the standard of living inevitably improves and the Occident is more and more drawn upon for new ideas and different products.

XV. Cargo Tonnage Changes, 1929–1932

The calendar or fiscal year 1930 has been utilized throughout this study as the most satisfactory single twelve-month
period from the standpoint of portraying typical conditions.
While no one year, or even series of years, is altogether
satisfactory for this purpose, the author has discovered that
a series of moving averages, based on the statistics of several
years, would not help materially in enabling the reader to
gauge the wide and irregular changes. In view of a probable
desire, however, for a record of the later years, it appears
worth while to devote this separate chapter to significant
cargo statistics for the past decade and especially for the
years 1929 to 1932, inclusive.[1]

This chapter is designed primarily to show the relative
and actual importance of the Pacific Coast district in the
maritime traffic of the United States.

The aggregate water-borne foreign and domestic commerce of the United States declined from 582,000,000 long
tons in the calendar year 1929 to 307,000,000 long tons in 1932,
a drop of nearly 50 per cent; while the Pacific Coast traffic
declined from 84,000,000 to 51,000,000 tons, or less than 40
per cent. By eliminating the Great Lakes ports, which suffered the greatest loss, the United States seaport tonnage
dropped from 316,000,000 to 220,000,000, or approximately
one-third. In the attempt to avoid duplication, primarily in
the coastwise statistics, the Shipping Board Bureau announced adjusted cargo movement tonnage of 346,000,000
tons in 1929 and 185,000,000 tons in 1932, again a drop of
almost one-half. Thus, the traffic of Pacific ports has had a
more favorable record, to the extent of 20 per cent, than
that of the United States as a whole.

Contrasting 1929 and 1932, one finds foreign commerce of
United States seaports declined 44 per cent, that of the

[1] The writer spent several days in Washington during January 1934 in
order to secure access to unpublished information. The material in this
chapter is based mainly upon data made available by the Bureau of Research of the Shipping Board Bureau and the Transportation Division of
the United States Department of Commerce. Official statistics for the calendar year 1933 were not expected to be available until late in 1934.

Pacific district 43 per cent; coastwise commerce 23 per cent for the United States and 37 per cent for the district; and the intercoastal commerce of the United States declined 45 per cent. The explanation for the marked drop in the Pacific cargoes lies in the abnormal amount of Western-originating tonnage which is represented by the preponderance of heavy bulk cargoes of petroleum and lumber products; these same trades suffered owing to sharp drop in the prices of these commodities in the Gulf region, and the latter region bene-fited at the expense of the Pacific seaboard. It is noteworthy, nevertheless, that the slump in the latter region was conspic-uous in the inbound movement: for instance, in the inter-coastal trade from 1929 to 1932, the inbound traffic into Atlantic Coast ports dropped 45 per cent compared to 70 per cent for Pacific ports, while the outbound cargoes de-clined 57 per cent for Atlantic ports compared to 44 per cent for Pacific ports. Regional aspects of industrial raw mate-rials and fuels will be considered later. Table 55 shows the foreign trade tonnage in 1930.

The traffic through the Panama Canal provides another important basis of comparison. The grand total of cargo tonnage moving from the Atlantic to the Pacific declined from 10,166,000 long tons in the calendar year 1929 to 4,887,000 long tons in 1932, a diminution of one-half. The even distribution of this slackening trade is shown by a total decline of from 4,434,000 to 2,249,000 long tons, respectively, to the West Coast of the United States from the following regions: the East Coast of the United States 3,467,000 and 1,798,000 long tons, respectively; East Coast to other parts of North America 329,000 and 173,000 tons; and from Europe to West Coast of North America, 1,024,000 and 431,000 tons in 1929 and 1932, respectively.

The eastbound Panama traffic from the Pacific to the At-lantic held up much better. This movement increased from 2.1 to 2.7 per cent of the total traffic; in other words, the west-east traffic became 30 per cent more important in the total movement. We learn that the Pacific-Atlantic move-ment declined from 21,284,000 tons to 13,211,000 tons, or 38 per cent; of these amounts the West Coast of the United States contributed 11,009,000 and 6,650,000 tons, respectively,

TABLE 55

CARGO TONNAGE OF WATER-BORNE IMPORTS AND EXPORTS, BY MAJOR
COMMODITIES, AND BY COASTAL DISTRICTS, 1930*

(Thousands of cargo tons)

Commodity	Total	North Atlantic	South Atlantic	Gulf	Pacific	Great Lakes
*Imports—*Total	47,562	31,477	1,748	4,801	2,905	6,631
Vegetable oils	502	374	1	50	77	...
Vegetables and vegetable products...	800	579	24	46	151	...
Animal, fish, and dairy products....	376	272	1	34	68	1
Bananas	1,535	811	36	613	75	...
Coconuts and copra...................	341	64	1	54	222	...
Sugar	3,104	2,240	157	597	110	...
Coffee	751	468	3	193	87	...
Vegetable fibers and grasses.........	332	190	3	53	62	24
Pulp wood and wood pulp............	2,731	1,710	...	18	51	952
Paper and manufactures.............	638	258	20	105	132	123
Coal and coke.........................	825	680	...	...	102	43
Gypsum	808	726	...	6	76	...
Non-metallic minerals	3,338	559	1	42	174	2,562
Iron and steel and manufactures.....	547	324	5	85	133	...
Copper and manufactures.............	513	296	...	...	217	...
Miscellaneous metals and manufactures	671	201	...	351	119	...
Logs and lumber......................	1,220	716	4	93	366	41
Nitrates	683	135	274	210	64	...
Pigments, chemicals, and manufactures	584	257	18	214	95	...
*Exports—*Total	49,731	13,132	810	14,228	11,965	9,596
Wheat	4,544	1,997	...	1,088	630	829
Barley	283	33	...	9	192	49
Wheat flour	1,290	647	3	314	323	3
Animal, fish, and dairy products.....	626	402	17	100	107	...
Fruits and nuts.......................	743	273	4	7	459	...
Cotton	1,501	40	158	1,234	69	...
Paper stock and manufactures.......	244	121	3	19	100	1
Petroleum and products...............	17,046	2,515	4	7,120	7,215	192
Iron, steel, and manufactures........	1,284	880	37	172	55	140
Copper and manufactures.............	318	240	...	15	60	3
Logs and lumber......................	4,169	150	168	1,582	2,265	4
Pigments, chemicals, and manufactures	510	282	...	114	109	5

* Data from United States Shipping Board. Some commodities are omitted.

thereby suffering a decline of 39 per cent. The distribution
of this eastbound United States tonnage in 1929 and 1932
was 7,545,000 and 4,706,000 tons to the East Coast of the
United States, 217,000 and 173,000 to the East Coast of other
parts of North America, 3,193,000 and 1,722,000 for Europe,

and 55,000 and 49,000 (including 1,422 tons for Asia) to Africa and South America.

That the United States Western littoral held its own in recent Canal traffic becomes perfectly clear with its contribution of 44 per cent in 1929 and 46 per cent in 1932 for the Atlantic-to-Pacific movement, and 50 per cent in both 1929 and 1932 in the instance of the Pacific-to-Atlantic movement.

California continues to rank second to New York State in the volume of the country's foreign commerce, and is improving her position in a striking fashion. In 1929, the ocean traffic of New York State was 27,000,000 tons (33,000,000 including the Great Lakes), and in 1932 only 15,000,000 tons (18,500,000 including the Great Lakes), a drop of 45 per cent. During the same period the foreign commerce of California consisted of 10,800,000 tons in 1929 and 7,000,000 tons in 1932, a drop of approximately 33 per cent. In 1929, California contributed 10 per cent to the foreign commerce of the United States, and New York (combining ocean and Great Lakes traffic) 30 per cent; in 1932 California contributed 12 per cent and New York State 30 per cent. If we confine the comparison to maritime traffic, the percentage attributable to New York remains fixed at 25 per cent, while California records a percentage gain from 10 per cent to 12 per cent, or a one-fifth relative increase.

Oregon and Washington have suffered severe declines from 1929 to 1932, owing to the depression in the lumber industry, which, in turn, provides the purchasing power for import needs. Total foreign cargoes dropped from nearly 2,000,000 to 750,000 tons in the case of Oregon, and from 4,000,000 to 1,700,000 tons for Washington between 1929 and 1932. The drop in exports was more pronounced than that for imports in each state. It is noteworthy that the decline in the volume of imports in Oregon and Washington was apparently the same as that for the United States as a whole, namely, 45 per cent, while the imports into California dropped less than 150,000 tons, or 12 per cent. The import trade is a vital factor in the prosperity of the American Pacific Coast.

The ranking of Pacific Coast ports is also pertinent. From 1929 to 1932, with respect to total foreign commerce, Los

Angeles changed from fourth to second place, San Francisco from seventh to eighth, Portland from fourteenth to eighteenth, Seattle from nineteenth to twentieth, and Tacoma from twenty-first to twenty-fifth. In 1932, the tonnage of Los Angeles was greater than that of New England, New Jersey, and Delaware combined. In terms of imports, San Francisco ranked seventh in both years, Los Angeles ninth in 1929 and eighth in 1932, Seattle sixteenth and seventeenth, Tacoma twentieth and twenty-seventh, and Portland forty-second and fortieth. With reference to exports, Los Angeles ranked second in both years, San Francisco rose from fifth to fourth place, while the other leading West-Coast ports dropped as follows: Portland from eleventh to fourteenth place among all United States ports, Seattle from twenty-first to twenty-fourth, and Tacoma from twenty-second to twenty-sixth. The total foreign commerce for all United States ports dropped from 108,000,000 tons to 60,000,000 tons from 1929 to 1932. It is noteworthy, therefore, to observe from the foregoing record that the Pacific Coast ports have at least held their own in American foreign trade.

The nature of the Pacific Coast cargo traffic can be well illustrated by a comparison of the commodities moving into coastwise commerce. Classifications based upon total water-borne traffic, foreign traffic, or intercoastal traffic would provide somewhat different pictures, but this three-fold comparison would add little to our stock of knowledge. For our present purposes the concentration upon the mutual significance of the three Coast states in the aggregate water-borne movement affords a satisfactory picture of the situation.

Upon the basis of commodities in which the Coast states figure to the extent of 10 per cent or more of the total water-borne "coastwise" (coastal) movement of the United States, the table on page 312 has been constructed from the statistics of the United States Corps of Engineers for the calendar year 1929, the calendar year 1932, and the average of the calendar years 1929 to 1932, inclusive.

It may be noted that, during recent years, the share of the Pacific district in the aggregate water-borne movement of asphalt, nitrates, barley, corn, gasoline, lubricating oil,

wood pulp, rice, and syrup and molasses has increased
greatly, while decreases are marked with respect to potash,

TABLE 56

AMERICAN WATER-BORNE COASTWISE RECEIPTS, PACIFIC DISTRICT
PERCENTAGES, 1929 AND 1932*

Commodities	1929	1932	Average 1929–32
Logs	89.5	89.6	87.9
Hay and feed......................................	79.2	61.5	65.4
Sugar	75.4	50.5	65.0
Lumber	60.2	72.0	58.2
Syrup and molasses..............................	45.0	59.3	54.1
Nitrates	38.1	69.6	46.8
Potash	49.2	10.7	46.6
Fuel and gas, oil.................................	41.5	39.4	45.0
Asphalt	25.3	65.8	43.6
Iron and steel, rolled............................	44.2	29.6	43.2
Wood pulp	6.0	11.5	39.9†
Fertilizer	35.9	46.3	39.5
Crude oil	36.0	38.6	37.9
Barley	11.7	66.8	36.8
Pulp wood	50.1	7.1	36.2
Marine products (fish)...........................	36.5	22.3	32.3
Gasoline	17.7	29.4	25.9
Rice	9.8	22.1	21.3
Lubricating oil	9.4	33.8	18.8
Flour and meal....................................	17.3	18.7	17.4
Cement	23.3	12.9	15.9
Grain, miscellaneous	13.0	9.8	14.9
Iron and steel, unmanufactured.................	30.4	2.9	14.9
Sulphur	13.4	15.7	13.3
Kerosene	14.4	10.6	13.1
Copper	4.6	6.5	11.7
Corn	...	17.3	10.3

* Data based upon figures of United States Shipping Board.
† The figure was 66.2 per cent in 1930, which accounts for this seemingly large
total average.

iron and steel, fish, miscellaneous petroleum products, pulp
wood, and sugar.

Contrasting the Atlantic and Pacific districts, the nitrate
receipts into the former region dropped from 47,641 to
24,951 tons, while those into the Pacific region gained from
29,293 to 66,279 tons. Potash is an inconspicuous factor in

maritime traffic. Unmanufactured iron and steel declined from 275,369 to 95,076 tons for the Atlantic district, but the drop was much heavier for the Pacific region; namely, from 276,768 to 23,316 tons. The receipts of logs at Pacific ports declined from 3,120,635 to 408,917 tons, and of lumber from 4,851,525 to 1,614,480 tons, although there was no decline in the percentage pertaining to the West Coast. The heavy drop in pulp wood is explained by the heavy movement to the Gulf ports. The drop in sugar receipts was due to a particularly heavy movement to the Atlantic States.

Pacific ports therefore can claim two-thirds of the receipts of miscellaneous grain, logs, and sugar, and over one-third of the receipts of asphalt, fertilizer, nitrates, potash, barley, rolled iron and steel, lumber, crude oil, fuel and gas, oil, pulp wood, wood pulp, and syrup and molasses.

Similarly, for outbound shipments from the Pacific district one may note conspicuous changes in commodity movements with particular reference to the years 1929 and 1932. The most conspicuous increases are for asphalt, unmanufactured copper, barley, fish, gasoline, lubricating oil and other petroleum products, wood pulp, and rice, while decreases are noted for hay and feed, crude oil, pulp wood, and syrup and molasses. Flour and meal cargoes have continued very steady; log and lumber shipments have declined heavily, an observation already noted above, since the other coastal ports figure so prominently as destinations; gasoline and other petroleum products have had an erratic recent movement, occasioned largely by the prevailing price levels in the Coast and Gulf districts, while the movement of sugar is unusually steady, not falling outside the range of 1,500,000 to 2,000,000 tons within the four-year period. Among outward shipments from all United States ports, the Pacific district accounts for over 80 per cent of those of wood pulp, logs, and lumber, 60 per cent of the sugar and the hay and feed, and over 30 per cent of the syrup and molasses, fertilizers, marine products (fish), pulp wood, fuel and gas, oil, crude oil, gasoline. Moreover, it is striking that in the majority of cases the same commodity appears among receipts and outbound shipments, which is a certain indication of the purely local movement, and furthermore there is a heavy predominance of agricultural products and raw materials in this water traffic.

A survey of the changes during the recent decade provides a broad barometer of Pacific Coast developments. Let us examine, therefore, the situation in 1932 compared to that in 1923 in order to discover the significance of the West-Coast cargoes in United States coastwise, intercoastal, and total water-borne traffic.

Applicable to inbound coastwise traffic, the Pacific district accounted for 12.3 per cent (19,800,000 tons) in 1923 and 16.6 per cent (18,500,000 tons) in 1932, or an average for the decade of 14.9 per cent (26,180,000 tons). The Atlantic district for this period increased its share from 25.5 per cent to 46.4 per cent, the Gulf district its from 1.8 to 5.1 per cent, while the Great Lakes traffic suffered a heavy drop from 60.4 to 31.9 per cent.

In the outbound coastwise traffic, the Pacific district accounted for 12.3 per cent (20,700,000 tons) in 1923 and 13.7 per cent (15,600,000 tons) in 1932, an average of 11.8 per cent (20,800,000 tons) for the decade. The relative changes in other districts correspond to those already given for inbound movements, with more weight, however, to be given to the petroleum shipments from the Gulf states at the expense of the Coast district.

In the inbound intercoastal traffic, the Pacific Coast contributed 22.4 per cent (2,800,000 tons) in 1923, and 28.1 per cent (1,600,000 tons) in 1932, an average of 25.9 per cent (2,400,000 tons) for the decade; this gain is equally at the expense of Atlantic and Gulf ports.

Applicable to outbound intercoastal traffic, the Pacific Coast accounted for the tremendous volume of 77.6 per cent (9,600,000 tons) in 1932, 71.9 per cent (4,100,000 tons) in 1932, or an average of 74.1 per cent (6,900,000 tons) for the decade; the slight drop in percentage is attributable, as noted, to the Gulf petroleum movement.

The share of the Pacific district in water-borne exports increased from 13.9 per cent in 1923 to 24.2 per cent in 1932, an average for the period of 20.5 per cent. The movement during this period was erratic, Gulf ports increasing from 23.0 per cent to 33.6 per cent, an average of 25.2 per cent, and the north Atlantic ports dropping from 43.2 per cent to 22.2 per cent, an average of 35.5 per cent during this decade. Similarly, in foreign imports, the share of the Pacific Coast rose from 4.9 per cent to 5.3 per cent, an average of 6.1 per cent (naturally due to heavy shipments during intervening years); other comparable figures are 60.7 per cent, 71.7 per cent, and 61.7 per cent for northern Atlantic ports and 21.3 per cent, 10.5 per cent, and 16.2 per cent for the Gulf ports. Combined export and import statistics show a gain for the Pacific district of from 9.5 per cent to 15.0 per cent, an average of 13.9 per cent, with comparable figures of 51.8 per cent, 46.1 per cent, and 47.4 per cent for northern Atlantic ports and 22.1 per cent, 22.5 per cent, and 21.1 per cent for the Gulf ports. During the decade of 1923–1932, inclusive, the ports bordering on the Great Lakes did not experience much change, for we find that the total foreign commerce percentage amounted to 14.2 per cent in 1923, 13.6 per cent in 1932, and an average of 14.9 per cent for the decade. Over this ten-year period, the total water-borne exports from the Pacific Coast amounted to 106,931,157 tons, imports were 26,319,737 tons, and the total traffic was 133,250,894 tons.

The grand total of inbound, water-borne foreign and domestic commerce of the Pacific district for the calendar years 1923 to 1932, inclusive, amounted to 352,000,000 tons. Its share of the aggregate United States traffic increased from 11.8 per cent in 1923 to 16.7 per cent in 1932, an average of 13.9 per cent for the decade. The movement on the Great Lakes is an overshadowing factor accounting for an average of 40.9 per cent for the ten-year period, exceeding that of the Atlantic districts, which amounted to 38.0 per cent for 1923 to 1932, inclusive. Similarly, for the outbound total movement the Pacific Coast contributed 17.2 per cent in 1923 (40,000,000 tons), 18.4 per cent in 1932 (28,000,000 tons), an average of 16.4 per cent (40,000,000 tons) for this decade. From these and other statistics it may be noted that the Pacific Coast has been increasing its importance in the water-borne commerce of the United States.

This survey would be incomplete without proper consideration of the maritime contacts between the Pacific district and the noncontiguous territories of the United States. Contrasting the years 1929 and 1932, the shipments into Alaska from the Pacific district dropped from 451,083 to 307,105 tons and their outbound shipments declined from 335,803 to 241,490 tons; the entire movement was with the Pacific district. The receipts at the Hawaiian Islands decreased slightly from 1,187,948 to 1,164,162 tons, with a rather sharp decrease in the shipments from the Pacific district amounting to 1,101,692 and 772,550 tons in 1929 and 1932, respectively. The outbound shipments from these Islands dropped from 981,138 to 783,012 tons, but in this case shipments to the nearest mainland showed relatively little change, namely, 883,991 and 685,765 tons, respectively, in 1929 and 1932.

A somewhat similar situation exists in the case of the Philippine Islands, where total imports[2] from the United States amounted to 1,116,819 tons in 1929 and 1,234,113 tons in 1932, with the Pacific district contributing 301,924 and 196,615 tons, respectively. The exports from the Philippine Islands to the United States amounted to 693,991 tons in 1929 and to 483,102 tons in 1932, of which the Pacific district received an even larger share, namely, 430,313 and 350,005 tons, respectively. The future status of these Asiatic Islands, therefore, has an important bearing on Pacific Coast affairs, since approximately one-sixth of the United States exports originate here and four-fifths of the inward movement arrives on the Western littoral.

To place our Pacific Coast situation in proper relief, it is worth while to observe that the Department of Commerce, using the year 1929 as equivalent to 100, has estimated "the quantity volume of activities for ocean-waterway traffic" as 100.1 for 1930, 83.3 for 1931, and 74.5 for 1932. The Economic and Financial Section of the League of Nations has reported that total world trade for this four-year period was as shown on the opposite page.

Finally, one can have the satisfaction of observing the changes during the years 1929 to 1932, inclusive, in order

[2] It may be recalled that our official statistics classify inbound and outbound cargoes between the Philippine Islands and the mainland as foreign commerce.

	Imports	Exports	Total
1929	$35,606,000,000	$33,035,000,000	$68,641,000,000
1930	29,083,000,000	26,492,000,000	55,492,000,000
1931	20,847,000,000	18,922,000,000	39,769,000,000
1932	13,885,000,000	12,726,000,000	26,611,000,000

to bring the situation more up to date. Yet these later de-velopments have been so irregular that the longer historical record, and particularly the most recent typical year of 1930, provide a satisfactory horizon. One should refer again to the chart constructed by the Harvard Economic Society, which appears as Figure 1, p. 4.

XVI. "Invisible" Shipping Activities

The portrayal of ships and shipping on the Western seaboard would be conspicuously incomplete without some mention of those direct and indirect activities which normally are not included in ships' cargoes. We are justified in classifying them as "invisible," from the standpoint either of trade statistics or of popular knowledge. Maritime shipping, far from being confined to the transportation of merchandise, may be as important for the carrying of passengers as for commodities; or it may serve outlying regions where the total commodity traffic is meager while other considerations, such as the developing of overseas connections for national defense or for trade strategy, may be of leading significance.

No money estimate has ever been made of the amount and character of marine business which obtains in addition to the transport of inbound and outbound commodities, but the totals must be enormous. Nor has the writer discovered anyone who has attempted a careful classification of what properly should be included, for example, among the "non-commodity cargoes." Human freight obviously cannot be neglected; hence the writer has included in this volume Appendix B, "Passenger Traffic on the Pacific Coast," and illustrative sailing schedules as necessary parts of the treatment of the West-Coast trade and shipping. Mails, too, are an important activity of shipping countries, and, in the case of the United States, possess as well a highly fictitious value in the popular imagination because they serve as the mask for shipping subsidies; the express business usually is included with the international postal services.

Gold and silver, whether in the form of ore, bullion, or coinage, may or may not be considered as commodities: the practices in this regard vary greatly among countries.

Bunker fuel, both coal and oil, is seldom included in trade statistics, and even when bunkers are later sold in a favorable market the producing country may receive no credit.

Ships' stores and supplies, while not to be placed in the

318

category of merchandise, are both an important factor in the business of each seaport and an inevitable adjunct to the operation of the merchant marine. A country's private shipping is never divorced wholly from naval, military, and civil national requirements. Yet official trade statistics take no account of transactions for government account which amount, on the American Pacific Coast, to many hundred million dollars annually.

The maintenance and operation of shipping involves a chain of auxiliary industries and businesses, notably with reference to materials and repairs of vessels, also those providing for personal needs of passengers and ships' officers and crew at each port of call, passenger and freight traffic departments scattered all over the world, clerical and accounting personnel and equipment, advertising, and supporting activities affecting numerous public and private organizations.

This chapter, therefore, while sketchy at best, helps to complete the panorama of ocean-borne traffic.[1]

Foreign Commerce and Navigation of the United States, the official publication of the United States Department of Commerce, lists separately the imports and exports of precious metals, but these movements are not recorded in the American foreign-trade totals. The United States omits entirely the precious metals, as matte, bullion, or specie, from both export merchandise and general imports. Some countries include all these items in their foreign commerce; others draw a distinction between them, such as including ore but not currency. In order to provide a basis for international statistical comparison, an analysis should be made of the practices followed by different countries with regard to the inclusion of gold and silver as merchandise exports and imports. For example, Australia includes gold and silver bullion and specie in the official trade returns, while others may include only currency. The distinction, therefore, is one resting upon public records rather than upon any difference in the physical handling of the precious

---

[1] Liberal use will be made of the pioneering research available in the author's *San Francisco's Trans-Pacific Shipping.*

metals. Furthermore, the navigation laws of the United States are stringent with regard to the transportation of bullion and coin offered to United States registered vessels.[2]

Since gold has played such a conspicuous part in the history of the Far West, it is surprising that this international movement is omitted from our official trade returns. The transactions still bulk exceedingly large. Thus for the calendar year 1930 the export of gold in its various forms through the San Francisco customs district totaled $405,000, the export of silver in its various forms nearly $14,000,000, the movement of silver from foreign countries through San Francisco over $4,000,000, the imports of silver over $2,000,000, and the imports of gold $161,000,000. The importance of these international transactions becomes evident by contrasting them with the total merchandise exports of $148,000,000 and the total general imports of $156,000,000 through this single customs district. In other words, during 1930 the gold imports exceeded the merchandise imports. These transactions for San Francisco are chiefly with the transpacific countries, principally China, Hong Kong, and Japan. Other Pacific Coast districts figure also, but to a far less degree than San Francisco, which normally ranks second to New York among American customs ports in this frequently unreported business. The movement in precious metals is particularly volatile.

Figure 35 depicts the actual and relative position of United States total merchandise exports, combined gold and silver exports, merchandise imports, and combined gold and silver imports. It is startling to note the statistics for the calendar year 1932, when the gold exports exceeded $800,000,000, silver exports $13,000,000, gold imports

---

[2] "All vessels belonging to citizens of the United States, and bound from any port in the United States to any other port therein, or to any foreign port, or from any foreign port to any port in the United States, shall, before clearance, receive on board all such bullion, coin, United States notes and bonds and other securities, as the Government of the United States or any department thereof, or any minister, consul, vice-consul, or commercial or other agent of the United States abroad, shall offer, and shall securely convey and promptly deliver the same to the proper authorities or consignees, on arriving at the port of destination . . . ."—*United States Revised Statutes*, 4204.

$360,000,000, and silver imports $19,000,000. The data, how-ever, are meager. Assistant Federal Reserve Agent Oliver P. Wheeler, of the Federal Reserve Bank of San Francisco, writes:

We are not familiar with any data showing the sources of pro-duction of gold and silver exported from the Far West. Practically all exports of gold and silver from Pacific Coast ports are of the refined metals, with the result that a large part of such exports have lost their identity as to locality of production by the time they are sent from this area. For example, a single exported gold or silver ingot may consist of metal produced from Twelfth District mines, derived from the melting of jewelry or silverware, and/or received from other parts of the United States or foreign countries.

In the precious-metal situation, the Far West, including Alaska, has surpassing national importance, since this re-gion furnishes nearly the entire United States domestic supply. (See Table 11, p. 59, above.)

Fig. 35.—United States imports and exports of merchandise, gold, and silver, 1921–33.

Publicized, three years ago, as a "treasure-trove to exceed the vision of a '49 bonanza king" was the arrival of a single shipment from Japan of 300 boxes of American gold "eagles" valued at $7,500,000, which had been stored in the specie vault of a Japanese liner. Another newspaper account tells of a record shipment from a single San Francisco bank on an American liner for Japan early in 1933 of 2,221 bars of silver, comprising 2,552,460 ounces valued at $640,000. Table 57 testifies to the outstanding position of San Francisco as a world shipper of silver.

TABLE 57

Silver Shipments from Important Ports, 1928–1932*

(American values in thousand dollars; British values in thousand pounds sterling)

	1928	1929	1930	1931	1932
San Francisco					
To China	62,637	57,711	45,340	15,719	13,642
To Japan	11	.....	.....	50	.....
To India	.....	.....	757	577	.....
To others	.....	.....	.....	4,491	674
New York					
To England	892	151	5,292	11,648	1,574
To Germany	4,269	2,774	2,637	7,719	2,404
To China	36,903	64,102	51,573	20,695	21,479
To India	35,599	16,819	24,554	20,610	652
To others	2,686	248	89	609	440
London to the East					
To India	4,012	3,948	5,648	3,137	639
To China	2,314	1,160	1,363	872	1,370
To Straits	198	.....	12	64	67

* Data from *Economic Handbook of the Pacific Area* (1934), Institute of Pacific Relations.

Surely, no community should be so careless or so modest as to overlook this maritime carriage of gold and silver, whether in the form of ore and base bullion, refined bullion, or coin.

Confusion and omissions, described in chapter vii with reference to oranges and dried fruits, appear again respecting petroleum exports from California. Statistics, it is true, are abundant, but their showing is far from clear. Michigan is credited as the leading customs export district for crude petroleum, with 1930 exports of nearly $12,000,000, out of a total of $32,000,000. Los Angeles is second with nearly $9,000,000. Similarly, in the case of petroleum products, the exporting district is frequently not synonymous with the producing section, with the result that it is impossible to learn from these official figures the state of origin. The attempt to secure trustworthy figures from any source is made more difficult because there is no uniform basis of classification of petroleum and its products and also the units used are seldom in agreement.

From a shipping standpoint, the importance of oil-bunkering facilities of Los Angeles Harbor can scarcely be exaggerated. What are the figures? The United States Department of Commerce does not consider bunker oil as merchandise, although the *Monthly Summary of Foreign Commerce* (for December only) does list bunker or fuel oil for vessels in foreign trade apart from the regularly reported trade figures. The 1930 totals for American vessels amounted to 23,000,000 barrels valued at $23,000,000, and those for foreign vessels to 28,000,000 barrels valued at $30,000,000, but the information stops there. The Bureau of Mines of the United States Department of the Interior reports exports on petroleum for the country as a whole, applicable to vessels engaged in coastwise, river, lake, and foreign trade, of which total 39,000,000 out of 94,000,000 barrels are tabulated as deliveries of fuel oil at Pacific ports. Figures furnished by the Bureau of Mines and appearing in the *National Survey of Fuel Oil Distribution* (1930), published by the American Petroleum Institute, show a distribution in California of 36,000,000 barrels of 42 gallons each to steamships, including tankers, with Diesel oil separated from bunker oil. Other pertinent data include the following: United States Shipping Board, 6,000,000 tons of crude mineral oil and products exported; United States Army Engineers and Bureau of Operations, United States Shipping Board,[3] foreign exports of bunker oil, 760,000 tons, and coastwise shipments of bunker oil 1,520,000 tons; the *Panama Canal Record* reports eastbound tanker traffic from Los Angeles as point of origin, 4,222,000 tons; and the Board of Harbor Commissioners, Los Angeles, gives the most complete data of bunker-oil intercoastal outbound shipments,

---

[3] United States Shipping Board, "The Ports of Los Angeles and Long Beach, California," *Port Series No. 13, Part I (revised, 1930).*

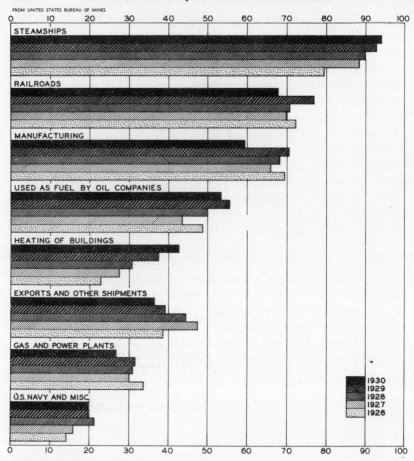

FROM UNITED STATES BUREAU OF MINES

STEAMSHIPS
RAILROADS
MANUFACTURING
USED AS FUEL BY OIL COMPANIES
HEATING OF BUILDINGS
EXPORTS AND OTHER SHIPMENTS
GAS AND POWER PLANTS
U.S.NAVY AND MISC.

1930
1929
1928
1927
1926

Fig. 36.—Gas and fuel oil deliveries (million barrels), by uses, 1926–30.

3,832,000 barrels, Hawaii outbound, 646,000 barrels, and coastwise outbound, 9,349,000 barrels, but with no figures for bunker oil received from foreign countries and later shipped. It is apparent, therefore, that the available sources of information provide unsatisfactory records of this great Coast industry.

The business of a port likewise is augmented by the in-transit and transshipment trade, the statistics of which are excluded from the maritime commerce credited to it. (This trade differs from foreign exports merely because it moves from one foreign country to another on a through bill of lading.) If Canadian grain is sent to New York by rail for shipment abroad, the export movement is the only one shown and there is no record whatever of the entry of the grain into the United States. However, Canadian grain entering the States via the Great Lakes appears in the records, so that, in the case of such grain as is really shipped from the Atlantic ports, both the inbound and outbound movements are reported. Grain loaded at a Canadian port in a ship which touches New York or other domestic ports en route to Europe does not enter into our records.

For the calendar year 1930, the value of in-transit and transshipment trade was given as $263,571,106 for the United States and $15,540,890 for the Pacific Coast, with the customs district of San Francisco credited with over a third of the latter total, followed by Alaska, Los Angeles, and Washington. No records are kept of the transit movement of commodities from the American Northwest through British Columbia and vice versa; the volume is small and probably is confined to concealed selling of American salmon and lumber as Canadian products, and the reverse, in order to overcome trade preferences. But contraband and shipments en route should not be discounted entirely.

The part played by the postal service in national and local shipping is grossly underestimated. Federal subvention is the most usual form of aid extended to initiate and maintain commercial shipping. The history of the Pacific Mail Steamship Company is the story of the pioneer transpacific line services.

The latest chapter in subsidies concerns the liberal contracts awarded under the Merchant Marine Act of 1928, whereby provision is made and required for the construction of more frequent and faster communications. The eight transpacific mail contracts effective in early 1929 (described further in chapter xx) do not cover all the mail carried across the Pacific, since it is the policy of the post office to expedite mails by sending them on foreign or non-contract American ships whenever an appreciable delay would result from holding them for the contract vessel.

But aside from the stimulation to shipping afforded by

mail subventions, there is the great asset which a port possesses in acting as an important mail-dispatching point. The weights of mail dispatched to transpacific destinations have been increasing more rapidly than to the transatlantic or the Central American–South American–West Indian destinations. The United States Post Office Department reports that the pounds of letters and postcards increased from 123,979 in 1910 to 680,642 in 1928, and the pounds of other articles increased from 1,710,108 in 1910 to 12,823,659 in 1928, for transpacific destinations. The United States Appraiser at San Francisco handled 298,842 parcel-post or mail packages during the 1928 calendar year.

The value of parcel-post packages entering and clearing through the federal post office is problematical. The handling procedure varies between localities. *Foreign Commerce and Navigation of the United States* reports parcel-post exports amounting to $21,000,000 in 1924 and to $28,000,000 in 1927, while no mention whatever appears among the general imports.

Figures are not at hand on incoming mails from transpacific regions, since they are under the jurisdiction of the several countries in which they originate.

Freight charges are another item to consider. Before the San Diego Chamber of Commerce, October 31, 1933, United States Shipping Board Commissioner Captain G. S. Lincoln, United States Navy (retired), remarked:

Trade routes are maintained and new ones developed as will best maintain and develop our commerce. In testimony before a Congressional committee it was asserted that but for the possession and operation of American ships an increase of at least 20 per cent in ocean freight rates would have been levied by foreign lines on American commerce since the war. As we have been paying an annual freight bill of approximately $900,000,000 an increase of 20 per cent would make the total paid out for mail contracts appear a small item. With one-third of our foreign commerce carried in American ships $300,000,000 of this annual freight bill is spent for American labor and materials and stays at home instead of being paid out to foreign countries. The money spent for the repair, maintenance and operation of ships and for building new ships is spent in the United States. This expenditure is not confined to shipyards or to ports, but finds its way to all parts of the country, for materials for shipbuilding and ship operation are drawn from every State in the Union.

Mr. Alfred H. Haag, Chief of the Division of Shipping Research, Shipping Board Bureau, wrote the author recently:

The total import traffic of the Pacific Coast for the calendar year 1932 amounted to 1,724,254 cargo tons with an average freight rate of $6.90 per ton, making a total of freights collected approximately $12,000,000. Of these imports American vessels carried 37%. The total export traffic of the Pacific Coast for the same period amounted to 7,847,662 cargo tons with an average freight rate of $6.75 per ton making a total of freight earnings approximately $53,000,000. Of these exports American vessels carried 26%.

It is interesting to note that here American ships carry a larger percentage of imports and a smaller percentage of exports than for the country as a whole.

American exports and imports are valued usually on an f.o.b. basis, whereby carrying costs are not included. Hence, the recorded foreign-trade statistics are out of line to this amount in comparison with statistics of other countries, and allowance should be made accordingly (Appendix D). This understatement should be clearly recognized.

No statistics are available showing the separation of domestic from foreign cargoes (consult chapter vii and Appendix D). Furthermore, no adequate records exist showing the domestic movement of commodities. Wool is a case in point. The intercoastal carriers carry eastward cargoes transshipped from Oceania and China along with the output of the Intermountain States. The "Golden Mountain" of the American-Hawaiian Steamship Company, in May 1933, carried the largest wool cargo ever to move out of San Francisco on a single vessel—3,700,000 pounds, representing the fleeces of 600,000 sheep, in addition to the hides of 20,000 cattle and the pelts of 5,000 sheep. Where can one learn how to keep track of the ceaselessly moving cargoes of a busy port?

From the standpoint of port and terminal facilities, statistics of this actual physical movement are greatly to be preferred to the present methods of computation. In 1912, the government made a trial schedule on this basis. The results obtained showed that 7 per cent of all United States imports were officially entered at ports other than the first place of arrival. No subsequent computation has been attempted, for reasons which are said to be due partly to the influence of sectional interests.

A picture of the merchandise moving into the San Francisco district from foreign countries would consist of the import entries at the local customhouse plus the goods moving by "immediate transportation" certificates. While no such computation has ever been compiled in the writer's knowledge other than in the 1912 experimental tabulation, nevertheless an exceedingly good index of a general character is available in the records of the State Board of Harbor Commissioners. For, by ascertaining the total tonnages from abroad which are landed at San Francisco on "immediate transportation" certificates, adding the remainder of the foreign tonnage entering the port, and then using a common money value based upon tonnage, a much more useful tabulation results. While this procedure at best cannot be more than a rough approximation, its application to the Pacific Coast ports should reflect an unusual degree of reality, since the incoming goods from transpacific countries are confined to a few products which move in a fairly steady volume.

The State Board of Harbor Commissioners reported for the calendar year 1927 total foreign imports amounting to 1,977,249 tons, and shipments en route to other United States points amounting to 102,222 tons, or a total of 2,079,471 tons. From these figures, however, should be deducted *all* tonnage from Alaska and the Hawaiian Islands, thereby reducing the totals to 975,505 tons and 102,222 tons, respectively. The shipments to other United States points, therefore, represent an additional 10 per cent tonnage. Now the imports into San Francisco for this same period were valued at $200,004,238. If we assume an even distribution of this 102,222 tonnage increase, then the real imports amounted to over $220,000,000.

But let us examine the situation for two particular import areas, namely (1) China, including Hong Kong, and (2) Japan. We shall utilize the tonnage figures compiled by the State Board, and the values made available by the Customs Service.

FOREIGN TONNAGE ARRIVING AT SAN FRANCISCO
(Calendar year 1927)

	China	Japan
Recorded imports (tons)	55,370	50,263
"I.T." shipments (tons)	29,525	32,481
"I.T." shipments (percentage to be added)	53.3%	64.6%
Recorded imports (value)...............	$19,910,908	$ 82,857,427
"I.T." shipments (equivalent value) increase (53.3% and 64.6%)............	$10,612,512	$ 54,525,827
Total adjusted value...................	$30,523,420	$136,383,325

If, then, the average tonnage figure for China and Japan is a fair basis for the unit value of imports from these countries, the statistics of imports for the San Francisco district should be increased over 60 per cent, or $65,138,339, for China and Japan alone. The percentage tonnage increases for other countries on a similar basis are East Indies 5.1 per cent, Oceania 10.8 per cent, and the Philippine Islands 9 per cent.

How much maritime commerce is incorrectly reported? Nobody knows. How much is unaccounted for? A similar answer. In certain instances commodities moving by interior waterways might more properly be included under the ocean trade: for example, since a vessel navigating between San Francisco and Monterey does not "clear" the San Francisco customs district, no record is kept of her cargoes or bunkers. Another illustration is the chained lumber raft which may move hundreds of miles in the open Pacific. During the calendar year 1927 the Chief of Engineers estimated that the commerce carried on the rivers, canals, and connecting channels of the Pacific Coast amounted to 5,932,797 short tons of miscellaneous bulk freight valued at $77,328,318, 14,505,290 short tons of floated and refloated timber valued at $67,992,479, 1,671,520 short tons of package freight valued at $158,728,156, or a total inland commerce of 22,109,607 short tons valued at $304,048,953. Although the writer recognizes the duplications, inaccuracies, and questionable items which the Corps of Engineers may have chosen to include, he is sure that much of this traffic is unquestionably maritime and should be so regarded.

The total commerce of Pacific Coast ports in the calendar year 1927 was estimated as follows: imports, 3,510,152 short tons valued at $571,565,327; exports, 17,350,535 short tons valued at $575,852,208; domestic, 93,281,501 short tons valued at $3,742,357,062; and a grand total of $4,889,774,597, or nearly five billion dollars. One observes that the value of "exports" and "imports" (the Corps of Engineers classification does not tally with that of the Bureau of Foreign and Domestic Commerce) is surprisingly close, and that domestic movements predominate.

One can couple with the foregoing inland-waterway statistics for the entire Pacific Coast a statement giving the total water commerce of San Francisco, which ranked, in the calendar year 1927, as second only to that of the port of New York. Table 58 classifies San Francisco Bay's traffic.

Shipbuilding and shipping are closely related in public policies and in private mercantile affairs. Therefore, an attempt to divorce entirely the non-traffic from the traffic activities can never be wholly successful. Professor Josef Grunzel of the University of Vienna (Wien) has been a leader in calling attention to the complete omission of the ships themselves from trade statistics, since they are built outside the customs zone, perform their transporting function outside of it, and beyond it pass out of existence.

Dry-docking and general repairs at shipyards figure prominently in maritime pursuits at well-equipped ports. In this connection, one feature of the American protective system deserves mention, and that is that, while services to foreign vessels are discouraged, those to American vessels are actively encouraged by the American tariff regulation that repairs, repair parts, and equipment furnished to American vessels in foreign ports are subject to an import duty of 50 per cent, unless it can be proved that these expenditures abroad were necessary for the safety of the vessel. Since it is exceptional for a ship engaged in foreign commerce not to make some of these purchases at each leading port of call, the expenditures for general repairs and sometimes dry-docking, by vessels of all nationalities, mean much to local port business.

In the tabulation of port business there is an almost en-

TABLE 58

WATER-BORNE COMMERCE, SAN FRANCISCO BAY, 1927*

	Tons (2,000 lbs.)	Value
Imports	1,134,792	$ 226,465,054
Exports	3,505,480	236,917,152
Total foreign	4,640,272	$ 463,382,206
Coastwise receipts	14,087,355	629,840,944
Coastwise shipments	8,168,429	502,268,361
Total coastwise	22,255,784	$1,132,109,305
Inland waterway receipts	6,054,231	$ 274,720,368
Inland waterway shipments	5,264,836	302,052,554
Total inland	11,319,067	$ 576,772,922
Total deep-water commerce	26,896,056	$1,595,491,511
Total inland-waterway commerce	11,319,067	576,772,922
Grand total of all commerce	38,215,123	$2,172,264,433
San Francisco City Docks	13,664,688	$1,427,318,572
Oakland	3,217,897	200,325,445
Richmond Inner Harbor	372,449	15,525,798
Richmond Outer Harbor	4,796,721	75,818,063
San Pablo Bay and Mare Island and Strait	3,850,694	202,610,398
Suisun Bay Channel	4,341,706	61,178,799
Carquinez Straits	6,571,958	144,642,217
Other San Francisco Bay shipping points	1,399,010	44,845,141
Grand total	38,215,123	$2,172,264,433

* Calendar year. Data from Corps of Engineers, War Department.

tire neglect of ship expenditures. In this respect, public and private agencies are equal offenders. Many of the separate items involved escape notice in any published form. The writer has been unable to obtain satisfactory estimates for the various charges involved in connection with this shipping traffic, a necessary element in port business, hence it is worth while to note the expenses involved in the actual performance of a large transpacific freighter.

This particular vessel operated from a California port to

Shanghai, Hong Kong, the Philippine Islands, then back to Hong Kong and the home port. The length of the voyage was 124 days. The expenses totaled $96,000, averaging $775 a day, including time at sea and time in port. An enumeration of the actual expenditures discloses that the amount paid for wages was $14,500, crew subsistence $2,500, shore subsistence $500, department stores $5,100, water $600, stevedoring $20,000, other cargo expense $6,000, port charges $4,000, repairs $5,000 (no expenditure for betterments), foreign repairs $300, and maintenance, the remainder. Administration, adjustments, canal tolls (if any), and miscellaneous expenses make up the remainder of the ship's expenses.[4]

Ships calling at the principal ports constitute big business. Wholesale houses, farmers, manufacturers, retailers, hotels, restaurants, and resorts profit greatly. Consider the required outlay for a single voyage in the Pacific offshore trades, where the journeys are of unusual length. When the "Lurline" of the Matson-Oceanic Line left San Francisco for a 25,000-mile maiden voyage on the Hawaii-South Seas run, the officials reported that over 850 item lots were purchased for this single trip. These included, not to mention extensive marine and manufactured supplies for mechanical upkeep and operation of the ship: 56,000 pounds of meat, 18,000 pounds of poultry and game, 7,400 pounds of fish, 154,000 pounds of vegetables, 84,000 pounds of fruit, 32,000 pounds of flour and meal, 14,000 pounds of sugar, 41,000 pounds of dairy products, 5,100 pounds of tea and coffee, and 140,000 pounds of ice. These figures, transferred into dollars, represent but 10 out of 850 items. Nor do they include salaries and incidental expenses. They represent money that has gone directly back to producers of Arizona, California, Delaware, Florida, Idaho, Iowa, Kansas, Massachusetts, New Jersey, Nevada, New York, Oregon, Pennsylvania, Texas, Washington, Wyoming, and practically every other state in the Union.

The Vancouver (British Columbia) Harbour Commissioners advertise that each deep-sea vessel brings to Van-

---

[4] A more detailed analysis of the foregoing expenditures appears on pages 77–80 of the author's *San Francisco's Trans-Pacific Shipping*.

couver approximately $4,000 in the form of wages and purchase of supplies, and that during 1933 ninety-four miles of such vessels were attracted to that port. "During the course of the year, this makes a colossal contribution to local business. No ship comes to port but some part of industry is stimulated; no vessel docks in Vancouver, but factories and retail stores become busier, transactions increase, new men are employed."

With the two hundred fiftieth sailing of the French Line from the Pacific Coast in May 1934, after a twelve-year period when the Pacific Coast–European trade has grown from a minor to a major trade, this one company has transported almost 3,000,000 tons of cargo between the North Pacific sector and Europe, for which revenues in excess of $30,000,000 were received; this averages $10 per ton, or $120,000 in freight revenues per round-trip voyage. The general agents report that on the Pacific Coast the French Line has spent $6,500,000 in operating expenses, including bunkers.

Another important unrecorded item is the purchase of supplies by governmental agencies. These annual totals aggregate many hundred million dollars on the Pacific Coast alone. To illustrate, during the calendar year 1931, the Navy used 840,000 pounds of sliced canned pineapple, the equivalent of nearly 450,000 large cans, or enough to provide about two million good-sized helpings. The U.S.S. "Virginia" of the Pacific squadron, during 1932, used nearly 16,000 pounds, equivalent to over 8,500 cans. The editor of the *Pacific Rural Press* is authority for the statement that the Navy on the Pacific Coast buys annually approximately $70,000,000 worth of dried and canned fruits and refrigerated fresh fruits and vegetables. Other purchases by the Navy and large outlays by the presidios, air stations, and various government departments mean a great deal to seaport towns. Purchases by the United States Navy in the Pacific district during the fiscal year 1934, according to latest information from Washington, totaled approximately thirty-five million dollars ashore and an equal amount on ships.

To summarize the situation regarding the "invisible" shipping business (enterprise which is not properly recorded—in fact is frequently unknown), the writer has prepared the following crude table which gives the outbound maritime traffic according to present methods of listing among the recorded exports of the San Francisco customs district (statistics applicable to the calendar year 1927):

	Included	Not Included
		(thousands)
Domestic merchandise exports	$199,708	?
Foreign merchandise exports	1,732	?
In-transit and transshipment trade (1927)	?	$ 6,122
Gold and silver	?	47,000
Domestic shipments credited elsewhere	?	?
Government account	?	?
Noncontiguous territories	?	52,605
Ship expenditures	?	?
Passenger business	?	?
Mails	?	?

In brief, the already published but separately classified official figures should credit San Francisco with additional outgoing maritime traffic amounting to over $100,000,000 more, or an increase of 50 per cent. The writer ventures the guess that the inclusion of the unknown amounts in the foregoing table would result in a total increase of 75 to 100 per cent.

In conclusion, then, as to the maritime trade of the Western United States hitherto, a few observations prompted by the longshoremen's strike of 1934 are in order.

A dock strike is a lamentable but wholly realistic demonstration of the vital importance of a harbor to every person, organization, and public body. Halfway through the period of the tremendous longshoremen's strike of May–July 1934 on the Pacific Coast, the *San Francisco Examiner* conducted an impartial survey of the situation at the Golden Gate, which is so graphic and pertinent that the report is reproduced here in detail.

The dock strike is costing San Francisco $700,000 every day.

And that means an average of $1 per day for every man, woman and child in this city.

Not only is every person in San Francisco affected directly or indirectly by the strike, but the striking men and their families are suffering a loss of over $10,000 for every day they are out of work.

While taking this loss the strikers and their families are costing city relief agencies $70,000 a month. Eventually the taxpayer is responsible for every cent of this relief expenditure. Director of Relief C. M. Wollenberg made this announcement yesterday.

Figures cast up by shipping statisticians yesterday showed that in 1932 a monthly average of 675,707 cargo tons moved in and out of the port of San Francisco.

This amount of cargo every month totaled $45,387,689.

Now, as possibly never before, San Francisco is being brought to the realization that its wealth, prestige and its very existence depend largely upon its harbor and the shipping which that harbor brings.

It is the bank debit figures which reveal graphically how the dock strike has affected every pocket-book in cold cash.

The bank debits represent all transactions made in San Francisco by check.

These bank debits for the first month of the strike were $55,000,000 less than the average for the similar period for four preceding years. That is nearly $2,000,000 a day.

For every ton of cargo moved in and out of San Francisco, shippers pay 50 cents as a handling charge.

That means striking stevedores and allied working groups are losing 50 cents a ton on each of the 675,707 tons that normally move in and out of this port each month.

In cold cash that means a loss to labor of $337,853.50 each month —over $10,000 a day.

Longshoremen and their families on relief total 521. It is estimated at least 500 more longshoremen are receiving relief aid at the single men's shelter. The money to care for these striking men is contributed by the taxpayer.

Yet not only the taxpayer is hit by the strike. There are the thousands of white-collar workers who handle office details connected with the shipping industry. There are, too, the banking houses, insurance companies, export and import offices, drayage companies and others who are an integral part of the shipping industry.

Then, too, there are the hotels which have lost tremendously in tourist trade. Two hundred tourists have entered San Francisco daily for the past six years as off-coast passengers. Each tourist, it has been estimated, spends $64.28 during his stay in the city.

Hotels, retail establishments, restaurants, amusement places are taking great losses.

The State income has been affected, since 12½ cents toll charge is paid for each ton of shipping. The monthly loss to the State in this port alone is over $84,000.

Definite figures on payroll cuts have not yet been compiled. But nearly 5,000 employes in the Bay district sugar refineries have been or shortly will be thrown out of work since raw sugar cannot be moved. Sugar prices are due to go up.

The provision market has also been hard hit. Chamber of Commerce statistics show the following provisions affected: Fruits and vegetables, candy, sausages, yeast, olive oil, poultry, shortening, fish, ice, meats, extracts, hams and bacon, coffee, spices, oysters, cocoa butter, catsup, flour and groceries.

The business losses of the great strike were estimated by the Associated Press at $200,000,000, without taking any account of the San Francisco Bay general strike losses, which were incalculable. Industrial associations in San Francisco and Seattle reported separately that conservative surveys indicated each port has lost $1,000,000 a day during the 74 days of the strike, and the total loss to the state of Oregon was declared to be in excess of $30,000,000. Los Angeles and Vancouver gained greatly through the diversion of cargoes and passengers. The strike furnishes conclusive proof that the Far West lives by the seaways.

In short, the subject-matter of this chapter is a largely overlooked yet necessary counterpart to an intelligent understanding of ships and shipping. It provides a direct answer to the query raised on page 80 of the author's *San Francisco's Trans-Pacific Shipping,* namely, "the direct significance to San Francisco of shipping in foreign trade can be appreciated most forcibly by attempting to discover what would be the theoretical effect of the closing of the Golden Gate for a period of twenty-four hours." Intangible factors are often the most important.

XVII. Shipping Conferences—British and American

The shipping of nations is primarily international in character. The problems involved are unique because of the pronounced nationalistic concern of governments in this essentially private enterprise. Not only must the shipowner conform in every respect to the navigation laws of his own country, even to the point of registration and periodical inspection, but also he must comply with the rules and regulations of each foreign port where his vessel enters and clears. Public interest and private operation are therefore closely intertwined. One of the best illustrations of this dual relationship appears in the organization by the steamship companies themselves into so-called "conference" agreements under the permissive direction of interested governments.

The conference system is a natural evolution—an attempt to better the cutthroat competition, slashing of rates, and general chaos which prevail on the free seas under an individualistic economy. There was no agency, national or international, which could govern the operations of the group; hence the shipping companies recognized that any improvement in the situation must come from their own efforts. Accordingly, companies competing in the same trades organized into groups, more or less informally, and formulated definite working agreements. Chronologically, the four main forms which these have taken are: (*a*) division of territory, (*b*) pooling of cargo, (*c*) pooling of profits, and (*d*) "conferences" or agreements of various kinds designed to provide for a better handling of their chief economic difficulties.

The hardships incurred under uncontrolled competition resulted in the early use of a territorial division of traffic among member lines serving the same territory. This practice, however, did not achieve adequate results, so that it was not long before freight pooling became a generally recognized practice. This second expedient was utilized under two different plans, namely, alternative sailings and the division of the actual business either on a percentage basis or according to the kind of traffic (for example, passenger and merchandise). The pooling of profits was a third device, less successful than the others however, since the confidential nature of shipping transactions as well as incomplete records concerning them often forbade a satisfactory accounting. Both freight pooling and money pooling have disappeared generally from shipping since the latter part of the nineteenth century; the reasons primarily are their reactionary character and the pronounced opposition to them expressed by the American government. The fourth type of informal agreement, the conference, is now a conspicuous feature of shipping operation in all seven seas. As a notable experiment in co-operation among nations, the historical basis for this system merits careful consideration.

Conferences, which were first developed by British steamship companies, did not originally include foreign lines. Later, however, it became apparent that considerations of mutual advantage required the inclusion of Continental lines in order that rates from British and Continental ports might be equalized, so that nowadays these agreements are less exclusively national than they were formerly. The conference system is said to date from 1875, when the Calcutta conference was organized to put a stop to the ruinous competition which had followed the great expansion of shipbuilding, the result of the successful development of iron and steel ships. The plan spread to other routes, also suffering from unrestricted competition, until it was quite generally adopted by the liner trades.

Growing up along with the conference system, although not a necessary feature, was the policy of deferred rebates. The origin of this policy was in the rate wars of the era of cutthroat competition when shipping companies were compelled to offer rebates to the largest and most powerful shippers in order to retain their patronage. Later, with the introduction of the conference system, deferred rebates were offered to all shippers as a means of keeping them "loyal" against the inroads of non-conference liners or tramps which offered lower rates.

Control of liner traffic by conferences and deferred rebates gradually spread to virtually all outward trade routes

of the United Kingdom except that to the United States.
While conferences existed on the North Atlantic, the system
of deferred rebates was not in force there, for the reason
that passenger traffic so dominated the situation that the
tonnage requirements in behalf of passengers produced a
great excess of cargo space and consequently very low cargo
rates. As a result there has been very little field for tramp
operation on this route.

The system of conferences, irrespective of the practice of
deferred rebates, is best adapted to trade routes where the
character of the demand for tonnage requires regular and
fixed sailings and where the bulk of the cargo is in small
parcels of relatively high value not suited to shipload-
handling by tramp steamers. Wherever the cargo moving
in one direction is very much greater than that moving in
the opposite direction and different from it in character, the
conference will be unable to impose the system of deferred
rebates on traffic moving in the direction of the greater
density unless conference shipping is offered in sufficient
amount to accommodate the larger volume. Even so, the
denser traffic is likely to be composed of bulky, low-grade
commodities which do not require and cannot afford the
faster, more expensive service of the liner, with the result
that tramp competition here makes itself felt. This fact
explains why conferences and deferred rebates have not
been so prevalent on homeward routes to the United Kingdom, since Great Britain is a large exporter of manufactures and consequently a large importer of raw materials
and foodstuffs.

The *Report of the British Royal Commission on Shipping
Rings,* which appeared in 1909, dealt exhaustively with the
effect of conferences and deferred rebates on British trade
and shipping. Alleged abuses were considered and both
shippers and shipowners willing to testify were heard. The
majority report was in large measure a vindication of both
conferences and deferred rebates. It was held that without
them, shipowners would be able neither to provide regular,
frequent sailings of fast ships nor to maintain rates on a
stable basis. It was further held that the monopoly acquired
under these was not complete, in that it was subject not only

to potential competition from without but also to competition in service from within the fold. "When regular and organized service is required, the conference system, fortified by some tie upon the shipper, is as a general rule necessary."[1]

The majority report, however, did recognize the existence of a number of abuses in connection with conferences and deferred rebates and recommended certain measures to safeguard the interests of shippers and of national trade generally. First, it recommended the formation, under Board of Trade approval, of associations of merchants and shippers to deal collectively with shipowners in order to make their bargaining power more effective. Further, the Board of Trade was to have certain powers of investigation into questions of national importance, but without express authority to enforce their conclusions. The report likewise recommended that conferences be required to file their agreements with the Board of Trade, this file to be confidential and for use of the government only. And, finally, it was suggested that the publication of steamship tariffs would be in the public interest.

For different reasons, as stated, a fairly high percentage of the members of this Commission did not sign the majority report. A number of them filed a detailed minority report, which was prefaced by the statement that, in their view, the majority report overstated the advantages and minimized the evils of conferences and deferred rebates. Their argument was to the effect that the real object of the combined system was to safeguard profits and to end ruinous competition with other liners as well as with tramps, and not, as stated in the majority report, to make possible improved service and more economic operation. They held that regular liner services existed before the inauguration of conferences and that improvements were taking place before their introduction; also that there was no special evidence to show that conferences tended to stimulate progress and improvements. On the other hand, conferences were held to create monopolies, the check upon which was

[1] Cd. 4668, p. 75.

often illusory or increasingly ineffective. They declared them to be injurious to tramps, at that time the strongest element in the great British merchant marine, and to the public also, by keeping rates above the competitive level. Conferences were likewise accused of leading to various forms of waste through interference with tramp operation and through inflation of tonnage.

Recommendations of the minority committee included the strengthening of the power of the Board of Trade in investigation, the requirement of full and regular reports on conference activity to Parliament, and the broadening of the scope of the associations of shippers.

Five years after the British report there appeared a report by the Committee on the Merchant Marine and Fisheries of the United States House of Representatives which had concluded an investigation into the subject of steamship agreements and affiliations.[2] A procedure somewhat similar to that of the British was adopted in the matter of hearings where testimony was given by the various interested parties, both shipowners and shippers. The conclusion reached was that it is necessary to permit lines to co-operate through some form of rate-and-pooling arrangement under governmental supervision and control.

It is the view of the Committee that open competition can not be assured for any length of time by ordering existing agreements terminated. The entire history of steamship agreements shows that in ocean commerce there is no happy medium between war and peace when several lines engage in the same trade. Most of the numerous agreements and conference arrangements discussed in the foregoing report were the outcome of rate wars, and represent a truce between the contending lines. To terminate existing agreements would necessarily bring about one of two results: the lines would either engage in rate wars which would mean the elimination of the weak and the survival of the strong, or, to avoid a costly struggle, they would consolidate through common ownership. Neither result can be prevented by legislation, and either would mean a monopoly fully as effective, and, it is believed, more so than can exist by virtue of an agreement. Moreover, steamship agreements and conferences are not confined to the lines engaging in the foreign trade of the United States.

[2] *Report on Steamship Agreements and Affiliations in American Foreign and Domestic Trade.* 4 vols. (House Document 805, 63d Congress, 2d Session, 1914.)

They are as universally used in the foreign trade of other countries as in our own. The merchants of these countries now enjoy the
foregoing advantages of co-operative arrangements, and to restore
open and cutthroat competition among the lines serving the United
States would place American exporters at a disadvantage in many
markets as compared with their foreign competitors.[3]

The conclusion reached by the American investigation
thus substantially agreed with that of the British report on
the question of permitting steamship conferences. The two
reports differed, however, on the matter of deferred rebates;
the American report recommended that deferred rebates as
well as all discriminations between shippers be declared
illegal and suggested specific legislation designed to subject
the lines to government supervision not only in the matter
of general policies but also in that of rates.

The House investigation also included the question of
traffic agreements between railways and steamship lines. It
was found that nearly all lines operating in transpacific
trade had effected agreements with leading transcontinental
railways. About half of these made provision for an exclusive working arrangement between the steamship line
and the railroad for traffic to and from the Far East. The
following shipping lines and railways were associated in
some form of traffic agreement:

Pacific Mail Steamship Co.	⎰Southern Pacific Railway ⎱Atchison, Topeka & Santa Fe Railway
Toyo Kisen Kaisha	⎰Western Pacific Railway ⎱ Company
Great Northern Steamship Co.	⎰Great Northern ⎱ Railway
Osaka Shosen Kaisha	⎰Chicago, Milwaukee & St. Paul ⎱ Railway
Ocean Steamship Co. China Mutual Steamship Co.	⎰Great Northern Railway ⎱Northern Pacific Railway

The House Committee's report pointed out that

when these agreements are considered in conjunction with the agreements and conference arrangements existing between the steamship lines themselves, it is apparent that the regular trans-Pacific
lines occupy a strongly entrenched position from a competitive point

[3] Report cited, Vol. 4, pp. 416–17.

of view, as compared with independent water carriers which have no such steamship conference or railroad connections.

The Shipping Act of 1916, which created the United States Shipping Board, put into effect most of the recommendations of the Congressional report, including the prohibition of deferred rebates. Section 14, which embodies this provision, reads as follows:

That no common carrier by water shall, directly or indirectly, in respect to the transportation by water of passengers or property between a port of a State, Territory, District, or possession of the United States and any other such port or a port of a foreign country, first pay, or allow, or enter into any combination, agreement or understanding, express or implied, to pay or allow, a deferred rebate to any shipper. The term "deferred rebate" in this Act means a return of any portion of the freight money by a carrier to any shipper as a consideration for the giving of all or any portion of his shipments to the same or any other carriers, or for any other purpose, the payment of which is deferred beyond the completion of the service for which it is paid, and is made only if, during both the period for which computed and the period of deferment, the shipper has complied with the terms of the rebate agreement or arrangement.

In amplification of this ruling and to assure American shipping all the advantages, not expressly declared illegal, of conference membership, the Merchant Marine Act of 1920 added the following provisions to Section 14:

The Board, upon its own initiative may, or upon complaint shall, after due notice to all parties in interest and hearing, determine whether any person not a citizen of the United States and engaged in transportation by water of passengers or property—

1. Has violated any provision of section 14, or
2. Is a party to any combination, agreement, or understanding, express or implied, that involves in respect to transportation of passengers or property between foreign ports, deferred rebates or any other unfair practice designated in section 14, and that excludes from admission upon equal terms with all other parties thereto, a common carrier by water which is a citizen of the United States and which has applied for such admission.

If the Board determines that any such person has violated any such provision or is a party to any such combination, agreement, or understanding, the Board shall thereupon certify such fact to the Secretary of Commerce. The Secretary shall thereafter refuse such person the right of entry for any ship owned or operated by him or

by any carrier directly or indirectly controlled by him, into any port
of the United States, or any Territory, District, or possession thereof,
until the Board certifies that the violation has ceased or such combination agreement or understanding has been terminated.

Considerable importance should be attached to the provision here requiring conferences to admit on equal terms,
if they apply for admission, all American lines engaged in
the same trade. While the law thus protects only American
lines seeking admission to conferences, this provision virtually compels the same treatment for all lines, and the
agreements filed with the Shipping Board in practically all
cases stipulate that any line engaged in the trade covered
by the several conferences may become a party thereto by
complying with its provisions, or upon consent of the members. The proviso is usually added that consent may not be
withheld except for good cause.

The admission of all lines to conference agreements tends
to keep in check the monopoly power which well-established
conferences are likely to acquire on routes dominated by
liner services. It has the further merit of eliminating one of
the leading causes of rate wars, so demoralizing to the
stability of rates and services and which yield no benefit to
the shipper commensurate with their burden. The precedent
elsewhere was that the only way in which a new line could
break into a trade was by inaugurating a rate war, which it
maintained, if financially able, until the conference was con-
vinced of the wisdom of admitting it to membership.
Naturally, only strong lines could hope to force their way
into conferences, so that the inevitable tendency was toward
more and more complete monopoly.

Section 15 of the 1916 Act provides that a copy of memo-
randa of all agreements must be filed with the Shipping
Board. As the result of *ex parte* proceedings decided August 16, 1927, the Shipping Board has ruled that agreements
relating to one or more of the following subjects must be
filed (and that unless they do relate to such subjects they
need not be filed):

1. Fixing or regulating transportation rates.
2. Giving or receiving special rates, accommodations, or other
special privileges or advantages.

3. Controlling, regulating, preventing, or destroying competition.

4. Pooling or apportioning earnings, losses, or traffic.

5. Allotting ports, restricting number and character of sailings between ports.

6. Regulating in any way the volume or character of freight or passenger traffic.

7. In any manner providing for exclusive, preferential, or co-operative working arrangements.

The Shipping Board is required to pass on all such agreements and may disapprove, cancel, or modify any agreement which it finds

unjustly discriminatory or unfair as between carriers, shippers, exporters, importers, or ports, or between exporters from the United States and their foreign competitors, or . . . . to the detriment of the commerce of the United States, or in violation of this Act.

The Shipping Act of 1916 likewise specifically exempts such agreements, when approved by the Board, from the provisions of the Sherman Act and subsequent anti-trust legislation.

Since the law includes in its scope all vessels engaged in trade touching ports of the United States, foreign steamship lines operating services to and from the United States are subject to its provisions equally with American lines. It follows, accordingly, that no conference agreement filed with the Shipping Board may contain any arrangement for the granting of deferred rebates and no such conferences may legally grant such rebates without including information as to this practice in the copies of agreements filed. The presumption therefore is that shipping conferences in American trade do not make use of the policy of deferred rebates which is employed so generally by conference lines in other parts of the world.

As a practical matter, however, it may be questioned how far existing legal machinery in the United States is able to prevent the granting of deferred rebates by conferences governing trades to the United States. In such cases headquarters are, or may be, on foreign soil, and the shippers to whom such rebates might be given would, in most cases, be citizens of foreign countries. Under the circumstances, on certain inward routes it is possible that deferred rebates are still granted, since a few years earlier there appeared considerable testimony before both British and American committees investigating the subject of steamship agreements, to the effect that deferred rebates have been utilized to keep shippers loyal, not only on inward trades but also in at least one outward trade of the United States.

Since the penalty for violation, however, is not only loss of right to enter United States ports but also a fine of $1,000 per day for Section 15 violations, it is quite certain that any deferred-rebate arrangements affecting American foreign trade which may still be in existence are so carefully guarded as to prevent their coming to the official notice of the Shipping Board. It is probably fair to state that, on the whole, conference lines operating both in and out of American ports do not rely on deferred rebates.[4]

The alternative method of inducing loyalty to conference lines on the part of the shippers had taken the form of contracts, either between individual conference lines and shippers or between the conference as a whole and shippers. In the early days of steamship liner services and of rate wars, the large and powerful shippers were often "tied" to the lines by contracts which granted them exceedingly favorable rates in return for their exclusive patronage. Testimony before the British Royal Commission on Shipping Rings indicated that on eastbound transatlantic routes the big American trusts consistently received enormous concessions from shipping lines, although the practice had been largely given up in other parts of the world in favor of the system of deferred rebates applicable to large and small

---

[4] This question of the organization of deferred-rebate conferences in the United States is not a dead issue. As recently as May 1932, Attorney Ira Campbell of the American Steamship Owners' Association advocated this new departure at Washington in an address delivered at a meeting of the American Conference for the Establishment of International Justice. Comment appearing in the *Pacific Shipper* (May 16, 1932) is in point: "Advocacy of rebate conferences from such a source was somewhat of a surprise to the shipping industry, for the reason that the American public has been considered as extremely hostile to rebates in any form because of the onus attached to railroad rebates. Steamship operators generally, on the other hand, long considered that rebate conferences were justifiable and logical, even though they have not openly espoused the cause. They have been operated successfully in foreign countries for many years."

shippers alike. The Shipping Act of 1916 expressly prohibited all rate discriminations, but the present practice of
granting lower rates to shippers who contract to send all
their goods by a given line or conference is not considered a
violation of the law, since no distinction is made between
large and small shippers. The contract rates apply not to all
merchandise but only to those commodities with respect to
which the conferences choose to establish such rates. The
deferred-rebate system likewise usually excepts from its
application certain commodities. The contract system has
many of the advantages, from the standpoint of the shipowner, of the deferred rebate, but it does not constitute, as
does the latter, a continuing tie on the shipper. It may be
explained that under the deferred-rebate system a rebate
earned by "loyalty" in one period is withheld until the end
of the ensuing period, so that any breach of loyalty in the
second period results in loss of rebates for both periods. A
shipper under the contract system may transfer his patronage at the end of a contract period without forfeiting anything except the right to the contract rate on shipments made
subsequent to the termination of the contract.

Shippers who do not patronize conference lines exclusively are protected by Section 14 of the 1916 Shipping Act,
which makes it illegal for shipowners to retaliate against
any shipper by refusing or threatening to refuse available
space or by discriminating in any other manner.

It is interesting to compare the methods developed in the
United States for curbing conference abuses and those favored in Great Britain. The former depend largely on
government control, the latter on voluntary measures. The
British Dominions, however, have been more inclined than
the Mother Country toward legislative restriction. A brief
recital of British official action since the *Report of the Royal
Commission on Shipping Rings* (1909) brings out clearly
these contrasts.

As far as may be judged, Great Britain took no definite
steps for some time to give effect to the recommendations
of the Royal Commission. Certain overseas parts of the
Empire, on the other hand, felt less satisfied with existing
shipping conditions and instituted measures designed to

improve the situation. In 1910 Australia amended its Industries Preservation Act so as to make rebates illegal on all outward trades from Australia. A year later South Africa, where the Royal Commission found conference abuses the most pronounced, attacked the system of deferred rebates through the medium of the mail contract; a new law provided that the Governor-General should not enter into any ocean-mail contract with any line giving rebates conditioned upon the exclusive shipment of goods by vessels of particular lines.

In 1912 the Dominions Royal Commission was appointed to conduct comprehensive studies of resources, development, trade, and communications of British overseas dominions. Their final report, issued in 1917, gave the results of a full consideration of all problems connected with Imperial transport, including recommendations on the question of government control of shipping, particularly in the matter of freight rates, a subject which had been brought before the Commission by the Canadian government.

The proposals of the Dominions Royal Commission involved a much larger measure of government control of conference rates than was recommended by the Royal Commission on Shipping Rings. It was proposed to give to the government the supervision of rates charged by all lines contracting for Imperial mail services and by all vessels whose construction or operation was in any way subsidized by the British or overseas governments.

This body likewise recommended the establishment of Dominions Boards to inquire into alleged abuses of shipowners, with full powers for taking evidence and for ordering the production of documents, to receive copies of all conference agreements and contracts with shippers or with other transportation companies, and to work for conciliation and amicable relations between shippers and shipowners. The Commission expressed the belief that some Dominions might consider it advisable to give their Boards power to enforce their decisions where conciliation has failed.

Following closely upon the final report of the Dominions Royal Commission (Cd. 8462) came the report of the Departmental Committee of the Board of Trade (Cmd. 9092), assigned to consider, among other things, the position of British shipping and shipbuilding after the World War. This committee did not find itself in full accord with the conclusions reached by the Dominions Royal Commission. In general its position was one of more complete *laissez faire* for the shipping industry. It did recommend, however, the establishment of a board of investigation, so constituted as to be in a position to appreciate the needs both of trade and of shipping, "and to give full weight to the position of this country as a maritime nation."[5] It is stipulated, however, that the Board's powers should not go beyond investigation, conciliation, and, where deemed expedient, publication of its findings. Its report likewise reiterated the recommendation made by the Royal Commission on Shipping Rings that strong trade associations among shippers be organized in order to meet conferences on equal terms. Belief was expressed that this development would be a more important influence than any other in curing whatever evils existed in conferences and deferred rebates.

In July 1918 the Imperial War Conference passed a resolution in favor of the appointment of an Imperial Investigation Board, with power to inquire into and report on all matters connected with ocean freights and facilities, and with the development and improvement of Imperial sea communications. In accord with this resolution the Imperial Shipping Committee was established in 1920, with functions described as follows:

1. To inquire into complaints from persons and bodies interested with regard to ocean freights, facilities, and conditions in the inter-Imperial trade on questions of a similar nature referred to them by any of the nominating authorities, and to report their conclusions to the Governments concerned;
2. To survey the facilities for maritime transport on such routes as appear to them to be necessary for trade within the Empire, and

[5] This sentence is a significant clue to the general attitude in England toward the shipping industry. It would seem to explain the repeated reluctance of each British body investigating shipping to recommend any legislative restrictions which might prove hampering to British shipping in the pursuit of its world-wide undertakings. The Dominions, as their policies show, have not fully shared this view.

to make recommendations to the proper authority for the co-ordination and improvement of such facilities with regard to the type, size, and speed of ships, depth of water in docks and channels, construction of harbor works, and similar matters.[6]

Under the first of the two groups of functions falls the problem of determining what, if any, government control should be imposed on shipping conferences.

It should be observed that the Imperial Shipping Committee antedates by three years the creation of the Imperial Economic Committee, although similarly this body receives its authority from and reports to the governments represented at the Imperial Economic Conference held in 1923. Sir Halford Mackinder, the well-known geographer, has served as its chairman from the outset.

At the request of the Australian government, the Imperial Shipping Committee early undertook an inquiry into the operation of the system of deferred rebates. The situation was that this government had in 1910 passed a law making deferred rebates on outward trades from Australia illegal. The commonwealth government later became the owner of a number of steamships, with which, after the World War, it started regular services in the Australian trades. The situation then arose that the government lines were precluded from becoming a party to the rebate system under which the conference continued to operate in the traffic to Australia, so that carriage by the government line involved the loss of rebates.

A final report on this question appeared in 1923.[7] To a very considerable extent it endorsed the original report on the same subject, namely, the *Report of the Royal Commission on Shipping Rings*. It stated that the conference system must be regarded as a necessary concomitant of modern commerce and, further, that there is a clear mutual obligation between shippers and operators of liner services whereby the latter are required to provide regular, dependable sailings, and the former to give the steady patronage that makes such service possible.

[6] *Report of the Imperial Shipping Committee on the Functions and Constitution of a Permanent Imperial Body* (Cmd. 1483, 1921).

[7] *Report on Deferred Rebate System* (Cmd. 1802, 1923).

As to whether the deferred rebate was the only or the best form of tie, the Imperial Shipping Committee was of the opinion that the "agreement" system, operating in South African trade since the relinquishment of rebates there, offered a workable alternative. This agreement system appears very similar to the contract rates in American foreign trade. Apparently, as applied in South Africa, the agreement system functions through an association of shippers who negotiate with the conference as a unit. Shippers who sign this contract agree to give their entire support to regular conference lines. In return, the latter undertake to maintain regular sailings at advertised rates adequate to meet the ordinary requirements of the trade, to maintain stable rates, which are definitely prescribed in the agreement, and equality of rates to large and small shippers. Proposed rate changes are discussed between the conference and the association.

The Imperial Shipping Committee proposed, as a solution to the Australian problem, that shippers be given the option of choosing to ship under either the agreement plan or deferred rebates. Both systems could thus operate simultaneously, provided care was taken that the net financial results to the shippers would be approximately the same in both cases. The suggestion was adopted with apparent success in the Australian trade, since most shippers elected the agreement system in preference to that of deferred rebates. Some time later the government line was purchased by private interests, so the original complications have now been eliminated.

The Imperial Shipping Committee reiterated the recommendation made by two of the earlier British commissions to the effect that shippers be organized into representative associations for every trade, these associations to be in a position to negotiate with the conferences for the amicable settlement of all differences and questions of mutual interest. The committee has called attention to the fact that during the period immediately following the World War British shipowners were organized in international conferences along practically all routes, but that there was no corresponding body acting for the shippers. The committee stated that the shipowners themselves had repeatedly said that they would welcome the organization of such associations, providing that they were of a thoroughly representative character. A significant step was taken as the result of the hearings in 1923, dealing with the East African Shipping Services, whereby there was created an East African Outward Shippers' Committee, composed of representatives of the Federation of British Industries and the Chambers of Commerce of Manchester, Liverpool, and London, which discusses rates and allied matters with the East African Steamship Conferences. In such cases the committee has taken the stand that a permanent Imperial Shipping Board to investigate complaints and to act in conciliation of differences was all such circumstances required.

The latest report of the Imperial Shipping Committee[8] indicates the general adoption by that body of a policy of acting only as intermediaries in disputes between ship operators and shippers when direct negotiations between the two parties have failed to develop an acceptable agreement. The importance of organizations of shippers related by common interests continues to be stressed, and apparently some progress has been made in that direction, although the obstacles inherent in this type of organization are apparent. The Imperial Shipping Committee has a record of restoring harmony between shipowners and shippers in spite of its lack of power to enforce decisions. In recent years the number of complaints has declined, with the result that the committee has been free to devote more attention to the broader aspects of Imperial shipping facilities.

[8] *Report on Work from June 1926 to May 1930* (Cmd. 3646, 1930), also article on the Imperial Shipping Committee by Sir Halford Mackinder in *Brassey's Naval and Shipping Annual* (1929).

XVIII. Pacific Shipping Conferences

The system of shipping conferences, which permits shipowners and operators to enter into loose or close agreements in order to modify the rigors of unrestricted competition, has existed on the Pacific as in most other important trades for many years. Principally but not solely because of the Panama Canal, it exists today over a much larger number of United States routes than ever before. The established economic belief in the universal beneficence of full competition is in active process of modification, on both land and sea, and the character of ocean services is such as to have called attention early to certain wastes to which unrestricted competition is prone to lead.[1]

Steamship conferences are extremely important in the Pacific Ocean traffic. Tramp shipping was not extensive in this region even before the World War, although, in contrast to the situation on the Atlantic, freight requirements were dominant and passenger traffic was of distinctly minor importance. As brought out elsewhere, one reason for the relative unimportance of tramp shipping is the fact that Japanese subsidized liners kept conference rates so low that tramp ships were not attracted to the field. For many years the Japanese lines virtually controlled the rate situation, since the subsidies which they received from their government obligated them to operate on a level which other lines were forced to meet if they wished to continue in the trade.[2]

Even the Japanese companies did not find the rates profitable, and occasionally faced a deficit in spite of the subsidies. While these rates were fixed by the conferences, the determining influence was the Japanese policy of building up Pacific trade in order to assure ready access to raw materials needed for her industrial development and to markets for the resulting manufactures, and to provide adequate communication with her overseas population.

[1] A brief historical résumé of the conference system and of governmental policies (particularly British and American) toward this system appears in the preceding chapter.

[2] P. C. Crockatt, *Trans-Pacific Commerce and Shipping* (1921).

353

As far as transpacific trade is concerned, many of the important conferences that exist today were also in existence and operating under similar agreements prior to the World War. Completion of the Panama Canal altered world trade routes, but the conferences applicable to the movement between Pacific North America and points in the Far East have not greatly changed in form, although their names are not always identical. Membership has been augmented by a number of new American lines and also foreign lines; agreements have been modified in accordance with the Shipping Act of 1916 and subsequent legislation; and several new conferences have been developed.

Transpacific conferences, discussed in the 1914 House Committee's report,[3] included two eastbound conferences, the Trans-Pacific[4] Tariff Bureau (China branch) and the Trans-Pacific Tariff Bureau (Japan branch); one westbound conference, the Trans-Pacific Bureau; and an agreement between the Pacific Mail and the Toyo Kisen Kaisha operating out of San Francisco, also for the Calcutta Trans-Pacific Conference. No separate passenger conferences were reported by the committee at that time, but the westbound conference agreement covered passenger rates and also included an understanding with the Pacific Mail for a mutual observance of territory with respect to Asiatic passenger traffic. Under this latter arrangement the Pacific Mail did not solicit business north of the California boundary, wherefore the conference lines promised not to encroach south of this line.

Transpacific conferences, particularly eastbound ones, appear to have had considerable difficulties in the past over alleged violations of conference agreements, a not surprising situation in view of the fact that eastbound traffic is much lighter than westbound. For example, in 1912 the Blue Funnel Line (British) withdrew from the Trans-Pacific Freight Bureau of China because of alleged rate-cutting.

[3] See chapter xvii for a discussion of the findings of the House of Representatives investigation into steamship agreements and affiliations in American foreign and domestic trade (1913–1914).

[4] The spelling of "transpacific" is according to the official name of the conference.

The chaotic experiences which sometimes confront the conferences usually have as their basis abnormally low rates offered shippers by non-members, the situation being perhaps merely temporary. Sometimes, however, the conferences themselves come into direct conflict, as in the instance of the Pacific Coast–Oriental Tariff Bureau of San Francisco and the Pacific Coast–Oriental Traffic Bureau of Seattle, respectively, established during the latter part of the World War. When the Seattle section of the conference disbanded in 1920, as a result of rate-cutting from the unorganized lines operating out of the Northwest, the southern conference sent an ultimatum on March 17, 1922, threatening to declare open rates. During the next six months Pacific Coast shipping was wholly disorganized, with the result that in August 1922 a meeting was called in Portland, Oregon, at which the Blue Funnel Line and the Osaka Shosen Kaisha Line signified their willingness to become full-fledged members; a truce was declared in September 1922 which formed the basis of the present Pacific Westbound Conference.

This question of steamship conferences is of vital significance not only as illustrating practical methods of co-operation among competitive lines of various nationalities but also as furnishing a striking example in good-will in one of the keenest fields of combined semi-governmental and private enterprise. Space does not permit an exposition of the history, special arrangements, and changes from time to time, with respect to each conference, but it is worth while to present the impressive list of agreements, classified according to destination (whether inbound, outbound, or both to and from United States Pacific ports), name of conference, and membership according to information verified by the Bureau of Regulation, United States Shipping Board Bureau, in July 1934 (a list which varies considerably from that of a year previously appearing in the author's *Regulation and Promotion of Pacific Shipping*).

SHIPPING CONFERENCES

Inbound:

Trans-Pacific Freight Bureau (*Hong Kong*). Members: American Mail Line; Barber-Wilhelmsen Line; Dollar Steamship Lines, Inc., Ltd.; Klaveness Line; Kokusai Kisen Kaisha; Maersk Line; Mitsui

Bussan Kaisha, Ltd.; Nippon Yusen Kaisha; Oceanic and Oriental Navigation Company; Osaka Shosen Kaisha; States Steamship Company; Tacoma Oriental Steamship Company.

The Associated Steamship Lines (Philippine Islands). Members: American Gulf Orient Line; American Mail Line; American & Manchurian Line; American Pioneer Line; Australian Oriental Line, Ltd.; Bank Line; Barber-Wilhelmsen Line; Ben Line, Ltd.; Blue Funnel Line; Canadian Pacific S.S., Ltd.; Dodwell-Castle Line; Dollar Steamship Lines, Inc., Ltd.; East Asiatic Company, Ltd.; Eastern & Australian S.S. Company, Ltd.; Fern Line; Hamburg-American Line; Holland East Asia Line; Java-China-Japan Line; Kawasaki Kisen Kaisha; Kellog Steamship Corporation; Kerr Steamship Company (Silver Line); Klaveness Line; Kokusai Kisen Kaisha; Koninklijke Paketvaart Maatschappij; Maersk Line; Mitsui Bussan Kaisha; Nakamura Gumi & Company, Ltd.; Nippon Yusen Kaisha; Norddeutscher Lloyd; Oceanic and Oriental Navigation Company; Osaka Shosen Kaisha; Pacific-Java-Bengal Line; Prince Line, Ltd.; Rickmers Line; States Steamship Company; Swedish East Asiatic Company, Ltd.; Tacoma Oriental Steamship Company; Tatsuma Kisen Kaisha; Wilh. Wilhelmsen (Norwegian Africa & Australian Line), Sir William Reardon Smith & Sons. Carrier Agrees to Observe Conference Rates: Isthmian Steamship Company.

Transpacific Freight Bureau (North China, except Tientsin). Members: American Mail Line; Barber - Wilhelmsen Line; Dollar Steamship Lines, Inc., Ltd.; Kawasaki Kisen Kaisha; Kokusai Kisen Kaisha; Maersk Line; Nippon Yusen Kaisha; Oceanic and Oriental Navigation Company; Osaka Shosen Kaisha; States Steamship Company; Tacoma Oriental Steamship Company.

Outward Continental North Pacific Freight Conference. Members: Compagnie Générale Transatlantique; East Asiatic Company, Ltd.; Hamburg-American Line; Holland-America Line; Deutsche Dampfschiffahrts—Ges. Kosmos; North German Lloyd; Royal Mail Lines, Ltd.

Straits-Pacific Conference. Members: Barber-Wilhelmsen Line; Dollar Steamship Lines, Inc., Ltd.; American Mail Line, Ltd.; Nippon Yusen Kaisha; Osaka Shosen Kaisha; Klaveness Line; Kerr Steamship Company, Inc.; Pacific-Java-Bengal Line; States Steamship Company; Oceanic & Oriental Navigation Company; Blue Funnel Line; Ben Line Steamers, Ltd.; East Asiatic Company, Ltd.

Trans-Pacific Freight Conference of Japan. Members: American Mail Line, Ltd.; Barber-Wilhelmsen Line; Canadian Pacific Steamships, Ltd.; Dollar Steamship Lines, Inc., Ltd.; Kawasaki Kisen Kaisha; Kokusai Kisen Kaisha; Nippon Yusen Kaisha; Osaka Shosen Kaisha; States Steamship Lines; United Ocean Transport Co., Ltd. (Daido Kaiun Kabushiki Kaisha); Maersk Line; Mitsui Bussan Kaisha.

West Coast South America—North Pacific Coast Conference. Members: (Grace Line) Grace Line, Inc.; Knutsen Line; Latin-America Line; Nippon Yusen Kaisha.

Calcutta Trans-Pacific Conference. Members: American Mail Line, Ltd.; Barber-Wilhelmsen Line; Canadian Pacific Steamships, Ltd.; China Mutual S. N. Company, Ltd.; Dollar Steamship Lines, Inc., Ltd.; Klaveness Line; Nippon Yusen Kaisha; Ocean Steamship Company, Ltd.; Oceanic & Oriental Navigation Company; Osaka Shosen Kaisha; States Steamship Company; Tacoma Oriental Steamship Company; Pacific-Java-Bengal Line; British India Steam Navigation Company, Ltd.; Indo-China Steam Navigation Company, Ltd.; Silver Line, Ltd.; Lykes Bros.–Ripley Steamship Co., Inc. (American Gulf Orient Line).

Dutch East Indies—Pacific Coast Conference. Members: Silver Line, Ltd.; Klaveness Line; Tacoma Oriental Steamship Company; Pacific-Java-Bengal Line.

Delhi–Pacific Coast Conference. Members: Silver Line, Ltd.; Klaveness Line; Pacific-Java-Bengal Line.

Outbound:

Pacific Coast–Australasian Tariff Bureau. Members: Canadian Australasian Line, Ltd.; Oceanic & Oriental Navigation Company; Oceanic Steamship Company; Transatlantic Steamship Company, Ltd.; Union Steamship Company of New Zealand, Ltd.

Pacific Westbound Conference. Members: American Mail Line; Blue Funnel Line; Dollar Steamship Lines, Inc., Ltd.; General Steamship Corporation; Kerr Steamship Company, Inc.; Klaveness Line; Nippon Yusen Kaisha; Oceanic & Oriental Navigation Company; Osaka Shosen Kaisha; Pacific-Java-Bengal Line; States Steamship Company; Tacoma Oriental Steamship Company; Canadian Pacific Steamships, Ltd. Carriers Agree to Observe Conference Rates: Bank Line, Ltd.; Barber Steamship Lines, Inc.; Kokusai Kisen Kabushiki Kaisha; Prince Line, Ltd.

Pacific–West Coast of South America Conference. Members: Compagnie Générale Transatlantique; Dollar Steamship Lines, Inc., Ltd.; (Grace Line) Grace Line, Inc.; (Grace Line) Panama Mail Steamship Company; Hamburg-American Line; Knutsen Lines; Latin-America Line; Nippon Yusen Kaisha; North German Lloyd; United Fruit Company.

Pacific Coast–Havana Conference. Members: Panama Mail Steamship Company; United Fruit Company.

Pacific Coast–Caribbean Sea Ports Conference. Members: Compagnie Générale Transatlantique; Dollar Steamship Lines, Inc., Ltd.; Hamburg-American Line; North German Lloyd; Panama Mail Steamship Company; United Fruit Company.

Pacific-Straits Conference. Members: Dollar Steamship Lines, Inc., Ltd.; Kerr Steamship Company, Inc.; Klaveness Line; Pacific-Java-Bengal Line.

Pacific Coast—West Coast Central America and Panama Canal Zone Ports Conference. Members: Compagnie Générale Transatlantique (French Line); Panama Mail Steamship Company; United Fruit Company.

Pacific–Dutch East Indies Conference. Members: Kerr Steamship Company, Inc.; Klaveness Line; Pacific-Java-Bengal Line.

Pacific Coast—Eastbound United Kingdom Conference Association. Members: Blue Star Line, Ltd.; Compagnie Maritime Belge (Lloyd Royal) S.A.; Donaldson Line; East Asiatic Company, Ltd.; Furness Withy & Co., Ltd.; Interocean Line; Johnson Line; North Pacific Coast Line (joint service of Royal Mail Lines, Ltd., and Holland-America Line); Fred Olsen Line; Reardon Smith Line, Ltd.

Pacific Coast–South and East African Lumber Conference. Members: American Mail Line; East Asiatic Company, Ltd.; Hamburg-American Line; Holland-America Line; Klaveness Line; Navigazione Libera Triestina, S.A.; Nippon Yusen Kaisha; North German Lloyd; Osaka Shosen Kaisha; Pacific-Java-Bengal Line; Royal Mail Lines, Ltd.; Silver Line, Ltd. (Kerr Steamship Co.); South African Dispatch Line.

Pacific Coast–European Conference. Members: Blue Star Line; Cascade Line; Compagnie Générale Transatlantique (French Line); Compagnie Maritime Belge (Lloyd Royal) S.A.; Donaldson Line Limited; East Asiatic Company; Fred Olsen Line; Fruit Express Line; Furness Line; Hamburg - American Line; Holland - America Line; Interocean Line; Johnson Line; Knutsen Line; Navigazione Libera Triestina, S.A. (Libera Line); North German Lloyd; Reardon Smith Line; Royal Mail Lines, Ltd. Parties Agree to Observe Rates: Anglo-Canadian Shipping Corp., Ltd.; Canadian Transport Co., Ltd.; and Isthmian Steamship Lines.

Pacific Coast–Puerto Rico Conference. Members: McCormick Steamship Company; Pacific Argentine Brazil Line, Inc.; Williams Steamship Corporation.

To and from United States Coast Ports:

Pacific Coastwise Conference. Members: American - Hawaiian Steamship Company; Chamberlin Steamship Company, Ltd.; (Grace Line) Panama Mail Steamship Company; Luckenbach Steamship Company, Inc.; Luckenbach Gulf Steamship Company, Inc.; McCormick Steamship Company; Nelson Steamship Company; (Pacific Coast Direct Line, Inc.) Weyerhaeuser Steamship Company; Pacific Steamship Lines, Ltd.; Sudden & Christenson Company and Hammond Steamship Line, doing business under the name of Christenson-Hammond Line; Williams Steamship Corporation; *Los Angeles Steamship Company; Los Angeles—San Francisco Navigation Company. *(This company participates in agreement as intra-state carrier only.)

Gulf Intercoastal Conference. Members: Gulf Pacific Mail Line, Ltd.; Gulf Pacific Line; Luckenbach Gulf Steamship Company, Inc.

Trans-Pacific Passenger Conference. Members: American Mail Line, Ltd.; Canadian-Australasian Line, Ltd.; Canadian Pacific Steamships, Ltd.; Dollar Steamship Lines, Inc., Ltd.; Kerr Steamship Company, Inc. (Silver Services); Matson Navigation Company; Nippon Yusen Kaisha; Oceanic Steamship Company; Osaka Shosen Kaisha;

Pacific-Java-Bengal Line; States Steamship Company; Transatlantic Steamship Company, Ltd.; Union Steamship Company of New Zealand, Ltd.

North Pacific Coast–Europe Passenger Conference. Members: Compagnie Générale Transatlantique; East Asiatic Company; Furness Line; Hamburg-American Line; Holland-America Line; Johnson Line; Libera Line; North German Lloyd; Royal Mail Lines, Ltd.

Pacific Coastwise Lumber Conference. Members: Beadle Steamship Company, Ltd.; Chamberlin Steamship Company, Ltd.; Hammond Lumber Company; J. R. Hanify Company; Hart-Wood Lumber Company; A. B. Johnson Lumber Company; Lawrence-Philips S.S. Company; Fred Linderman; A. F. Mahony Company; McCormick Steamship Company; Nelson Steamship Company; Oliver J. Olsen & Company; Pacific Spruce Corporation; Pacific Steamship Lines, Ltd.; Paramino Lumber Company; Schafer Bros. Lumber & Shingle Company; Schafer Bros. Steamship Lines; Sudden & Christenson; Tacoma Shipping Company; E. K. Wood Lumber Company.

United States Intercoastal Conference. Members: American-Hawaiian Steamship Company; Argonaut Steamship Line, Inc.; (Arrow Line) Sudden & Christenson and Los Angeles Steamship Company; Dollar Steamship Lines, Inc., Ltd.; (Grace Line) Panama Mail Steamship Company; Isthmian Steamship Company; Luckenbach Steamship Company, Inc.; McCormick Steamship Company; Nelson Steamship Company; (Panama Pacific Line) American Line Steamship Corporation; (Pacific Coast Direct Line, Inc.) Weyerhaeuser Steamship Company; (Quaker Line) Pacific-Atlantic Steamship Company; Williams Steamship Corporation.

Puget Sound Carriers Conference. Members: Border Line Transportation Company; Puget Sound Freight Lines; Puget Sound Navigation Company; Skagit River Navigation and Trading Company.

Pacific Coast–River Plate–Brazil Conference. Members: Pacific Argentine Brazil Line; Westfal-Larsen Company Line.

A brief description of the organization and scope of various shipping agreements governing Pacific liner services as they now exist indicates the manner in which the carrying trade is being handled by joint action on the part of competing lines flying the flags of different nations. Irrespective of the merits and demerits of the question whether or not conferences are desirable from the separate points of view of the operator, the shipper, and the public, at least this co-operation suggests that commerce is not necessarily war and that national differences do not constitute an insuperable barrier to harmony in the shipping world in spite of occasional rough seas on which some agreements have been wrecked.

An examination of various Pacific conference agreements filed with the United States Shipping Board reveals many elements in common. From the very nature and purpose of conferences, it follows that each makes provision for joint action on certain matters in which the members have a mutual interest. The freight conferences provide, with certain agreed exceptions, for a uniform scale of rates and, in most cases, for uniform charges for other services given or received in connection with shipping. A standardized procedure for weighing and measuring commodities is likewise considered in so far as it constitutes a necessary element in uniform freight rates. The passenger conferences deal with fares, agencies and their commissions, and allied subjects.

Notable is the Pacific Westbound Conference, organized to cover liner freight services from or via Pacific Coast ports of North America to Japan proper, Korea, Formosa, Siberia, Manchukuo, China, Hong Kong, Indo-China, Siam, the Philippine Islands, and the Straits Settlements. Through shipments from transcontinental freight bureau territory in the United States and Canada, destined westward through Pacific ports, are thus included in its scope.

Among these lines the agreement in force embraces regulation of rates, tariff brokerage, and related matters. Members bind themselves to observe strictly the schedule of charges established by the conference, and to refrain from any form of discrimination against, or rebate to, any shipper, contractor, broker, consignee or other receiver of merchandise. Action agreed to by two-thirds of the members is binding on all. Questions of breach of agreement are left to arbitration by impartial outsiders, and each member deposits $25,000 in cash in government or surety bonds as protection to other members. A member may be expelled for breach of agreement on a two-thirds vote, and new members may also be admitted by a two-thirds vote.

Perhaps the most interesting feature of this conference agreement is the detailed plan for adjudication of disputes by arbitrators appointed to serve in accordance with the laws of the state or province involved, with full authority to examine records and to enter judgments which have the force of court awards.

Furthermore, the Pacific Westbound Conference had an agreement with the Far East Conference,[5] which operates to the same region from the United States Atlantic and Gulf ports, "to provide for understanding and co-operation between said conferences and the members thereof for the better promotion of trade and commerce." Joint action on rates, tariffs, brokerage, and related matters was made possible by mutual consent, but the agreement did not require that the two conferences act in unison on such matters except as they jointly elected to do so. When such action was agreed on, however, by two-thirds or more of the members present at a joint conference (two-thirds of all members constituting a quorum), it became binding on all, and any member line proved guilty of breach was subject to damages imposed according to the rules of the conference to which the offending member belonged.

Operating to regulate traffic westward from or via United States and Canadian ports on the Pacific to ports in Australasia is the Pacific Coast–Australasian Tariff Bureau. Rate maintenance is required of members except as unanimously agreed to, and all discriminations or concessions are expressly forbidden. In the memorandum filed with the Shipping Board the duty of the Secretary to investigate cases of alleged rate cutting is set forth, but no mention is made of machinery for settling disputes, nor, apparently, is any bond required of members.

One of the newest agreements is that covering trade from Pacific Coast ports to Netherlands India. Members of this conference undertake to maintain strict uniformity in rates and charges and to refrain from all discriminations against shippers or receivers. Deferred rebates are specifically prohibited. Conference action is by unanimous vote as long as member lines do not exceed three in number, and by unanimous vote less one in the event of a larger membership.

The Gulf Intercoastal Conference, after consultation with the Shipping Board Bureau, has recently attempted the furthest step ever taken toward the extension of steamship conference control in this country, at least during recent history. Amendments to its organic agreement have

[5] Revoked December 15, 1930, but historically important.

been filed with the Board by the Conference which, if sanctioned, would require: (1) that a member line hold what is tantamount to a certificate of necessity and convenience; (2) that the Board be the arbiter of the certificate; (3) that the line guarantee to maintain a minimum of two sailings a month, for not less than one year, between New Orleans, Houston, Mobile, and Pacific Coast ports; (4) that each member post a fulfillment bond of $100,000.

Eastbound conferences include the Trans-Pacific Freight Bureau of North China, a similar organization for South China, and a third for Japan. Membership in the first two is almost identical, while the third has an independent list of members. The majority of members in the eastbound conferences also belong to the Pacific Westbound Conference. Terms of the first two conferences are practically the same, and those of the Japan conference closely similar. Joint action on rates is provided, and proof of breach may lead to expulsion. All kinds of concessions, the effect of which is violation of the agreed tariff, are specifically prohibited.

Jurisdiction of the Trans-Pacific Freight Bureau of North China covers shipments from or via Shanghai, Tientsin, Newchang, Chefoo, Wei-Hai-Wei, Tsingtao, Ningpo, and all Yangtze River treaty ports to or via Pacific Coast ports and Hawaii. Two tariffs are provided, one for through shipments to interior points in North America, and one for shipments terminating at Pacific ports. The parallel conference for ports of South China, called simply the Trans-Pacific Freight Bureau, originally included in its scope Indo-China, Siam, Straits Settlements, Federated Malay States, Java, and Ceylon.

Since the consummation of the foregoing agreement a separate conference for shipments from the Straits Settlements to North American Pacific ports has been created. The agreement for the observance of rates set forth in joint tariffs is enforced only by the statement that "any line quoting lower rates than those shown in the tariff is under moral obligation to notify the other lines of intention to do so." Membership of the eastbound Straits Conference only partly duplicates the membership of the westbound conference.

The Trans-Pacific Freight Tariff Bureau of Japan has jurisdiction over shipments carried by member lines from Japanese ports to North American ports. This agreement includes transpacific shipments from Japan to the Pacific Coast and Hawaii, to any transcontinental freight bureau territory, or to any overland point via Pacific Coast ports.

A conference entitled the Associated Steamship Lines has been established for the announced purpose of looking after "matters pertaining to ocean transportation to and from the Philippine Islands, also to provide united action in dealing with matters affecting the interests of members of the Association as a body." For tariff matters the Association is divided into five groups; namely, the Atlantic Coast service, the Pacific Coast service, the China-Japan service, the Saigon-Straits-Java-India service, and the Australia–New Zealand service. Group affiliations are determined by the services operated by members. Although not specifically stated in the agreement, the implication is that uniform rates are observed within each group. Tariff matters are voted by a majority of two-thirds of the members voting; on all other questions a majority vote is sufficient. The Association maintains a weighing-and-measuring department under the direct supervision of the secretary, who keeps account of expenditures for this service and sends bills to the members accordingly. Failure to observe regulations renders the offending member liable to expulsion.

Another conference, the Calcutta Trans-Pacific, was organized to effect a working agreement between lines operating services between Calcutta and Hong Kong, on the one hand, and lines operating between Hong Kong and Pacific ports of North America, on the other. The former are also designated in the agreement as the Calcutta lines, the latter as the Pacific lines. The United States Shipping Board lines were originally a party to this agreement under a separate category, but since all these Shipping Board services have been sold to private operators, the agreement stands as between the two groups mentioned. The chief purpose of the organization is an arrangement for mutually exclusive transfer at Hong Kong of through cargo moving between Calcutta and the Pacific Coast of North America (including Hawaii), and for a division of the through rate, one-third going to the Calcutta lines and two-thirds to the Pacific lines. Both eastbound and westbound traffic is covered; through rates are fixed by unanimous action of the conference. Further, each group of lines agrees not to invade the territory of the other by instituting services therein. Thus this agreement differs from others in that it is concerned with transshipment of through cargo between two groups of lines operating on different routes.

There are a number of other conferences concerned with trade between the United States Atlantic and Gulf ports and Far Eastern regions, their agreements covering the transpacific route via the Panama Canal or alternative routes via either Panama or Suez. The Japan–Atlantic Coast Freight Conference, composed of lines operating from Japanese ports, including Formosa and Dairen, to the Atlantic Coast of the United States via the Panama Canal is one of these.[6] Another governs shipments from the Straits Settlements to North Atlantic and Gulf ports of the United States via either the Panama or Suez Canal.[7] Still another conference, the New York Freight Bureau (Shanghai branch), with jurisdiction over shipments from Shanghai, Yangtze River ports, and coast ports north of Shanghai to North Atlantic and Gulf ports of the United States, stipulates the alternative routes of the Suez Canal, the Cape of Good Hope, or else the Panama Canal, either direct or with transshipment at Pacific Coast ports of the United States to intercoastal steamers.[8]

[6] Terms of this agreement are very similar to those covering eastbound transpacific trade to Pacific Coast ports, rates being determined by joint action of all members who agree to abide by the adopted scale. All concessions and discriminations whose effect is a departure from the conference tariff are prohibited, violations rendering members liable to expulsion.

[7] This agreement also stipulates the maintenance of rates published in joint tariffs by stating that "any line quoting lower rates than those shown in said tariff is under moral obligation to notify the other lines of its intention to do so." This provision would seem to indicate a somewhat less rigid enforcement of adherence to conference rates than exists in most of the other freight agreements.

[8] The memorandum covering this agreement is very brief and consists chiefly in an undertaking by the signers to maintain rates agreed on in joint conference by a majority vote. Neither bonds are stipulated nor penalties provided, and all liners in the trade are invited to participate by complying with the terms of the agreement.

All passenger traffic, through and local, entirely on or via the Pacific Ocean is covered by the Trans-Pacific Passenger Conference.[9] Half of the members participate in two of the three groups included in the conference, namely, Hawaiian, through-Orient, and through-Australasian traffic. Comparatively detailed agreements cover questions pertaining to regular fares, concessions in fares, commissions, agencies, advertising, and various other matters. While the conference does not undertake specifically to fix fares, its rules are designed to facilitate their stabilization. Each member is obligated to file with the conference all fare sheets, circulars, and rules and regulations pertaining to passenger traffic, and to give advance notice of all rate cuts or other departures from the tariff. The conference likewise sets itself the task of receiving, compiling, and disseminating passenger-traffic data for the benefit of all the members.

Pacific-Australasian passenger traffic is governed by another conference which specifically excludes from its jurisdiction questions of fares and all other charges, but members are bound to give thirty days' notice of reduction in through fares. Promotion and improvement of direct passenger traffic between North America, New Zealand, and Australia is undertaken by the conference. In addition, it endeavors to record and centralize proceedings of member lines, and to facilitate the interchange of passengers in order to provide diversity of routing and service.

Availability of the Panama Canal route has brought with it the development of services from Pacific Coast ports to ports on the Caribbean and the Atlantic. These services, in turn, have led to the organization of conferences to cover the several trades thereby created. From the point of view of tonnage the Pacific Coast–European route is the most important, but the conference agreement covering this service applies to eastbound movement only. Its main provision is for co-operation in the maintenance of uniform rates and practices agreed to by unanimous vote of all members pres-

---

[9] The passenger conference and freight conferences act independently of each other even if they have the same membership. Each has its own secretary and separate office force, and maintains distinct headquarters.

ent at a meeting. Membership consists of some sixteen lines at the present time, and is open to all carriers.[10]

A passenger conference is likewise in operation on the Pacific Coast–European route, which includes both eastbound and westbound traffic between Pacific Coast ports of the United States and ports of the United Kingdom, the Continent, Scandinavia, and the Mediterranean. It embraces as well northbound and southbound traffic between Pacific ports of the United States and West Coast ports of Central America and the Panama Canal, and traffic in both directions between Pacific United States and British Columbia. Uniform rates, rules, and regulations are in force subject to such amendment from time to time as the conference decides upon.

The Pacific Coast–River Plate–Brazil Conference undertakes to establish uniform freight and brokerage rates on traffic moving between Pacific ports of the United States and Canada and those of Argentina, Uruguay, and Brazil, and territories adjacent thereto. Another conference operating through the Canal applies to freight traffic moving between Pacific ports of the United States and a considerable number of listed ports in the West Indies, Colombia, Venezuela, and adjoining territories. Members of this conference also bind themselves to abide by rates unanimously adopted by all members present at a given meeting, although withdrawal from the conference requires only ten days' notice in place of the more usual 60 or 90 days.

Because the domestic intercoastal route is heavily overtonnaged, creating a constant temptation to rate-cutting, the history of the United States Intercoastal Conference has been a stormy one. Membership in the protected coastal trade is, of course, confined to American lines, but at no time have all the companies using the Canal route joined the conference. Complicating the surplus-tonnage problem is the existence of several industrial carriers whose interests do not always accord with those of independent shipping lines. Further difficulties have been created by the overlap-

---

[10] Shipping lines operating on this route include a larger number of nationalities than are involved in any other United States Pacific trade.

ping of coastwise and intercoastal services on the Pacific. Intercoastal carriers, in the course of calls at various Pacific ports, have picked up more or less cargo for purely coastwise movement.

After months of complete disruption the Intercoastal Conference was again reorganized in February 1932. The agreement did not include the industrial carriers, but the latter agreed to abide by the rates and practices of the conference, and one such carrier has voluntarily joined the conference. Member lines are required to post a $25,000 bond, and penalties for violations are to be determined by member lines other than the complainant and the accused.

Undoubtedly the threat of stringent regulatory legislation contained in bills introduced into Congress hastened the reorganization of this conference. The present agreement, however, does not wipe out the memory of the long succession of short-lived conferences, and the movement on foot to subject intercoastal traffic to greater federal regulation is likely to gain support. Since this trade is confined by law to ships of American registry, it is quite conceivable that some administrative body such as the Shipping Bureau or the Interstate Commerce Commission may eventually be designated to control intercoastal shipping affairs somewhat as interstate commerce by land is now regulated.[11] If the present conference breaks down it is almost certain to precipitate legislation of this sort, and some shipping interests that are affected are already favorably disposed toward submitting their affairs to government regulation.

[11] The Intercoastal Regulation Act (S. 4491) was signed by the President on March 3, 1933. This legislation specifies that if rate schedules are not filed within 90 days from the date of enactment, no common carrier may operate through the Panama Canal in intercoastal traffic until its schedules have been properly filed and approved. Under this new law changes in rates, fares, or regulations, which have been filed with the Shipping Board and posted publicly, may not be effective earlier than a period of not less than 30 days after a new filing and posting. No carrier shall charge, demand, collect, or receive a greater, less, or different compensation than specified in the schedules filed, posted, and in effect; nor shall any carrier refund or remit in any manner or by any device any portion of the rates, fares, or charges specified, nor extend or deny to any person any privilege or facility except in accordance with such schedules. Violators shall be punished by a fine not less than $1,000 or more than $5,000 for each act of violation and/or each day such violation continues.

The Pacific Coastwise Conference also has been in difficulties, partly for the same reasons. A reorganization agreement, effected simultaneously with that of the Intercoastal Conference, plans a considerable degree of dictatorship on the part of the directing head. Although it has a separate identity, it is under the same control as the Pacific Coastwise Lumber Conference.

Two Pacific Coast international coasting conference agreements are filed with the United States Shipping Board. One covers traffic northbound from Pacific ports of South America to Pacific ports of the United States and Canada. By "gentlemen's agreement," members undertake to abide by rates established through unanimous vote of all lines party to the conference. The other coasting conference applies to traffic between Pacific ports of the United States and Canada and Pacific ports of Central America, including the Canal Zone. Here, too, co-operation in the maintenance of uniform rates is agreed upon.

In addition to the various conferences proper which relate to Pacific Coast shipping activities, and which are severally organized so as to include carriers engaged in the same trade, certain so-called "tandem" and similar agreements are also in force between conferences. The latter involve connecting trades and cover matters pertaining to joint through billing, through rates, routes, absorption practices, and co-operative terminal arrangements. One agreement similar in nature, known as the Calcutta Trans-Pacific Conference, has already been noted. Others cover through transpacific shipments from Atlantic ports with transshipment at Pacific ports, shipments from United States Pacific ports to points in Atlantic Canada, the West Indies, etc., with transshipment at United States Atlantic ports and shipments on similar through routes.[12]

Shipping companies are availing themselves more and more of the facilities offered by Section 15 of the Shipping

[12] Intermediate between conference and tandem agreements are numerous other arrangements for mutual action of one sort or another, varying enough in kind and purpose to make classification difficult. While they are important as a whole, they are individually much less important than the conference agreements.

Act. The number of agreements examined and recommended by the Bureau of Regulation to the Board increased from 275 in 1929 to 425 in 1930, 530 in 1931, 563 in
1932, and 630 in the fiscal year 1933. One hundred and
thirteen of these 630 agreements, or over a fifth of the total,
were conference agreements. On June 30, 1930, the number
of active conferences functioning in the foreign and interstate commerce of the United States totaled 101, contrasted
with 86 at the close of the fiscal year 1932. The trades
covered, and the number of conferences operating in each
one, appear in Table 59.

TABLE 59

Aᴍᴇʀɪᴄᴀɴ Sʜɪᴘᴘɪɴɢ Cᴏɴꜰᴇʀᴇɴᴄᴇꜱ, ʙʏ Tʀᴀᴅᴇ Rᴇɢɪᴏɴꜱ, 1930*

Trades	From United States North Atlantic and South Atlantic Ports	To United States North Atlantic and South Atlantic Ports	From United States Gulf Ports	To United States Gulf Ports	From United States Pacific Coast Ports	To United States Pacific Coast Ports
United Kingdom	8	5	3	1	3	1
Continental Europe, including Spanish Atlantic, Scandinavian, and Baltic ports	9	10	2	..	2	1
Mediterranean ports, including Adriatic, Black Sea, and Levant ports	8	5	2	..	2	..
Far East, including Indo China, Philippine Islands, Siam, Straits Settlements, and India	2	9	2	8	4	7
Dutch East Indies	1	1	1	1	2	3
South Sea Islands	..	..	..	..	2	2
Australasia	1	..	..	..	2	1
Africa	2	1	..	..	2	..
West Indies and Caribbean Sea ports...	6	4	5	4	2	..
South and Central America and Mexico	4	6	3	2	5	4
Between Philippine Islands and foreign ports	..	..	3	..	..	..
Between Puerto Rico, Virgin Islands, and Europe	..	..	1	..	..	..
Intercoastal and coastwise, including Great Lakes, Hawaii, and Alaska.....	..	..	11	..	..	..
To Panama Canal Zone from foreign ports	..	..	3	..	..	..

* Fiscal year. Data from United States Shipping Board.

The most arresting feature of the foregoing conferences is
the demonstrated practice of private companies, operating

under flags of leading maritime powers, in merging their spheres of enterprise and business secrets into semi-voluntary, international groups.[13] Membership, open to all participating lines, is applied for and secured by most carriers. All ocean lanes to and from United States ports are included within these powerful regional bodies. The majority in these conferences is strikingly that of foreign lines. A surprising feature is the far more co-operative and established order of affairs in the conferences of many flags than in those to which only United States lines can obtain membership. This fact is another demonstration that economic factors rather than national protectionism provide the real basis for efficient operation of commercial vessels. And yet patriotism, chauvinism, and pride are more closely associated with a country's shipping than with any other form of national enterprise.

[13] The apportionment of sea trade upon a predetermined quota basis is receiving now a great deal of attention. In a recent issue of *Fairplay* a correspondent signing himself "Realist" proposes this method of apportioning trade on an equitable basis. To the best of the writer's knowledge, the first definite proposal of this kind appeared in a brief paper presented by Captain I. N. Hibberd, of San Francisco, at the Pan-Pacific Commercial Conference (1922), at which the author was present, when this retired sea master suggested this provisional division of transpacific traffic: "A fair division of the traffic of that ocean to and from both the Americas would be apportionment of fifty per cent to the United States, thirty per cent to Japan, and the balance to the various other maritime nations of the world. This division would affect the North and South Pacific and the eastern seas as far as the 95th degree of east longitude, and would cause very little dislocation of existing conditions. An exception should be made of the trade between Australia and England, which is a separate unit belonging to those two countries in which other nations have very little interest."

An item in the *Trans-Pacific* (April 26, 1934) carries this significant news item: "The Java Freight Conference, consisting of the Nippon Yusen Kaisha, Osaka Shosen Kaisha, Nanyo Yusen Kaisha, Ishiwara Industry Company, and Java-China-Japan Line, has decided on a quota system for the volume goods carried by ships of member companies. The quota is 73 per cent for the four Japanese companies and 27 per cent for the Dutch concern. Objection has been raised by the Dutch interests, who insist that the ratio should be more than 33 per cent and that the matter be submitted to the coming Japanese Dutch East Indian Conference in Batavia, Java, next month." In December 1934 a 60-40 basis was under negotiation.

XIX. Government Subsidies—British and Japanese

Merchant shipping engaged in foreign trade presents a paradox. On the one hand, it is primarily national in character; no economic activity is more susceptible to state supervision and political maneuvers. On the other hand, the international merchant marine is basically international. National and international policies are nearly certain to conflict with each other, because even under the most favorable circumstances they cannot be in complete harmony; hence the situation immediately involves uncertainty as to the wise formulation of maritime policies. One can believe the statement that external shipping is a half-domestic industry, for, while official regulations can be set up for the inbound movement of vessels and their cargoes, little can be done to control their outbound movement. And yet shipping, more than any other known business activity, is inherently worldwide in all of its aspects. Neither one-way traffic nor one leg of a journey can stand the costs of an entire voyage; nevertheless the intrusion of a strictly nationalistic program unfortunately appears practical and not academic to politicians and to millions of educated persons.

The facts are surprisingly difficult to discover. Propaganda of the most flamboyant and flimsy type, unsatisfactory statistics, secrecy, and a just pride in past achievements greatly confuse the fundamental issues. No subject which the writer has investigated is so surfeited with contradictory and ill-advised discussions, for reasons which are altogether apparent. There is the failure, first, to distinguish public from private policies; second, to decide upon feasible private policies; third, to formulate proper public policies; and, fourth, to co-ordinate all these. As a result, one often wonders whether or not it is possible to bring together on a world basis a representative array of men of affairs and trained students both willing and able to think and act internationally. Yet such meetings do have a constructive value, if for no other reason than to clarify divergent issues.

The barriers to maritime navigation are described in the

following extract from the *Report of the Sea Transport Committee of the International Chamber of Commerce:*

The right of every country to its due participation in world maritime trade must be recognized. The existence of any extraneous conditions which in effect prevent or obstruct the national shipping of a country from such participation must be seriously deprecated as hindering freedom of trade and resulting in retaliation. . . . . As regards maritime navigation, certain grave hindrances indicated in the report presented by the International Chamber to the World Economic Conference still persist. At the request of the merchants and shipowners associations of the various countries, the International Chamber has thoroughly inquired into these difficulties and in particular into those arising out of:
  I. Flag discrimination.
  II. Customs and Consular practices.
  III. Sanitary requirements.[1]

That report singles out as of prime importance that "active effort must be continued to secure the final abandonment of flag discrimination." Happily, this expression of national protectionism is largely absent from the Pacific countries. On a trip from one port to another, there is no kind of flag discrimination in the handling of cargo, port charges, purchases of fuel and supplies, or remission of taxes. Although the United States has not been a party to the various conventions held since the World War dealing with freedom of transit, simplification of customs formalities, railways, navigable waterways, and maritime ports, the Presidents of the Republic have taken a firm stand against the levying of discriminatory duties on ships flying foreign flags or their cargoes; President Wilson resisted the pressure to enact different dues for American and foreign ships at Panama; and he and his successors have not chosen to put into effect certain enabling provisions in the Merchant Marine Act of 1920, such as the application of American coastwise laws to vessels operating between United States and Philippine ports. Accordingly, the scope of this chapter is limited to the use of a general form of official aid, namely, subsidies in the shipping industry, with prime reference to the Pacific trades.

Conditions are nowhere the same. No two countries are

[1] *World Trade*, January 1931.

alike. No one country has uniform internal development. Sectional interests, based principally upon differences of resources, occupations, and the relative importance of land and sea influences, determine the broad outlines of economic policy. When the geo-economic forces become meshed with political, military, and naval policies, which is an inevitable evolution, the national interests become increasingly internally and externally dynamic. Is shipping protectionism to be wielded upon a national or upon an Imperial grouping? Can naval strategy be separated from purely trade motives? Are common-sense methods of transacting general business alien to the best interests of the shipping industry? Now these questions, fundamental though they are, cannot be more than hinted at by the writer in the following exposition of concrete practices in the Pacific shipping world.

As an introduction to the situation today, let us first gain a brief perspective by quoting an authority who has served both as Chairman of the war-time Inter-Allied Maritime Transport Council and as the peace-time head of the Economic and Financial Section of the League of Nations, Sir Arthur Salter, of Oxford University. He says:

> Merchant shipping has throughout history occupied both in the public mind and in the economic system of the world a place altogether out of proportion to either the human effort or the capital which it represents. . . . . But the steamships by which the communications of the world are maintained and its products and manufactures exchanged have never exceeded in number some 8,000. The men employed in manning them amount to some 450,000 and those in building them to perhaps another 250,000, small numbers compared with the 8,000,000 persons occupied in agriculture in a single country such as France. The total value of all the ocean-going ships in the world before the war was not more than some £300,000,000, that is, less than the capital invested in two English railway companies.[2]

Shipping was, of course, closely allied with political power long before the rise of nationalism, but modern states have made this inherited tradition their own in seeing in the ocean-shipping industry an instrument of national power.

[2] *Allied Shipping Control,* Carnegie Endowment for International Peace, "Economic and Social History of the World War," British Series, 1921.

In consequence of this emphasis the maritime shipping industry has perhaps been more frequently the subject of economic protectionism than any other industry throughout the world. Even in countries which have accepted in principle the policy of free trade, shipping has not generally been allowed entirely to fend for itself, although the extent of protection in some cases has been narrowly confined and its effect on the prosperity of the national merchant marine, as a whole, has been correspondingly small.

Two decades ago, world shipping presented a picture vastly different from what it does today. In 1931 the commercial fleet aggregated 70 million gross tons, compared to 47 million gross tons in 1913, or a gain of nearly 50 per cent; of these amounts tonnage available for international trade increased from 33 to 52 million gross tons, or 57 per cent, which was one-seventh faster than all shipping. During the same period world trade increased from 3,300 million pounds sterling to 4,000 million pounds sterling, or a gain of only 21 per cent. Sir Norman Hill, in a discussion at Chatham House in 1933, declared: "The whole of that increase has since disappeared, and there is therefore in the world today an unused surplus of 19 million tons gross of shipping. There is no work for one out of every three of the ocean-going steamships."[3] Thus, the world commercial fleet increased nearly three times as fast as world freight. That this unequal development of vessels in relation to cargoes is responsible for overtonnaged trades, ships tied up, and perhaps the lowest freight rates on record cannot be denied. And this basic maladjustment has greatly aggravated the popular clamor for public funds and startling nationalistic proposals.

The premier maritime nations in 1913 were ranked in this order by *Lloyd's Register of Shipping,* according to their percentage of total world tonnage: Great Britain and Ireland, 40 per cent; United States, 17 per cent; Germany, 11 per cent; Norway, 5 per cent; France, 5 per cent; Italy, 3 per cent; Japan, 3 per cent; and the Netherlands, 3 per cent. In 1931 the comparative statistics were: Great Britain and Ireland, 29 per cent; United States, 19 per cent; Japan, 6 per cent; Germany, 6 per cent; Norway, 6 per cent; France,

[3] *International Affairs,* May–June, 1933.

5 per cent; Italy, 5 per cent; and the Netherlands, 4 per cent. The size of the fleets of the United States, Japan, Italy, and the Netherlands more than doubled. The most striking change for the last decade has been the growth in the German merchant marine from 673,000 gross tons in 1920 to 4,255,000 gross tons in 1931, a gain of over 500 per cent, or only 16 per cent less than her pre-war status.

TABLE 60

MERCHANT MARINE OF THE WORLD AND THE UNITED STATES, 1895–1932*

(In thousand tons)

Year	World Total	United States
1895	25,086	2,165
1900	28,957	2,750
1905	35,998	3,996
1910	41,913	5,059
1915	49,262	5,893
1920	57,314	16,049
1925	64,641	15,377
1929	68,074	14,633
1930	69,608	14,046
1931	70,131	13,642
1932	69,734	13,547

* Data from *Lloyd's Register of Shipping.*

NOTE.—Vessels of 100 tons and over. Prior to 1919 tonnage figures are gross for steamers and net for sailing vessels, thereafter gross for both. Wooden vessels on the Great Lakes and vessels on the Caspian Sea are not included. Japanese sailing vessels and most sailing vessels belonging to Greece, Turkey, and southern Russia are not included. Figures for Philippine Islands are included with United States beginning with 1910.

The leading flags in Pacific shipping today are the British, the American, and the Japanese. To the totals for the British Isles should be added the statistics for the British dominions located on the Pacific littoral. *Lloyd's Register* includes these returns among "all other countries" in 1913, but a statistical comparison of 1920 with 1931 reveals a total increase (not Pacific only) for Australia and New Zealand combined, of from 649,000 to 681,000 tons, and for Canada of from 171,000 to 1,438,000 tons, or gains of 5 per cent for Australasia and 741 per cent for Canada. The tonnage of the U.S.S.R., somewhat less than that of the South Pacific dominions, is located outside the Pacific Basin. There are no other countries bordering the Pacific which have a significant merchant fleet.

The following table shows the relative order of national flags in the shipping of the British Pacific dominions, China, Japan, the Philippines, and the United States, according to the relative capacity of vessels entering the country:

TABLE 61

RANKING OF LEADING FLAGS IN FOREIGN TRADE BY COUNTRIES (BASED ON SHIP TONNAGE ENTRANCE, 1930–1931)*

Flag	Australia	New Zea-land	Canada	China	Japan	Philip-pines	United States
British							
United Kingdom	1	2	1	2	2	2	2
Canada	–	4	–	–	–	–	–
Australia	5	1	–	–	–	–	–
New Zealand	2	–	–	–	–	–	–
German	–	–	5	5	4	5	4
Japanese	6	–	4	1	1	3	5
Norwegian	3	–	3	6	5	4	3
United States	4	3	2	4	3	1	1

* Data from various government statistics and yearbooks. Chinese vessels rank third in her own foreign trade. Corresponding ranking for vessels entering the United Kingdom would be the United Kingdom, Germany, Netherlands, France, Norway, United States, Sweden.

The dominance of the United Kingdom, the United States, and Japan in Pacific maritime shipping is unquestioned. The position of the Norwegian and German merchant marines is also noteworthy. Other leading maritime powers play a minor rôle in the Pacific, thus: France is first in French Indo-China, sixth in Japan, and seventh in the United States; Netherlands, together with Netherland India, is first in the latter colony, sixth in the United States, the Philippines, and Canada, and seventh in Japan; Denmark is seventh in Canada and the Philippines and eighth in Japan; Italy is eighth in Canada and the United States; and Sweden is ninth in Japan and the United States. What this table does not show is that Germany and Norway rank along with Japan and the United States as the chief gainers in recent commerce. On the Pacific, therefore, the concentration of shipping flags is much more marked than on the Atlantic Ocean or the adjacent Mediterranean.

The Pacific is the chief theater of British overseas enterprise, and markedly so when the contiguous Indian Ocean is included. Located on the Pacific are three of the four dominions, also Hong Kong, British Malaya, certain islands in the South Sea, and perhaps British India, which may well be considered as the geographical center of the Empire. The link with London is always the sea, never the land; hence it is but natural that the great British shipping interests should treat the dominion in the North Pacific and the two in the South Pacific as integral sections of Imperial transport and communications.

The maritime developments in Canada, Australia, and New Zealand reflect this world point of view. These dominions, each less than a century old in the British federation, have always leaned heavily upon the Mother Country to provide commercial vessels and warships, while devoting themselves primarily to the building up of a well-rounded internal economy. Despite the abortive adventures by Australia and Canada into government-owned merchant marines, the situation remains true today that these interests in the Pacific region attach the greatest importance to the British naval and shipping fleets. Approximately only 3 per cent of the navigation in Australian waters is by Australian vessels, somewhat less than 30 per cent is of foreign nationality, and the rest other British; New Zealand shipping is outstandingly British, with Australia first and the United Kingdom second, even though the number of vessels recorded for the United States and for the United Kingdom is nearly identical; approximately three ships of every five entering Canadian ports fly the British flag, with the United Kingdom in the lead and Canadian vessels credited with about one-sixth of the cargo movement.

Aid to shipping from the public coffers is based upon both the national defense and the commercial requirements. In theory, a separation of function can be made; in practice, the dividing-line is a shadowy one. Dependence upon the Mother Country explains the willingness of Australia, New Zealand, and Canada to forego the seeming luxury of a large mercantile marine. To date, China, on the other hand, is so little interested that she is content to leave her foreign shipping largely to the Japanese and the British. Japan recognizes a maritime destiny which prompts a studied and far-sighted plan in her sea services. The United States likewise has the leading part of her foreign shipping under vessels flying the national flag, with the British ensign in second place here, outnumbering all the other flags put together. The vast tonnage in the protected coastal trade of the United States is valuable as an auxiliary in time of war, also for carrying war materials.

Insular countries require adequate sea tonnage to provide communication for the transport of people, mails, import deficiencies, and surplus products. The United Kingdom and Japan, the latter consisting of thousands of islands, are leading examples. It is noteworthy that other outstanding islands—Australia, New Zealand, and Tasmania—not alone are diminishing their fleets but also, unlike the two greatest Island kingdoms, are located far off the main trade routes. The feverish war-time activity in shipbuilding in the United States and Canada has now subsided; furthermore, both North American countries as well as Australia have experimented with government control and have pronounced it a signal failure. Shipping protectionism is still practiced in Japan and the United States, in one form or another; on the other hand, the shipping interests of the British Isles appear to be promoted best by the minimum of trade barriers, if for no other reason than because one out of every four British vessels is employed in trades between foreign countries.[4]

[4] The Chamber of Shipping of the United Kingdom includes this declaration of policy to the Government for consideration at the World Economic Conference (London, 1933): "Tested both by tonnage entrances and earnings, we estimated that inter-Empire trade finds employment for only a little over one-third of the British tonnage available for overseas trade, and that employment would not be substantially increased if the whole of the inter-Empire trade were reserved exclusively for British shipping. The remainder of such British tonnage—nearly two-thirds—finds employment in trade between the Empire (including the United Kingdom) and foreign countries, or between foreign countries. Unless those trades are re-established there can be no future for the British Mercantile Marine as it exists today. It follows, therefore, that the primary concern of the British shipping industry at the World Economic Conference must be the removal of the trade barriers of every description that have played such an important part in bringing about the deplorable diminution in the world's trade, including that of the United Kingdom."

Subsidies take various forms. Some are direct, notably favorable borrowing and interest rates for construction of ships or excess remuneration beyond normal charges for the carrying of mails. Some subventions are indirect, certainly less direct, illustrated by exemption from federal taxes or import duties on materials needed for shipbuilding, a sliding scale of port charges depending upon the nationality of the vessel, special use of national credit, and political favors. The reservation of the coasting trade to national vessels is an example of preferential legislation, but this subject is divorced from any consideration of direct or indirect financial assistance. A factor always to be borne in mind is that subsidies and bounties extended by one's government frequently cause greater injustice at home between shipbuilders or shipowners than exists even between competitive nationals: to illustrate, the domestic shipping conferences discussed in the preceding chapter certainly are more subject to strife and disagreement than are the international conferences; again, the harshest critics of the Emergency Fleet Corporation of the United States Shipping Board were not the foreign lines but certain of the private American companies which were in an unenviable competitive position with their own government.

Let us consider, briefly, some of the pertinent applications of the public subsidies to British, Japanese, and United States shipping in the Pacific Basin.

At no time has the British government granted a general subsidy or bounty to shipping. While its policy of postal subventions dates from 1839, ten years before the repeal of the navigation laws, this policy never applied to more than 5 per cent of the tonnage under the British flag, a proportion represented by specialized fast steamers, more important for rapid communication with colonial possessions and as potential naval reserves than as cargo carriers.

In all, there have been three forms of direct financial aid extended to British shipping: (1) postal subventions, (2) admiralty subventions, and (3) colonial subventions. Of these the first has been the most important. Before the war there were two transoceanic lines under postal subvention. One of them, the Cunard Line, received also an admiralty

subvention and another a subsidy charged to colonial services. The Canadian Pacific Railway was the only recipient
of a subvention covering a transpacific route. This Canadian
company was originally subsidized by the United Kingdom
for services between Liverpool and Hong Kong, via Halifax
and the transcontinental railway to Vancouver. In 1914,
however, the Dominion of Canada assumed this contract
including an annual subvention of $375,000, a substantial
increase over the sum granted by the British government.

It can be stated that the prime purpose of the British
policy of postal subventions was Imperial rather than commercial, designed to encourage the maintenance of fast mail
services and regular routes between Great Britain and all
parts of the Imperial domain, and to provide transportation
for emigrants and troops. In addition, of course, this policy
provided ships well adapted by size and speed for use as
naval auxiliaries in time of war. Other factors, such as promoting foreign trade and shipbuilding, were of secondary
importance. Steamers with mail contracts were of special
design, little adapted to ordinary commerce. The actual
commerce carriers in the British Merchant Marine were vessels which received no financial support from the government.

During 1914–1918, Great Britain acquired a very large
government-owned fleet and jointly with her allies assumed
direction over the employment of 90 per cent of the seagoing
tonnage of the world. Yet the traditions of private enterprise were so strong and the British shipowning interests so
insistent that the government withdrew very rapidly not
only from ownership but also from control over shipping in
the years immediately following the war.

The world-wide economic depression in 1920–1921 was severe in the highly industrialized United Kingdom, where so
many of the basic industries depend heavily upon foreign
outlets. British unemployment conditions became so acute
that the government felt it necessary to take steps to stimulate industrial activity, both to provide employment and to
keep alive important industries. In 1921 was passed the British Trade Facilities Act, which authorized the treasury to
guarantee loans made for the manufacture or purchase of

articles which would promote employment in the United Kingdom. Since the prime object was unemployment relief, the Act applied to work undertaken on foreign as well as on British account.[5]

A number of shipping companies availed themselves of the facilities of government credit thus extended by ordering new ships to be built in British yards. The government looked with special favor on these loans, for they not only provided employment but also maintained shipbuilding yards for meeting future requirements of the merchant marine and the navy. Loans aggregating some 23,500,000 pounds sterling were guaranteed on behalf of shipbuilding, on terms ranging from five to twenty years.[6] Interest rates varied considerably, but averaged around 5 per cent.

Previous to the passage of the Trade Facilities Act of 1921, the only instance of government aid in the form of loans to shipowners was in the instance of the Cunard Line, which has been the frequent recipient of special favors from the British government. In order to provide for large and fast steamers for transatlantic service these subsidies have included unusually large postal subventions, admiralty subventions, and loans at half the commercial rate of interest. Relations of the Cunard Line to the government have been duplicated by no other line; but they have no direct bearing on British shipping activity in the Pacific.

The British stake in transpacific shipping is mainly through her Pacific dominions of Canada, Australia, and New Zealand, and it has devolved upon these dominions directly to give whatever support, through either postal subventions or other means, is deemed necessary for the maintenance of adequate transportation facilities on the various transpacific routes.

The general Canadian policy with regard to shipping has

[5] As originally passed, the Act provided that the total amount to be so guaranteed should not exceed 25,000,000 pounds sterling; this maximum was later increased to 75,000,000 pounds sterling by the final Act passed in 1926, which extended the period of the facilities one year.

[6] The government of Northern Ireland passed a similar act in 1922, which was extended from time to time up to March 31, 1931. Total loans guaranteed aggregated about 11,500,000 pounds sterling for shipbuilding.

been a part of the wider Imperial policy. Before the war there were a large number of lines operating under contract postal subventions, and also two operating under authority of statute. Transpacific services included lines to China and Japan, to Australia and New Zealand, the former by the Canadian Pacific Railway, and the latter by the Union Steamship Company of New Zealand. Between 1914 and 1917 the Canadian Pacific Railway received $375,000 annually from the Canadian government for twenty-six trips to China and Japan. (Previous to that time, as noted, Great Britain shared the expense of this postal subvention.) The contract stipulated that neither passenger nor freight rates should be in excess of the rates charged on ships of a similar class from United States ports on the Pacific. A similar clause appeared in the contract with the Union Steamship Company, which received $180,000 annually for its monthly service to Australasia. All contracts provided general government supervision over rates and fares, as well as over types and equipment of vessels.

Since the war, Canadian expenditures on mail subventions have been reduced to about one-third the pre-war level. Economic conditions have rendered curtailments necessary, and the partial elimination of Germany as a naval power has altered the political aspects of the question for the entire British Empire. The contract with the Canadian Pacific Railway, originating in 1890–1891 as a part of the Imperial defense plan, is no longer in force.

Since April 1921, Canadian mails to the Orient have been paid for at uniform rates without regard to nationality of the carrying ship. For example, the Canadian Pacific Line now carries Canadian transpacific mails on exactly the same basis as any other vessel. The Union Steamship Company of New Zealand now receives $100,000 annually from the Canadian government, in return for which it is required to carry Canadian mails free to Australia and New Zealand, and must likewise carry gratuitously Canadian trade representatives and their families.

In 1929 a new subsidized service owned by the government was inaugurated between British Columbia and Australia by Canadian vessels. The purpose of this subsidy was to stimulate the outbound movement of lumber from Canada. An annual subsidy of $92,500 for twelve trips was reduced in the 1931–1932 budget to $73,920. The stipulation regarding free carriage of mails and government officials applies also to this service. An interesting feature has been that the contracting lines were prohibited from joining the Trans-Pacific Conference. Owned by the Canadian government, operated under the name of the Canadian Government Merchant Marine, this service has suffered the usual fate of government in the shipping business. At the end of 1922 the government-owned fleet consisted of 64 ships of 778,000 deadweight tons, costing over $86,000,000, including interest. There remained undisposed 30 vessels of 239,170 tons at the end of 1930.

About half of the original Canadian Government Merchant Marine had been sold by June 1933, with the expectation that the remainder will be disposed of should there be reasonable offers. The latest data available indicate a cumulated deficit of over $60,000,000, apart from the fact that the vessels are still carried on the books at a value far in excess of their actual worth.

Canada occupies a dual position in the transport world. Her vessels are regarded in their rightful place as service agencies in the dominion's transportation system, illustrated by a two-thirds ownership or control of the commercial fleet by the two railway companies—the Canadian Pacific under private operation, and the Canadian National under government control. For the fiscal year 1931, British Columbia outranked all other provinces in ship tonnage, although Ontario recorded a larger number of vessels, so it is not surprising that Pacific Canada enjoys an enviable position not only in national development but also as the shortest Imperial link across North America to eastern Asia and Australasia.

Turning now to the south Pacific Ocean, one discovers that as long ago as 1869, the date of the completion of the first transcontinental railway in the United States, a transpacific service to San Francisco from Sydney via Auckland was inaugurated. This service was operated jointly on a monthly schedule by the Union Steamship Company and the Pacific Steamship Company, for which New South Wales paid $125,000 annually and New Zealand $55,000. The contract expired in 1890 and was replaced by one reducing the subsidy and fixing the remuneration on the basis of the weight of mail carried. Since 1907 the Australian government has made no payments which could be classed as subsidies to shipping companies serving Pacific North American ports, since Australian mails were carried at Universal Postal Union rates. New Zealand, on the other hand, made a new contract with the Union Steamship Company for monthly mail services to Vancouver and to San Francisco. Recent payments on account of these services have been 20,000 pounds sterling annually for the former, and 25,000 pounds sterling for the latter. The 1931–1932 budget reduced these items to 18,000 pounds sterling and 22,500 pounds sterling, respectively. In addition, certain harbor dues are waived to these subsidized ships, which in effect increases the remuneration. The mail-contract subsidies paid by the Australian government, which amounted to 174,000 pounds sterling in 1929, were four-fifths of the pre-war allotment.

Between 1916 and 1928 the Australian government owned and operated a merchant fleet, acquired, as were those of Canada and the United States, as an incident to the prosecution of the war. Australian experience was not greatly different from Canadian, except that Australia brought an end to its shipping venture and the losses thereon in 1928, with the sale of seven liners to the White Star Line. Her shipping economy, now divorced from any direct operation, centers about the securing of cheap and adequate carriage of seasonal commodities.

An interesting transport feature appears in the marked influence of railways on the development of Australia and New Zealand, with seemingly little direct regard to shipping activities. Australia is given due credit for having the greatest railway mileage per capita of any country. In New Zealand, there appears to be no public resentment over a diminishing employment of ships and men and a heavy loss in passenger and goods transport, the natural result of splendid new railway and highway connections.

In marked contrast to the British policy, which has been generally one of unusually moderate subsidies to a few lines (in fact, some of the payments on account of mail services hardly can be called subsidies), Japan has enacted far-reaching programs of official aid to national shipping. The reasons are clear. Like Great Britain, the Nipponese Empire is on the northern fringe of a great continent, limited in area, densely populated, poor in natural resources (more so than the British Isles), forced to seek external markets, and far from being self-sufficient. Political aspirations as well as economic dependence are logical reasons for the ideal that the country become a great shipbuilding as well as ship-owning nation. But there are these two fundamental points of difference, namely, that Britain succeeded the United States as the leading shipping nation three-quarters of a century ago through her skill in supplanting oak construction by steel and iron, and also that an early political start has resulted in the world being one-quarter British on the basis of either area or population. Japan has no far-flung dependencies.

Japan emerged from her centuries of isolation at the time of Commander Perry's visit to Japan in 1853. Her subsequent strides have been remarkable.

Prior to the war with China, Japan's merchant fleet consisted largely of native junks for trade near by. The need of transports in this war, and also in the war a decade later with Russia, compelled the purchase of a large number of modern, European-type steamers. The laws passed in 1896, one covering shipbuilding bounties and the other navigation bounties, constituted the first assistance given Japanese shipping other than mail subventions, the latter totaling approximately $470,000 annually from 1890 to 1895.

Construction bounties were granted exclusively to Japanese companies building ships of over 700 gross tons entirely of Japanese materials except as specifically authorized. Ships under 1,000 tons received a bounty of 12 yen per gross ton, while those over 1,000 tons received 20 yen per ton. An amendment passed in 1909 increased the minimum size of eligible ships to 1,000 tons and also provided for two classes of ships of four grades each, on which the subsidy varied from 11 yen to 22 yen per gross ton. These ships were also required to be of steel, constructed under the supervision of and in accordance with regulations of the Ministry of Communications.

Through conditions engendered by the World War, Japanese shipbuilding received so great an impetus from both Japanese and foreign orders that by 1918 the output of her shipyards had reached 489,924 tons, as compared with 85,861 tons in 1914. The financial burden of greatly increased construction bounties, as well as the fact that the purpose of the bounty law was being accomplished by the war demand for tonnage, led Japan to suspend its operation in 1918. This type of bounty has proved of questionable value. A Japanese student of public finance, Professor Gotari Ogawa, expresses the situation aptly in these words: "when the demand for steamships increased with the increase in trade, the shipyards prospered; but the promotion of shipbuilding failed to encourage the development of shipping."[7] The far-reaching New Construction Facility Act of late 1932 will be described later.

A subsidiary bounty, however, in the form of state aid to the steel industry was adopted in 1917, primarily to encourage the output of steel for shipbuilding purposes. This law was amended in 1921, and again in 1926. Subsidies paid to manufacturers of pig iron and steel have varied from three to six yen per metric ton. In addition, subsidies were payable to makers of steel plates and other steel articles in so far as they are used in the building and repair of ships.[8]

Navigation bounties were confined to iron and steel steamships owned exclusively by Japanese subjects and engaged in trade between Japanese and foreign ports; foreign-built ships under five years of age, if owned by Japanese, were eligible for the bounty. The basis of the bounty

[7] V. G. Ogawa, *The Effect of the World War upon the Industry of Japan*, Carnegie Endowment for International Peace, "Economic and Social History of the World War," Japanese Series, 1929.

[8] A Japanese writer in *The Far Eastern Review* (February 1933) remarks: "It is cynical that Japanese scrappers are still importing a considerable quantity of old ships for scrapping in order to deliver them up to the steel furnaces owing to the somewhat high prices of Japanese steel, and they can still make a profit from scrapping of imported old ships, whilst Japanese shipowners are not inclined to sell their old ships at such low quotations as are accepted in foreign countries. In this connection Japan may be considered as scrapping old ships for other countries."

was 25 sen per gross ton per mile for a ship of 1,000 tons capable of a speed of ten knots. The rate increased with the size and speed of the vessel. Fifteen subsidized routes were established in 1896, including two to the United States of America.

The combined effect of the construction and navigation bounties was such a rapid expansion of shipping that the resulting burden on the Japanese treasury led in 1899 to a modification of the act. As amended, the law reduced by one-half the bounty on foreign-built ships and limited the annual subsidies on the specified postal routes to fixed amounts. The Toyo Kisen Kaisha was granted about $475,000 annually for a service to San Francisco, for which it was required to operate three steamers of not less than 6,000 tons and at a speed of seventeen knots. This company made an arrangement with the Pacific Mail Steamship Company, then under the American flag, whereby the two companies made their voyages alternately.

In 1910 the subsidy policy with regard to lines operating to Europe, Australia, North America, and South America was modified. The minimum size for vessels coming under the plan was increased to 3,000 tons and the minimum speed to twelve knots. Rates on vessels over five years old declined with each additional year, while ships built according to plans approved by the government were entitled to a bounty 25 per cent higher than the normal rate. Although it materially increased certain rates, the 1910 law is not to be interpreted as a substantial advance in navigation bounties.

This legislation, furthermore, gave the Minister of Communications considerable control over the operation of subsidized lines. Passenger and freight charges were made subject to his approval and revision, as were the arrangements for maintaining regular services, the routes to be followed, number and type of vessels to be employed, frequency of services, and allied matters. Subsidized ships were required to carry free of charge certain government officials and all Japanese mail.

As far as transpacific trade is concerned, the law of 1910 resulted in three subsidized services to Pacific North

America: the Nippon Yusen Kaisha was required to operate
a service every four weeks to Seattle, using 6,000- to 6,500-
ton vessels, of 13- to 14-knot speed; the Osaka Shosen Kaisha
was scheduled in March 1910 for a fortnightly service to
Tacoma with vessels of size and speed similar to those employed on the Seattle route; and the San Francisco line was
to be operated by the Toyo Kisen Kaisha once every four
weeks with 13,000- to 14,000-ton steamers capable of from
18 to 20 knots per hour. The three great Japanese shipping
companies had a paramount place in this pre-war transpacific trade.

Though the war inevitably involved certain changes in
Japanese subsidized shipping services, in the main there
was no important alteration in the policy pursued or in the
manner of its execution during the actual period of the
war. In 1914 and 1915, navigation allotments on the North
American route amounted to nearly $2,000,000.

Subsequently all Japanese shipping involving the national interest has been subject to the Department of
Communications, which enters into contracts with the several lines specifying such matters as the routes, type of
vessels, and frequency of sailings. For the most part, a
system of fixed payments for specified services is in effect,
although the routes to Europe and to Australia are operated
on a system by which the compensation varies with the mileage and weight of Japanese mail carried. For example, the
approximate subsidies for the three transpacific services of
the Nippon Yusen Kaisha, which absorbed the Toyo Kisen
Kaisha in 1926, are: from Japan to Seattle, $850,000; one
from Japan to San Francisco, $1,400,000; and from the west
coast of South America calling at American Pacific ports,
$1,100,000. Contracts for these services, also those entered
into by the Osaka Shosen Kaisha to the east coast of South
America as a part of its round-the-world service via South
Africa and the Panama Canal, are for five-year periods.

The developed North American services, ordered by the
Japanese Department of Communications, consisted of the
San Francisco and Seattle lines under contract to the Nippon
Yusen Kaisha. The San Francisco service called for three
vessels less than fifteen years old, 13,000–14,000 tons, 18–20

knots speed, and sailings at least once every three weeks; the Seattle service called similarly for three vessels less than fifteen years old, but of 10,000–12,000 tons, 17–19 knots, and sailings at least once every four weeks. The contracts expired in December 1934 and December 1933, respectively. New contracts on an apparently reduced scale were in process of decision late in 1934.

From 1918 to late 1932, when the Japanese government did not pay construction bounties to encourage shipbuilding, it fostered construction activity through maritime credits extended through selected banks rather than by the government directly.[9] In general, during recent years, the overseas liner companies have felt less need of official financial backing than the charter-tonnage and tramp-ship owners. Owing to favorable conditions in the money market, recent building by these companies has apparently been financed without resorting even to construction subsidies in the form of loans offered at low interest rates.

Effective in June 1930, however, a new measure was adopted by the Japanese Diet to facilitate cargo ship construction by lines not then enjoying subsidies. This act provides for a loan fund limit of approximately $15,000,000 to be advanced through the Industrial Bank of Japan for ships of not less than 5,000 gross tons and 14 knots speed. Interest rates may not exceed 6 per cent, of which the government is to contribute from 1.5 to 2 per cent. Owing to the economic depression and the marked surplus of shipping, little interest was shown by shipping companies in this measure.

Japanese policy with regard to merchant shipping has undergone, then, three phases of development: construction bounties, which insured an active shipbuilding industry up to the time that war conditions made the bounty unnecessary; general navigation bounties; and then special subsidies

[9] French experience in this regard is illuminating in its possible implications. Despite losses incurred by the Compagnie Générale Transatlantique amounting to 400 million francs during the year 1931, the construction costs on the super "Ile de France" more than duplicated this huge sum. Late in 1932 the French Ministry of Shipping agreed to provide an annual allotment of 90 million francs toward the indebtedness of the company, which amounted to 1,142 million francs, but only after writing off 60 per cent of this debt as inadequately secured.

to individual lines on specified routes have provided quick and regular communication with all regions in which Japan's political or economic interest was pronounced. In all cases, maritime power, which Japan feels indispensable to her progress as an island empire with meager domestic resources, has been the principal object sought and attained. Commercial aims were perhaps subordinate to naval and military considerations, although Japan's commercial interest in shipping is also great.

Without governmental support it seems unlikely that Japan would have made great progress, certainly before the war, either as a shipbuilder or as a shipowning nation plying overseas routes. Prior to 1914, the three largest trans-oceanic companies often failed to show an operating profit, but national subsidies enabled them to pay dividends. With Europe completely preoccupied for the period of the war, however, Japanese shipping as well as shipbuilding made enormous advances, so that between 1914 and 1922 the merchant fleet was doubled in size. On July 1, 1931, the Japanese merchant marine consisted of 1,024 vessels of 1,000 tons or over, aggregating 3,951,399 gross tons. According to the *Japan Year Book* (1932), this figure represents a 44-fold increase over the 90,000 tons of Occidental-type ships in the merchant marine of 1880, a half-century before. This splendid growth now gives Japan rank as the third shipping power in the world.

Events of an epoch-making character, at home and abroad, have produced a rapid and radical change in the shipping and shipbuilding situation of Japan. As late as the autumn of 1932 the shipbuilding and allied industries, together with shipping, were in the doldrums. The military activities on the Asiatic mainland, boycotts, depressed silver prices in the East, abandonment of the gold standard by most Occidental countries, including Great Britain, and the widespread economic crisis hit shipping severely. It was thought, apparently, that new bounties for construction were a forlorn hope, since prospects of an early shipping revival seemed remote. However, something had to be done, or else Japanese-built vessels and possibly her merchant marine would suffer an eclipse. The net result was the passage of the New Construction Facility Act, which included as an important feature the organization of a society known as the Ship Improvement Institution composed of government officers, shipping firms, business men, and such other persons as are vitally concerned with national shipping.[10]

No picture of Japanese shipping and shipbuilding would be complete without a brief reference to the Osaka shipbreaking industry. There has been for some time past a considerable importation for breaking up, one of their principal uses being to furnish scrap metal of good quality for iron and steel foundries. The ships are broken up "in bond" and since the metal thus obtained is classed as iron and steel "waste or old, fit only for remanufacturing," it comes to the foundries duty free. There is of course a good deal of idle, semi-obsolete tonnage in Japan and it would seem more profitable to break up only Japanese ships, but most of them are heavily mortgaged and their owners cannot dispose of them without lifting the mortgage.

The New Construction Facility Act was passed at the special session of the Imperial Parliament in the fall of 1932. The prime purpose is to substitute new tonnage for old, under an approved arrangement whereby a bounty is created for 200,000 gross tons of new ships, while the owners of 400,000 tons of ships to be scrapped will be compensated by specified subventions. The "scrapping ship" should be of steel or iron, 1,000 gross tons or over, and at least twenty-five years old (with possible exceptions approved by the Ministry of Communications). The new vessel, called the

[10] The sweeping scope of activities of this newly created body is enumerated by Y. Taji (*The Far Eastern Review*, February 1933) thus: "The demand and supply of scrapping ships and replacing ships and their adjustments as well as mediation between shipowners and builders. The provision of plans for carrying the annual programs into effect and fixing the order for scrapping and building; the issue of verifications for various contracts between the owners of scrapping ships and of new ships and the shipbuilders; the procedure of the application for and payment of the subsidy allowance from the Treasury in charge of the shipowners; the distribution of the subsidy between the owners of scrapping ships and of new ships; giving encouragement for carrying out the terms of the Facility Act; the negotiations as a group between steel makers, ship scrappers and others, the prevention of the importation of foreign ships; the investigations of the qualifications of scrapping ships; and other various matters deemed necessary by the institution."

"replacing ship," should be a steel-fabricated modern vessel of over 4,000 gross tons, capable of at least 13½ knots (unless a lower speed is approved by the Ministry), and built in a shipyard located in Japan proper. It is further provided, with reference to the replacing ship, that "her gross tonnage should not be less than one-third of the gross tonnage of the scrapping ship." Also, when the total gross tonnage of the replacing ships is 50 per cent or more of the corresponding tonnage of the scrapping ships, the subsidy allowance is not available for this excess. The subsidy rates are on a sliding scale according to speed, with the minimum payment of 45 yen per gross ton for vessels below 14 knots and the maximum of 54 yen for vessels of 18 knots.

The Facility Act grants a total subsidy of 11,000,000 yen, allocated as follows: first fiscal year, 1,250,000 yen; second year, 5,500,000 yen; third year, 4,250,000 yen. The term of the legislation is three years, while the term of existence of the society is five years. It is noteworthy that all subsidy applications must be approved by the Ship Improvement Institution before the required documents are submitted to the Minister of Communications.

The results have been immediate.[11] The American Com-

11 The wonderful growth of the Japanese mercantile marine, which received its first great impetus during the Sino-Japanese war, is described graphically by the Tokyo correspondent of the *Daily Commercial News* (July 16, 1934) : "When I arrived in Yokohama after an absence of 11 years I was not prepared for the change. In 1923 the harbor was cluttered with a great assemblage of old cargo hulks, cast-off British, French and German vessels that had outlived their usefulness years ago. A shipping man said that there were only two things that kept them afloat—the strength of hand-hammered rivets and the gentleness of God's anger.

"But Yokohama today is a different sight. Gone are those old dowagers of the sea and in their place riding at anchor and moored to the modern piers are beautiful, 1934 models, express freighters. The hulls of these cargo ships look more like sleek transatlantic liners than cargo carriers. These new ships of the Japanese merchant marine average 17 and 18 knots and only one ship of a specific fleet of 30 new carriers is as slow as 15 knots.

"Yesterday's *Japan Advertiser* carried a story of a new 18-knot oil tanker being open to public inspection. The M.S. 'Toa Maru' is 13,500 tons, 500 feet long, 65-foot beam, 18.5 knots and after her shakedown cruise for a load of Sakhalin oil she will become a unit in the fleet of tankers that runs between California and Japan.

"The latest development to startle the shipping world is the announcement less than a week ago by the Tokyo Bay Steamship Company that it had let a contract to the Mitsubishi Shipbuilding Company at Kobe for

mercial Attaché at Tokyo reported in March 1933 that the operation of the law has proved highly beneficial to the ship-building yards; that total building applications have reached 95,150 tons, with additional new plans for 13 ships of 81,200 tons (mostly 5,000–7,600-ton freighters); that the amount of dockyards business has resulted in declining orders from Soviet Russia; and that the barometers of employment, freight loadings, the imports of scrap iron and steel, and un-filled steel orders are decidedly improved. Approximately 80 per cent of the new tonnage built since October 1932 is of motorships with a capacity of at least 6,000 gross tons. It should be understood, too, that this entirely up-to-date tonnage will be placed in Pacific waters, notably on the important runs to Pacific North America.

The shipbuilding industry in Japan has shown remarkable activity due to (1) improvement of the shipping market, (2) larger naval budget, (3) the Better Ships Act. As a result of the Better Ships Act the tonnage of ships under construction since April 1933 has been over twice as large as that eighteen months previously. The Japanese draft budget provides for the scrapping of further obsolete vessels and a construction bounty for 50,000 tons to be built in 1935–36.

The realism of the world maritime subsidy situation is admirably depicted in the following editorial note appearing in the *Shipping Register* (May 19, 1934):

American ship owners who have complained of competition by British interests which have an advantage because of lower wage costs, may find a grain of comfort in reading how the British ship owner is being underbid by his continental competitors. According to *Foreign Trade News,* a British ship carrying a crew of thirty men was sold at Rotterdam to a Finnish operator. The new owner immediately reduced the crew to twenty-four men, and cut crew wages from an aggregate of forty-four dollars to sixteen dollars a day. The latter figure averages about seventy cents a day per man, which means that some members of the crew must work for a fraction of this figure.

Another instance of low operating costs is found in the food allowance of twenty cents a man per day, given to the new captain. British owners say that they are unable to survive such competition.

---

the construction of the first 100 per cent streamlined passenger liner in the world.

"America may have her streamlined trains and automobiles, but Japan will be the first nation to use the principles of aero-dynamics at sea."

XX. Government Subsidies—American

The best introduction to the subject of American shipping protectionism is a knowledge of the nationality of ships which transport our exports and imports. The percentage of the foreign trade carried in American vessels amounted to 10.1 per cent in 1913, and to 33.8 per cent in 1930, and has fluctuated between 32 per cent and 37 per cent since 1921; in 1933, this percentage was 35.4. Thus American ships carry about one-third of the nation's foreign commerce, as shown by Table 62 (p. 396).

The joint statement, prepared during the severe Coast maritime strikes of May to July, 1934, by the thirty-six foreign-owned or -operated ship lines engaged in the off-shore trade from the Pacific Coast to all regions of the world, is in point:

Over 95 per cent of the Pacific Coast–European trade is conducted by vessels owned or operated under foreign flags, and over 50 per cent of the transpacific trade is conducted by vessels owned or operated under foreign flags. A substantial part of the foreign trade to all the other areas enumerated is served by vessels owned or operated under foreign flags.

Of the above 36 lines, 11 of the lines fly the British flag, two the Danish, two the Dutch, one the French, two the German, one the Italian, seven the Japanese, eight the Norwegian, and two the Swedish. The total deadweight tonnage of the vessels of these lines exceeds 2,523,800 tons.

This does not include the offshore tramp steamers from the Pacific Coast ports to ports throughout the world, a substantial part of which is engaged in by foreign-owned vessels. A preponderance of all the offshore foreign trade from the Pacific Coast is engaged in by vessels flying foreign flags.

Extension of aid by the United States government toward the upbuilding of a national merchant marine has been more or less spasmodic in the one hundred and fifty-odd years since the formation of the republic. Forms of assistance, both direct and indirect, have been successively granted and withdrawn. In name, at least, subsidies have never been part of any merchant marine legislation enacted by Congress, although the direct financial aids extended have in effect been subventions.

Earliest government assistance took the form of postal subventions to certain lines operating on specified routes in ocean trade. The original law of this type was passed in 1845. Provision was made for the awarding of mail subventions to lines operating in the transatlantic, West Indian, and coastwise trades. Soon after its passage, the acquisition of Oregon and California made satisfactory intercoastal communication doubly important, and a contract for a monthly coastwise service from Astoria to the Isthmus, with calls at San Diego, Monterey, and San Francisco, was entered into with the Pacific Mail Steamship Company. The contract called for three steamers, two of them of at least 1,000 tons each, and provided an annual compensation of $199,000. The connection at the Isthmus was made with another contract line operating to New York. This intercoastal joint service was inaugurated in the latter part of 1848, almost coincident with the rush to Californian goldfields. Largely as a result of this fortuitous development the line was highly successful. A supplementary contract in 1851 increased the subvention to $348,250 and placed the service on a semi-monthly basis.

In 1865 a law was approved authorizing a ten-year contract with the Pacific Mail Steamship Company for a monthly service between San Francisco and certain ports in China and Japan. The company was obligated to operate ships of not less than 3,000 tons built in American yards under naval supervision, and the government agreed to pay the company $500,000 annually for the service, which was begun in 1867. Shortly thereafter, in return for a $75,000 annual subvention, the California, Oregon, and Mexican Line was awarded a contract calling for the operation of a service to Hawaii.

The Pacific Mail Steamship Company obtained another contract for a second steamship service to China and Japan, payment for which was also set at $500,000 annually. Discovery of bribery in connection with the passage of the act, which authorized the contract, caused its cancellation in 1875. The first contract was allowed to stand until its expiration in 1877, but was not renewed. All together, the Pacific Mail Steamship Company received some $5,000,000

TABLE 62

VALUE OF EXPORTS (EXCLUDING RE-EXPORTS) AND IMPORTS OF MER-
CHANDISE, BY METHOD OF CARRIAGE AND NATIONALITY OF
VESSEL, 1914–1930*

(Thousand dollars)

Method of Carriage	Calendar Years					
	1914	1920	1925	1928	1929	1930
Exports, excluding re-exports	2,071,058	8,080,481	4,818,722	5,030,099	5,157,083	3,781,172
American vessels	186,926	3,116,440	1,458,199	1,459,913	1,475,569	1,107,549
Foreign vessels:						
Belgian	7,763	76,370	37,792	36,825	31,345	26,774
British	1,011,691	2,587,813	1,423,507	1,341,764	1,348,593	946,641
Danish	......†	71,841	94,980	93,654	90,986	62,616
Dutch	83,895	157,957	166,413	164,090	163,326	110,823
French	70,037	166,232	137,218	123,183	126,237	103,747
German	158,640	9,671	163,767	252,283	268,807	201,735
Italian	44,544	215,441	146,858	143,614	122,733	76,328
Japanese	23,957	208,876	173,205	158,532	163,847	110,584
Norwegian	89,821	236,696	172,324	236,005	266,073	205,015
Spanish	......†	113,291	62,167	50,505	48,638	27,677
Swedish	......†	54,074	53,598	83,504	83,186	61,003
All other	126,611	130,515	89,975	86,338	94,456	95,839
Total foreign	1,616,959	4,028,671	2,721,804	2,770,298	2,808,228	2,028,782
Parcel post	......	......	26,052	29,014	26,656	20,510
Cars and other land vehicles....	267,173	935,370	612,667	770,873	846,630	624,331
Aircraft	......	......	......	......	......	......
Imports	1,789,276	5,278,481	4,226,589	4,091,444	4,399,361	3,060,908
American vessels	216,199	1,987,861	1,151,242	1,132,598	1,205,008	897,973
Foreign vessels:						
Belgian	24,404	24,736	10,211	11,309	11,867	7,385
British	808,344	1,600,697	1,384,926	1,120,985	1,163,519	751,085
Danish	......†	40,767	54,142	57,452	48,084	30,070
Dutch	90,840	187,478	122,278	135,495	144,137	100,567
French	82,945	141,181	147,809	140,621	145,788	91,710
German	151,613	14	85,945	199,154	243,318	171,524
Italian	39,796	60,618	70,663	65,170	68,400	50,425
Japanese	57,545	454,180	390,393	377,108	437,914	265,061
Norwegian	82,679	111,811	164,095	150,157	164,409	139,997
Spanish	......†	36,148	15,886	16,926	17,710	11,408
Swedish	......†	27,663	36,102	50,173	50,837	43,276
All other	77,410	57,959	82,624	93,085	106,035	74,540
Total foreign	1,415,576	2,743,252	2,565,074	2,417,633	2,602,017	1,737,048
Parcel post	......	......	125,133	110,153	123,309	75,786
Cars and other land vehicles....	157,501	547,368	385,140	431,061	469,027	350,101

* Data from the Bureau of Foreign and Domestic Commerce.
† Included in "All other."

in postal subventions, of which $500,000 was for its line to Panama and the balance on its transpacific contracts. Its transpacific service was continued without subvention until 1915.

Corruption connected with the Pacific Mail contract militated against this form of government aid for some years and it was not until 1891 that the policy of postal subventions was renewed. Under the act of that year the Postmaster-General was authorized to invite bids, and to enter into contracts for five or ten years with American citizens for carrying mail between the United States and foreign ports in American-built and -owned ships. Compensation was on a mileage basis, and the rate increased with the size and speed of the ships employed. All except the lowest class of ships were to be built under naval supervision and were to be adaptable as auxiliary cruisers. Pacific Coast shipping shared in the benefits under this law through two mail contracts, one from San Francisco to Australia and one from San Francisco to Tahiti. Both lines were operated by the Oceanic Steamship Company. The Australian service was receiving $200,000 annually in the years immediately preceding the war; the Tahiti service, operating from 1902 to 1912, received sums varying from $21,000 to $46,000 per year.

While the mail subventions granted under the act of 1891 were regarded as liberal at the time, being considerably in excess of the non-contract rates for American ships,[1] and several times the amounts which would have accrued to foreign ships carrying United States mails under Universal Postal Union rates, they did not preserve an effective merchant marine. At the outbreak of the World War, American shipping was unimportant except in the coastal trades.

The tremendous emphasis upon shipping which inevitably accompanied the waging of an overseas war immeasurably strengthened the position of advocates of government aid for the maintenance of a large American merchant marine. As a result, the war and post-war era

[1] In 1914, for the first time, the contract service cost was less than would have been incurred had the mails all been carried on American ships under non-contract rates. It was, however, still in excess of the cost under Universal Postal Union rates.

has witnessed a succession of acts designed to foster American shipping, with its culmination in the Merchant Marine Act of 1928.

A very small number of mail contracts under the Act of 1891 were still in force at the end of the war. The last Pacific contract was with the Oceanic Steamship Company for service to Hawaii and Australia. This contract expired on June 30, 1922, and while not renewed under the terms of the Act of 1891, approximately $5,000,000 had been paid to the line during the life of the contract.

The Merchant Marine Acts of 1920 and 1928 separately reaffirmed the principle of the earlier act, namely, that of granting subventions to specified lines on designated routes by means of mail contracts. Each sought, however, to provide terms more suitable to post-war shipping conditions. The Act of 1928 greatly liberalized the payment to such lines for the operation of ships of larger size and greater speed. The Postmaster-General was authorized to invite bids for contract postal services on specified routes with American ships of types approved by the Shipping Board. Maximum remuneration per mile of outward voyage allowed under the law is as follows:

			Remuneration per Nautical Mile
Class	I	(20,000 gross tons or over, 24 knots per hour)	$12.00
Class	II	(16,000 gross tons or over, 20 knots per hour)	10.00
Class	III	(12,000 gross tons or over, 18 knots per hour)	8.00
Class	IV	(10,000 gross tons or over, 16 knots per hour)	6.00
Class	V	(8,000 gross tons or over, 13 knots per hour)	4.00
Class	VI	(4,000 gross tons or over, 10 knots per hour)	2.50
Class	VII	(2,500 gross tons or over, 10 knots per hour)	1.50

A direct comparison with rates established by the law of 1891 is not possible, since the classifications adopted are dissimilar. Under the earlier act, however, maximum compensation per mile was fixed at $4 for ships of at least 8,000 gross tons and capable of a speed of twenty knots.

At the close of the fiscal year 1931, forty-four contracts were in operation under the Act of 1928. Among these only one called for Class I ships, five called for the operation or construction of Class II ships, and ten for either present operation or construction of Class III ships. By far the greater number of contracts provide for the operation of ships in Classes V and VI. No contract is in force calling for the use of the lowest class ships, but many of the routes are operating under contracts which specify the use of ships of two classes, for either current or prospective operation.

Sixteen contract routes cover mail services from Pacific Coast ports. Table 63 (p. 400) shows that half of these operate out of San Francisco. Eleven of these provide for current operation of Class VI ships, although ultimately all but three will use ships of higher classes, in whole or in part. These contracts run for ten years and call for an estimated total payment of $97,000,000, almost one-third of the aggregate payments to be made on account of all existing mail contracts under the Act.

Assistance given to American ships by means of payment for the carriage of mails is not confined to contract lines. While other payments are gradually diminishing in aggregate amount as the contract service is expanded, they are still of considerable proportions. Non-contract service is paid for on the basis of weight of mails carried. The rates authorized for service by ships of American registry are 80 cents per pound for letters and cards and 8 cents per pound for other articles. Foreign vessels carrying United States mails from American ports, on the other hand, receive only 6.57 cents per pound for letters and cards and 0.87 cents per pound for other articles on routes up to 300 miles; for routes from 300 to 1,500 miles the corresponding rates are 17.5 cents and 2.2 cents, and for all routes over 1,500 miles, 26.3 cents and 3.5 cents, respectively.

That these differences are of substantial benefit to the American ships is evidenced by the fact that in the fiscal year 1931, although American vessels carried only 60.8 per cent of the mails, they received 91.6 per cent of the pay. American ships on the Pacific Coast carried 74 per cent of the total weight and received 96 per cent of the pay. On the Atlantic the discrepancy was much greater; American ships carried only 46 per cent of the mails but received 82 per cent of the pay.[2]

[2] The low percentage of mails carried across the Atlantic is due to there being faster ships under other flags, particularly, in the last year or so, the fine new German ships.

TABLE 63

FOREIGN MAIL CONTRACTS LET UNDER MERCHANT MARINE ACT OF 1928 ON PACIFIC ROUTES, UP TO JUNE 30, 1931*

Port and Route	Name of Line	Class of Ships	Construction Required			Construction Conditionally Required			Reconstruction Required			Voyages per Year	Approximate Pay for the Term
			No.	Class	Approximate Tonnage	No.	Class	Approximate Tonnage	No.	Class	Approximate Tonnage		
San Francisco													
To Sydney	Oceanic S.S. Co.	IV	2	II	40,000	1	II	20,000	..	..	....	17	$ 9,863,436
To Manila	Dollar Line	III	..	..	....	..	..	....	..	..	....	26	14,731,080
To Colombo	Dollar Line	V	4	III	92,000	..	..	....	4	VI	23,000	26	14,570,032
To Buenos Aires	Pacific-Argentine-Brazil	VI	..	..	....	..	..	....	..	..	....	18	3,005,323
To Puerto Colombia	Panama Mail	V	2	III	18,000	..	..	....	..	..	....	26	7,132,570
To Puerto Armuellas	United Fruit Co.	VI	3	IV	21,600	..	..	....	..	..	....	52	7,348,246
To Dairen	Oceanic and Oriental Nav.	VI	2	V	16,000	..	..	....	..	..	....	14–19	3,565,775
To Saigon	Oceanic and Oriental Nav.	VI	2	V	16,000	..	..	....	..	..	....	..	4,014,516
Seattle													
To Manila	Admiral Oriental	III	..	..	....	..	..	....	..	..	....	26	14,731,080
To Tampico	Gulf Pacific Mail	VI	1	V	3,200	..	..	....	..	..	....	12–24	3,393,130
Portland													
To Manila	Admiral Oriental	VI	..	..	....	..	..	....	2	V	10,600	24	4,341,518
To Dairen	States S.S. Co.	VI	..	..	....	..	..	....	1	V	5,300	12	2,053,632
To Manila and Dairen	Tacoma Oriental S.S. Co.	VI	..	..	....	..	..	....	2	V	10,000	24	3,933,519
Los Angeles													
To Auckland	Oceanic and Oriental Nav.	VI	..	..	....	..	..	....	..	..	....	12	1,711,545
To Melbourne	Oceanic and Oriental Nav.	VI	..	..	....	..	..	....	..	..	....	..	2,109,600
Tacoma													
To Valparaiso	Grace Line	VI	1	III	9,000	..	..	....	..	..	....	17	2,708,000

Total approximate payments for ten-year period................ $96,969,502

* From *Annual Report of the Postmaster-General for 1931*, pp. 129–30.

In addition to postal subventions, other financial aid is extended to the American shipping and shipbuilding industries. Among the most important of these is the revolving loan fund available at low interest to shipowners who order vessels of approved types to be constructed in American yards. The Act of 1928 established the fund at $250,000,000 (an increase of 100 per cent over the amount specified in the 1920 Act), and provided that the interest rate on loans for ships for foreign service should be the lowest appearing on any government obligation issued later than April 1917. Early in 1931 a ruling appeared stipulating that interest rates on inactive ships, or those employed in domestic trade, should be not less than 5.5 per cent, while loans to ships in process of construction or remodeling or engaged in foreign trade should be not less than 3.5 per cent. The amount loanable on any one vessel is three-quarters of its cost of construction or remodeling, and the period of the loan may be as long as twenty years.

Up to June 30, 1931, the Shipping Board had authorized loans to 25 steamship companies for the construction of 56 new ships and for the reconditioning of 19 others. While the total of these loans is $145,000,000, only $72,000,000 had been advanced up to the end of the fiscal year. The Dollar Line has taken advantage of this fund for the construction of two passenger-and-cargo vessels of approximately 23,000 gross tons each and a speed of twenty knots. Loans on these two vessels total something over $11,000,000. The same company has also financed, through the construction loan fund, the reconditioning of five of its "President" liners. Sums advanced by the government on this account have aggregated $1,750,000.

The Oceanic Steamship Company, operating a contract mail service from San Francisco to Australia, under the construction loan fund, built three cargo-and-passenger vessels of 20,000 gross tons each and twenty knots speed. Loans on these vessels amounted to $5,850,000 each. One vessel is already in service and the other two will shortly be completed.

The Panama Mail Steamship Company has obtained loans of approximately $3,000,000 each on two combination cargo-and-passenger vessels of about 11,500 gross tons and 18.5 knots speed. These ships are designed for use on the company's contract route from San Francisco to the Caribbean. The United Fruit Company, which holds a mail contract for the route from San Francisco to Central America, has also financed through the loan fund the construction of four 7,000-ton ships for this service, which have been subsequently placed in operation. Loans on these vessels approximated $2,500,000 each.

In the Merchant Marine Act of 1920 there was included a provision which amounted to a construction bounty for American-built ships, through the waiving of certain income taxes when at least three times the amount of such taxes was invested in new American-built ships of approved types. As a result of a technical ruling by the Treasury Department this section was largely inoperative during much of the ten-year period over which the provision was made to extend. The "Malolo," built for the Matson Navigation Company, was constructed with the assistance of this provision. A number of tankers for Pacific Coast operation also came within the provisions of the section. On June 5, 1930, the provision automatically became void.

No information is published in the annual reports of the Shipping Board indicating the rate of interest, which usually corresponds to the lowest commercial quotations, borne by these several loans; but since the subsequent government borrowing rate has been extremely low, these shipowners are able to finance fleet additions and improvements at very much less than present commercial rates.

Between 1923 and 1928 the Shipping Board disposed of all of the government-owned services on the Pacific. The Pacific Coast was therefore the first to emerge from the war-imposed conditions of government ownership and operations. The "President" ships, which were combination cargo-and-passenger type vessels of 10,500 and 14,200 gross tons, were sold at prices ranging from $50 to $80 per ton, a small fraction of their original cost. To the extent that serviceable ships have been sold to American shipping companies at prices well below their replacement cost, such companies have been relieved of a portion of their overhead burden and hence have been assisted in the competitive struggle with both American and foreign operators. Eventually, the question will be raised as to the replacement of these vessels when they are no longer to be classed as modern.

The *Annual Report of the United States Shipping Board* to Congress for the fiscal year 1932 includes the important information that during that year 37 vessels were sold for $2,644,687, and that there were then over 96 ships in commission and 240 laid up out of the original total of 2,546 vessels. This total shipping expenditure, most of which relates to "the bridge of ships" considered essential to the conduct of the World War, has been reckoned in various ways, and usually in the range of three billion dollars.[3] Where does a war-time subsidy end and a peace-time subsidy begin? The practical answer to this underlying question furnishes a clue to the American subsidy programs.

The United States government makes use of ocean mail contracts in order to compensate for the inability, otherwise, to maintain a satisfactory merchant marine. Even with the subsidies, there is almost no activity at the American shipbuilding yards.

According to a bulletin issued by the National Council of American Shipbuilders in May 1933, not a single seagoing merchant vessel, as distinguished from bay and harbor craft, was under construction in American private shipyards. And then there are the operating costs which vary from time to time. To quote a public address in 1924 by a leading

[3] The best estimates available appear in Dr. J. M. Clark's volume, *The Cost of the War to the American People* ("Economic and Social History of the World War," American Section, 1931). Analyzing American war outlays, he concludes (p. 55): "The largest single item of property carried over consisted of the ships and shipbuilding plant of the Shipping Board and Emergency Fleet Corporation. These organizations had expended, to June 30, 1921, $3,316,100,000; most of it for ships, shipyards, houses, transportation facilities, and other durable productive assets. The real economic value of these assets carried over is a doubtful quantity; certainly only a very small portion of their cost, and in many cases a minus quantity." The actual ship costs, he says (p. 251), might be expressed thus: "The whole budget of the Shipping Board, spread over the total tonnage acquired, gives a comprehensive cost in the neighborhood of $250 per deadweight ton, though costs of construction alone were nearer $200, equivalent to perhaps $300 per gross ton."

Pacific Coast ship operator, Vice-President J. E. Cushing, of the American-Hawaiian Steamship Company:

Steamers, cargoes, trades, and voyages are so materially different that it is impossible to translate these handicaps into a measure of money except by the roughest kind of a rule of thumb. Inaccurate as it must needs be, it is interesting to try it in order to get a crude idea of just what our much-discussed operating disadvantages mean.

Out of every hundred dollars spent on an ordinary cargo voyage, thirty-five will go for fixed charges, wages, feeding, and repairs, and sixty-five for fuel, port charges, agencies, and handling of cargo. On the first or competitive item, British wage costs are about thirty-five per cent under ours. The fixed charge element is harder to figure, but on a newly constructed steamer, there is probably thirty per cent against us. In other words, where we spend one hundred dollars, our competitor's outlay is about eighty-five. With the Japanese, the comparison is worse. At the highest, their wages are less than half of the American scale. On a low freight market—and in times of peace its chronic state is low or lower—we must work under a heavy handicap.

Unfortunately, this handicap, severe as it is on cargo carriers, is even worse on passenger liners where, relatively, first costs and wages are greatly increased. So that, competitively speaking, we are up against our hardest problem on the class of vessel which we need the most.

There is no concerted attempt to disguise the subvention feature, despite the aversion of Americans to anything which might be labeled a bounty or subsidy. It is recognized that construction-and-operating costs are doubtless higher than for other maritime nations. As to the costs involved, the government has estimated that for the fiscal year ending June 30, 1931, the amount paid for the mail contracts totaled about seventeen million dollars more than would have been required under the poundage rate; unofficial estimates are somewhat lower, reckoning payments of $18,544,000 under contracts against $2,696,000 under poundage rates, or a difference of $15,847,000. Whether one believes that this extra compensation is high or low begs the question relative to the double purpose of this subsidy, namely, provision for the national defense and the development of foreign and domestic trade. The Merchant Marine Act of 1928, generally referred to as the Jones-White Law, reaffirms the authority for mail contracts and loans and their plain purpose as defined in the Merchant Marine

Act of 1920: "That it is necessary for the national defense and for the proper growth of its foreign and domestic commerce that the United States shall have a merchant marine of the best-equipped and most suitable types of vessels sufficient to carry the greater portion of its commerce and serve as a naval or military auxiliary in time of war or national emergency . . . . and it is hereby declared to be the policy of the United States to do whatever may be necessary to develop and encourage the maintenance of such a merchant marine."

The foregoing analysis of the principal steps taken by the three leading Pacific maritime powers to foster national shipping has omitted several aspects of the question which any detailed study of the merchant marine problem should include. Each country has a long and complicated set of national and local navigation laws which in many ways affect ship operation and, more particularly, ship-operation costs. Laws on the manning of vessels, in regard to both the number of seamen required and their qualifications, have involved endless discussion but little agreement on the comparative handicaps or advantages of sailing under one flag or another. It is generally admitted, as has been said, that labor costs, both wages and subsistence, are higher on American than on other ships; but while there has been much testimony at Congressional hearings, the amount of the difference is open to dispute.[4] National rules on ship measurement, load lines, safety at sea, inspection, etc., also influence ship-operating costs. The net effect of these provisions on international competition in shipping is considerable, but not always so great as many shipowners would have us believe. Of far more importance are the underlying economic forces at work in the several countries. It is pos-

---

[4] Statistics compiled by the United States Bureau of Navigation and Steamboat Inspection, appearing in the annual Merchant Marine Statistics, give the following average monthly wages of ordinary seamen on American ships during 1930: American $45, Swedish $30, British $28, Norwegian and Spanish $23, Danish $21, Dutch and French $20, Italian $19, and German $17. Similar data for the year 1932, somewhat less satisfactory because of the greater variances in exchange values, are: American $41, Swedish $22, Dutch and French $20, British $18, Italian $17, Spanish $16, Danish $15, Norwegian $14, and German $12.

sible, therefore, in a brief survey of shipping protectionism, to ignore these other related matters without presenting a picture that is seriously distorted.

Exactly fifteen years ago there appeared a careful shipping analysis and forecast. Although war was in progress when the investigating committee was appointed, evidence taken, and a report rendered, the general findings are vital and true today. The British Board of Trade Departmental Committee, "appointed to consider the position of the Shipping and Shipbuilding Industries after the War," emphasized the dual needs of maintaining the sea supremacy of the Empire and of repairing the war wastage of shipping. Reference was made to the "nearest and most formidable rival —the German mercantile marine," and to the coming competition of two new rivals, Japan and the United States. A brief quotation is pertinent:

> Neutral shipowners have been able to amass large profits which will enable them to engage in serious competition after the war. Japanese encroachment on our Eastern trades is already serious and will become more serious. Competition of the most formidable character is also to be anticipated from the United States where marine enterprise has received a great stimulus during the war.
>
> Unless British shipping is enabled at the outset of the reconstruction period to take full advantage of the situation, it may fall behind in the competitive race and definitely lose the ascendency which has been the keystone of the Empire and the condition of our industrial existence.[5]

Shipping competition has become more keen than was anticipated. Profits have declined severely, owing to higher wages and prices, the demand for more commodious ships, and the concurrent lack of cargo. The British position, for example, is shown in the statistics released by the British Shipping Federation: as between 1913 and 1932, traffic had declined 18 per cent, operating costs were 50 per cent higher, more than one-third of the seamen and nearly two-thirds of the men in all branches of the industry had become unemployed, and profits had been halved even between 1930 and 1932.

World maritime conditions resulted in the decision by the Preparatory Commission of Experts for the Monetary

[5] Cd. 9092 (1918), p. 78.

and Economic Conference at London (1933) to include the following statement in the draft agenda:

In the case of shipping, the most urgent questions arise in connection with direct or indirect subsidies to national mercantile marines and premiums on national shipbuilding. This policy has certainly contributed towards the creation and maintenance of a much greater tonnage than is required by existing international trade, so that in many countries shipping has become a burden on the national economy instead of a contribution to its prosperity.

We agree with the meeting of shipowners recently held at the International Chamber of Commerce that it is impossible to return to sound conditions in the shipping industry so long as the uneconomic policy of Government subsidies continues. This policy of excessive intervention requires to be checked by agreement between the Governments. At the same time, certain possibilities of agreement might be considered with regard to the scrapping of old tonnage, the utilisation of existing tonnage and the laying down of new ships.

Events have moved rapidly since the failure of the Monetary and Economic Conference. European countries have taken the lead in setting up new governmental aids. Thus, in May 1934 the French Chamber of Deputies by a vote of 575 to 10 passed a subsidy bill providing for (1) a national bonus to crews ranging up to 30 per cent of their wages, depending upon the size of the vessel, (2) a daily operating subsidy up to 19 centimes per gross ton, depending upon the size and speed of the ship, and also (3) requiring shipowners who enjoy an annual subsidy of more than one million francs to set aside 20 per cent for building new tonnage in French yards, the money to be refunded in the event that orders are not placed within a five-year period. The funds required for this program, amounting to about 150,000,000 francs, have been budgeted from the higher import duties.

The British proposals follow an entirely different slant and are much more far-reaching. Thus, in March 1934 the President of the Chamber of Shipping of the United Kingdom and the Chairman of the Liverpool Steamship Owners' Association prepared a joint statement to the President of the British Board of Trade, which included this momentous recommendation:

H.M. Government, after consultation with the Dominions, should announce:

That Imperial preferences will be enjoyed only by goods imported in ships belonging to countries which gave fair play to British exports and British shipping as indicated above.

That pending the revival of trade and the effective operation of the measures, subsidy will, where necessary, be met by subsidy. Accordingly, when any section of the British mercantile marine can show that a temporary subsidy is necessary and will ensure its preservation for the time, H.M. Government should favorably consider the granting of such a subsidy, taking care not to prejudice other sections of British shipping thereby.

In their desire to help the industry in a crisis, H.M. Government should study and should prune the various burdens of taxation and regulation which have been laid upon British shipping over the periods of prosperous trade.

During 1934 the changes have come rapidly. The huge Cunard and White Star fleets have become merged; several million pounds sterling have been appropriated by the government to complete the giant Cunarder, "No. 534"; and in July President Walter Runciman of the Board of Trade announced that the government is prepared to spend up to $10,000,000 for "defensive subsidies for vessels carrying tramp cargoes under tramp conditions." Competition with the tramps of other seafaring countries, especially Scandinavian, has caused this latest move, which, however, does not solve the vexing problems of liner-tramp competition under the national as well as foreign flags. At the close of the year, legislation passed by the House of Commons provides for the subsidizing of tramp vessels upon a unique "ton-days" basis, and for the modernization of British cargo vessels.

The existing governmental activities with reference to shipping hark back to the British navigation acts laid down in principle in the Middle Ages, made definitely more stringent by Cromwell in the middle of the seventeenth century, and later repealed in 1849. It seems a far cry back to the words of Adam Smith in his *Wealth of Nations,* chapter ii:

The Act of navigation, therefore, very properly endeavors to give the sailors and shipping of Great Britain the monopoly of the trade of their own country, in some cases by absolute prohibitions, and in others by heavy burdens upon the shipping of foreign countries.

How hard it is to remove the popular delusion that British sea supremacy has been directly traceable to the navigation acts! Actually, while they did contribute to later supremacy, in the process they nearly brought British shipping to utter and absolute disaster. This lesson should be learned by all countries.

The position of American private shipping interests regarding government aid was expressed at a conference held under the auspices of the United States Shipping Board in Washington on January 10–11, 1928, when the American Steamship Owners' Association, the Pacific American Steamship Association, and the Shipowners Association of the Pacific Coast jointly recommended: (1) replacement of obsolete and worn-out ships; (2) meeting the differentials in operating costs; (3) retirement of the government from the shipping business; (4) amendment of the navigation laws to make them no more burdensome than the laws of other maritime countries. Secretary R. J. Baker of the American Steamship Owners' Association, after calling attention to the situation that the American people are still paying approximately $90,000,000 in interest on the cost of the war-built fleet, which consisted of 2,000 vessels costing $3,000,000,000, makes this trenchant statement:

The U.S.A. supplies a goodly part of the freight and 70 per cent of the passengers on the North Atlantic. Two-thirds of the freight and about 90 per cent of the passengers go to foreign ships. Any recrudescence of national feeling that would increase the participation of American vessels in the business would make secure the future of our shipping structure. A similar situation, although to a lesser degree, prevails in the Gulf and on the Pacific Coast.[6]

With special reference to subventions in Pacific shipping (a topic which in 1918 was apparently of little more than academic interest to the British Board of Trade Departmental Committee), the general situation may be summarized as follows:

1. The dominant flags in the Pacific are those of Great Britain, Japan, and the United States. There appears no legitimate reason to prophesy any other alignment in the near future.

2. Other noteworthy flags are German and Norwegian. Before the war the German government gave one of the

[6] *The Nautical Gazette*, January 20, 1934.

main shipping subsidies to the North German Lloyd for services to the East Indies, Australia, and China, although there is no evidence that the funds were in excess of actual services rendered. The striking comeback of German shipping presages a return to the western Pacific, and probably an extension to all Pacific ports. Scandinavian shipping is economical and reliable, concerned more with freight vessels than with a distinctive passenger-cargo type of service. The U.S.S.R. is an uncertain factor.

3. British shipping is on an Imperial basis. Except for one line in Canada and one in New Zealand, British shipping is confined mainly to vessels registered from the Mother Country, which in the past have had the advantage of low building and operating costs, principally because of the following three causes as summarized in the 1918 report: (*a*) the strong industrial position of the United Kingdom itself, based on free access to the markets of the world for foodstuffs and raw materials; (*b*) a world-wide Empire with well-distributed coaling-stations and ports of call; and (*c*) a large coal export trade which provided ships with outward freights which would otherwise have been lacking. The strength of the British Commonwealth was never so great as it is today, but the drop in the United Kingdom coal exports from 76,687,000 tons in 1913 to 45,909,000 tons in 1931 and to 41,895,000 in 1932 (the published statistics of the Liverpool Steam Ship Owners' Association) is a disturbing feature in the maintenance of low building and operating costs. The rapid increase in the number of oil-burning vessels upsets the former ratio of inbound merchandise to coal exports in such a way that British marginal profits and foreign subsidies are thrown into a close relationship.

4. Japanese shipping is concentrated in the Pacific. The most important foreign maritime connections are with Pacific North America. Military operations on the Asiatic mainland during 1931 to 1933 have tended to accentuate the depression in the shipbuilding and shipping industries, coincident with the world economic crisis, with the double effect, however, of replacing the old tonnage by new owing to important shipbuilding subsidies, and the creation of the integrated Ship Improvement Institution. There is persist-

ent rumor of a merger of the three leading shipping lines. From an international point of view it is questionable whether Japan has not embarked permanently on a significant subsidy program, because shipbuilding materials must continue to be imported and her geographical position is not too attractive.

5. The United States is in a decidedly disadvantageous position compared to more than one foreign country with respect to shipbuilding costs, yet a foreign-built ship cannot enter the coastwise or intercoastal service of the United States, or, except under certain conditions, obtain American registry. There is the further handicap that the combination of unusually favorable building costs and postal subventions is limited to vessels built in American yards. These navigation acts, therefore, increase ship-purchase costs to the extent of the difference between the home and the foreign market (30 per cent to 50 per cent higher in the United States than in Europe is not unusual), which is an extra expenditure to be absorbed in the protected trades but far more burdensome in the open trades. Add to this extra investment, which must be amortized sooner or later, the much higher operating costs of vessels under the American flag, and the necessity for a continued subsidy becomes economically understandable. As long as the United States adheres to her policies of protecting private shipyards and maintaining a high standard of seamen's wages and conditions— and no prospect whatever of reversal of policy appears— then some kind of substantial subsidy is needed to keep the merchant marine on the long sea trades. The connection between the commercial and the naval fleets of the United States is unmistakably expressed in the Merchant Marine Acts.

6. Everywhere, direct and indirect taxes of nearly every kind show a marked tendency to increase appreciably. Although the shipowner possibly may reduce the operating costs somewhat by lower salaries, wages, and material costs, scant relief is possible with respect to port charges, taxes, and official payments of various description.

7. Private ownership of shipping is the rule on the Pacific. The experiments of the United States, Australia, and Canada have been universally acclaimed as failures. At best, treas-

ury accounts are not easy to unravel. Subventions are less veiled and less objectionable under government control than under government ownership.

8. Uniform rates are characteristic of Pacific shipping. Tramp vessels are relatively unimportant, and most liners are members of regional conferences. These stabilized conditions are distinctly helpful features in removing the economic justification for additional subsidies.

9. Because of the long voyages, the competitive features, the undeveloped resources, and tremendous potentialities of Pacific lands, this sea region is more likely than any other to invite subsidy schemes.

XXI. Résumé

The maritime future of the American Pacific region is most promising. The achievements to date, after less than a century under the régime of the United States, have been without historical parallel. A virgin region of great productivity has been exploited in its early stages, industries characteristic of the frontier stage of development have been conspicuous, people from other sections of the country and abroad have entered in an unprecedented fashion, and the new lands have already become a rich, distinctive entity. The growth, however, has not been at the expense of that of the rest of the country; indeed, the contrary has been the situation. And André Siegfried appropriately concludes his penetrating analysis in *America Comes of Age,* with a chapter entitled "The United States, the Dominions and the Pacific."

The shipping and foreign-trade development of the Pacific Coast appears clearly and succinctly in the two accompanying tables. Table 64 (p. 414) enumerates the total value of exports and imports since 1860 by customs districts; Table 65 (p. 415) records the number of vessels entered and cleared at the American natural frontiers during this century. It will be noted that the growth in Pacific Coast trade and shipping has not only been striking but also more rapid than that of any other coastal region of the United States.

Charting the information which appears in Tables 64 and 65, Figure 37, page 417, enables us to visualize the importance of Far Western maritime trade in American affairs.

The present, and the past, may be viewed in retrospect by turning back to that classic volume, *The American Commonwealth,* wherein (p. 219) the farsighted Englishman, James Bryce, writing half a century ago, gave as his candid judgment:

Western America is one of the most interesting subjects of study the modern world has seen. There has been nothing in the past resembling its growth, and probably there will be nothing in the future. A vast territory, wonderfully rich in natural resources of many kinds; a temperate and healthy climate, fit for European labor, a soil generally, and in many places marvellously fertile; in some regions mountains full of minerals, in others trackless forests where every tree is over two hundred feet high; and the whole of this virtually unoccupied territory thrown open to an energetic race, with all the appliances and contrivances of modern science at its command,—these are phenomena absolutely without precedent in history, and which cannot recur elsewhere, because our planet contains no such other favored tract of country.

Thus far, Western America is greatly underpopulated. Despite the rapid rate of influx to the West Coast district, no phenomenon of the United States is more impressive to the traveler than the extremely low man-land ratio. Thus,

TABLE 64

EXPORTS (INCLUDING RE-EXPORTS) AND GENERAL IMPORTS OF MERCHANDISE, BY GROUPS OF CUSTOMS DISTRICTS, 1860–1933*

(Thousand dollars)

Year or Yearly Average	Atlantic Coast		Gulf Coast		Mexican Border		Pacific Coast		Northern Border	
	Exports	Imports	Exports	Imports	Exports	Imports	Exports	Imports	Exports	Imports
1860.......	160,216	304,577	153,680	22,303	1,012	528	4,981	7,372	13,688	18,836
1865.......	257,459	193,741	3,622	1,476	...	...	10,905	15,948	16,228	27,580
1870.......	293,440	370,614	146,020	16,506	2,213	959	14,647	16,241	15,043	31,639
1871–1875..	390,885	501,968	122,677	20,099	2,719	1,440	21,581	26,039	22,318	28,328
1876–1880..	533,477	425,404	107,452	12,430	3,114	1,707	33,466	30,326	25,028	22,703
1881–1885..	589,552	572,760	114,719	13,834	4,431	2,200	50,742	40,285	32,649	37,141
1886–1890..	548,775	594,176	112,611	14,204	3,640	6,413	42,352	46,455	31,000	48,514
1891–1895..	655,100	651,233	140,229	21,407	8,597	9,619	44,260	46,683	44,235	48,245
1896–1900..	813,139	611,207	188,587	18,356	15,051	4,579	60,712	49,627	79,727	50,247
1901–1905..	923,383	776,744	297,581	37,652	25,364	12,931	81,029	55,747	126,276	76,141
1906–1910..	1,058,483	1,052,156	408,656	60,901	33,074	16,980	86,229	82,813	192,242	112,757
1911–1915..	1,364,246	1,278,953	513,960	100,153	22,785	24,708	135,718	128,019	333,493	159,878
1915–1920†.	4,234,998	2,245,780	946,560	185,341	49,361	41,471	449,906	429,557	840,366	432,185
1921–1925..	2,207,280	2,296,418	1,088,592	233,228	73,826	17,117	374,062	421,082	653,761	456,922
1926–1930..	2,224,224	2,675,493	1,082,472	275,442	92,606	30,003	526,059	485,671	825,539	535,040
1930–1931..	1,167,773	1,461,408	502,108	139,074	47,959	13,857	303,038	194,948	389,335	264,791
1932.......	665,222	914,138	467,085	93,621	32,794	7,827	203,026	130,018	233,689	168,175
1933.......	723,791	1,037,594	502,046	100,713	41,852	4,031	197,670	121,063	209,624	176,752

* Data from the Bureau of Foreign and Domestic Commerce.

Fiscal years to and including 1915; thereafter, calendar years. All figures except export figures for 1865 and 1870–1878 represent specie values; exports for those years represent mixed gold and currency values and hence do not agree with the specie values given for total exports in other tables. Exports and imports of the interior districts, a small percentage of the total, are not included in this table.

† Period July 1, 1915, to December 31, 1920.

TABLE 65

VESSEL ENTRANCES AND CLEARANCES, BY COASTAL REGIONS, 1901–1933*

(Thousand ship tons net)

Yearly Average or Year	Atlantic Coast		Gulf Coast		Pacific Coast		Mexi- can Border, Total	Northern Border	
	Total	With Cargo	Total	With Cargo	Total	With Cargo		Total	With Cargo
Entrances:									
1901–1905...........	17,427	15,149	4,056	1,770	3,068	2,286	....	5,939	2,602
1906–1910...........	20,921	18,494	5,159	2,420	3,570	2,707	...	8,072	3,207
1911–1915...........	24,293	20,708	6,635	3,377	5,055	3,649	52	11,879	4,564
1915–1920†.........	24,581	16,094	7,939	4,646	5,487	4,329	64	13,440	5,646
1921–1925...........	30,979	27,133	12,390	8,243	9,562	6,070	28	13,334	6,475
1926–1930...........	36,884	33,003	11,634	7,415	15,100	8,247	150	15,293	7,700
1928...............	35,678	33,438	11,629	7,020	15,292	8,249	210	17,402	8,571
1929...............	38,190	35,438	12,120	7,703	16,278	8,734	265	15,749	7,558
1930...............	38,382	35,594	10,932	6,932	17,015	9,674	171	14,753	7,418
1931...............	35,155	31,812	9,144	5,697	15,938	9,653	190	12,355	5,980
1932...............	32,482	28,755	8,136	5,078	14,452	8,808	159	9,607	4,869
1933...............	30,013	27,299	7,142	4,050	14,216	8,990	211	9,371	4,444
Clearances:									
1901–1905...........	17,077	15,714	4,499	4,328	3,057	2,418	...	5,918	3,825
1906–1910...........	20,162	18,659	5,477	5,187	3,517	2,922	...	8,036	5,673
1911–1915...........	23,608	21,765	7,193	6,414	5,104	4,643	50	12,060	8,567
1915–1920†.........	25,921	23,168	8,528	6,915	5,626	4,762	62	13,511	9,637
1921–1925...........	30,837	24,284	12,833	9,589	9,880	8,360	28	13,075	9,236
1926–1930...........	36,361	28,696	12,326	10,641	15,658	13,148	95	15,319	10,504
1928...............	35,118	27,488	12,437	10,879	15,715	13,184	61	17,336	11,898
1929...............	37,424	28,776	12,802	11,220	16,545	13,877	260	15,313	10,917
1930...............	36,969	28,379	12,019	10,594	17,385	14,406	127	14,808	9,809
1931...............	34,293	26,182	10,244	9,138	16,564	14,382	103	12,297	8,644
1932...............	30,778	22,966	9,143	8,086	14,875	12,753	104	9,547	6,799
1933...............	28,819	22,684	8,294	7,601	14,837	12,781	132	9,204	6,629

* Data from the Bureau of Foreign and Domestic Commerce.
† July 1, 1915, to December 31, 1920.

the three states of California, Oregon, and Washington have a combined density of less than thirty to the square mile, which drops to ten to the square mile through the inclusion of Alaska and the Hawaiian Islands, and to seven by adding the Mountain States. Compare the New England States with 132 inhabitants to the square mile, the Middle Atlantic States and Switzerland with exactly double this concentration, the United Kingdom with nearly 500, and Belgium and the Netherlands with in excess of 600 persons to the square mile. While the great Western commonwealth has vast areas of desert, arid land which cannot be made productive, and commercially inaccessible timber stands, there is no sane and unprejudiced person who would hazard a prediction that this virgin territory has anywhere near reached its ultimate destiny.

The size of the political units contiguous to the Western seaboard merits attention. California is larger than Japan, Oregon than the United Kingdom, Washington than Czechoslovakia, and the Mountain States greater than France, Spain, Portugal, Germany, Italy, Austria, and Hungary combined. Alaska is over twice the size of the three Scandinavian countries. Tiny Hawaii is only one-seventh as large as Cuba, but nearly twice as large as Puerto Rico; it is significant to note that, with a population density less than that of Cuba, and one-eighth that of Puerto Rico, the marvelous fertility of these islands makes them the sixth ranking market of continental United States. This total Western Empire, comprising 49 per cent of the superficial area of the United States (excluding the 114,400 square miles in the Philippine Islands), aggregates over a million and three-quarters square miles: this region is a quarter as large as all South America, and three-quarters that of Europe (excluding the U.S.R.R.). And the potentialities of any commonwealth are set by the riches of the region even more than by the number of possible inhabitants.

To discover and study the shipping cargoes properly belonging to our Western America, the Coast States of the mainland have been regarded as a region by itself. The Mountain States are tributary mainly to the Pacific littoral; Alaska is related wholly to the nearest United States mainland; and the Hawaiian Islands, despite the notable New England traditions, are linked now almost entirely with the Golden State. In a larger sense, and a real one, the whole world is the hinterland with "the Seven Seas" providing an unlimited and exclusively non-political highway. Where can one say that a maritime hinterland begins, or ends? But some degree of localization is necessary. Even in the case of commodities moving by sea, we are impelled to single out these above-cited complementary land boundaries embracing the Western continental states and their noncontiguous territories.

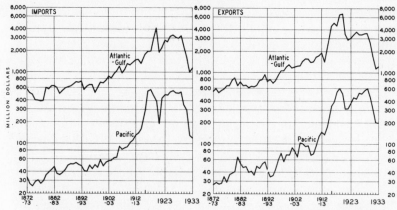

Fig. 37.—Value of United States exports and imports by groups of customs districts, 1872–1933.

Maritime commerce is a subject involving both trade and shipping, but primarily the former. Ships move in response to available cargoes. Although vessels can and do promote interchange of commodities through changes in schedules, ports of call, and types of carriers, in the last analysis it is always the demand and supply of cargo, reflected in commodity and handling costs which regulates and promotes the seaways. The writer's approach, therefore, is that of treating the vessel as a transporting unit in the same way that the bank might be thought of as a financing unit, the engineer a technical unit—each one serving as a handmaid to production and trade. In this volume we have limited ourselves to water rather than land transport, and to sea rather than interior waterways. Furthermore, there have been omitted many closely related topics, notably naval and military needs, competition of railways, trucks, and aëroplanes, and details of port facilities and charges. But even with these limitations, the subject of water-borne commerce has not been presented other than in broad outline.

Statistics, history, and geography have provided the chief tools of investigation. Neither one alone has proved sufficient; the same situation is true of any dual combination of these three approaches. Moreover, it was not wise to pass over the application of certain features of marine engineering, port economics, municipal planning, and business organization, even though they have not constituted main approaches to our subject-matter. How, then, have we utilized to advantage the interlocked force of statistics, history, and geography?

Tangible yardsticks are necessary in order to ascertain the amount, quality, type, direction, and stowage of ship's cargo. General descriptions based upon other than unit standards afford only a limited usefulness. It is absolutely essential, therefore, to discover, to group, and then to analyze carefully all the best data available; there is no alternative. Statistics are valuable to the extent that they gauge short-time and long-time movements. Yet maritime developments become thereby unusually difficult to utilize because nowhere are they fitted into a composite system. For instance, in the United States, where the statistics are the most complete (and probably the best) to be found in any country, separate organizations publish figures covering presumably the same commodities which differ hopelessly, however, with respect to (1) the period involved, (2) the classification of sea "trades," (3) the classification of commodities, and (4) the units. To illustrate, there are the confusion of fiscal year and calendar year, the definition of "exports" and of "foreign" commerce, the commodities included under textiles, and the failure to distinguish between the various tons (short, long, gross, net, and deadweight).

There is always the question of the value of statistics (since their raw material is almost never 100 per cent correct), and also of the faithful interpretation of what the statistical tables are intended to convey. It is an utter impossibility for any table or series of tables to tell the story behind the individual voyage of a ship loading and discharging at several ports. How can one segregate points of origin, shipment and perhaps transshipment, unloading, and ultimate destination? The problem is complicated indeed and calls for the thought of the persons best informed on the subject of shipping. In spite of present deficiencies in statistics published by maritime countries, these different records constitute the one indispensable basis for observing the movements in merchant shipping.

The maritime history of the Pacific Coast lends itself to ready analysis. Prior to the American occupation, the exploration and settlement of the three states is a chronicle of romance and adventure, yet devoid of activity upon a scale to influence greatly the later events. The Territory of Hawaii, then the Sandwich Islands, settled over a century ago by missionaries from New England, developed a score of decades before the mainland coastline, and her schools were patronized by ambitious youths living in California. Alaska was purchased in 1867. Less than a hundred years may appear to be an exceedingly brief span to the historian, yet here the problems are rendered relatively simple by the virtually uninhabited condition of this vast, inaccessible region. The vessels navigating the coast were few and far between, and their cargoes were made up of a few well-known articles of merchandise.

The gold rush to California and the settlement of the Oregon Territory are logical starting-points for the present development. The student of shipping history will find interest and profit in researches into the early voyages, briefly touched upon in chapter v, but his chief rewards will come in treating almost as a unit the two periods, 1849–1914 and 1914–1918, the latter noteworthy for the completion of the Panama Canal and for the World War. While it has become a truism that the great world conflagration caused a sweeping revolution in political, social, and economic thought, from the standpoint of our particular study the most significant changes were in the trade routes and in the new domestic and foreign traffic stimulated by the opening of the Canal in 1914, the startling inroads of oil over coal as the ship fuel (a great boom to the Californian petroleum fields), and the displacement of ships of pre-war standards by fast, commodious, modern carriers. The writer does not discount in the slightest the importance of historical study when he concludes that the present and the future maritime history of the Pacific Ocean really dates from the severing of the land barrier at the Isthmus. Dr. F. L. Paxson admirably characterizes the changes in the Far West as due to the passing of free and cheap land, the passing of the frontier, and the rise of industrialism. While the history of the frontier is a necessary precursor to existing knowledge, lack of space has compelled the omission of so many pertinent, earlier chronicles. Thus the historical approach has been confined to comparatively recent events.

The sailing-ship has practically disappeared from coastal shipping. The "tramp" has been largely replaced by freighters and combination passenger-cargo ships on an almost regular schedule. Practically all leading foreign lines provide the Coast with regular services. The motorship and the Diesel-ship are now far more prominent than the coal-burner. A great many vessels calling at Pacific ports are equipped with the most up-to-date refrigeration facilities. Government transports and industrial carriers benefit by the Panama route. Most striking of all, the tremendous development in the southern California oil fields has been abetted by the new uses for petroleum and petroleum products as fuel for ships, railroads, automobiles, and aircraft, and auxiliary uses of varied character in manufacturing and public utility operation. The reader is referred to chapter ix, "Types of Vessels and Services," and Appendix A, "Directory of West Coast Services, 1934," for a vivid picture of present classes of vessels and regional services applicable to every part of the world. Developments are so rapid, particularly with respect to new companies and additional vessels operating on this coast, that complete and up-to-the-minute information is difficult to secure.

The harbors on the Pacific rim are distinguished by splendid, modern vessels. To the best of the writer's knowledge, there is no seacoast which can boast such a predominance of commodious ships. To illustrate, statistics published by the Bureau of Navigation and Steamboat Inspection for the fiscal year 1932 substantiate this impression, since from them we learn that the vessels documented at San Francisco are two-thirds larger than those claiming New York as their home port, while the average for the Pacific Coast ports is twice that of the country's average. The open Pacific requires strong vessels of medium and large size, while the heavily tonnaged route via the Panama Canal also requires ships of ocean-navigating type. Among the finest American merchant ships afloat are the electric-turbine vessels of the

Panama Pacific Line operating between New York and San Francisco, the luxurious "Santa" vessels of the Grace Line, the United Fruit Company "Great White Fleet" operating between the Canal and San Francisco, the round-the-world "President" type of the Dollar Line, and the Hawaiian–South Seas–Oceania vessels of the Matson Line–Oceanic Line.

The Pacific Coast ports are outstanding examples of the working of economic specialization based upon geographical influences. The absence of a coastal plain anywhere along the littoral not only prevents the development of new ports of consequence but tends as well to stimulate the development of existing water terminals. The phenomenon of decentralizing maritime activities, characteristic of localities where the hinterland is readily accessible and the approach to the sea easy, is decidedly unlikely in this Western commonwealth, owing to the physical and economic barriers of a rugged coastline and the unfavorable land connections with the Intermountain area. There appears to be no sound basis for the promotion of significant harbors anywhere outside of the regions of Puget Sound, Columbia and Willamette rivers, San Francisco Bay, Los Angeles, and San Diego. Likewise, no marked changes can be expected in the outlying territories. The West Coast ports are favored with deep water and freedom from ice; they are scarcely influenced by tides, are not subject to extreme weather conditions, and remain open for traffic every day in the year. Their future growth is limited only by the wise exploitation of rich natural resources by an alert, expanding population.

From the Canadian to the Mexican border, the harbors are few in number and distinctive in character. On the northwestern coast Seattle and Tacoma are the leading ports of Puget Sound; then, for over two hundred miles there are no ports of consequence until we reach the Columbia River, with Astoria near the mouth, and Portland, approximately 100 miles away, on the tributary Willamette; 350 miles to the southward we pass Eureka, and after a further 250 miles come to San Francisco Bay, where San Francisco and Oakland are the leading ports, with minor ports on the Sacramento and San Joaquin rivers in the offing; man-made Los

Angeles Harbor is reached after another 368 nautical miles
south, and nearly 100 miles farther, adjoining the Mexican
border, is the natural, protected port of San Diego.

Partly for geographical reasons, and partly because of
late development, river ports on the Pacific Coast have an
importance far less striking than one usually finds in most
maritime regions, as illustrated by such ports as London,
Glasgow, Antwerp, Hamburg, and Bremen. On the American western coastline there are no important tidal, delta,
or canal ports. Puget Sound provides natural interior waterways, San Francisco Bay and San Diego offer the advantages
of splendid natural seaports, the Columbia, Willamette,
Sacramento, and San Joaquin provide river ports, and Los
Angeles has an artificial harbor.

There are no West Coast ports which are primarily passenger ports like Southhampton, mail ports like Harwich,
ports of call like Honolulu or Singapore, or coal ports like
Cardiff; however, Los Angeles is a great fuel oil port and
one of increasing importance for passengers and freight,
Portland is a leading wheat-exporting port, San Diego and
Puget Sound are important naval districts, and San Francisco is the ranking port with many of the problems which
confront the port of New York. The *Port Series No. 12,* issued
jointly by the War Department and the United States Shipping Board (1933), is justified in printing the following statement: "San Francisco Bay is the best harbor on the Pacific
coast and one of the finest in the world, with a long commercial history. The large sheltered deep-water area and
the great amount of shore line offer almost unlimited opportunities for terminal and industrial water-front development." The history of San Francisco, together with its mid
position on the Western Slope, makes this region the focal
point for future Pacific Coast maritime development.

The spatial distribution of Coast ports is a large factor
in reducing to a minimum their competitive features, a strik-
ing contrast to the situation prevailing on the Atlantic and
Gulf coasts where Boston, New York, Philadelphia, and
Baltimore, or New Orleans, Galveston, Houston, and Port
Arthur do not enjoy such exclusive positions. On the Pacific
Coast, significant results of this greater geographical isola-

tion are to be discerned in the relatively small amount of outbound cargo originating outside the immediate hinterland, the greater importance of transshipment by all-water routes, and the minor influence of rail rates in the location and activities of ocean terminals. Competition does exist, of course, between all Pacific ports, since the whole Western territory is subject to blanketed transcontinental freight rates, yet except between Seattle and Portland, and to far less extent within California, overland freight rates are minor factors. Geographical conditions, particularly the lofty mountain ranges and sparsely populated areas, exert the prime influence upon Western traffic territory.

It is somewhat surprising, nevertheless, that scarcely any Canadian traffic passes through Seattle, or corresponding American traffic through Vancouver. Between the American Pacific ports, the struggle for superior advantage will continue to center not only about commercial gain but also around the securing of naval and military establishments: no greater calamity could befall San Diego than to be deprived of its naval stations, and similarly other ports stand to gain or lose through the location of strategic battleship, aëroplane, dirigible, and presidio establishments. But turning from the political to the business phases, we are also impressed by the signs of geographical specialization.

The economic destiny of the Far West is absolutely dependent upon the nature of the future demands (local, national, and international) for primary products, of which there appears to be an almost inexhaustible local supply. Vast power resources are available through the utilization of waterpower, petroleum, and coal (on the extreme northern and eastern fringes), hence, the industrial prospects are of real and growing importance; however, despite the superior advantages of cheap power and ideal working conditions, it is the natural resources and agricultural products in raw or simply converted forms which will prove to be the deciding factor in the region's development. To illustrate, of the total exports from the United States, the Pacific Coast states are among the leaders in petroleum products, lumber, wheat and flour, barley, dried fruits, citrus fruits, apples, canned goods, and metals of various kinds.

But leading questions arise. Will petroleum continue to hold its present economic position? How badly will the lumber industry suffer for the use of substitute products for building and construction purposes? What is the future of the Coast wheat and flour industries? Will present consumers still retain their liking for oranges, lemons, apples, raisins, wine, prunes, apricots, peaches, asparagus, lettuce, cantaloupes, and canned fish? Will suitable methods of conservation be practiced in the petroleum and timber industries and, more important still, in the proper use of land and water resources? And finally, assuming that the Western States enjoy wise agricultural, industrial, and financial policies, can they individually and as a group withstand intensified competition from favored regions abroad and within the country's borders? While he disclaims the gift of prophecy, the writer is nevertheless a cautious optimist.

The most intimate external relations exist between the Canadian and the American sides of the international frontier. Propinquity is a sufficient reason, but similarity of products is not less important. The three Coast states benefit immensely because they are situated along the shipping route between British Columbia and the countries washed by the North Atlantic Ocean. The remarkable maritime achievements of British Columbia, dating from the opening of the Panama Canal, have resulted in new and frequent sea traffic with lands located on both sides of the Atlantic Ocean. These shipping connections, although often designed to serve primarily the British Columbia–European trades, have greatly stimulated inward and outward cargo traffic with reference to intervening American ports of call. Thus, during the first four months of 1934 there were 47 vessels operating under the regulations of the North Pacific Coast–Europe Passenger Conference which called at Vancouver or Victoria and stopped en route at American West Coast ports (usually Seattle-Tacoma, Portland, San Francisco, and Los Angeles) before proceeding direct to the United Kingdom–Continental ports. These services, provided by vessels of leading European lines, have been made possible to these United States ports in many instances merely because the latter are situated along this route.

Since the coastwise laws of the United States forbid vessels under foreign flags from operating between our ports, a considerable percentage of these European-owned ships otherwise would not find sufficient inducement to terminate or originate their business south of the Canadian frontier. Therefore, the political line between West Coast Canada and the United States, while resulting in a loss of some traffic to American-flag vessels, has meant a much greater movement of sea-borne trade from British Columbia to the American West Coast and vice versa, and from Europe to the American West Coast and vice versa. Much new tonnage has become available because of the low rates offered by these carriers, which are anxious for any additional revenues even though the latter may not be more than "out-of-the-pocket" contributions to the expenses of the entire voyage.

A study of the region's commercial geography discloses a strongly competitive position in the North Pacific sector. The outstanding maritime outbound cargoes of both British Columbia and Washington-Oregon are grain and lumber; other noteworthy commodities of both regions are canned fish, apples, and metals. Similarity of products tends to restrict mutual trade possibilities in spite of the growing interdependence in certain lines, notably in the pulp and paper industry. A further factor contributing to the promotion of intercountry interests lies in the heavy investment of American capital in British Columbia enterprises, especially in the lumber, paper, pulp, and mineral industries. In Canada, wheat originates in the outlying prairie provinces; in Washington and Oregon, the production of these coast areas is supplemented by the output of Idaho and Montana. In both countries, the timber stands are situated in the coastal districts, while vast mineral deposits are located both on the littoral and in the interior. The apple-growing situation is decidedly competitive. The salmon fisheries are present all the way from Alaska to the Columbia. In short, the products of the Canadian and American Pacific coasts are similar in nature and grade, which places them in a strongly competitive position locally and in the world's markets. It is especially fortunate, therefore, that there exists, in the vessels of various nationalities and types, an instrument for equalizing supply and demand of products by providing the facilities for carrying them at low rates to the world's markets.

Between these Northern Pacific ports and California, the trade is complementary rather than competitive. Even in the instance of similar commodities, the climatic variations result in seasonal movements. Flour is the most competitive product. By and large, however, the products are dissimilar, a fact well illustrated by exports of wheat from the Northwest and barley from California. Little competition exists between the timber grown in these two areas. Numerous leading horticultural products of California, such as citrus fruits, grapes, almonds, and melons, are not produced in the North. Precious metals are mined in both California and British Columbia, but they are not competitive. Coal is available in the Northwest but not in California, while California has a monoply of fuel oil and allied products. Accordingly, it is not surprising that there is a vast and growing commerce between California and the American–Canadian Northwest, with petroleum, citrus fruit, and dried fruit bulking large in exchange principally for products of the timber industry. Other commodities, in addition to those already mentioned, moving northward in considerable volume are sugar, cement, salt, and, in the return coastwise movement, feed, potatoes, and copper are conspicuous. The future possibilities of the entire West Coast are heavily dependent upon this reciprocal trade between these prosperous Pacific customers.

Pacific Canada, East Asia, and Northwestern Europe are the outstanding regions exchanging merchant cargo with the Pacific ports of the United States; Latin America, Australia, and the East Indies are of lesser total importance. A marked difference, however, exists with reference to the various classes of cargoes. Based upon cargo statistics covering the fiscal year 1930, the total import tonnage from British Columbia, amounting to over one-quarter of the aggregate inward movements, exceeded that from Europe, East Asia, or Latin America. The low-grade freight from Pacific Canada exceeded that from Europe and Asia combined and was double the amount received from Latin America. With respect to high-grade freight, the receipts from Pacific Canada were similar in volume to those from Latin America or from the Havre-Hamburg Range (Northwestern Europe) and the United Kingdom combined; East Asia contributed three and a half times as much as British Columbia, or approximately 50 per cent of the total imports. Reckoned in terms of either low-grade or high-grade imports, it is noteworthy that Pacific Canada, East Asia, and the Havre-Hamburg Range contributed approximately three-quarters of the aggregate.

East Asia, the United Kingdom, the West Coast of South America, and Pacific Canada, in the order named, are the leading destinations of the Coast exports. Somewhat over half of the total exports consists of tanker cargo, with the United Kingdom and Canada absorbing equal amounts, East Asia taking twice and Latin America two and a half times as much as either of the foregoing regions, and Australia accounting for one-twelfth. With regard to low-grade exports, the ranking order is East Asia, United Kingdom, Australasia, Havre-Hamburg Range, and the West Coast of South America; in the case of high-grade exports, the corresponding order is East Asia, the United Kingdom, Havre-Hamburg Range, and Pacific Canada. Three-quarters of the low-grade freight is destined for East Asia, the United Kingdom, and Australia, and a similar percentage of the high-grade freight for East Asia, the United Kingdom, and the Havre-Hamburg Range.

In passing, attention should be called to the international character of the United States fisheries, which is a subject closely related to shipping. The cosmopolitan aspect of the West Coast industry, illustrated by the foreign ownership of vessels, is graphically shown in Figure 38, p. 429.

On a tonnage basis, the volume of exports is over four times that of imports, but this net difference is attributable largely to tanker cargoes which require a separate type of carrier. Outward movement by tanker is ninety times greater than similar inbound traffic, outgoing low-grade freight is three times that of the inbound movement, while the high-grade freight shows a 10 per cent increase in the inward over the outward traffic. Looking to the future, the writer is unable to discover any logical reasons why the recent tendencies with respect either to foreign customers or the nature of cargoes will be greatly altered.

Foreign and domestic commerce, however, represents only a part of the sea-borne trade. The Bureau of Research, United States Shipping Board, has published statistics covering the calendar year 1929, from which this summary table is prepared:

TABLE 66

VOLUME OF UNITED STATES SEA TRADES, PACIFIC DISTRICT, 1929*

(In million long tons)

	Inbound	Outbound	Total
Foreign	3.2	13.6	16.8
Intercoastal	3.2	7.4	10.6
Coastwise	30.5	23.7	54.2
Noncontiguous	1.5	1.2	2.7
Total	38.4	45.9	84.3

* Data from United States Shipping Board. Coastwise figures, obtained from Board of Engineers for Rivers and Harbors, War Department, should properly have a deduction of 50 per cent, since each transaction is presumably counted twice.

In order to evaluate the share of the Pacific ports in the total of United States seaports, the following table of percentages gleaned from the same source gives a fair picture:

TABLE 67*

PERCENTAGE OF UNITED STATES SEA TRADES, PACIFIC DISTRICT, 1929

	Inbound	Outbound	Total
Foreign	7	28	18
Intercoastal	30	70	50
Coastwise	30	24	27
Noncontiguous	70	60	65
Total	24	29	27

* See note to Table 66.

The foregoing table depicts admirably the maritime significance of the American West Coast. Worthy of marked attention are the heavy shipments of foreign, intercoastal, and noncontiguous cargoes, and the regional concentration of Hawaiian and Alaskan commerce. Comparative statistics

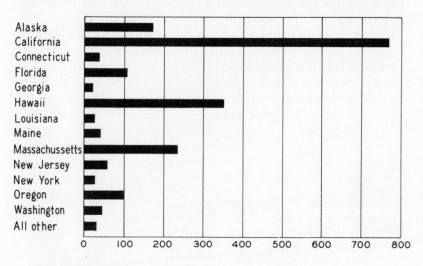

Fig. 38.—Number of American fishing vessels owned by aliens, 1929.

for the subsequent years are far less satisfactory, chiefly on account of the temporary slump in the building industry; the only noteworthy changes are an increase in maritime inter-

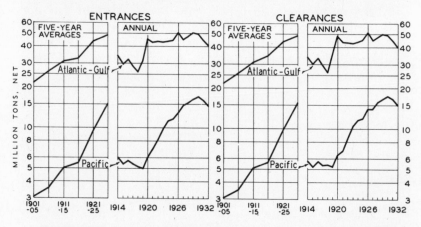

Fig. 39.—Tonnage of vessels entered and cleared in United States foreign trade, 1901–33.

course between the Atlantic Coast and Hawaii, and a higher percentage of Coast exports in the United States total.

Applicable to the aggregate inbound water-borne foreign commerce for the fiscal year 1930, the Pacific district contributed 3,200,000 out of 49,800,000 tons, or 6.4 per cent, contrasted with North Atlantic ports 66.8 per cent, South Atlantic 3.3 per cent, Gulf 11.3 per cent, and Great Lakes 12.2 per cent. The regional distribution of United States imports, classified by the percentage of the total received at West Coast ports, for selected commodities, follows:

	Percentage		Percentage
Copper ore	85	Vegetables and products...	19
Silk manufactures	70	Animals, fish, and dairy products	19
Miscellaneous metals and manufactures	49	Miscellaneous textiles and manufactures	17
Cotton manufactures	43	Coal and coke	16
Clay manufactures	40	Cotton	11
Logs and lumber	28	Fruits and nuts	11
Iron and steel manufactures	25	Coffee	11
Paper manufactures	24		
Miscellaneous	20		

With regard to the total outbound foreign commerce for the same period, the Pacific Coast accounted for 13,300,000 out of 54,700,000 tons, or 24.4 per cent, compared with the North Atlantic ports 26.6 per cent, South Atlantic 1.7 per cent, Gulf 28.4 per cent, and Great Lakes 18.9 per cent. The relative importance of West Coast ports in total American trade according to percentage of commodities received was the following:

	Percentage		Percentage
Fruits and nuts	67	Grain	18
Logs and lumber	58	Animal, fish, and dairy products	18
Tanker cargoes	44	Rubber and manufactures.	16
Paper and manufactures...	41	Copper and manufactures.	16
Pigments, chemicals, manufactures	30	Non-metallic minerals	15
Petroleum products	29	Miscellaneous	12
Sugar	27	Miscellaneous ores and metals	11
Hides, skins, and manufactures	19	Vegetables and products...	10

Finally, a ten-year summary of the foreign and domestic water-borne commerce, excluding the Great Lakes district which is devoid of seaports, presents the following complete

TABLE 68

FOREIGN, INTERCOASTAL, AND COASTWISE WATER-BORNE COMMERCE, BY U.S. COASTAL DISTRICTS, 1923–1932*

	Inbound Long Tons	Percent-age	Outbound Long Tons	Percent-age
Great Lakes	95,849,524	41	100,098,043	41
Atlantic	88,948,501	38	58,615,357	24
Pacific	32,503,887	14	39,728,803	16
Gulf	12,518,319	5	40,974,146	17
Noncontiguous territory	4,089,793	2	3,355,577	2
Total	233,910,024	100	242,771,926	100

* Data from United States Shipping Board.

picture of the water-borne foreign, intercoastal, and coast-wise movements.

XXII. A Forecast

Despite the superabundance of Coast optimism relative to the great future of the Pacific area, there is a manifest dearth of bona fide concrete information concerning it. While this lack is not surprising in view of the impossibility of making tangible estimates regarding prospective developments, the rôle of the sagacious prophet, hazardous though it is, should be essayed. The bold task is now before us.

In the welter of published and unpublished literature, the writer discovered only one carefully devised, tangible forecast of shipping traffic. Under the able direction of the late Captain W. P. Cronan, U.S.N., retired, there was prepared a study dealing with the future economic situation of San Diego, with special reference to the possibilities inherent in local port development. In this connection, the estimated annual commerce of the Pacific Coast was calculated for the then ensuing two decades of 1927–1946, inclusive. Like *all* statistical prophecies viewed in retrospect, the prognostications appear out of line—in this instance over-optimistic; however, all the prophets of 1927, while we remain in their debt, encountered national and international conditions which they could not well foresee. The San Diego study concluded that Pacific Coast shipping would grow from 111,000,000 tons in 1926 to 307,000,000 tons (plus an undetermined amount arising from Northwestern Mexico) in the year 1946.

It is interesting and worth while to note the basis for this computation. First, there is the "present" trade of Pacific Coast ports which would presumably be retained: the figure of 111,000,000 tons (to which might be attributed the estimated value of nearly five billion dollars) is derived from the only public record, namely, the Corps of Engineers of Rivers and Harbors. Next comes future trade to be diverted from railroads, or 75,000,000 tons. The third element is the increased commerce as a result of population growth, or 111,000,000 tons (it is a coincidence that this is the identical figure for "present" trade). Finally, there is increased trade with the Orient, or 10,000,000 tons. Applicable to the calendar year 1926, the Chief of Engineers estimated the commerce of the Atlantic Coast at 325,000,000 tons, the Gulf Coast 72,000,000, the Great Lakes 254,000,000, or a total traffic, including the Pacific Coast, of 761,000,000 tons (or 479,000,000 tons on an adjusted basis). It appears, therefore, that the San Diego forecasters looked forward to a West Coast business in 1946 nearly as large as the Great Lakes and Gulf commerce combined, or the Atlantic Coast commerce alone, of the year 1926.

A world economic debacle has resulted in a substantial drop in actual commerce. The shipping of United States ports declined 40 per cent between 1926 and 1932, both inclusive, with the Pacific district dropping 31 per cent or much less than the national average; the reported statistics for the Pacific district for the calendar year 1932 were 2,500,000 so-called "export" tons valued at $170,000,000 and 9,500,000 so-called "import" tons valued at $213,000,000 and 65,000,000 domestic tons valued at $2,311,000,000, making a grand total of 77,000,000 cargo tons valued at $2,695,000,000. The writer believes that the pre-depression totals will be regained within from two to five years.

From the standpoint of the railways, the recent loss of traffic (particularly eastbound) to motor trucks and vessels is alarming. Pipe lines also have reduced freight-car loadings. While it was recognized that the truck was an exceedingly formidable competitor for short hauls, there was scant realization that transcontinental highways and good roads would make possible its considerable use in the long hauls. There was no illusion regarding the potential competition of water carriers in the coast-to-coast traffic, but again there was no adequate comprehension, for instance, that Pacific lumber could be transported profitably via the Atlantic ports as far inland as Chicago in competition with the far shorter rail haul. To the territory east of the Mississippi River, the West Coast Lumbermen's Association shipped through the Canal 64 per cent of their lumber in 1929, 75 per cent in 1931, and 80 per cent in 1932.

Serious as is this situation, to the extent that it represents a business which otherwise would move by land, the railroads have suffered far more from the transfer to the water carriers of high-grade commodities which provided the most desirable traffic and revenues. Maritime refrigeration has stimulated regular, heavy water shipments of dairy products and fruits of various descriptions. Canned goods are moving by both water and rail. Automobiles owned by tourists are sent usually by the intercoastal lines. Transcontinental railways have made their complaint before the Interstate Commerce Commission that owing to lower rates by water their automobile freight had declined 85 per cent, while the intercoastal carriers were increasing theirs 233 per cent between 1929 and 1933. Perhaps most serious of all within the past three years, the tremendously profitable raw silk imports from China and Japan have been transshipped at an American or Canadian port to an intercoastal vessel, instead of being transported by the well-established transcontinental rail movement. During the spring of 1934 the railroads made drastic rate reductions in order to try to regain this valuable business, for which action the steamships are ready to retaliate. All high-grade traffic which is sensitive to freight-rate charges will continue to be strongly competitive. Although the San Diego analysis has allowed nothing for a diversion of trade from ships to railways or motor trucks, this latter factor can be largely forgotten since the commodities affected are few in number and the amounts not large. The railways have lost, probably permanently, much of their former freight; the water carriers have profited thereby even more than the motor trucks—in fact, their comparative gains have been not so much in diversion of traffic as in the securing of new business which is adapted only to transit by sea. A moderate percentage of the estimated 75,000,000 tons of diverted railway freight has become an actuality.

Population increase in the Far West is certain to make heavy demands for additional sea tonnage, since more people require a larger volume and more varied kinds of commodities handled by sea, land, and air, both inward and outward bound. Although the rate of population increase is markedly slowing down in North America and Europe, with the Pacific Coast no exception to this recent trend, the influx, particularly from the Mississippi Valley and the Eastern states, will not end in the near future and may not even greatly slacken.

The population growth in the Far West during the twentieth century far exceeds that for the country as a whole or that of any other section: from 1900 to 1930, the number of persons in the United States increased 61.1 per cent, while the corresponding statistics for the Mountain and Pacific divisions were 121 per cent and 239 per cent, respectively. That the saturation-point appears a long way off may be judged by the low man-to-land ratio. Thus, in 1930, the density of population per square mile was 41.3 for the country at large, 262.6 for the Middle Atlantic States, 131.8 for New England, 4.3 for the Mountain States, and 25.8 for the Pacific States. The Pacific States, in particular, are destined to have an increase of many million persons in the next few decades, and, while numbers are a less satisfactory economic gauge than their quality, upon the basis of numbers alone incoming and outgoing freight by water is bound to assume far larger proportions than at present. The underdeveloped West will continue to attract a virile, progressive, and ambitious population of much higher than average purchasing power. To illustrate, the Pacific Coast now ranks foremost among the nine geographical divisions of the United States with respect to retail sales per capita. The San Diego forecast of 111,000,000 additional tons by the late 'forties will suffer a postponement of perhaps two or three decades, in view of the tightening of American immigration regulations and the slowing down of the nation's birth-rate, but no one can doubt that the larger population, year by year, is promoting greater maritime business.

The estimated increased trade with the Orient, set at 10,000,000 tons, is possible of fulfillment. The advance in American-Oriental commerce since 1910 has been without precedent, in spite of conditions of unrest on the continent of Asia and a severe earthquake in Japan. While the United States increased the value of her aggregate exports 11.9 per cent and her imports 23.8 per cent between the period 1910–14 and 1931, the corresponding exports to China and Japan combined increased 252 per cent and the imports from these countries 126 per cent. The most conclusive testimony ap-

pears in an exhaustive study by the Economic and Financial
Section of the League of Nations issued in 1927, which summarized the world trade movements in these words:

> In comparing 1925 with 1913 figures, the United States and India
> now buy less from Europe and more from Asia; China and Japan
> buy less from Europe and more from North America; Australia less
> from Europe and more from both North America and Japan. Recipro-
> cally, India sends a greater proportion of her goods to North America
> and Asia, China to North America; Japanese exports to Europe have
> dropped from 23 per cent to only 7 per cent of her total exports,
> while those destined for North America have risen from 30 to 45
> per cent. Australian imports from Europe have dropped from 71 to
> 54 per cent of her total imports.[1]

While the trend away from Europe to Asia has not been
so pronounced since 1925, yet in spite of the troubled conditions in the Far East during the past decade, that region
absorbs 20 per cent of the entire merchandise exports from
the United States. The continual shifting of the world's
civilization westward is certain to enhance greatly the development of Pacific Basin trade. As the Orient assumes a
growing position in world economy, the American Pacific
region will be the prime gainer because of its greater interest
in Pacific affairs and because it sometimes saves several
thousand miles in transportation as contrasted with the
Atlantic Coast.

A conservative feature of the San Diego forecast is the
lack of consideration of possible gains to Western shipping
from developments in Europe, Africa, Oceania, and Central and South America. Mention is made of the advantages
to southern California ports resulting from the probable
large development of Northwestern Mexico. It is altogether
likely that the Pacific Coast will enjoy a considerably larger
trade than at present with the continent of Europe and with
the vast undeveloped regions of the earth, not alone in Asia
but also in Africa, Australasia, and the Americas. European
countries and Japan are exceedingly active in promoting the
transport of cargoes to and from the United States on all
coasts, even to the point where the entire, direct, common-

[1] League of Nations, *Memorandum on International Trade and Balances
of Payments, 1911–25* (Geneva, 1927).

carrier service between the Pacific Coast and Europe is handled by European companies (the Isthmian line is an industrial carrier). The advent of so many new lines and more frequent services in Pacific shipping, scarcely anticipated half a dozen years ago, has greatly widened the markets for Western products.

Leaving now the forecasting problem, we may make brief reference here to the exceedingly important place of shipping conferences in Pacific sea-borne foreign trade. Regional agreements, designed to stabilize rates and regulate services, exist on all routes and are participated in usually by all lines maintaining regular sailing schedules. It is noteworthy that not only most shipping companies but also many shippers are in favor of this regulated type of competition among the carriers. These organizations, loosely knit and not standardized in pattern, have, as one of their most important functions, the machinery for adapting themselves quickly to current conditions, as exemplified by the ever-changing schedule of freight rates.

The domestic intercoastal and coastwise conferences have had a far less harmonious existence; however, the economic justification for shipping conferences is applicable no less to domestic than to foreign cargoes. Whether or not "codes" may be promulgated by the federal government to usurp many of the functions of existing conferences is a question which cannot be answered during the fall of 1934. However, there is a pronounced trend in this country as well as abroad for the national government to assume a more active control of shipping activities, with the probability that in the United States all kinds of carriers will be subject to a greater degree of regulation under some form of unified, federal administration. How far the United States government can and will go relative to foreign shipping conferences is debatable, but, in the domestic trades, legislation is needed to safeguard and promote this public interest. The conference question, nevertheless, is related more to ships than to ships' cargoes.

Shipping protectionism, likewise, is primarily a feature of transport rather than of trade. Each enabling measure of this type, whether the government acts in co-operation with shipping interests or independently, is designed to aid shipping interests rather than trade, for example, to subsidize shipyards at the expense of water commerce. Such political measures actually are more likely to deter than to promote the untrammeled carriage of international cargoes. Irrespective of whether the expressed governmental purpose is to subsidize the shipbuilding industry, to provide auxiliary naval power, or to keep the national flag on the seas at any cost, the special subsidies or favors are uneconomic, since they fall mainly upon potential cargoes which are prevented thereby from moving. The promotion of new vessel routes inevitably does stimulate the movement of certain commodities, notably to and from isolated regions, but the net result of such forced rivalry does not tend to enhance industry and trade or to make it more profitable; the reverse is more likely the case. However, the writer despairs of the hope that public and private interests may divorce propaganda from fact or be willing to recognize that nations differ greatly with respect to their geographical, commercial, and political welfare.

Domestic and foreign shipping policies of any single country are closely related, yet distinct. It has been the established tradition in the United States, for example, to reserve the purely domestic shipping to vessels flying the American flag; Australia and Canada have similar policies. Leading maritime nations, notably Great Britain and Japan, while admitting the perfect right of these North American countries to reserve their internal trade to themselves, are eager to participate in the continental coastal trade or that between the mainland and the outlying territories. In the Western empire, the shipping between Hawaii and the Pacific Coast is a tempting prize. The United States has not seen fit to extend "coastwise" regulations to the Philippine Islands, even though the Shipping Act of 1920 provides for this new departure. Virtually all countries make reservations upon the state of open competition for their domestic business, and even where specific laws are not in existence, joint action by the government and private interests is frequently just as effective.

The spectacle of widespread demands for shipping subsidies is now being presented. Belgium, France, Germany, Great Britain, Italy, and the United States are among the countries actively considering fresh legislation. The most significant instance is the United Kingdom, which, after unexpectedly abandoning the century-old tradition of laissez faire in favor of protectionism, is now definitely planning various types of subsidies for her merchant marine in spite of the contrary declaration of principle at the recent World Monetary and Economic Conference. A grant of three million pounds sterling has already been made for finishing the mammoth Cunarder No. 534 on the Clyde, a temporary subsidy of a similar two million pounds sterling for tramp shipping has been overwhelmingly passed by the Chamber of Shipping, the Cunard and White Star Companies were merged on July 1, 1934, and definite proposals are being made to reserve intra-Empire trade to British ships. Even the partial translation of such measures into practice would revolutionize the relation of world trade to shipping, for, at the present time, 15 per cent of the world trade is British intra-Empire trade, 39 per cent is between the British Empire and foreign countries, and 46 per cent is between foreign countries alone. British shipping carries 90 per cent of the intra-Imperial trade, 60 per cent of the trade between the Empire and foreign countries, and 25 per cent of the trade between foreign countries alone. Hence, one can discern easily why maritime activities are of such overshadowing importance in British home and foreign policies.

In the Pacific Basin, the merchant ships are predominantly American, British, and Japanese. Governmental subsidies and bounties by the British Commonwealth and Japan, therefore, would place a distinct handicap on the profitable operation of American ships, particularly if the trade features were invoked by such expedients as limiting the application of Imperial preferential tariffs to goods carried in British ships. Under these proposed conditions, shipping protectionism would affect adversely the immediate trade and shipping development of countries outside the British Commonwealth.

The United States is continually being held up to censure because of the practically silly but politically expedient guise of the subsidy in the form of mail pay. The name, a clear misnomer, was adopted since the war by Congress because the idea of a "subsidy" was so repugnant to the American people. Obviously, the international postal service was used as an excuse for providing taxpayers' money for the further-ance of the American merchant marine. Fortunately the situation is being clarified through an analysis of the needs of the American merchant marine based upon the distinct elements of construction differentials, operating differen-tials, trade penetration needs, and special aid extended by other shipping countries to be countered. It is too much to expect that the executive and legislative branches of the gov-ernment will pursue the best policy as applied to each of the foregoing factors, but at least an encouraging start has been made in stating the problem more clearly and intelligently.

In the absence of any known form of protectionism which can confer equal benefits upon shipping and trade, every act devised must be of a prejudicial character. For example, during the Seventy-third Congress (1934), bills introduced affecting the shipping industry included measures designed to modify the naturalization of alien seamen, regulate the freight - forwarding business, tax commodities imported through a contiguous country from a third country, promote shipbuilding on the Pacific Coast, subject coastwise traffic to regulation by the Interstate Commerce Commission, es-tablish a National Maritime Labor Board, reorganize the accounts of the Panama Canal, increase the Panama Canal tolls, re-define "fighting ships," remit income taxes against American ships engaged in foreign trade, increase tonnage dues on ships of nations which have defaulted on debt pay-ments, require the carriage by American ships of exports financed by the American government, and establish foreign trade zones or "free ports." Except for the last measure cited, business would stand to lose more than gain by these proposals.

American federal policies which are of far greater signifi-cance to maritime trade relate to the relations with Canada, the independence of the Philippines, monetary policies, pay-ment of war debts and reparations, and the more strictly domestic policies of land utilization, relations between government and production, conditions of employment, and taxation. The specter of high future taxes affecting all kinds of transportation is a clear deterrent to individual enterprise. The railways have to contend with their heavy fixed investment in right of way, equipment, and terminals; public motor-trucking companies are being subjected to increased taxes for highway maintenance; and while the situation for the water carriers is somewhat less unfavorable than for the land carriers, their taxes, too, show no tendency to lessen. Scant hope can be held out for the diminution of marine operating costs except by reducing cost of materials and ship stores, wages, and salaries; little hope of relief appears with regard to port and canal dues, stevedoring expenses, and federal, state, and municipal payments.

To the Pacific Coast, the relatively more favorable situation of ocean carriers produces a differential of much significance. Under the most favorable circumstances the Western railways, which have been the country's leaders in reducing passenger rates and making adjustments to new conditions, are helpless in face of the still-sustained long-and-short haul provision of the Transportation Act, and the consequent difficulty of reducing transcontinental freight rates. The greater flexibility of water transport, manifested not only in the cheaper rates but also in a greater degree of freedom from centralized political authority, is a decided asset in Pacific Coast development. But the same situation does not prevail in the instance of the Mountain States, because their isolation from the seaboard prevents them from securing the lower rail-freight rates which would result from water competition.

The world is the market for any seacoast, even as it is the source of incoming cargoes. This condition is strikingly apparent on the Pacific Coast, where direct steamship service is available to all seas and to all commercially important countries of the earth. But there is ever the danger of greater economic barriers between nations, serious enough from the point of view of trade but even worse for ships plying foreign routes. Vessels serving the West Coast fly flags of all maritime nations—American, British, Chilean, Danish, Dutch, French, German, Italian, Japanese, Mexican, Norwegian,

Swedish, et cetera. These ships go where cargo is offered. On the Pacific seaboard the individual commodities which fill the entire cargo space or constitute the bulk of the stowage are principally petroleum, lumber, barley, wheat, flour, fruits, canned salmon, dairy products, paper, and copper.

Applied to California alone, the world markets normally absorb over two hundred million dollars worth of the output of its ranches, forests, oil fields, fisheries, and manufactures. It is the appreciation of this vital contribution to the Coast's prosperity which has resulted, on the Pacific Coast, in a saner, better-balanced, and more understanding attitude toward foreign trade than is true of other sections of the United States. The latest evidence of the necessity of two-way trade appeared in the great storm of protest by chambers of commerce, steamship lines, and other business interests over the pending action by Congress to place an import tax upon Philippine-produced coconut oil.

On the American Pacific Coast a more cosmopolitan attitude exists toward foreign-owned shipping than in any other region known to the writer. A single quotation suffices to illustrate the foregoing point. In 1928, a period when American confidence in its ability to engage in a profitable world trade by exporting alone was so pronounced, the Pacific Foreign Trade Council unanimously voted this resolution at the annual meeting held in Los Angeles:

> We urge the development of import trade by
>   A removal of prejudice against foreign manufactured goods;
>   Encouragement of utilization of imported raw materials;
>   Concentrated efforts to use the Pacific ports as entrepôts for imported commodities, not only for the Pacific Coast, but for the Middle West and Eastern United States;
>   Removal of regulations which handicap imported goods, and are of no particular benefit;
>   Encouraging trade with Pacific Coast importers.

This declaration was a spontaneous action, emanating from this informal body which truthfully labels itself "a nonpartisan and non-political organization, composed of industrial and commercial interests of the Pacific Slope, including leading manufacturers, merchants, agriculturalists, transportation men, bankers, importers, and exporters."

It is undoubtedly fortunate for the development of Pacific Coast foreign commerce that the existing American tariff structure does not happen to weigh so heavily on our trade with the Orient as it does on that with Europe. An advantage which the Pacific ports enjoy is that a larger percentage of products entering here are duty-free than is characteristic of other ports of the country. In 1900, of Pacific Coast imports, 69.5 per cent entered duty-free; in 1913, the figure was 76 per cent; and the preliminary 1933 estimate is approximately 80 per cent. To a considerable extent, raw materials and a wide variety of exotic products, non-competitive with American goods, constitute our imports from the Far East. Such products do not encounter the opposition of powerful, organized tariff lobbies in the United States. Our tariff policy has consequently been to admit these commodities duty-free. The result is a reciprocal trade far less heavily unbalanced than that with countries whose chief products encounter the high tariff walls of this country. The leading export markets for American products are the highly industrialized countries of northwestern Europe, Canada, and Japan. This is true not only of raw materials and foodstuffs but also of factory products. Within this American foreign trade sphere, moreover, the Pacific Coast is the most favored to benefit by this trade specialization because of its distinctive and mainly non-competitive commodities.

The heavily unbalanced cargo movement between the Pacific Coast of the United States and northwestern Europe, including the United Kingdom, means that every three cargo ships sailing to Europe with holds filled must divide among them, on the return trip, an amount of freight not large enough to fill to the load line even one of the three. Though such a large percentage of sea traffic does not move on a reciprocal basis, considerable disproportion is doubtless inevitable from the character of the products moving in the two directions. This, however, is not the complete explanation. Europe is an industrial region which produces, in the main, exactly the type of goods against which American tariff rates are the highest. For the most part, however, these articles are goods in the production of which the Pacific Coast is not self-sufficient. The tariff, then, clearly aggravates the unbalanced movement, and hampers exports not only by reducing the amount of reciprocal purchasing-power of the importing countries but also by necessitating freight rates on these exports high enough to finance return voyages in ballast. In consequence, one discovers that the Pacific Coast shipping journals are keen to approve the diminution or abolition of restrictions which interfere with the unrestrained, natural flow of commodities to their logical markets.

The Far West Coast is dominated by leaders in banking, industry, shipping, and trade who are notable for individuality, independence of thought and action, and a large degree of freedom from national and international prejudices. An intense pride in regional development, amounting at times to almost religious fervor, coupled with a sense of freedom divorced from set business traditions and practices, makes for a cosmopolitan and progressive commonwealth. It is striking to discover that a large percentage of the outstanding men and women are natives of other lands, exemplified so outstandingly by the late Captain Robert Dollar, the Canadian-born Scot, who had the undaunted courage to pioneer the round-the-world services which have now been imitated by shipping companies abroad.

The Matson Company, founded by Captain Matson, has supplemented the excellent services between Hawaii and the Pacific Coast, with the de luxe liners, "Lurline," "Mariposa," and "Monterey," on the Australasian–South Seas voyage. The intercoastal vessels, necessarily of ocean type and traversing 12,000 miles on the coast-to-coast round trip, are operated by such able and far-sighted companies as the American-Hawaiian, Luckenbach, McCormick, and Panama-Pacific Lines (the first three are Western organizations), and more recently by the Grace Line and the United Fruit Line (the latter joins the Pacific Coast and Central America and provides connections at Panama). The chronicle of the coastwise trade is filled with stories of romance and adventure. Without discounting in any way the great tradition of early sea vessels in Pacific Coast development—for example, hardly one of the famous New England clippers failed to visit San Francisco Bay on her maiden voyage or early voyages—the writer has been impressed by the qualities of initiative and independence which characterize Coast shipping tradition.

This Western spirit of self-initiative is of immeasurable consequence in Western business enterprise. But how far will governmental agencies go in regulating or virtually controlling regional development? To the extent that any area can maintain freedom of action, its American individualism will not be sacrificed to questionable political forces operating three thousand miles away from the first-hand conditions. In shipping affairs, the West Coast was the first to free itself from the shackles of government ships operating in competition with private merchant lines. Foreign-flag vessels receive the same consideration as American-flag vessels on the part of American shippers and commercial bodies. The attitude is this: " 'Buy American' is all right, but how about the shipping business?" The inhabitants of the Coast States appear instinctively to know that their future is tied up with maritime trade, hence they patronize the carriers which provide the most satisfactory services. Trade is the thing.

What is the future of public ownership and regulation of American transport agencies? Will the carriers be treated as unrelated units, or will they be subject to unified federal control? Will the distinctions between interstate and intrastate business be preserved? Will there be created several regulating bodies, or will maritime rates and services be grafted upon the Interstate Commerce Commission? What will be the eventual functions of the Shipping Board Bureau of the United States Department of Commerce? What will be the policies relative to foreign and domestic shipping conferences? Will railways, motor trucks, and pipe lines remain exclusively under private control, while vessels and aëroplanes continue to be operated along certain routes under competitive conditions of public and private ownership and regulation? Will important changes be made in transcontinental railway rates or the Panama Canal tolls? While it is reasonably certain that ships will be the least likely of any carriers to come under the ban of severe regulation or ultimate national ownership, there remains, nevertheless, the vexing problem of the prospective relations of the government to private business.

As we consider the future of Pacific Coast shipping, there are several points in conclusion which seem to deserve strong emphasis.

First, the maritime trade of Western United States is significant and of rapidly growing importance. The merchandise imports increased from $60,000,000 in 1900 to $129,000,000 in 1913, to $523,000,000 in 1929, and then declined to $121,000,000 in 1933; correspondingly, merchandise exports gained from $72,000,000 in 1900 to $147,000,000 in 1913, to $595,000,000 in 1929, and declined to $198,000,000 in 1933. The recent abnormal slump in foreign trade, which has affected the whole world as well as the Pacific Coast, is to be viewed as a temporary phenomenon.

Second, all classes of ocean commerce will grow. The important coastwise trade not only gives no signs of lessening but also shows the steadiest, gradual increase of the American sea trades. The tremendous increase in transshipment of Oriental cargoes at mainland ports is certain to enhance the magnitude of intercoastal shipping. The internal expansion of the United States, which has been typically east and west, will now probably develop mainly along the Great Lakes and the coastal fringes. There will be increased coast-to-coast business for both railways and ships. Both domestic and foreign ships and shipping are necessary forces in the future expansion of the Pacific Coast.

Third, the domestic trade of the Far West will parallel the internal expansion of the United States of America, but at an accelerated rate, owing to the superior conditions of climate, soil, power resources, raw materials, foodstuffs, and a virile, cosmopolitan population. The satisfying conditions of living will continue to attract people from less attractive climes. Conditions of natural resources, production, trade, wealth, and population are distinctly favorable.

Fourth, the foreign trade must depend at least one-half upon conditions abroad. Isolation is impossible for either trade or shipping. Irrespective of temporary conditions of war or strife, the world's mutual needs are certain to increase. The focal point is the rising standard of living which is taking place in all countries, which makes imperative the need for securing articles of luxury and non-luxury from every continent.

Fifth, despite the number and variety of federal measures which are surfeiting public and private shipping and trade policies, many of which are certain to prove uneconomic in the long run even if not now, commerce can be thwarted but never wholly denied. Shipping is the most international activity in existence; nationalism cannot be carried out to the ridiculous extent of stipulating that most incoming and outgoing cargoes shall be carried in one's own vessels, unless unloading and loading take place in mid-ocean. Happily, measures of economic protectionism are seldom as drastic as their opponents fear, for the reason that other circumstances and financial considerations are of larger consequence. The potential wealth of Western United States will likely continue to be administered by a virile, progressive people who are accustomed to depend upon themselves for their welfare and progress. The region is certain to respond to the unusually favorable features of physical geography and human geography.

Sixth, ships exist for trade, and not trade for ships. Ships, like banks and other financial institutions, have an important place in assisting trade, but they are to be thought of primarily as the handmaids of trade. They serve the demand-and-supply function by transferring commodity surpluses, and mail and passengers, from one place to another. While the number and type of merchant vessels available at any one time is fixed, the demand for their services varies according to the season, the price-level of commodities, economic conditions, and the state of a region's development; in other words, despite an increase in world vessel tonnage of 45 per cent between 1913 and 1932 without any larger world trade, at any one time, the supply of tonnage is inelastic, while the demand for tonnage is relatively elastic. Can any one of us question that future industry and trade will confer their choicest favors upon those forms of transportation, whatever they may be, which provide the greatest flexibility of rates and services at the lowest cost? Our sea-going ships will secure additional business by reason of new cargoes rather than by diversion of traffic from existing agencies serving our Coast.

Seventh, the Coast's location on the extreme western frontier of Occidental civilization, its propinquity to the vast, unexploited resources and markets of the Far East which represent a large percentage of the world's coming business, and the intimate and tremendous maritime intercourse between peoples dwelling by the Pacific constitute the dominant trade influences. There is every assurance that in the persistent geographical march of history the era of the Pacific is definitely looming ahead.

Appendix

A. Directory of West Coast Services*

THE ORIENT

Dollar Steamship Line and American Mail Line
Weekly from Los Angeles and San Francisco to Honolulu, Yokohama (fortnightly), Kobe, Shanghai, Hong Kong, and Manila.
Fortnightly from Los Angeles and San Francisco to Oriental ports, Singapore, Penang, Colombo, Bombay, Suez, Port Said, Alexandria, Naples, Genoa, Marseilles, Boston, New York, Havana, and Cristobal.
Fortnightly from Seattle—Victoria to Yokohama, Kobe, Shanghai, Hong Kong, Manila.

Nippon Yusen Kaisha
From San Francisco, Los Angeles to Yokohama, Kobe, Nagasaki, Shanghai, and Hong Kong.
Fortnightly from Seattle via Vancouver to Yokohama, Kobe, and Moji.

Canadian Pacific
From Vancouver and Victoria to Yokohama, Kobe, Nagasaki, ("Empress of Canada" omits), Shanghai, Hong Kong, and Manila.

States Steamship Company
Every 21 days from Portland to Yokohama, Kobe, Shanghai, Hong Kong, and Manila.

Prince Line—Silver Line
Los Angeles to Manila, Shanghai, Hong Kong, and around the world.

Barber Line
Los Angeles to Manila and Shanghai.

Osaka Shosen Kaisha
Los Angeles to Yokohama, Kobe, Hong Kong, Saigon, Singapore, Colombo, Durban, Cape Town.

Oceanic and Oriental Navigation Company
For Los Angeles and San Francisco to North and South China ports. (Limited passenger accommodations.)

Silver–Java Pacific Line
Pacific ports to Philippine Islands, Dutch East Indies, Straits Settlements, Burma, and India.

East Asiatic Company, Ltd.
Monthly to China and Manila.

* From *Pacific Shipper*, June 18, 1934. See chapter x, above, for other lists of coastwise and intercoastal vessels, also chapter xviii for members of the various regional conferences.

† Although actually listed under "passenger services," most of these vessels obtain their chief revenue from the carriage of freight. This grouping is useful and convenient for reference purposes.

Klaveness Line
From Pacific Coast ports to Shanghai, Hong Kong, Singapore, and Dutch East Indies ports.

Blue Funnel Line
From Vancouver and Victoria to Yokohama, Kobe, Hong Kong. (Six first-class passengers only.)

Maersk Line
Los Angeles to Yokohama, Kobe, Shanghai, Hong Kong, and Manila.

MEXICO AND CENTRAL AMERICA

Grace Line
Fortnightly to Mazatlan, San Jose, La Libertad, Canal Zone, Cartagena, Puerto Colombia.
Fortnightly to Ensenada, Manzanillo, Acapulco, Champerico, Acajutla, La Union, Amapala, Corinto, San Juan del Sur, Puntarenas, Canal Zone.

Mexican Mail Steamship Company
Every three weeks to Ensenada, Mazatlan, La Paz, Guaymas, Manzanillo, Acapulco, Salina Cruz.

Barber Line
From San Francisco and Los Angeles to Canal Zone.

United Fruit
Weekly to Balboa and Puerto Armuelles.

Gulf Pacific Mail Line
Pacific Coast to Panama Canal, Puerto Colombia, Kingston, Tampico.

Nippon Yusen Kaisha
Monthly from San Francisco and Los Angeles to Manzanillo and Balboa.

Navigazione Libera Triestina
Monthly to Acajutla, La Libertad, and Corinto.

SOUTH AMERICA

WEST COAST

Nippon Yusen Kaisha
Monthly from San Francisco and Los Angeles to Callao, Pisco, Mollendo, Arica, Iquique, and Valparaiso via Manzanillo and Balboa.

Grace Line
From Pacific ports to West Coast South America.

EAST COAST

Pacific Argentine Brazil Line
From the Pacific Coast to Montevideo, Buenos Aires, and Santos. (Limited accommodations.)

Westfal-Larsen Line
Monthly from the Pacific Coast to Montevideo and Buenos Aires.

AUSTRALASIA

Matson Navigation Company (Oceanic Steamship Company)
Every 28 days to Honolulu, Pago Pago, Suva, Auckland, Sydney, and Melbourne.

Transatlantic Steamship Company, Ltd.
From the Pacific Coast to Australia and New Zealand.

Canadian Australasian
Monthly from Vancouver and Victoria to Honolulu, Suva, Auckland, and Sydney.

Union Steamship Company of New Zealand
Monthly from San Francisco to Papeete, Rarotonga, Wellington, and Sydney.

HAWAII

Los Angeles Steamship Company
From Los Angeles to Honolulu, Hilo, or Kahului.

Matson Navigation Company
From San Francisco to Honolulu, Hilo, or Kahului.

Canadian Australasian
Monthly from Vancouver and Victoria to Honolulu.

Dollar Steamship Line
Weekly from San Francisco and Los Angeles to Honolulu.

SOUTH AFRICA

Osaka Shosen Kaisha
Monthly from Los Angeles to Durban and Cape Town, via the Orient.

Silver–Java Pacific
Monthly from Pacific Coast to Cape Town, Durban, and Lourenco Marques.

COAST-TO-COAST

Grace Line
Weekly via Spanish Americas to Havana and New York.

Panama Pacific Line
Bi-weekly to Havana and New York.

Dollar Steamship Lines
Bi-weekly to Havana and New York.

United Fruit
Weekly to New York and New Orleans via Havana.

Nelson Line
(Limited passenger accommodations.)

Shepard Line
(Limited passenger accommodations.)

Luckenbach Line
Every five days to Philadelphia, New York, and Boston. Fortnightly to New Orleans, Mobile, Houston. (Limited passenger accommodations.)

ALASKA

PUGET SOUND–ALASKA

Alaska Steamship Company
From Seattle to Ketchikan, Wrangell, Petersburg, Juneau, Haines, Skagway.
From Seattle to Ketchikan, Wrangell, Juneau, Cordova, Valdes, Seward.

Northland Transportation Company
From Seattle every Monday to Ketchikan, Wrangell, Juneau, Petersburg, and Douglas.

Wills Navigation Company
From Seattle to Ketchikan, Metlakatla, Prince of Wales Island ports, Douglas, Juneau, and wayports.

Canadian Pacific
To Alert Bay, Prince Rupert, Ketchikan, Wrangell, Juneau, and Skagway.

EUROPE

East Asiatic Company
Pacific Coast to Southampton, Hamburg, Copenhagen.

French Line
From Pacific Coast ports to Havre, Dunkirk, Antwerp, Bordeaux.

Furness Line
From Pacific Coast ports to London, Liverpool, Manchester, and Glasgow.

Hamburg-American Line
Every ten days from Pacific Coast ports to Hamburg, Bremen, and Antwerp.

Holland-America Line and Royal Mail (North Pacific Coast Line)
Fortnightly from Pacific Coast ports to Liverpool, London, and Rotterdam.

Interocean Line
Fortnightly to France, Belgium, Holland, and United Kingdom.

Johnson Line
Monthly from Pacific Coast ports to Plymouth and Gothenburg.

North German Lloyd
Every three weeks from Pacific Coast to Hamburg, Bremen, and Antwerp.

Cascade Line
Monthly to London, Rotterdam, Antwerp.

Fred Olsen Line
Pacific Coast ports to Liverpool, London, Hull, Bergen, and Oslo.

Fruit Express Line
Pacific Coast ports to United Kingdom and Continent.

MEDITERRANEAN

Dollar Steamship Line
Fortnightly to Port Said, Alexandria, Naples, Genoa, and Marseilles, via Orient and Suez.

Navigazione Libera Triestina
From Pacific Coast to Gibraltar, Barcelona, Marseilles, Genoa, Leghorn, Naples, Venice, and Trieste via Central America, Panama Canal.

B. Passenger Traffic on the Pacific Coast

Until comparatively recent years the phrase "to go abroad" was synonymous with visiting Europe. Great Britain and the Continent have been the focal centers of cultural and recreational interests to all Americans who could afford and were bent upon making a transoceanic voyage. This state of affairs naturally grew out of the circumstances which dictated that the New World was to be settled and possessed in modern times almost entirely by peoples of European origin. Hence ethnic and political bonds early made close ties between America and the mother countries of Europe. While the political bonds have long since been dissolved, those which depend on a common European ancestry have remained and have added their force to the economic developments growing out of the Industrial Revolution, by which the European and American continents have become steadily more interdependent.

Before the present drastic legislation restricting immigration, moreover, the westbound transatlantic movement of European people seeking homes in the New World added tremendously to the volume of passenger travel on that ocean. In fact it may be said to have dominated this traffic and to have been one of the strongest supports of the great transatlantic steamship lines. This movement was so great as to necessitate shipping services more than adequate to take care of cargo requirements, thereby making the formation of a transatlantic freight conference difficult or impossible.

On the Pacific, on the other hand, immigration by sea has been slight. Special restrictions on Oriental immigration have long been in force, and those arriving from or via Canada and Mexico have had the choice of a land or a sea route. Needless to say, before the opening of the Panama Canal, the number of European immigrants arriving at American Pacific ports was extremely small. Nevertheless, the statistics of pre-war passenger movements in and out of American ports as recorded by the United States Commissioner of Immigration indicate that immigrant travelers constituted decidedly the largest class of arrivals at Pacific ports, although their number was negligible in comparison with total immigration for the country, and of much less relative importance in Pacific Coast passenger movements than the corresponding figures for the Atlantic.

The three ports of San Francisco, Portland, and Seattle recorded, in the fiscal year 1914, arrivals of approximately 15,000 aliens and 6,000 American citizens. Among the former group 9,500 were classed as immigrants (see Appendix Table A, p. 458). In addition nearly 16,000 aliens (mostly immigrants), and 1,700 American citizens were recorded as arriving at Mexican border seaports, besides the land-border movement from Mexico. Arrivals at Canadian Pacific seaports were only 2,300 of all classes. Outgoing passenger traffic naturally included a much smaller number of aliens than incoming traffic, although the outward movement of non-emigrant aliens was as great as the number of incoming non-immigrant aliens. Arrivals and departures of American citizens were not far from balanced.

Hawaii likewise enjoyed a substantial passenger traffic in 1914, including the arrival of some 7,000 aliens (of whom 5,500 were immigrants) and 8,000 American citizens. Nearly 4,000 aliens departed, together with about 2,000 Americans. Passenger traffic, according to the same records, was extremely small.

To gain a perspective of passenger traffic at American Pacific ports, as compared with that on the Atlantic, it should be noted that in 1914 the Commissioner of Immigration reported the arrival of 1,200,000 immigrant aliens, 185,000 non-immigrant aliens, and 286,000 American citizens at all United States ports. Two-thirds of this number landed at New York, and less than 100,000 were overland arrivals. Departures included 630,000 aliens and 368,000 American citizens. Clearly, ocean-borne passenger traffic on the Pacific was almost negligible in comparison with that of the country as a whole. In the post-war period immigrant travel has, of course, dropped off very precipitously on both the Atlantic and the Pacific as a result of stringent restrictive legislation. For the country as a whole the arrival of immigrants in 1930 was reduced to about 20 per cent of the 1914 level, and the arrivals by sea declined to an even greater relative extent because the quota restrictions do not apply to Mexico and Canada. On the Pacific the number of immigrants arriving by sea is approximately half what it was in 1914, except in Hawaii, where the movement has almost disappeared.

In other categories of ocean travel, however, there has been a substantial growth above the pre-war level. This growth has been relatively greater on the Pacific than for the United States as a whole. The increase in the number of non-immigrant aliens and American citizens arriving at Pacific Coast ports is more than sufficient to counteract the declining immigration movement, except at Mexican border seaports. Among the several categories of departing passengers every group registers substantial gains except emigrants. Including Hawaii, total inbound passenger movement in 1930 on the American Pacific Coast amounted to approximately 45,000 persons and outbound movement to about 53,000 persons.

These figures are still extremely small compared with those for the United States as a whole. Approximately 168,000 immigrant aliens and 172,000 non-immigrant aliens were admitted into the United States in 1930, excluding those entered via the Canadian and Mexican borders. About 460,000 American citizens arrived at all seaports. Departures, except in the emigrant-alien class, were of substantially the same volume. All told, therefore, some 800,000 passengers arrived by sea at American ports in 1930, of whom scarcely more than 5 per cent arrived at Pacific ports, including Hawaii. In spite of its somewhat greater relative increase above the pre-war

TABLE A
Passenger Traffic at Pacific Coast Ports*

Port, and Year Ending June 30	Entered				Departed				Aliens Debarred
	Immigrants	Non-Immigrants	United States Citizens	Total	Emigrants	Non-Emigrants	United States Citizens	Total	
San Francisco									
1914	6,716	3,084	5,404	15,204	2,228	6,582	6,303	15,113	338
1929	2,590	7,646	7,530	17,766	2,364	6,125	7,318	15,807	184
1930	3,344	6,818	7,812	17,974	2,767	7,757	8,941	19,465	138
Mexican border seaports									
1914	12,695	3,206	1,706	17,607	1,385	1,313	730	3,428	2,396
1929	1,063	1,563	7,026	9,652	607	2,129	7,275	10,011	47
1930	1,384	2,096	9,543	13,023	681	2,903	9,798	13,382	56
Seattle									
1914	2,842	2,531	938	6,311	634	2,460	1,024	4,118	141
1929	584	2,091	2,277	4,952	1,579	1,669	2,190	5,438	120
1930	716	2,284	2,580	5,580	1,279	1,866	2,425	5,570	77
Canadian Pacific									
1914	352	1,029	906	2,287	629	1,215	892	2,736	10
1929	169	2,944	1,194	4,307	754	3,009	1,463	5,526	61
1930	...†	...†	...†	...†	948	3,025	1,607	5,580	10
Portland									
1914	47	3	—	50	—	—	—	—	—
1929	6	6	8	20	12	32	213	257	8
1930	6	3	16	25	18	40	58	116	3
Hawaii									
1914	5,575	1,468	1,073	8,116	744	3,117	2,029	5,890	219
1929	164	3,633	3,976	7,773	234	4,106	3,333	7,673	20
1930	220	3,715	3,686	7,621	392	4,494	4,102	8,988	24

* Data from Annual Reports of the Commissioner General of Immigration.　† Not reported separately after 1929.

level, it will certainly be many years before passenger travel through Pacific ports even approaches the volume of that on the Atlantic.

The United States Shipping Board is likewise concerned with the volume of ocean-borne passenger travel, and publishes reports in some detail on this traffic. No distinction is made between aliens and American citizens, but the statistics classify travelers arriving at and departing from the several ports on the basis of region from which arrived or to which departed. This makes it possible to segregate the local traffic from the transoceanic (see Appendix Table B).

TABLE B

FOREIGN AND DOMESTIC OCEAN-BORNE PASSENGER TRAFFIC OF THE UNITED STATES PACIFIC COAST FOR FISCAL YEARS 1926–1930*

Classification	1926	1927	1928	1929	1930
Foreign—Total	395,891	387,586	375,641	434,539	427,180
Overseas	50,310	55,417	57,781⎱	432,934†	425,869†
Near-by	345,581	332,169	317,860⎰		
Tourist	......‡	......‡	......‡	1,605	1,311
Domestic—Total	87,733	95,548	101,364	125,202	110,261
Noncontiguous	77,784	81,318	86,910	103,378	87,877
Noncontiguous tourist..	......‡	......‡	......‡	1,953	1,369
Intercoastal	9,949	14,230	14,454	19,871	21,015
Total traffic.............	483,624	483,134	477,005	559,741	537,441

* Data from United States Shipping Board.
† Near-by and overseas foreign reported together, beginning with 1929.
‡ Not reported separately prior to 1929.

Quarterly reports have been issued beginning with 1925. The Board of Engineers for Rivers and Harbors of the War Department compiles statistics showing the passenger traffic at American ports, but it does not show origin and destination.

The majority of Pacific Coast travelers by sea are those who are going between United States and Canadian ports. Approximately three-fourths of the number included in the foreign travel class have sailed from or for Pacific Canada. Most of these are credited to the port of Seattle (see Appendix Table C, p. 460). Eastern Asia accounts for much the largest transoceanic group, with a total of about 50,000 passengers embarked for or landed from that region in 1930. On this route San Francisco takes first place, with considerably over half the total, and twice as many in 1930 as were reported for Seattle, second in importance. Eliminating local Mexican and Canadian travel, San Francisco ranks first in passenger traffic on every foreign route. Los Angeles, however, appears to be overtaking San Francisco on the European route, for which its location and bunkering facilities, as well as its greater population, render it a more important port of call.

TABLE C

PASSENGER TRAFFIC THROUGH PRINCIPAL PACIFIC PORTS OF THE UNITED STATES TO AND FROM FOREIGN REGIONS, FOR FISCAL YEAR 1930*

Port	Total	Mexico	Europe	Austra- lasia	East Asia	Pacific Canada	All Others
Los Angeles..........	26,782	10,068	1,729	40	7,217	2,943	4,785
Port Angeles, Wash.	50,860	....	....	....	....	50,860	....
Portland	151	....	131	....	11	....	9
San Diego............	1,302	868	11	....	....	266	157
San Francisco........	45,487	867	2,176	5,431	28,506	3,264	5,243
Seattle	257,969	....	112	....	14,345	243,497	15
Tacoma	2,609	....	2	....	....	2,606	1

* Data from United States Shipping Board.

In intercoastal passenger travel there has been an uninterrupted increase for the five fiscal years for which statistics are available. In fact the growth within this short period has been more than 100 per cent. Los Angeles and San Francisco are the major ports on the Pacific which handle intercoastal passengers. In this branch of service Los Angeles nearly equaled San Francisco in the number of passengers embarking and landing, as shown by Appendix Table D.

TABLE D

FOREIGN TRAFFIC FOR THE YEAR 1932*

Port	Arrivals	Departures
Seattle	61,952	67,092
Port Angeles, Washington	14,434	12,278
Los Angeles	14,363	16,549
San Francisco (including all ports within San Francisco Bay)	12,191	20,261
Others	6,230	4,742
	109,170	120,922

* Data from United States Shipping Board. Tourist cruises not included.

There is also a growing volume of ocean-passenger travel between Pacific continental ports and the noncontiguous territories of Alaska and Hawaii, including both regular travel and tourist cruises. This movement is four or five times as great as that of intercoastal passenger travel, since there is no alternative land route to Hawaii and no practical one to Alaska. Both territories have approximately the same volume of passenger traffic. Almost the entire movement to and from Alaska is through the port of Seattle, while Hawaiian trade is divided between San Francisco and Los Angeles, with the former predominating.

Shipping Board figures for the entire United States bring out what has already been noted, the minor importance of passenger traffic on the Pacific as compared with the Atlantic. These figures, however, give the Pacific Coast a much greater share in the total (about 20 per cent) than do those of the Commissioner of Immigration, for the reason that the latter undertakes to eliminate those habitually entering from contiguous foreign countries, such as commuters, tourists, etc. Since there is a large movement of this kind through Seattle, the Shipping Board total for the Pacific Coast is thereby considerably augmented. Elimination of the major item of essentially local traffic, both for the Pacific Coast and for the entire country, results in the former constituting about 10 per cent of the latter.

The steamship lines serving Pacific Ocean travel have, in recent years, undertaken at once to meet the demands which increased travel has imposed on existing facilities and to stimulate further demand by the provision of ships which offer comfort and speed meeting the requirements of the most exacting traveler. On the routes to Asia, to Australasia, and to the South Seas, as well as on those turning eastward to Atlantic destinations, almost any type of passenger accommodation is now available in ample volume. In so far as physical facilities are capable of stimulating Pacific travel the way is paved for a great increase in this branch of commerce.

There are indications of a growing interest in the Pacific area on the part of Americans. Passenger travel is of two kinds: business, and cultural or recreational. Economic involvement with Pacific lands has increased greatly since the Philippines came under American rule, and along with it has occurred an increase in the volume of travel incident to the furthering of these economic interests. This force has by no means spent itself. For the growing cultural interest in Pacific regions a variety of causes appear to be responsible. First of all the commercial ties themselves are a contributing factor, just as they were in European travel. Also to be considered in this connection has been the great prosperity of the United States, which created a large leisure group free to travel, not only to Europe on a hasty, long-planned tour, but also to the far ends of the earth. The Orient, with its fundamentally different social institutions and philosophies of life, offers exotic sights and experiences to the American which European travel cannot match. The steamship companies have been alive to these influences in fostering world tours and travel off the beaten track of European travel.

The Orientals now resident on the Pacific Coast add another element to transpacific travel. Second- and third-generation Chinese and Japanese, many of whom have attained a considerable degree of economic well-being, travel to the Orient and back, both on business and for visits to relatives. Similarly those still residing in the Orient are induced to visit this country for pleasure or for business. In this way a growing volume of passenger travel is built up between American Pacific ports and the Far East.

There is a genuine growth, also, in interest in Latin America from Mexico southward and an awakening appreciation that our neighbors in the Western Hemisphere have something more to offer us than opportunities for economic exploitation. While Latin America was settled by Europe, its culture has been strongly modified by the Indian population, which in many regions had attained a remarkable and still little understood civilization before the advent of the white races. In this growing interest in Latin America, the American Pacific Coast shares intimately.

The recent available traffic figures are interesting. Of the 655,544 ocean-borne passengers arriving at United States ports in the calendar year 1932, the North Atlantic district led with 485,737, followed by 142,283 for the Pacific district, 28,385 for the Gulf district, 7,902 for the South Atlantic district, and 8,763 credited to the intercoastal movement. Similarly, in the case of departures, of the 769,142 passengers, the North Atlantic district accounted for 587,415, the Pacific district for 153,421, the Gulf district for 28,562, the South Atlantic district for 7,241, and 7,497 are credited to the intercoastal movement. Thus, the Pacific district had over one-quarter the number for the North Atlantic district, and four times that for the Gulf and South Atlantic districts combined. A noteworthy feature, however, is the established character of high-grade traffic through the West Coast ports, which do not cater greatly to cabin, second-class, third-tourist and third-class passengers, but the first-class travelers are half as numerous as on the North Atlantic coast: "first-class" arrivals totaled 115,900 for the Pacific district and 219,366 for the North Atlantic, departures 114,814 for the former and 222,230 for the northeastern coast.

According to trades in the calendar year 1932, the intercoastal movement, amounting to 16,260, was naturally an offset between Atlantic and Pacific ports. The North Atlantic district had a total of only 18,765 noncontiguous passages, as compared to 48,297 for the Pacific district (a further evidence of unity of the Western Empire); and the foreign tourist tabulated the large number of 147,342, as contrasted with only 1,455 for the Pacific district. The foreign movement bears testimony to the outstanding rank of the North Atlantic ports with a total of 890,811 passengers, compared to 230,092 for the Pacific district, 56,360 for the Gulf district, and 13,946 for the South Atlantic district out of a total of 1,192,209 ocean-borne passengers; however, here again attention should be called to the superior type of travel upon Pacific vessels, which accounted only 29,681 third-class passengers compared with 281,206 for Atlantic vessels, while the number of first-class passengers tabulated 187,574 compared with 322,658 in the case of Atlantic ports.

It is noteworthy that during the past few years intercoastal travel has greatly increased. Also coastwise passenger traffic was far heavier during the summer of 1934 than ever before and more and better vessels are being put on this run. There is every indication that sea trips to Alaska, Hawaii, and the west coasts of Canada, Mexico, Central America, and South America will prove increasingly popular. Practically all the European lines operating between the Pacific Coast and the continent of Europe carry a limited number of passengers, and increasing use is being made of these new services. Another new departure in the last three or four years has been the inauguration of cruises operating from the Pacific Coast to the South Seas, the Antipodes, and eastern Asia, with such fine vessels as the "Lurline" and the "Malolo" chartered for these trips.

C. American Merchant Fleets, 1934 *

Owner and State of Incorporation	No.	Gross Tons
Pittsburgh Steamship Company (W.Va.)	87	489,426
Standard Shipping Company (Del.)	69	373,945
Standard-Vacuum Transportation Company (Del.)	136	300,146
Interlake Steamship Company (Del.)	49	288,586
Lykes Brothers–Ripley Steamship Company (La.)	43	263,366
Dollar Steamship Lines, Ltd. (Del.)	22	255,172
Gulf Refining Company (Texas)	65	213,410
Texas Company (Del.)	60	175,001
Pan American Foreign Corporation (Del.)	26	172,618
Isthmian Steamship Company (Del.)	28	164,137
Matson Navigation Company (Calif.)	26	158,070
Luckenbach Steamship Company (Del.)	22	149,004
Export Steamship Corporation (N.Y.)	25	147,421
Standard Oil Company of California (Calif.)	33	135,961
Southern Pacific Company (Ky.)	60	134,780
United States Lines Company (Nev.)	10	128,975
Oceanic and Oriental Navigation Company (Del.)	21	128,517
Munson Steamship Line (N.Y.)	28	122,842
American-Hawaiian Steamship Company (N.J.)	21	115,973
United Fruit Steamship Corporation (Del.)	26	112,695
Pioneer Steamship Company (Del.)	19	108,935
Atlantic Refining Company (Pa.)	28	108,518
Great Lakes Steamship Company (Del.)	19	101,003
Pacific Atlantic Steamship Company (Del.)	17	99,353
A. H. Bull Steamship Company (N.J.)	32	97,372
Cities Service Transportation Company (Del.)	13	96,547
Mystic Steamship Company (Trustees)	52	95,939
Great Lakes Transit Corporation (N.Y.)	23	90,328
Cleveland-Cliffs Steamship Company (Del.)	14	86,769
Charles Nelson Company (Calif.)	32	86,134
Portland California Steamship Company (Calif.)	25	82,598
Ford Motor Company (Del.)	33	80,186
Merchants and Miners Transportation Company (Md.)	25	78,968
American Steamship Company (N.Y.)	15	78,079
Grace Steamship Company (Del.)	13	77,265
Eastern Steamship Lines (Maine)	48	76,428
Union Oil Company of California (Calif.)	28	75,100
Sun Oil Company (N.J.)	19	71,616
Clyde-Mallory Lines (Maine)	59	71,404
American Mail Line (Nev.)	5	70,730
Waterman Steamship Corporation (Ala.)	13	70,060
Calmar Steamship Corporation (Del.)	12	69,161
Los Angeles Steamship Company (Calif.)	12	67,957
Sinclair Navigation Company (Del.)	12	65,154
Columbia Transportation Company (Del.)	10	64,694
Standard Transportation Company (Del.)	10	63,075
Motor Tankship Company (Del.)	7	63,042
Wilson Transit Company (Del.)	11	62,721
Southern Transportation Company (N.J.)	94	62,282
States Steamship Company (Nev.)	11	62,045
Ore Steamship Corporation (Del.)	9	61,739
American Scantic Line (Del.)	11	56,866
Associated Oil Company (Calif.)	19	56,566
Bethlehem Transportation Corporation (Del.)	8	55,206
American Line Steamship Corporation (Del.)	3	54,331
Reiss Steamship Company (Del.)	10	53,458
American Diamond Lines (Del.)	10	52,736
Alaska Steamship Company (Nev.)	16	52,700
Pacific Argentine Brazil Line (Del.)	9	50,550

* Data from Bureau of Navigation and Steamship Inspection. These fleets, of 50,000 gross tons and over, total 6,907,660 gross tons, or 46 per cent of the American documented merchant marine as of January 1, 1934.

D. Official Statistical Sources

The chief source of information as to the movement of ships in the foreign commerce of the United States is the report of the Bureau of Foreign and Domestic Commerce on entrances and clearances of ships in American foreign trade. Collateral to this are the reports of the Chief of Engineers, War Department, on vessel movement in and out of United States ports. The United States Shipping Board likewise prepares one summary table on the same subject. The entrance and clearance statistics of the Bureau of Foreign and Domestic Commerce will be examined first.

The annual publication, *Foreign Commerce and Navigation of the United States,* includes two statistical tables entitled, "Number and tonnage of vessels entered and cleared in the foreign trade, by customs districts and countries," and "Number and tonnage of vessels entered and cleared in the foreign trade, by nationalities and countries." How are these figures compiled, and what significance therefore attaches to them? In the first place, it is necessary to note the meaning of the term "tonnage," as used in these tables. The ship "ton" of entrance and clearance statistics is a net ton, which is calculated for each ship by measuring the internal carrying capacity, after deducting space for crew and engines, allowing 100 cubic feet to represent one such ton. Since the rules for vessel measurement, which are not standard throughout the world, influence the calculation, American net tons cannot be assumed to be the equivalent of all other net tons. Usually these differences are small, but this is not always true.

Furthermore, if the net tonnage of vessel entrances and clearances be used to indicate comparative maritime commercial activity, consideration must be given to the wide variations in the amounts of cargo loaded or discharged from the same ship or ships of the same size. A vessel "with cargo" may be burdened to the load line, or perhaps may be entering or leaving with her hold only a fraction filled. Again, a vessel clearing with cargo may or may not have loaded any cargo from the port of clearance.[1]

[1] While it is not within the province of this discussion to make comparisons of corresponding shipping statistics published by other countries, it may be interesting to point out that even so apparently simple a distinction as that between a vessel with cargo and one in ballast is capable of diverse interpretation. In British statistics, for example, a ship entering a British port from abroad to take on or discharge only passengers or to obtain only further supplies or repairs is recorded among the "in ballast" figures, even though the ship may be loaded to the marks. Since this type of call of British ports is much more common for foreign than for British ships, the figures for British and foreign ships are not truly comparable. A much higher percentage of British than of foreign ships reported as entering or clearing in ballast are really empty ships.

As a result of the International Conference on Economic Statistics, held

The most serious limitation on the entrance and clearance statistics compiled by the Bureau of Foreign and Domestic Commerce is felt equally by those interested in vessel movements from a transportation standpoint and those interested from a commercial standpoint. The following is quoted from the explanatory text supplied for these tables:

A vessel is reported as entered at the first port in the United States where the whole or part cargo is unladen, or where she enters in ballast, and as cleared from the port where her outward cargo is completed, or where she clears in ballast. A vessel is credited as entered from the country in which is located the first foreign port where she took on cargo for the United States unless the bulk of the cargo was taken at some other port, when the vessel is shown as entered from the country in which that port is located. In clearing, the vessel is credited to the country with the first port for discharge of cargo as shown on the clearance papers, but if the bulk of the cargo is destined for another foreign port the country where that port is located is shown.[2]

Noteworthy, as far as American published summaries are concerned, port statistics are available for only the forty-seven customs districts, which embrace a total of several hundred distinct ports of entry. Of these forty-seven districts only thirty-three are so situated

---

under the auspices of the League of Nations in 1928, data of great value to those interested in using international trade statistics were computed. The report of this conference includes tabular statements showing methods employed by most countries of the world in compiling foreign-trade reports. Information was presented as to methods or systems in use relative to trade valuation, transit trade, improvement and temporary trade, bunker fuel and ship stores, fish from extraterritorial waters, gold bullion, countries of provenance and destination, statistical year, and periodicity of interim tables.

The *Annual Statistical Year-Book* of the League of Nations provides a valuable, but exceedingly brief, compendium of international shipping.

[2] It is interesting to note that the British system tabulates arrivals according to the first foreign port at which cargo was taken on for the United Kingdom and departures according to the last foreign port at which cargo from the United Kingdom is discharged. Vessels calling in the course of a single voyage at more than one British port are recorded among the arrivals at each one, but the summary tabulation for the United Kingdom (as a whole) eliminates duplication by counting the vessel as an entrance at only one of these ports. Entrances and clearances, unlike arrivals and departures, are shown only for the United Kingdom as a whole, and not for individual ports. The particular port at which the vessel is recorded as entering or clearing is determined by the nature of the voyage.

It should be admitted that this method gives a better picture of port activity than the one followed in American statistics, which eliminates a considerable tonnage of shipping at the individual ports in order to avoid duplications in the total tabulations. Nothing of great value is lost in the British report by failure to show the volume of official "entrances" and "clearances" at each port.

geographically as to make possible entrances and clearances in foreign trade. In fact, scores of these official "ports" are devoid of water transport. These customs districts correspond strictly neither to economic nor to political boundaries, although, for purposes of convenience, a state is frequently the entity; in some instances two states are grouped together. It is without significance to compare off-hand the respective trade and shipping activities of American customs districts without at the same time taking into account that these boundaries are changing. (San Diego appears and reappears, for example.) The areas are far from comparable. Thus, the customs statistics for the port of New York include not alone all of New York state, except for the northwestern Buffalo, Rochester, and St. Lawrence districts, but also most of New Jersey.

What, then, do the detailed statistics of entrances and clearances really represent? It is clear that they do not show the actual vessel movements for individual domestic ports, for customs districts, or for foreign countries.

It should be stated that the method results in an understatement for each coastal district taken separately, but, unfortunately, an understatement that is not uniform among the several ports. An important factor is the geographic location of the domestic and foreign ports with respect to established trade routes; hence these figures may not safely be used to compare the activities of the various districts. They can be used, however, with reasonable accuracy to measure the growth from year to year of the same district, providing the territory has not changed, although even here one should be on guard against overlooking the effect of any new development, for example, the Panama Canal, on trade routes and the precise order in which ships touch at their ports of call.

In regard to the foreign side of the picture the situation is even less satisfactory, since the one and only method of tabulation may be either the "first foreign port" or that port "where the bulk of the cargo" was loaded or unloaded. It is greatly to be regretted that there is no satisfactory way of ascertaining the extent to which either of these two methods is employed, or even whether or not there is uniformity in practice as among the reports at the various districts.

This method of tabulating countries of destination and departure is particularly misleading for long trade routes, of which the half-dozen or more round-the-world services are the most extreme examples. Take the case of a westbound round-the-world liner, loading cargo first at Japanese ports and then proceeding to call at other Asiatic ports, the East Indies, and the Mediterranean region; on the basis of "first foreign port" this movement will appear in the statistics as an entrance from Japan, unless an unusually diligent clerk who handles the record decides that the bulk of cargo was probably loaded elsewhere and that it should be classed accordingly. The wide discretionary power left to a poorly paid clerk is nowhere better exemplified than when, as a result of the writer's visit to the New York Customhouse a few years ago, he ascertained that a leading round-the-world liner touching Japan first after leaving American shores and entering New York direct from a Spanish port was credited as a clearance from Italy, since the clerk inferred from an inspection of manifests that calls at two Italian ports provided a predominant cargo.

Thus the actual movement of vessels between individual United States ports or customs districts and foreign countries cannot be ascertained from these reports. Nor can even the movement between the United States as a whole and any given foreign country be determined. Unless a person were sufficiently interested to follow the painfully laborious task of noting the actual movements as reported in Lloyd's *List* or the *Maritime Register,* there is no method known to the writer of estimating the percentage of understatement for each individual port, customs district, or foreign country. The unsatisfactory method of consigning the statistics of foreign commerce to the method of computation adopted by the Bureau of Foreign and Domestic Commerce has been alleviated in a striking way by the supplementary statement prepared by the Collector of Customs at the Port of New York. This special statement, prepared monthly and appearing regularly in the *Journal of Commerce,* records not alone direct entrances and clearances but also movements via other ports; thus for the month of August 1927 there were 100 vessel entrances in addition to the 440 credited as direct entrances, and 62 clearances via other ports in addition to the 443 direct clearances, or an increase of 23 per cent and 14 per cent, respectively. Without question the figures for other ports would be increased to a far greater extent, because New York is outstanding as the first port of entrance and final port of clearance. These two statements issued for the Port of New York, both based upon the same data, are naturally confusing. Similarly, the Collector of Customs at New York issues separate figures for direct and indirect entrances and clearances in the intercoastal trade.

There are several other official sources of information on vessel movements in and out of American ports. The annual report of the Chief of Engineers, War Department, publishes tables showing the number and net tonnage of inbound and outbound vessels at each American port. If these figures may be taken as accurate they supply a measure of total vessel movements, and so make possible comparisons of port activity in these terms. They do not, however, give any details as to origin or destination of the ships included in the tabulation, and hence make it impossible to distinguish between foreign, coastwise, and intercoastal movements. There is also no indication as to whether the vessels were with cargo or in ballast. It must be admitted, furthermore, that there are some grounds for questioning the "official" nature of these reports. The actual procedure is for the port engineer in charge to send out a questionnaire once a year to local transportation companies asking them to furnish the record of their ship movements for an entire year, including cargo carried. The engineer or his clerk then has the task of recording prices over the entire twelve-month period, a procedure which is not less difficult than questionable because of the changing value of commodity prices. Cases have come to the writer's attention where the entire collecting and tabulating of figures has been handed over to the local Chamber of Commerce. Since the engineers are interested in commercial statistics only in so far as they bear upon the improvement of harbors and waterways, it is only fair to state that their published figures are subject to considerable query. It should be added, however, that data for recent years are much more dependable than formerly.

The figures published by the United States Shipping Board on vessel entrances and clearances contribute little to those already discussed. They throw no light on individual port activities, since they show, by nationality of ship, totals for the entire United States. They are not comparable with those of the Bureau of Foreign and Domestic Commerce, since they are in terms of deadweight tonnage instead of net tonnage, cover the fiscal rather than the calendar year, and include only vessels of 100 gross tons and over. Since little detail is attempted, however, they fail to encounter certain of the complications which attend the tabulations of the Bureau of Foreign and Domestic Commerce; they are doubtless accurate for what they purport to cover. Further, the deadweight ton is probably a closer approach to the carrying capacity of the ordinary cargo vessel than is the net ton.

The *Panama Canal Record* likewise publishes certain statistics of vessel movements in American maritime commerce. As transits are classified by trade route, considerable information is here available on the movement from and to the main coasts of the United States on trade routes which utilize the Panama Canal. Here again the classifications are broader than those attempted by the Bureau of Foreign and Domestic Commerce, with consequently more accurate presentation. For example, no separate data by ports are shown, but American terminals are classed as either East-Coast or West-Coast of the United States. Foreign terminals are grouped into broad trade regions, corresponding, as far as possible, with customary routes of ocean carriers. This procedure largely does away with the difficulty of naming, among a series of ports of call, either the American or the foreign end of the movement.

Even so, a small percentage of commercial transits fails to fall wholly within any trade route. In such cases the trade route is determined by taking the original port of loading and the ultimate port of discharge.[3] For example, an intercoastal vessel stopping at Central and South America en route is classed among the intercoastal

[3] Information based upon a letter from Executive Secretary J. H. Smith, the Panama Canal Executive Department, May 5, 1931.

movements. This means a small understatement of the vessel movements on intermediate routes, but the figures as a whole furnish good indices of the utilization of the Canal for the important trade routes.

No one as yet has been able to devise a satisfactory or even greatly informative set of statistics for vessel movements. The Interstate Commerce Commission has never attempted to compile statistics of freight loaded and unloaded in each locality by the various railway lines of the United States, yet the problem is far more difficult for vessels engaged not only in noncontiguous but also in foreign trade on the same voyage.

A much more important category of water-traffic statistics is found in the official reports covering movements of commodities. Cargo statistics include both foreign and domestic commerce. Domestic water-borne commerce is of two kinds, maritime and inland-waterway. The former includes coastwise, intercoastal, and trade with noncontiguous territory, all of which are legally classed as "coastwise," their carriage restricted to ships of American registry. Movements by inland waterways are outside the scope of this study. Only foreign-trade movements are covered with any attempt at completeness and accuracy.

As far as foreign water-borne and domestic ocean-borne trade statistics are concerned, there are available annual reports from the same four governmental agencies which contribute statistics of vessel movements. The reports of the Chief of Engineers are the only ones issued which show all three types of domestic ocean-borne trade. On inland-water traffic, likewise, these War Department reports constitute the only annual source of information in existence. The Bureau of the Census makes a decennial report on transportation by water, but the figures contained therein appear to be taken from other governmental reports, and the inland-waterway tables are based on War Department records. The latest Census report applies to the year 1926.

Annual figures of cargo movements published by the Bureau of Foreign and Domestic Commerce include the most detailed reports available on commodity movements in foreign trade, and the only commodity statistics published on trade of, as well as with, noncontiguous territory. (The Shipping Board report, which includes noncontiguous regions, does not contain details by commodities.) The Philippines and the Virgin Islands are treated as foreign countries, so that their trade with the United States only is reported. For purposes of foreign trade the territories of Alaska, Puerto Rico, and Hawaii are recognized customs districts of the United States, so that their trade with the rest of the world is reported in all tables giving details by customs district.

Imports and exports are published annually (*a*) by article and country, (*b*) by country and customs district, and (*c*) by article and customs district. Biennially, they are published (*d*) by country and article. Since figures for two years are given, the latter record is continuous. The only difference between (*a*) and (*d*) lies in the tabular arrangement of data, which makes it possible to analyze both the geographic origin or destination of any given commodity and the commodity make-up of the trade between the United States and any given country.

It will be observed that nowhere do the published reports of the Bureau of Foreign and Domestic Commerce on foreign trade afford a threefold classification showing article, customs district, and country.[4] In other words, if one is interested in a full analysis of the commerce of any district he is at once face to face with the impossibility of following to their countries of origin and destination the commodities imported and exported through that district or of determining the commodity make-up of its trade with the principal countries with which it exchanges goods. Providing such a three-fold classification would obviously increase the complexity of the problems of collection and tabulation and would correspondingly increase the occasions on which present methods fail to produce results that accurately reflect the facts. Nevertheless, the lack of such a classification has been felt by every student who attempts a regional study of American foreign commerce.

Examining more particularly the methods of compilation and tabulation of these reports, one finds that statistics of imports and exports are based on the returns made under oath by importers and exporters to the collector of customs of the district involved in the transaction. These documents state the kinds and quantities of merchandise, its value, and its origin or destination. There is, of course, a persistent bias in the case of imports subject to ad valorem duty toward understatement of value and merchandise classification so as to make it fall in the lowest possible duty group. The check to this tendency consists of rigid customshouse supervision and heavy penalties for deliberate undervaluation. The values reported in the published tables are those appearing in the original import entries, before review by customs officials, since it would be impracticable to hold up compilation and publication until all disputed cases for any period are adjudicated. Accordingly the published figures on imports doubtless somewhat understate actual amounts and values, but this understatement would presumably not invalidate comparisons between years or between customs districts. It would probably be small enough in percentage to occasion little concern on the part

---

[4] Monthly mimeographed reports of foreign commerce by article and country in great detail are available for each customs district but not for the separate ports. These tabulations, known as "blotters," since the fresh entries are taken directly off the consular invoice-and-export declarations, are prepared for all districts in the section of customs statistics located at New York. These statistics, discontinued since May 1933, provide the only combined source of information with respect to the customs district, import-and-export commodity, and foreign point of origin or destination.

of students using these figures in any economic analysis to which this type of information contributes.

There is, however, another complicating factor in the "value" figures of imports into the United States. The present tariff laws make provision for five alternate methods of determining the value of imports subject to ad valorem duty. (See Article 694, *Customs Regulations of the United States,* 1923, reprinted without change in 1929, and not substantially altered in valuation bases by the Smoot-Hawley Tariff.) This situation naturally creates uncertainty, particularly if it is desired to compare these figures with those emanating from foreign countries where the bases for determining value often do not correspond. It would seem not unreasonable to hope that the makers of tariff laws might settle on one method of valuation without jeopardizing the attainment of the objects for which such laws are passed. The principal bases for valuation of imports into the United States are foreign value or export value, whichever is higher. It is thus an f.o.b. value at some foreign point. The commoner method of fixing value is at the frontier—a c.i.f. basis.

In 1916 Dr. Frank R. Rutter, then Assistant Chief of the Bureau of Foreign and Domestic Commerce, expressed the view in the *Journal of the American Statistical Association* that "there is considerable error in the statistics of dutiable imports; more in the statistics of free imports; and most of all in the statistics of exports." The reason for this statement is that export declarations are markedly subject to errors from carelessness, since they are not closely scrutinized by customs officials nor are penalties imposed for misstatement. The task of making out export declarations is frequently assigned to minor employees, with the result that returns are often flagrantly erroneous. In a notice sent out some years ago asking for the co-operation of exporters in eliminating these errors the Department of Commerce cited numerous extreme instances of both undervaluation and overvaluation. For example, hoes and rakes were so reported as to give them an average unit price of $132, while denatured alcohol was valued at 1¼ cents per gallon. Accordingly, figures for any small item among commodity returns may thus be subject to a wide percentage of error. But great groups, or even single classes moving in large volume are probably not seriously wrong as a rule, owing to the tendency toward compensating errors. The statistics, on the whole, are remarkably free from misrepresentation.

Quantity units for both exports and imports, when appearing in the statistics of the Bureau of Foreign and Domestic Commerce, are those commonly employed by the trade for the specified articles. This makes the figures of more interest and use to the trade than it would be if a homogeneous unit, like weight, were employed. But those concerned with ocean-cargo movements from the transportation angle, such as steamship lines, find it difficult to gain from these data an idea of the volume of movements sufficiently definite to be of great practical use. Likewise, totals of great classes reported in different quantity units may be readily compiled only in terms of value, which, over a period of years, must be corrected for changing prices.

The United States is almost alone among nations in reporting the value of both exports and imports on an f.o.b. basis. Exports are declared in accordance with their value at the port of export and when exported, while the value of imports is normally recorded as that then obtaining in the country from which shipped. Neither basis includes, presumably, the items of ocean transportation and insurance, while both include costs of packing; recorded exports include internal freight charges to the port of shipment. Comparison of trade statistics with other nations becomes somewhat of an enigma, especially since they normally quote values c.i.f. port of landing.

Before turning to other problems connected with the method of tabulation of export and import returns one should remember that the Bureau of Foreign and Domestic Commerce has two categories of imports, those entered for "consumption" and "general imports." The latter covers all goods brought into the country during the period shown, including those placed in bonded warehouses. The former includes only those finally cleared through the customs, a portion of which may or may not have had physical entry among general imports in a previous period. Some of the goods entered for consumption may later be re-exported either in the same or in modified form. If they are exported in the same condition they reappear in the statistics as exports of foreign merchandise; while if they are exported after change in form or enhancement in value by further manufacture they are included with other domestic imports. These two classes of exports, domestic and foreign, together make up the total export movement of commodities from the United States. The detailed tables of imports by countries and by customs districts are tabulations of general imports only. The tables of imports for consumption show only the quantity, value, rate of duty, and amount of duty for each article entered.

We have now to consider how cargo movements are tabulated in accordance with origin and destination. Taking up first the American end of the movement, one finds that imports and exports by customs districts are treated differently. Exports are credited to the customs district where the goods are actually loaded on vessels for transportation to foreign countries or where exports by land cross into foreign territory. Thus these figures tell nothing regarding the actual origin within the country of the commodities exported through the several districts; therefore, as far as the individual customs districts are concerned, the method of compilation makes them appear as transportation statistics rather than as trade statistics.

The Bureau of Foreign and Domestic Commerce distributes a mimeographed statement purporting to show exports by states of origin.

These figures, however, are based on movements on through bills of lading and take no account whatsoever of shipments made on local bills of lading to primary markets and wholesale centers, with subsequent movement to foreign destinations. In the case of staple raw materials, such as grain and cotton, for which the existing marketing organization calls for concentration at certain centers, these statements of exports by states are particularly misleading. The "exports" from Illinois, for example, are swelled by enormous quantities of grain which originate in Kansas, Iowa, and the Dakotas and are shipped to Chicago on local bills of lading. Or, goods may be shipped to seaboard on a local bill of lading and later exported; in this case the seaboard state would appear as state of origin. These tabulations by states show only where the through bill of lading was preferred, and unless the trade details are known the statistics are meaningless.

Imports are credited to the frontier port of physical entry only when that is also the point at which the technical "entry" for consumption or warehouse is made. The choice of the "port of entry" is wholly within the discretion of the importer. While the majority of goods brought into any port are recorded as imports of that district, a varying percentage are forwarded inland and appear among the imports of other customs districts. After goods have been "entered" at any particular district they may be shipped elsewhere at will, so that the district of "entry" may not be the district of landing nor that of wholesaling nor that of final destination. This fact imposes a palpable limitation on the use of such statistics, both from the standpoint of transportation and from that of either immediate or ultimate trade.[5]

Furthermore, comparisons from year to year for the individual districts are more or less invalidated because one cannot be certain how far the apparent variations arise from changes in transportation routes, from location of import entries, and from trade practices. A case in point is the shift in route followed by raw silk from the Orient, largely obscured by the present method of tabulating imports. What has been said in chapter vii regarding silk and the customs districts involved applies to a greater or less degree to all

[5] At one time, summary figures were published showing the value of imports entered in districts other than those of landing. These figures indicated that in 1912, the latest year for which they are published, 7 per cent of the aggregate value of all imports were not "entered" at the port of landing. Such goods move on "immediate transportation" orders, and are consequently known as I.T. shipments. Unfortunately, there is no proper record of these movements, a statement confirmed by a letter to the writer from the Section on Customs Statistics, New York, dated April 3, 1933, as follows: "In reply you are advised that we do not prepare a compilation of immediate transportation shipments entering the various customs ports in the United States. It is our understanding that these entries are retained by the Collectors of Customs in their files, but no statistical tabulation of them is prepared."

commodities and all customs districts, because there is no sure ground for assuming any uniformity in the degree to which the tabulated facts correspond to the actual economic situation for the different customs districts.[6] As a result, one may not gain from the standpoint of transportation, from that of immediate trade, nor from that of ultimate trade a correct picture of the foreign-trade activity of the several customs districts. No system of tabulation would, of course, satisfy the requirements of all types of economic inquiry, but the statistics by customs districts, as now reported, are open to misinterpretation.

The foreign end of the cargo shipments in and out of ports of the United States may now be considered. Foreign commerce statistics are available by country and customs district, by article and country, and, every two years, by country and article. What is the significance of the terms "exports to" and "imports from" the various countries?

Foreign-trade data by countries are compiled from import entries and export declarations filed with collectors of customs. These papers show countries of invoice for imports and countries of consignment for export. While this method of tabulation aims at presenting, as far as possible, statistics of actual origin and destination rather than of transportation or immediate trade, it is only partially successful in this respect.

The "origin" of imports is often merely the country from which the commodities are immediately shipped rather than the country of production. The figures of imports and exports between the United States and Hong Kong, or any other great center of trade, do not represent the exchange of goods mutually produced and consumed by these two regions. They are thus statistics of transportation and of immediate trade. The same situation arises with respect to a considerable volume of transit trade passing through seaport countries to or from interior points.

Instructions for making out export declarations require that the country of final destination, when known, be recorded as the country of consignment. Exporters or their employees often misinterpret these instructions, however, and report as country of consignment the country in which is located the port of unloading. Errors of this type are inherent in any system of collecting reports from a large number of individuals who have varying capacity for understanding written instructions or for accuracy.

Furthermore, the complexity of commercial relationships, with

[6] It is not unwise to repeat here that the geographic boundaries of the customs districts have been altered from time to time, so that any study covering a period of years will encounter the difficulty of obtaining comparable figures. The make-up at each customs district is published annually in *Foreign Commerce and Navigation,* so that it is possible to ascertain what changes have been made, though not always possible to adjust figures accordingly.

reconsignments, resales, etc., frequently renders knowledge of actual origin and ultimate destination difficult or impossible to obtain. Unfortunately, in this case, errors are only slightly compensatory, if at all, since the geographic relationships which affect trade routes are fixed and countries containing the major seaports will consistently show larger movements than would be the case if all reports were made out according to the intended method. The resulting figures, therefore, do not represent in strict accuracy the direct transportation movement between the ports of the United States and those of the several countries, the immediate trade relationships, or the exchange of goods produced by the countries specified.

For countries with important ports, which are either gateways or entrepôts, the figures will be an understatement of the transportation and immediate trade movements and an overstatement of the ultimate trade. For interior countries, or those without great trading centers, the reverse relationship will prevail. But the probable margin of error in any given case is not known.

This type of difficulty cannot be avoided under any plan of collecting trade statistics by countries, and is accordingly encountered by all commercial nations. The table of in-transit and transshipment trade, published by the Bureau of Foreign and Domestic Commerce, showing value of such trade from and to each country, does not provide a satisfactory adjustment to this error, since it covers only goods moving on through bills of lading. Further, it gives no details by commodities.

There are also to be considered certain categories of water-borne commerce which are a part of the international shipping and commercial activities of the country but are not included in the statistics of foreign trade by the Bureau of Foreign and Domestic Commerce. Among these may be considered the imports and exports of gold and silver. Neither ore, bullion, nor coin of either precious metal is regarded as a merchandise item, but all three forms of both metals are listed in a separate table showing their movement from and to the several foreign countries.

Other essentially merchandise transactions not included among exports and imports are the sale of ship supplies of all kinds to foreign vessels in American ports and the purchase abroad of similar supplies by American vessels, provided, in both cases, all such supplies are for use on voyage and are not unloaded for disposition on land. The situation regarding bunkers (coal and oil) is discussed in chapter vii. Fish caught in extraterritorial waters are likewise excluded from the merchandise account, as are sales and purchases of ships. Repairs to American ships in foreign ports, except such as are necessary to render the vessel seaworthy for its ensuing voyage, are subject to duty. The transactions mentioned above are essentially commodity transactions, yet so far as official records go they are invisible items, along with tourist expenditures, emigrant remittances, and capital transfers.

Statistics of exports and imports by parcel post are incomplete. For the former, export declarations are not required for shipments to private customers. Since it is difficult in practice to distinguish between an individual in business and a private individual, large numbers of packages are undoubtedly posted unchallenged. Further, packages less than $25 in value addressed to business concerns need not be declared. Parcel-post import statistics include all mail shipments valued at more than $100 per shipment. There are no separate statistics of parcel-post imports, but parcel-post exports by commodities are shown in the condensed table showing exports by articles and customs districts. In the general tables of imports and exports by commodities, such parcel-post shipments as are recorded are included with freight shipments.[7]

The Bureau of Foreign and Domestic Commerce touches the subject of ocean-borne domestic commerce only in its reports on trade of continental United States with its noncontiguous territories of Alaska, Hawaii, and Puerto Rico, which are not published in the annual *Foreign Commerce and Navigation,* but only totals by twelve-month periods, which appear in the June and December issues. Since these reports are based on trade with continental United States as a whole, they avoid defects inherent in the tabulation of foreign trade by customs districts and by countries. There are, accordingly, no special qualifications to bear in mind in utilizing these data, and as immediate trade statistics they serve their purpose with reasonable adequacy. As ultimate trade statistics, however, they are not complete; for example, they do not show what percentage of Hawaiian sugar is exported after arrival at mainland ports.

The most ambitious program of transportation reports on waterborne commerce, other than on rivers and canals, ever undertaken by a governmental agency was inaugurated by the United States Shipping Board beginning with fiscal year 1922.[8]

The two most voluminous annual reports are, first, one showing the long tons of cargo moving in foreign trade between each port of the United States and each foreign port, and, second, one showing the foreign cargo-shipments between the United States coastal districts and foreign-trade regions. The first has a limited commodity classification, because of the extremely detailed form of its geographic classification. The second has a considerably more detailed commodity list, while, in addition, it shows separately the large

[7] The limited appropriations for the statistical section charged with compiling and publishing export and import returns have made it impossible for this section to handle the large number of additional records involved in the numerous small shipments and receipts.

[8] The Shipping Board's first annual report on the water-borne foreign commerce of the United States ports by ports of origin and destination covered the fiscal year 1921. This report, however, gives no details by commodities, dividing movements into bulk and general cargo only, so that the present series may properly be said to commence with 1922.

groups of tanker cargo, high-freight-rate cargoes, and low-freight-rate cargoes. It also distinguishes between shipments carried in American and those in foreign vessels; these two classes are again subdivided, respectively, into United States Shipping Board and independent American vessels, and British and other foreign vessels.

Taking up first the report on port-to-port cargo movements, this publication is, as far as the writer is aware, the only source of information on such movements in the world. From it may be obtained the tonnage of cargo moving between any United States port and any foreign port.[9] Likewise, because of a double tabulation, one may trace the trade of any foreign port with any or all United States ports. This makes it extremely convenient for use in studying port-to-port movements of American foreign trade from either the American or the foreign angle.

Obviously such data are in the field of transportation statistics, since only the seaport (and Great Lakes ports) terminals are considered. The exports from all United States ports to all ports in China, for example, do not constitute an accurate index of the amount of goods sold to the Chinese for their use. These figures tell nothing concerning the first origin or the ultimate destination of the goods whose movement is recorded. Canadian grain loaded at New York for Liverpool appears as an export from New York exactly as if it were Kansas grain. This method of compilation is not surprising, since the natural emphasis of the United States Shipping Board is on data primarily of interest to ship owners and ship operators. As ocean-transportation statistics, however, they are a great advance over anything heretofore available.

The other Shipping Board report of major size on water-borne foreign commerce is an attempt to give, in geater commodity detail, the volume of cargo moving on the various foreign trade routes of the United States. For this purpose American ports are grouped under five coastal districts—North Atlantic, South Atlantic, Gulf, Pacific, and Great Lakes. Foreign ports are divided among twenty trade regions, which correspond, as far as practicable, with routes of es-

---

[9] Assistant Director Virgil C. Miller, Bureau of Research, United States Shipping Board, in a letter to the writer dated May 11, 1931, stated:

"As far as we are able to ascertain, and I feel warranted in stating that the average applies to ninety-nine and some hundredths per cent of the tonnage shown, the ports of origin and destination are exact. I do not know of any instances in which we have not been able to ascertain exact ports of loading, but at rare intervals we do receive a report indicating an optional or split destination. In such cases we pursue the matter by correspondence until we can determine the actual ports of unloading, and in the exceedingly rare cases in which it is impossible to arrive at a positive destination for all or part of a cargo such tonnage is assigned to a port which past experience indicates as the logical destination. Cases of this kind are, however, so rare that they do not have any appreciable effect upon the integrity of the reports as issued."

tablished steamship lines. The result is a fairly close picture of the amount and character of the flow of foreign commerce between each specified coastal district and the several foreign trade regions.

With some exceptions, these data make possible the study of ocean-trade routes and their comparative importance from the transportation standpoint. The exceptions concern the problem raised by alternate routes between terminals such as those offered by Panama and Magellan for goods moving between the east coast of the United States and Australia, for example, or by Panama or Suez for goods moving between the east coast of the United States and transpacific ports as far south as Hong Kong or Manila, or by Suez or Good Hope for ships between Atlantic ports of North America and Europe on the one hand and India and the Far East on the other. There is widespread interest in such questions as determining the actual flow of maritime commerce in and across the Pacific Basin, but even the highly detailed Shipping Board figures cannot fully answer that question as far as American foreign commerce is concerned. Other governmental statistics fall short even more.

The question now arises as to how far these statistics are comparable with, and supplementary to, those published by the Bureau of Foreign and Domestic Commerce previously discussed. As already pointed out, the former are entirely in the realm of transportation, while the latter are sometimes transportation, sometimes immediate trade (these two uses are almost identical for seacoast terminals), but more often a combination of immediate and ultimate trade statistics which makes them wholly satisfactory for neither.

More than this, the Shipping Board reports are in terms of tons of 2,240 pounds, while the quantity units of the Bureau are not always reducible to a weight basis without great labor. Besides, only cargoes carried by vessels of 100 gross tons and over are included in the Shipping Board reports, and the weight reported includes weight of containers as well as of the commodities themselves.

The first of these differences would not of itself be serious, particularly for transoceanic movements, but the second might introduce considerable discrepancy in figures on commodities of certain types. Commodities carried in quantities of less than ten tons per shipment are reported by the Shipping Board as "general cargo." Land-borne foreign commerce with or through contiguous countries is included by the Bureau of Foreign and Domestic Commerce but excluded by the Shipping Board. Finally, the Bureau reports are for the calendar year, and those of the Shipping Board are for the fiscal year ending June 30.

In addition to statistics of foreign commerce the Shipping Board also publishes reports on the exchange of commodities between ports on the Pacific Coast of the United States and those on the Gulf and Atlantic coasts. The report of intercoastal traffic, like that of foreign traffic, is a transportation record which is tabulated as port-to-port movements, by commodities, measured in long tons. Returns are published for both the fiscal and the calendar years. For the water-borne exchange of commodities between the east and west coasts of the United States these reports constitute a valuable record. They do not, however, include any coastwise, as distinguished from inter-coastal, traffic.[10]

Doubtless some goods are carried between intercoastal ports which have previously been, or are later, forwarded coastwise from or to other ports. One cannot be certain, therefore, that all the ship-ments from and to the several ports which are really a part of inter-coastal trade are credited to the ports at which they actually originated or to which they were ultimately delivered. The absence of satisfactory statistics of domestic commerce is everywhere felt and makes itself apparent in the realm of water-borne commercial statistics through lack of adequate records of coastwise commerce.

Before leaving the reports of the Shipping Board one may say a few words on the commodity classifications which are there used. The prime object of such reports has been not to overlap the work of the Bureau of Foreign and Domestic Commerce in its detailed import and export statistics but rather to provide ship owners and operators with the type of information on cargo movements most useful to them. When this fact is kept in mind, certain limitations of the commodity classifications must be expected.

Use of the gross ton as a unit of quantity results in a great em-phasis on articles of large bulk, hence of relatively low value. Con-sequently, only goods moving in very large quantities are reported separately, since the number of commodity classes is not great. The restricted classification likewise leads to a grouping of different commodities within the same class, which often obscures the facts regarding the movement of individual articles of some importance.

Statistics of Panama Canal traffic reported in the weekly publica-tion, the *Panama Canal Record,* have already been mentioned in connection with the discussion of vessel movements. Monthly and annual statements of cargo traffic through the Canal are reported in considerable detail, both as to commodity and as to origin and desti-nation. There are nineteen regional groups, of which eleven include either the east or the west coast of the United States as one terminus. These reports show the tons (of 2,240 pounds) of cargo, moving in each direction through the Canal between the points designated in the nineteen regional groups. The data are compiled from special cargo declarations prepared by masters of vessels for the use of the Panama Canal authorities.

[10] Starting with the calendar year 1925, a brief summary report, pub-lished by the Shipping Board, of all sea-borne commerce (including the Great Lakes as inland seas) of each United States port shows separately the tonnage of intercoastal, coastwise, and noncontiguous domestic com-merce. The coastwise figures are obtained from the Board of Engineers for Rivers and Harbors, War Department. No details by commodities are included.

Except for the fact that there is a relatively large undistributed item called "general cargo," which is nowhere broken up into its constituent elements, these commodity statistics show the actual movement of all specified articles on the routes indicated. The report, earlier referred to, showing movement of vessels on the several trade routes through the Canal, also gives tons of cargo carried by these ships, but since some of that cargo has another origin or destination than that within the route in which the vessel is classed, the tabulation is not so accurate for origin and destination as the commodity statement just described.

It is necessary in passing only to point out that these statistics, like those of the Shipping Board, are primarily transportation statistics and that the terms "origin" and "destination," as used in the table, refer merely to origin and destination with respect to the particular voyage for which the cargo declaration is made. Nevertheless the tables of Panama Canal traffic seem admirably well adapted, on the whole, to bring out the more important facts regarding commercial utilization of that waterway.

Statistics on American waterways have appeared in the reports of the Chief of Engineers since 1866 and have been published as a part of his annual report starting approximately with 1870. The remaining source of information on water-borne commerce of the United States is the annual, *Commercial Statistics,* published as Volume II of the *Report of the Chief of Engineers, War Department.* In 1891, Congress authorized the Board of Engineers for Rivers and Harbors to collect traffic statistics on waterways under improvement by the federal government in order to throw light on probable commercial needs of proposed and in-process channel and port improvements. Until 1920 the statistics so collected and published were more or less fragmentary, unreliable, and without uniformity among the numerous engineering districts as to methods of compilation and presentation. Places not under improvement by the federal government were not included. Beginning with 1920, however, standard forms for compilation and presentation of data were introduced, and attention was extended to include all regions having water traffic of any commercial importance, whether or not federal projects were in process.

At the present time, accordingly, these reports undertake to cover the entire water-borne commerce of the United States, foreign, intercoastal, coastwise, and inland waterway. As to the last two categories of traffic, as already mentioned, they are the only existing official source of information. The published reports distinguish between foreign, coastwise, and internal movements, but the "coastwise" figures presumably include all types of traffic legally so called. Statistics are given for each port, waterway, or section of waterway for a fairly detailed list of commodities wherever the nature of the traffic makes that possible; value of traffic is shown for totals only; figures are in short tons.

There is no information as to either origin of incoming goods or destination of outgoing goods with respect to the cargo movement of these ports. Summary tables attempt to report, including value as well as tonnage, the entire volume of water-borne commerce of the United States by type of traffic, both with and without elimination of duplications caused by double reporting of domestic shipments. These data are given for the principal coastal districts and inland waterway systems, as well as for individual seaports, Great Lakes ports, and rivers, canals, and other inland water routes.

What has been said regarding the War Department reports as a source of statistics on entrances and clearances applies equally to their figures of cargo movements. So much uncertainty surrounds their bases of tabulation that it does not appear safe to classify them as accurate indexes of either trade or transportation. For example, there is no way of knowing whether in-transit and transshipment cargoes are included in the figures of foreign trade as they are by the Shipping Board or excluded as they are by the Bureau of Foreign and Domestic Commerce. Since the general point of view of the organization is one of transportation, however, it is probable that all goods actually handled are normally included in one or another category of commerce reported by them. The most serious sources of error probably arise out of the machinery for collecting these facts, which is the result of inadequate appropriations for this work, underpaid and not especially trained personnel, inadequate private records, and perhaps reluctance on the part of private companies to prepare this voluntary statement for public use.

Nevertheless, in any attempt to measure the total water-borne traffic of a port, a region, or the United States as a whole it is necessary to turn to these reports before it is possible to derive even an estimate. It is to be hoped that the future will be marked by continued improvement in these reports, in both form and reliability, as well as in the publication of more details regarding methods of collection and tabulation. Without this improvement, the reports will remain subject to varying interpretations.

Before closing this section on official statistical sources, some mention should be made of local water-traffic reports issued either by municipal port authorities or by unofficial bodies such as Chambers of Commerce. Because of the geographic focus of the present study, attention is called here only to such reports as are issued for the major seaports of the Pacific Coast.

The California Board of State Harbor Commissioners, which administers the port of San Francisco, publishes an annual tabulation of the principal commodities entering and leaving the San Francisco customs district, showing foreign trade, in short tons, by principal country or foreign region, intercoastal trade, and trade with Hawaii and Alaska. Figures are based on federal customs records, which are converted to a tonnage basis and then combined into fewer classes both of commodities and of foreign countries. This statement likewise gives the total volume of imports entering the district en route to other United States customs districts (i. e., goods landed at San Francisco, but officially "entered" elsewhere), and the volume of in-transit shipments of foreign merchandise moving to a foreign destination. Since the report is based on customhouse records, it is subject, in the main, to the same qualifications as those of the Bureau of Foreign and Domestic Commerce. The conversion to a tonnage basis, however, makes it more usable for certain purposes, and the inclusion of the immediate transportation statement provides a desirable correction to the import total.

Seattle, Tacoma, Portland, Los Angeles, and San Diego ports are under municipal control or supervision, and each governing body prepares an annual report which includes water-borne-traffic statistics in greater or less detail. These statistics do not appear to be taken from any of the federal sources already discussed but are presumably compiled from records of local origin. Statistics of trade of Seattle are compiled from the port warden's reports; those of Los Angeles, issued by the Los Angeles Board of Harbor Commissioners, are stated to be "from tonnage reports received from all available sources." The Port of Portland Commission issues statistics "compiled from data obtained through sources deemed most authentic." Likewise, the city of San Diego Harbor Department issues a statistical report without an accompanying explanation of source or method.

Each of the reports named above contains data which purport to embrace all water-borne commerce of the specified port. Each distinguishes, under one caption or another, foreign, intercoastal, coastwise, and noncontiguous-domestic water traffic. The quantity unit is usually the short ton, and considerable detail is available in each report as to both commodities and countries or regions of origin and destination. Some figures in terms of value are likewise reported, as are vessel movements, usually by nationality.

In so far as statistics from these sources may be accepted on faith, they constitute a useful addition to regional traffic data. They are much more detailed for the individual ports than any federal statistics published; they undertake not only to include all types of water-borne traffic but to distinguish among them as well. It is obvious, however, that one cannot feel too comfortable about accepting them at their face value in the absence, as a rule, of any specific knowledge as to how they are collected or tabulated.

E. Statistical Tables

TABLE I

PACIFIC COAST STATES, ECONOMIC STATISTICS, 1930*

	Washington	Oregon	California	Pacific States	Percentage Pacific States of Continental United States
Land area (square miles)...	66,836	95,607	155,652	318,095	11
Population	1,563,396	953,786	5,677,251	8,194,433	7
Density of population per square mile*a*	23.4	10.0	36.5	25.8	
Number of cities over 50,000 inhabitants*b*	3	1	11	15	
Percentage urban population*c*	56.6	51.3	73.3	67.5	
Persons in gainful occupations:					
Agriculture	104,077	81,879	332,024	517,980	5
Forestry and fishing.......	31,921	18,632	12,944	63,497	26
Extraction of minerals....	5,720	2,167	39,745	47,630	5
Manufacturing and mechanical industries......	188,411	107,166	636,564	932,141	7
Transportation	60,234	36,491	199,228	295,953	8
Trade	93,536	55,449	436,619	585,604	10
Public service	15,996	6,241	60,741	82,978	10
Professional service	48,988	31,947	235,386	316,321	10
Domestic and professional service	64,480	39,153	294,074	397,708	8
Clerical occupations.......	51,367	30,520	253,320	335,207	8
Amount of income tax returns:					
Corporation	$2,686,000	$1,517,000	$36,114,000	$40,317,000	5.7
Individual	$2,750,000*d*	$1,074,000	$27,136,000	$30,960,000*d*	6.7
Taxes—amount per capita*ef*	$47.13	$49.55	$48.97	$48.61	
Total assessed valuation of property subject to general property tax..........	$1,253,000,000	$1,125,000,000	$8,809,000,000	$11,187,000,000	7
Banks—number reporting...	259	169	363	791	4
Total resources	$426,983,000	$241,125,000	$3,505,619,000	$4,173,727,000	7

* Data from *Statistical Abstract of the United States* and the Fifteenth Census of the United States.

a Population density for the United States, 41.3.
b Number of cities in United States with population of 50,000 or over, 191.
c Percentage for United States, 56.2.
d Includes figures for Alaska.
e Figures for 1922.
f Per capita taxes for United States, $32.23.

TABLE I (Continued)

	Washington	Oregon	California	Pacific States	Percentage Pacific States of Continental United States
Wealth[e]					
Real property and improvements	$3,257,299,000	$2,089,511,000	$8,360,722,000	$13,707,532,000	8
Live stock	$60,918,000	$75,176,000	$191,108,000	$327,202,000	5
Farm implements and machinery	$40,416,000	$31,242,000	$102,632,000	$174,290,000	7
Manufacturing, machinery, tools, and implements	$203,604,000	$83,651,000	$438,775,000	$726,030,000	5
Railroads and their equipment	$390,042,000	$365,252,000	$710,573,000	$1,465,867,000	7
Street railways, shipping, waterworks, etc.	$247,806,000	$184,070,000	$1,057,560,000	$1,489,436,000	10
All other	$922,320,000	$590,557,000	$4,170,364,000	$5,683,241,000	8
Total wealth	$5,122,000,000	$3,419,000,000	$15,032,000,000	$23,573,000,000	7
Total wealth per capita[g]	$3,600	$4,182	$4,007	$3,934	
Wholesale trade:[h]					
Number of establishments	2,631	1,439	9,751	13,821	8
Net sales	$1,147,136,000	$466,831,000	$4,159,323,000	$5,773,290,000	8
Retail trade:[h]					
Number of stores	22,110	14,570	85,691	122,371	8
Net sales	$761,808,000	$455,931,000	$3,216,863,000	$4,428,602,000	9
Per capita sales[i]	$487	$478	$566	$540	
Gross postal receipts	$8,719,000	$5,436,000	$37,223,000	$51,378,000	8
Telephones per 1,000 population[j]	190	207	268	242	
Production of electric power:					
Generated by water power[k]	2,290,000,000	772,000,000	6,804,000,000	9,866,000,000	30
Generated by fuel power[k]	265,000,000	447,000,000	2,144,000,000	2,856,000,000	5
Developed water power[l]	766,000	299,000	2,301,000	3,365,000	25
Potential water power available					
90 per cent of the time[m]	7,145,000	3,665,000	4,603,000	15,413,000	40
50 per cent of the time[m]	11,225,000	5,894,000	6,674,000	23,793,000	40

[g] Total per capita wealth of the United States, $2,918.

[h] Figures for 1929.

[i] Per capita retail sales for United States, $400.

[j] Figures for 1927. Number per 1,000 population of United States, 155.

[k] Production in kilowatt-hours.

[l] January, 1930. Data cover capacity of actual installation of water wheels and turbines in plants of 100 horsepower or more.

[m] Figures in horsepower.

TABLE I (*Concluded*)

	Washington	Oregon	California	Pacific States	Percentage Pacific States of Continental United States
Rural road mileage:					
All types...................	43,881	51,617	76,964	172,462	6
Surfaced roads.............	16,870	13,931	25,647	56,448	8
State gasoline taxes (total gross receipts).............	$7,253,000	$6,199,000	$34,870,000	$48,322,000	10
Motor vehicle registrations[n]	446,062	273,625	2,041,356	2,761,043	10
Railway mileage.............	5,542	3,456	8,240	17,238	7
Irrigation:					
Area included in enterprises (acres)[o]	915,379	1,478,128	8,075,895	10,469,402	34
Capital invested...........	$40,562,000	$38,755,000	$450,968,000	$530,285,000	51
Lumber — reported production (board feet)..........	5,502,000,000	3,654,000,000	1,514,000,000[p]	10,670,000,000[p]	41
Fisheries—value of products	$8,334,800	$2,256,300	$12,433,000	$23,064,100	24
Mineral production (value)..	$20,076,000	$6,170,000	$479,050,000	$505,296,000	12
Crude petroleum production[q]	....	....	227,329,000	227,329,000	25
Manufacturing industries:[h]					
Number of establishments	3,672	2,463	12,019	18,154	9
Wage-earners (average for year)	114,830	65,505	290,911	471,246	5
Value of products.........	$795,562,000	$411,769,000	$3,103,350,000	$4,310,681,000	6
Value added by manufacture	$367,149,000	$206,542,000	$1,349,191,000	$1,922,882,000	6

[n] Includes passenger cars, motor trucks, and road tractors.
[o] Irrigable area.
[p] Figures include Nevada.
[q] Figures in barrels of 42 gallons.

TABLE II

ALASKA AND HAWAII, ECONOMIC STATISTICS, 1930*

	Alaska	Hawaii
Area (square miles)	586,400	6,407
Population	59,278	368,336
Density of population per square mile	0.1	57.5
Number of cities over 50,000 in population	....	1
Persons in gainful occupations	27,752	154,270
Agriculture	1,198	63,907
Forestry and fishing	5,187	1,785
Extraction of minerals	4,787	250
Manufacturing and mechanical industries	3,034	21,028
Transportation	3,006	10,780
Trade	1,746	13,141
Public service	915	21,387
Professional service	1,406	8,533
Domestic and personal service	6,099	12,595
Industry not specified	374	864
Amount of income tax returns:		
Corporation	$35,000	$3,858,305
Individual	....[a]	972,000
Reporting banks:		
Number of banks	16	19
Total resources	$12,390,000	$114,035,000
Gross postal receipts	$104,000	$774,000
Developed water power[b]	36,000	32,000[c]
Potential water power available:		
90 per cent of the time[c]	1,000,000	19,000
50 per cent of the time[c]	2,500,000	28,000
Motor vehicle registration[d]	3,002	47,824
Railway mileage	790	232
Fisheries—value of products	$37,679,000	......
Mineral production	$13,707,000	......

* Data from *Statistical Abstract of the United States* and the Fifteenth Census of the United States.

[a] Figures combined with Washington.
[b] Capacity of actual installation, horsepower.
[c] Capacity in 1928, horsepower.
[d] Passenger cars and motor trucks combined.

TABLE III

MARITIME COMMERCE OF PRINCIPAL UNITED STATES PACIFIC PORTS,
1925–1930*

(All figures in thousand long tons)

Ports by Calendar Years	Total Commerce			Foreign		Intercoastal		Coastwise[a]		Non-contiguous	
	Total	In-bound	Out-bound	In-bound	Out-bound	In-bound	Out-bound	In-bound	Out-bound	In-bound	Out-bound
San Francisco											
1925.........	26,223	15,499	10,724	958	1,860	881	1,035	12,704	7,321	956	507
1926.........	25,104	15,272	9,832	1,016	2,097	1,038	1,111	12,247	6,149	971	475
1927.........	24,281	14,254	10,027	981	2,282	997	1,372	11,581	5,921	694	453
1928.........	25,747	16,215	9,532	1,139	2,542	971	1,386	12,989	5,145	1,115	460
1929.........	28,310	19,251	9,059	1,194	2,482	1,131	1,286	15,903	4,848	1,023	441
1930.........	23,274	15,452	7,822	1,127	2,060	916	1,151	12,400	4,212	1,009	398
Los Angeles											
1925.........	18,316	3,748	14,568	393	3,231	825	3,153	2,491	7,954	39	230
1926.........	20,981	4,498	16,483	452	4,435	962	3,873	3,039	7,888	44	287
1927.........	22,978	5,031	17,947	511	5,663	989	3,968	3,485	7,936	46	379
1928.........	23,152	5,041	18,111	601	5,739	1,100	2,600	3,290	9,537	50	235
1929.........	27,276	6,162	21,114	685	6,054	1,373	3,400	4,026	11,341	79	318
1930.........	28,122	7,471	20,651	647	5,855	1,038	3,017	5,722	11,328	64	451
Seattle											
1925.........	7,685	5,457	2,228	428	546	242	370	4,593	993	195	319
1926.........	8,349	5,833	2,516	403	786	258	306	4,924	1,103	247	321
1927.........	8,293	5,679	2,614	455	804	251	326	4,809	1,164	163	319
1928.........	8,638	6,168	2,470	449	720	284	342	5,184	1,078	250	330
1929.........	7,904	5,142	2,762	445	718	315	357	4,042	1,380	340	307
1930.........	6,251	4,129	2,122	360	520	262	280	3,117	1,015	390	307
Tacoma											
1925.........	3,888	2,541	1,347	336	455	22	370	2,072	493	111	29
1926.........	4,454	2,959	1,495	359	528	27	442	2,471	494	102	30
1927.........	4,314	2,920	1,394	391	587	33	359	2,394	417	102	31
1928.........	5,038	3,541	1,497	386	601	37	342	3,043	522	76	32
1929.........	3,761	1,737	2,024	391	667	50	356	1,220	972	77	29
1930.........	2,754	1,470	1,284	364	486	52	296	980	472	73	30
Portland											
1925.........	3,634	2,002	1,632	106	746	204	352	1,691	508	2	7
1926.........	4,377	2,073	2,304	113	1,527	225	378	1,729	388	6	10
1927.........	4,500	2,153	2,347	126	1,644	193	350	1,832	349	3	3
1928.........	4,550	2,315	2,235	122	1,304	208	473	1,981	447	4	11
1929.........	4,765	2,480	2,285	109	1,377	234	419	2,132	478	6	11
1930.........	4,521	2,576	1,945	95	1,117	209	341	2,264	476	8	10

* Data from United States Shipping Board.

[a] These figures apparently include a large volume of purely local traffic, particularly within the Puget Sound area. They are generally much larger than the corresponding figures published by the several reports.

TABLE III (*Continued*)

Ports by Calendar Years	Total Commerce			Foreign		Intercoastal		Coastwise[a]		Non-contiguous	
	Total	In-bound	Out-bound	In-bound	Out-bound	In-bound	Out-bound	In-bound	Out-bound	In-bound	Out-bound
Everett											
1925........	1,660	875	785	9	165	3	375	863	234	1	11
1926........	1,566	911	655	10	145	6	500	896	...	...	8
1927........	1,782	975	807	16	187	2	418	956	185	...[b]	18
1928........	2,287	1,433	854	4	235	2	434	1,427	180	1	5
1929........	1,829	878	951	8	217	2	405	867	325	1	3
1930........	1,195	297	898	15	202	7	312	277	377	...	7
Grays Harbor											
1925........	1,613	90	1,523	1	466	1	315	88	732	...	10
1926........	2,279	101	2,178	3	489	1	356	98	1,120	...	13
1927........	2,336	120	2,216	1	652	2	486	117	1,079	...	19
1928........	2,140	157	1,983	2	602	4	492	151	874	...	16
1929........	1,871	168	1,703	2	611	8	446	159	618	...	28
1930........	1,197	166	1,031	2	347	6	263	159	405	...	15
Other Pacific ports											
1925........	8,855	3,588	5,267	311	838	53	400	3,205	3,881	19	148
1926........	10,105	4,331	5,774	238	1,177	55	557	3,910	3,896	28	144
1927........	11,159	4,765	6,394	306	1,501	61	585	4,383	4,166	14	142
1928........	11,542	4,657	6,885	323	1,671	70	617	4,239	4,443	26	154
1929........	8,628	2,627	6,001	351	1,467	52	717	2,194	3,697	29	120
1930........	9,074	2,837	6,237	295	1,377	54	842	2,467	3,909	21	109
Total Pacific											
1925........	71,874	33,801	38,073	2,542	8,326	2,231	6,371	27,706	22,117	1,322	1,260
1926........	77,215	35,978	41,227	2,693	11,385	2,573	7,524	29,314	21,039	1,399	1,290
1927........	79,643	35,897	43,746	2,786	13,321	2,529	7,844	29,557	21,218	1,025	1,363
1928........	83,093	39,527	43,566	3,026	13,412	2,675	6,687	32,304	22,226	1,521	1,241
1929........	84,345	38,447	45,898	3,185	13,593	3,164	7,387	30,543	23,659	1,555	1,259
1930........	76,387	34,399	41,988	2,905	11,965	2,542	6,502	27,387	22,194	1,565	1,327

[b] Less than one thousand long tons.

TABLE IV

Tonnage of Principal Commodities in Foreign Trade, Leading Pacific Ports, 1922–1930*

(All figures in thousand long tons)

	1922	1923	1924	1925	1926	1927	1928	1929	1930
					LOS ANGELES				
Imports, total	182.5	322.4	578.2	418.1	425.5	505.1	530.7	645.8	674.1
Provisions	17.5	31.2	13.2	14.1	22.8	43.9	55.4	64.9	53.1
Lumber	50.4	82.6	193.4	88.1	74.3	99.7	78.8	75.2	93.9
Paper	30.3	43.9	60.4	62.7	36.1	54.4	53.9	47.2	66.0
Non-metallic minerals	...ᵃ	29.9	36.5	34.0	78.0	61.1	55.1	91.8	93.6
Metals and manufactures.....	15.4	55.1	47.6	46.1	60.8	85.3	72.5	82.8	60.0
Fertilizer	8.5	28.6	31.3	19.7	35.5	36.3	42.0	46.3	38.7
Rubber	...ᵃ	...ᵃ	...ᵃ	...ᵃ	...ᵃ	5.3	5.5	28.7	30.3
Exports, total	372.3	1,522.9	2,737.1	3,333.8	3,734.2	5,052.4	5,895.9	5,664.7	6,421.5
Petroleum	315.4	1,429.0	2,636.3	3,223.1	3,619.5	4,857.0	5,658.8	5,331.0	6,035.7
Total exports except petroleum.....	56.9	93.9	100.8	110.7	114.7	195.4	237.1	333.8	385.8
Fruits	6.1	23.3	11.8	10.7	11.2	26.5	28.9	41.7	49.4
Cotton	12.3	7.7	4.9	14.4	12.8	38.2	25.5	59.2	61.7
Paper stock and manufactures.....	...ᵃ	9.8	13.7	18.6	21.8	27.3	33.8	40.6	43.4

* Data from United States Shipping Board. All commodities not included.

ᵃ Not reported separately.

TABLE IV (Continued)

	1922	1923	1924	1925	1926	1927	1928	1929	1930
	SAN FRANCISCO—OAKLAND (including other Bay ports)								
Imports, total	762.2	1,092.2	847.3	901.6	973.8	1,000.2	1,071.4	1,179.6	1,189.1
Provisions	...[a]	85.0	55.3	83.2	83.8	84.1	117.4	118.7	110.1
Nuts	71.9	98.7	88.8	101.7	132.5	140.4	154.6	187.1	131.1
Vegetable oils	49.1	...[a]	28.4	64.1	40.5	61.1	29.3	50.7	57.2
Coffee	59.3	61.1	69.3	58.2	61.8	55.7	64.8	62.6	62.8
Sugar	49.0	108.8	67.6	93.2	86.9	70.3	103.0	105.5	111.5
Textiles	58.4	77.8	68.1	69.3	85.6	74.0	79.6	94.7	121.8
Lumber	...[a]	...[a]	38.0	41.7	46.7	41.2	39.9	48.2	45.7
Paper	...[a]	...[a]	58.5	57.9	54.3	76.7	70.2	73.4	76.1
Non-metallic minerals	125.6[b]	175.8[b]	83.7	80.0	82.6	76.5	135.2	121.2	119.9
Metals and manufactures	...[a]	...[a]	84.9	58.4	97.6	124.2	95.7	87.3	103.8
Chemicals	...[a]	...[a]	43.6	56.7	60.4	63.7	66.5	84.3	75.4
Exports, total	1,338.8	1,986.6	1,891.5	1,779.6	2,085.0	2,214.2	2,410.4	2,602.7	2,218.8
Fish	...[a]	...[a]	21.9	20.8	29.0	33.0	28.4	33.6	35.5
Grain	442.5	420.2	312.5	225.0	344.4	353.1	279.8	346.6	287.5
Fruits and vegetables	129.7	...[a]	167.7	187.7	243.0	237.4	314.7	365.0	228.9
Lumber	34.8	70.5	60.3	62.2	103.4	105.2	93.1	100.8	84.5
Paper	...[a]	...[a]	30.4	26.9	31.3	27.5	29.9	23.0	26.0
Petroleum	435.3	1,004.1	1,048.7	936.6	1,006.4	1,154.1	1,356.1	1,387.8	1,230.5
Salt	...[a]	...[a]	29.8	29.6	35.3	29.3	35.7	40.9	28.2
Metals and manufactures	82.1	102.4	45.0	46.1	63.4	54.5	71.9	65.4	68.1
Chemicals	...[a]	25.5	25.7	42.7	55.7	26.7	27.2	25.0	22.9

[b] Listed as "coal" in 1922, 1923.

TABLE IV (Continued)

	1922	1923	1924	1925	1926	1927	1928	1929	1930
PORTLAND									
Imports, total	45.9	83.7	95.1	98.7	103.2	119.8	139.2	106.3	108.6
Copra	...[c]	23.9	22.3	14.7	17.9	21.0	31.4	32.0	28.1
Provisions	2.8	6.7	...[a]	13.4	6.8	12.2	17.6	14.4	12.3
Metals and manufactures....	2.1	5.4	8.4	15.7	15.4	20.6	13.0	10.7	14.9
Exports, total	1,504.9	931.6	1,464.7	910.7	1,111.2	1,355.5	1,717.4	1,416.6	1,304.9
Grain	1,011.7	511.0	804.3	390.3	511.0	761.6	1,071.3	646.8	618.0
Lumber	425.9	377.7	622.8	459.3	517.3	467.6	587.4	663.9	599.0
Fruit	11.1	25.4	23.5	42.2	33.9	77.7	32.2	72.0	52.1
Metals and manufactures....	8.6	5.4	2.8	4.9	31.5	29.7	12.2	8.3	12.9
TACOMA									
Imports, total	199.0	250.2	355.0	322.0	343.8	382.9	392.2	379.8	404.7
Gold and silver ore........	...[d]	...[d]	...[a]	107.7	104.6	110.9	115.9	104.6	91.0
Copper	...[d]	...[d]	206.5	168.5	180.9	235.3	230.4	223.0	245.4
Lumber	...[a]	...[a]	...[a]	...[a]	5.4	5.4	13.7	10.9	17.8
Provisions	...[a]	6.3	...[a]	...[a]	7.8	8.9	13.4	...[a]	...[a]
Exports, total	446.1	400.9	646.7	432.0	534.6	549.9	582.0	646.5	590.2
Grain	184.0	141.4	211.2	78.5	96.2	98.7	107.4	152.7[e]	122.0[f]
Lumber	202.2	197.7	334.1	271.8	325.7	327.8	374.9	394.4	403.0
Metals and manufactures....	46.5	35.0	74.2	59.3	24.1	90.6	80.3	78.0	48.8

[c] Nuts, largely from the Philippines (probably coconuts), 9,994 tons.
[d] Not reported separately. "Ores and metals" totaled 126,274 tons in 1922; 184,411 tons in 1923; and 84,474 tons in 1924.
[e] Listed as wheat and wheat flour.
[f] Flour (wheat).

TABLE IV (*Concluded*)

SEATTLE

	1922	1923	1924	1925	1926	1927	1928	1929	1930
Imports, total	196.9	346.9	337.8	424.9	400.2	448.1	448.8	455.5	423.3
Provisions	13.7	50.5	18.6	29.6	15.6	22.9	41.9	33.6	26.6
Vegetable oils	8.1	24.8	21.8	34.0	29.3	36.2	23.9	24.6	22.1
Vegetable fiber	...[a]	...[a]	34.7	24.9	24.9	25.5	31.1	23.1	23.5
Silk	26.2[b]	57.6[b]	16.2	19.8	17.4	18.9	19.4	19.5	14.8
Lumber	18.0[a]	23.4[a]	29.7	36.0	8.5	21.8	30.4	23.4	24.1
Paper	18.0	23.4	26.7	19.1	34.3	22.7	24.6	20.0	24.2
Coal	65.0	69.7	53.7	77.8	82.3	78.6	59.2	53.6	54.8
Non-metallic minerals	9.2	19.1[a]	34.2	...[a]	...[a]	97.1	83.1	101.1	81.7
Chemicals	...[a]	...[a]	6.0	26.7	14.0	18.6	29.3	33.0	33.4
Exports, total	653.0	526.9	781.6	607.9	663.5	768.0	817.8	744.2	628.5
Animal, fish, and dairy products....	211.3[a]	190.2[a]	254.6[a]	54.0	47.8	46.2	30.6	37.6	32.0
Grain	...[a]	...[a]	...[a]	148.0	109.8	243.4	332.7	234.5	189.6
Fruits and nuts	...[a]	...[a]	...[a]	26.4	38.0	48.3	39.4	104.8	66.9
Lumber	285.8	180.6	320.4	224.8	274.7	255.7	277.6	224.5	189.7
Metals and manufactures.......	50.0	39.3	57.0	47.8	45.1	46.8	47.3	38.8	51.7

[a] Listed as "textiles" in 1922 and 1923.

TABLE V

VALUE OF FOREIGN TRADE BY PRINCIPAL COUNTRIES, PACIFIC DISTRICT, 1927–1930*

(All figures are in thousands of dollars)

LOS ANGELES[a]

Country	1927			1928			1929			1930		
	Total	Exports	Imports	Total	Exports	Imports	Total	Exports	Imports	Total	Exports	Imports
All countries[b]	167,714	120,574	47,140	196,250	141,899	54,351	230,014	166,329	63,685	198,543	146,455	52,088
United Kingdom	31,209	28,545	2,664	29,859	27,099	2,760	43,471	40,225	3,246	36,797	34,530	2,267
Japan	15,672	13,290	2,382	21,917	18,968	2,949	31,129	27,498	3,631	28,352	23,590	4,762
Mexico	15,042	7,407	7,635	17,143	8,712	8,431	23,598	13,463	10,135	17,573	11,414	6,159
China	8,129	7,425	704	17,008	16,124	884	12,555	11,236	1,319	13,065	10,463	2,602
Canada	11,635	7,812	3,823	12,489	9,380	3,109	11,350	8,642	2,708	10,813	7,799	3,014
Germany	12,422	8,695	3,727	11,645	6,605	5,040	13,031	7,845	5,186	12,315	8,111	4,204
British Malaya	6,832	1,192	5,640	8,297	1,018	7,279	12,594	1,835	10,759	8,704	1,048	7,656
Philippine Islands	5,730	2,672	3,058	8,205	4,637	3,568	9,470	5,007	4,463	9,543	5,443	4,100
France	4,671	2,502	2,169	7,479	5,517	1,962	7,863	5,911	1,952	5,597	4,152	1,445
Australia	5,204	5,176	28	6,408	6,372	36	10,019	9,952	67	9,063	8,766	297
Argentina	7,014	6,385	629	5,786	5,286	500	5,177	4,454	723	4,834	4,284	550
Hong Kong	3,162	2,784	378	4,254	3,961	293	2,246	1,949	297	2,997	2,744	253
Netherlands	2,223	1,686	537	2,832	2,010	822	1,655	829	826	1,320	700	620
Brazil	3,003	2,096	907	2,217	60	2,157	2,125	10	2,115	1,331	101	1,230
Colombia	1,650	521	1,129	1,492	398	1,094	1,703	382	1,321	1,698	386	1,312

* Data from *Foreign Commerce and Navigation of the United States.*

[a] San Diego, made a separate customs district on June 20, 1930, is included in this table with Los Angeles for that year in order to preserve comparability with preceding years.

[b] Included a number not enumerated below.

TABLE V (Continued)

SAN FRANCISCO

Country	1927			1928			1929			1930		
	Total	Exports	Imports	Total	Exports	Imports	Total	Exports	Imports	Total	Exports	Imports
All countries[b]	374,554	174,555	199,999	399,540	201,265	198,275	418,696	206,018	212,678	303,132	147,568	155,564
Japan	104,402	21,540	82,862	97,427	23,648	73,779	113,362	24,025	89,337	71,950	15,909	56,041
United Kingdom	42,920	39,920	3,000	45,316	41,728	3,588	42,515	39,614	2,901	33,930	30,125	3,805
China	25,201	10,680	14,521	37,681	19,659	18,022	36,442	16,421	20,021	24,310	10,241	14,069
Philippine Islands	33,308	11,826	21,482	35,398	13,606	21,792	32,273	16,087	16,186	24,962	12,127	12,835
Australia	23,757	22,371	1,386	24,975	23,038	1,937	28,720	27,258	1,462	18,371	16,680	1,691
Germany	11,550	8,449	3,101	15,444	12,339	3,105	13,648	9,943	3,705	10,682	7,650	3,032
Colombia	13,049	1,493	11,556	14,541	1,971	12,570	19,203	1,702	17,501	14,313	950	13,363
Canada	11,043	6,900	4,143	10,780	6,646	4,134	10,992	7,695	3,297	10,239	5,301	4,938
Brazil	9,130	82	9,048	9,983	54	9,929	5,501	255	5,246	5,129	262	4,867
Hong Kong	9,075	3,681	5,394	9,620	4,530	5,090	6,919	3,738	3,181	4,755	2,513	2,242
Netherlands	5,106	3,583	1,523	6,128	4,967	1,161	4,535	3,256	1,279	3,992	3,085	907
France	4,878	2,112	2,766	5,639	3,444	2,195	4,931	2,321	2,610	5,398	3,771	1,627
Argentina	4,923	2,526	2,397	4,642	3,568	1,074	5,632	4,598	1,034	2,628	1,689	939
Mexico	4,923	3,665	1,258	4,317	3,259	1,058	4,934	3,652	1,282	2,722	2,078	644
British Malaya	5,380	2,283	3,097	4,138	2,117	2,021	6,262	2,089	4,173	4,519	2,076	2,443

TABLE V (Concluded)

Country	1927			1928			1929			1930		
	Total	Exports	Imports	Total	Exports	Imports	Total	Exports	Imports	Total	Exports	Imports
OREGON												
All countries^b	92,940	78,732	14,208	76,003	63,879	12,124	85,760	66,060	19,700	57,764	46,787	10,977
United Kingdom	25,664	25,265	399	15,676	15,056	620	15,141	14,568	573	12,392	11,967	425
Japan	10,544	10,074	470	13,881	13,437	444	21,101	13,869	7,232	8,864	7,154	1,710
Philippine Islands	5,788	1,387	4,401	5,500	1,692	3,808	4,877	1,797	3,080	3,827	1,605	2,222
China	4,481	4,116	365	5,468	5,218	250	9,125	7,953	1,172	4,920	4,765	155
Germany	3,657	2,956	701	2,807	2,297	510	3,882	3,301	581	3,380	2,786	594
Netherlands	4,118	3,827	291	2,650	2,469	181	1,460	1,374	86	2,250	1,914	336
Australia	2,642	2,639	3	2,129	2,124	5	3,509	2,769	740	1,369	1,157	212
Hong Kong	973	859	114	1,314	1,247	67	1,270	1,217	53	932	894	38
WASHINGTON												
All countries^b	368,797	129,513	239,284	379,841	150,817	229,024	370,648	153,874	216,774	216,363	102,655	113,708
Japan	184,510	30,477	154,033	193,369	38,613	154,756	169,139	30,017	139,122	82,116	16,921	65,195
Canada	48,995	19,026	29,969	50,010	21,542	28,468	56,823	25,363	31,460	41,502	19,094	22,408
China	39,586	6,578	33,008	37,634	13,106	24,528	36,058	12,772	23,286	15,146	6,469	8,677
United Kingdom	20,844	19,755	1,089	18,664	17,516	1,148	22,644	20,936	1,708	18,898	18,150	748
Germany	12,565	11,713	852	15,572	14,703	869	15,307	14,364	943	7,673	6,899	774
Philippine Islands	10,572	8,760	1,812	11,747	9,660	2,087	11,926	9,922	2,004	8,668	6,583	2,085
Hong Kong	9,469	6,517	2,952	8,945	6,387	2,558	7,600	5,895	1,705	4,886	4,777	109
France	5,239	4,763	476	8,134	7,877	257	10,383	9,884	499	6,859	6,649	210
Netherlands	4,464	3,882	582	4,907	4,078	829	3,850	3,573	277	3,491	3,146	345
Mexico	3,901	794	3,107	4,000	763	3,237	5,320	1,081	4,239	4,292	579	3,713
Australia	4,626	4,585	41	3,259	3,232	27	3,880	3,817	63	1,281	1,187	94
Brazil	1,226	51	1,175	1,553	330	1,223	1,285	397	888	671	160	511
Argentina	2,289	881	1,408	1,452	1,342	110	2,104	1,923	181	1,469	1,154	315
British Malaya	656	390	266	724	546	178	543	374	169	247	162	85
Colombia	398	174	224	417	145	272	408	135	273	411	42	369

TABLE VI

INTERCOASTAL TRAFFIC AT PRINCIPAL PACIFIC COAST PORTS, BY COMMODITIES, 1926–1930*

(All figures in thousand long tons)

	1926 Atlantic	1926 Gulf	1927 Atlantic	1927 Gulf	1928 Atlantic	1928 Gulf	1929 Atlantic	1929 Gulf	1930 Atlantic	1930 Gulf
Los Angeles										
Inbound, total	754	115	899	127	778	120	1,124	198	941	269
Canned goods	13	...[a]	17	1	16	1	3	1	3	1
Paper	25	...[a]	36	1	32	1	35	2	33	3
Cotton and other textiles	20	...[a]	22	1	22	1	27	1	31	2
Sulphur	...[a]	34	...[a]	21	...[a]	34	...[a]	22	...[a]	30
Iron and steel manufactures	450	55	563	73	448	54	745	103	528	148
Machinery	23	...[a]	35	1	32	2	29	3	27	3
Chemicals	42	1	53	1	50	1	54	2	49	4
Outbound, total	3,306	163	3,815	39	3,138	44	2,811	79	3,212	204
Canned fish	18	2	10	2	16	2	16	4	15	5
Beans	17	2	26	4	27	5				
Cotton	11	1	24	1	9	...[a]	15	...[a]	16	...[a]
Petroleum and products	3,169	148	3,638	25	2,950	22	2,605	55	2,989	176
Chemicals	20	1	16	1	23	2	24	1	18	3
San Francisco										
Inbound, total	823	107	902	128	803	130	868	176	854	191
Tobacco	20	...[b]	17	...[b]	15	...[a]	22	...[a]	21	1
Textile manufactures	26	2	29	3	37	3	34	4	28	4
Paper	38	1	48	3	41	1	50	2	46	4
Sulphur	...[a]	33	...[a]	32	...[a]	30	...[a]	30	...[a]	29
Iron and steel manufactures	374		434	36	371	20	389	69	358	96
Machinery	32	1	46	2	31	2	32	6	27	3
Chemicals	59	3	64	9	62	8	66	7	66	7

* Data from the United States Shipping Board. Not all commodities included.

[a] Less than one thousand long tons.　　　[b] Not reported separately.

TABLE VI (Continued)

	1926		1927		1928		1929		1930	
	Atlantic	Gulf	Atlantic	Gulf	Atlantic	Gulf	Atlantic	Gulf	Atlantic	Gulf
Outbound, total	866	115	1,153	99	1,243	187	1,130	228	996	186
Canned fish	18	...	21	...[a]	16	1	17	1[b]	22[b]	2
Beans	22	6	20	7	29	11	...[b]	...[b]	...[b]	...[b]
Canned vegetables	52	6	74	8	88	8	...[b]	...[b]	...[b]	...[b]
Dried fruit	107	5	123	6	168	5	148	7	118	6
Canned fruit	151	26	203	26	238	29	270	42	234	27
Sugar	...[a]	4	...[a]	33	17	74	16	98	11	100
Lumber	11	...[a]	12	11[a]	...	48	15	51[a]	9	21[a]
Petroleum and products..	334	56	510	...	496	...	306	...	268	...
Copper	30	...	52	...	46	...	21	...	30	...
Portland										
Inbound, total	177	44	161	44	153	38	154	48	183	68
Sulphur	...	17	...	19	...	13	...	18	...[a]	20
Iron and steel manufactures.	82	12	72	12	69	10	66	14	88	29
Chemicals	10	...[a]	11	...[a]	11	1	10	1	10	1
Outbound, total	364	22	327	10	428	10	421	13	364	18
Wheat and flour	35	5	27	1	26	3	43	4	31	2
Canned fruit and vegetables.	8	1	19	1	17	1	32	2	32	2[c]
Lumber	249	15	210	5	310	4	296	3	228	11
Paper	6	...[a]	10	1	22	1	19	2	23	2
Grays Harbor										
Inbound, total	1	...	...[a]	1	1	2	2	5	...[a]	7
Outbound, total	354	13	378	1	496	1	462	2	383	2
Lumber	354	12	378	1	496	1	453	2	367	2

[a] Reported "vegetables and vegetable products" in place of "canned vegetables" in 1928.

TABLE VI (Concluded)

	1926		1927		1928		1929		1930	
	Atlantic	Gulf	Atlantic	Gulf	Atlantic	Gulf	Atlantic	Gulf	Atlantic	Gulf
Seattle										
Inbound, total	222	28	224	29	229	30	244	54	258	43
Iron and steel manufactures	104	13	108	15	92	12	108	30	118	17
Chemicals	15	...[a]	17	1	25	1	16	...[a]	23	...[a]
Outbound, total	297	29	298	24	290	14	351	29	315	19
Fish and products	51	11	57	12	43	5	46	11	43	9
Lumber	162	5	129	6	118	2	156	10	135	6
Magnesite	5	...	20	...	19	...	...[b]	...[b]	...[b]	...[b]
Tacoma										
Inbound, total	18	3	21	12	23	9	37	10	45	13
Iron and steel manufactures	6	1	6	7	9	3	9	2	7	3
Outbound, total	421	17	387	8	368	4	338	4	325	5
Lumber	375	15	341	6	332	2	267	3	220	2
Copper	9	...	12	...	16	...	18	...	22	...
Everett										
Inbound, total	5	...	3	...[a]	2	...	2	...	1	2
Outbound, total	488	4	427	6	431	1	418	1	372	3
Lumber	483	4	425	5	427	1	414	1	365	3

TABLE VII

PACIFIC COAST WATER-BORNE COMMERCE BY FOREIGN REGIONS, TOTAL
AND NON-TANKER CARGO, 1922–1930*

(All figures in thousand long tons)

Foreign Regions	1922	1923	1924	1925	1926	1927	1928	1929	1930
Total cargoes, all regions........	6,653	8,866	12,057	11,038	12,518	14,819	16,810	16,610	16,521
United Kingdom	1,149	1,246	1,324	1,359	1,602	1,816	1,904	2,090	2,333
North Atlantic and Baltic Europe	61	80	137	145	103	137	155	103	126
Havre-Hamburg range	461	339	467	715	799	1,020	1,217	1,385	1,401
South Atlantic Europe...........	39	37	13	15	22	85	33	60	71
West Mediterranean	96	94	43	79	30	14€	307	192	89
East Mediterranean	...	2	...ᵃ	3	8	3	1	11	19
West Indies	14	46	19	26	64	112	198	137	142
Mexico	135	420	636	316	254	276	322	389	447
Central America	126	521	594	469	720	1,114	1,229	758	753
South America									
North Coast	3	2	2	6	11	31	24	28	28
East Coast	39	238	398	372	530	910	1,213	571	413
West Coast	318	580	890	1,013	1,152	1,024	1,112	1,470	1,244
Africa									
West	11	...	...	...	...	...	...	...	3
Southeast	...ᵃ	29	16	24	20	26	25	36	51
Australasia	312	565	587	754	987	1,069	1,280	1,385	1,359
East Indies	72	113	124	101	157	213	213	283	267
East Asia	3,091	3,293	5,005	3,987	4,114	4,658	5,666	5,726	5,538
India, Persian Gulf, Red Sea.....	73	26	102	14	50	7	39	80	151
Pacific Canada	653	1,169	1,574	1,560	1,623	1,857	1,845	1,929	2,057
Atlantic Canada	...	66	126	78	273	315	27	13	29
Non-tanker cargoes, all regions..	5,660	6,103	7,938	7,008	7,929	8,844	9,888	10,171	9,576
United Kingdom	1,061	1,028	949	853	1,079	1,075	1,270	1,276	1,301
North Atlantic and Baltic Europe	61	80	137	137	97	137	150	103	119
Havre-Hamburg range	447	313	421	621	677	824	1,029	1,051	1,010
South Atlantic Europe...........	39	9	11	12	10	57	26	45	24
West Mediterranean	96	86	43	27	31	129	307	158	90
East Mediterranean	...	2	...ᵃ	3	8	1	1	2	8
West Indies	14	23	19	26	48	73	75	87	46
Mexico	80	98	130	109	187	182	204	219	215
Central America	96	127	123	129	150	150	206	284	248
South America									
North Coast	3	2	2	6	10	30	18	22	28
East Coast	39	94	82	118	135	230	263	244	209
West Coast	264	287	359	424	407	456	402	436	482
Africa									
West	11	...	...	...	...	...	...	...	...
Southeast	...ᵃ	29	16	24	20	26	25	36	41
Australasia	312	555	526	634	827	784	769	831	758
East Indies	55	73	56	64	130	135	156	228	211
East Asia	2,656	2,520	3,954	2,702	3,070	3,389	3,848	3,956	3,566
India, Persian Gulf, Red Sea.....	73	15	2	2	4	7	39	81	143
Pacific Canada	353	748	1,097	1,061	1,035	1,146	1,073	1,099	1,059
Atlantic Canada	...	18	11	79	4	13	27	13	18

* Data from the United States Shipping Board.

ᵃ Less than one thousand long tons.

TABLE VIII

Pacific Coast Imports and Exports by Foreign Regions, Total Tanker and Non-Tanker Cargo, 1922–1930*

(All figures in thousand long tons)

Foreign Regions	1922 Im-ports	1922 Ex-ports	1923 Im-ports	1923 Ex-ports	1924 Im-ports	1924 Ex-ports	1925 Im-ports	1925 Ex-ports	1926 Im-ports	1926 Ex-ports	1927 Im-ports	1927 Ex-ports	1928 Im-ports	1928 Ex-ports	1929 Im-ports	1929 Ex-ports	1930 Im-ports	1930 Ex-ports
Total cargo, all regions	1,431	5,222	2,322	6,544	2,559	9,500	2,534	8,505	2,610	9,909	2,815	12,004	2,885	13,926	3,112	13,498	3,176	13,345
Non-tanker cargo, all regions	1,385	4,276	2,308	3,796	2,552	5,886	2,534	4,474	2,503	5,336	2,745	6,069	2,796	7,093	3,014	7,158	3,099	6,477
United Kingdom																		
Total	103	1,046	204	1,042	158	1,165	96	1,263	92	1,510	71	1,745	81	1,823	93	1,996	84	2,249
Non-tanker	103	958	204	824	158	791	96	757	92	987	55	1,020	68	1,202	63	1,213	66	1,235
North Atlantic and Baltic Europe																		
Total	10	50	44	36	106	31	83	62	44	59	52	85	55	100	56	47	74	53
Non-tanker	10	50	44	36	106	31	83	55	44	52	52	85	55	95	56	47	74	45
Havre-Hamburg range																		
Total	128	334	183	156	301	166	376	338	389	410	439	552	423	794	462	923	505	897
Non-tanker	128	319	183	130	301	120	376	245	389	288	417	406	388	646	428	623	468	542
South Atlantic Europe																		
Total	2	37	5	31	7	6	5	10	4	18	5	80	4	29	3	58	4	67
Non-tanker	2	37	5	3	7	4	5	7	4	6	5	52	4	22	3	42	4	20
Western Mediterranean																		
Total	1	95	4	90	3	40	5	74	15	15	18	128	16	291	25	167	26	64
Non-tanker	1	95	4	82	3	40	5	74	15	15	18	112	16	291	25	132	26	64
Eastern Mediterranean																		
Total	...	...	...	2	...[a]	...[a]	...[a]	3	...[a]	8	...[a]	3	...[a]	1	...[a]	11	...[a]	19
Non-tanker	...	...	...	2	...[a]	...[a]	...[a]	3	...[a]	8	...[a]	1	...[a]	1	...[a]	2	...[a]	8
West Indies																		
Total	...[a]	14	6	40	1	19	...[a]	26	16	47	26	87	58	140	65	72	22	121
Non-tanker	...[a]	14	...[a]	23	1	19	...[a]	26	...[a]	47	26	48	28	47	58	28	22	24
Mexico																		
Total	60	75	21	399	33	603	27	289	97	156	68	208	117	205	143	246	101	345
Non-tanker	19	61	21	78	33	97	27	82	97	89	67	115	116	85	141	78	99	116
Central America																		
Total	56	70	81	440	71	522	64	406	66	654	54	1,060	85	1,145	131	628	122	631
Non-tanker	56	40	81	46	71	52	64	66	66	83	54	96	85	122	131	153	122	126

* Data from the United States Shipping Board.

[a] Less than one thousand long tons.

TABLE VIII (*Continued*)

Foreign Regions	1922 Im-ports	1922 Ex-ports	1923 Im-ports	1923 Ex-ports	1924 Im-ports	1924 Ex-ports	1925 Im-ports	1925 Ex-ports	1926 Im-ports	1926 Ex-ports	1927 Im-ports	1927 Ex-ports	1928 Im-ports	1928 Ex-ports	1929 Im-ports	1929 Ex-ports	1930 Im-ports	1930 Ex-ports
South America, North Coast																		
Total	3	...a	2	1	1	1	3	3	4	6	11	19	11	13	16	12	23	5
Non-tanker	3	...a	2	1	1	1	3	3	4	6	11	19	11	7	16	6	23	5
South America, East Coast																		
Total	35	4	69	170	57	341	63	309	76	454	125	785	137	1,076	73	498	62	351
Non-tanker	35	4	69	23	57	25	63	55	76	59	125	106	137	127	73	171	62	147
South America, West Coast																		
Total	123	195	156	424	160	730	132	880	143	1,009	179	844	142	970	160	1,309	212	1,082
Non-tanker	123	141	156	129	160	199	132	292	143	264	179	277	142	260	160	275	212	269
West Africa																		
Total	...a	11	...	...	...	...	...	...	...	...	...	...	...	...	...	...	...	3
Non-tanker	...a	11	...	...	...	...	...	...	...	...	...	...	...	...	...	...	...	...
Southeast Africa																		
Total	...	...a	...	29	...	16	...	24	...	20	...a	26	...	25	...	36	...a	51
Non-tanker	...	...a	...	29	...	16	...	24	...	20	...a	26	...	25	...	36	...a	40
Australasia																		
Total	114	198	163	401	60	528	45	709	45	943	27	1,042	37	1,243	58	1,291	64	1,295
Non-tanker	114	198	163	392	60	466	45	589	45	783	27	756	37	732	58	773	64	694
East Indies																		
Total	37	34	29	84	18	106	20	81	47	110	29	184	43	170	119	164	77	189
Non-tanker	33	22	27	46	18	37	20	44	47	83	29	107	43	113	95	133	77	134
East Asia (Orient)																		
Total	453	2,638	739	2,554	668	4,338	741	3,246	688	3,426	734	3,924	760	4,906	784	4,942	845	4,692
Non-tanker	453	2,204	733	1,788	661	3,293	741	1,961	688	2,383	705	2,684	756	3,091	784	3,175	826	2,741
India, Persian Gulf, Red Sea																		
Total	26	48	...	26	1	101	...a	13	...a	50	...a	7	18	21	39	42	65	86
Non-tanker	26	48	...	15	1	1	...a	2	...a	4	...a	7	18	21	39	42	65	78
Pacific Canada																		
Total	279	373	614	555	915	659	871	688	882	742	977	879	884	961	872	1,058	871	1,186
Non-tanker	279	73	614	135	915	182	871	189	881	154	977	169	884	189	872	227	871	188
Atlantic Canada																		
Total	...	...	3	63	...	126	...	79	...	273	...	315	14	13	13	...	18	10
Non-tanker	...	...	3	14	...	11	...	79	...	4	...	13	14	13	13	...	18	...

TABLE IX

PACIFIC COAST FOREIGN TRADE CARRIED IN AMERICAN, BRITISH, AND OTHER FOREIGN SHIPS, ACTUAL AND PERCENTAGES, 1922–1930*

(All figures except percentages in thousand long tons)

Fiscal Years	American	British	Other Foreign	Percentage American	American	British	Other Foreign	Percentage American
	TOTAL CARGOES				TANKER CARGOES			
Exports								
1922.....	1,979	888	2,235	38	633	188	135	67
1923.....	2,110	2,293	2,141	32	796	1,543	410	29
1924.....	3,059	3,191	3,249	32	1,412	2,106	596	34
1925.....	3,138	2,586	2,781	37	1,834	1,696	501	45
1926.....	3,369	3,521	3,019	34	1,939	2,119	514	42
1927.....	4,088	4,035	3,881	34	2,443	2,604	859	41
1928.....	4,310	4,931	4,684	31	2,678	2,954	1,202	39
1929.....	4,072	3,973	5,453	30	2,241	2,023	2,076	35
1930.....	4,191	3,598	5,556	31	2,456	2,038	2,375	36
Imports								
1922.....	608	298	525	42	23	8	15	49
1923.....	923	725	674	40	13	2	..	86
1924.....	1,098	734	736	43	7	..	..	100
1925.....	904	818	812	36	..	..	..	100
1926.....	952	880	778	36	17	..	..	100
1927.....	1,131	875	809	40	37	29	3	53
1928.....	1,200	845	840	42	57	24	8	64
1929.....	1,320	768	1,023	42	49	..	49	50
1930.....	1,277	816	1,082	40	28	29	20	36
	NON-TANKER CARGOES, LOW FREIGHT RATE				NON-TANKER CARGOES, HIGH FREIGHT RATE			
Exports								
1922.....	1,032	566	2,025	28	313	134	206	48
1923.....	967	536	1,505	32	347	215	226	44
1924.....	1,272	846	2,391	28	375	239	262	43
1925.....	940	591	1,999	27	364	299	281	39
1926.....	1,021	1,113	2,177	24	409	288	327	40
1927.....	1,270	1,102	2,687	25	376	329	335	36
1928.....	1,283	1,638	3,059	21	350	340	424	31
1929.....	1,417	1,479	2,811	25	414	471	566	29
1930.....	1,340	1,190	2,708	25	395	371	474	32
Imports								
1922.....	267	125	194	45	318	165	315	40
1923.....	396	380	209	40	515	343	465	39
1924.....	508	300	188	51	574	434	548	36
1925.....	365	404	261	35	538	414	551	36
1926.....	345	449	264	33	590	431	514	38
1927.....	573	509	338	40	521	336	468	39
1928.....	635	499	372	42	508	322	460	39
1929.....	653	517	444	41	617	252	530	44
1930.....	663	535	513	39	586	252	550	42

* Data from the United States Shipping Board.

TABLE X

PACIFIC COAST IMPORTS AND EXPORTS BY TRADE REGIONS, TONNAGE OF CARGO CARRIED IN AMERICAN, BRITISH, AND OTHER FOREIGN SHIPS, 1925–1930*

(All figures in thousand long tons)

Region	1925		1926		1927		1928		1929		1930	
	Im-ports	Ex-ports	Im-ports	Ex-ports	Im-ports	Ex-ports	Im-ports	Ex-ports	Im-ports	Ex-ports	Im-ports	Ex-ports
United Kingdom, total	96	1,263	92	1,510	71	1,745	81	1,823	93	1,996	84	2,249
American	4	254	3	187	10	205	5	210	19	167	12	267
British	61	613	57	974	55	1,108	45	1,188	32	1,183	29	1,249
Other foreign	31	395	32	348	7	437	31	425	42	646	43	734
North Atlantic and Baltic Europe, total	83	62	44	59	52	85	55	100	56	47	74	53
American	...	...[a]	...	...	...	...[a]	2	5	...	...	...	...
British	...	8	...	7	...	...[a]	...	8	...	...[a]	3	1
Other foreign	83	55	44	51	52	85	53	87	56	47	71	52
Havre-Hamburg, total	376	338	389	410	439	582	423	794	462	923	505	897
American	49	52	26	50	47	51	27	36	28	7	14	44
British	77	84	115	115	93	153	91	291	78	265	80	225
Other foreign	250	203	249	244	298	377	305	468	356	650	411	628
South Atlantic Europe, total	5	10	4	18	5	80	4	29	3	58	4	67
American	1	...	...	...	...	9	...	...[a]	...	...	...	...
British	...[a]	6	...	8	...[a]	44	2	14	...[a]	33	...	4
Other foreign	4	4	4	10	5	27	2	15	3	25	4	63
West Mediterranean, total	5	74	15	15	18	128	16	291	25	167	26	64
American	5	...[a]	6	...[a]	6	...[a]	4	...[a]	6	...[a]	5	...[a]
British	...[a]	8	...	...[a]	...	45	...	161	7	54	7	8
Other foreign	...	65	9	15	12	83	12	130	12	113	14	56

* Data from the United States Shipping Board. Horizontal and vertical totals may vary in the last digit.

a Less than one thousand tons.

TABLE X (Continued)

Region	1925		1926		1927		1928		1929		1930	
	Imports	Exports	Imports	Exports	Imports	Exports	Imports	Exports	Imports	Exports	Imports	Exports
West Indies, total	...ᵃ	26	16	47	26	87	58	140	65	72	22	121
American	...ᵃ	21	16	18	3	78	35	111	15	32	2	31
British	...ᵃ	4	...ᵃ	20	5	...ᵃ	14	16	23	29	16	36
Other foreign	...ᵃ	1	...ᵃ	8	18	8	8	13	27	11	4	54
Mexico, total	27	289	97	156	68	208	117	205	143	246	101	345
American	3	48	38	58	32	116	71	119	84	156	74	243
British	1	164	24	2	13	1	20	1	1	1	8	3
Other foreign	22	77	36	96	24	91	26	85	35	90	19	100
Central America, total	64	406	66	654	54	1,060	85	1,145	131	628	122	631
American	26	268	18	449	21	904	49	947	89	539	76	537
British	9	93	8	155	7	114	11	140	15	21	17	45
Other foreign	29	45	40	50	25	42	24	58	27	68	30	49
North Coast South America, total	3	3	4	6	11	19	11	13	16	12	23	5
American	...ᵃ	1	2	4	5	11	4	12	12	10	17	5
British	...ᵃ	...ᵃ	1	1	2	3	1	...ᵃ	...ᵃ	...ᵃ	1	...ᵃ
Other foreign	3	2	2	2	5	5	6	1	4	2	5	...
East Coast South America, total	63	309	76	454	125	785	137	1,076	73	498	62	351
American	46	130	60	84	71	215	54	281	36	127	50	89
British	7	113	7	342	...	445	32	691	...	243	...	80
Other foreign	9	66	9	28	53	125	50	104	36	127	12	182
West Coast South America, total	132	880	143	1,009	179	844	142	970	160	1,309	212	1,032
American	67	319	68	398	120	341	107	534	109	670	123	631
British	...	440	...	400	...	294	4	293	3	320	...	204
Other foreign	65	121	75	211	59	210	31	144	49	319	89	197

TABLE X (Concluded)

Region	1925 Im-ports	1925 Ex-ports	1926 Im-ports	1926 Ex-ports	1927 Im-ports	1927 Ex-ports	1928 Im-ports	1928 Ex-ports	1929 Im-ports	1929 Ex-ports	1930 Im-ports	1930 Ex-ports
Australasia, total	45	709	45	943	27	1,042	37	1,243	58	1,291	64	1,295
American	6	210	11	178	8	216	17	188	32	260	33	228
British	21	135	22	358	13	411	12	508	19	590	23	520
Other foreign	17	364	12	407	6	415	8	451	7	441	8	546
East Indies, total	20	81	47	110	29	184	43	170	119	164	77	189
American	18	57	33	64	10	81	17	47	25	65	25	95
British	1	21	5	39	15	81	19	74	35	46	16	52
Other foreign	1	2	9	7	4	22	7	50	59	53	37	42
East Asia, total	741	3,246	688	3,426	734	3,923	760	4,906	784	4,942	845	4,692
American	396	1,292	381	1,248	457	1,235	450	1,271	462	1,346	473	1,255
British	48	633	49	663	36	757	44	1,001	14	755	37	641
Other foreign	297	1,321	257	1,515	241	1,931	266	2,633	308	2,841	335	2,796
Pacific Canada, total	871	688	882	742	977	880	884	961	872	1,058	871	1,186
American	280	460	290	467	341	454	354	453	395	682	364	734
British	591	228	592	273	636	426	530	507	476	363	507	426
Other foreign	...a	1	...a	2	...	...a	...a	1	...a	12	...	26
All regions[b]	2,534	8,505	2,610	9,909	2,815	12,004	2,885	13,926	3,112	13,498	3,176	13,345
American	904	3,138	952	3,369	1,131	4,068	1,200	4,310	1,320	4,072	1,277	4,191
British	818	2,586	880	3,521	875	4,035	845	4,931	768	3,973	816	3,598
Other foreign	812	2,781	778	3,019	809	3,881	840	4,684	1,023	5,453	1,082	5,556

[b] "All regions" include East Mediterranean and Black Sea, West Africa, South and East Africa, India, Persian Gulf and Red Sea, and Atlantic Canada, not here shown separately.

F. References for Further Study

The sources of information utilized by the author are mainly of two kinds, namely, statistics, and the articles appearing in current periodicals. Most useful have proved to be the tabular reports issued by federal departments and local harbor boards; news items appearing principally in the Coast shipping and trade periodicals, notably the *Monthly Review of Business Conditions* issued by the Federal Reserve Bank of San Francisco, *Daily Commercial News* (San Francisco), *Harbour and Shipping* (Vancouver), *Pacific Shipper,* and *Shipping Register,* have been of immeasurable aid in supplementing reports and studies appearing in countless sources. Although considerable use has necessarily been made of references in checking historical and technical data, the author has discovered nowhere any volume or series of volumes which cover adequately the maritime developments of the West Coast starting with the completion of the Panama Canal; hence, there is scant reference in the preceding pages to authorities.

For the student, however, who desires access to a list of published works which would serve as a broad, suggestive basis for further research, the writer has compiled the following selected bibliography dealing with important phases of subjects treated in this volume.

AMERICAN ASSOCIATION FOR THE ADVANCEMENT OF SCIENCE, PACIFIC COAST COMMISSION, *Nature and Science on the Pacific Coast* (1915)
AMERICAN ASSOCIATION OF PORT AUTHORITIES, *Bibliographic Notes on Ports and Harbors* (1926)
———. *Port Glossary* (1927)
AMERICAN BUREAU OF SHIPPING, *The American Merchant Marine* (1933)
ANDERSON, J., *The Last Survivors in Sail* (1933)
ANSTEY, V., *The Trade of the Indian Ocean* (1929)
BAIN, H. F., *Ores and Industry in the Far East* (1933)
BAKER, J. N. L., *A History of Geographical Discovery and Exploration* (1932)
BAKER, O. E., *Agricultural Regions of North America,* from *Economic Geography*
  Part VIII, *The Pacific Subtropical Crops Region* (April and July, 1930)
  Part IX, *The North Pacific Hay and Pasture Region* (April 1931)
  Part X, *The Grazing and Irrigated Crops Region* (October 1932)
  Part XI, *The Columbia Plateau Wheat Region* (April 1933)
BANCROFT, H. H., *History of the Pacific States* (1884)
———. *The New Pacific* (1900)
BEAZLEY, C. R., *The Dawn of Modern Geography* (3 vols., 1897–1906)
BENSON, W. S., *The Merchant Marine* (1923)
BERGLUND, A., *Ocean Transportation* (1931)
BOGART, E. L., *Economic History of the American People* (1930)
BOLTON, H. E., *History of the Americas* (1928)
———. *Outposts of Empire* (1931)
BONE, S. C., *Alaska, Its Past, Present, and Future* (1925)
BOWEN, F. C., *The History of the Canadian Pacific Line* (1928)

507

BOWMAN, I., *Forest Physiography* (1911)
————. *The New World: Problems in Political Geography* (4th Revised Edition, 1929)
————. *The Pioneer Fringe* (1931)
BREBNER, J. B., *The Explorers of North America, 1492–1806* (1933)
BRIGHAM, A. P., *The United States of America* (1927)
BROOKINGS INSTITUTION, "Service Monographs of the United States Government":
  No. 8, *Steamboat Inspection Service* (1922)
  No. 15, *Bureau of Navigation* (1923)
  No. 18, *Interstate Commerce Commission* (1923)
  No. 27, *Office of the Chief of Engineers* (1923)
  No. 29, *Bureau of Foreign and Domestic Commerce* (1924)
  No. 44, *Panama Canal* (1927)
  No. 63, *United States Shipping Board* (1931)
BRYCE, JAMES, *The American Commonwealth* (2 vols., new ed., 1922–1923)
BUREAU OF RAILWAY ECONOMICS, *An Economic Survey of Inland Waterway Transportation in the United States* (1930)
————. *Statistics of Waterways, United States* (1934)
CALVIN, H. C., and STUART, E. G., *The Merchant Shipping Industry* (1925)
CHAPMAN, C. E., *A History of California: The Spanish Period* (1921)
CLARK, A. H., *The Clipper Ship Era* (1911)
CLARK, G., *Economic Rivalries in China* (1932)
CLELAND, R. G., *A History of California: The American Period* (1926)
CLELAND, R. G., and HARDY, O., *The March of Industry* (1929)
CLOWES, E. S., *Shipways to the Sea* (1929)
COFFEE, F., *Forty Years on the Pacific* (1920)
COMMITTEE ON RECENT ECONOMIC CHANGES OF THE PRESIDENT'S CONFERENCE ON UNEMPLOYMENT, *Recent Economic Changes* (2 volumes, 1929)
CONDLIFFE, J. B., *A Pacific Bibliography* (1927)
CORNFORD, L. C., *A Century of Sea Trade* (1924)
CROCKATT, P. C., *Trans-Pacific Commerce and Shipping* (1921)
CUNNINGHAM, B., *Port Economics* (1926)
Customhouse Guide (annual)
DAGGETT, S. R., *Principles of Inland Transportation* (1928)
————. *Railroad Consolidation West of the Mississippi River* (1933)
DANA, R. H., *Two Years Before the Mast* (1840, and numerous later editions)
DENNETT, T., *Americans in Eastern Asia: A Critical Study of the United States with Reference to China, Japan, Korea in the Nineteenth Century* (1922)
DENTON, V. L., *The Far West Coast* (1924)
DOBIE, C. C., *San Francisco: A Pageant* (1933)
DOLLAR, R., *One Hundred Years of Steam Navigation* (1931)
DUBOSCQ, A., *Le Problème du Pacifique* (1927)
DUGGAN, S., *The Two Americas* (1934)
DULLES, F. R., *The Old China Trade* (1930)
DURAND, E. D., *American Industry and Commerce* (1930)
ELDERTON, W. P., *Shipping Problems, 1916–1921* (1928)
ELY, R. T., HESS, R. H., LEITH, C. K., and CARVER, T. N., *The Foundations of National Prosperity* (1920)
ETHERTON, P. T., and TILTMAN, H. H., *The Pacific: A Forecast* (1928)
FAYLE, C. E., *The War and the Shipping Industry* (1927)
————. *Short History of the Shipping Industry* (1931)

Fox, F., *The Mastery of the Pacific* (1928)

Fuller, G. W., *A History of the Pacific Northwest* (1931)

Gilbert, E. W., *The Exploration of Western America, 1800–1850* (1933)

Gillespie, J. E., *A History of Geographical Discovery, 1400–1800* (1933)

Golder, F. A., *Behring's Voyages* (1922)

Grady, H. F., and Carr, R. M., *The Port of San Francisco* (1933)

Great Britain, Admiralty, *Alaska (south-east) Pilot* (1920 and supplements)

———. *America (Central) and United States (West coasts) Pilot* (4th edition, 1925, and supplements)

———. *British Columbia Pilot* (2 volumes, 1923, and supplements)

Great Britain, Imperial Shipping Committee, *Final Report on the Deferred Rebate System* (Cmd. 1802, 1923)

Great Britain, Royal Commission on Shipping Rings, *Report* (Cd. 4668, 1909)

Greely, A. W., *Handbook of Alaska, 1924* (3d edition, 1925)

Hallberg, C. W., *The Suez Canal: Its History and Diplomatic Importance* (1932)

Hardy, A. C., *American Ship Types* (1927)

———. *Oil Ships and Sea Transports* (1931)

———. *Seaways and Sea Trade* (1927)

Henry, A. K., *The Panama Canal and the Intercoastal Trade* (1929)

Hittell, T. H., *History of California, 1885–1897* (4 volumes, 1898)

Hoskins, H. L., *British Routes to India* (1928)

Huntington, E., *Climate and Civilization* (1924)

Huntington, E., and Williams, F. E., *Business Geography* (2d edition, 1926)

Hurley, E. N., *The New Merchant Marine* (1920)

Hutchinson, L., *The Panama Canal and International Trade Competition* (1925)

Innes, H. A., and Plumptre, A. F. W., eds., *The Canadian Economy and Its Problems* (1934)

Institute of Pacific Relations, *Economic Handbook of the Pacific Area* (1934)

———. *Problems of the Pacific* (1927, 1929, 1931, and 1933 biennial conferences)

International Chamber of Commerce, Report of the Subcommittee of American Section, *Thirty Years of Europe–United States Trade* (1931)

Johnson, E. R., *Panama Canal Traffic and Tolls* (1912)

———. *The Panama Canal and Commerce* (1916)

Johnson, E. R., Huebner, G. G., and Wilson, G. L., *Principles of Transportation* (1928)

Johnstone, J., *A Study of the Oceans* (1926)

Jones, E., *Principles of Railway Transportation* (1924)

Keiler, H., *American Shipping, Its History and Economic Condition* (1913)

Kidd, H. C., *Regulation of Intercoastal Commerce* (1932)

Kirkaldy, A. W., *British Shipping: Its History, Organisation and Importance* (1914)

Latourette, K. S., *The History of Early Relations between the United States and China, 1784–1844* (1917)

Lawson, W., *Pacific Steamers* (1927)

League of Nations, *World Economic Survey* (annual)

Lewis, H. T., and Miller, S. I., editors, *Economic Resources of the Pacific Northwest* (1923)

Lippincott, I., *Economic Resources and Industries of the World* (1930)

Lloyd's Register of Shipping (annual)

LYMAN, G. D., *The Saga of the Comstock Lode* (1934)

MACARTHUR, W., *Last Days of Sail on the West Coast, San Francisco Harbor* (1930)

MacELWEE, R. S., *Port Development* (1925)

———. *Ports and Terminal Facilities* (1926)

McKEE, M. M., *The Ship Subsidy Question in United States Politics* (1922)

McKENZIE, R. D., *The Metropolitan Community* (1933)

MAHAN, A. T., *The Problem of Asia and Its Effect upon International Policies* (1900)

MAXWELL, L. W., *Discriminating Duties and the American Merchant Marine* (1926)

MEARS, E. G., *Regulation and Promotion of Pacific Shipping* (1933)

———. *San Francisco's Trans-Pacific Shipping* (1929)

MEARS, E. G., and TOBRINER, M. O., *Principles and Practices of Coöperative Marketing* (1926)

MEYER, B. H., and OTHERS, *History of Transportation in the United States before 1860* (1917)

MILLER, G. J., and PARKINS, A. E., *Geography of North America* (1928)

MITCHELL, J., *Shipbuilding and the Shipbuilding Industry* (1926)

MORISON, S. E., *The Maritime History of Massachusetts, 1783–1860* (1923)

MOULTON, H. G., *Japan; an Economic and Financial Appraisal* (1931)

———. *Waterways versus Railways* (1926)

MOULTON, H. G., and ASSOCIATES, *The American Transportation Problem* (1933)

NATIONAL CONFERENCE ON THE MERCHANT MARINE, *Annual Proceedings* (1928–33)

NATIONAL FOREIGN TRADE COUNCIL, *Ocean Shipping* (1917)

NATIONAL FOREIGN TRADE COUNCIL (Convention Headquarters), *Official Report of Annual Conventions* (especially San Francisco, 1920, Seattle, 1925, Los Angeles, 1930, and Honolulu, 1932)

NATIONAL INDUSTRIAL CONFERENCE BOARD, *The American Merchant Marine Problem* (1929)

———. *Trends in the Foreign Trade of the United States* (1930)

NEWTON, A. P., *The Great Age of Discovery* (1932)

ORCHARD, J. E., *Japan's Economic Position: the Progress of Industrialization* (1930)

PAINE, R. D., *The Old Merchant Marine* (1921)

PAXSON, F. L., *History of the American Frontier, 1767–1893* (1924)

———. *The Last American Frontier* (1910)

PRATT, E. E., *International Trade in Staple Commodities* (1928)

PRESIDENT'S COMMITTEE ON RECENT SOCIAL TRENDS, *Recent Social Trends in the United States* (2 volumes, 1933)

RICHARDSON, A., and HURD, A., editors, *Brassey's Naval & Shipping Annual*

RIEGEL, R. E., *The Story of the Western Railroads* (1926)

RITTER, A. H., *Transportation Economics of the Great Lakes–St. Lawrence Ship Canal* (1925)

ROGERS, S. R. H., *The Pacific* (1931)

ROOSEVELT, N., *The Restless Pacific* (1928)

ROWLEY, R. C., *The Silk Industry and Trade* (1919)

ROYCE, J., *California* (1886)

SALTER, J. A., *Allied Shipping Control: An Experiment in International Administration* (1921)

SARGENT, A. J., *Seaways of the Empire* (1918)

SCHMECKEBIER, L. F., *The Statistical Work of the National Government* (1925)

SEMPLE, E. C., *American History and Its Geographic Conditions* (1903)

———. *Influences of Geographic Environment* (1911)

SHALER, N. S., *The Geological History of Harbors* (U.S. Geological Survey 13th Annual Report, 1891)

———. *The United States of America* (1894)

Shipping World Year Book (annual)

SIEGFRIED, A., *America Comes of Age* (1930)

SMITH, J. R., *Industrial and Commercial Geography* (1925)

———. *Influence of the Great War upon Shipping* (1919)

———. *North America* (1925)

SPEARS, J. R., *The Story of the American Merchant Marine* (1910)

SPURR, J. E., *Political and Commercial Geography* (1920)

STEPHENS, H. M., and BOLTON, H. E., editors, *The Pacific Ocean in History* (1917)

SULLIVAN, J., *A History of the C. Brewer & Company, Limited* (1926)

TAYLOR, A. P., *Under Hawaiian Skies* (1922)

TODD, J. A., *The Shipping World* (1929)

TREAT, P. J., *Japan and the United States, 1853–1921* (Revised Edition, 1928)

TURNER, F. J., *The Frontier in American History* (1920)

———. *The Significance of Sections in American History* (1932)

UNITED STATES, *Annual Report of the Governor of the Panama Canal*

UNITED STATES BUREAU OF CENSUS, *Water Transportation* (1926)

UNITED STATES BUREAU OF FOREIGN AND DOMESTIC COMMERCE, *Commerce Yearbook* (annual)

———. *Commercial and State-Aided Ship Scrapping*, Supplement No. 3 to Trade Promotion Series 129 (1934)

———. *Commercial Survey of the Pacific Northwest*, Domestic Commerce Series 51 (1932)

———. *Commercial Survey of the Pacific Southwest*, Domestic Commerce Series 37 (1930)

———. *Foreign Commerce and Navigation* (annual)

———. *Government Aid to Merchant Shipping*, Special Agents Series 119 (revised edition, 1925)

———. *Hawaii: Its Resources and Trade*, Trade Information Bulletin 473 (1927)

———. *Inland Water Transportation in the United States*, Miscellaneous Series 119 (1923)

———. *Liner Predominance in Transoceanic Shipping*, Trade Information Bulletin 448 (1926)

———. *Ocean Routes in United States Foreign Trade*, Trade Promotion Series 96 (1930)

———. *Shipping and Shipbuilding Subsidies*, Trade Promotion Series 129 (1932)

———. *Statistical Abstract* (annual)

———. *Trade of Pacific Coast States with West Coast of South America*, Trade Information Bulletin 525 (1928)

———. *Transcontinental and Intercoastal Trade of the Pacific Southwest in 1926*, Domestic Commerce Series 25 (1929)

———. *Trans-Pacific Shipping*, Miscellaneous Series 44 (1916)

———. *Transportation of Pacific Coast Perishables*, Trade Promotion Series 12 (1924)

UNITED STATES BUREAU OF MINES, *Minerals Yearbook* (annual)

UNITED STATES BUREAU OF NAVIGATION AND STEAMBOAT INSPECTION, *Measurement of Vessels* (occasional)

———. *Merchant Marine Statistics* (annual)

———. *Merchant Vessels of the United States* (annual)

———. *Navigation Laws of the United States* (quadrennial)

———. *Amendments to the Navigation Laws* (annual)

———. *Regulations for the Establishment of Load Lines for Merchant Vessels* (occasional)

———. *Seagoing Vessels of the United States* (annual)

UNITED STATES COAST AND GEODETIC SURVEY, *Alaska Coast Pilot* (Parts 1 and 2, 1932, and supplements)

———. *Hawaiian Islands Coast Pilot* (1933)

———. *Pacific Coast Pilot: California, Oregon, and Washington* (1926 and supplements)

UNITED STATES COMMISSIONER OF CORPORATIONS, *Report on Transportation by Water in the United States* (4 volumes, 1909–13)

UNITED STATES CONGRESS, *Hearings*

UNITED STATES DEPARTMENT OF THE INTERIOR, *General Information Regarding the Territory of Alaska* (1931)

———. *Report of Governor of Alaska* (annual)

———. *Report of Governor of Hawaii* (annual)

UNITED STATES FEDERAL TRADE COMMISSION, *Report on the Pacific Coast Petroleum Industry* (2 parts, 1921)

UNITED STATES GEOLOGICAL SURVEY, *Boundaries, Areas, Geographic Centers, and Altitudes of the United States and the Several States*, Bulletin 817 (1932)

UNITED STATES HOUSE OF REPRESENTATIVES, COMMITTEE ON MERCHANT MARINE AND FISHERIES, *Report on Steamship Agreements and Affiliations in American Foreign and Domestic Trade*, 4 volumes, House Document 805, 63d Congress, 2d Session (1914)

UNITED STATES HYDROGRAPHIC OFFICE, *The Development of the Great Circle Sailing* (1899)

———. *Table of Distances between Ports via the Shortest Navigable Routes*, No. 117 (1931)

UNITED STATES INTERSTATE COMMERCE COMMISSION, *Various Rate Hearings*

———. Bureau of Statistics, *Growth of Traffic on Steam Railways of the United States, 1900–1928* (1929)

UNITED STATES NAVY DEPARTMENT, *Annual Report*

UNITED STATES NAVY DEPARTMENT, OFFICE OF NAVAL INTELLIGENCE, *The United States Navy as an Industrial Asset* (1924)

UNITED STATES SHIPPING BOARD, *Annual Report*

———. *Relative Desirability of Ships Operating in Four Trade Routes* (1919)

———. *Report on the History of Shipping Discriminations and on Various Forms of Government Aid to Shipping* (1922)

UNITED STATES TARIFF COMMISSION, *Colonial Tariff Politics* (1922)

UNITED STATES WAR DEPARTMENT, *Annual Report of the Chief of Engineers* (2 volumes, annual)

———. *Panama Canal and Its Ports*, Port Series 22 (1928)

———. *Ports of Los Angeles, Long Beach, San Diego, and San Luis Obispo*, Port Series 13 (Parts 1 and 2, Revised Edition, 1930)

UNITED STATES WAR DEPARTMENT, *Ports of Portland, Astoria, and Vancouver,* Port Series 11 (2 volumes, 1931)

———. *Ports of San Francisco, Oakland, Berkeley, Richmond, Upper San Francisco Bay, Santa Cruz, and Monterey,* Port Series 12 (1933)

———. *Ports of Seattle, Tacoma, Bellingham, Everett, and Grays Harbor,* Port Series 7 (Revised Edition, 3 volumes, 1931)

———. *Ports of the Territory of Hawaii,* Port Series 17 (1926)

UNITED STATES WEATHER BUREAU, *Climatology of the United States,* Bulletin Q (1906)

———. *Summaries of Climatological Data by Sections,* Volume 1, Bulletin W (1912)

UNIVERSITY OF OREGON, *Studies in Business. Analysis of Overseas Markets for Oregon and Washington Dried Prunes* (1929)

———. *Import Traffic through Atlantic and Gulf Ports of Selected Far Eastern Commodities in 1927* (1928)

———. *Import Traffic through Pacific Ports of Selected Far Eastern Commodities in 1927* (1928)

———. *Oregon Exportable Surplus* (1930)

———. *Oregon's Share in Import Traffic from the Far East* (1928)

———. *Pacific Coast Wheat Flour Exports, January–April, 1928 and 1927* (1928)

———. *Portland's Share in Export Traffic from North Central United States to Trans-Pacific Markets* (1930)

———. *Veneers, Plywood and Doors Exported from the Pacific Coast, January to August, 1927 and 1928* (1928)

UYEHARA, S., *The Industry and Trade of Japan* (1926)

VAN HISE, C. R., and HAVEMEYER, L., *Conservation of Our Natural Resources* (1930)

VAN METRE, T. W., *Tramps and Liners* (1931)

WARD, R. DE C., *The Climates of the United States* (1925)

WARE, E. E., *Business and Politics in the Far East* (1932)

WICKSON, E. J., *Rural California* (1923)

WILLIAMS, B. H., *Economic Foreign Policy of the United States* (1929)

WILSON, A. T., *The Suez Canal: Its Past, Present and Future* (1934)

WILSON, G. L., *Traffic Management* (1926)

WOOD, G. L., *The Pacific Basin* (1930)

WRIGHT, P. G., *The American Tariff and Oriental Trade* (1931)

ZIMMERMAN, E. W., *Ocean Shipping* (1921)

———. *World Resources and Industries* (1933)

Periodical sources are notably *Annals of the American Academy of Political and Social Science, Business Week, California Historical Society Quarterly, Commerce Reports, Daily Commercial News, Fairplay, Far Eastern Review, Federal Reserve Bank of San Francisco— Monthly Review of Business Conditions, Harbour and Shipping, Journal of Commerce, The Log, Marine Digest, Nautical Gazette, National Geographic Magazine, Official Steamship Guide, Oregon Historical Quarterly, Pacific Historical Review, Pacific Marine Review, Pacific Shipper, Panama Canal Record, Shipping Register, Trans-Pacific, Washington Historical Quarterly, World Ports.*

Publications of the following organizations will be found of value: American Association of Port Authorities; Association of Pacific and

Far Eastern Ports; Chamber of Commerce of the United States—Western Division; Institute of Pacific Relations; Federal Reserve Bank of San Francisco; Institute of World Affairs; Pacific Coast Economic Association; Pacific Coast Transportation Advisory Board; Pacific Foreign Trade Council; United States Bureau of the Census; United States Bureau of Foreign and Domestic Commerce; United States Bureau of Mines; United States Department of Agriculture; United States Geological Survey; United States Naval Institute; United States Shipping Board Bureau (formerly United States Shipping Board).

Index